OXFORD CLASSICAL

Published under the supervisi...
Faculty of Classics in the University of Oxford

The aim of the Oxford Classical Monograph series (which replaces the Oxford Classical and Philosophical Monographs) is to publish books based on the best theses on Greek and Latin literature, ancient history, and ancient philosophy examined by the Faculty Board of Classics.

Singing for the Gods

Performances of Myth and Ritual in Archaic and Classical Greece

BARBARA KOWALZIG

OXFORD
UNIVERSITY PRESS

OXFORD
UNIVERSITY PRESS

Great Clarendon Street, Oxford OX2 6DP

Oxford University Press is a department of the University of Oxford.
It furthers the University's objective of excellence in research, scholarship,
and education by publishing worldwide in

Oxford New York

Auckland Cape Town Dar es Salaam Hong Kong Karachi
Kuala Lumpur Madrid Melbourne Mexico City Nairobi
New Delhi Shanghai Taipei Toronto

With offices in

Argentina Austria Brazil Chile Czech Republic France Greece
Guatemala Hungary Italy Japan Poland Portugal Singapore
South Korea Switzerland Thailand Turkey Ukraine Vietnam

Oxford is a registered trade mark of Oxford University Press
in the UK and in certain other countries

Published in the United States
by Oxford University Press Inc., New York

First published 2007
First published in paperback 2012

British Library Cataloguing in Publication Data
Data available

Library of Congress Cataloging in Publication Data
Data available

Typeset by RefineCatch Limited, Bungay, Suffolk
Printed and bound by
CPI Group (UK) Ltd., Croydon, CR0 4YY

ISBN 978–0–19–921996-4 (Hbk)
ISBN 978–0–19–963950-2 (Pbk.)

To my family

αὐτίκα γᾶ πᾶσα χορεύσει

Acknowledgements

To set the Greek world singing and dancing is, like the *khoros* itself, a communal activity. And like the Greek chorus, it forges bonds going beyond the actual practice. I have had many fellow-dancers in the production of this book. The sensitivity, wisdom, and rigour of Robert Parker have accompanied it at every stage, and I owe more to him, and his humanity, than to anyone else. Simon Hornblower oversaw the process of turning the thesis into the much larger book, and has generously and committedly brought his exactitude, breadth of knowledge, and intellectual open-mindedness to my ideas. Chris Pelling heroically read the near-completed manuscript and has throughout been a wonderful and stimulating colleague. Oliver Taplin's good intuitions and optimism have encouraged this book from the very beginning, and he imperceptibly drew me into performance and theatre studies. My closest synkhoreut for many years now has been Peter Wilson, whose expertise, imagination, and boldness have unswervingly supported this project; another *athlon* in choral matters goes to Ian Rutherford, whose range of knowledge and friendship has been a great source of inspiration. I have been much stimulated by lively discussion with Leslie Kurke and Giambattista D'Alessio; they both allowed me to see their brilliant articles long before their publication. Emily Mackil shares my enthusiasm for tramping around the Greek landscape in search of its social topography, ancient and modern, and has been a careful and acute reader of my work. Ewen Bowie and Pat Easterling have examined the thesis and have shown continued interest in this project. Nicholas Purcell was enthusiastic for my adventures in the Mediterranean. Katherine Clarke has been an invaluable friend personally and academically. I further thank Lucia Athanassaki, Lisa Bendall, Bruno Currie, John Davis, Gunnel Ekroth, David Fearn, Catherine Holmes, Nikolaos Papazarkadas, Tim Rood, and Scott Scullion. I have learned a lot about the English language from my close friends—especially Erika Milburn and Philomen Probert—who with admirable patience and reliability kept smoothing my sentences. Annelies Cazemier and Theodora Jim kindly assisted me with the proof-reading, and Nigel James's technical expertise has been essential in the map production. I am much indebted to the members of the Centre Louis Gernet in Paris, where the book took its final shape in a highly inspiring atmosphere and in perfect working conditions. François Lissarrague made this stay possible in the first place, and has been indefatigably generous and inspirational. Claude Calame, Pauline Schmitt, and François de Polignac offered me the chance to present my work in their seminars: this set off a host of new ideas at that late stage. I would like to thank particularly Jean-Claude Schmitt for instructing me on the anthropology of music and ritual, as well as Rosine Adda, Vincent Azoulay, Renée Piettre, Gabriella Pironti and Agnès Tapin. I finally owe thanks to Heather Watson and

Kathleen Fearn who did an excellent job at copy-editing and overseeing the production of this book.

The arguments of various chapters have been inflicted on audiences at numerous seminars and conferences throughout the UK and in Oxford in particular, as well as in Washington, Berkeley, Paris, and Athens; all these occasions contributed to shaping my ideas. A responsive student population played an important part in the experimentation with, and eventual crystallization of, many ideas presented in this book. I owe further thanks to a number of archaeologists in Greece for sharing and discussing with me material from their more and less recent excavations, particularly Dr B. Wells (Swedish Archaeological Institute at Athens), Dr H.-R. Götte (Deutsches Archäologisches Institut), Prof. A. De Vita (then Scuola Archeologica Italiana di Atene), Dr I. Papachristodoulou and Mrs A. Giannikouri (Ephorate of the Dodekanese), Dr V. Mitsopoulos-Leon and Dr C. Schauer (Österreichisches Archäologisches Institut, Athens). Many thanks also to the staff of the British School at Athens, who were very hospitable and helpful during my numerous stays in Greece. The librarians of the Ashmolean and now Sackler libraries have offered inestimable help for many almost impossible quests, for which I am very grateful. I completed the research for this book during the summer of 2005 and have therefore not systematically taken account of literature published after that date.

The original D.Phil. research was generously supported by the Studienstiftung des deutschen Volkes, the Deutscher Akademischer Austauschdienst, and the British Academy. I am very grateful indeed to the Craven Committee at Oxford for their grant of the Craven Fellowship 1997–9, lucrative support of my extensive travels in Greece and Italy, as well as to St John's College, where I had a very happy time as a graduate. I was fortunate to be elected to the Moses and Mary Finley Research Fellowship by Darwin College Cambridge, in 1999. My colleagues at University and The Queen's Colleges provided much help and lively company while I was a Tutorial Fellow there between 2000 and 2005. I am extremely appreciative of the Fondation Maison des Sciences de l'Homme Paris and the Deutscher Akademischer Austauschdienst for offering me a fellowship during 2005–6 to do research at the École des Hautes Études en Sciences Sociales and the Centre Gernet.

Much stimulation has over many years come from two very close friends, Elena Pallantza and Stefania De Vido. Last but not least, my family has always been there to provide healthy distractions, and I look forward to their reaction when they realize that this book is actually dedicated to them. Despite the dithyrambic array of people with greater or lesser involvement in the affairs of this book, all errors are my own.

B.K.

Oxford
September 2006

Contents

List of Illustrations

Photographs are the author's unless indicated otherwise.

List of Maps

All maps are created by the author from digital map data © Collins Barthlomew (2004) 2007.

Conventions and Abbreviations

All quotations from Pindar and Bacchylides follow the standard editions by Snell and Maehler (SM) unless indicated otherwise: B. Snell and H. Maehler, eds., *Pindari Carmina cum Fragmentis*, i. *Epinicia* (Leipzig, 1987). H. Maehler, ed., *Pindari Carmina cum Fragmentis*, ii. *Fragmenta, Indices* (Leipzig, 1989); *Bacchylidis Carmina cum Fragmentis* (Leipzig, 1970 (^{10}1992)). The text of Pindar's paeans is that of Rutherford (as Ruth below). Simonides is quoted according to *PMG*; the Scholia vetera to Pindar according to Drachmann (as Dr below). Greek authors are referred to as in LSJ, occasionally elongated, hence 'Bacch.' not 'B.' while Pindar remains Pi. Latin authors appear as in *OLD* or unabbreviated. Journals bear the acronyms used by *Année Philologique*, occasionally adapted. The spelling of Greek names is Hellenized or Latinized according to a random criterion of familiarity, that is 'Herodotus', but 'Philokhoros'.

Commentaries are referred to in the notes by author only, for example, 'Maehler on Bacch. 11.37'. Translations are my own unless otherwise indicated.

ATL	B. D. Meritt, H. T. Wade-Gery, M. F. MacGregor, *The Athenian Tribute Lists*, 4 vols. (Princeton, 1939–53)
AttTar	*Atti del . . . Convegno di studi sulla Magna Grecia*. Istituto per la Storia e l'Archeologia della Magna Grecia, Taranto
Bergk	Th. Bergk, *Poetae Lyrici Graeci* (4th edn., Leipzig, 1878)
Bernabé	A. Bernabé, ed., *Poetarum Epicorum Graecorum. Testimonia et Fragmenta* (Leipzig, 1987). Corrected edn. (Stuttgart, ^{2}1996)
BMI	E. L. Hicks, G. Hirschfeld, F. H. Marshall, C. T. Newton, eds., *The Collection of Ancient Greek Inscriptions in the British Museum*, 6 vols. (Oxford, 1874–1916)
CA	J. U. Powell, ed., *Collectanea Alexandrina: reliquiae minores poetarum graecorum aetatis ptolemaicae, 323–146 A.C.* (Oxford, 1925; repr. 1970)
Campbell	D. A. Campbell, ed., *Greek Lyric*, 5 vols. (Cambridge, Mass., 1982–93)
CEG	P. A. Hansen, ed., *Carmina Epigraphica Graeca*, 2 vols. (Berlin, 1983–9)
Chios	D. F. McCabe and J. V. Brownson, *Chios Inscriptions. Texts and List* (Princeton, 1986)
Chronicle	C. Blinkenberg, ed., *Die lindische Tempelchronik* (Bonn, 1915)
CID	*Corpus des inscriptions de Delphes* (Paris, 1977–)
CIG	*Corpus Inscriptionum Graecarum*, 4 vols. (Berlin, 1828–77)
Clara Rhodos	*Clara Rhodos. Studi e materiali pubblicati a cura dell'Istituto storico-archeologico di Rodi*, 10 vols. (Rhodes, 1928–41)
DGE	E. Schwyzer, *Dialectorum Graecarum Exempla Epigraphica Potiora* (Leipzig, 1923)
DK	H. Diels and W. Kranz, *Die Fragmente der Vorsokratiker*, 3 vols. (Berlin, ^{6}1951–2)
DNP	H. Cancik and H. Schneider, eds., *Der Neue Pauly: Enzyklopädie der Antike* (Stuttgart, 1996–2003)

Dr	A. B. Drachmann, ed., *Scholia Vetera in Pindari Carmina*, 3 vols. (Leipzig, 1903–27)
ED	*Exploration archéologique de Délos*. École française d'Athènes (Paris, 1909–)
FD	*Fouilles de Delphes*. École française d'Athènes (Paris, 1902–)
FGrH	F. Jacoby, ed., *Die Fragmente der griechischen Historiker*, 3 vols. (Berlin–Leiden, 1923–58). Part 4 ed. G. Schepens (Leiden, 1998)
FHG	C. Müller, ed., *Fragmenta Historicorum Graecorum*, 5 vols. (Paris, 1843–70)
Fornara	C. W. Fornara, *Archaic Times to the End of the Peloponnesian War*. Translated Documents of Greece and Rome 1 (Cambridge, ^{2}1983)
GGM	C. Müller, ed., *Geographi Graeci Minores*, 2 vols. (Paris, 1855–61)
HG	R. Herzog, *Heilige Gesetze von Kos* (Berlin, 1928)
HN^{2}	B. V. Head, *Historia Numorum. A Manual of Greek Numismatics*. New and enlarged edition (Oxford, ^{2}1911)
IC	M. Guarducci, ed., *Inscriptiones Creticae*, 4 vols. (Rome, 1935–50)
ID	*Inscriptions de Délos*, 7 vols. (Paris, 1926–72)
IG	*Inscriptiones Graecae* (Berlin, 1873–)
IGASMG	R. Arena, ed., *Iscrizioni greche arcaiche di Sicilia e Magna Grecia*, 5 vols. (Milan, 1989–98)
IK	*Inschriften griechischer Städte aus Kleinasien* (Bonn, 1972–)
Inventory	M. H. Hansen and T. H. Nielsen, eds., *An Inventory of Archaic and Classical Poleis: An Investigation Conducted by the Copenhagen Polis Centre for the Danish National Research Foundation* (Oxford, 2004)
Iscr. Cos	M. Segre, *Iscrizioni di Cos*, 2 vols. Monografie della Scuola archeologica de Atene e delle missioni italiane in Oriente 6 (Rome, 1993)
Kock	T. Kock, ed., *Comicorum Atticorum Fragmenta*, 2 vols. (Leipzig, 1880–8)
KP	K. Ziegler, W. Sontheimer, H. Gärtner, eds., *Der Kleine Pauly: Lexikon der Antike*, 5 vols. (Munich, 1964–75)
Lazzarini	M. L. Lazzarini, *Le formule delle dediche votive nella Grecia arcaica* (Rome, 1976)
LGPN	E. Matthews, P. M. Fraser, *et al.*, eds., *A Lexicon of Greek Personal Names* (Oxford, 1987–)
LIMC	H. C. Ackermann, J.-R. Gisler, L. Kahil, eds., *Lexicon Iconographicum Mythologiae Classicae*, 8 vols. (Zurich, 1981–97)
Lindos I	C. Blinkenberg, *Lindos. Fouilles et recherches, 1902–14, I. Les Petits Objets*, 2 vols. (Berlin, 1931)
Lindos II	C. Blinkenberg, *Lindos. Fouilles et recherches, 1902–14, II. Inscriptions*, 2 vols. (Berlin–Copenhagen, 1941)
Lindos III	E. Dyggve, *Lindos. Fouilles et recherches, 1902–14 et 1952, III. Le Sanctuaire d'Athana Lindia et l'architecture lindienne*, 2 vols. (Berlin, 1960)

LSAG	L. H. Jeffery, *The Local Scripts of Archaic Greece: A Study of the Origin of the Greek Alphabet and its Development from the Eighth to the Fifth Centuries B.C.* Revised edition with a supplement by A. W. Johnston (Oxford, 1990)
LSCG	F. Sokolowski, *Lois sacrées des cités grecques* (Paris, 1969)
LSCGS	F. Sokolowski, *Lois sacrées des cités grecques. Supplément* (Paris, 1962)
LSJ	H. G. Liddell, R. Scott, R. Mackenzie, eds., *A Greek–English Lexicon*, revised and augmented throughout by H. S. Jones. With a Supplement (1968) (Oxford, ^{9}1940; repr. 1990)
Maiuri, *Nuova Silloge*	A. Maiuri, *Nuova silloge epigrafica di Rodi e Cos* (Florence, 1925)
ML	D. Lewis and R. Meiggs, eds., *A Selection of Greek Historical Inscriptions to the End of the Fifth Century B.C.* Revised edition (Oxford, 1969; repr. 1988)
N^2	A. Nauck, *Tragicorum Graecorum Fragmenta* (Leipzig, ^{2}1889)
Nomima	H. van Effenterre and F. Ruzé, *Nomima: recueil d'inscriptions politiques et juridiques de l'archaïsme grec* (Rome, 1994–)
OCD	S. Hornblower and A. Spawforth, eds., *The Oxford Classical Dictionary* (Oxford, ^{3}1996)
OGI	W. Dittenberger, *Orientis Graeci Inscriptiones Selectae: Supplementum Sylloges Graecarum*, 2 vols. (Leipzig, 1903–5)
OLD	*Oxford Latin Dictionary* (Oxford, 1968–82)
Olympia V	W. Dittenberger and K. Purgold, eds., *Die Inschriften von Olympia.* Olympia V (Berlin, 1896)
Osborne–Rhodes	R. Osborne and P. J. Rhodes, eds., *Greek Historical Inscriptions, 404–323 BC* (Oxford, 2003)
Paroem. Gr.	E. L. von Leutsch and F. G. Schneidewin, *Corpus Paroemiographorum Graecorum* (Göttingen, 1839–51). Supplementum (Hildesheim, 1961)
PCG	C. Austin and R. Kassel, eds., *Poetae Comici Graeci* (Berlin, 1983–)
PH	W. R. Paton and E. L. Hicks, *The Inscriptions of Cos* (Oxford, 1891)
PLF	E. Lobel and D. Page, eds., *Poetarum Lesbiorum Fragmenta* (Oxford, 1955). Corrected edn. (Oxford, 1963)
PMG	D. L. Page, ed., *Poetae Melici Graeci* (Oxford, 1962)
POxy.	B. P. Grenfell, ed., *The Oxyrhynchus Papyri* i – (London, 1898–) (roman numbers refer to volumes; arabic numbers to individual papyri)
RE	*Real-Encyclopädie der klassischen Altertumswissenschaft*, ed. A. Fr. von Pauly, rev. G. Wissowa *et al.* (Stuttgart, 1894–1980)
Ruth	I. C. Rutherford, *Pindar's Paeans. A Reading of the Fragments with a Survey of the Genre* (Oxford, 2001)
SEG	*Supplementum Epigraphicum Graecum* (Leiden and Amsterdam, 1923–)
SFP	C. Collard, M. J. Cropp, K. H. Lee, eds., *Selected Fragmentary Plays. Euripides*, 2 vols. (Warminster, 1995–2004)

SGDI	E. Bechtel *et al. Sammlung der griechischen Dialekt-Inschriften*, ed. H. Collitz, 4 vols. (Göttingen, 1884–1915)
SH	H. Lloyd-Jones and P. Parsons, eds., *Supplementum Hellenisticum* (Berlin, New York, 1983)
Slater	W. J. Slater, ed., *Lexicon to Pindar* (Berlin, 1969)
SLG	D. Page, *Supplementum Lyricis Graecis* (Oxford, 1974)
Syll.^{3}	W. Dittenberger, *Sylloge Inscriptionum Graecarum* (Leipzig, ^{3}1915–24)
ThesCRA	*Thesaurus Cultus et Rituum Antiquorum* (Los Angeles, 2004–)
Tit. Cal.	M. Segre, *Tituli Calymnii* (Bergamo, 1952)
Tit. Cam.	M. Segre and G. Pugliese-Carratelli, 'Tituli Camirenses', *ASAA* 27–9, NS 11–13 (1949–51) 141–318
Tit. Cam. Suppl.	G. Pugliese-Carratelli, 'Tituli Camirenses. Supplementum', *ASAA* 30–2, NS 14–16 (1952–4) 211–46
Tod	M. N. Tod, ed., *A Selection of Greek Historical Inscriptions*, 2 vols. (Oxford 1933–48)
TrGF	B. Snell, R. Kannicht, S. L. Radt, eds., *Tragicorum Graecorum Fragmenta*, 5 vols. (Göttingen, 1971–2004).
W	M. L. West, ed., *Iambi et Elegi Graeci ante Alexandrum Cantati*, 2 vols. (Oxford, ^{2}1989–92)

Prelude to the *khoros*

φέρε δή, πῶς ἄν τις μὴ θυμῷ λέγοι περὶ θεῶν ὡς εἰσίν; ἀνάγκη γὰρ δὴ χαλεπῶς φέρειν καὶ μισεῖν ἐκείνους οἳ τούτων ἡμῖν αἴτιοι τῶν λόγων γεγένηνται καὶ γίγνονται νῦν, οὐ πειθόμενοι τοῖς μύθοις οὓς ἐκ νέων παίδων ἔτι ἐν γάλαξι τρεφόμενοι τροφῶν τε ἤκουον καὶ μητέρων, οἷον ἐν ἐπῳδαῖς μετά τε παιδιᾶς καὶ μετὰ σπουδῆς λεγομένων καὶ μετὰ θυσιῶν ἐν εὐχαῖς αὐτοὺς ἀκούοντές τε καὶ ὄψεις ὁρῶντες ἑπομένας αὐτοῖς ἃς ἥδιστα ὅ γε νέος ὁρᾷ τε καὶ ἀκούει πραττομένας θυόντων, ἐν σπουδῇ τῇ μεγίστῃ τοὺς αὐτῶν γονέας ὑπὲρ αὐτῶν τε καὶ ἐκείνων ἐσπουδακότας, ὡς ὅτι μάλιστα οὖσιν θεοῖς εὐχαῖς προσδιαλεγομένους καὶ ἱκετείαις ἀνατέλλοντός τε ἡλίου καὶ σελήνης καὶ πρὸς δυσμὰς ἰόντων προκυλίσεις ἅμα καὶ προσκυνήσεις ἀκούοντές τε καὶ ὁρῶντες Ἑλλήνων τε καὶ βαρβάρων πάντων ἐν συμφοραῖς παντοίαις ἐχομένων καὶ ἐν εὐπραγίαις, οὐχ ὡς οὐκ ὄντων ἀλλ' ὡς ὅτι μάλιστα ὄντων καὶ οὐδαμῇ ὑποψίαν ἐνδιδόντων ὡς οὐκ εἰσὶν θεοί . . .

Well now, how can one argue for the existence of gods without getting angry? You see, one inevitably gets irritable and annoyed with these people who have put us to the trouble, and continue to put us to the trouble, of composing these explanations. If only they believed the stories which they had as babes and sucklings from their nurses and mothers! These almost literally 'charming' stories were told partly for amusement, partly in full earnest; the children heard them related in prayer at sacrifices, and saw acted representations of them—a part of the ceremony a child always loves to see and hear; and they saw their own parents praying with the utmost seriousness for themselves and their families in the firm conviction that their prayers and supplications were addressed to gods who really did exist. At the rising and setting of the sun and moon the children saw and heard Greeks and foreigners, in happiness and misery alike, all prostrate at their devotions; far from supposing gods to be a myth, the worshippers believed their existence to be so sure as to be beyond suspicion. (Plato, *Laws* 887c–e, tr. T. J. Saunders)

The scene is the tenth book of Plato's *Laws*, that ancient work which like no other singles out religion as the set of collective practices forming the overarching framework within which alone a society can work. Plato's 'Athenian' is just about to launch into a defence of the basic convictions in support of these practices: that the gods do exist, do care, and are incorruptible, the premises under threat in the *Laws*' setting. The guarantee of a functioning religious system is a working set of practices directed towards the gods, the mere conduct of which is proof enough of these gods' existence. Paradoxically, it was probably precisely those practices that motivated the stance the 'Athenian' seeks to combat: the sceptic would claim that it is those practices that mislead the gullible into false belief.

This fundamental passage teaches us something about how the Greeks themselves imagined they had come to believe in their gods. Myth has an important share in this, but not by itself: it is the ritual orchestration of myth, the theatricality of myth-telling that is supposed to generate belief. The ceremonial embedding of myth-telling is essential for the efficacy of myth. We can identify here four different 'ritual' frameworks for the performance of myth: small children being told fairy-tales by their nurses and mothers; religious spectacle; intense prayer; and ritualized situations evoked by awe of natural phenomena, here the beauty of the rising and setting sun. In other words, myths are there to be believed in, and the best way to generate belief is to put them into 'practice', that is, into religious ritual, or a form of ritualized behaviour. The emphasis on practice also explains why the recitation of, and listening to, myth is an acquired habit, something that one learns as a child, that forms part of one's education and socialization.

It has become a truism to say that ancient Greek religion cares far less about belief than about ritual practices. This is, however, not exactly what emerges from the religious self-assessment offered in this passage. Belief here is established through practice. Belief and practice are intrinsically intertwined in the constant interplay of myth and ritual.

What interests me in this study is also what, according to Plato, seems to fascinate children most, the second of his 'methods' of inculcating belief. It is the simultaneity of myth and ritual, myths 'which together with the sacrifices they hear in prayers' (μετὰ θυσιῶν ἐν εὐχαῖς αὐτοὺς ἀκούοντες) and 'see as performances' (ὄψεις ὁρῶντες), that makes ritual participants believe in active gods. Plato makes reference here to religious spectacles on a grand scale, and more precisely to the great festive pageants involving song, music, and dance—to what anthropologists call 'song-culture'.[1] Plato's 'Athenian' deems this the most efficacious method to make people believe in active gods, because it offers the most intense emotional and aesthetic experience through its sensory orchestration: words and sounds are intertwined with gestures, movement, and sacrificial action, and they are perceived by spectators and performers alike as a whole. The telling of myth belongs to the ritual; it is as much a part of ritual activity as is the sacrifice. It is their combined operation that for Plato's 'Athenian' seems to ensure the gods' reality.

Greek ritual, on this view, has a vital narrative and a performative aspect, put together as myth and ritual. In singling out the aesthetic contextualization of myth—to 'hear' and to 'see' the stories in performances—as essential in enhancing the gods' credibility, Plato smoothly glosses over what has perhaps been one of the greatest stumbling-blocks for the modern way of dealing with the apparent ubiquity of myth in ancient cultures: that myth's entertainment value may complement rather than contradict its serious content. Is it not precisely the excitement of myth that makes religion accessible to the Greeks themselves and so omnipresent in their society? Not only do myths have more validity when enacted in ritual, but it is myth that makes ritual interesting, and perhaps meaningful. Reading between the lines, Plato's 'Athenian' may have gauged the underlying

[1] Herington (1985) was perhaps the first to stress the continuity of song-culture in ancient Greece.

force driving the extremely ritualistic character of Greek religion, which because of its intangibility has been one of the greatest obstacles to the study of ancient religions. He thereby identifies a basic mechanism for the operation of myth and ritual within Greek polytheism, and also spots the social and political potential of song-culture to propel a community into a shared belief.

In this book I am concerned with the role of such ritual performances of myth in archaic and classical Greek religious song: I am interested in how this 'theatrical' interaction of myth and ritual works in actual performance situations, and what it does to the community of worshippers involved. This implicates a very old question: that of the relationship between myth and ritual. It is a central issue in the study of Greek religion, and a satisfactory explanation is very hard to pin down. The relationship between myth and ritual, two fundamentally social categories, is theoretically and conceptually intricate, and scholarship on the subject seems to come down to a long-standing tradition of *aporia*. That this relationship continues to be elusive can in part be attributed to the fact that one has rarely looked for the concrete situations in which myth and ritual operate together. More often myth and ritual have been tackled in the abstract, as two interrelated systems of thought, without ever rooting them in actual social contexts.

Choral performance is the one realm of Greek religious practice offering such direct access: hymns, paeans, dithyrambs, the sacred chants and tunes performed in honour of the gods. Religious choral song features the telling of myth as part of a ritual performance. Evidence for such songs crops up frequently throughout antiquity, but the largest and most varied corpus dates from the early- to mid-fifth century BC. Famous poets such as Pindar, Bacchylides, and Simonides composed cultic songs that featured aetiological myths in specific ritual contexts. Aetiological myths are local tales reciting the origins of cults: how Apollo set up his temple at Delphi, or how Herakles established the Zeus precinct at Olympia, for example. Choruses sang of the myths of gods in their own cult: singing for the gods entailed singing *about* the gods.

Of this kind of fifth-century material we possess the equivalent of two volumes of Pindar, one of Bacchylides, somewhat less by Simonides. Victory odes, too, belong for the greater part, if not entirely, in the category of religious song, as performances often staged in the context of public festivals and sharing many formal features with the songs addressed to the gods alone.[2] There are other contemporary figures whose surviving oeuvres are slimmer and more fragmentary, for example the Boiotian poetess Korinna, or the patriotic Argive lady Telesilla, who was also active in this period. In reality the whole Greek world is full of song composed and performed in local religious contexts, often presented in

[2] D'Alessio (1994*a*) discusses the comparability of formal features of 'cult' song and victory odes. Currie (2005) argues for epinikian performance in religious settings while Cairns (2005) makes a case for how individual and *polis* interest merge in Bacchylides' *Ode 11* (see Ch. 6 below). Kurke (1991) and Mann (2001) firmly root athletics in a public context.

choral performance such as the poetry of the Spartan Alkman, of Stesikhoros of Himera or of Sappho on the island of Lesbos. But in the work of these figures there is less detailed cultic aetiology than we have in our fifth-century poets, for good reason as we shall see.

These communal chants were commissioned by Greek cities, or by their powerful individuals, to be performed in specific ritual contexts, such as celebrations or festivals at local, regional, or Panhellenic sanctuaries, nearly everywhere in Greece except for mainland Asia Minor, a tantalizing exception.[3] The choruses are thus neatly tied to verifiable milieux: these are concrete performances taking place within circumscribed historical and social frames (the latest possible date for Bacchylides' lifetime has been established as the 430s, while he is more widely thought to have died towards the end of the 440s BC).[4] Strictly linked to the communities for which it was composed, religious choral song thereby provides a framework and a privileged context within which the much-contested relationship between myth and ritual may be investigated, and a background against which myth can be seen in action within a cult community.

That myth and ritual, choral performance, and the workings of the society in which they were produced were closely interlinked was well known to the ancients themselves. In a much-quoted passage on the social functions of song and dance, the Arkadian Polybius proudly explains that his compatriots used to train their children in choral performances right from the cradle:

Ταῦτα γὰρ πᾶσίν ἐστι γνώριμα καὶ συνήθη, διότι σχεδὸν παρὰ μόνοις Ἀρκάσι πρῶτον μὲν οἱ παῖδες ἐκ νηπίων ᾄδειν ἐθίζονται κατὰ νόμους τοὺς ὕμνους καὶ παιᾶνας, οἷς ἕκαστοι κατὰ τὰ πάτρια τοὺς ἐπιχωρίους ἥρωας καὶ θεοὺς ὑμνοῦσι.

Everyone is familiarly acquainted with the fact that the Arcadians are almost the only people among whom boys are by the laws trained from infancy to sing hymns and paeans, in which they celebrate in the traditional fashion their local heroes and gods. (Polybius 4.20.8, tr. Shuckburgh, adapted)

Polybius then continues to explore the different kinds of choral education, demonstrates the uses of choruses at military parades and public festivals, and eventually comes up with an explanation for such intense choral life: indulging in the smooth and pleasant activity of collective chorus-singing and of public festivals compensates for the tough reality of everyday life in rural Arkadia, which produces otherwise highly individualistic characters.[5] The element of geo-

[3] Hornblower (2004) 144–59 doubts whether we should really take east Greece more generally as an exception; differently Hutchinson (2001) 322–3. See Ch. 2 below.

[4] Schmidt (1999), esp. 82 ff.

[5] Plb. 4.21.3–4: *βουλόμενοι δὲ μαλάττειν καὶ κιρνᾶν τὸ τῆς φύσεως αὔθαδες καὶ σκληρόν, τά τε προειρημένα πάντα παρεισήγαγον καὶ πρὸς τούτοις συνόδους κοινὰς καὶ θυσίας πλείστας ὁμοίως ἀνδράσι καὶ γυναιξὶ κατείθισαν, ἔτι δὲ χοροὺς παρθένων ὁμοῦ καὶ παίδων, καὶ συλλήβδην πᾶν ἐμηχανήσαντο, σπεύδοντες τὸ τῆς ψυχῆς ἀτέραμνον διὰ τῆς τῶν ἐθισμῶν κατασκευῆς ἐξημεροῦν καὶ πραΰνειν.* 'And it was with a view to softening and tempering this natural ruggedness and rusticity, that they not only introduced the things which I have mentioned, but also the custom of holding

graphical determinism introduced here need concern us less than the fact that song-culture and society are perceived as being closely intertwined. Choral song and dance is held to be socially integrative and fundamental to the community's well-being, and it affords a social cohesion in which the common reference system of local gods and heroes plays an important role. Choral singing is something traditional, handed down from generation to generation with the implication of unchangeability, and it shapes the relations of the participants, both with one another and with their past. Choral performance of myth and ritual is a vehicle for social interaction and guarantees stability.

The Arkadians were not the exception to the rule, despite Polybius' claims to their unique socialization through *mousike*. Ancient Greece abounded in local choral performances of this kind. Choral song was everywhere in the Greek world, and even if we attempt to avoid the risk of viewing the entirety of Greek civilization through the choral lens, it is nevertheless clear that dancing in the Greek *khoros* was a ubiquitous, and culturally highly prolific, social practice.[6] One reason for this ubiquity lies no doubt in the chorus being a representation of 'community' and closely related to questions of group identity on many possible levels: local civic identity within the framework of the ancient city, but also on the Panhellenic stage and even beyond. Class, gender, and age identity are also formulated within the chorus. Singing in the chorus is often seen as typical of the archaic *polis* world and as much a feature of the aristocratic community as a way of handling conflict arising from it, for example in the way it commands ambitious individuals to dance along to a common tune. However, the *khoros* is bound to the same type of dynamic in the Greek city from the archaic to the Hellenistic period and later.[7]

The role of choral song in social integration has long been established by the pioneering work by Claude Calame, *Les chœurs de jeunes filles* (1977). This book is still a mainstay of the subject for the way in which it argues for the Greek chorus as a means of socialization of the young and a performative forum in which rites of passage into adulthood are conducted. The Greek chorus has since been much explored as a social institution enacting community roles. Choruses' references to their own performance are often intimately tied to values and attitudes, especially in cities that kept tenaciously constructing social roles from very early on, that is for example Sparta. But also for Athens we now possess a brilliant

assemblies and frequently offering sacrifices, in both of which women took part equally with men; and having mixed dances of girls and boys: and in fact did everything they could to humanize their souls by the civilizing and softening influence of such culture' (tr. Shuckburgh, adapted). For joint sacrifice and choruses together see also [Plut.] *De Mus.* 1135f. Plato's *Laws* are particularly fervent about propagating such truths about the interrelation between choral dance and social order, and also choruses' entertainment value: note esp. 653c–667b; 795d–802e; 803d–804b; 814d–17e; 840b–c. I discuss some of these passages in Kowalzig (2004).

[6] Greek cultic songs are now collected in Bremer and Furley's edition (2001). Bremer (1998) gives an overview of religious settings in which cultic song was composed. Rutherford (2001) 3–136 is a detailed analysis of paeans in their social and religious contexts.

[7] Nagy (1990) 339–81 discusses many of these aspects.

study showing how one's commitment to the civic chorus was an important element in a successful political career: Peter Wilson's *The Athenian Institution of the Khoregia* demonstrates how in classical Athens the practice of 'leading the chorus' openly exploited the image of collective representation in the *khoros* and turned communal dancing into a fierce and vain competition over staging one's engagement for the city's welfare. The chorus was thus by no means purely an instrument of community representation but also a field of social competition, which allowed the conspicuous demonstration of social hierarchies within the group.[8]

This was true not only within individual *poleis*: choruses sent as representatives of their city travelled across the Mediterranean in order to participate at festivals elsewhere in the Greek world, often in the context of the fragmented phenomenon recently termed 'choral *polis-theoria*', the most intense manifestation of which is on the island of Delos (Chapter 2).[9] Dancing *polis*-delegations at such festivals tend to assert local identities while at the same time demonstrating that they are part of a wider worshipping community. *Theoria* was one of the practices the Greeks invented for themselves to mediate the constant tension felt between locality and something more 'Hellenic', and was an important factor in inter-state relations.[10] Tellingly, the *khoros*, and choral singing and dancing, forms a musical metaphor regularly used by Greek authors to picture civic accord. If it also turns into a political image of the city itself, and is even more widely deployed to describe harmony or a harmonic formation, this is not only proof of how all-pervasive the Greek chorus was, but ultimately a testimony to how Greeks' social and other imagination was stamped by religious practices.[11]

But, it must be noted, the great majority of ancient cult choruses come without text, and they only survive in antiquarian literature. Extant pieces of cult song are tantalizingly few compared to the extent of choral activity that must actually have taken place. The reason is probably that (as Polybius' passage strongly suggests) the everyday format of choral songs took the shape of traditional oral hymns which were only picked up by tradition when they presented peculiar features, such as the crow songs mentioned by Athenaios.[12] That said, the production of songs was continuous and prolific throughout. The striking series of cultic poems set on stone for performance at Delphi suggests a constant demand for new hymns, as if the traditional ones were not appropriate for all occasions. This was a matter on which opinions could diverge: Aeschylus allegedly refused to write a paean for the reason that a certain Tynnikhos had composed a better one long before.[13]

[8] Calame (1977) (rev. edn. Eng. 1997); Stehle (1997); Wilson (2000).

[9] For choral polis-theoria Rutherford (2004), but the topic appears already in Rutherford's study of Pindar's paeans (2001), *passim*, esp. 293–8.

[10] Kowalzig (2005).

[11] Bowie (2006) collects such passages, focusing especially on the Second Sophistic.

[12] *PMG* 848 (= Ath. 8.360b–d).

[13] *PMG* 707 = Pl. *Ion* 534d, NB a paean 'sung by all' (ὅν πάντες αἴδουσιν). For the paeans inscribed on stone see Ch. 4 n. 14.

Since the poetry that survives is almost exclusively that composed by the great choral poets—Alkman, Simonides, Pindar, Bacchylides—we tend to think of their work as representative of mainstream cult song. It is a more reasonable assumption, however, that these outstanding figures did not normally compose for routine religious business but were asked to do so on specific occasions to mark a special festival, to make a point about a particular performance or otherwise to label an event as important and different. The post-classical cult songs composed especially for Delphi indicate that prominent religious centres regularly asked eminent poets to write for their major festivals. On the other hand, it is also worth noting that many commissioning communities appear only once in the corpus of choral songs and particularly so in the early fifth century; if they decided they could afford a Pindar it is more likely than not that his chorus responded to a particular situation.

Similarly, we know that remuneration of these poets was costly, and their legendary greed might suggest that they preferred to work selectively, on commissions well worth their talent. The 'perks' that poets often received in exchange for their works, such as life-long privileged seats at festivals (*proedria*) or priority in consulting the oracle (*promanteia*) at Delphi, and other honours such as proxeny, suggest that their services were regarded as highly relevant to the community.[14] They thus fit Polybius' idea that choral song, with its myths and rituals, is performed both by and for the worshipping group as a social entity. This practice makes the poet a remarkably central member of society, but in a way different from the modern concept of a lyric genius. These poets were surely remarkable for their creative energy; but above all they must have been strangely capable of putting a society's concerns in order through their music. This ability—and presumably the demand for it too—can perhaps best be explained by the role these poet-composer-performer figures played in the oral society of archaic Greece. They were not only the people who could provide access to the past, but also the only ones who offered a creative way of dealing with it.[15] It is a reasonable assumption, therefore, that these songs were tied to specific performance situations, even—or especially—if these were moments or periods of great change. This consideration confers on choral performances much more of a rooting in

[14] e.g. Kleokhares of Athens received *promanteia* ('right to consult the oracle first'), *proedria* (right to a front seat at festivals), *prodikia* ('priority in courts'), *asylia* ('inviolability'), *ateleia* (exemption from tax), and 'what else is normally granted to *proxenoi* ('public guest') and *euergetai* (benefactors)', for having composed a paean, a *prosodion*, and a *hymnos* taught and staged by a ?local teacher (*didaskalos*) at Delphi (*FD* iii. 2. 78 (= *Syll.*^{3} 450) (230–225 BC)). Hermokles of Chios is honoured for among other things writing a hymn to the god (*FD* iii. 3. 224); cf. *FD* iii. 3. 217 (*Syll.*^{3} 447, *c.*257 BC): the Chian Amphiklos, a 'poet of epics' (*ποιητὴς ἐπῶν*). Cf. similar honours for 'stage directors' *FD* iii. 1. 49 (date unknown): Thrason and Sokrates of Aigeira put on a performance of lyric poetry; *Syll.*^{3} 703 (*c.*118 BC) honours two brothers from Pheneos for training the local chorus for a performance at Delphi, and in particular for staging 'the tunes of the ancient poets'.

[15] On the social roles of the archaic poet see Maehler (1963); P. Murray (1981); Calame (1983); Martin (1989).

contemporary historical processes than we are inclined to admit, as a form of social practice operating in the here and now.[16]

For when thinking 'hymn', one thinks 'traditional religious chant'; when 'myth', 'traditional tale', when 'ritual', 'traditional religious practices'. By contrast, I hope to show in this book that myth, ritual, and religious song in action form an ensemble that is highly dynamic, extremely malleable and productive in the contemporary social process. Taking individual choral performances as the starting point from which we can sensibly examine the relationship between myth and ritual, I shall argue for a pattern, or a set of patterns, characteristic of Greek cult in which aetiological myth, when communicated through ritual choral song, is central to an incessant process of forging and re-forging religious communities over time, and to expressing relations between the different groups involved in a cult. It is in this role that performance of myth and ritual can take on an active share in social and historical developments of their time and effect cultural change.

Neither aetiology itself and its relation to ritual, nor the nature of the working of religious performances in Greece, have been properly explored before. Aetiological myth tends to be overlooked as a sub-group within the broad but vague category of the great Greek myths. This book will suggest that the relationship should be reversed and that aetiological myth is the primary form through which myth plays a function in ritual, and thence in society. Similarly, while one might think of the study of myth and ritual as rather orthodox in the field of Greek religion, no one has ever attempted to pin down their relationship through the medium in which they act. Older studies of Greek myth tend to isolate it from religious activity altogether; more recent investigations look at individual rituals mostly provided by antiquarian sources; and while performance has been a popular category in the study of choral poetry, few attempts have been made to tie performance to mythical content.[17]

By contrast, each and every particular performance shapes the social and political function of the ritual. The key to understanding the social efficacy of myth and ritual lies in the collapse of the distinction between mythical past and ritual present in choral performance, allowing for a continuous reformulation of the worshipping group that any given song delineates. Myth-ritual performances thus lend themselves to radical redefinitions of social and power relations within the worshipping group that myth and ritual claim to embrace. So if, for example, Argives in the fifth century perform as masters of the Heraion in the Argive plain, a song may give the impression that Argos' sacred authority was long-standing, when in actuality their highly controversial control of the sanctuary was at the

[16] Many studies tend to place choral performances in social structures and given historical milieux, rather than as part of historical processes and change: Calame (1997); Stehle (1997); Krummen (1990); Lonsdale (1993); Mullen (1982). Ceccarelli (1998) is an exception. Various facets of the social power of the chorus in the Athenian democracy are discussed in Wilson (2000) *passim* and (2003*b*). Gentili (1988; orig. 1984) and Rösler (1980) explore the social setting of lyric poetry.

[17] See Chapter 1 for detailed bibliographical references.

time of performance still emerging. While maintaining the fiction of being rooted in religious tradition, such sacred performances effectively encompass social change in their own time.[18]

The fact that most myth-ritual performances stem from the first half of the fifth century is not at all accidental. This is the period we tend to associate with rapid and pivotal changes throughout Greece, and with the grand transforming events of classical Greek history: these choruses of myth and ritual are set in, and form part of, the period of the Persian Wars and the emergence of the Athenian empire, a Greek world hovering between local, regional, and Panhellenic identities, aristocratic rule and democracy, and the social and economic consequences that follow in their train. In this milieu, for which, incidentally, the songs are also the only contemporary literary evidence, choral rituals emerge as a medium through which social relations between potential and real worshipping communities are established—that is created, maintained, and confirmed, but also negotiated, contested, and possibly dissolved. By showing the mechanics through which social conflict is handled (usually resolved or pinpointed) in song for the gods, I suggest that cult served as a forum in which central issues concerning the interaction and socialization of participating communities were carried out.

It is important to keep in mind that none of the cult songs, and only some of the victory odes, featuring in this book are dated. And that is good: the social processes of which they are a part are themselves undatable and not those of accurately squared historical chronology. We can place the performances in a *milieu* but it would defy the validity of the thesis in this book if they could be pinned down to the day of their performance. Though multiple facts and dates will feature at various places throughout the study, they serve to orchestrate the historical climate in which the songs were presented and could stake the claims they make. The performances form part of structural change, which can but need not be long-term. In the case of Rhodes, for example, *Olympian 7* (Chapter 5), through the way it configures myth and ritual in the song, evokes an image of a unified island and gives it an identity that—certainly not by chance—contains elements of that of the unified Rhodian state coming into existence over half a century later. The majority of myth-ritual performances put on stage issues that are relevant specifically to the *Pentekontaetia*, the fifty-year period leading up to the Peloponnesian War which began in 431 BC. So, for example, a series of songs presents Argos' intertwined political and religious restructuring of the Argolid and the Argive plain (Chapter 3). The performance of Pindar's *Paean 6* at Apollo's all-Greek centre at Delphi emerges as set in the midst of definitions of what it means to be a Greek, characteristic of the post-Persian War period. Both *Olympian 7* and *Paean 6* deal with economic issues of concern to members of the Athenian empire. What is fascinating about these performances is that they pick up, in religious song, on tendencies and fashions, issues concerning and worrying individual Greeks or a collection of *poleis* or other groupings, and sometimes suggest solutions.

[18] Pindar, *Nemean 10*; see Ch. 3, Section 2 below.

The world of early fifth-century song has long been considered a prerogative of the local, and aristocratic, Greek world. Athens was thought to renounce such elitist forms of choral representation, having already come up with drama as its solution to how best to represent the whole city in the chorus. This vision has thankfully been redressed: Athens perhaps staged bigger shows involving more people performing or watching, but was not so different in continuing a tradition of archaic song-culture.[19] Indeed, it is gradually becoming clear that drama itself travelled the Greek world and was performed outside Athens much earlier than we used to think.[20] The precise consequences of this for the world of choral song are yet to be worked out. But as we shall see through much of this book, epichoric religious poetry interacts with Athens and also bits and pieces of Athenian performance culture at every point, and myth-ritual performances often give expression to things that are not said in what survives of the prose sources.

However, the rapprochement in matters choral between Athens and others may in fact be a result of more widely shared transformations: 'community poetry' was in existence in some form from very early on. But the proliferation of local choral commissions across the Greek world in this period is, I think, no coincidence. It forms part of the phenomenon of a pronounced awareness and construction of local identity intimately linked to the big developments in the early fifth century, especially the Persian Wars followed by the emergence of the Athenian empire and democracy, all of which put a big question mark over what it meant to be a *polis* in a wider Greek context. The fact that choral song performed at local festivals had a share in the creation and transformation of novel and constantly changing senses of community is well set to be part of this bigger picture. Chapter 7 for example exposes the Boiotians' response when religious choral song seems gradually to create something like a notion of 'Boiotia', a regional identity, while Chapter 6 observes a similar phenomenon related to the forging of an ethnic 'Akhaian' identity in Megale Hellas.

Last but not least, therefore, I am interested in the ways in which social and power relations are explored, defined, and asserted within and between communities through religious practices and in a manner complementary, or alternative, to more recognized forms of the wielding of power, such as brute military force, institutional authority, or economic exploitation. Cultic aetiology, intricately linked to choral ritual, will be revealed as central to the process by which authority in these communities is contested and competed for. I aim to explore the extent to which myth and ritual receive a social dimension through the medium in which they act, the choral performance: in this manner, they become an agent in society, sometimes a tool, but probably more often a dynamic that

[19] e.g. Hornblower (2004), 247–62 discusses the role of Athens, as part of the wider study reinterpreting the social contexts of epinikian song. Kurke (1991), introduction, places epinikian song somewhere in between private aristocratic and public democratic culture and has since further studied interactions between contemporary fifth-century lyric and dramatic poetry. Cf. Kowalzig (2004).

[20] Taplin (1999) and (2007); Csapo (2004); Revermann (2006) esp. 66 ff.

shapes the relations between the people exercising them. 'Myth and ritual' may turn out to be something different from what we think they are, and the performances of myth and ritual will reveal how the eminently social character of Greek religion is bound to its role in the historical process.

The substantial introduction to this study establishes the conceptual framework that underlies the set of unorthodox observations made in the main body of the book, which will deal with actual instantiations of aetiological myth in choral ritual. I begin by formulating why I think the study of myth and ritual has turned into something like deadlock, where little progress is made in the conceptual debate, and why I think historical and geographical rooting in actual performance can make a difference to the question. One underlying idea in the argument is that aetiological myth and ritual come to interact in a performative context due to an inherent similarity in their workings, specifically with respect to their relationship to 'time' and 'place'. I discuss both myth and ritual in this perspective, and engage with the specific qualities of 'performance' as a third category of social activity. The primary goal of Chapter 1, then, is to lay out the conceptual underpinning, assumptions, and possibilities on which the later argument is made. But I also hope to open up wider perspectives on these three types of social pursuits, informed by recent approaches to ritual found in anthropology, theatre studies, and medieval and modern history, with a view to establishing Greek ritual as a dynamic and productive force in Greek society.

The main body of the book will then present some of what is still traceable of the web of early fifth-century myth-ritual performances which once, I believe, enveloped the entire Greek world. The argument is on the whole not 'progressive', and the case rests on cumulative evidence and the pattern that arises from it. That said, Chapter 2, examining choral performances on Delos, a centre of *theoria*, the peculiar form of state-pilgrimage mentioned above, sets out the fundamental case of how aetiological myth is re-enacted in choral performance, and how the breakdown of mythical past and ritual present in choral performances allows a constant reformulation of worshipping communities. Delian myth and ritual, shaping the cultic community of choral *polis-theoria* over time, create an alternative network, heavily exploited by the fifth-century Delian League, to that of political allegiances. The chapter thus establishes a basic paradigm for the reconfiguration of mythical pasts and ritual presents through sacred performances taken for granted in later chapters. I shall then follow the keen performers of myth and ritual all over the Greek world and delineate whole myth-ritual landscapes for this period, travelling through the island world, the Argolid, the Saronic Gulf, central and northern Greece, the Dodekanese, and engage with the complex sets of identities in Megale Hellas, southern Italy. But I should also single out early on what my web does not cover: Kyrene in North Africa, for example, will not feature, despite the fact that Pindar's *Pythian 5* has a beautiful aetiology for Apollo Karneios in this city, and we have much evidence for the early fifth-century Kyrenaika. However, Apollo Karneios and his Theran settlers have been abundantly treated in inquiries related to mine, to which I can happily refer the reader.[21] But the real reason for confining myself to a set of major performance landscapes, often linked to each other, lies in the book's thesis as it gradually emerged in writing it: that the phenomenon examined is so universal to choral song that it would be vain to aspire to completeness. Pindar's and Bacchylides' fragmented scraps of cult poetry, many quietly hidden away in their respective editions, are goldmines for the field of myth, ritual, performance, and Greek *mousike* that have only just begun to be exploited. If this book can go some way toward piecing together the picture of the Greek world set on *khoroi* of myth and ritual, then something significant will have been achieved.

[21] Calame (1996*b*); Dougherty (1993); Krummen (1990); Bremmer (2001*b*), and others.

1

Introduction

1. MYTH AND RITUAL

Plato's hints in the *Laws* have not been taken very seriously in the study of this subject. Myth and ritual have always been treated in isolation from the medium in which they interact and the social implications arising from the performative situation. The question of the relationship between myth and ritual is a very old one, and a whole army of anthropologists, classicists, theologians, and orientalists have been concerned with it. There are several basic problems in traditional approaches, which taken together make for slow progress in the debate. The explicit or implicit search for the primacy of myth or ritual is one such unbroken premise. Even when no longer looking for the origin, these approaches have tended to privilege the one over the other as more 'original' or more 'interesting'. Studies of myth and ritual, moreover, almost universally aim at pinpointing their relationship using the somewhat dubious dichotomy of thought and action. Myth and ritual are seen as two different, yet intrinsically interrelated, modes of communication, and ultimately they are supposed somehow to convey the same message. Approaches are based on the a priori assumption of a certain parallelism (that is, myth and ritual are mutually reflective, complementary, even exclusive) and concern themselves with how best to describe this mutuality, of how to say that myth and ritual actually achieve the same thing in different ways.[1]

But the search for parallels of this kind has not been able to solve questions such as why there survive myths without rituals and vice versa, or why there are quite so few detailed myth-ritual sequences; or why in the majority of cases we find merely allusions of the one to the other, some broken reflections. And finally, why myth and ritual change over time, and do so independently of each other, leaving individual myth-ritual ensembles full of anachronisms. Traditional anthropological approaches in particular cannot account for how and why myths and rituals attach themselves to new historical contexts and migrate geographically as they so easily do in ancient Greece. Not least because the distinction between 'myth and ritual' and the cultural phenomenon 'myth in ritual'

[1] Bell (1997) 3–21; R. Segal (1980) and (1998) give cross-disciplinary overviews over the debate. The fundamental essay on myth and ritual in antiquity is Versnel (1990); rev. (1993) 15–88, n. 1 for a comprehensive bibliography on the history of scholarship. Excellent recent surveys can be found furthermore in Burkert (2002); Bremmer (2005*a*). Calame (1991) discusses the lack of ancient categories of 'myth' and 'ritual'; cf. Bremmer (1998). Older studies include Kirk (1970) 8–31; (1974) 66–8; 223–53; Burkert *passim* but esp. (1979*a*) 34–9; 56–8; (1980) 172–82; Graf (1993*a*) 35–43; Schlesier (1994); Segal ibid. For myth especially see now Csapo (2005).

has not normally been drawn, the role of actual myth-telling in and for cult activity has remained little explored.

The latter contention is only partially true: the old myth-ritualists did conceive of a role of myth in ritual. We tend to associate the study of myth and ritual with the long-superseded views of the so-called Cambridge school of myth-ritualists revolving around William Robertson Smith, James George Frazer and, for classicists, above all Jane Ellen Harrison. Much ink has gone into surveying their thinking and their legacy, so that a little may suffice here. I am interested not so much in what previous scholarship did or did not contribute to the issue, or in why those concepts do not work, but in how the theories used are characteristic of the problems in dealing with myth and ritual.[2]

But I must start from further afield. The Cambridge myth-ritualists were foreshadowed by one scholar. For the anthropologist Edward Tylor (1832–1917) myths were equal to primitive philosophical attempts at explaining the world, rather than metamorphoses of men's fantasies. A mirror of the primitive mind, myths exist in their own right and are part of an evolutionary scheme underlying humanity, elements of which survive into the age of rationality. Although Tylor does not have an explicit view on myth's relation to ritual, it is worth mentioning him as one of the first to engage with myth as an explanatory mode, a line that the Cambridge ritualists would later develop.[3]

Tylor's concentration on myth forms a marked contrast to the well-known student of Near Eastern religions, William Robertson Smith (1846–94), who focused on ritual. Robertson Smith was indeed probably the 'father' of the view still resounding in classical studies that ancient religions had no explicit 'creed': beliefs were either entirely non-existent, or subsumed in ritual. Anticipating what would become the much-repeated Durkheimian notion, he sought the origins of religion in society. Ritual is the prominent communal activity through which deified images of society itself are worshipped. Myth is relegated to the back-bench, to an unsubstantial role, in this conception, as an explanation of ritual that arises when the magical meaning of ritual has been forgotten. Myth is explanatory, but only as an afterthought.[4]

It is from these conceptual premises that anthropology's most controversial figure emerged. Motivated by Robertson Smith's concept of ritual as the source of all cultural and social activity, James George Frazer's *Golden Bough* argued that all

[2] For the Cambridge myth-ritualists see, other than the works listed in the preceding note, Ackerman (1991). Specifically on Jane Harrison, Beard (2000); Robinson (2002).

[3] Tylor (1958; orig. 1871).

[4] Robertson Smith (1889) 1–28; e.g. 16–18: 'antique religions had for the most part no creeds; they consisted entirely of institutions and practices . . . So far as myths consist of explanations of ritual, their value is altogether secondary, and . . . in almost every case the myth was derived from the ritual and not the ritual from the myth; for the ritual was fixed, and the myth was variable, the ritual was obligatory and faith in the myth was at the discretion of the worshipper.' 28: 'religion did not exist for the sake of saving souls but for the preservation and welfare of society'. The totem theory expounded in the *Lectures* was picked up by Durkheim on whom see pp. 34–5 below.

rituals enact a world-wide diffused model of the death and resurrection of a god or divine king whose sufferings ensure the fertility of his land and welfare of his people. It is out of this patterned process that myths (and indeed all other customs and cultural activities) arise in a variety of forms, but all following the same underlying model, functioning not so much as an explanation, but rather as an expression of the universal concern with sacral kingship and fertility in the relevant society.[5]

Both Robertson Smith and Frazer (1854–1941) heavily influenced the so-called Cambridge myth-ritualists, concerned chiefly with the religions of the Graeco-Roman world and the Near East and adopting the primacy of ritual. This group of scholars' view crystallized in the various voluminous works of Jane Ellen Harrison (1850–1928). In Harrison's initial conception, Frazer's sacred king shaped the sequence of most rituals in ancient Greece too. Myth always derived from 'practical ritual' (rather than 'poetic imagination'—something hotly debated to the present day)[6] enacting the recurrent pattern, but over time the 'meaning' of those rituals was forgotten and 'myth' became 'ritual misunderstood'. Though building upon Frazer's somewhat monolithic explanatory model, Jane Harrison achieved more than is normally attributed to her. She was, for example, puzzled by the fact that myths claim to explain without actually explaining anything, hence her solution that the original meaning of myths must have slipped out of memory, that they became 'professed explanations', and thus a rather poor attempt by humanity to cope with its own customs and their change over time.[7] Her interpretation also accounted for the fact that many myths at first sight seem to have no accompanying rite, and for the many versions and many figures of Greek mythology, myth, she maintained, is longer lived than ritual and tends to attach itself to new rituals and other figures of the heroic cycles once the original rite has died out. Her myths in fact vividly regenerate themselves, reflecting what she thought the mythical figures themselves did at the time of mythopoiesis: 'When the Kouretes lose faith in their (ritualistic) power to rear a child yearly they go on uttering their myth but they put it in the past and interpolate an explanatory function marking the decay of faith.'[8] Her manner of coping with the awareness that myths can have a life of their own unwittingly introduces the issue that myths and rituals live and develop over time, and that part of the difficulty in dealing with their relationship may lie in the changes they undergo independently of each other. Though many interesting observations on the role of myth in cult originate with Harrison's work, all these early scholars

[5] Frazer (1890), the first edition, expanded in later ones.

[6] The discussion on the relation of traditional ritual practice and creative poetic imagination in the classical world is most vigorously carried out in scholarship on ancient tragedy. Studies adopting a view somewhere in between two extremes include Krummen (1998); Henrichs (2000); Parker (1997).

[7] Harrison (1890) iii (generally): 'My belief is that in many, even in the large majority of cases, *ritual practice misunderstood* explains the elaboration of myth'; then e.g. xxxii–xxxiii 'There is no more fertile source of absurd mythology than *ritual misunderstood*.' The view is also maintained in her *Prologomena* (1903), harshly criticized by Kirk (1970) 8–31.

[8] Harrison (1912) 330.

dismissed straightaway what should have been their figurehead: while Harrison thinks that myths can 'become' aetiological 'when the emotion that started the ritual has died down and the ritual though hallowed by tradition seems unmeaning', Samuel Hooke remarks about aetiological myth that '[it had] no magical potency, and does not seem to satisfy any more fundamental need than curiosity'.[9]

Despite, or perhaps because of, her pronouncedly evolutionist stance, Harrison's rather intuitive theories seem indirectly to acknowledge that the much sought-for original relationship between myth and ritual is in fact poorly reflected in surviving Greek myths or rituals. Harrison then grew dissatisfied with her initial concept and changed her theory into what has become known as the first of many models of myth and ritual arising 'pari passu' ('in parallel'), with both myth and ritual having a common starting point in a particular social situation. Myths function as the spoken part of ritual, *to legomenon*, as contrasted with, or rather as related to, *to dromenon.*[10] Harrison thus was perhaps the first to look for a common derivation of both. One should also note that, though her concerns clearly lie with the origins of a relationship of myth and ritual, she thought about them under the functionalist influence of Émile Durkheim, who states that myth and ritual are the mutually evocative product of contemporary social activity and cannot be separated from each other. In a remarkable transfer of methodology, Jane Harrison eventually combined all of her intellectual legacies by adding a social dimension to the Frazerian model of sacral kingship: the narrative of death and rebirth of the vegetation god was enacted symbolically in a ritual of initiation into society.[11]

Just how influential this broad conception was is revealed by its many followers, only some of them classicists.[12] Close to Harrison as well as Frazer, the Old Testament scholar Samuel Hooke acted as a hub for the now emerging Myth-and-Ritual School. Taking an explicitly synchronic viewpoint, he was the first to argue systematically for the idea of myth as 'the spoken part of ritual', that is a precise description of what is being done in ritual, the 'story which ritual enacts'—myth is the 'ritual text'.[13] The long-lasting idea of their both being linear sequences of thought and action probably has its origins here. Though harshly criticized for the random way in which narrative and ritual sequences were believed to reflect each other, the great popularity of Frazer's ritually dying and rising priest-king

[9] Harrison (1912) 16; Hooke (1956) 43.

[10] In *Themis* (1912) esp. 16; 327–31. The words *dromenon* 'the done thing' and *legomenon* 'the said thing', which are often elliptically used to describe myth and ritual, in the ancient texts actually only occur in the context of mystery cults: Calame (1991) 201–3.

[11] Harrison (1912) 27–9; 46–7 introduces a new interest in the social component of the development of myth *à la* Durkheim (see below): myths are products of spontaneous, collective emotions. In Frazer's view, by contrast, man is a manipulator, believing he can control external processes by magical methods, that is, rites.

[12] Harrison's best-known contemporaries are e.g. Murray (1912); Cornford (1912).

[13] Hooke (1933) 3; see also (1935) v–vi; (1956); (1958*a* and *b*). See also Harrison (1912) as n. 10 above for myth as the 'spoken correlative' to ritual.

among folklorists occasioned adventurous applications to many peoples' lore—reaching as far as the saga of the Danish king Hamlet. The fantasies of the myth-ritualists are astonishing intellectual constructs, often composing myth on no evidence for ritual and vice versa.[14] With a bit more focus, the archetypal myth-ritual complex of the Near Eastern New Year royal ritual sacrifice, in a diffusionist approach, was taken to amount to a kind of cultural and religious *koine* among Semitic religions of the Near East.[15] Only as late as 1966 did the rigorous critique by the classical scholar Joseph Fontenrose cause the dying and rising god's universality to be dismissed. The question of origins, meanwhile, had been abandoned by Clyde Kluckhohn, who pointed out what Harrison may already have sensed with her second theory: the question of primacy of either myth or ritual could not be solved.[16] The Myth-and-Ritual School demonstrates well the dangers of excessive comparativism, and draws attention to the problems in making exact correspondences between *legomena* and *dromena* the only quest in investigations of the relationship between myth and ritual.

Bronislaw Malinowski (1884–1942), despite his strong myth-ritualist sympathies, was the first to abandon the evolutionary model in favour of an understanding of myth and ritual as operative within society. The function of myth for Malinowski is neither magical nor explanatory of human concerns but social. Myth comes onto the scene when rite and ceremony, social institutions or kinship systems, belief or morality demand a 'justification, a warrant of antiquity, reality, and sanctity'—the notion known as the 'charter' function of myth. Oddly, the perceived father of functionalism in the study of myth saw ritual as profoundly rooted in personal experience and belief rather than as a social phenomenon. Rituals satisfy emotional and psychological needs, while myths uphold society by kindling feelings towards phenomena of social value.[17] So, for example, in ritual death is addressed as a human preoccupation, but myth treats death as a social institution. Though uninterested in the particulars of myth-ritual, by postulating a dichotomy between the social apprehension of myth and the individual apprehension of ritual, Malinowski addresses their relationship by recognizing a social function for both, expressed as a typically Durkheimian convergence of individual and collective experiences.

While the dichotomy between the individual and the collective might have suggested that myth and ritual form an indissoluble and mutually dependent ensemble, structuralism, from Claude Lévi-Strauss (1908–) to Stanley Tambiah (1929–) and other twentieth-century anthropologists, tends to treat them separately and only sometimes looks at their relationship. Though the question of

[14] Widengren (1969) 150–7. For *Hamlet* see Murray (1914).

[15] Babylonia: the Enuma Elish myth recited during New Year festivals, which, complemented by a spurious 6th-cent. BC tablet, accounted for a dying and rising god Marduk: see esp. the exuberant studies of Engnell (1943) and Widengren (1955); see also Mowinckel (1921–4).

[16] Fontenrose (1966); Kluckhohn (1942).

[17] Malinowski (1948 (1926)) 84–5; cf. 122. He features as a functionalist in the scholarship of classical myth (Burkert (1979*a*) 23; Graf (1993*a*) 42), but among the intellectualists/psychologists among the ritual theorists (Bell (1997) 50–1; 25; 28).

'primacy' had long been buried, not so were views on which is the more important category. Lévi-Strauss famously privileges myth over ritual, and this resounds in what he says about their relationship. As a condensed form of cultural expression myth disassembles the coherence of continuous experience of reality into structural units. Ritual discharges into ecstasy in a desperate and notoriously unsuccessful attempt to put back together the fragmented pieces into continuous lived human experience: ritual is after all only the degenerated form of human thought expressed in myth.[18] The relationship is expressed like a little war between the different types of representations of the human mind. Ritual here is the inferior and scattered echo of the deep intellectual structures contained in myth. Lévi-Strauss strongly privileged myth over ritual, but still put them in a dialectical relationship where both account for different mental transformations of reality. Whatever one thinks of the pure intellectualism of myth,[19] the notion of continuity or fragmentation in myth or ritual respectively is useful. The opposition of a happily disjointed and non-sequential myth and a ritual vainly searching for unity is especially appealing: it suggests, above all, that the relationship is not linear.

Nevertheless, the irresistible search for parallels prevails in the Lévi-Straussian model as well and recurs tenaciously in scholarship influenced by him, as if the best hit in defining the relationship between myth and ritual lay with models of their greatest possible correspondence. Edmund Leach (1910–89) for example accentuated their interdependency insisting that 'myth implies ritual and ritual implies myth', and in Lévi-Straussian fashion then resorted to myth as the patterning device for their relationship.[20] For the influential anthropologist Stanley Tambiah, myth and ritual shape, or as he would say, 'frame', the 'two sides of an insoluble paradox and both may attempt alternative kinds of mediation'.[21] The legacy of Lévi-Strauss is felt when we read in Tambiah that myths and rituals in Buddhist Thailand are related to each other like an image and its—now vastly distorted—mirror. As part of the process of attaining priesthood in the community he observes, myth validates the religious status and power of a given person, while the rite enacts just the opposite, the domestication and subjection of the future priest to the religious authority with which the myth empowered him—a system of oppositions expressed in myth and ritual which recalls the thought-world of the classical *Black Hunter*.[22] Though Tambiah insists on the effect of mutual mirroring, he unintentionally introduces a processual aspect into the relationship: the rite leads towards what is a fact in myth; in order to become a religious authority, you must first be subject to this authority. But the wider social

[18] Lévi-Strauss (1981) 679 (= French edn. (1968) 607): 'while myth resolutely turns away from the continuous to segment and break down the world . . ., ritual moves in the opposite direction: . . . it strives to get back to the continuous, although the initial break with lived experience effected by mythic thought makes the task forever impossible'.

[19] Lévi-Strauss (1970) 12: 'I therefore claim to show not how men think in myths but how myths operate in men's minds without their being aware of the fact.'

[20] Leach (1954) 13 ff.

[21] Tambiah (1970) 307.

[22] Vidal-Naquet (1986) (Eng. 1981).

context to which this belongs is also telling: as Tambiah perceptively acknowledges, underlying this process of becoming a priest through myth and ritual is a set of principles characteristic of religious life in the Thai village, by which ritual is a form of spiritual self-castigation to overcome the weakness of sensuality, while mythical characters form part of the pantheon of benevolent moral agents. The two most basic ethical attitudes of this community are thus reflected in myth and ritual. Though Tambiah himself does not then draw these theoretical conclusions, it seems that here for the first time myth and ritual appear as complementary to, rather than coextensive of, each other, perhaps geared towards 'the same thing', but without the essence of each being contained in the other. And—as late as 1970—the notion of the priority of one over the other was finally ruled out.[23]

While the relationship between myth and ritual has never ceased to be of interest in classical studies, it is above all Walter Burkert (1931–) who has incessantly engaged with the conceptual issues involved, formulating a model that though well known has perhaps not elicited as much further debate as it should. He initially embarked on searching for parallels in narrative and rite with two seminal articles, in which he established myth as the 'plot' of ritual while avoiding judgement on when and under what circumstances the relationship came about.[24] Burkert subsequently borrowed more and more from a wide range of disciplines to trace what there is in the human constitution to allow myth and ritual to represent two sides of the same thing. Influenced by the Russian formalist Vladimir Propp on the one hand and by the biological anthropology of Konrad Lorenz on the other, Burkert argued that myth and ritual are the verbal and pragmatic expressions of fundamental behavioural patterns predetermined by biological 'action programmes': that is to say, recurrent patterns in myth pick up on corresponding rituals which in turn are emphatic and externalized expressions of biological drives and crises: the story of the young hero driven out of the city (myth) recurs in initiation ceremonies (ritual) all of which underlies biologically programmed transition into adulthood ('action programme'). The core idea is that some form of ritual action lies at the basis of any group integration and cohesion among humans, and animals.[25]

Classical scholars hesitate to accept this view whole-heartedly—less perhaps because it is implausible than because it is unverifiable.[26] Though professedly not

[23] Tambiah (1970) esp. 308–9.

[24] Burkert (1966) and (1970) 14, cf. Martin (1987) for a subsequent study on the same myth. Other classical scholars explicitly interested in the concrete workings of myth and ritual are Versnel (1970); (1987); (1990); Bremmer e.g. (1978); (2001*a*); (2005*b*); Calame e.g. (1996*a*); (2006*b*); Sourvinou-Inwood e.g. (1988); (1991*a*); (2003*a*); (2005) to name just a few landmark studies. For individual rituals and their relation to myth see e.g. Graf (2000 (1978)).

[25] Burkert (1983) but esp. (1979*a*) and (1979*b*); (1996). The pattern applies to human preoccupations such as puberty, menstruation, defloration, pregnancy, and birth—see esp. (1979*a*) 6–7; 57.

[26] Burkert's thinking has nevertheless influenced the study of myth and ritual in a major way: Graf (1993*a*) and Versnel (1990); Bremmer (1978), but see now his critique in (2005*a*) 36–9.

interested in origins, Burkert really looks at the fundamentals underlying social action, few of which can be either denied or proven. While it is perfectly possible, and indeed likely, that a pattern similar to that of initiation, profoundly concerned with group integration, lies at the heart of the social animal's behavioural design, this model too finds it hard to account for what has puzzled scholars from the beginning: the perplexing questions that Burkert himself chooses to single out, how myths and rituals are 'isolated' in the tradition, how myths can 'become' seemingly independent of ritual, or why some myth-ritual sequences seem to have survived while in many more cases their relationship is reduced to either relics of the myth in the ritual, or mythical references to evidently ritual elements[27]—problems which have led certain classicists to declare that ritual was after all no interesting component of the workings of myth.[28]

Looking for behavioural patterns, however, meets the pitfall in studies influenced by structuralism, of ignoring development over time and place, while at the same time the fact that myth and ritual have moved so far from these 'origins' (note that Burkert's own phrasing is 'becoming') is recognized to be a problem. In his view, myth and ritual express intrinsic human values, such as men's ideas on birth, death, or marriage, which are transmitted in history from generation to generation through religious rites:

> we should venture to see it [sc. Greek mythology] in the greater context of the tradition of humanity, and to perceive through the Greek form the antecedent, dynamic structures of experience which have formed human life and molded the human psyche in the vast realm of the past.[29]

Strictly speaking, though, this model does not allow for the perceived changes in myth or ritual over the course of the history of a practised religion, especially since underlying human behavioural patterns and programmes of action, such as male and female initiation, are unlikely to change over a short period of a couple of centuries. Such discussion of myth and ritual by definition limits itself to the mere interpretation of myth on a synchronic rather than a diachronic level, and therefore cannot cope with change in either myth or ritual. Part of the problem lies in the adoption of certain aspects of a functionalist-structuralist position, postulating that a myth can only be fully understood if considered in the complexity of its variations as maintained, for example, by the French scholar, Marcel Detienne:

> Ces différents récits mythiques, l'analyse structurale revendique le droit de les combiner . . . sans constrainte d'espace ni de temps . . . un mythe ne peut être défini que par l'ensemble de ses variantes . . .

[27] Burkert (1966): 'Myth, being the plot, may indicate connections between rites which are isolated in our tradition' (14); 'myth may *become* independent of ritual' (14); 'only the myth carries, in phantasy, to the extreme what, by ritual, is conducted into more innocent channels' (16).

[28] Kirk (1970) esp. 31; (1974). Similarly, his treatment of aetiology (1972) bears little relation to ritual.

[29] Burkert (1979*a*) 141–2.

L'histoire événementielle ou sociale n'a donc aucun privilège à l'explication des mythes, elle n'est qu'une donnée parmi toutes celles qui font partie de la réalité dont la mythologie fait son profit . . .[30]

It is perhaps under the influence of such definitions of myth, so important and productive in understanding many aspects of ancient Greek religion, that classical scholarship has never really liberated itself from certain elements of the Cambridge myth-ritualists.[31] The Dutch scholar Henk Versnel makes a challenging observation in this respect: the diffusionist model of the early twentieth-century myth-ritualists—Frazer's sacred king dying and rising in myth and ritual—has found a replacement in classical studies in the fashion of making initiation rites the underlying pattern of much human ritual action. Probably the most popular subject in Greek religion for the last half-century, the wave of initiation based on van Gennep's convenient three-stage 'séparation'—'marge'—'agrégation',[32] a broad enough template to be mapped happily onto a number of myth-ritual sequences, has swallowed their specificity by reducing to a repetitive scheme a phenomenon which in reality shows great variety.[33]

Indeed, hardly a word has ever been spoken against the notion that myths and rituals exist in timeless clusters, and yet here may lie one of the central problems in dealing with myth and ritual. In the more recent history of the problem, the Cambridge anthropologist Stephen Hugh-Jones (1945–), though a professed Lévi-Straussian, has advanced a few tentative conclusions relevant to how the specificity of time and place of either myth or ritual ties into their relationship. Although the study stands out as a unique attempt among anthropologists, historians, and classicists, it has not prompted much discussion in classical or other fields. Hugh-Jones explores myth and ritual in a smallish set of Amazonian communities. The group of attested myths and rituals gives important insights into how myth and ritual work practically in a (then) contemporary society. Starting from the analysis of a single festival, concerned mainly with fertility, Hugh-Jones puts myth back into its place in ritual and develops the notion of a grid of interrelated and inseparable myths and rituals. Myths can only be understood if they are systematically related to ritual; many facts of ritual can only be understood in relation to myth, or, in his words, only 'in the context of ritual is their [i.e. myths'] potential meaning made actual'. The important difference from most scholarship to that date is to observe myth in a ritual setting—in a performative context just as Plato suggested—rather than putting the two in a relation in a somewhat abstract way. And the study vividly suggests (though never says it) that all myths and all rituals are inherently connected in a network of

[30] Detienne (1977) 76; 86.

[31] Besides Burkert one might also name Versnel (1987); Graf (1993*a*) and elsewhere among those with certain sympathies for the Cambridge school.

[32] Van Gennep (1909) 14.

[33] Versnel (1990). See e.g. Jeanmaire (1939); Brelich (1961); Burkert (1966); (1970); Graf (1980); Bremmer (1978); Sourvinou-Inwood e.g. (1988); Calame (1997), to name some prominent representatives. Robertson is perhaps the most fervent diffusionist, e.g. (1995); (1996).

myths and rituals in which even myths that superficially have nothing to do with a specific ritual may end up having a bearing on it if investigated in the appropriate context. So a single myth-ritual complex may involve a whole group of myths and rituals with no apparent relation to each other.

This surely should not be taken as a charter for the structuralist method of joining together all myths relating to a given phenomenon with the aim of finding one structure underlying them all.[34] Hugh-Jones makes another remarkable observation. Between versions of the same myth the degree of variation was, among the people asked, very low; rather, myth tellers were eager to remain consistent and precise in details. They were also keen to distinguish between their own and alien myths, suggesting that the chosen corpus at a particular point in time was clearly circumscribed and agreed upon among people of a certain locality. In other words, every single one of the existing versions is to be taken in its own right—there is always someone with an interest in producing the variation.[35]

To conclude, what is the thrust of this century-long discussion? The study of myth and ritual has perhaps for an unusually long time suffered from a certain type of evolutionist approach. The search for the primacy of myth over ritual and vice versa, as formulated by the Cambridge myth-ritualists of the late nineteenth and early twentieth century, mutated into the claim that myth is the more dominant, even the more sophisticated of the two, while Burkert re-established ritual as a category in its own right at least for Greek antiquity. By contrast, the search for parallels, based on the old idea of myth being the text for ritual, has been tenacious, perhaps not least in consequence of the methods meanwhile developed to see ritual as a form of 'communication', suggesting the analogy (on which see below). The search for such parallels in the classical world has yielded some insights, but on the whole has proved only moderately successful. Detailed myth-ritual sequences exist: certain mystery cults, for example, clearly show parallel mythical and ritual processes, but they are in the minority.[36] Anthropological studies allow us safely to agree that, for the most part, myth and ritual do not reflect each other on a one-to-one basis as the original myth-ritualists argued, and as is often unwittingly still assumed. They may be 'drawing upon a common set of cultural categories, classifications and ideas'[37] through two different media, but it is impossible to argue that ritual literally depicts in action what myth tells in a story.

34 e.g. Detienne (1986) 65: 'a myth must never be interpreted individually, but in its relationship to other myths which, taken together, constitute a transformation group', a claim that is fundamental but can only be part of the story when it limits itself to a synchronic analysis. See Detienne's quotation pp. 20–1 above.

35 Hugh-Jones (1979) esp. 252–60.

36 Graf (1993*a*) 116.

37 Hugh-Jones (1979) 260; superficially alluded to by Rappaport (1979) 134–9; but see already Harrison: pp. 15–16 above.

Instead of searching for parallels in a closed system, we might look at myth and ritual as an open texture where there is not an exclusive relationship between one myth and one ritual: I should like to air the notion of a network of interacting myth*s* and ritual*s*. Hugh-Jones's is the first tentative approach to work with the idea that myths and rituals build a system of relations which invites thinking about myth and ritual not as in a fixed relationship but as consisting of a creative network of complementary traditions related to time and place. Myth and ritual are part of a bigger ensemble of traditions and are obscure in isolation.[38]

This ties in with another problem. All of the above approaches to myth and ritual are synchronic-functionalist. Few consider that myth and ritual develop over time and change places. Myth and ritual do evolve, and this may account for part of the problem in pinning down their relationship. The simple observation that myth and ritual pose all the problems they pose because of the way they relate to change over time should encourage us to introduce a diachronic dimension into the study of myth and ritual, that is, one in which local and temporal variation interacts with particular social circumstances.

Hugh-Jones's study, and to a lesser degree that of Tambiah, suggest, though they do not elaborate on, a further valuable insight, that myth and ritual may do something quite different when they work together in the same setting, which means for us the performative setting of ritual choral song. It may then become apparent that myths do not 'say' the same as ritual but that myths in fact say more if related to ritual and vice versa. 'It is through ritual that the categories of thought can be manipulated to produce effects.'[39]

So instead of mutual reflection, exclusion, or complementarity the notion of interaction might be more helpful: this entails looking at the strategies that myth and ritual deploy in order to 'put their case across'. As I shall argue in the following section, the most conspicuous of these strategies are myth and ritual's relationship particularly to 'time', but also to 'place' and notions of 'space'. The analysis will serve as a starting point for further reflections on how religious performance functions as the medium in which these strategies become active; myth and ritual start interacting and constantly reformulate their relationship. It is on such a basis that the issue of 'myth and ritual' may turn out to embrace far more than the examination of narrative versus enacted sequences: myth and ritual could work as strategic modes of human action which establish, maintain, challenge, and transform social and power relations between the members of the community in which they are performed, and as such are fundamentally related to historical processes.

[38] But see already Lévi-Strauss (1978) 598 indicating the possibility that a number of isolated myths may contribute towards one ritual ('implicit myth'), as opposed to a fully fledged connected narrative ('explicit myth').

[39] Hugh-Jones (1979) 260.

2. AETIOLOGY

It is curious that the theoretical study of 'myth and ritual' has been little concerned with the kind of myth that lends itself most easily to such an examination: aetiological myths with their intrinsic relation to religious practice.[40] Aetiologies, local tales explaining the origin of specific cults, temples, rites, or sacred objects, were central to religious life. The institutions of Greek religion are almost all imagined to have been invented and authoritatively created in Eliade's famous *illud tempus*, in a timeless period of origins. This beginning has supreme authority, and linking oneself to the creative moment offers a share in this authority.[41] Aetiology thus by definition oscillates between mythical past and ritual present, and this circumstance is pivotal for its role in a social context. I shall look here at the strategies aetiology uses in order to configure the relationship between these two spheres.

Religious aetiology creates a map of Greece entirely shaped by itinerant gods, heroes and humans from a distant past, who establish cults and rituals, and set up and carry around cult images and other spoils from a time long ago. Apollo founded his shrine at Delphi, Demeter hers at Eleusis; Herakles established the mysteries at Thasos and the cult of Zeus at Olympia; and Diomedes carted around the Palladion of Trojan Athena in the Italian West. Aetiological myths also account for popular customs or features of geography, often related to a cult as well, through reference to the activities of a mythical predecessor. Few are the cult places in Greece which are not either themselves the product of an individual story or linked into a mythical cycle: the Athenian hero Theseus travels around the Aegean on his way to and from the Minotaur on Crete and litters the island world with cults giving testimony to his journey, even if he is not himself always and in all versions mentioned as a cult's founder.[42] If we traced all the voyages of the gods and heroes on a giant map of the Mediterranean, positioning little figures where they left behind a cult, few spots would remain blank, some would be rather crowded, and certain protagonists would cluster in certain areas. Apollo would feature as a big traveller in the Aegean island world, Hera in southern Italy, Poseidon in the Dodekanese; the Samothracian mysteries would dominate northern Greece, while Artemis sits around the Gulf between Attika and Euboia. If in addition we gave each story-set of cult foundations or divine journeys their own colour, this would very quickly teach us something fundamental about religious aetiology: it lends a place a role in a bigger system, tying the different localities to each other. Aetiology constructs a notion of individual

[40] Graf (1993*a*) 110–18 is a rare treatment of some basic features of aetiological myth, though even he feels the need for justification in treating them in relation to ritual: 'Cult aitia occur most frequently among etiological myths, and for that reason alone the connection between myth and ritual deserves a special consideration' (113).

[41] Eliade esp. (1949; Eng. 1955); also (1969) but the idea is also found in many of his other writings.

[42] Calame (1996*a*) esp. Chs. 3 and 5; Parker (2005) 208–13.

religious 'places' as much as shared 'spaces' in which religious activity can happen.

Aetiology creates a religious world that is tied to visible localities and lived local customs. It is always engrained in the physical world, linked to a tangible reality of cults and rituals, shrines and objects of cult. Unlike what at first sight seems to be 'Panhellenic' mythology—stories of how the Greek gods came into existence, such as those of Hesiod's *Theogony*—cult aetiology is always geographically bound: it is what one sometimes hears referred to as the *hieros logos* of a particular place of importance in local religion. Aetiology thus has a share in everyday religious practice; and it creates social explanations of items in use by a community of myth-tellers. More than any other type of myth, it justifies Burkert's conception of myth as bearing with it concrete, applicable social relevance: 'myth is a [sc. meaningful] traditional tale with secondary, partial reference to something of collective importance [sc. for the present]. Myth is traditional tale applied; and its relevance and seriousness stem largely from this application.'[43]

There is a widespread perception that aetiology accounts for queer things: it preferably picks up on features of the real world that strike the human eye as being particularly odd, rare, or remarkable. This assumption used to go along with the romantic idea that aetiology is a primitive form of wisdom, reflecting man's ever-developing propensity for rational thinking; aetiology showed man's inborn desire for an explanation of the world around him.[44] It is probably true that aetiologies tend to have a particular grip on unusual features of the human surroundings; it is equally true, however, that, as modern Greek parallels show,[45] aetiology picks up on things because they are characteristic of, and relevant to, the community in which they serve. The point of having an extra story for a feature in local religion lies in being able to distinguish one's own cult or ritual from others, in making a special case for the cult involved. It might not have occurred to anyone to ask for the mythical origins of the reformed Areopagus in mid-fifth-century Athens, so powerfully staged in Aeschylus' *Oresteia*, had it not received a new social importance. In this sense, aetiology of course picks up on remarkable features of a cult, but not primarily because they are intrinsically striking but because they are different. Only in this sense is it true to say that 'if the thing lost its distinctive feature, the aetiology got forgotten'.[46] In stronger terms, aetiology is the narrated form of diversity in Greek religion. In accounting for diversity, giving an identity to a place and a community of myth-tellers, lies aetiology's greatest potential for acting as a tale of social relevance in the Burkertian sense.

The rhythms by which aetiologies appear and disappear already suggest that there is something rather idiosyncratic about how these stories provide

[43] Burkert (1979*a*) 23; cf. the even more explicit German formulation in Burkert (1979*b*) 1–34, esp. 29; similar concepts in Graf (1993*a*) 1–8, and (1993*b*) 42–3.

[44] For the older view of aetiology as a scientific explanation that grew out of the naive mind of as yet undeveloped peoples see e.g. Gunkel (1910) xx; Dähnhardt (1907–12) i, vii.

[45] Many examples of this can be found in Polites' collection (1994 (1904)) (vol. i).

[46] Graf (1993*a*) 113.

explanations for human institutions. Aetiology's handling of time is a key strategy in the aetiological logic. The word 'aetiology'—αἴτιον λέγειν 'to give a reason'—suggests a means of explanation. Effectively, however, aetiology reduces the connecting of cause with effect to connecting mythical past directly with the present, thereby achieving a transcendence of time. Aetiology thus engages with history by abolishing it, by denying change through time. It often does so by postulating the continuity of a religious locality, of a circumscribed religious space, a structured ritual environment—of what I shall call in shorthand religious 'place'.

Aetiology does work causally, but develops a very special form of causation. Broadly speaking, the Greek world distinguishes between three associated forms of thinking in which aetiology features as a concept of causation, that is aetiology in science, in history, and in mythology.[47] Scientific aetiology from Democritus to Aristotle comprises the search for the principle of causation based on logical or empirical deduction.[48] A kind of historical aetiologizing is sometimes associated with Herodotus' ideas of causation and his deductive methods.[49] His handling of aetiology introduces an important temporal component into the causative character of aetiological thinking. For Herodotus, aetiology seems to be a particular way of connecting historical processes of different time frames, and especially a way of relating events of the past with the narrator's present. To name a striking example, in the excursus on Aiginetan history, which seeks to account for the παλαιὴ ἔχθρη, the 'ancestral hatred' between Athens and Aigina, a series of aetiological *logoi* from Greek local history is recounted. Grouped one after the other, these stories approach Herodotus' present step by step. They constitute a continuous chain of causes that connect a past that lies further away with one closer to hand and, ultimately, with the present.[50] What emerges here is that an older time is always responsible for a younger time; the past is thought to be causative, and the chain of causes develops into a chain of pasts. The past in itself becomes explanatory, if not to say authoritative—one of the features through which oral history and myth-telling has left its stamp on the *Histories*.

It is the tendency to identify causal and temporal explanation that is significant for the workings of 'mythical' (= religious) aetiology. The distinction between the

[47] For such a general distinction see e.g. Cancik-Lindemaier (1988); Loehr (1996) 1–31.

[48] The term 'aetiology' is usually applied both to Democritus' division of natural phenomena into single 'causes' and, on the other end of the scale, to Aristotelian teleology and its separation between φαινόμενα and αἰτίαι; see, among many treatments of the issue, Regenbogen (1931); Kullmann (1974). It is known in medical analysis from Hippokrates to the present day, and in the Thucydidean distinction between two different levels of causes, even if his differentiation between *prophasis* and *aitiai* works in a different way. See Rechenauer (1991).

[49] Schmid and Staehlin (1934) 571 and n. 3; 604 and n. 8; 606 n. 3 on Herodotus' aetiology, though their general idea of history (601–2) is problematic.

[50] Hdt. 5.82 ff. The story-chain relates how the Aiginetans slowly but securely turned from being intimately tied to Athens to political and cultural independence, involving the gradual appropriation and reinterpretation of the cult of the heroines Damia and Auxesia, which originally symbolized the bond. A good analysis of the passage, with some details regarding its 'aetiological' nature, can be found in Figueira (1993*d*): see below, Ch. 4 pp. 211–12.

Herodotean search for causes and 'mythical' aetiology can of course not be clearly drawn. Mythical aetiology explains a present state of affairs entirely in mythical terms; the authority of the mythical time period alone is explanatory, there is no more 'chain of pasts'. Any other causal dimension is lost entirely in favour of the authority of the mythical world: myth *is* the cause. What in science, and to a certain degree in history, has a multifaceted causal relationship is now reduced to a temporal one. The distinction becomes visible when one considers the methods of deduction underlying the three types of aetiologizing. In natural science, the 'truth' of the aetiological deduction can be proved by multiple repetition of the same experiment or the same observation. If we asked Herodotus how he went about finding his truths, the answer would probably be that he spoke with various independent sources who reported one and the same event. Mythical aetiology, however, as long as it is an 'applied tale' emerging from given social contexts, denies the possibility of multiple deduction. The accountability of the repeated experiment or repeated story-telling is fully taken over by the authority of the mythical world. Such mythical causation cannot be questioned beyond the subjective belief of a group of myth-tellers: if and when it is being told, a working aetiology aims to be the only credible tradition, to be entirely authoritative. That many Greek cults boast a host of competing cult legends is a product of aetiology's claim to veracity and ultimate unverifiability.

So mythical aetiology, while pretending to connect cause with effect, really relates present with a mythical past. It seems to establish a timeless continuity from the moment of origins to the present day, and claims that things have remained unchanged throughout. All aetiology's principal features and techniques are geared towards achieving this transcendence of time—most conspicuously through banking on the continuity of religious 'place'. Aetiological thinking is thus fundamentally circular; mythical past and ritual present interact at every stage. If aetiology's transcendence of time seems to oscillate in a contradictory way between denying the progress of time and asserting continuity, this is precisely due to the constant interaction of past and present in aetiology. This interaction comes to bear particularly on aetiology's relationship to place, time, and its narrative shape.

There is first and foremost, aetiology's love for the physical world, integrating features of an existing religious environment, temples, heroic graves, sacred ways, mountain-top shrines into its narrative (hence the frequent appearance of a seemingly unchanging landscape). The visible locality or the ritual space where the story happens or a rite is still to be observed form the most important link between the events portrayed in the aetiological tale and the religious reality which the myth seeks to explain. The whole story quite literally revolves around this locality or object, inferring from its object in the present a likeness in a tale set in the past, in order to explain its present shape by reference to this past. After this one point of metamorphosis in a primordial time, the *aition* claims, the state of affairs has always remained the same. If the story's object is physical, a temple or a monument, its appearance has not changed since; if it purports to account for a rite or habit, a kind of aetiological clock ensures continual repetition of the same processes or the same ritual journey at regular intervals. And so the mere existence of the aetiologized object or custom in the present functions as the guarantor for the truth of this continuum.

The connection to the real world importantly suggests a degree of objectivity in the circular process of aetiologizing: it is the temple of Demeter with the funny akroteria for which an explanation is sought, but the old temple is there to prove what is being told about it: the continuity of 'place' furnishes the proof for the sought-for temporal continuity. Aetiology's visible object is inherently ambiguous: quite often in the mythical narrative a cult place or a ritual already function in the way they are only about to be set up to work; the stories are full of anachronisms. So an aetiological tale seeks to elicit belief in its story by presupposing continuity through time of the locality that is its object: time-travelling localities—not just temples, but also lakes, mountains, islands—are one of the narrative strategies that aetiology applies in order to achieve its transcendence of time.[51]

Aetiology thus transcends real (historical) time by postulating a physical or local continuity of religious place. In reality, therefore, aetiology does not even deal with time other than by transcending it. This feature obviously determines its relationship to 'history' ('history' as I understand it entailing change through time): aetiology lacks differentiation in time through the abolition of the historical process. Studies concerned with the anthropology of time have often found that the 'time of the ancestors', and the authority going with it, remains unaffected by the passage of real time.[52]

This has certain ramifications. Aetiology and the degree to which it may represent historical processes was at one point a hotly disputed issue in Old Testament studies, the only discipline ever to have explored features of aetiology in greater detail.[53] The controversy arose over aetiology's relation to archaeological remains of cult places. Surviving traces of the Israelites were thought either to have stimulated aetiological myth in the first place, or, on the contrary, to have supported a transmission of hard facts over time. The theological discussion rather unsurprisingly ended in an aporia, that while elements of a past may survive, actual historical processes cannot be sought in aetiology's narrative alone.[54] What makes this debate intriguing for us is that aetiology's most effective tool, its play with the illusion of continuity, for a long time puzzled these students.

This is not to say that aetiology is devoid of historical meaning—quite the contrary. But it confirms another fundamental in the study of Greek religion: myth does represent a truth, and that is the truth believed by the people who care about telling it. A working aetiology makes statements about history bound to the

[51] The 'materialization' of social memories in archaeological remains is a related phenomenon: see e.g. Alcock (2002); Alcock and Van Dyke (2003).

[52] Gell (1992) gives an interpretative overview of approaches to social conceptions of time. Cf. also the critical essay by Munn (1992).

[53] See Golka (1970); (1972); (1976); (1977); B. O. Long (1968) and briefly Loehr (1996) 4–8.

[54] Physical remains as a mnemotechnic device: Albright (1946) 39; (1939) 11–23. Alt (1953) 21 denies *any* history coming from aetiology.

moment in which it is being told.[55] Though claiming to be explanatory of the past, aetiology accounts for the significance of its object for the present, its role in a living and myth-telling, local community. It offers a plan, an outline of belief for the present backed by mythical authority. Thus aetiological myths constitute no more, and no less, than a charter for the particular interpretation of their object, delivering proof for how things are written into the religious landscape. Aetiology acts out truths of the present in the mythical past, telling us a lot about the present in which it is being narrated and in which it is culturally relevant; about the past that it pretends to describe, however, it conveys very little.

But aetiology is still more shrewd than this. In offering a perceived past that is believed, or claiming a truth that should be believed, it deliberately plays with the unverifiability of its contention. Its subjective relation to historical truth thus invests it with great potential: in a world where right, privilege, or obligation to worship in a particular cult were rarely uncontested, this yields interesting battles for the truth, expressed in the almost infinite number of competing myths.[56] It is not so much the fact that everybody may have believed something different as the social and political consequences of the plurality of acclaimed truths that make this observation fruitful for understanding some of the workings of Greek religion. While the multiple truths competing with and accommodating each other are generally seen more as a problem than as an opportunity, it is exactly this plurality that makes aetiology so much a part of social negotiation. Greek mythology, and aetiology in particular, is not codified; it is competed over and disputed.

Next, aetiologies come in stories. This may sound like a truism, but the nature of aetiology's narrative is more delicate than a superficial glance might suggest. Here, too, we see the mythical past and the ritual present crisscrossing, transcendence of time achieved through stipulating a continuity of religious place. The narrative builds the formal framework for aetiology's transcendence of time: it makes possible the connection between mythical past and narrative present. Aetiology's inherent circularity and its anchor in the present are conspicuous formal features of aetiological myth. Typically structured as a *Ringkomposition*, every aetiological myth works on at least two interconnected time levels, that of the narrator telling the story, and that of the event that is being told. The object (temple, rite, cult image) for which an *aition* is being told is the centre of attention in both time spheres; both time levels seem to converge in this object. As a consequence, a continuous aetiological narrative allows the narrator to connect smoothly the present with the narrated past and to establish that very same continuum between the first cause and the present state of affairs that achieves the transcendence of time.

[55] This is a view taken by some Old Testament scholars but not explored further: Noth (1960) 279–80; Smend (1968) 15.

[56] Just as multiple beliefs compete within the individual (Veyne (1988; Fr. 1983)): this is perhaps something inherent in the 'eminently social' character and shape of Greek religion. For comments on Veyne see e.g. Méheust (1990) and Buxton (1994) 155–65.

Aetiology in all cultures develops a set of formulae to express this relationship exactly. These phrases occur in historiographical and antiquarian texts, and are a conspicuous stylistic feature in religious song.[57] Both entry to and exit from the aetiological tale are clearly marked. The object of aetiological interest is typically introduced by a main clause followed by a relative construction, often qualified by a temporal particle. Bacchylides' *Ode 11* (Ch. 6), for instance, introduces the myth dealing with the shrine of Artemis at S. Biagio near Metapontion as νῦν δ' Ἄρτεμις . . . νίκαν ἔδωκε. τ]ᾶι ποτ' Ἀβαντιάδας β]ωμὸν κατένασσε πολύλλ[ι]στον εὔπεπλοί τε κοῦραι; 'and now Artemis . . . has granted victory, for her once upon a time the son of Abas [sc. Proitos] and his beautifully robed daughters founded a much-frequented altar'. *Olympian 10* starts Herakles' institution of the Olympian games with ἀγῶνα δ' ἐξαίρετον ἀεῖσαι θέμιτες ὦρσαν Διός, ὃν ἀρχαίῳ σάματι πὰρ Πέλοπος βωμὸν ἑξάριθμον ἐκτίσσατο 'the ordinances of Zeus have prompted me to sing of the choice contest, which [Herakles] founded with its six altars by the ancient tomb of Pelops'. The implicit change of time level is accompanied by a discreet change of narrative tense, through which the story quietly catapults its audience from a ritual present into the mythical past.[58]

Similarly, at its close the myth can end in the way it started, by various pronoun references, as in a paean fragment by Bacchylides, recounting the story of Apollo's cult at Asine (Ch. 3): κεί]νας ἀπὸ ῥίζας τὸ δὲ χρ [– – ⏑ – – ἐξό]χως τίμασ' Ἀπόλλων ἄλσο]ς, ἵν' ἀγλαΐαι τ' ἀνθ]εῦσ[ι] καὶ μολπαὶ λίγ[ειαι 'from that root Apollo honoured this [oracular shrine ab]ove all, where there blossom festivities and lucid voices'.[59] In many if not most cases, the narrative states the continuum from the first establishment of a custom through phrases such as ἐκ τότε, νῦν γάρ, and, especially καί νυν 'since then', 'for now', 'and so even now'.[60] But a local reference such as the ἵνα 'where' of the paean is just as frequent. And, subsequently, the change from past to present tense within the same sentences beams the listener back from the mythical past into the ritual present.

Aetiology's formulaic features aim at transcendence of time in the most comfortable way. The boundary formulae help to regulate the narrative jetlag bound to arise in every aetiological tale. These idioms are comparable perhaps to the 'once upon a time', or to the 'and they lived happily for ever after' of fairy-tales. Little investigation of Greek cult myths (as opposed to heroic tale) has been conducted with respect to its formulaic character: most Greek mythical narrative is preserved in 'literary works' full of such features of an ultimately oral tradition

[57] This may be due to the degree of imitation of authentic myth-telling that is attempted in religious poetry.

[58] Bacch. 11. 37–42; Pi. *Ol.* 10. 24–5 (tr. Race; βωμόν). Pelliccia (1989) makes some interesting remarks on the 'syntax' of aetiology, which often combines past and present tenses in the same sentence to indicate the aetiological 'punch line'.

[59] Bacch. fr. 4.54–6.

[60] Other such formulae include νῦν δέ, ἐξ οὗ. E.g. Pi. *O.* 1.90; 3.34; 6.71; 10.78; or more generally to relate mythical examples to a victor: *P.* 3.66; or simply past to present: *N.* 6.8. A list of occurrences of e.g. καὶ νῦν in Greek literature would be infinite. For example Plut. *Thes.* is notorious for the number of editorial comments on Theseus' many cult foundations.

of religious myths. The aetiological formula is only the most obvious of traces of the rather set nature of Greek mythology, which also characterizes Greek literature.[61]

Aetiological myths are not always consistent in their usage of these formulae, and the idea that only myths ending in these formulae are aetiologies cannot be maintained. Such phrases, often called 'editorial comments', have served both to identify aetiological tales and to distinguish different strands of narration in the Old Testament as they do in Herodotus' network of local tales. In the Old Testament, the formula 'until this day' tags deviation from the main narrative into the believed origins of religious customs, institutions, and, most often, names.[62] Those literary signposts do not, however, justify separating the aetiological tale from the context in which it is being told.[63] Aetiological myths do not normally exist in a narrative vacuum, as the very biography of Theseus suggests. Independent aetiological myths eventually find entry into the antiquarian tradition, at the latest at the time of Callimachus. Neither a Euripidean nor a choral aetiology is bereft of its narrative, or rather performative, context. And in some ways one is inclined to think that the nature of aetiological myth with its inherent circularity forbids an absolute *aition* without social relevance. What is crucial in aetiological myth, then, is not formal shape but social relevance.

It is a consequence, and this brings us back to the opening, that aetiology does not, in fact probably cannot, exist without a wider religious reference system. Gods and heroes employed in aetiological myth make sense only through an overarching framework that defines their relations to each other. Mythical causality can only work if the plot is acted out by people who matter. 'Panhellenic mythology' might provide such a reference framework, but in reality Greek mythology is constituted of a number of interconnected such frameworks which exist on various levels, local, regional, Panhellenic, with many fluid stages in between. Damia and Auxesia, for example, are local heroines of Epidauros, but their cult spreads over various locales in the area of the Saronic Gulf and reflects the way participant *poleis* relate socially and politically to one another. Cult founders are often itinerant heroes who cover a wide range of attached or adjacent localities, as Melampous pervades the Argolid and Messenia, but unless they are a universal Herakles they are irrelevant in other sacred geographies. The cultic landscape of Epeiros and southern Italy is the product of a particular

[61] This set of issues has been explored more for epic and lyric poetry, much less for drama: Martin (1989); Nagy (1990).

[62] See e.g. Childs (1963); Golka (1972); (1976); (1977). In Old Testament studies it is a recurrent issue whether the biblical aetiologies were originally independent local tales and were welded into the overarching narrative framework. A comparison between the formulae of biblical and Greek historiography is conducted by Seeligman (1961) 141–69; see also folklore studies such as Baumann (1959) 9: 'aitiologische Schlußformeln haben eine oft nicht mit dem Mythos, Märchen oder Sage zusammenhängende Funktion'; 'explanatorisches Element . . . als "after thought" '.

[63] In Old Testament and folklore studies the formulae were the formal criterion for identifying an aetiological tale: Westermann (1964) 39–47 and Schuir (1930–40).

set of figures of the *Nostoi* tradition such as Odysseus, Diomedes, Epeios, and Philoktetes, who hardly affect mainland Greece.[64]

Aetiology brings to the fore the largely unexplored phenomenon of the 'diffusion' of mythic figures and the cults they found. Heroes and gods act as unifying figures for entire areas; they are definitely more than local but they do not spread randomly. It would thus be wrong and unproductive to reduce the issue to an opposition between 'the local' and 'the Panhellenic'. Rather, aetiology is socially especially active in the space in between, in those intermediate realms that characterize the local histories of Greece. Aetiology functions as a connective both within a local religious framework and in its relation to others: heroes and gods related to each other in intricate networks constitute a valid reference system through which relations between cults and their worshipping communities are expressed. The thing to keep in mind for the moment is that aetiology is a way of connecting individual localities to a wider framework of religious activity. The resulting dynamic is one of the themes in this book.

To summarize, aetiology emerges as possessing a set of intricately linked attributes. A cultic *aition* is a mythical story pretending to be an explanation for the nature of things visible in the ritual present of the narrator and audience. Using the authority of the mythical world, it develops a strategy to that effect, a strategy of pretence. Aitia are characterized by a notorious argumentative circularity: the *aition* replaces a chain of causal relationships with a timeless continuum that effects the transcendence of real time, and thus of history. In its object or locality it has an anchor to the real world that, functioning as a hinge element, serves to connect past and present in a timeless continuum. It does not therefore explain the past but offers an explanation of the myth-tellers' present. Most importantly, therefore, aetiology derives its charter value from its ability to bring the mythical past into the ritual present, while at the same time this past is anachronistic, a product of the present. Mythical past and ritual present thus at any stage interact in aetiology. Finally, it is bound to locality, not to isolate it from, but rather to connect it with, others; aetiology is a phenomenon that has to do with the creation not just of religious place, but more dynamically, of religious space.

3. RITUAL

One reason why the theoretical debate of myth and ritual has advanced methodologically so little since the Second World War may lie in the fact that, since Lévi-Strauss at least, myth and ritual have developed as different areas of study and have, with a few notable exceptions, not been considered as an

[64] Damia and Auxesia: Aigina, Epidauros, Troizen (Ch. 4 n. 78). For Melampous see Ch. 6. below; similarly wandering seers: Scheer (1993) 153–271. For the *Nostoi* traditions see Malkin (1998*b*) Chs. 6–8, who attaches these legends to native populations.

ensemble. The result of this is that our ideas about both myth and ritual have significantly changed since the Cambridge ritualists first initiated the discussion, but changes in the one area have had few repercussions on the other. In anthropology the study of ritual for the last three decades has been flourishing while myth lags behind. Conversely, Lévi-Strauss's preference for myth has stimulated classicists to concentrate particularly on the workings of myth. Studies by Jean-Pierre Vernant, Pierre Vidal-Naquet, Marcel Detienne, and in the wider orbit of the Centre Louis Gernet in Paris have produced sophisticated approaches towards myth and the way religious imagination worked in archaic and classical Greek society.[65] More recently, work such as that of Irad Malkin or Jonathan Hall has engaged with the charter value of myth. Moving away from myth's concern with human preoccupations (such as initiation) and taking myth as a means of mapping out territorial and kinship claims has stimulated a fashionable, if slightly dispersed, field.[66]

What is common to many of the interesting new ways of looking at classical myth is that they bear little or no relation to ritual. This is reflected in a more general trend. Paradoxically, while from the late nineteenth century actual rituals came to dominate the existing textbooks on Greek religion,[67] ideas about ancient ritual have, despite Walter Burkert's courageous advances, remained rather static. By contrast, the discipline of ritual studies in anthropology has moved on considerably from the assumptions on which many classical studies are still built. The potential of what we now think ritual can do has been little exploited for antiquity.[68] If the particular dynamic of aetiological myth is related to that offered by ritual, that might also change our ideas about the possibilities of exploring myth and ritual in ancient Greece. Part of the aim of this section is therefore to convey a sense of the multifold and intricate range of communicative possibilities emerging from ritual.

This task may sound easier than it is. 'Ritual studies' is a wide-ranging, popular discipline that reaches from anthropology via theology to modern history. The literature on the subject is vast and diffuse, a feature that finds reflection in a recent book on the socio-cultural phenomenon of 'ritual', which stands at a proud 650 pages.[69]

Ritual has long been recognized as a heuristic tool for social history, either as one of many systems of cultural knowledge, or as a form of social activity itself:

[65] Vernant (1983; Fr. 1965); (1979; Fr. 1974); Vidal-Naquet (1986; Fr. 1981); Detienne (1977); (1986; Fr. 1981) to name just the landmark studies.

[66] Malkin (1994); (1997); (1998*b*). Cf. e.g. Scheer (1993); J. Hall (1997); (2002); but see already Nilsson (1951). Csapo (2005) is a recent study examining the different concepts of myth often applied to classical mythology.

[67] e.g. the various works by Usener (1912–13), or Nilsson (1906/95).

[68] Some (often recent) exceptions: Price (1984) esp. 9–11 on Sperber's approach to symbols (1975; Fr. 1974); Scheid (2005) 275–84; cf. Chaniotis (2002) and (2005). Graf's *Gray Lectures*, Cambridge 2000, on late antique Roman festivals in Asia Minor, addressed problems of power and representation that will be relevant here. Similarly, Beard's paper on the Roman triumphus (Oxford, 2001) was concerned with ritual's strategies of communication; see also *ead.* (1988) and Elsner (1998).

[69] Rappaport (1999).

ritual produces a picture of society, rituals make statements about society, give ideas about how society is, could, or should be, and what the relations between individuals or groups in that society are. However, it is ritual's relation to 'time', especially the past, that has really changed the subject, and made the study of ritual—among many other things—a subdiscipline, and a tool, of the study of culture through time, that is history. For a long time rituals were examined as something static and unchanging, confirming a given social order. Especially in Classics, ritual is still relatively rarely studied as a productive force, a dynamic agent, which derives its power not from a fixed relation, but from a dialogue, with its own past. Traditional anthropology, in the sway of functionalism, adopted a purely synchronic approach. It is only recently, with growing interest in anthropology in the historical disciplines, that ritual has received a diachronic dimension, and been thought of as creative in historical processes. Work on the formation of the modern nation-state, where unified pasts had to be invented often with the help of a reconfiguration in ritual of figures from a 'mythical' past, have paved the way for more flexible reflection. The thinking about ritual has moved away from the idea that ritual is something fixed and inflexible towards a view that sees in ritual a dynamic and efficient element of social activity, firmly rooted in the present rather than the past. Rituals are constantly renewed and reformed in performance, oscillating as they are between ossification and creativity. A powerful tool for creating and maintaining social relations, ritual emerges as a medium for accommodating change.[70]

The late recognition of this truth may at first sight seem extraordinary: the anti-positivistic rebound that dominated much of twentieth-century scholarship certainly contributed to depriving ritual of that dimension that crucially determines its workings, that is 'time'. The fault lies in a simple truism. For ritual is a false friend: rituals are old. They are traditional, they have remained the same over years or decades or centuries, for the Greeks since the mythical period. They are intrinsically non-changing, guardians of a past with which participants would like to associate themselves. From the common-sense idea of what ritual seems to be, they must therefore be resistant to change. The whole common-sense notion that religions are notoriously 'conservative' largely derives from the basic—and as will emerge misconceived—idea that rituals are of necessity ancient. By contrast, being antique is a strategy of ritual. Ritual convinces, ritual persuades by its antiquity. Rituals have to be ancient in order to be accepted and to be effective. All rituals only work on the assumption that they continue old practices. Being old is an appearance of ritual, but more importantly it is a technique, something that ritual aspires to. All the characteristics of ritual are geared towards this goal—its formality, archaism, symbolism, repetition.

[70] This is the necessarily superficial impression arising from a survey of the literature. Bell (1992) and (1997) works the history of the subject into her own theory of ritual and is central to the field. Other recent approaches include Asad (1993); also J. Z. Smith (1987); Buc (2001); Schmitt (1999); Muir (1997); Trexler (1980) for changes in and through ritual in early modern Europe; Hobsbawm and Ranger (1983) with a wider notion of 'ritual'. Problems of the definition of 'ritual' recur in all these studies, first aired by Goody (1977).

I can anticipate myself here in saying that aetiology and ritual behave similarly both in their professed and real relation to time. Both have to be ancient to be believed. They use comparable strategies for making their case, and both are jugglers of time levels. Just as aetiology has the authority of a mythical past to prove the truth of its story, ritual banks on the authority of a traditional practice handed down from the past. The past has a similarly sanctifying authority in granting the truth (or the significance) of what is being carried out in the ritual. Through continuous enactment ritual purports to establish a continuum with the past, and the implication that the world has remained unchanged ever since the rite was first enacted. Because of its perennial existence in practice, in producing an image of an unchanged society ritual too transcends real time. Rituals, just as aetiological myth, therefore have something of an atemporal and universal character.[71]

The idea that rituals claim to transcend time in this way, that their enactment creates an illusion of a timeless continuum from a distant model of society, poses no problems to a functionalist theory and what followed from this theory. In fact it goes to the very heart of how rituals work. At the bottom lies an idea shared by most ritual theorists: ritual transcends social reality by creating a sense of community. Ritual is a form of representational behaviour, in ritual you behave not as you do in real life; you mark a particular occasion as special. The bulk of ritual theories in anthropology work on the assumption that ritual overcomes the problems of social reality. Rituals maintain social cohesion through a common emotional experience sanctified by a common tradition.[72] The synchronic approach to ritual has difficulty in accounting for what rituals do to a community that *believes* in this continuum while the community itself is continuously changing—no community exists in a historical vacuum.

It is this sense of community that I shall engage with first. Looking for the universally underlying cognitive and behavioural structures of society, this approach goes back at least to the nineteenth-century scholar William Robertson Smith, and finds its most prominent expression in Durkheim's functionalist interpretation of ritual as a mirror of society itself. Ritual's collectively projected representations of society are a basic function in the process by which religion sacralizes the structure of, and social relations within, the worshipping community. A form of hyperindividual, emotionally highly charged experience, ritual thus serves to generate and support communal identification, ensuring and maintaining social cohesion.[73]

[71] Cf. e.g. the formulation by Leach (1966) 411–13: '[performing ritual] implies to be . . . guided by rules whose claim to validity is based upon the general acknowledgement of those who practise them that these rules are theirs and proper to them, ancient and to be observed because things should be done in that way, as they were done before by their forebears: tradition justifies their practice'.

[72] Representatives of this line of thought are most prominent post-Durkheimians, such as Radcliffe-Brown (1964 (1933)); Evans-Pritchard (1974 (1957)); Geertz (1966); Turner (1969); (1974*a*), etc.

[73] Tylor (1958; orig. 1871); Robertson Smith (1889); Durkheim (1915, Fr. 1912).

Although Durkheim himself was interested in the 'origins' of religion in society and his approach may be described as vaguely evolutionary, the idea of religion as collectively projected representations of society shaped the more developed forms of largely ahistorical functionalism and later structuralism.[74] Much subsequent ritual theory kept working on the assumption that ritual was largely supportive of balanced social interaction and a given world order, and on the premise of a closed, static society lacking exchange with others. To account for the nevertheless visible dynamism in society, however, a certain number of cultural and other contexts have been introduced to the intrinsically stable community. Ritual ecologists, for example, see ritual as a means to regulate and maintain the relationships between social systems, and between social systems and the natural resources of the environment. Other such neo-functional approaches include those of ethologists who derive ritual forms from processes of natural selection modelled on the animal world; or attempts to ground ritual behaviour in society in fundamental psychological experiences that lie at the base of human relations such as that between mother and new-born child,[75] ideas which have been taken up by Walter Burkert in his recent work.[76]

The idea that ritual is essentially conservative when constraining and maintaining the social status quo also resurfaces in the attempts made to supersede it. In a series of approaches culminating in the important work of Victor Turner, ritual appears not any more as a forum in which a static unity of society is celebrated, but as one in which a society constantly disassembles and reassembles itself in a social drama that enacts the extremes between normality and crisis. This should account for the frequent dissolving of social boundaries during ritual time. With its emphasis on process, Turner's model takes up something of Van Gennep's three stages of initiation ritual mentioned earlier (separation—transition—reintegration). Ritual ecstasy expresses the tensions within society while the ritual procedure pieces back together elements of conflict into the old equilibrium of social relations. Such 'ritual process' entails not only the reconfirmation, but above all the recreation of a given society every time through the experience of what Turner termed *communitas*: the notion of a fruitful dynamic between structure and anti-structure, the turning of the obligatory into the desirable.[77]

Turner's ideas of the ritual channelling of social conflict through the invocation of *communitas* singles out liminality, a temporary distance from the accustomed social order, as a factor actively determining the dynamics of society. This vision has become very dear to classical scholarship: classicists have notoriously been interested in the opposing forces acting within society and its cultural system, expressed in rituals of change of status such as initiation or

[74] For critique see B. Morris (1987) 186–203, 122–31; Aron (1967); Lukes (1973); Pickering (1984).

[75] Ecologists: Rappaport (1979); M. Harris (1977); ethologists: the basic work is in J. Huxley (1966*a*) esp. his introd. 1966*b* and Lorenz (1966); psychologists: Erikson (1966).

[76] Burkert (1996).

[77] Turner (1969); (1974*a*); interesting is also (1974*b*).

marriage, many of which involve rituals of liminality and reintegration.[78] To take a known example, a popular (though not uncontested) interpretation of the City Dionysia at Athens understands the festival as a temporary dissolution of a series of social boundaries, between men and women, *oikos* and *polis*, or, more abstractly, the visible and the invisible (hence the carrying of masks), thereby actually confirming the social order and hierarchies in the Athenian democracy.[79] The fusion of boundaries between social statuses that are discrete in social reality is typical of such rituals. Perhaps, however, because it is almost too convenient a theoretical framework, Turner's influential insights have to a certain extent prevented, rather than stimulated, the exploration of more complex and varied social uses of ritual. What therefore has become prominent in the classicists' notion of ritual is the concept of liminality in rituals of change of status and the experience of social solidarity or *communitas*.

Both ritual's potential and its grammar for regulating social conflict have been exploited much beyond the immensely popular model of Turner, and in a variety of disciplines. But what these approaches all share, with sophisticated differentiation, is a view of ritual ultimately maintaining social stability. Ritual on this view often acts as the purifier of the impending pollution of imminent social chaos. The anthropologist Max Gluckman, for example, corrected the idea of ritual merely expressing social cohesion by introducing the notion of 'rituals of rebellion' (on which a little more below). Ritual temporarily turns upside down the hierarchy of everyday social relations, for example in transvestite rites when women take on the role of men, but do so in a hyperbolic way, being 'excessively male'. Ritual thus enacts tensions within society through wild exaggeration of the real issues of life in representative behaviour, but is ultimately geared at the continuity and cohesion of the community.[80] Edmund Leach saw the trick in symbolism: symbols, through their fluidity, help to achieve the transition from one social state to another: only ritual can transfer boy to warrior. Even a writer of such extravagance as Pierre Bourdieu sees rituals as strategic practices to transgress and reshuffle cultural categories in order to meet the conflicts arising from situations in real life.[81]

Approaches working on the notion of ritual holding up social cohesion make many fine observations. They mark out ritual as a special event, hyperindividual, often turning reality upside down and teasing out the very limits of human

[78] I pick randomly, Vidal-Naquet's *Black Hunter* (1986, Fr. 1981); or Winkler (1990); Seaford (1988); Goldhill (1986) 177–9; Kurke (1991) part i on the rituals of 'return' after victory. Turner's model underlies the work of many outstanding religious historians, most prominently perhaps that of F. Graf.

[79] I simplify for the sake of clarity an interpretation of Dionysism most persistently defended perhaps by Seaford (1994); (1996). Facets of this view can often be traced in the interpretation of tragedy and its relation to its ritual context: e.g. Goldhill (1986); Zeitlin (1996).

[80] Gluckman (1962*b*) esp. 42. A good summary of Gluckman's important ideas can be found in Bell (1997) 38–40; 52–5.

[81] Bourdieu (1977); Leach, esp. (1976).

relations. Above all, they bring out the role of 'community' invoked in ritual. If scrutinised in more detail, however, the social cohesion theory has a number of problems. And those problems lie precisely in this idea of the image of *communitas* called up in ritual representations which are thought to maintain a (sense of) community. One problem, which affect anthropological studies more than historical anthropology, is that it is essentially idealistic—it starts from a concept of society as an ideal, harmonious grouping of people as conservative as the rituals it performs and denying change. Another is an implicit or explicit assumption of a strong authority and the notion of a powerful apparatus supporting the pomp that inculcates a set of values, and the identity of 'state' and 'religious' authority. For archaic and classical Greece, neither of these things are given, or are only partly granted: this is a society undergoing rapid and intense social transformation, and what and how homogeneous an authority there was to back the festival culture is a much-debated question.[82]

Viewing ritual in terms of social unity curiously overlooks the workings of the very medium that it studies: the fact that ritual *stages* a model of the world and sets up a claim to a reality without necessarily fulfilling it. The power of ritual lies exactly in the kind of powerful suggestions it makes about social reality under the aegis of divine authority. How are we to assess, for example, the fact that Athens' allies turned up at the fifth-century Panathenaia, and thereby demonstrated their solidarity with their radiant mother city, while at the same time they devised secession back home? Ritual pictures a differentiated worshipping group in which as many relations are depicted as there are ritual participants. But it gives a picture of social relations within the worshipping community whose bearing on reality might lie somewhere between full correspondence to reality and total lie. The community depicted is just as likely to be imagined as real. Ritual invents a social reality and hopes that this proposal may appeal. It claims a truth but it defies any means of verification of this truth. The ceremonial invocation of *communitas* is therefore a tool in the creation, maintenance and transformation of social relations between participants. The idea of Turner's *communitas* as illusion or even 'deception' affords ritual a character much more dynamic than one might at first think. And this is where I believe the potential of ritual in social situations lies.

What is at stake can perhaps be illustrated by a few more ritual variations. Mikhail Bakhtin's studies on carnival traditions in early modern France have prompted a vivid interest in 'rituals of reversal' and the potential for subversion. Carnival is a populist, utopian vision of the world, a critique of authority through the inversion of social hierarchies.[83] But such rituals of reversal were

[82] On the question of ritual and strong/weak institutional authorities supporting it, see the interesting considerations in Buc (2000).

[83] Bakhtin (1968) 11–12: 'As opposed to official feast, carnival celebrates temporary liberation from the prevailing truth of the established order; marks the suspension of the hierarchical rank, privileges, norms, prohibitions. Carnival was the true feast of time, the feast of becoming, change and reversal. Hostile to all that was immortalised and complete.'

often appropriated by the ruling powers as a way to control, not to instigate the potential for rebellion.[84] This set of ideas has been popular in the study of Greek religion and drama performed at the Dionysia at Athens, a festival with elements of reversal and inverse hierarchy. Especially in Old Comedy sharp satire and subversive humour are a constitutive element in the self-image of free speech and democratic discourse that Athens fabricated for itself.[85] Rituals of reversal, featuring fancy cross-dressing and transvestism, are popular beyond Athens. At the festival of the Argive Hybristika, for example, women dressed as men, remembering a time when Argive men were unable to defend the city against the Spartans; women took to arms and chased out foreign forces. The name of the festival—'The festival of Hybris'—makes clear that this ritual was surely not an orchestration of a feminist revolution in sixth-century Greece, but one where patriotic values were inculcated by the temporary loosening of the then developing civic order.[86]

However, ritual occasions or festivals do often give rise to strife, though this does precisely not happen in rituals of reversal. Michel Foucault's case of an audience revolting during heavily ritualized public executions provides perhaps the most striking example of a political ritual turning into an expression of dissent.[87] It is no coincidence that social transformation in Greece has a long history of having taken place during religious events. One of the *aitia* of the Messenian War, the conflict of much consequence for Greek history between Sparta and its Messenian neighbours to the west in the Peloponnese, tells of a shared festival of Artemis Limnatis at which celebration either Messenians attacked Spartans or vice versa. Another rebel group at Sparta, the so-called Partheniai, supposedly sparked off their revolt at the Hyakinthia, a major festival for the city's divine patron Apollo. Democratic tradition at Athens held that Hipparkhos, the degenerate son of the tyrant Peisistratos, was murdered at the city's greatest civic pageant, the Panathenaia. These revolutionaries too work with the notion of ritual's community-creating power, but evidently with a different set of ideas about ritual's potential in mind: the ritual frame, precisely because it evokes an image of peaceful social relations, provides the forum for the reshuffling of social relations and hierarchies.[88]

What marks out all these occasions is ritual as something temporary: 'ritual time' is special time, where there is a licence to disassemble a given order—but it is not always clear in what way it is reconfigured. It is in this ambiguous, highly

[84] Davis (1975).

[85] See e.g. Goldhill (1991) 176–88; Carey (1994); for the Dionysiac context e.g. Riu (1999); Lada-Richards (1999).

[86] Examples of 'rites of rebellion' in antiquity: Argive Hybristika: Plut. *Mul. Virt.* 245e–f. 'Mocking' festivals occur frequently: mocking women's *khoroi* (χοροῖσι γυναικηίοισι κερτόμοισι) for the local heroines Damia and Auxesia (Hdt. 5.83.3); Apollo's aiskhrology on the island of Anaphe (A.R. 4.1717–28; Apollod. 1.9.26; Konon *FGrH* 26 F 1 (il)); Demeter at Pellene (Paus. 7.27.10).

[87] Foucault (1975) 61–8.

[88] Messenian War: Paus. 4.4.1–3; Partheniai: Timaios *FGrH* 555 F 13; Hipparkhos: Th. 1.20; the synoikism of Korinth and Argos in 392 BC was introduced during a festival: Xen. *Hell.* 4.4.2–3.

flexible space that some of the Greek myth-ritual performances that I am going to consider are set. Throughout this book I am interested in the way some Greek ritual celebrations work with the notion of ritual affording *communitas*, while this *communitas* is only in the process of constituting, or possibly reconfiguring, itself.

Our attention thus must be drawn to those features of ritual that contribute to making Turner's *communitas* creative rather than static, and it is in this context that ritual's relationship to time and the past is an important factor. For surely in the Greek world, as in many other cultures, the sense of community invoked by ritual is that of a religious community defining itself by its relation to the past, and the social and power relations between participants are staged as those deriving from a past. Ritual's strategies, the techniques for evoking the past therefore need to be examined.

In this context, the notion of 'ritualization' is helpful. In the more recent history of the field of ritual theory, ritualization surfaces repeatedly as an analytic tool for the understanding of ritual. Ritualization means nothing other than making something a ritual, giving it the status of a rite or ritual. It lies at the basis of all ritual, and, so many people claim, it is the degree and kind of ritualization of some, and not all, social activity that makes certain forms of social interaction different from others. Ritualization came to prominence in connection with the study of cultural activities that bore some resemblance to religious ritual, such as sporting events and theatre; it greatly helped to extend the notion of ritual to any kind of ceremonial behaviour.[89]

In a wonderfully lucid theory of ritual developed through close observation of Jain religion in India, Caroline Humphrey and James Laidlaw have offered a conceptual underpinning for making ritualization the fundamental issue of ritual. They go some way towards explaining why and how ritual does achieve a sense of community, and, so I believe, how *communitas* may be generated as illusion or deception. On this view, acts of any kind can be ritualized, and thus acquire a ritual quality. These ritual acts do not per se carry meaning. Because of a set of socially agreed attitudes on the part of the performer of ritual, they are treated as if they were meaningful. When committing themselves to a 'ritual stance', people performing ritual acts choose to attribute a socially agreed significance to them. Ritual is non-intentional though prescribed; because meaning can easily be given and taken away by society, purpose (content) and form of ritual acts are unrelated or at best vaguely connected.

Much of Humphrey and Laidlaw's proposal, dealing with personal ritual attitude (emotion; stances of the self; individual commitment), can only be cited as a

[89] See esp. the volume by Moore and Myerhoff (1977*a*) on 'non-religious' rituals; MacAloon (1984*b*) on the Olympic Games. Moore and Myerhoff (1977*b*) draw a helpful distinction between types of rituals; in modern history e.g. François, Siegrist, and Vogel (1995) esp. 'Vorwort'. Already Gluckman (1962*b*) discussed ritualization of social relations in tribal societies, cf. (1965) esp. 250–9; cf. also 265, on how tribal rituals entail dramatization of the moral relations of the group, as 'performance of roles in social relations is believed to release beneficent power'; more recently especially Humphrey and Laidlaw (1994, see below) and Bell (1988); (1989); (1992).

prerequisite to the understanding of collective ritual here. We shall nevertheless repeatedly stumble upon some wide-ranging consequences of their ideas: the fact that ritual actions have 'their own facticity'; they are like an object that can be ascribed meaning and deprived of it at any time and in any context. Since they can have entirely different and new meanings if applied in a different situation, rituals are thus flexible types of action that can be applied purposefully. The degree to which a particular interpretation can be sustained depends on the institutional authority that supports this meaning. In the case of the Jains this leads to ever-conflicting interpretations of ritual acts, and it will be interesting to see what it yields for early fifth-century Greek *polis* communities and other groupings where institutional authority is low and rituals constantly seem to change sides between different owners: ritualization may well point to a way of coping with the problem mentioned above as basic in the study of myth and ritual in ancient Greece, that both myth and ritual easily attach themselves to different religious phenomena. Ritualization finally entails that there are as many meanings of ritual as there are actions, and that every action can be ascribed an indefinite number of meanings, leading to the observation that was implied already long before the heights of the popularity of ritualization by the anthropologist Max Gluckman: it is the always-changing ritualization of social relations in ritual that makes ritual a powerful agent within, rather than a static representation of, society.[90]

If ritual depicts society by creating a real or ideal image of social relations among its participants, how is that meaning, ascribed and volatile as it may be, created in ritual acts? Ritual's relation to time comes in here. The ability to transcend time is not only a feature of ritual, but one of its strategies. Now if ritualization is a principal feature of ritual, then ritualization must work as a technique for evoking the past through the imitation or adaptation or invention of ancient practices. This is why rituals strive to appear old and the most prominent features of ritual are all ultimately directed towards that goal. That rituals are believed to be traditional, literally handed down from one generation to another, is inherently part of the strategy: ritual is regular, recurrent action or sequence of action. The idea of repetition itself suggests that rituals are modelled on the past. But more technical features, too, such as formality, archaisms, and symbolism, all derive their force from a link with past occurrences or images associated with a time long past.[91] And finally, a point that will be discussed more in the next section, ritual binds cult places and sacred spaces into the construction of a tradition by constantly redefining and adapting the role of religious locality in the ritual process, imbuing them with new roles in the past according to

[90] Humphrey and Laidlaw (1994); Gluckman (1962*b*) *passim* and e.g. 28–9 on the many roles any individual can take within a system of multiply ritualized relations; Gluckman (1965) 256–7 in relation to space rather than time: the same space can serve various forms of ritualized interaction.

[91] The idea of 'traditionalism' has lately been popular in ritual studies: see Bell (1997) 145–50 for a recent theoretical analysis (cf. already Moore and Myerhoff (1977*a*)), though this is inherent in many applied studies of ritual, first perhaps explicitly in Hobsbawm and Ranger (1983).

present circumstances. The correlation of spatial or geographical progression with ritual processes in rites of passage already underlies van Gennep's concept of initiation. The ritual delineation of sacred space and its relation to time is perhaps best explored by Jonathan Z. Smith: ritual activity cuts up a 'controlled environment' into different stations that even determine the progress of ritual in time itself.[92] The chopping up, enlarging, manipulation, and redirection of ritual spaces and voyages in ritual plays a big role in how the Greeks created such 'controlled environments'.[93]

So traditionalism, the conscious attempt to appear ancient, is perhaps the most pertinent ritual strategy and embraces much ritual activity, and often all of it. Ritual itself is in such cases nothing other than the ritualization of contemporary social relations through traditionalizing, to construe a worshipping community as if it derived from ancient times. As the present day is continuously changing, however, this relationship between present and past is constantly redefined, recreated, and readapted. This procedure takes as its starting-point the present, not the past, so that a past is constructed on the assumption of the present state of affairs, or at any rate must have a strong bearing on the present. The process of linking present with past is nothing other than the creation of a tradition: the opposite of what the popular conception of ritual is, a mode of behaviour transmitted from a past. But ritual is constructed towards the past rather than from it.

Paradoxically, we now end up with the idea that our old, traditional ritual is a matter of saying something about change, and more precisely the constantly changing relationship of a contemporary ritual community to its own past, about changing traditions. It is evident how theories working on the premise of structure alone, of a model of society that remains and aims to remain essentially stable, encounter some difficulty. The necessary travelling between different time spheres makes ritual a historical phenomenon, of a particular society belonging to a particular place at a particular time in history simply because society cannot avoid change because it exists through time.

If ritual is a product of the present, ritual will both reflect change, and, more dynamically, also become itself a forum in which social change is enacted, since the present is never stable but always entails a form of change. Such links between tradition, ritual, and social change are the hobby-horses of 'practice' theorists such as Marshall Sahlins who maintains that a community's forms of ritualization embrace *all* social change: ritual, by its very nature, embeds and integrates any new situation in a performative tradition, providing a context within which cultural change is both comprehended and accepted. A much-cited example of his is Captain Cook's disembarking on the Sandwich Islands (Hawaii), where the

[92] Van Gennep (1909) Ch. 2, 19–33; 275; Eliade e.g. (1965) 21–59; Turner (1974*a*); J. Z. Smith (1987) 74–96.

[93] Little has been done along these lines for Greek religion. Cf. J. Z. Smith (1998) 18: 'The activity of transposition is one of the basic building blocks of ritual and a central object of ritual thought. The capacity to alter common denotations in order to enlarge potential connotations within the boundaries of ritual is one of the features that marks off its space as "sacred".'

islanders seamlessly turned the arrival of a stranger into the epiphany of a native god who came to visit them.[94] Whatever one thinks of Sahlins's claim to account universally for *all* cultural change, the idea that enduring patterns of social relations staged in ritual are brought to bear on real-life situations presents a useful framework for assessing the creative rather than conservative force of ritual. While it is questionable whether ritual embraces all change, it is something quite different to say that ritual always has a potential or enacted element of social change.[95]

I have tried to come to grips with some aspects of what I think underlies all social activity embedded in ritual, its relation to time. A central implication of the view presented here is that rituals are always related to a particular time and a particular place. A second is that rituals constantly engage in a discourse with their own past, and a third, that ritual's perceived traditionality is a factor that crucially shapes the sense of community that it creates. Ritual's moving between present and past in the effort to create a transcendence of time lies at the basis of how it works in society, and its diachronic dimension will turn out as indispensable for an understanding of what ritual action can achieve. While societies' attitudes towards time and the mythical past vary, in a society whose entirety of ritual traditions are believed to be rooted in the mythical past, as is the case in Greece, the aspect of 'changing traditions'—the fact that every ritual is both a product of the past and of the present—inevitably turns the study of ritual into a study of myth and ritual, and the two into effective social agents.

4. THE POWER OF PERFORMANCE

To turn back to the consideration of aetiology conducted above, aetiological myth and ritual seem to proceed, and act out their power, in strikingly similar fashion, in that the primary strategy of both is to invoke a timeless continuity from a time of origins. Both base their claims on the perceived superiority of the past, which acts as an authority for the present. Both myth and ritual are characterized by a circularity in the way they argue their case; both integrate features of the present, tangible world, objects or places, into either narrative or practice while pretending to be traditional; they offer a suggestion of how to see the present, they both tell us more about the present than about the past. Both claim to be explanatory, but are essentially suggestive and non-explanatory. Aetiology and ritual thus share the basic strategies through which they claim to convey truth. How then will they react when they work together?

[94] Sahlins (1976), on Captain Cook's death and divinization.

[95] For ritual related to social change cf. e.g. for the contemporary world, Cohen (1993) on how the Notting Hill Carnival has shaped identities of different ethnic and social groups in the London area. Peacock (1968) is also interesting in this respect.

This brings us back to the medium through which they act. I have omitted thus far discussing what ritualists have long acknowledged as the main feature of ritual: its performativity. The potential of ritual lies in the fact that it is not read or told but acted out; it is ritual's performative aspect that makes it a powerful agent in society, and that invests with a certain kind of power those who enact rituals.

A relation between power and performance has always been made, because it was felt that ritual is a special kind of power. Because of its unreal, merely representative character, ritual was long regarded as a mere expression of power and its legitimation that really lay somewhere else: processions in Asia Minor underscore the authority of the emperor; the pomp and circumstance of the Doge's entry mirror his exalted position in the Venetian republic. Such rituals reflect the powerful position of a monarch or of a constitutional authority.

Some time ago, Clifford Geertz challenged the view that ritual is a mere expression and reflection of a power more crudely exerted elsewhere. He argued that ritual is itself a form of power rather than something external to it, questioning the traditional view of what power was about beyond the idea of one group imposing its will on another by a threat of violence.[96] The idea that ritual itself is power rather than a representation of it has gained great applause from many schools of thought, but especially from scholarship in medieval and modern history. David Cannadine, for example, looked at the way ritual created both a new image of and novel authority for the British monarchy at the end of the nineteenth century.[97] The view has subsequently established itself that ritual is a strategic form of practice through which power structures are revealed, and social control is exerted in a particular way. Modern historians are typically interested in secular rituals and incline to the idea that ritual inculcates the dominant political ideology, often engendered through a subtle interweaving of political with religious symbolism, a view representatively summarized by David Kertzer: 'By repetitively employing a limited pool of powerful symbols, often associated with emotional fervor, rituals are important molders of political beliefs.'[98] To give a somewhat crude generalization, both traditional anthropology and modern historians tend to see the power of ritual in the degree to which it gives definition, or indeed reality, to the way the existing social order reflects and maintains rhythms and rules of humanity. Because rituals offer models of a working society they do not challenge the existing social order, even if, as in the case of carnival, they sometimes masquerade as a challenge.[99]

[96] Geertz's theatre-state (1980) esp. 122–3, also 136, and the much-repeated pronouncement at 13: 'Mass ritual was not a device to shore up the state, but rather the state . . . was a device for the enactment of mass ritual. Power served pomp, not pomp power.'

[97] Cannadine (1983); (1987); for the French and German 19th-cent. context see François, Siegrist, and Vogel (1995).

[98] Kertzer (1988) 95.

[99] Promoting 'schematic thinking': Kertzer (1988) 175. See e.g. Hanawalt and Reyerson (1994) for the medieval world; but also modern 'civic' secular rituals work in this way: Cannadine (1982) quoting Skinner (1981) 37; or on ritualized cultural events: La Fontaine (1986).

Some form of confirmation is ready to hand. As Edwin Muir argued in his study of Venice's Renaissance festivals, the stability of the city's mixed constitution relied heavily on public religious rituals to create an overarching sense of community. The sacralization of civic space built upon the existing social order and functioned as a key to broader civic control that left the existing hierarchies undisturbed: *nobili* and *cittadini* did not interfere with each other in either real or ritual life but both had a clear-cut position within the ritual activities that showed their role in the community. Through an intricate network of interrelating public activity between the community's urban spaces and sacred figures, Venetian civic identity was constantly celebrated, reaffirmed, and recreated through repeated invocation of a common past and a common tradition—the management of myth and ritual. Other Italian cities such as Naples, whose civic life was divided between royal and papal authorities, lacked the kind of civic patriotism created, established, and maintained through the sacralization of civic life—and were torn apart with civil strife.[100]

The behaviour of Muir's Republican Venice looks dangerously like that of the Athenian democracy, and studying the religious orchestration of public ideology risks encountering some of the same stumbling blocks: an analysis on the unargued assumption that many and frequent public displays fostered an 'indigenous civic identity and ideology based upon a broad consensus about social values' when there is no attempt at verifying the claim.[101] More differentiated perhaps is Richard Trexler's animated ritual history of Renaissance Florence which aims to show how ritual *transforms* a society into a unified whole against all the odds of institutional unsteadiness: ritual and ceremony were creative forces in their own right, potent enough to make peace between factions and even to keep the whole commune going, to resuscitate it when it was almost dead.[102] The idea of rituals as stimulating growing social consciousness, civic pride, and urban solidarity rather than as messages passed down from rulers only in one direction has in fact since been a fashionable line to take, chiefly amongst early modern historians.[103]

Ritual, it seems evident, functions as an alternative kind of power, one that works with special strategies. Rite commands more surely than physical brutality.[104] Power structures depicted in rituals are at all times taken extremely seriously. At a festival of Corpus Christi in early eighteenth-century Piedmont the

[100] Muir (1981). The idea is that old Venetian traditions are successfully incorporated into contemporary civic ideology.

[101] Muir (1981) 5 with the review by T. Kuehn in *Journal of Modern History* 55 (1983) 149–50. On comparable approaches for democratic Athens see e.g. Connor (1987); Boedeker and Raaflaub (1998).

[102] Trexler (1980) xix on ritual being 'at the core of the city's identity'; 128, 198, 216 on ritual's power to transform.

[103] Cf. e.g.: MacKay (1985) for 15th-cent. Castile; Torre (1985) for 18th-cent. Piedmont; Prodi (1987) for the collaboration of clergy and local elite in the papal monarchy; Davis (1981*b*) for 16th-cent. Lyon; Terpstra (1995); (2000) for the intersection of civic and religious power structures at and through individual shrines in Renaissance Bologna.

[104] Bendix (1978) 17: 'legitimation [through ritual] achieves what power alone cannot'.

baldachin, core of the sanctity of the entire procession, proved an especially fat bone of contention for the competitors: the ensemble of the public bodies were eager to arrange themselves around it in a way which commended their respective position within the local social hierarchy.[105] Because rituals involve and postulate participation in a given world order, as a form of indirect power an effective ritual can be more influential than the outcome of a battle, or for that matter a trial in court. What is more important, rituals often communicate things that it would be unwise or even ineffective to convey in any more direct fashion—and we shall see examples of this on various occasions through this book.[106]

While ritual's role as an alternative, even creative power is firmly established precisely because of its theatrical character, the actual relation of power to performance is much more difficult to pin down. That ritual's 'power' lies in its aesthetic appeal is an old observation, which only recently has been embellished with some conceptual underpinnings. 'Performance theory' was first developed to account for the strategies, many of them visual, by which drama manages to involve its spectators, in other words, to come to terms with theatre's representational character and sensual strategies. By suggesting an active rather than a passive role for participants in the theatrical ritual and the simultaneous involvement of both acting and watching participant, performance theory deals with just how the audience is persuaded into participation in the play. (One should perhaps add that performance theory was also developed with a view to a specific problem of anthropological ethnography: in making even the analyst a participant, the perennial problem of ritual studies, the gap in perception between performer and spectator, is annulled.) Performance models thus develop a kind of reader-response theory for performed arts.[107]

Because of the evident similarities between theatre and ritual in their representational character performance theory has been reapplied to ritual, where it has

[105] Torre (1992).

[106] Foucault's 'programme' (1982) 188–90, 198–201 of studying power relationships as ways of behaving that indirectly influence action—rather than directly exert physical force—perhaps best describes the phenomenon, though he himself is not interested in the specific modalities of religious ritual: ritual and ritualization are merely 'techniques' serving the display of power relations (1980).

[107] Schechner first in (1988; orig. 1977), initiated by the earlier works of Turner (1969); (1974*a*); (1982) (1986); Moore and Myerhoff (1977*a*); Goffman (1967); see also Sullivan (1986). Rappaport (1979) 176–7: performance is the 'sine qua non' of ritual. Prominent more recent representatives are assembled in Appel and Schechner (1990); Wirth (2000) includes semiotics and linguistics in his collection of landmark essays. A German school has developed with Fischer-Lichte (2004) esp. 127–239 on the materiality of 'body', 'space', 'sound', 'time' in performance. Already Singer (1959) xii–xiii had maintained that cultural performances are 'the ways in which the cultural context of a tradition is organised and transmitted on particular occasions through specific media'. An early forerunner is also Langer (1953) 163 ff., who talks of a principle of assimilation in music. Singer (1959) xiii ff. was the first to address the problem of the spectator's = theorist's involvement; cf. Grimes (1990). The volume by MacAloon (1984*a*; see 1984*b*) looks at performative elements in all kinds of ritualized activity. The performative dimension of cultural activity has recently become popular with classicists: see Goldhill and Osborne (1999) with Goldhill's introduction; Bierl (2001) 22–30; cf. Pelling (2005).

achieved at least as much as the medium for which it was developed.[108] Performance theory in ritual studies attempts to grapple with the long-felt recognition that ritual's effectiveness lies in its non-intellectual aspects: rituals are felt and experienced, not understood.[109] At the basis of the definition of the register in which 'understanding' is generated through emotional and behavioural, rather than intellectual, involvement, lies the recognition that it is predominantly the simultaneous presence of many media in ritual, employed redundantly, that allows for aesthetic understanding and accounts for ritual's complex potential in society.[110] Ritual's dramaturgy is intricate, often simultaneously employing elements such as role play and text, music, song, and dance. All of these are geared towards the same thing, though none of them acts in the same way as another, nor would any of them make the same sense if performed on their own. Anthropology has borrowed from psychology the term 'synaisthesia' to describe the multifarious cooperation of many communicative means that compose ritual's highly representational character on the one hand, and its bold concreteness on the other.[111]

How is one to make the medium a message? There is no such thing as a consistent 'theory of performance', just as there is no 'ritual theory' that unproblematically accounts for all the aspects of the phenomenon.[112] The anthropologist Stanley Tambiah has contributed to a model that helps to describe some basic processes of performative action.[113] He is concerned mainly with ritual's formality, the basic feature of ritual that responds to the demand of conventionalism inherent in any ritual activity: a ritual is only validated if a libation, a sacrifice, or a prayer is carried out in a particular prescribed way, or improvises within the boundaries of a prescriptive formal framework of action. Tambiah's template perhaps adequately reflects the problem intrinsic to all ritual studies, ritual's almost uncontrollable dynamic balance between content and form.

Tambiah applied to ritual the terminology of speech-act theory fashionable at the time. Ritual acts are similar to Austin and Searle's 'performative utterances' found in speech, employed in situations when 'saying is doing': what is said in words really implies an action. Unlike the original linguistic approach, for Tambiah social conditions are what attribute meaning to particular ritual actions. Part of the ritualist's job, then, is to excavate the particular conditions under which 'ritual saying' is a form of action, of doing; ritual's performative utterances would only work in this context.

108 Tambiah (1985 (1981)); Rappaport (1999); already Bloch (1974).

109 Myerhoff (1977); G. Lewis (1980) 33–4: 'not decoding but affecting'.

110 e.g. Rappaport (1999) and earlier.

111 The term already occurs in Leach (1976) 25.

112 See e.g. the definitional problems met by (most recently) Diamond (1996) (with more bibliography), and the problems in defining how universal a category it is: Turner (1990); Blau (1990).

113 Tambiah (1985 (1981)) esp. 127 ff. and already (1968).

The starting point for Tambiah's reflections on the pragmatics of ritual action was the formalism of ritual speech. In an acclaimed article, he argued against the Malinowskian view that spells and prayers were intrinsically meaningful. Instead their magical power and efficacy derived from a use of symbolic forms of expression in ritual language, in particular metaphor and metonymy. Such imagery makes use of the real world as it is culturally experienced and thus relates it to people's real use of language in which activities such as sowing and harvesting are symbolically expressed in terms of 'pregnancy' and 'childbirth'. Ritual language, he suggests, is not a different category of language altogether; rather it is a form of verbal expression based on the available cultural system of knowledge abstracted from normal communication through the formality of a performative situation in which many such symbols act contemporaneously in many different ways.[114]

Tambiah's inference from this, borne out particularly in his later essays, is that ritual says things by creating a 'fused sense of communication': the variety of performative modes mixed with the variety of sequences of ritual action dissolves the boundaries between their individually inferred meanings. According to Tambiah, the two basic mutually dependent performative strategies of ritual include 'economy' and 'redundancy', terms deriving from information theory. Costly newspaper pages or minutes on television require the weather map always to appear in the same corner, while short items of news on TV are often accompanied by pictures, thus both abbreviating and multiplying parts of the communicative process. Similarly, he observes, by its intrinsically representative (symbolic) character ritual abbreviates meaning, while at the same time it tends to say many things more than once. Stereotype and redundancy are thus key features of ritual—a strategy of ritual performances that will become relevant when we look at the ever-the-same patterns of ritual song on Delos (Chapter 2).

To create meaning, ritual, according to Tambiah, moves between the horizontal level of sequenced acts on the one hand and the vertical level of inferred values on the other. So-called 'indexical values', another linguistic category, are attached to and inferred by actors during the performance. (An 'index' is a variety of sign that is connected to its object by a quite specific relationship—for example, footprints would be an indexical sign of presence, smoke an index of fire.)[115] As the two varieties of values inferred from ritual action, Tambiah distinguishes between a 'cosmic' representation that is related to aspects of human life such as birth, marriage, and death, and a representation that 'legitimises and realises social hierarchies'.[116] This breaks down the often-felt dichotomy between the 'human' and the 'charter' value of rituals. To take an ancient example, this would

[114] Tambiah (1968), in which Austin's (1962) theory of performative utterances is complemented by the social context; an essential corrective to Malinowski's view (cf. Tambiah (1990)): it is not the ritual which effects the harvest but the community who performs it. See Bell (1992) 282 n. 29.

[115] 'Indexical' is used here in order to account for what long before had been recognized as the 'representative' nature of ritual, thereby avoiding the complicated terminology of, for example, symbolism.

[116] Tambiah (1985 (1981)) 153–4.

mean that through ephebic initiation ('cosmic') the public festival of the Athenian Oskhophoria directed by the *genos* of the Salaminioi could express the status of the clan within the *polis* (charter value). Very particular inferences about a social reality are made by actors during the performance of 'cosmic' representations.[117]

It is Tambiah's 'condensation' or 'fusion of meaning' creating an intensified, 'heightened' way of communication through the merging of form and content that ultimately puts its finger on what makes ritual ritual. The blurring of the communicative modes converging in the same message, for example the parallelism of text in song, a particular formal dance, and a specific musical tune all geared towards the same specific occasion, make rituals what they are: a rather diffuse non-linear sequence of images and symbols relating to values and realities of a society and its mental projection of these. None of the elements would make sense in isolation, and none of them would work outside the performative situation. The formality of the performance combined with a host of interacting social values inferred from it create the atmosphere through which ritual's discourse intensifies and eventually persuades into belief and propels a community into a conviction about truth emerging from the ritual action.[118]

Sorting out the workings of this long-observed forest of fusing symbols is perhaps one of the greatest merits of Tambiah's performative approach to ritual. Tambiah's formulation comes closest to the effect of ritual's awkward if exceptionally forceful persuasiveness: 'ritual is not just an alternative way to express things but is about things that cannot be expressed in any other way'.[119] This implies that the manner of saying or doing something is intrinsic to what is said or done in ritual, the 'medium itself becomes a message'.[120] In other words, certain things can only be expressed ritually.

On the curious psychological phenomenon that may lie behind the compelling nature of this 'heightened form of communication', it is ultimately Maurice Bloch and not Tambiah who has made the most pertinent observations. In a much-quoted article, Bloch is especially interested in the medium of song and dance, an almost unexplained social performative category of any, and certainly of Greek, religion.[121] Starting from the idea that 'symbols in ritual cannot be understood without studying the communicative medium of ritual in which they are embedded, in particular singing and dancing',[122] Bloch himself first came

[117] The simultaneous operation of cosmic and charter dimension is just another way of relating (conflicting) longevity and immediacy in ritual: see pp. 52–3 below.

[118] Cf. e.g. Rappaport (1979) 174–8 and (1999) 29–32; Myerhoff (1977), promulgating the idea that 'doing is believing' in ritual; more recently Myerhoff (1990).

[119] Tambiah (1985 (1981)).

[120] Rappaport (1999) 38.

[121] But see Ceccarelli's admirable study of the *Pyrrhike* (1998). Naerebout (1997) attempts to set out a cross-culturally valid approach to dance. In anthropology see the dated work by Hambly (1926), more recently the volume by Spencer (1985). Lawler (1978 (1964)) deals especially with visual evidence.

[122] Bloch (1974) 56. 'Symbols' for Bloch seem to be what metaphor and metonymy are for Tambiah: those elements that connect to real-life experience in an abbreviated form.

up with some thoughts on ritual recitation to introduce the subject matter, but these ideas were not further developed. On his view, formalization of speech in ritual is a medium characterized by impoverished, and therefore limiting, linguistic creativity: whereas everyday language, deployed freely and naturally, offers a choice of acceptable answers, stylized speech reduces the range of possible responses. Ritual language, because it forces both speaker and audience into established roles of communication, has no propositional force at all; on the contrary, ritual language—in speech and song—is a kind of force that becomes more totalitarian with increasing perfection. 'There is no argument in song, no linguistic adaptation to reality possible.' Because participants do not challenge the routine formulae or conventions, formalization is thus very effective in promoting a loose compliance with the social roles depicted in the ritual: acceptance of the mode of presentation coincides with acquiescence in the content. Ritual participants are therefore effectively maintaining the implicit assumptions, apparently sanctified by tradition, that underlie the depiction of authority staged in the ritual. Ritual is an especially forceful system of communication because the range of what can be said in content (propositional force) is reduced while the degree of persuasiveness of what is said (illocutionary force) is heightened the more formalized a ritual is: *You cannot argue with a song.*[123]

Bloch came to the radical conclusion that ritual is entirely deprived of content and has no explanatory force at all.[124] Nowhere is it a speculation about humanity, about good and evil, or about man's place in social structure,[125] because ritual rules out the very tools of explanation. He inferred that ritual is not a necessary component of social life per se but, in a formula resembling Geertz's, is 'the exercise of a particular form of power' that makes 'a power situation appear a fact in the nature of the world'.[126] Bloch's views, extreme and shaped by his contemporary political climate, bring out, and seek to account for, the undeniable social constraints imposed by ritual action, and it is for this reason that they deserve to be treated here.

Through the effect of formalization, according to Bloch, ritual does not determine people's individual emotion but rather effects an emotional distance allowing institutionalized communication to come to the fore. Trexler puts the issues more positively: ritual is 'a formal behaviour, those verbal and bodily actions of humans that, in specific contexts of space and time, become relatively fixed into those recognizable social and cultural deposits we call behavioural forms'.[127] That ritual coerces its participants into a position of acceptance is an old observation: Durkheim too perceived the supra-individuality of ritual. Already Radcliffe-Brown had casually noticed the curious social strait-jacket that, for example, dance rhythm imposes on one's movement: agreeing to participate

123 Bloch (1974) 71.

124 Tambiah argues against Bloch's (1974) contention of loss of semantic content of ritual words.

125 Man (Lévi-Strauss); good and evil (Evans-Pritchard); man's place in society (Radcliffe-Brown, Durkheim).

126 Bloch (1974) 79.

127 Trexler (1980) xxiv.

in a ballroom dance reduces the personal rhythmical impulse by requiring conformity to the movements prescribed by collective performance; private emotions are submitted to a public morality and participation in the dance goes imperceptibly along with consenting for example to established gender roles or their rejection.[128] Humphrey and Laidlaw imply the same thing when they invent a kind of mental condition in which ritual is performed, their 'ritual stance' or 'commitment' that entails acceptance of meaning. Attending rituals that are not one's own puts the issue to the test—in an aesthetically involving religious procession I easily adopt feelings commanded by an alien tradition: an important condition in the constant process of creation and recreation of worshipping communities in Greek antiquity.

Such a consent-model forms an attractive counterweight to earlier conceptions of ritual acting primarily on the psyche of the individual.[129] While the Blochian model is itself rather static, it can produce a fruitful dynamic among participants in ritual who constantly move between resistance and consent. Compliance and defiance, so it is argued more recently, determine both ritual's efficacy and its limitations. If I participate in the political rituals of a totalitarian state, I may find myself balancing certain (often material) considerations against each other with the effect that my body attends while my mind is absent. There is an illusion of consensus presumed among the participants of ritual, not unrelated to personal advantages that may lie in participation, from which it is inferred that rituals above all objectify dominating power structures.[130]

Even if one does not agree with the extremes of this view (which reflects the still prevalent puzzlement of scholars at the workings of mass enthusiasm and its exploitation by totalitarianism), the type of intentional non-intentionality, between Humphrey and Laidlaw's 'ritual stance' and coercion, presupposed for ritual participation, may pose interesting questions for Greek religion. Do we think that participation by Athens' allies in the Greater Panathenaia was merely agreed to as a necessary condition for survival, or may we also leave some room for Athena's divine charisma? Or, more briefly, do I owe my tribute of a panoply to the Athenians or to Athena? The answer to such questions will be considered on various occasions in this book, for example in connection with cults imperial powers such as Athens or Argos share with smaller cities, where the perceived *communitas* of equals plays a major role in the configuration of relations between participants (Chapters 2 and 3).

[128] Radcliffe-Brown (1964 (1933)) 247.

[129] e.g. through the appeal to universal human events such as birth, death, or marriage: Malinowski and others (see above).

[130] Objectification: 'The orchestrated construction of power and authority in ritual, which is deeply evocative of the basic divisions of the social order, engage the social body in the objectification of oppositions and the deployment of schemes that effectively reproduce the divisions of the social order': Bell (1992) 215. Rappaport (1979) 193 draws a curious distinction between myths which can be believed, and rituals which must be: the very situation of myth in performance, however, makes such a distinction untenable.

It is this intertwining of performance and power that I am interested in. Though Bloch's views were rejected,[131] their essence was absorbed by most anthropologists at the time, and they are still among the more convincing models developed to account for a tie between performance and power. While Bloch sees in ritual a fixed representation of (a totalitarian) society whose formalism is sanctified by tradition, I believe that the performative dimension of ritual is its most malleable and most creative aspect, and the nub of negotiation over social and power relations between ritual participants. Bloch's essay is the first and only attempt to get to grips, by allowing 'form' as a determiner of 'content', with why ritual does not allow dissent, in other words why you somehow have to agree with what ritual suggests. It is in this coextensive relation between form and content that ritual's modalities of 'seeming old' and 'being old' crucially overlap, because there is no mode of differentiation afforded by ritual itself. The involvement in ritual does not allow for participants to make that distinction.

A more general—and less extremely formulated—way of describing the same thing is to say that a ritual tradition is sanctioned by the widespread belief in its continuous practice. It derives its persuasive power precisely, and solely, through being believed to be transmitted through uninterrupted performance. While someone might think that they are enacting a religious tradition that already has a long history of transmission, it is often very clear that there is no such continuity—or, more importantly, not the same continuity. While a perceived continuity is at the centre of how ritual performances work in society, it really says nothing about who continues what, nothing about the nature of this continuity. In other words, a performative tradition is not a product of a direct linear descent through time but instead presents a creative handling of the past.[132]

But the real past nevertheless must not be entirely neglected. For in this conundrum, religious localities—cult places with their associated aetiological myths and rituals—do have a more complex relationship with the past than we have so far been able to establish. They do feature as an element of a perceived continuum through time in a changeable world as was argued above, but the professed continuity is in itself intricate. Once a particular place has started to be associated with worship in a certain way, it is very difficult, if not impossible, to free that locality of these 'traditional' ritual forms. For example, it turns out to be impossible to rid the Greek hero Neoptolemos of the bad reputation he once acquired, no matter what the reformulation of his myth (Chapter 4); or to abandon the crucial but enigmatic role of Artemis, the older and more venerable deity on Delos, in the myths and rituals whose stated aim in the later period is to worship Apollo (Chapter 2). The phenomenon is in the end similar to the much more accessible symptoms of continuity between pagan cults and Christian

[131] See Tambiah's critique (1985 (1981)) 151–3.

[132] The very recent discussions on reperformance of poetry or drama address some of this issue of 'performance through time': see e.g. Revermann (2006) 66 ff.; Currie (2004); the performative dimension is important for Alcock (2002). But cf. Chaniotis (2002) 43 'one cannot celebrate the same festival twice'—the reasons for which are given in note 134.

worship. Attributes of the Christian Saint *Διονύσιος* on early twentieth-century Naxos still involved ivy and wine, and a similar parallel can be drawn between *Ἅγιος Δημήτριος* and his ancient female namesake. All rituals carry with them if not elements of a real past, certainly of a perceived one.[133]

It follows that traditional associations of a cult—that is who used to be related to whom in what way through the worship of a particular god—shape a ritual experience, and its role within the specific religious group. It also follows that creative, productive rituals will necessarily engage in a dialogue with their own, often only nebulously preserved and/or perceived, past. Song and dance are determined by their own tradition: there is no such thing as an isolated ritual performance; every performance carries with it the tradition of previous performances, the burden of its own past. The reason for this lies, again, in the same problem of practice mentioned above: most of the rituals considered here use their own tradition, and derive their force from the fact that they draw from their own perceived history. Precisely here lie both problems and opportunities for a recurrent reinterpretation of cult places and their myths and rituals. Ritual performances in Greece lie at every moment between tradition and immediacy, between the past and the present.[134]

This means that no ritual can be understood in its social significance without the unwrapping of its tradition, without us engaging what is thought to be a ritual's previous life. It is a central fault of the existing models of performance theory that they are not interested in the diachronic dimension of ritual, while in fact the history of a ritual significantly determines its role in a performative present. And perceiving history in ritual, with history meaning 'change' in ritual, makes an approach via individual performances helpful. Religion in Greece is so spectacularly incremental precisely because there is some form of (real and perceived) continuity. To counteract the alleged intractability of this interaction between myths and rituals and their own past is one of the methodological aims of the book.[135]

So what I shall offer here is a tentative approach towards studying how the notion of continuous—choral—performance helps the redefinition and reinterpretation of religious practices over time and ties it to the social uses of these practices. The material, a series of quite specific performances, each of them composed for a particular community for a particular type of ritual occasion, offers to myth and

[133] Cf. Lawson (1910).

[134] Chaniotis's recent concept of 'ritual dynamics' is targeted at similar phenomena: (2002) studies the Boiotian Daidala through their multiple reorganizations, concluding e.g. that they integrate 'tensions between traditional ritual and actions, which have to be performed in a particular way, and continually changing communities of performers, participants and receptors or spectators that invest the rituals with new meaning'. The 'blurring of meanings and the understanding of their performance permits reinterpretations and new associations'. See esp. 38–43.

[135] The problem is shared, though not identical, with that addressed in the stimulating approaches on the construction of social memories in antiquity through performances in traditional sacred spaces: Alcock and Van Dyke (2003); Alcock (2002).

ritual an anchor in an actual present of participants in such performances. It will emerge that, because ritual performances by definition bear in themselves an element of change, they are a medium through which change can be, and often is, enacted; and perhaps they are even a particularly powerful means through which to generate change precisely because they exploit the notion of ritual's unchangeability.

While I believe that the mechanics of the interrelation between power and performance suggested here are in principle transferable to other religions, the specific situation of the archaic and classical Greek world of city-states and other groupings, such as *ethne* 'peoples (of an imagined blood relationship)' and *koina* ('federations'), multiplies and intensifies their dynamic role in the fifth-century historical climate. To judge from perhaps the majority of studies in modern history and anthropology, one might think that the greater the institutional authority, the greater the degree of active shaping of religious and secular rituals.[136] Greek rituals, however, public or not, had little to do with indoctrination or repression through an authoritative ritual that includes drilled modes of behaviour or the engendering of mass enthusiasm. On the contrary, the dispersed Greeks had much power to be negotiated, and little authority to focus it. The fragmented power structures of the Greek *polis*-world are intriguingly reflected in the variety of social relations established through myth and ritual, and the number of conflicting and variable authorities determine the quantity of competing traditions in circulation. Ritual in Greece will have been a form of social control as in many other places but there is a multiplicity of highly flexible mutual social controls between the parts of a community that is expressed in ritual. If, as is likely, the ancient city-state had anything like the same degree of dispersed liturgical authorities as, for instance, the early modern Italian city-state, not only does the making of tradition through ritual become controversial but so also does the question of social and power relations between and within all these groups become indefinitely complex, and in some ways more interesting and intricate than for a totalitarian state.[137]

So while it is uncontroversial that Greek ritual performances embrace some kind of power, it is not always clear whose power it is and who exerts it on whom. Nor is it clear from where it is generated: the power of tradition in religious practice and the creation and exertion of social and/or political power are inextricably intertwined. If myths and rituals change in an area, it is very possible that a particular authority intrudes by conscious design into a myth or ritual where it was previously absent. On the other hand, a change in power relations can equally make it natural for anybody involved in this changed power

[136] See n. 82 above.

[137] Cf. for example Torre's (1985) illuminating analysis on parish formation in medieval Piedmont, which gives a fascinating account of power negotiations between clergy, confraternities, and laity through liturgy. It is also clear from this study that priests and laymen were united in the use of religious discourse and religious practices as a way of defining identities of social groups and the nature of the relations between them.

configuration, that is to say not necessarily just the beneficiaries, to reshape a particular religious tradition and retell myths in a new way, possibly even without elements of conscious design, and the performances of myth and ritual by island states in Chapter 2 will lay open some such phenomena. This is an essential corrective to the possible view that the manipulation of myth, ritual, and religion in archaic and classical Greece was always the primary instrument of public policy. By contrast, it is a characteristic of myths and rituals that they reshape themselves whenever the relations between the people who practise them change; it is the dynamic of social and power relations expressed in ritual that generates myths.

It is perhaps in the Greek *polis*-world that ritual's delicacy and social work—contrasted with the bold concreteness it often seems to have—can be best observed, and not only because it is often only through rituals that structures of authority are revealed in the first instance. Ultimately, therefore, one aim of this study is to illustrate how religion is a form of power, but a power that lies in the medium itself, and not always, and not necessarily, in the hands of those who have it rather than in the power of tradition that lies behind it. It may in the end contribute to a more differentiated picture of how and why power lies with whom in archaic and classical Greece, and perhaps why it is so inconsistent in its sympathies, and, finally, why it always resides somewhere between parties, and not with the one or the other. The myth-ritual performances investigated constitute one of the many ways in which religion, qua cultural activity, is a way of sounding out, exploring, asserting, and sometimes exerting power.

2

Dancing on Delos: *Δαλίων θύγατρες* between Myth, Ritual, and *theoria*

Ἀστερίη θυόεσσα, σὲ μὲν περί τ' ἀμφί τε νῆσοι
κύκλον ἐποιήσαντο καὶ ὡς χορὸν ἀμφεβάλοντο.
οὔτε σιωπηλὴν οὔτ' ἄψοφον οὖλος ἐθείραις
Ἕσπερος, ἀλλ' αἰεί σε καταβλέπει ἀμφιβόητον.
οἱ μὲν ὑπαείδουσι νόμον Λυκίοιο γέροντος,
ὅν τοι ἀπὸ Ξάνθοιο θεοπρόπος ἤγαγεν Ὠλήν·
αἱ δὲ ποδὶ πλήσσουσι χορίτιδες ἀσφαλὲς οὖδας.
δὴ τότε καὶ στεφάνοισι βαρύνεται ἱρὸν ἄγαλμα
Κύπριδος ἀρχαίης ἀριήκοον, ἥν ποτε Θησεύς
εἵσατο, σὺν παίδεσσιν ὅτε Κρήτηθεν ἀνέπλει.
οἱ χαλεπὸν μύκημα καὶ ἄγριον υἷα φυγόντες
Πασιφάης καὶ γναμπτὸν ἕδος σκολιοῦ λαβυρίνθου,
πότνια, σὸν περὶ βωμὸν ἐγειρομένου κιθαρισμοῦ
κύκλιον ὠρχήσαντο, χοροῦ δ' ἡγήσατο Θησεύς.
ἔνθεν ἀειζώοντα θεωρίδος ἱερὰ Φοίβῳ
Κεκροπίδαι πέμπουσι, τοπήια νηὸς ἐκείνης

(Callimachus, *Hymn to Delos* (4) 300–315)[1]

With this picture Callimachus rounds off the fine imagery that shapes and frames the entire *Hymn to Delos*, evoking a profound familiarity with long-lived religious traditions converging in these verses' antiquarianism. The dancing Kyklades setting up their *khoros* around the island of Delos is one of those powerful images of antiquity that persist to the present day.[2] Delos was home to the great sanctuary of Apollo and Artemis and throughout antiquity a centre of *theoria* ('pilgrimage'), the practice whereby places participated in central cults by sending

[1] Fragrant Asterie, round and about you / the islands made a circle, a dancing choir. / Never are you silent, never hushed / when curly-headed Hesperos / passes over you, but always he can hear / the sound of voices then—of boys / singing the song of Olen, the old man / of Lykia, who came as sacred envoy / from the Xanthos, and of girls / who make the solid ground / reverberate beneath their dancing feet. / And then it is the holy statue of Kypris / so ancient, so famous, / bows under heaps of garlands. / Theseus erected it, on his way from Crete / with children aboard. Remember: / they escaped the menacing bellow / of Pasiphae's brute son and left behind / his coiled lair, the labyrinth, / to dance around your altar, Lady, / circling to the tune of harps / as Theseus led the way. / And ever since, the Kekropidai / have sent to Phoibos the rigging of that ship, eternal / tribute to their sacred mission (tr. Nisetich).

[2] N. Gatsos, *Ὁ Χορὸς τῶν Κυκλάδων* in the collection *Τὸ κατὰ τὸν Μάρκον* (1964).

sacred delegations. To Delos cities dispatched choruses as part of such delegations, a singing tribute to the twin gods. This custom shaped the ways in which the locality was imagined, and the *khoros* the island's history. Even the ancient etymology of the name 'Kyklades' is related to the choral tributes that *poleis* delivered.[3] Callimachus' hymn develops a picture in which Delos is the fixed anchor in a sea of (dancing) traditions surrounding it. But while the songs of Olen, the choral traditions, and the dances of Theseus' *geranos* merge into one and the same floating movement, they represent a number of different stages in Delos' musical history. How the set of choral customs interacted with contemporary Greek history will be the subject of this chapter.

The fifth century was a period of particularly intense activity for choruses sent to Delos. At least a dozen early fifth-century religious songs were intended for performance on Delos and in a Delian context, and more candidates float among the fragmented splinters of song, surviving as mere numbers in the modern editions. Commissioned by individual localities, the majority are 'paeans' (*παιᾶνες*), sometimes 'processional paeans' (*προσοδιακοὶ παιᾶνες*), or 'processional songs' (*προσόδια*).[4] There is also a possibility that dithyrambs were sung at Delos earlier than in the fourth century, when musical competition became normal.[5] Pindar's *Paeans 5*, *7b*, and so-called *Paean 12* are certainly dedicated to Delos; *Paean 4* is likely to have been conceived for a Delian performance, while the surviving fragments of the so-called 'Hymn to Zeus' (fr. 33a–d) contain essential elements of local Delian cult myth and have most recently even been attributed to a hymn to Apollo.[6] Pindar's fr. 140a involves the foundation of a cult of Apollo Delios on Paros, and at least a handful of short fragments have a good chance of having been sung on Delos.[7] Bacchylides contributes a rarely noted longer text (fr. 65); and *Ode 17* was in all likelihood composed for performance at

[3] The image of the *khoros* of islands floating around Delos recurs in Call. *Del.* (4) 18, 93, 198, 250, 300–1, 325. Dion. Per. 525–8 for the ancient etymology. Calame (1997) 104–10 is the most detailed discussion of the traditions of choral song on Delos; see Graf (1993*a*) 102–10 on Delian aetiology.

[4] See D'Alessio (1997) for the generic classification of Pindaric song surviving on papyrus, especially the so-called paeans. He calls into question several attributions in the authoritative Snell-Maehler edition. Pi. *Pae.* 1–6, 7, 7a–d, 8, 8a–d, 9, 10, are all paeans beyond reasonable doubt. Maehler's classification will be used throughout here, with an indication of the generic ambiguities where appropriate, i.e. the central song Pi. *Pae.* 12, is 'so-called *Paean 12*'. Attribution to a literary genre on formal grounds is not of primary relevance for the argument of this book, and cultic song may even require differently formulated criteria of classification.

[5] Simonides of Keos is supposed to have composed a book of dithyrambs called *Δηλιακά* (Sim. *PMG* 593 = Str.15.3.2 = *Dith.* test. 131 Ieranò and 279–83); and so is Timotheos. A 4th-cent. choregic dedication to Dionysos on Delos is *IG* xi.4 1148 = *CEG* 2. 838 = *Dith.* test. 132 Ieranò. A further choregic monument dedicated to Apollo on the island of Keos attests a victory gained in an agon on Delos: *IG* xii.5 544 A2, 35–48 = *Dith.* test. 142a Ieranò; cf. Wilson (2000) 293–4; 390 nn. 138–9; 191 n. 143. For Athenian *kyklioi khoroi* sent to Delos (as well as at the Athenian Thargelia) see Wilson (2007).

[6] D'Alessio (2005) and (forthcoming *a*).

[7] Pi. *Pae.* 12(a) (= G2 Ruth); 16 (= G3 Ruth); fr. 60 (b) (= G4 Ruth); 7(a) (= G5 Ruth); 8b (a) 1–4 (= G6 Ruth); 8b (a) 5 ff. (= G7 Ruth); possibly fr. 215 (a) (= G10 Ruth). See p. 99 below.

Delos.[8] Most remarkably, however, we can include in this category half a dozen of Simonides' confirmed and likely paeans. Only a few lines per fragment survive, and not a single complete poem is preserved, but the remaining scraps contain enough text to show that they must have been closely connected to Delian cult, and very probably were Delian *paianes* as well.[9]

The Delian songs constitute a unique body of evidence, though the reality of Greek song culture that they reflect was probably not unique: they make up a whole collection of contemporary songs belonging to a single religious context, revolving around the cult centre of Apollo and Artemis and the practice of public *theoria* on Delos in the first half of the fifth century.[10] The songs for the most part turn, in gracious repetition, around the same theme. They narrate, in greater or lesser detail, the aetiological myth leading to the establishment of the Delian cults: Leto's delivery of her children Apollo and Artemis on the island.[11] Their relative uniformity is part of the phenomenon to be investigated. Performance on Delos in a theoric chorus seems beyond reasonable doubt for the majority of the poems; the verses commissioned for identifiable communities tend to link their own locality to the central Delian cult. All songs seem to form part of the same religious sphere and custom, possibly even in a milieu where serial performances in several localities could be imagined.[12]

The examination of the Delian set of choruses in this chapter will make the fundamental case for choral performance as the requisite medium for the interaction of myth and ritual. It will reveal, first, how aetiological myth comes to life in a cultic context, that is to say how myth and ritual begin to work together once put into the performative setting of religious song. It will also suggest how this interaction, through its manipulation of mythical time and ritual space, was active in the creation, maintenance, and transformation of a large worshipping community centred on Delos.

[8] Maehler (1982–97); Calame (forthcoming). See n. 83 on the discussion of whether this song was a dithyramb or a paean.

[9] Sim. *PMG* 519 frr. 32, 41, 55, 84, also 37, 47, 70, with Rutherford (1990). I print the three fragments 70, 47, and 37 here primarily because they are too insubstantial to be discussed at a later stage, but also because the image—not least in a presentation in a note—is one of a procession of paeans 'to Delos' (*ἐς Δᾶλον, πρὸς Δᾶλ[ον*; cf. *προσοδιακοὶ παιᾶνες*). The text follows Rutherford (1990):

PMG 519 fr. 37	fr. 47	fr. 70
] . . . . [	]μακα . [	]αν ἐς Δᾶλον]
]. οισιν ἅλι[	]ό̈ . ᾽ἐς Δαλ[	́]π̣ο̣νται[
]ν πρὸς Δᾶ[λον		
]. χαις ὀρι̣δρόμο̣[		
]δ̣εν[ ] [		

[10] For *theoria* as a context for song-dance and the idea of the 'theoric chorus' see Rutherford (2004).

[11] Some aspects of the divine birth are discussed in Rutherford (1988); Simon (1997); Laager (1957).

[12] See e.g. on Pi. *Pae.* 4 and fr. 140a below. Currie (2004) discusses the mechanics of reperformance in the case of victory odes.

The second, and third, longest, portions of this chapter discuss how the songs, individually and as a group, operate within this malleable system in actual theoric interaction on Delos in the first half of the fifth century. Delos was at this time the centre of the 'Delian League', at an early phase the Athenian empire. Our songs very likely belong to this historical milieu, but their relationship to the most powerful contemporary organization on the same small island is very far from clear. This chapter will show how performances of myth and ritual in the context of *polis-theoria* forged and severed ties to the larger cult community on Delos, oscillating delicately between compliance with and defiance of the growing Athenian hegemony. Choral *theoria* emerges as a flexible practice alternative to, and by no means identical with, political and military alliances, yet highly active in the definition of relations between participants through the constant interplay between local and central identities.

Finally, as we dig further into the choral past of the island, it will become apparent that fifth-century practice was itself a product of continuous interaction between myth and ritual on the island over a long period of time. Traces of this interaction can be perceived through somewhat antiquarian pieces of information starting at least as early as Herodotus, and some suggestions from archaeology. The role of this fourth, much shorter, section is to alert us to the phenomenon postulated in the introduction, that myths and rituals in an observable, contemporary milieu, in this case the fifth century, themselves emerge from multiple reworkings of long-standing practices and the continuous manipulation of mythical times and the religious spaces created by theoric practice. So the Callimachean image of islands floating around this most musical of islands reflects the fluid choral configurations, the changing relationships between participants in choral song, a key constituent in the creation of worshipping communities in ancient Greece and their workings in a social context.

1. MYTH AND RITUAL, TIME AND SPACE: FORGING TIES IN CHORAL SONG

Transcending *time*: the divine birth on Delos

It is well known how Apollo and Artemis came to be worshipped on Delos: it was their birthplace. The Delian part of the *Homeric Hymn to Apollo*, composed in the sixth century, is the first of many songs to tell the story of how Zeus impregnated Leto with the seeds of a twin birth.[13] When the time came for Apollo and Artemis' arrival on earth, Leto roamed the Aegean in search for a place of sufficient size and dignity to deliver her divine burden. All the places she called on, shuddering at the prospect of such responsibility, refused her hospitality. This is how the twins came to be born on Delos: a small, rocky island in the middle of the Aegean,

[13] *H. Ap.* 1–178.

barely equipped to nourish its own people, offered its soil in return for fame and prosperity. At once it became the hub of the Aegean island world, thenceforth home of the great cult of Apollo and Artemis; the hymn ends with a description of the splendid festivals held there ever since.[14] This aetiology for the cult of Apollo and Artemis explains the otherwise seemingly bizarre choice of Delos as one of the major cult centres of the Greek world. It turns an apparent paradox of reality into the punch line of the story: the image of Delos as a helpless little insignificant place is nowhere true. Delos, in every period of its traceable history, was well-frequented and notoriously overpopulated; its barrenness and small size contrast oddly with the island's centrality in Aegean communications since at least the Bronze Age. At all times it was central to the physical layout of Aegean history, the orchestra, the dancing floor for the enactment of this history.[15]

It is this aetiological story of the divine birth on Delos that our songs tell over and over again, indefatigably rehearsing, or alluding to, the self-same plot. The account of the birth lies at the heart of the *Homeric Hymn*'s tale, where it marks the beginning and end of the mythological section;[16] the moment of the divine twins seeing the light of day draws the unswerving interest of our paeans. It is the moment of the birth that is central to the interaction of myth and ritual in Delian cult, and the starting point for all further considerations on how myth and ritual in Delian song came to work in the cultic community performing them. The most detailed of these birth-reports is given in Pindar's *Paean 12*, which may be cited in full to serve as the frame of reference for all the other songs.

. . . θαμὰ δ' ἔρ̣[χεται
Να]ξόθεν λιπαρο̣τ̣ρ̣όφων θυσί]ᾳ
μή]λων Χαρίτεσσι μίγδαν
Κύ]ν̣θιον παρὰ κρημνόν, ἔνθα [
κελαινεφε̂ ἀργιβρένταν λέγο[ντι
Ζῆνα καθεζόμενον
κορυφαῖσιν ὕπερθε φυλάξ̣ᾳι π̣[ρ]ονοί[ᾳ,
ἁνίκ' ἀγανόφρων
Κοίου θυγάτηρ λύετο τερπνᾶς
ὠδῖνος̣· ἔλαμψαν δ' ἀελίου δέμας ὅπω̣[ς
ἀγλαὸν ἐς φάος ἰόντες δίδυμοι
παῖδες, πολὺ̣ν̣ ῥ̣ό̣θ̣[ο]ν̣ ἵ̣εσαν ἀπὸ στομ[άτων
Ἐ]λείθυιά τε καὶ Λ̣ά̣[χ]ε̣σις· τ̣ελέ[σ̣]αι δ' ολ[
κα]τελάμβανον . [. . .]
. .]εφθέγξαντο δ' ἐ̣γχ̣ώ̣ριαι
ἀγ]λ̣αὸς ἅς ἀν̣' ἑρκε̣[.] . . .

17 *ὀλ[ολυγαί* Deubner (1941)

[14] *H. Ap.* 146–64.

[15] Delos was one of a series of sanctuaries located at places nodal to maritime communication, and, as is typical for islands, a centre of commodity production: see Horden and Purcell (2000) 346; 608 (on Delos as a long-term bronze-working centre); 440; 456 on sanctuaries placed at convenient points of communication.

[16] *H. Ap.* 25–9; 115–19 (cf. already 14–19).

. . . often there comes . . .
from Naxos for the sacrifice
of richly-fed sheep, together with the Graces,
to the slope of Kynthos, where
they say dark-clouded, thunder-flashing
Zeus, sitting
above the heights, kept watch with forethought,
when the gentle-minded
daughter of Koios was being released from her sweet
birth-pains. The twin children shone like the sun
when they came into the splendid light,
and Eleithyia and Lachesis sent forth
much shouting from their mouths . . .
were taking
and the local women cried out
the splendid . . .

(Pindar, *Paean* 12.5–20 = G1 Ruth,
tr. adapted from W. H. Race)

Unlike the *Homeric Hymn*, which only alludes to the birth of Artemis on the fictitious island of Ortygia, the paeans make a point about a double birth on Delos itself, an observation well worth noting: it contrasts with the general notion that on Delos everything revolved around Apollo alone. This emphasis on the double birth reappears elsewhere in choral song: twins who 'shone like the beams of the sun when they appeared in the splendid light' (*Pae.* 12.14–5) are taken for granted throughout when Delos is the place 'where Leto produced and beheld her blessed progeny', her 'quiver-bearing offspring'. In the one Simonidean fragment where we can actually identify a mythical narrative, it refers to both deities. Even in the victory odes, whenever Leto features, the twins appear along with her.[17] Incidentally, the tradition of the twin-birth dominates early representations on vases.[18]

Correspondingly, both deities are the divine addressees in the majority of songs composed for performance on Delos, against the common notion that this song ought to be reserved for Apollo.[19] Pindar's *Paean 5* ends with the poet's plea to Leto's children to welcome him and his song. Artemis appears in the fragmented beginning of *Paean 12* relating to simultaneous cult activity (l. 3).

[17] *PMG* 519 fr. 84; Pi. fr. 33d.9–10: *ἔνθα τεκοῖσ' εὐδαίμον' ἐπόψατο γένναν* (typically referring to collective offspring) and *Pae.* 7b.52: *τοξοφόρον τελέσαι γόνον*. Pi. *N.* 9.4 contains an exhortation to give honour in song to 'the mother and the twin children' (*ματέρι καὶ διδύμοις παίδεσσιν*).

[18] Cf. *LIMC* s.v., e.g. no. 10, a black-figured depiction of Leto with her two children emerging from her shoulders (dated to 540–520 BC). Cf. the Aegean pictorial tradition on a kind of mother goddess with two children on the 7th-cent. relief pithoi from Tenos (Schaefer (1957) 79–82; the current state of the debate features in Caskey (1998)). Cf. Riccioni (1966).

[19] On the 'Apolline' nature of paianic song see Rutherford (2001) 23–36, who also draws attention to paeans jointly addressed to Artemis and Apollo, as in Eur. *IA* 1467–80, cited n. 25 below.

And *Paean 7*b, another song alluding to the double birth in some detail, starts off by invoking Apollo, calls upon his mother in the third line, and very likely would have contained a reference to Artemis in the second.[20] The same can be observed in some Simonidean pieces: *PMG* 519 fr. 41.1 describes Artemis; fr. 37 apparently connects the ritual movement of a chorus πρὸς Δᾶ[λον with Artemis referred to by ὀρίδρομο̣[('running on the mountain'), as in fr. 35 (b).[21] Fr. 84 talks about Apollo and might contain a reference to Artemis too, as implied by the epithet εὐέθειρα, though this is uncertain; even fr. 55 could have had an allusion to Artemis especially should the epithet for the goddess mentioned be χρυσ]ῶπις rather than γλαυκ]ῶπις.[22] Finally, Bacchylides' fr. 65, which has never really drawn the attention of scholars at all, features Delos, Artemis, and *khoroi*, and was probably a paean like all the others.[23] Despite the commonly held view that paeans were for Apollo only, this set of poems was evidently sung for both Apollo and Artemis.

But our main focus should be the event of the birth. The moment is carefully and elaborately orchestrated, deploying the full repertoire that aetiology has to offer. Aetiological strategies can be exceptionally well observed because the well-excavated site of Delos allows us to identify the references to individual sacred and geographical localities, confirming a certain literal-mindedness of the myth. A tangible Delian reality is delicately interwoven into the narrative through recurring formulae and a fixed set of topographical references, as if there were a ready-made way of talking about this particular mythical event. Leto's negotiations with the island are spun out at great length in the *Homeric Hymn*, pinpointing the locality very precisely; Pindar's songs, too, dwell on Delos' search for identity, leaving the island drifting across the sea, even granting Delos a speech all to herself which contrasts the tribulations of her floating fate with the attraction of becoming a steady place.[24] Once the place of the mythical birth is fixed, the ritual procession *Paean 12* moves towards the 'Kynthian cliff' (Κύ]ν̣θιον παρὰ κρημνόν (*Pae.* 12.8)), switching into myth and placing the birth on the side of Delos' spiked Mount Kynthos, just as the *Hymn* imagines Leto 'resting against the great mass of the Kynthian hill' (κεκλιμένη πρὸς μακρὸν ὄρος καὶ Κύνθιον ὄχθον l. 17, κλινθεῖσα πρὸς Κύνθου ὄρος l. 26). The pining *khoros* in Euripides' *Iphigenia in Tauris*, dreaming itself away from its 'barbarian' exile on the Krimea to typically 'Greek' cult places, similarly refers to the place as παρὰ Κύνθιον ὄχθον ('by the Kynthian hill'), and situates it at the nearby sanctuary of Artemis Λοχία

[20] Pi. *Pae.* 7b.1–3: Ἄπολλο[ν . . . / σὲ καὶ . . . / ματ̣έ̣ρ̣[.

[21] Cf. Eur. *IA* 1593, in which the sacrificial victim for Artemis is the ἔλαφος ὀρειδρόμος ('deer running on the mountains').

[22] *PMG* 519 fr. 84.6; fr. 55.7 as printed by Rutherford (1990).

[23] Bacch. fr. 65.6, 9, 11. Typical paean themes, like a wish for ὄλβος 'good fortune' (l. 7), occur e.g. in Pi. *Pae.* 2.60; 6.133; 9.9; Bacch. fr. 4.59 (for the concept of *olbos* in Pindar and Bacchylides see Gonzáles de Tobia (2004)). Cf. the Muses or Charites at the beginning of poetical paeans: Pi. *Pae.* 3; 6; 7.10; 12.

[24] Pi. *Pae.* 7.38–47.

('of childbirth') and the lake on Delos.[25] The lake is itself relevant to the story: its 'meadows' feature in the *Homeric Hymn*, and the same word λειμών also assists Simonides in picturing the scene.[26]

The birth itself, at the height of all this narrative build-up, is equally portrayed in a conspicuously set manner. Leto's birth pangs, ὠδῖνες, recur with remarkable consistency in the *Homeric Hymn*, Simonides, and Pindar: in the *Hymn*, Leto for as long as nine days and nights is 'pierced with unhoped-for birth-pangs' (ll. 91–2 ἀέλπτοις ὠδίνεσσι πέπαρτο). Simonides creates an image of the enormous weight she is carrying (fr. 32.4 ἐβ̣άρυνον ὠ̣[δ]ῖ̣νες 'the birth-pangs weighed her down'), while Pindar speaks of the 'birth-approaching pain' (ὠδίνεσσι ἀγχιτόκοις fr. 33d.3–4). Even Zeus in *Paean 12* appreciates the intensity of the procedure when he 'guards with foresight' from his vantage point on Mount Kynthos how Leto is being released from her 'sweet labour' (τερπνᾶς ὠδῖνος̣ *Pae.* 12.13–4).[27]

But the ritual moment is not quite there yet: the event of the birth does not attract Zeus' interest alone, but features a whole chorus of birth-attendants. In the *Hymn*, all female deities instantly rush around the scene save Eleithyia: the goddess of birth is held back theatrically by Hera, fearing yet another prominent offspring not hers, and Eleithyia receives her own entry just in time for the event.[28] The goddesses together mark the delivery with a cry: 'the goddesses all shouted with joy' (θεαὶ δ' ὀλόλυξαν ἅπασαι l. 119). The scene features in *Paean 12* in virtually the same setting: Eleithyia and Lakhesis shout at the moment of birth, probably also in *ololyge* (ll.16–17: πολὺν̣ ῥ̣ό̣θ̣[ο]ν̣ ἵ̣εσαν ἀπὸ στομ[άτων . . . τ̣ελέ[σ̣]αι ὀλ[]). And the scene recurs with the same force in one of the fragmentary representations of the birth by Simonides:

[25] Eur. *IT.* 1094–1105 (tr. D. Kovacs):

Χο. ἐγὼ σοι παραβάλλομαι	I, a bird with no wings
θρηνοῦσ' ἄπτερος ὄρνις	vie with you in lamentation,
ποθοῦσ' Ἑλλάνων ἀγόρους,	longing for the Greeks' gathering places,
ποθοῦσ' Ἄρτεμιν λοχίαν,	longing for Artemis, goddess of childbed,
ἃ παρὰ Κύνθιον ὄχθον οἰ-	who dwells by the Kynthian hill
κεῖ φοίνικά θ' ἁβροκόμαν	and the date palm with its tender tresses
δάφναν τ' εὐερνέα καὶ	and the lovely slip of laurel
γλαυκᾶς θαλλὸν ἱερὸν ἐλαί-	and the sacred shoot of the gray-green olive,
ας, Λατοῦς ὠδῖνι φίλον,	dear to Leto's offspring,
λίμναν θ' εἱλίσσουσαν ὕδωρ,	and the lake that swirls its water
κύκλιον, ἔνθα κύκνος μελῳ-	in a circle, where the melodious swan
δὸς Μούσας θεραπεύει.	renders his service to the Muses.

The sanctuary of Artemis Lokhia is thought by its French excavators to be a cult building right to the east of the summit of Mount Kynthos, though the identification is not certain: Bruneau–Ducat (1983) no. 108; cf. *ED* xi, 293–308.

[26] *H. Ap.* 118: λειμῶνι μαλακῷ 'in the soft meadow'; Sim. *PMG* 519 fr. 32.3.

[27] Cf. Call. *Del.* (4) 209 ff. The depiction of the actual birth is equally formulaic: ἐκ δ' ἔθορε πρὸ φόως δέ 'he leapt out into the light' in *H. Ap.* 119; ἔλαμψαν . . . ἀγλαὸν ἐς φάος ἰόντες 'they flashed into the splendid light' Pi. *Pae.* 12.14–15.

[28] *H. Ap.* 97–114.

]ντο Καρῶν ἀ̣λκίμων.[
ἀμ]φὶ ῥέεθρα καλὸν ἔστασαν [χορόν
]λ̣ειμῶνας· ἤδ̣η γὰρ αἰδοῐ̣[αι
ἐ]β̣άρυνον ὠ̣̓[δ]ῖ̣νες· ἄυσ̣ε
] . υος ἀθαν[άτ]ας· ἧκε
κλ]ῦθί μοι ασ .[. .]ω̣σ̣.

. . . of the doughty Karians
. . . on the banks of . . .'s streams they set up
a fair [dance in the] meadows; for now [the goddess]
was burdened with the private toils of birth
. . . cried out . . ., of the . . . divine, and sent forth
Hear me . . .

(Simonides *PMG* 519 fr. 32, after Rutherford (1990), tr. West, adapted)

Here a group of people seems to assemble on the banks of some water in a manner typical of a female *khoros* surrounding a mythical scene. A cry of some sort is indicated (*ἄυσε*), while *ἀθαν[άτ]ας* suggests the collection of female divinities. The divine guests, however, are not alone: Pindar's *Paean 12* has more attendants to follow and speaks of some native women: *ἐ̣γχ̣ώριαι*, local women, who mix with the divine circle in shouting and singing in honour of the divine arrival (*Pae.* 12.17–20 . . . *ὀλ[ἐφθέγξαντο*), in the same way as the goddesses of the *Hymn* cry out in *ὀλολυγή* at the event. What is this *ololyge* for the twins? Who are these local women, shouting and singing for Apollo and Artemis? The scenes of the gathering *khoros* are tellingly placed at the end of the paeans' mythical sections, and it is the ensuing performative parts that give some clues as to what is going on here. For exactly such local women appear in other paeanic fragments. But they are now the real girls who are actually singing the choral songs in the ritual in progress. Simonides' fr. 55 conspicuously calls upon certain 'daughters of the Delians', the *Δαλίων θύγατρες*,

(a)

]τυχαι Λύκιον [
]σα κάλλιστον υἱόν· ἰη[
[ὀλολύ-]ξατε, Δαλίων θύγατ[ρες
] σὺν εὐσεβεῖ· [
]ντ' . ἐν τᾷ̣δε γὰρ δ̣ικα[(b)
]μ̣ε πλαξιάλοι' ἀπ Ἀ[. . .
΄]α̣ρ μόληι· ποτνία χ[ρυσ]ῶπι δ[
]αείδοντες ὀλβο̣[.] . [. . .
] . οις ὕπο̣ μ̣ενο̣[
]εφερον[

3 fort. Rutherford

. . . the glens . . . Lycian [Apollo]
her finest of sons. Ie, ie!
Cry the olol]yge, Delian maids,
with reverent [dance]

. . . for in this . . . just . . .
near battering water . . . A[rtemis?
when . . . comes. Lady of D[elos, gold of] face,
. . . we in song . . . fortune . . .
. . .
they carried

(Simonides *PMG* 519 fr. 55, after
Rutherford (1990), tr. West, adapted)

These *Δαλίων θύγατρες* are summoned to show due reverence in cult and song, to give the paean cry (*ἰή*) and presumably to shout the *ololyge* (*]ξατε*). The Lady of Delos is probably Artemis, whose turn it is then to be surrounded by the *khoros* 'who sings' (*ἀείδοντες*) for someone's good fortune (*ὄλβος*). The scene is a place near water, as elsewhere. The 'choreography' suggests that the first and second surviving lines sing of the birth itself, in a story ending, for example, as *τεκοῖ]σα κάλλιστον υἱόν*.[29] The paean thus summons the girls in the same role as the 'goddesses' mixed with 'local women' appear in *Paean 12*, at the transition between mythical and performative part of the song.

Singing and dancing *κοῦ[ραι* of some sort are also involved in Simonides' *PMG* 519 fr. 41. Here Artemis features in typical attire of a bow and is 'deep [girdled]', someone's instrument is taken from the hook and musical *σ]άματα* are given to the girls who recur as *αἱ δὲ* at the beginning of the following (missing) line.

(a)
Ἀρ]τέμιδός τε βαθυ̣[
]όν τε τόξον [. (b)
ἄν]αξ ἀπὸ πασσάλο̣[. . .
]ἐν οἴκῳ Διὸς ἀ̣θαν[
σ]άματα κού̣[ραι]ς· αἱ δ̣[
᾿] . [. . .
. . .

of both Artemis, the deep-[bosomed?]
. . . and the bow
lord, from the hook
in the house of Zeus . . . immortals
signals to girls. And they . . .

(Simonides *PMG* 519 fr. 41,
after Rutherford (1990))

Who is this chorus singing so conspicuously at the interface of myth and ritual? As is well known, in the Delian panegyris in the *Homeric Hymn to Apollo*, there features a set of singing women as *Δηλιάδες*. These Deliades praise Apollo, Artemis, and Leto, and sing of past heroic events, and do so in many dialects

[29] Cf. Pi. fr. 33d.9–10.

('voices').[30] In Hellenistic times, the Deliades were a standing chorus on Delos, which features in the inventories of the island's temples. There is no evidence for the actual institution in the classical era, but it is clear that the Deliades were widely known as a local chorus of singers and dancers of paeans to Apollo and Artemis on Delos. The chorus of old men in Euripides' *Herakles* compares its song to theirs.

> παιᾶνα μὲν Δηλιάδες
> ναῶν ὑμνοῦσ' ἀμφὶ πύλας
> τὸν Λατοῦς εὔπαιδα γόνον,
> εἱλίσσουσαι καλλίχοροι·
> παιᾶνας δ' ἐπὶ σοῖς μελάθροις
> κύκνος ὣς γέρων ἀοιδὸς
> πολιᾶν ἐκ γενύων
> κελαδήσω· τὸ γὰρ εὖ
> τοῖς ὕμνοισι ὑπάρχει.
>
> A paean about their temple gates
> the maidens of Delos sing
> to the fair son of Leto,
> weaving their lovely dance steps.
> And paeans about your house
> I, an aged singer, swan-like
> from my hoary throat
> shall pour forth. For the power of right
> is in my hymns.
>
> (Euripides, *Herakles* 687–95,
> tr. D. Kovacs)[31]

The paean-singing here, incidentally, is also concerned with the actual birth of Apollo and Artemis from Leto, just as in the real paeans by Pindar and Simonides. Simonides' Δαλίων θύγατρες, the 'local women' of Pindar's paean, must therefore

[30] *H. Ap.* 156–64:

> πρὸς δὲ τόδε μέγα θαῦμα, ὅου κλέος οὔποτ' ὀλεῖται,
> κοῦραι Δηλιάδες, ἑκατηβελέταο θεράπναι·
> αἵ τ' ἐπεὶ ἂρ πρῶτον μὲν Ἀπόλλων ὑμνήσωσιν,
> αὖτις δ' αὖ Λητώ τε καὶ Ἄρτεμιν ἰοχέαιραν,
> μνησάμεναι ἀνδρῶν τε παλαιῶν ἠδὲ γυναικῶν
> ὕμνον ἀείδουσιν, θέλγουσι δὲ φῦλ' ἀνθρώπων.
> πάντων δ' ἀνθρώπων φωνὰς καὶ βαμβαλιαστὺν
> μιμεῖσθ' ἴσασιν· φαίη δέ κεν αὐτὸς ἕκαστος
> φθέγγεσθ'· οὕτω σφιν καλὴ συνάρηρεν ἀοιδή.

'And besides, this great wonder, the fame of which will never perish: the Maidens of Delos, the servants of the Far-shooter, who, after first hymning Apollo, and then in turn Leto and Artemis profuse of arrows, turn their thoughts to the men and women of old and sing a song that charms the peoples. They know how to mimic all people's voices and their babble; anyone might think it was he himself speaking, so well is their singing constructed' (tr. West).

[31] See Henrichs (1996) on the role of the Deliades in this passage; Calame (1997) 75–7 and 104–10 on the Deliades on Delos.

be the same Deliades, those girls who in the songs are imagined to perform the paeans, and their singing is closely related to the coming into existence, the epiphany, of the two gods. And we can conclude that, similarly, the local women (ἐγχώριαι l. 19) at the end of the mythical narrative of *Paean 12* must be a reference to the Deliades.

Ἐγχώριαι, Δαλίων θύγατρες, κοῦραι, are all the same local women, singing and shouting for Artemis and Apollo. They seem to do exactly the same as the female goddesses in the mythical accounts: they welcome the divine twins with birth-shouts. The birth-shout in myth becomes the paean imitating the birth-shout in the ongoing ritual, and the local women who cried out in myth become a local female chorus in the ritual, the so-called Deliades. It appears that singing the cultic hymn to Artemis and Apollo was singing their birth-shout. The myth also gives the *aition* for the type of cult song: with the ritual shout at the birth, the paean as a song of greeting for Artemis and Apollo was introduced.[32] Myth and ritual, past and present, blend here in the actual performance of the chorus, prompting the sensation that the birth was happening as the chorus was singing, in the here and now of the performance. That is to say, the choral dance is the medium in which myth and ritual merge, become one and the same thing.

It is crucial to realize that the same Δαλίων θύγατρες simultaneously perform in both time spheres, as companions of the female deities in the mythical tale, and as the chorus of women in the current festival. They are at once narrators of, and actors in, the story, performing in ritual what they are narrating in myth. In this double role, the chorus of the Δαλίων θύγατρες bridges the time gap, linking the mythical past to the present ritual; the two spheres smoothly blend into one another, so that mythical time and present time are no longer clearly separate. For the spectator or singer, there is no longer a distinction between the 'local women' in myth and those in ritual.

It is in the service of this fusion of myth and ritual in the choral dance that songs at this stage move from the telling of myth into the performative mode. In *Paean 12*, the chorus of the Deliades appears for the first time at the end of the mythical narrative, but the surviving text stops here. Simonides' fragment 32 quoted above, however, offers a direct transition from the birth to the performance in progress, and the song continues with an invocation to a divinity, a reference to the ritual present: κλ]ῦθί μοι . . . The mythical narrative terminates at this point, and it is now the function of the chorus to address the god in, for instance, prayer. The *khoros*-singing thus features in both mythical past and ritual present; it stands at a point of transition, forming the hinge between the two.

Through the merging of the two different time levels, of performing and performed time, the chorus achieves the abolition and transcendence of real time. Creating something close to Tambiah's fused sense of communication, the performance works like a pool into which associations of either myth or ritual, related to their relevant time spheres, are thrown and jumbled up. Through their

[32] This is consistent with the tradition that Apollo received offerings on Delos on his birthday, 7 Thargelion: D. L. 3.2.

presence at the divine birth, the timelessly performing Deliades partake in these authoritative times of origins, which set up 'the order of things in the world'. Every single performance thus has a share in the mythical beginnings of the cult where the ritual not only reproduces but, in the minds of those in the ritual, actually takes place at that same creative moment.

The fuzzy aesthetic boundaries of these combined ritual acts and the consequent sense of atemporality are not unusual features of rituals that contain elements of re-enactments. Until relatively recently, strongly plotted ritual sequences like the Orthodox Easter ceremony projected onlookers into the events of the sacred narrative. The Easter story was staged through tricks, such as constant theatrical shifts between a narrative told in the past and the ritual speech and chants of the present. Together with vital visual effects this evoked spontaneous crying at the staged crucifixion or joyful shouting at the resurrection, the known effects of this intensified and highly sensual experience. The specific ways of performing the cult song work as orchestration to achieve the mythical projection.[33]

Performance—in the case of Greek cultic song, choral performance—is therefore a chief medium through which myth and ritual can interact. Rather than through parallels between myth and ritual, where ritual repeats step by step what the myth narrates, it is through a hinge element such as the Deliades that an association is formed. The relation of myth and ritual to each other is therefore not one of mutual reflection but of interface. In the Introduction I looked at the shared strategies of myth and ritual in the way they construe their relationship to time and the past. We can now conclude that choral performance is one of the media for these strategies to come into action: it affords the trick of transcending time that is necessary for myth and ritual to start communicating with each other.

All this is an illusionary strategy to make things real, in other words to propel participants in a ritual into a conviction, even to create 'belief' in the way postulated by Plato's Athenian in the *Laws* cited at the beginning. Performances of this kind therefore make it possible to transfer claims, associations, and also emotions relevant to the situation of the past into the present. What is said in the mythical sphere is valid for the present as well. This is a characteristic effect of these performances, and historically perhaps the most prolific: it is the workings of this effect within the community singing these myths that allow myth-ritual choral performances to operate in society in a given time and place, by creating authoritative views and ideas about a past. More generally, performance, staging, and theatricality emerge as fundamental to how myth and ritual can act. The result is a prolific paradox that will follow us through this book: for ritual can validate for the present what the myth claims for the past. And conversely, myth can validate for a present what ritual claims for the past. The play with time is one of the features of the myth–ritual interaction that allows performances to operate within a given worshipping community.

[33] An older generation of modern Greeks described former Easter ceremonies to me in such a way.

Mapping out religious *space*

In the fifth century, *khoroi* came from all over the Greek world to the Delian festival, performing what must have been an overwhelming number of songs. None of the existing pieces to be performed on Delos was in fact composed 'for the Delians', but for islands such as Keos, Paros, Naxos, for Athens, and for half a dozen more commissioners of uncertain identity. A closer look at the Delian festival itself will reveal that choral song had a key role in Apollo and Artemis' rituals. The choruses sent there were a distinct item on the ritual agenda without which the ritual would be incomplete and invalid; places marked their participation in the cult by embarking a chorus on the journey to Delos. In what follows we shall see how the interaction of myth and ritual in the songs is central to how a theoric worshipping community was forged. The songs travelling between locality and centre were mapping out the religious space shared between places participating in the worship of the twin gods. In particular, performances of myth and ritual not only affect our choruses' relationship to time and the past, but also to place and the spaces in which they act.

It is from Thucydides' brief history of the Delian celebrations that the role of the choral songs in the festival is best understood. Quoting the relevant passage of the *Homeric Hymn*, he thinks, first, of an indefinite point in the past of a 'great gathering' (*μεγάλη σύνοδος*) when 'Ionians and surrounding islanders' participated in what he describes in the following terms:

ἦν δέ ποτε καὶ τὸ πάλαι μεγάλη ξύνοδος ἐς τὴν Δῆλον τῶν Ἰώνων τε καὶ περικτιόνων νησιωτῶν· ξύν τε γὰρ γυναιξὶ καὶ παισὶ ἐθεώρουν ὥσπερ νῦν ἐς τὰ Ἐφέσια Ἴωνες, καὶ ἀγὼν ἐποιεῖτο αὐτόθι καὶ γυμνικὸς καὶ μουσικός, χορούς τε ἀνῆγον αἱ πόλεις. δηλοῖ δὲ μάλιστα Ὅμηρος ὅτι τοιαῦτα ἦν ἐν τοῖς ἔπεσιν τοῖσδε, ἅ ἐστιν ἐκ προοιμίου Ἀπόλλωνος . . .

There had also been in the distant past a great gathering of the Ionians and neighbouring islanders at Delos. They used to come there to the festival with their wives and children, just as the Ionians now go to the festival at Ephesos, and they used to hold contests there in athletics, poetry, and music, and the cities sent choruses there. That this was so is made perfectly clear by the following lines of Homer, from his hymn to Apollo . . .

This stage in the history of religious gatherings involves the full festival armada of musical and athletic contests as well as choral performances sent by cities. Thucydides attributes to this phase some extraordinary acts on the part of Delos' rich supporters, such as the Samian tyrant Polykrates' preposterous dedication of the neighbouring island Rheneia to Apollo Delios, and above all Delos' purification initiative by Peisistratos. This act was famously emulated by the Athenians in 426/5 BC when they 'reinstated' the Ionian panegyris as a penteteric festival. For the period between the *μεγάλη ξύνοδος* and the second purification, Thucydides notes that the festival was carried out on a smaller scale:[34]

[34] It remains questionable whether the purification was a ritual act related to the divine birth on the island too; cf. C. R. Long (1958); Picard (1959).

τοσαῦτα μὲν Ὅμηρος ἐτεκμηρίωσεν ὅτι ἦν καὶ τὸ πάλαι μεγάλη ξύνοδος καὶ ἑορτὴ ἐν τῇ Δήλῳ· ὕστερον δὲ [i.e. between *H. Ap.* and 425] τοὺς μὲν χοροὺς οἱ νησιῶται καὶ οἱ Ἀθηναῖοι μεθ' ἱερῶν ἔπεμπον, τὰ δὲ περὶ τοὺς ἀγῶνας καὶ τὰ πλεῖστα κατελύθη ὑπὸ ξυμφορῶν, ὡς εἰκός, πρὶν δὴ οἱ Ἀθηναῖοι τότε τὸν ἀγῶνα ἐποίησαν καὶ ἱπποδρομίας, ὃ πρότερον οὐκ ἦν.

We thus have evidence from Homer that in ancient times also there was a great gathering and festival at Delos. Later the islanders and the Athenians still sent choruses and sacred offerings, but the contest and most of the other ceremonies were discontinued, probably because of the difficulties of the times, and remained out of use until this occasion when the Athenians celebrated the games, including in them horseracing, which was a new event. (Thucydides 3.104, 3–4, 6, tr. Warner, adapted)

The festival in this intermediate phase was reduced to its bare bones, but *khoros* singing was strikingly still part of it. While it may feel natural to tie the *khoroi* to a choral contest in honour of the god, just as dithyrambic competitions formed part of the worship of Dionysos at Athens, in both passages the agonistic part of the festival is clearly distinct from the choral performances, as if they did not quite fall into the same category of rites: in the 'Ionian' period, a gymnic and musical contest was held 'and furthermore the *poleis* sent *khoroi*' (χορούς τε ἀνῆγον αἱ πόλεις). The second formulation makes the separation between the agonistic and the ritual component even clearer: while the musical and athletic part were abolished, 'islanders and Athenians sent the *khoroi* together with the *hiera*' ('sacrificial offerings'). This implies that the *khoroi* came with the sacrifices, integral, or at least very closely connected, to them, and made up what characterized the worship of the Delian deities. Hence they were the only items left at the time of the festival's reduction in scale and expenditure.

Another peculiar passage confirms that there was something special about these *khoroi* on Delos' ritual agenda. In his *Life of Nikias*, Plutarch reports that the great general led the Athenian *theoria* to Delos, in either 421 or 417 BC (but in any case after the renewal of the festival and the reinstitution of the contests). As *arkhitheoros* he mounted his own very particular procession to Delos, including a *khoros*.

The choruses which cities used to send thither to sing the praises of the god (ᾀσομένους τῷ θεῷ) were wont to put in at the island in haphazard fashion. The throng of worshippers would meet them at the ship and bid them sing, not with the decorum due, but as they were hastily and tumultuously disembarking, and while they were actually donning their chaplets and vestments. But when Nikias conducted the festal embassy (ὅτε τὴν θεωρίαν ἦγεν), he landed first on the neighbouring island of Rheneia, with his choir, sacrificial victims, and other equipment (τὸν χορὸν ἔχων καὶ τὰ ἱερεῖα καὶ τὴν ἄλλην παρασκευήν). Then, with the bridge of boats which he had brought along with him from Athens, where it had been made to measure and signally adorned with gildings and dyed stuffs and garlands and tapestries, he spanned during the night the strait between Rheneia and Delos, which is not wide. At break of day he led his festal procession in honour of the god (τήν τε πομπὴν τῷ θεῷ καὶ τὸν χορὸν ἄγων), and his choir arrayed in lavish splendour and singing as it marched, across the bridge to land. After the sacrifices and the contests and the banquets were over, he erected the famous bronze palm-tree as a thank offering to the god. (Plutarch, *Nikias* 3.4, tr. B. Perrin)

The *khoros* is part of the theoric *pompe* arriving not simply by sea, but quite physically processing by boat from island to island, leading up to the sacrifice, to be followed by separate contests and banquets. The juxtaposition of ἀρχιθέωρος and χορηγός, positions which Nikias effectively merges, recurs in the list of officials that the *Athenaion Politeia* specifies for the Delian *panegyris*, neatly tying the chorus to the cult obligation to be fulfilled on Delos. All these passages suggest that theoric songs on Delos were an intrinsic part of the ritual but not performed as part of a musical competition—yet there was a competitive element to them, to which I shall return.[35]

For Thucydides, '*khoroi* and *hiera*' were thus intimately connected to each other on Delos. The peculiar combination of words occurs elsewhere and suggests that *khoroi* at festivals had a specific ritual function and were constitutive of what related a deity to his or her rites.[36] Certain instances of the ancient record make this relation closer than others. Mocking *khoroi* were the main element in the worship of Damia and Auxesia on Aigina; the aetiological myth discloses that the essence of this festival was to overcome social conflict in ritual laughter. The integral role of *khoros*-singing in worship is implied in the fact that Kleisthenes of Sikyon, as part of his social reform, could famously divide up the traditional honours for Adrastos, attributing the 'sacrifice' to the newly introduced hero Melanippos, while his *khoroi* went to Dionysos.[37]

Once the ritual role of the *khoros* is established in this way, it also becomes clear why cities shipped their choruses to Delos. Sending a *khoros* formed part of the religious tribute to the god. It almost seems that sending a (theoric) *khoros* was 'obligatory' for membership in the worshipping community; the 'choral tribute' marked, along with the offerings, participation in the cult. Interestingly, ἀνάγειν, if used in a ritual context as in the passage from Thucydides quoted above, seems to describe a typically religious 'contribution'.[38]

That this participation was expressed in choral song is the really remarkable observation here. For, given the myth–ritual interaction unfolded in the previous section, it means that all these communities came to Delos in order to celebrate the birth of Apollo and Artemis through hymnic re-enactment. The Naxians performing *Paean 12*, the key song discussed above, themselves become, as it were, the Deliades, taking on the role of the birth-helpers. Naxians, in the 'logic' of the performative illusion created, therefore have the same 'claim' to worship of

[35] The standard view is that cultic songs were principally not performed in competition (Bremer and Furley 2001); Bremer (2000) 61–6, but it seems now clearer than ever that the boundaries between 'competitive' and 'ritual' song were fluid: e.g. Calame (forthcoming); Wilson (2007).

[36] e.g. Pl. *Leg.* 804a; Plb. 4.20.5–21.9; Luc. *De Salt.* 16 and 17; [Plut.] *De Mus.* 1135a etc.

[37] I discuss more instances of a firm rooting of choral song in communal rituals all over Greece, always tied to a cultic aetiology, in (2004); the choral reform of Kleisthenes of Sikyon (Hdt. 5.67) is treated in (2007).

[38] ἀνάγειν 'produce' in religious circumstances: chorus/dance: Hes. *Sc.* 280: ἄναγον χορόν; Eur. *Troad.* 332–3: χόρευμ' ἄναγε; festival, sacrifice *vel. sim.*: Hdt. 2.48: τὴν δὲ ἄλλην ἀνάγουσι ἑορτὴν τῷ Διονύσῳ; 60 μεγάλας ἀνάγοντες θυσίας; *OGI* 764.47 (2nd cent. BC) ταυρούς; cult songs: Soph. *Trach.* 210–14: ὁμοῦ δὲ παιᾶνα παι / ἂν' ἀνάγετ', ὦ παρθένοι, / βοᾶτε τὰν ὁμόσπορον / Ἄρτεμιν Ὀρτυγίαν; Eur. *El.* 126 of a lamentation: ἄναγε πολύδακρυν ἁδονάν [for song]; *Ph.* 1350: ἀνάγετ' ἀνάγετε κωκυτόν.

Apollo and Artemis on Delos as the local Delian women. All the island choruses flocking to Delos do just the same, identifying themselves with the Deliades and one by one re-living the birth of the twins. Any of the choruses giving their welcoming shout to Apollo and Artemis would thus have had their own role in the origins and establishment of the cult: the birth story is a mythical past shared by them all. The process of identification in cult song is crucial for how places construe their participation in the cult, marking their share in this particular religious community. The ritual song thus ties the worshipping community to the centre.

This is interesting because the magnetic power of Delos in attracting worshippers from abroad is only one side of the picture. At the same time, Delos seems to have worked as an epicentre for the spreading of cults. What purports to originate as Delian local religion unfolds into a most amazing network of cults covering substantial parts of the Aegean. That Delian cults bounce back to the islands shows how fundamental the staking of a claim to participation through myth-ritual performance is for the creation of a theoric worshipping community, as well as the delineation of a common religious space in which this community could interact. A sacred landscape unfolds through performance (Map. 2.1).

The Delian pantheon itself is a patchwork of the birth legend's mythical figures, proving once again how intimately cult aetiology is linked to the tangible world of religious practice. The focus is on the divine twins with a series of temples for Apollo *Δήλιος* erected successively from the seventh century onwards, and a huge, much older complex for Artemis *Δηλία*. Artemis is also believed to have had a little precinct as *Λοχία* close to the lake. Despite the emphasis on the twins in the paeanic myths, their precincts are kept separate, a point to which I shall return. Birth-giving Eileithyia was present on the slopes of Mount Kynthos, which yielded a respectable number of votive offerings; Zeus Kynthios and Athena Kynthia, the first of whom we remember from Pindar's *Paean 12*, are placed high up on the top of Mount Kynthos, overlooking the entire sanctuary. At the foot of the hill, a fifth-century *Ὅρος Λητοῦς* has been located. Even Hera, who was so eager to prevent the birth, finds herself on Delos (Fig. 2.1).[39]

Sailing around the neighbouring island world quickly reveals that this happy family was frequently reproduced.[40] The nearby Kyklades are particularly prone

[39] See Bruneau–Ducat (1983) for a general overview; Jockey (1996) is a very useful survey of the religious monuments and their recent literature in the archaic period. More recent finds and studies include the altar of Artemis: Étienne–Fraisse (1989). The debate over the so-called Oikos of the Naxians as a possible first temple for Apollo is still ongoing: Roux (1977/9); Courbin (1979), (1980), (1987); Gallet de Santerre (1984); Kalpaxis (1989); Picard (1992). Eleithyia's cult, well-attested from the 3rd cent. onwards, has not been located; it used to be thought to be in the precinct now attributed to Artemis Lokhia: *ED* 11.293 ff.; Bruneau–Ducat no. 108. Leto's *horos*: *ED* 11.283; cf. Gallet de Santerre (1946).

[40] An early collection of the cults of Apollo Delios in the Aegean was put together by Jessen, *RE* iv (1901) 2443–6; cf. Rubensohn (1962) 39–43. It is possible that some islands had sanctuaries of Apollo Delios which were local cult centres, whilst individual cities still had their own shrine of Apollo Delios, for example on Euboia, or Amorgos (nn. 45, 47 below). The Dalion on Kos may have had

Figure 2.1 View from Mount Kynthos over the sanctuary and harbour on Delos; the island of Rheneia lies to the left, Syros appears in the distance; Zeus watched the birth of Apollo and Artemis on Delos from here

to adopting the Delian pantheon. Paros is the most striking instance of this phenomenon: here the late sixth-century complex called *Δήλιον*, overlooking the bay of Paroikia, assembles together Artemis Delia and Athena Kynthia, and the likely hypothesis is that the same complex also hosted their male partners, Apollo Delios and perhaps even Zeus. Of Geometric origin, the sanctuary experienced a major monumentalization around 530 BC, comprising a small temple to Artemis, an altar and a so-called *hestiatorion*. Eileithyia is found only a couple of miles further away, in a cave cult dating from the Geometric period that has produced a host of votive offerings.[41] Stray finds of a sixth-century BC seated

a regional, amphiktyonic function: n. 51 below. Constantakopoulou (2005) 15–16 discusses pan-island cults. Pingiatoglou (1981) 32–7 on the disproportionate spread of Eileithyia on the islands.

[41] On the Delion on Paros see Rubensohn (1962); Schuller (1982); Schuller and Ohnesorg (1991). Artemis Delia: *IG* xii.5 211 (4th cent. BC); Apollo Delios: *IG* xii.5 214 (4th cent. BC); 211 (4th cent. BC); 215. Athena Kynthia: *IG* xii.5 210 (archaic?). The triad of Apollo, Artemis, and Leto: *Horos* 10–12 (1992–8) 438 no. 2; possibly *IG* xii.5 271. Artemis is also Ephesia (*IG* xii.5 218, 3rd cent. BC) and Kynthia (*IG* xii.5 390; Add. p. 313), epithets tying Paros into the fluid Delian worshipping community as argued below. Eleithyia (Call. fr. 7.10 Pf) was located on the Kounados hill opposite (*IG* xii.5 189–205 (3rd cent. BC and later, but the archaeology goes back to the Geometric period: Rubensohn (1949)). *IG* xii.5 183 is a 5th-cent. *horos* stone from the sanctuary of Eileithyia forbidding women entry into the apparently adjacent shrine of Zeus Hypatos. *ID* 53 (with *BCH* 50 (1926) 572) is a Parian dedication to Artemis Delia on Delos.

image of Artemis, the beautiful *kore* of Naoussa and a rich set of further *kore* statues suggest that the same divine figures were popular in several, unexcavated, parts of the island too.[42]

Moving on from Paros in the direction of Delos, the traveller is greeted by the incomplete silhouette of another major temple of Apollo, at Naxos, built over Geometric remains. The Hellenistic poet Parthenios has a romantic story revolving around Apollo's Delion on Naxos, and in any case Artemis is not far away, with inscriptional evidence from the nearby ancient *agora*, and possibly some 300 metres along the northern coast just outside the ancient city, where archaic remains of a temple for a female deity have been found. *Kouroi* scattered all over the island suggest that an Apollo may well have been present in other localities, reflected among other things in the modern place-name Apollonias in north-eastern Naxos.[43] Apollo figured prominently in all cities of the *tetrapolis* on Keos, the Kykladic island closest to Athens and the commissioner of Pindar's *Paean 4*, Bacchylides' *Ode 17*, and in Herodotean times a place boasting a *hestiatorion* for its *theoroi* on Delos.[44] Amorgos, to the east of Delos, offers cults dedicated to Apollo Delios in all three cities, Arkesine, Minoa, and Aigale, of which that at the island's most important city, Minoa, dates back to the classical period. Artemis and Eileithyia dwelt in Arkesine, too, in the immediate proximity of the Apollo sanctuary, and the goddess of birth joined Apollo in the third city of Amorgos, at Aigale.[45]

One could proceed in this fashion, noting cults of Apollo Delios and his associates, through much of the Aegean island world. Tenos had a Delios and a tribe called after the cult at least as old as the third century. Mykonos has

[42] See e.g. Kostoglou-Despini (1979). Most of these *korai* can be seen in the museum of Paros. The collection is well accessible in Zapheiropoulou (1998) 28–88.

[43] At Naxos, the temple of Apollo Delios (Plut. *De Mul. Virt.* 17. 254b-7; Parthen. 9; Andriskos *FHG* ii p. 156; iv p. 302) was started in the 530s BC under the tyrant Lygdamis but was never finished: Gruben (1984) 344–8 is still authoritative here. Cults of Artemis in the centre of town: Zapheiropoulou (1988). Apollonia in the north-east faces Delos; cf. the series of *kouros* colossi found on Naxos; Paros and Naxos were chiefly responsible for the production of marble *kouroi* and *korai* circulating on Delos, Naxos, and Paros. See Kostoglou-Despini (1979); Kokkorou-Alewras (1975).

[44] Keos: no actual Delion has been discovered, though Keos had very close links to Delos: see n. 87 below. Ioulis: Apollo *IG* xii.5 615 (4th cent.); 616; *IG* ii^2 111.22 (363 BC, Apollo Pythios). Koresia: *IG* ii^2 1128.16 (mid-4th cent.; no epithet; cf. Ath. 10.456f); cf. Str. 10.5.6 (Apollo Sminthaios); Poiiessa *IG* xii.5 1100 (late 5th cent. BC, Pythios); 571.5–6; 12–13; 20 (3rd cent. BC); *SEG* xiv 547 (no epithets). Karthaia: *IG* xii.5 528 etc. (no epithet). Artemis certainly had a cult at Ioulis (*IG* xii.5 617; 618) and possibly at Karthaia (Pi. *Pae.* 4.1). All these precincts were architecturally expanded towards the end of the 6th cent.: see Schuller (1985) 361–82 for the development of Doric monumental architecture in the Kyklades, at Keos.

[45] Amorgos: Apollo Delios seems attested in Minoa: *IG* xii.7 220 (5th–4th cent.); later attestations with the epithet, not all of them dated, are 221b; 222–4; 226 (3rd cent. BC); 225 (3rd cent. BC without epiklesis). This shrine apparently lies at the harbour, today's Katapola. Arkesine: *IG* xii.7 50 (cf. *MDAI* 11 (1886) 112 for the *naos* mentioned here); Aigale: *IG* xii.7 388 (200–150 BC; cf. 389); Artemis: Arkesine *IG* xii.7 71–4. Eileithyia: Aigale: *IG* xii.7 420 (Vigla, 4th cent. BC); Arkesine: xii.7 82–5 (4th–2nd cent. BC; *BCH* 12 (1888) 327).

Map 2.1 The Delian pantheon in the Aegean: cults of Apollo Delios and Artemis, Leto, and Eileithyia spread across the island world. Created from digital map data © Collins Bartholomew (2004) 2007

Figure 2.2 The akropolis of Arkesine on Amorgos, seat of cults of Apollo Delios, Artemis Delia, and Eileithyia; the island of Donousa lies in the background

a modern place-name Apollonion situated on the western promontary of the island, the part closest to Delos, and on Syros, too, the god is reflected in a modern place-name.[46] Euboian Eretria's Apollo bore the name Delios, and the Euboians were throughout keen worshippers of the triad.[47] More distant from Delos, Chios had an ancient Delion well worth seeing.[48]

[46] Tenos: *IG* xii.5 863–6 (Apollo); 865; 872.104, 875.31; 901 (tribe, all 3rd/2nd cent.); *IG* xii.872.102, 120; 944 (cult/locality). Mykonos: I owe this piece of information to Ewen Bowie. In Hellenistic times, the god had land on Mykonos and a festival called τὰ Χερσονήσια, perhaps suitable for a promontory: *ID* 328.10; 353 B 44–5f; 366 A 132, with Herbst, *RE* xvi (1925) 134. On Syros the top of the higher of the two hills in today's Hermoupolis was called Δήλι until the 1870s: *IG* xii. 5 test. 1500 p. xxxi.

[47] On Euboia the triad of Apollo, Artemis, and Leto appears regularly in the cities of Eretria, Amarynthos, and Tamynai: Eretria: *IG* xii.9 191 A1, 48; 54 (4th cent. BC); 266 (3rd cent. BC); 276–8 (2nd cent. BC). Amarynthos: 140–3 (mid-2nd–early 1st cent. BC). Tamynai: 97–9 (end of 2nd cent. BC). Eileithyia: *IG* xii, suppl. 572 (4th cent. BC). For the close Euboian links to Delos see n. 74 below.

[48] Chios: *DGE* 688 = *Chios* 76, A ll. 5–6: ἀπὸ τούτο μέχρι τô Δηλίο 'from here to the Delion'. The cult of Apollo is not located, but is believed to equate with that of Apollo Phanaios by some scholars, both ancient and modern (cf. St. Byz. quoted n. 58 below). Plut. *De E ap. Delph.* 385b. Cf. Kontoleon, *AEph* 1952, 209–10. On Anaphe Apollo is Αἰγλήτης 'the Shiner': Str. 10.5.1 = Call. fr. 7.23 Pf; A.R. 4.1713–18; *IG* xii.3 248–9; 254; 259–60; 412. cf. Corn. 67.2 for a link between Delios, Phanaios, and Anaphe.

The most astounding and intriguing pieces of evidence, however, come from the Dorian islands of the Dodekanese. Here less full versions of the Delian pantheon have come to light, but these are all the more significant because of their unexpected location in the Dorian insular world.[49] Kalymnos especially offers scarce, but spectacular, traces of an old sanctuary of Apollo *Δάλιος*—Dorian rather than the Ionian *Δήλιος*—with finds dating back to the Geometric period and hence pre-dating some of its Kykladic counterparts.[50] Similarly Kos, intensely involved in the worship of Apollo on Delos in Hellenistic times, had an ancient *Δάλιος*. Apollo and Leto appear together in a Hellenistic Koan inscription, and there is also a local Artemis *Λοχία*. The fourth-century Koans, tantalizingly, had a chorus named *Δαλιάδες* that was quite possibly sent to Delos as a representative of several Dodekanese islands.[51] Dalios touched upon other nearby Dorian islands such as Nisyros and Syme, though the evidence here starts much later; and on Rhodes and Telos he has only left faint traces in a month-name.[52] Kasos, a little-known island on the way from Crete to Karpathos, had strong links to Delos in the Hellenistic period.[53] On Astypalaia, placed where the Kykladic and Dodekanesian spheres overlap, there is fourth-century evidence for the triad of Apollo, Artemis, and Eileithyia, suggesting a further Delion there. It is worth noting that Apollo Delios-Dalios is seemingly absent from

[49] Delos' appeal to Dorian islanders is rarely considered, e.g. in studies on the early Delian League: Hornblower on Th. 3.104 refers to PH xxiv already making this point; contrast Meiggs (1972); Santi Amantini (1977); Sealey (1966); Robertson (1980*a*); Steinbrecher (1985); Roussel (1987); Smarczyk (1990), or in treatments of the *Homeric Hymn to Apollo* such as Miller (1986).

[50] Kalymnos: Bean–Cook (1957), mentioning among other things (129 n. 285) a Geometric bronze griffin part, and an archaic marble head. Cf. *Tit. Cal.* 7 and n. 2; for the epiklesis Dalios see test. xiii; xiv; xxviii (1st cent. BC); 52.9; 130B.2 (3rd cent.); cf. 108; 109 (Roman). Inscribed 6th- and 5th-cent. sherds from the temple are recorded ibid. nos. 235, 245a, 247.

[51] The cult of Apollo Dalios on Kos was apparently the most important on the island, and of some antiquity; it was probably located at Halasarna: Sherwin-White (1978) 299–301. A *Δάλιον* is attested in *Iscr. Cos* 45 (= PH 43 = *HG* 9 = *LSCG* 165; 2nd cent. BC). *Iscr. Cos* 55 B (= PH 40 = *HG* 5 = *LSCG* 156.1 = *SGDI* iii.1 3639) records a late 4th-cent. *theoria* to Delos and the dispatch of boys' and girls' choruses; ll. 15, 18, 23, name Apollo Dalios, Artemis, and Leto. The Koan *Δαλιάδες* occur in an unpublished inscription (*HG* p. 18), to be edited by K. Hallof in *IG* Cos, and have been restored in *HG* 5B 5: Rutherford (forthcoming) suspects a mini-amphiktyony centred on Apollo Dalios on Kos that gathered the delegations from the neighbouring islands (Knidos, Kalymnos, possibly Kasos; see already *HG* p. 18; Sherwin-White (1978) 299 f.) before dispatching a ?shared one to Delos (ll. 11 ff.). For a list of Hellenistic *theoriai* from Kos to Delos see Sherwin-White 91 n. 50. Cf. Herod. *Mim.* 2.98; Tac. *Ann.* 12.61, according to whom tradition placed the birth of Leto, daughter of Koios (Hes. *Th.* 404 ff.; Pi. fr. 33d.3), on Kos.

[52] Apollo Dalios on other Dorian islands: Nisyros: *IG* xii.3 92 (Apollo Dalios, 3rd cent. BC, possibly located near the island's volcanic lake: Rubensohn (1962) 42–3). Syme: *IG* xii.3 2 (Apollo Dalios, Artemis, Leto (2nd cent. BC)). The month name Dalios is attested on Telos (*IG* xii.3 85); and many times on Rhodes: *IG* xii.1 1237 etc. *Rhodes IK Peraia* 204.4 (Hell.) is a dedication of someone from Patara in the Rhodian Peraia to Apollo Dalios. Rhodes receives an oracle from Delian Apollo in D.S. 5.58.4–5.

[53] Apollo Temenites of Kasos is attested on Delos: *IG* xi.2 144 B, 11–12 (4th cent. BC, Bruneau (1970) 164); 3rd-cent. *theoria* from Kasos to Delos: *ID* 199, B, 14 (Bruneau 97).

those islands with strong cultic relations elsewhere, for example, Thera to Sparta.[54]

The Delian cults thus spread out like a spider's web over much of the Aegean. Strikingly, a new Delion is in the process of being discovered, neat confirmation of the validity of this kind of myth–ritual interaction. On absolutely minuscule Despotiko, the island south of Antiparos, off Paros, a new sanctuary has recently been found and with it classical sherds inscribed *ΑΡΤΗΜΕ*[and *ΑΠ*[, *ΑΠΟΛ*[, and similar. The significance of this find for the argument presented here can hardly be overstated: Despotiko is in the immediate proximity of a whole host of insular Delian sets, and this new site is likely to certify the importance of the Delian configuration in the island world, a myth-ritual network reaching to the tiniest places of this community.[55]

It is not only in cultic practice in participating localities, but in associated myth too, that the network of Delian cults finds its reflection. I have deliberately paid little heed to diachronic considerations in my assemblage of Delian pantheons travelling the Aegean island world. There is an important suggestion to support a substantial distribution of Delian cults in the Aegean long before the epigraphical or archaeological evidence for the cults of the Delian twins just listed. The sixth-century *Homeric Hymn* has a splendid catalogue of cities and places which refused their hospitality to the desperate Leto. It notably starts at Athens, covers the northern Aegean mainland, crosses to the northern Aegean islands, drifts down the coast of Asia Minor and its large off-shore islands of Chios, Lesbos, and Samos, jumps to the Dodekanese with Kos, Karpathos, Knidos, and ends at the Kyklades.[56] This is obviously not a random lining up of cities; more likely it forms a catalogue of future cult places. The implication is that *none* of the communities with a future share in the cult dared (or cared) to welcome the divine birth except the 'insignificant' island of Delos. The catalogue, then, not only orchestrates the designation of the geographical centre of Delos as the *omphalos* of the Aegean, but specifically spells out what seems important in this network of myths and rituals in the Aegean: surely an Imbrian islander would 'remember' that Leto had once passed his island's shores, and so would a Lesbian, or someone from Miletus. What I mean to imply is that it is through the aetiological myth of the birth-story that places associated themselves, or—should we take the *Homeric*

[54] Astypalaia: *IG* xii.3 185 (Apollo, 4th cent.); *IG* xii, suppl. 151. *IG* xii.3 192; 192 [1] (Eileithyia, early 4th cent. BC). The museum on Astypalaia exhibits an inscribed 4th-cent. dedication (?) to Artemis (Apollo is Pythios in *IG* xii.3 201; 217 (no date)). Thera: *IG* xii.3 326 on works in the *hieron* of Eileithyia in the Antonine era.

[55] Kourayos (2005), according to whom the shrine was a major cult place in the late archaic period (esp. 130–3). See now id. (2006).

[56] The catalogue in *H. Ap.* 30–44: Crete, Athens, Aigina, Euboia, Aigai, Eiresiai, Peparethos, Athos, Pelion, Samothrace, Mount Ida, Skyros, Phokaia, Autokanes, Imbros, Lemnos, Lesbos, Chios, Mimas, Koryx, Klaros, Aisagea, Samos, Mykale, Miletus, Kos, Knidos, Karpathos, Naxos, Paros, Rheneia.

Hymn as a piece of Polykratean propaganda—were associated with, the Delian cults.[57]

Cities in fact made every effort to link themselves to Delos (and indeed many other cult places) in this manner. Hypereides, when establishing Athenian claims to Delos in the fourth-century dispute over the island, points out that it was at Cape *Ζωστήρ* (where there is an evocative sixth-century temple for Apollo) that Leto loosened her 'girdle' and was guided by local Athena Pronoia to Delos. Or the Delion on Chios with its cult of Apollo *Φαναῖος* claimed that it was from here that Delos 'appeared' to Leto.[58] Just as Delian cults branch out, these aetiological myths for local cults (and more could be cited) are developments of the central Delian myth.

The interaction of aetiological myth and ritual thus leaves a very tangible imprint on the places participating in the cult on Delos. A great number of cult places spread all over the Aegean for the same set of central deities, foremost among them Apollo Delios, appear to be part of the same intricate network of entwined myths and rituals. The recurrent configuration of Apollo, Artemis, Leto, and Eileithyia suggests that the birth carried special significance: surely these communities worshipped 'Apollo Delios' and 'Artemis Delia' not as the ones 'on Delos' but as the twins 'born on Delos'—just as Apollo Pythios in Delphi would be identified as the one 'who slew the dragon Python'. The relevant conclusion is that people worshipped not their own, exclusive Apollo and/or Artemis, but precisely the one(s) 'born on Delos'; in having such a cult of the deities 'born on Delos,' places indicated that they were part of the wider cult community of all those who worshipped Apollo and Artemis in this way. Local cults were connected with the centre through a shared network of myths and rituals.

The repercussions on the local pantheons of the sanctuary's catchment area, with what should be seen as the physical manifestation of the myth-ritual nexus in Delian worship, indicate the central role of myth-ritual performances for those who were part of this theoric landscape. The role the theoric *khoroi* fulfilled in this network becomes clear: their performances of myth and ritual created and constantly renewed the web spanning much of the Aegean island world. In other words, the choruses singing birth-shouts were indispensable in forging a religious community and in delineating the catchment area of Delian *theoria*. Theoric *khoroi* were sent by all those communities celebrating the birth of Apollo and Artemis on the island and thus claiming a share in the cult; by sending a *khoros* to Delos, a community marked its membership of this religious group.

[57] Polykrates had famously aimed to celebrate the Delia at the same time as the Pythia, thus tying to himself the two principal Apolline cult centres of the Greek world: Burkert (1979*c*).

[58] Delian aetiology abroad: Attika: Hyperid. fr. 67; cf. Semos of Delos *FGrH* 396 F 20 (birth of Apollo at Cape Zoster); the temple belonged to the deme of Halai Aixonides: Parker (2005) 69–70 and fig. 6; 59 n. 35. Athena Pronoia at Prasiai: *Anecd. Bekk.* 1.299.6–7, possibly on Delos: Macr. 1.17.55. Chios: St. Byz. s.v. *Φάναι: ἀπὸ τοῦ ἐκεῖθεν ἀναφανῆναι τῇ Λητοῖ τὴν Δῆλον* 'from there Delos appeared to Leto'; cf. Lykia: Ov. *Met.* 6.317–81; Ant. Lib. *Met.* 35 after 4th-cent. Menekrates of Xanthos.

On a more general level, we can conclude that the interaction of myth and ritual in choral song is fundamental for the creation of a worshipping community. This interaction makes strong claims about how a sense of religious community was forged: through repetition, multiplication, redundancy, and in many localities—and, most importantly, through the evocative power of religious song. On Delos multiple choruses from all around the chorus of islands constantly reaffirm their link to the central worshipping core, thus formulating a shared religious space, the theoric landscape. Above I discussed how these paeans manage to create an illusion of mythical re-enactment in their performance through the abolition of time. We can now go a step further and state that the choruses' relationship to 'place' is also affected. Through the constant merging of the associations of local and central worship in the performances, one's sense of how myth and ritual relate geographically is also fused. A pivotal effect in the dynamic of myth and ritual in performance is therefore not only a transcendence of time, but also of place.

So let us once again return to the useful concept of a 'fused sense of communication' (pp. 48–9), but reformulate it in a way that suits the theoric context of archaic and classical Greek religion: choral performance seems to jumble the associations of myth and ritual to time and place, allowing for a transcendence of both. It thus creates a fuzzy notion amongst performers or spectators about their own localization vis-à-vis the mythical past and religious space. In the next section, looking at the songs whose commissioners can be identified, we shall see how choruses do indeed lose their sense of locality in performance: whether myth told and ritual practised are central or local, whether a performance enacted on an individual island or on Delos, is something that is as ambiguous in the songs as it will have been in reality. What seems to happen is that local practice becomes supra-local in the theoric chorus, and central practice becomes localized. What is more, we shall see that not only are performances of myth and ritual temporally and spatially disorientating, but they also pool notions of time and space in order then to reconfigure them. Myth-ritual performance can be seen to allow a continuous restructuring of the mythical past in relation to current ritual practice, while maintaining the fiction of traditionality, and a continuous redefinition of religious space by inserting individual localities into a larger sacred geography.

The relationship between myth and ritual thus emerges through the interaction of ritual space with mythical time, in a network of manifold relations between these four factors, myth, ritual, time, and place. It is here that power and the possibilities of myth-ritual performance as a social tool lie, and it is the resulting dynamics in actual fifth-century social contexts that I shall investigate for Delos in the next section, and in general through much of this book.

2. ISLANDS AND IONIANS BETWEEN COMPLIANCE AND DEFIANCE IN THE DELIAN LEAGUE

The capacity of choral performances to reconfigure time and space in relation to a worshipping community is fundamental to how these choral shows come to work in historical processes. The choral tributes of our paeans are the medium through which this network of myths and rituals is continuously recreated, challenged, and transformed. It is in forging and unforging relations to and from the central Delian cult and its catchment area in ritual performance that singing for the Delian gods becomes a form of social interaction by which to create, maintain, and dissolve bonds and power relations between cities over time. The Delian myth-ritual network, from early on until the Hellenistic period, comes to be the language places use to make these kinds of statements. Choral *theoria* to Delos will thus emerge as an additional, and often very subtle, way to express social and power relations between places within this worshipping community.

Delos at the time of our songs, the first half of the fifth century, is intimately associated with the Delian League and the Athenian empire. It is here that the Delian League had its initial seat at the time of its foundation in 477 until the 450s BC, when the treasury was moved to the Akropolis at Athens, the moment most often associated with the notorious change from 'league' to 'empire'.[59] In particular, it is often thought that Delos was picked as the synedrion for the Delian League because it was a traditional religious meeting place, as we know from the *Homeric Hymn to Apollo* notably for the Ionians, the ethnicity of such high currency in the later Athenian empire. Any Delian festival could thereby be conveniently turned into a league occasion and vice versa. Likewise, it is tacitly assumed that the choruses, the theoric landscape just sketched, and the phenomenon of fifth-century Delian *theoria* are theatrical expressions of sympathies on levels other than religious, the songs instruments of crude and direct political propaganda. Our paeans were no doubt composed in that context, but their relationship to the league is not straightforward.

Rather, theoric song on Delos represents an excellent demonstration that religious and political communities are related, but not always identical, and probably even in principle not identical. Though *theoria* is as yet an under-researched if fashionable topic in Greek religion, we are in a position to state that a theoric worshipping community is essentially an egalitarian gathering, explicitly designed to counteract the hierarchies of political and military alliances or enmities. The self-portrayal of *theoria* in the Greek sources suggests just that, a wish to keep peaceful relations amongst otherwise fiercely argumentative groups of cities competing for political power and leadership. There is therefore an expressed desire to maintain this worshipping community in defiance of

[59] On this much-discussed topic, see most recently Hornblower (2002) 15.

individual cities' ambitions. This reflects more widely the manner in which Greek cults interacted with political history. Religious communities seem to be different structures with their own dynamics and a considerable draw and force that was in no way less powerful than politico-military alliances. A salient example is the Panionion, the shared sanctuary of the 'Ionians' in Asia Minor, where the relationship between religious gathering and politico-military action is continuously problematic.[60]

The theoric choruses of this period, our cult songs, will reveal that to assume an identity between Delos' religious community on the one hand, and the political community of the Delian League on the other, is far too simple. There is an undeniable attempt at their identification—obviously, but not exclusively, undertaken by Athens. Notably, there is the effort to exploit the possibilities of *theoria* for the creation of community—the making of the imperial *communitas.* But the songs lay open just as much the ambition as the failure of this aspiration. The myth-ritual network proved to be a highly flexible, manipulable, and dynamic system of interaction between communities and the Athenians. For myth-ritual choruses and the associated cultic phenomena are not an exact means of community-building. Rather, they work on a level that is suggestive, often compellingly suggestive, but basically always pushing the boundaries of an anyway vague notion of who used to be there in the past dancing for Apollo and Artemis, who could be there in the present, or who should be in the future. That is not to say that myth-ritual performances on Delos are politically useless, quite the contrary: as we shall see, singing on Delos subtly undermines the egalitarian aspect of the theoric worshipping community through powerful suggestions arising from contrived interactions of myth and ritual in individual songs. Likewise, through the interweaving of local and central mythology, these songs have a creative share in establishing the definition of local identities, thus identifying the type of relationship between locality and the wider religious and political networks of the Athenian empire.[61]

So what follows will explore these gliding boundaries between the religious and the allied chorus cruising around in a dangerously overlapping theoric and imperial Aegean world. Two groups will emerge as the particular targets of the efforts to bring about the identification of the religious and the political: 'islanders' and 'Ionians', both participants in the Delian Festival in Thucydides, but also, as we shall see, two particularly prominent groups in the admission and recruitment policies especially of the early Delian League. The assumption and/or memory of traditional *theoria* sent to Delos by both sets of people plays a central

[60] For the wider phenomenon of pilgrimage see now Elsner and Rutherford (2005); *theoria* is the subject of a major research project by Ian Rutherford. I discuss the Greeks' perception of *theoria* as maintaining harmonious relations between cities in (2005): cf. e.g. Phlegon of Tralles *FGrH* 257 F 1 (Olympia); Heniokhos *PCG* fr. 5; Th. 5.18 (the peace of Nikias being closely associated with *theoria*). Sacred laws for the Hellenistic Panionion and the cult of Athena at Ilion, reassessing the contributions of individual cities, seem related to crisis situations when the theoric community was under pressure.

[61] Rutherford (2004) 69 makes a few general remarks about *theoria* as a privileged context for the display of local, and often civic, identity.

role in this contemporary dynamic. The myth-ritual network was a system cities exploited both to become part of the Athenian orbit and to distance themselves from it. Conversely, for the Athenians it was a convenient system for tying communities to them through a bond that was perceived to be both mutually beneficial and desired. Theoric choruses thus tell us things about this period in history that we would otherwise not know: about various communities' relationships to Athens; about those who did join the league or the festival, those who did not, and for what reasons.

Islanders in an Athenian mythic *kyklos*

Islands were particularly keen dancers on Delos, and I shall start with how their role in the wider network of *polis-theoria* was construed. We know that early in the century, both prior to and after the end of the Persian Wars, Athenians aspired to conscript islands into what was then still the 'Hellenic League'. Places that feature there are Andros, Keos, Karystos on Euboia, and 'other islanders'.[62] Cult song on the one hand confirms this picture, but on the other reveals the malfunctioning of this attempt to identify the religious and the politico-military.

Euboia

Pindar's *Paean 5* recounts the Athenian colonization of Euboia and the Kyklades (here the *sporades*), culminating in the Athenian settlement of Delos. On the pattern established for the *Homeric Hymn to Apollo*, such catalogue-type myths typically delineate a community of some sort; the song gives the illusion of Athens and the island world jointly worshipping the Delian gods.[63]

[– ⏑ ⏑ – ⏑ ⏑ *Εὔ*-]
βοιαν ἕλον καὶ ἔνασσαν·
ἰήϊε Δάλι' Ἄπολλον·
καὶ σποράδας φερεμήλους
ἔκτισαν νάσους ἐρικυδέα τ' ἔσχον
Δᾶλον, ἐπεί σφιν Ἀπόλλων
δῶκεν ὁ χρυσοκόμας
Ἀστερίας δέμας οἰκεῖν.

They
took Euboia and settled there:
Ieie Delian Apollo—

[62] Athenian conscription of islanders just before and just after 479 BC (end of Persian Wars): Hdt. 8.111–12 (cf. Plut. *Them.* 21.1–2); 121–2; in 9.101 (cited n. 147 below) islands together with the Hellespont feature as the 'prize' (*ἄεθλα*) in case of a Greek victory; in 9.106 Chios, Samos, Lesbos, and 'other islands' are admitted to the Hellenic League.

[63] Cf. the Delian part of *H. Ap.* 30–44 (n. 56 above); but similarly also the 'Delphic' part, where Apollo visits one by one his cults located around the Kopais basin (Ch. 7 below).

and they colonized the scattered, sheep-bearing
islands, and they took widely famed
Delos, when golden-haired Apollo
gave them the body
of Asteria to dwell on.

(Pindar, *Paean* 5.35–42 = D5 Ruth, tr. W. H. Race)

It used to be argued that this passage referred to the Euboians themselves.[64] This is unlikely for, despite powerful colonial activity elsewhere, the Euboians did not establish themselves on Delos. *Paean 5*, rather, refers to Athenian settlement in the Aegean islands, here concluding with their colonization of Delos.[65] The paean is generally quoted as a not necessarily very remarkable song that the Athenians carried with them on one of their regular *theoriai* to Delos.[66] But it is clear that the Athenians took *theoria* to Delos very seriously indeed. *Deliastai* were thought already to have featured in Solon's *kyrbeis*, taking the tradition back a very long time. Be it as old as it may, during the fifth and fourth centuries, much effort was put into strengthening the theoric link to Delos and tying Athens firmly to the island.[67] While for a long time this evidence had not been assembled, it is now clear that, by the mid-fifth century, there were probably at least a handful of Delia in Attika.[68]

It is in this context that *Paean 5* also needs to be seen, not as a routine theoric *khoros* sent to Delos, but as a special mission fostering the role of Athens in the existing theoric network. The short song quite possibly airs claims much greater than is at first sight suggested by the delicacy of the few lines that survive. Athenians putting in at Euboia and a set of islands on a primordial trip to Delos is

[64] von Wilamowitz-Moellendorff (1922) 327–8.

[65] The scholiasts to the paean remark ἀπ' Ἀθηναίων 'from the Athenians' (Σ 35). Σ 45 mentions Pandoros and Aiklos as founders of Chalkis and Eretria respectively; cf. [Skymn.] 571–7 (= *GGM* 1.218–19); in Str. 10.1.8; Plut. *QG* 296d–e Kothos replaces Pandoros. Aiklos and Kothos later become sons of Xouthos like Ion: West (1985) 58; cf. Hdt. 7.94.

[66] Most recently Parker (2005) 81 n. 7; Rutherford (2004) 82–6; Wilson (2000) 44–6; Smarczyk (1990) 472 n. 184.

[67] *Deliastai* at the time of Solon: Polem. fr. 78 Preller *ap.* Ath. 6.234e–f. Peisistratos heavily invests in Delos: Hdt. 1.64.4. In the 4th-cent. mythical imagination *theoria* went back to Athens' earliest times: its founder was King Erysikhthon, who settled the island as it 'had a good harbour' (*euormos*), died on the way back and was buried at Prasiai in north-east Attika, the departure point for the Athenian *theoria* to Delos (n. 58 above; Phanodemos *FGrH* 325 F 2 = Ath. 10.392d; Paus. 1.31.2 (his grave at Prasiai)). He dutifully dedicates the first Athenian image of Apollo on Delos (a wooden statue ξύλινον Plut. fr. 158, l. 4 Sandbach), and in return takes to Athens the cult and image of Eileithyia (Paus. 1.18.5); Eus. *ap.* Hier. Chron. 43b Helm (builds temple of Apollo); Paus. 5.7.7. In Pl. *Crit.* 110a E. is one of Kekrops' sons. The *genos* of the Erysikhthonidai on Delos: *ID* 2517–18. Rutherford (2005) 111–14 suspects that the Erysikhthonian tradition may have come to Athens from Thessaly and was the same that also linked Kos to Delos (see below).

[68] See Parker (2005) 82, who now thinks that the Solonian *Deliastai* had a shrine at which they dined at Athens (Polemon as preceding n.; cf. Harpocr. D 26 = Lyc. fr. 87 Conomis), possibly also venue for the 'dancers' of Theophr. 119 Wimmer *ap.* Ath. 10.424e–f. Further Delia are at Phaleron (n. 164 below); Prasiai (n. 58 above); the *tetrapolis* at Marathon sent its own *theoria* to Delos, though their shrine has not been found (Philokhoros *FGrH* 328 F 75). For Cape Zoster see n. 58 above.

central to this construction. Traditions do report that the Athenians went to live in Euboian cities and the '*sporades*' (the term in antiquity did not denote the Northern Sporades of Modern Greece—Skopelos, Halonisos, Skiathos—but the Kyklades).[69] However, fifth-century texts tend to keep Euboia suspiciously discrete from Athenian aspirations in the wider Aegean island world. Herodotus and his contemporaries on many occasions mention that Athenians had come to settle a series of Kykladic islands, among which feature Keos, Andros, Tenos, and Naxos, as well as Siphnos and Seriphos.[70] Euboians never appear amongst this group; this seems to have been a separate expedition.[71]

What is more, we know that the fifth-century Boiotian *mousikos* Pronomos composed a processional song—a so-called ᾆσμα προσόδιον—for the city of Chalkis in Euboia to perform on Delos.[72] Usually taken as belonging to the context of the Athenian empire, it has sometimes been suggested that this song should rather be dated to a time after 411 BC, when the Euboians revolted from Athens, as a first and powerful statement of independence.[73] This idea matters because it brings out a triangular relationship between Athens, Euboia, and Delos that is perhaps more strained than is normally perceived. On the one hand, Euboia has its own set of stories linking it to the sacred island, while, on the other, Athenian vase painters are happy to join Delos and Euboia as dancing nymphs.[74] *Paean 5* is the first piece of evidence to integrate Euboia into Athenian settlement on the islands in a joint mythography: this looks as if it were a problematic claim.

Moreover, one might be inclined, as is most common, to read into the Athenians' travel the narrative of the Ionian migration, as if the islands, and particularly the Kyklades, were taken in passing on the way to Asia Minor. The paean would thus represent one of the earliest records of the big-scale settling

[69] See V. *Aen.* 3.126–7 and Deubner, *RE* vi.a (1871) s.v. Sporades. This is a bit of a paradox: did the 'cycle around Delos' only emerge from the 'scattered' group of islands once Delos was established as a (cult or other) 'centre'? In the late geographical tradition the *sporades* are all islands other than the Kyklades: Deubner (as above).

[70] Hdt. 8.46 (Keos, Naxos); 8.48 (Siphnos, Seriphos); Th. 7.57.4 (Keos, Andros, Tenos); Nikolaos of Damaskos *FGrH* 90 F 40–1 (Siphnos founded from Sounion, Skyros by Pelasgians); Dion Chr. *Or.* 30.26: (Siphnos, Kythnos; in Hdt. 8.46 the Kythnians are Dryopians). Cf. for Naxos: Xenomedes *FGrH* 442 F 1 (5th cent. BC); Call. fr. 67.7; 75.32; 38 Pf (Prometheus, son of Kodros exiled to Naxos); Paus. 7.3.3; Ael. *VH* 8.5 (on the difficulties at Naxos); Zenob. 5.17 (Mykonos); *Σ* Dion. Per. 525: where only Hippokles, settler of Mykonos, belongs to the Kodridai.

[71] Euboia's colonization a different tradition altogether: Str. 10.1.3–10, esp. 8. Paus. 1.5.3; Vell. 1.4.1–3 (first Euboia, then the rest from Athens); Dio Chr. 64.12: Euboia. See also n. 65 above for Athenian colonization of Euboia.

[72] Paus. 9.12.6.

[73] D'Alessio (forthcoming *b*); Wilson (2007), arguing for a performance after 411 BC. Note that Chalkis is the city that 'suffered' a decree according to which certain legal cases were to be tried in Athens, favouring 'democratic' justice (ML 52, *c.*446–5 BC).

[74] The Euboians are curiously close to Delos in some traditions: Hdt. 4.35 where the Hyperborean tribute stops off at Karystos on Euboia before continuing to Delos, a journey the Athenians came to intercept: Paus. 1.31.2. Cf. Call. *Del.* (4) 20 and a black-figure cup showing Tethys (Call. ibid. 17) and the dancing maenads Euboia and Delos: *LIMC* iii (1986) s.v. Delos ii (440 BC, on which also a satyr Lemnos).

movement. A closer look at the evidence, however, reveals, similarly, that the fifth-century texts in particular, referring either to mainland or island settlements, insist on keeping these quite distinct. No classical text quotes the Athenian colonization of the islands as transit stops on the route to Ionia. It seems rather that islands were an entirely different category of settlements and that two different traditions are working in parallel.[75] Islands seem to have had closer relations to Athens, while the first evidence for Greek settlement in Asia Minor ignores Athenian origins.[76] In the same vein, the paean's journey too stops on Delos. If this were meant to be the final destination of Athenian island hopping then surely something was implied other than the ethnic conquest of Ionia. And if this paean was meant to recreate the Ionian universe of the early Delian League, one would have thought that this particular myth was not exactly well-placed.[77] One even begins to wonder whether such a myth, with its focus on island communities, did not deliberately exclude non-islanders.

The song produces an image of Delos as a centre of island *theoria*, to which Athenians at the head of the island chorus deliver the first ever tribute of song. The Athenian journey, taking in the rest of the insular catchment area on the way, is not representative, it is provocative; it does not depict an existing worshipping community, but creates a new configuration of participating communities. The integration of Euboia in this myth of Athens' settlement of Delos and the islands is especially striking. This seems to be a song, as we shall see one of many, active in forging, rather than confirming or maintaining, a theoric community on Delos. Similarly, the separation of Ionians and islanders may not be traditional, but could well be a fifth-century innovation, or at least a vision that was particularly laboured in this period. *Paean 5*, singing of a myth not attested elsewhere, may well present an important key to our understanding of the early fifth-century Delia: it was part of a special effort to create a tradition of Athenians and islanders jointly serving the Delian gods—including the Euboian neighbour and the Kykladic islands, but to the exclusion of the Ionians.

[75] 'Ionians and islanders' remain strangely discreet in the same formulaic way as in Thucydides 3.104, even when related to the alleged large-scale Ionian movement from Athens, part of aggressive Athenian ideology in the later 5th cent.: Th. 1.12.4; 6.82.3; 7.57.4; Eur. *Ion* 1581–4 ('Kyklades' and 'coastal cities'); Isocr. 4.35; 12.43–4 (where Athenian colonization is directed against the 'barbarians'); Arist. fr. 76 (Rose). Ael. *VH* 8.5; Zenob. 5.17; Himer. *Or.* 6.117: Athenians first free the islands of pirates, then settle on the mainland 'lying across'; Nonn. 13.180–2; St. Byz. s.v. *Ἴος*; *Σ* Eur. *Phoen.* 208. Str. 8.7.1 mentions Kodros' expedition to Ionia only, not to the islands. Th. 6.76.3, a difficult passage, also intriguingly separates Athenian domination of the Ionians from other 'symmakhoi', here probably the islanders (*ἀπὸ σφῶν* should be taken to refer to the Athenians). I thank Simon Hornblower for this reference.

[76] Unlike Ionia, Athenian island settlements have Pelasgian predecessors: Hdt. 6.137; 7.94–95.1, although the Ionians were called 'Pelasgians' when still living in the Peloponnese. Interestingly, some islands continued faithfully to deliver religious tributes to Athenian Athena in the wake of the Second Athenian Confederacy: *SEG* xxxiii 67.8–9; only after the end of the Second Confederacy did Ionian mainlanders make such statements of loyalty: Parker (1996) 221 and nn. 13 and 14. The earliest traditions associate Greek settlement in Asia Minor with Messenian Pylos and the Neleids: Mimn. fr. 9, 10 W; cf. Str. 8.7.1.

[77] As was argued e.g. by von Wilamowitz-Moellendorff (1922) 327–8.

Andros

But that insular illusion did not always work. The ambiguity arising over Pronomos' Euboian poem, as a piece of, alternatively, compliance or defiance, already suggests that a song to Delos dispatched or withheld in itself conveyed a stance towards those seen to control the sea across which the theoric chorus would have travelled. Indeed, how communities escaped participation may have been just as important to the system as their conscription. Sending or not sending a choral *theoria* could be turned into a rather demonstrative statement. There is for example the case of resilient Andrians, admittedly scarcely documented but suggestive of a wider issue. The Andrians are routinely present on Delos and some think they even had a treasury there.[78] Andros was a highly desirable target for recruitment into the chorus of Athenian allies as it tried to resist dancing to Athenian tunes: when the Athenians attempted to recruit the island into the Hellenic League, it flatly refused to pay tribute on the grounds of poverty (*penie*) and necessity (*anagke*).[79] And—we might immediately add—in this period they sent a (presumably rather expensive) cult song not to Delos, but to Delphi: amidst several of Simonides' samples of choral songs composed for *theoria* to Delos, we find a cult song 'for the Andrians to Delphi'.

] **Ἀνδρίοις εἰς Πυθώ** [
]μοι α[ἴ]σιον κελαδεῖ ἀμφι .[
(Simonides *PMG* 519 fr. 35b)

We know of a fifth-century Andrian *theoria* to Delphi, a rare epigraphic testimony to the practice at this early date, though no *khoros* is mentioned.[80] The Andrians later pay a hefty tribute, starting with 12 talents, into the league treasury.[81] So summoning *penie* for their cause in the first instance may well have been a plain lie. This was a rich island, happy to defy Athenian hopes, and, we may provokingly suggest, which stopped sending the traditional choral *theoria* to Delos. Although the argument from silence is of course uncertain, it is attractive to surmise that one way to express opposition was by the withholding of one's traditional chorus to Delos. That an attested song should have gone to Delphi instead may not be a coincidence. Delphi seems to have been a kind of choral centre 'of resistance': in Chapter 4 we shall see how the Aiginetans, who were in great trouble with Athens in this period, were very much present there with Pindar's *Paean 6*. It is tempting to speculate that the quick and/or demonstrative

[78] Bruneau and Ducat (1983) no. 43 suspect an Andrian treasury on Delos. In 376/5 BC the Andrians were the only non-Athenians with a share in the amphiktyonic council on Delos: *IG* ii^2 1635. Eileithyia has a cult on Andros: *IG* xii, suppl. 264 (4th cent.); *IG* xii.5 192.

[79] Hdt. 8.111; the same story in Plut. *Them.* 21.1–2.

[80] *CID* 1.7. I only know of Rutherford's discussion of the poetic fragment (1990) 176–7: someone 'sings' of something 'auspicious' perhaps 'about' a locality. Andrian choral customs are noted in Philostr. *Im.* 1.25.

[81] *IG* i^3 262.i.19 (451/50 BC), then reduced to six (*IG* i^3 263.iv.22; 450/49 BC), raised again to seven (*IG* i^3 289.i.21; 416/15 BC).

(re)direction of a long-standing tradition from Delian to Pythian Apollo represented the interest of the wealthy Andrian maritime elite who had little to gain from the emerging Athenian empire, just as commercially ambitious Aiginetans resisted the Athenian grip.[82] The Andrians' behaviour would thus represent an example of cult song forming part of a community's redefinition of its standing in relation to its neighbours, while at the same time it hints at the Athenians' incomplete grasp of the insular world. Below I shall discuss the important role that the discourse of 'island poverty' came to have in defining the relations between Athens and the islanders. Scant and speculative as the evidence for Andros may be, it makes good sense in a larger picture: quite apart from the elusive Euboian song, in the case of the Ionians (pp. 102–10 below) we shall meet another group traditionally part of the Delian theoric cult community whose non-attendance was just as important to the system as the choral presence: contributing or not contributing a choral *theoria* could be turned into a rather open statement. Andros was a defiant island.

Keos

Not so another island, Keos. This is an interesting case of an island that complies, but seemingly refuses to acknowledge its own submission to Athens' control of the island circle. The issue revolves, not surprisingly, around Theseus and the most difficult and probably latest poem belonging to the Delian set. Bacchylides' *Ode 17*, notoriously impossible to classify as either a paean or a dithyramb, seems to have been composed for performance on Delos by the Keans: a group of young men from the island invoke Apollo Dalios himself (ll. 130–1).[83] As usual, the song is undated, but as we shall see it has a good chance of belonging to the early years of the Delian League.[84]

These Keans, singing in honour of Apollo Delios, were wooed by the powerful illusions that song-dance can create, through a contrived fusion of myth and ritual in the performance. For although sung by Keans, the ode deals with an episode of a familiar Athenian story: Theseus' journey to Crete with the *Δὶς Ἑπτά* (*Twice Seven*), the seven Athenian boys and girls destined to be sacrificed to the Minotaur, which turned out to be a trip liberating the Athenians from this hefty human tribute paid to King Minos. The familiar story tells of how Theseus met

[82] Andros had a long-term history of being at the node of communications: Horden and Purcell (2000) 134 (Zagora). Andros' colonies in the northern Aegean are well known to Thucydides, leading one to suspect that these links were actually active in the 5th cent. (Th. 4.84.1; 88.2; 103.3; 109.3; 5.6.1, on Stagiros, Argilos, Akanthos, Sane). Andrians also supported the 400 at Athens during the oligarchic coup in 411 BC (Th. 8.69.3).

[83] The attribution to Bacchylides' dithyrambs goes back to the Alexandrian editors (see e.g. Serv. *Aen.* 6, 21 (II.1, p. 9 Thilo) thinking of Bacch. 17 as a dithyramb). Bacch. 17 features in *PLond. Inv.* 733 after Bacch. 15, classified under *dithyramboi* (*POxy.* vii, 1091): see Maehler (1982) 36–8 and 43; and (1997) 167–70. Käppel (1992) 156–8 and 187–9. See now Calame (forthcoming) and Wilson (2007) on the complementarity of Apolline and Dionysiac cult songs.

[84] For a discussion of the circumstances of performance see Maehler (1982–97) ii. 167–70.

Ariadne, deceived and killed the Minotaur with her help, thereby forever freeing Athens from the tie of Minos' capricious demands. Bacchylides' ode does not recount this story, but stages the conflict as a warrior's contest, in which King Minos orders Theseus to dive for a ring at the bottom of the sea.[85] Theseus plunges into what seems a hopeless mission, and returns with cloak and crown bestowed by Amphitrite instead. When he miraculously resurfaces, the fourteen Athenian youths greet him in song and dance:

. . . ἐπεὶ
μόλ' ἀδίαντος ἐξ ἁλός
θαῦμα πάντεσσι, λάμ-
πε δ' ἀμφὶ γυίοις θεῶν δῶρ', ἀγλαό-
θρονοί τε κοῦραι σὺν εὐ-
θυμίαι νεοκτίτωι
ὠλόλυξαν, ἔ-
κλαγεν δὲ πόντος· ἠίθεοι δ' ἐγγύθεν
νέοι παιάνιξαν ἐρατᾶι ὀπί.
Δάλιε, χοροῖσι Κηΐων
φρένα ἰανθείς
ὄπαζε θεόπομπον ἐσθλῶν τύχαν.

. . . when
he [Theseus] came unwet from the sea,
a marvel for all, and the gods' gifts shone
on his limbs; and the splendid-throned
maidens cried out with the
new-founded joy and
the sea resounded, and the nearby youths
raised a *paian* with a lovely voice.
God of Delos, rejoice
in your heart at the choirs of the Keans
And grant a heaven-sent fortune of blessing.

(Bacchylides 17.121–32, tr. Campbell, adapted)

The Athenian youths welcome the hero just at the moment when the narrative and performative modes fuse in the song—and in an intriguingly familiar way: as if they were accompanying not the 'epiphany' of Theseus but rather the birth of Artemis and Apollo on Delos![86] The Kean maidens' *ololyge* and the youths' paean cry and praise strikingly recall the birth-shouts for Apollo and Artemis in the fragmentary songs. Their greetings for the emerging Theseus imperceptibly blend into the welcome shout for Apollo Delios and the blessings of the Kean *khoros*. And so a curious triangular relationship emerges: the account of an *Athenian* myth unwittingly turns into a celebration in honour of *Delian* Apollo, performed and re-enacted by a *Kean* chorus.

[85] On the mythical narrative see Maehler (1982–97) ii. 174–84; Ieranò (1989) 174–6; Calame (2003) 13–23 with further bibliography.

[86] Theseus' 'epiphany': Calame (forthcoming), also referring to the hero 'baigné de lumière'—just as the twin gods 'sprang forth into the splendid light' (n. 27 above).

Keos, we are led to believe from Herodotus onwards, had strong theoric links with Delos: Herodotus knows of a Kean *hestiatorion* on Delos, a kind of hostel where Keans would stay when on *theoria*. We know of choruses sent to Delos from Keos in the fourth century, and *Paean 4*, to be discussed below, is another chorus for this island.[87] We have to assume then, that for a fifth-century Kean chorus, *theoria* to Delos was a tradition. Identifying with an Athenian myth, however, was not: while a habitual ritual is being performed, its perceived meaning receives some additional slants. That Athenian myth and Kean interest should merge in quite such blunt fashion might strike us as odd in the first instance, but it actually furnishes a clue to how Athenians seem to have handled their choral tribute policy on early to mid-fifth-century Delos.[88]

To grasp the full picture we need to look a little more closely at Theseus' feat. As already stated, his journey releases the Athenians from a heavy obligation. The mythical dispatch of the ἠΐθεοι, the Twice Seven, is symbolic of a former, long-standing obligation to, and dependence on, Minos and the Cretans, and it is this burden that Theseus heroically manages to lift. The tribute of the *Twice Seven* had been instituted as an oracularly ratified compensation to gratify Minos for the death of his son Androgeus, an athlete so fantastically superior that he happened to be killed in a primordial edition of the Panathenaia.[89] Many details in the stories of how the δασμός ('tribute') came about reveal a close and competitive relationship between Athens and Minos and his family. Theseus in the myth releases the chain to mythical Cretan power.[90]

However, Theseus ended up killing two birds with one stone: Bacchylides' song is a dazzling example of how in fifth-century myth-making Theseus did not just become Athens' liberator, but released the whole of Greece from this supposed 'Cretan' domination, by curiously taking over what Minos had famously left behind—a naval empire that covered much of the Aegean island world.[91] The myth-ritual nexus of Bacchylides' *Ode 17* operates exactly at the point of transition from Minoan to Athenian sea-empire: the blend of mythical actors and

[87] Hdt. 4.35.4. *IG* xii.5 544 A2, 35–48 (4th–3rd cent. BC) mentions a *khoregos* and a boys' chorus taken to Delos (n. 5 above). *ID* 253.9 (?1st cent. BC) attests a public Kean offering to Delos. Pi. *I.* 1.1 ff. with Σ for a sacred song by Pindar to Delos. For the expressed song-dance tradition on Keos see n. 104 below.

[88] Wilson (2007) 179, citing colonial links between Athens and the island, suspects that the song was performed by Athenian citizens on Keos.

[89] Apollod. 3.15.7 ff.: the fateful Panathenaia, following which Minos goes against Athens in a protracted war. His prayer for revenge (to Apollo?) prompts a plague upon the Athenians, which can only be lifted through the tribute of the *Dis Hepta* to the Minotaur. Note that the word used for the performance of group-tribute is ἱλάσ(κ)ομαι (Kowalzig (2004)). Calame (1996*a*) 314 cities Helladius *ap.* Phot. *Bibl.* 534a, implying that the killing of Androgeus forms the mythic nexus for purification at the Thargelia. Note that D.S. 4.61 relates the story to the drought that Aiakos lifted from all Greeks except the Athenians: see Ch. 4.

[90] Plut. *Thes.* e.g 15.1. The intensity of the obligation is exposed when Minos himself came to choose which youths had to die for him (Hellanikos *FGrH* 4 F 164) and the rather gruesome details, for example that the young people were killed and sacrificed, or adopted by Minos himself into his kingdom.

[91] Calame (1996*a*) discusses this point: 213–19; 424–9; and now (2006*a*) 184–7.

ritual performers is deliberate, and what the Keans are celebrating here is precisely what the myth is about: Theseus' successful abolition of the tribute to Crete. But because the song was performed by Keans (and not Athenians for example, for whom it would make more sense), it unnoticeably turns the Keans into the beneficiaries of the feat, as if it were they who had been freed from the compelling Cretan imposition. The Keans here are subject to the finest ideological trick: they celebrate release from an oppressor's tribute—to Minos—by paying, with or without realizing it, a new tribute—to Athens.

Actually, behind this lurks a much wider redefinition of the mythical Aegean, part and parcel of an Athenian formulation of the Theseus cycle, in which the Minoan thalassocracy presents both mirror and prefiguration of the Athenian hegemony in the Aegean. Thucydides makes the point about sea-empires from Minos to Athens following each others' routes of maritime communication, and in singling out Minos' *Pax Cretica*, liberating the Aegean from piracy, he reflects the Athenians' own self-perception as the rightful successors of the Cretan thalassocracy. Plutarch sets the story of Theseus' journey to Crete at the time 'when the Athenians were not yet devoting themselves to the sea'.[92] Theseus' own heroic temple, at Athens, unlocated but dedicated shortly after his bones were repatriated from the island of Skyros in 476 BC, was decorated with scenes of his very dive in the Cretan sea.[93] How important yet problematic the Thesean take-over was to Athenian self-understanding is clear from the fate the ousted thalasso-dynast Minos himself underwent in the process. Turning the model into the villain features as a prime strategy in justifying Athenian action, tellingly illustrated by the verve with which fifth-century Athens pits Minoan against Athenian power, in the picture of a harsh and uneducated Minoan king 'who was at enmity with a city that had a language and a literature', so much so that he was constantly 'reviled and abused' in the Athenian theatre.[94]

This is in stark contrast to Minos' image amongst the earlier Greeks, where he featured as a wise man with a special zeal for education. In effect, tradition held that he was popular particularly with the islanders, a fact revealed, significantly, in reference to Athens: when Androgeus was killed at Athens Minos himself happened to be sacrificing to the Graces on Paros. The islanders were so affected

[92] Hdt. 3.122; Th. 1.4; 8; Plut. *Thes.* 17.6: μηδέπω τότε τῶν Ἀθηναίων προσεχόντων τῇ θαλάττῃ.

[93] Paus. 1.17.2–3; 6 for the dedication of the shrine (on which see Wycherley (1957) 113–19), with Calame (1996*a*) 154; 259–66; 430–43 (with bibliography); Plut. *Cim.* 8.5–7; *Thes.* 36; Paus. 3.3.7 on the repatriation of Theseus' bones. Cf. Parker (1996) 168–70, notably on Theseus' steep rise at Athens from the 470s BC onwards; (2005) esp. 208–10; 211–13 for his being aetiological to the festivals in Athens' religious calendar.

[94] Plut. *Thes.* 16.3 The surviving plays do not refute the accusation of ridiculing and vilifying Minos: Aesch. *Ch.* 612 ff. (showing a lovesick king); Polyidos' story (Hyg. *Fab.* 136) may have been alluded to in Aesch. *Cret. TrGF* 116; Eur. *Polyidos TrGF* 634–46, esp. 640 ff. (wanton luxury). In Eur. *Cretans TrGF* 472e esp. 32 ff. Minos gets bad press from Pasiphae. The Minotaur story was possibly treated by Sophokles: *TrGF* 730a–g (Theseus?). Giesekam (1977) 240–2 discusses the changing attitude towards Minos in 5th-cent. Athenian culture from a more positive 6th- and early 5th-cent. image; Bacchylides, *Ode 17* is located at the transitional point, when the image of Minos started to worsen (ll. 88–9). See also Maniet (1941).

by the tragedy that to Apollodorus' day they held a mourning festival for the king's son.[95] Athenian culture's vivid interest in this personality stands in the service of a formulation of the take-over of this empire, in which claiming to have ousted the whimsical tyrant turned into the justification of Athens' own rule of the sea. It also shows a remarkable awareness amongst the ancients as to what 'poets' could do to a mythical character, and hence the patterns of mythical belief.[96]

These strikingly divergent traditions about Minos, Theseus' Aegean travels, and choral *theoria* to Delos are inextricably linked to each other and surprisingly productive in the mapping out of a Delian dance to Athenian tunes. For what has not been realized is that our paeans and fifth-century island *theoria* to Delos have a dynamic share in the process by which the island world was wrapped into a network of myths and rituals reformulating the mythical past of the Aegean in a way centred on Delian Apollo. The exchange of Minoan rule for a tribute to Apollo Delios as in the Kean case recurs frequently: Athenian *theoria* to Delos is itself so motivated, for Theseus' tour liberating the Aegean is the same journey during which the hero also disembarked on Delos. There, according to Plutarch, he set up the 'altar of horns', the *keratinos bomos* around which the famous 'crane dance', the *geranos* was performed, an imaginary world that has been well investigated, while it cannot be linked directly to fifth-century paeans composed for performance on Delos.[97] The Athenian *theoria* to Delos was seen as re-enacting Theseus' trip, and the poetic or hieratic word ἠΐθεοι of Bacchylides' Kean poem normally labels the actual Athenian chorus sent to Delos. Finally, the fact that in the classical period Athenians used the often-repaired original ship of Theseus himself for their Delian *theoria* attests not only a spectacularly physically orchestrated sensation of mythical re-enactment in ritual, but also an indispensable link between *theoria* to Delos, the Thesean liberation trip, and the Athenian claim to a legacy of thalassocracy.[98]

It is a fascinating trip to follow the Delian songs through the Aegean and observe how they managed to force out the Minoans as lords of the island world

[95] n. 112 below. The tradition of a good Minos: *Od.* 19.178 f.; 11.568–71; Hes. fr. 144 MW, alluded to in Plut. *Thes.* 16.3–4; Pl. *Min.* 318d; 320d. According to Zenis of Chios (*FGrH* 393 F 1 = Ath. 13.601f), Minos befriended Theseus and married his daughter Phaidra to him (cf. Apollod. 3.15.8). Pl. *Min.* 319b ff.: zeal for education/sophist educated by Zeus. The ancient tradition is well aware that Minos underwent repeated reinterpretation by the Athenians: Plut. *Thes.* 15: 'most writers agree that the Athenians treacherously killed Minos' son . . .'. Str. 10.4.8: 'but again the earlier writers have given a different account of Minos, which is contrary to that of Ephoros, saying that he was tyrannical, harsh and an exactor of tribute, representing in tragedy the story of the Minotaur and the Labyrinth, and the adventures of Theseus and Daidalos' (tr. Jones). On Plutarch's literary interaction with Thucydides see Pelling (2002) Ch. 5, 117–41.

[96] Pl. *Min.* 320e: 'for poets have great influence over opinion, according to as they create it in the minds of men by either commending or vilifying. And this was the mistake that Minos made, in waging war on this city of ours, which besides all its various culture has poets of every kind, and especially those who write tragedy.'

[97] Calame (1996*a*) Ch. II. 7. It is likely that Bacchylides' *Ode 17* is *not* an *aition* for the crane-dance.

[98] Parker (2005) 81, noting especially the rarely observed point about the ship: Pl. *Phaed.* 58a–b; Plut. *An. Sen. Ger. Rei Publ.* 786f; Arist. *Ath. Pol.* 56.3; Plut. *Thes.* 23.1. Bacch. 17 refers to the ἠΐθεοι several times: 43, 93, 128.

and establish, or cultivate, worship of Delian Apollo: such evidence survives for Keos (Pi. *Pae.* 4), Paros (Pi. fr. 140a), and indirectly for Kos (Pi. fr. 33a). There are indications that even Chios and Naxos were part of this world of reformed mythical connections expressed in cult song. The songs show well how *theoria* supports local identity within the wider theoric framework, and in the service of an overarching ideology. Drifting as they do in that vast and floating space between locality and theoric centre created by the Delian myth-ritual network, localities crystallize within a theoric worshipping community whose liaison with the Delian League was dangerously ambiguous throughout. The creation of local selves in theoric song is exploited in the definition, and sometimes also the execution, of social and power relations between contributing localities.

Inserting oneself into the illusion of 'liberation', like the Keans of Bacchylides' *Ode 17*, is part of the process. The Cretans so successfully ousted by Theseus are conspicuously present on those islands that dutifully send their choral representatives to Delos or otherwise construe a relationship to Apollo Delios. Pindar's *Paean 4*, also composed for the Keans, is a good example of how a Minoan presence and rule on the islands is at once acknowledged and denied. This paean has incited some debate on where it was performed, though everything considered, a performance on Delos is certainly preferable.[99] That said, a definite case for its travelling to Delos rather than staying in Kean home territory need not even be made, as the poem presupposes the theoric practice. The ambiguity of its local references—Kean mythology on the one hand, devotion to Delian Apollo and Artemis on the other—helpfully situates the paean between locality and central hub, in the religious space created by the theoric network.[100]

Building on typical 'island' themes towards a 'Kean' identity, the paean sings of the mythical king Euxantios, a bastard son of Minos born of his union with the local nymph (?) Dexithea. Euxantios rejected a fertile seventh share in his father's Cretan kingdom in favour of his own barren island.[101] This myth acknowledges in splendid fashion the presence of strong Cretan links that it is at the same time eager to dismiss. Behind the varnish of local island pride, the selfless rejection of Minos' offer reveals a commitment to island hardship instead: the island is a 'narrow stretch of land' (ἐλα]χύνωτον στέρνον χθονός l. 14), a rock (σ[κόπ]ελον l. 21) bare of plains (πεδίων l. 16) but surrounded by fish (ἰχθύσιν l. 20). On it people grow vines but they cannot work oxen (i.e. perform

[99] Rutherford (2001) 280–93 and (2000) argues for a performance on Keos, while D'Alessio (1994*b*) 64 prefers the paean to have been sung abroad; see also *id.* (forthcoming *b*). Cf. n. 87 for a sacred song for Keans to Delos by Pindar.

[100] Pi. *Pae.* 4 = D4 Ruth. The paean's performative parts have both local and Delian references: Artemis (l. 1); 7–8 talk about ἡσυχία ('peace') on Keos; 11–13 link 'famous Delos and the Charites' with the Kean city Karthaia in the south-east. That only Karthaia is mentioned has prompted speculation about whether this was a paean sent by a single one of Keos' four cities (Rutherford (2001) 283 n. 1), but note that all other songs for Keos seem to be composed for the whole island. Brun (1989) thinks that Keos was a federated state already in the 5th cent. BC.

[101] The myth is known from Bacch. 1 and the 5th-cent. historian Xenomedes of Keos (*FGrH* 442 F 1 = Call. *Aet.* fr. 75.64 ff. Pf).

agriculture) or raise horses.[102] One's 'home town' is praised as satisfactory while only foolish men would strive for things afar (ll. 32–4). But it nevertheless has many athletic victories to boast (*δια-/γιγνώσκομαι μὲν ἀρεταῖς ἀέθλων/Ἑλλανίσιν* ll. 21–3) almost as if giving itself a function on the Panhellenic stage through symbolic rather than actual capital.[103]

The small island of Keos had as many as four cities, a collection of successful athletes, a proverbial number of victories, and two poets of Panhellenic renown to praise them and with this a strong tradition of choral dance.[104] During the Persian Wars, it sent as many as seven ships to Salamis and had its participation recorded both on the Serpent Column at Delphi and at Olympia, while later paying a regular tribute of up to six talents to the Delian League and assessed at as much as ten in the 420s BC.[105] The chances are that, like the Andrians, the Keans—or rather, certain Keans—lacked neither urbanity nor wealth. Ever-recurring island poverty and barrenness is the chief ingredient in insular representation during the fifth century, a topos that was, I suggest, instrumental to and exploited by Athenian imperial ideology to inculcate among islanders a sense that it was necessary to tie themselves into a wider imperial network in the first place. While the Andrians used the topical poverty to escape the Athenian grip, in the case of Keos the image of the poor island is part of the song's strategy, ultimately to make Theseus' journey worthwhile. Depicting the insular world in this way quite possibly suited the purpose of recruitment. This may well have been correlated with the creation of a civic ideology: in *Paean 4* we should note the (fragmentary) appeal to *ἡσυχία* ('peace') and the island's claim to have 'no lot in sorrow and strife', elements which we shall come across again in the case of Paros. Poverty recurs in gnomic traditions about Keos, often related to social harmony, leading us to suspect a civic ideology trying to reconcile rich and poor.[106] We shall hear more of this as we call in at other islands.[107]

[102] Pi. *Pae.* 4.25–7: *[ϵ]ἰ καί τι Διω̣[νύσ]ο̣υ ἄρο̣[υρ]α φέρει/βιόδωρον ἀμαχανίας ἄκος,/ἄνιππός εἰμι καὶ βουνομίας ἀδαέστερος* 'although my earth produces Dionysos' life-giving remedy against distress, I am without horses and rather ignorant of tending oxen'.

[103] The topos is known from Bacch. *Ode* 2. The paean thus exploits the frequent motif of contrasting an island's downsides with its virtues: passages are listed in Rutherford (2001) 285–6. For a complex history of paradoxical island self-representation see Brun (1993).

[104] A considerable number of victory odes survive from this island: Bacch. *Ode* 1, 2, 6, 7. Cf. the prosodion *SLG* 460 = *POxy.* 2625 fr. 1 (b). The antiquarian record for dance on Keos is sizeable: Ath. 10.456 f mentions Simonides and a *khoregeion* ('place where the *khoros* trained') at Karthaia. In Ant. Lib. 1 (= Nic. *Met.* 3 fr. 49 + 50 Gow) Hermokhares spots Ktesylla of Ioulis dancing at Karthaia; see n. 87 above.

[105] Hdt. 8.1.2; 46.2; ML 27.7; Paus. 5.23.2. The Keans started at 1 talent in 451/0 BC (*IG* i^3 262.v.22), raised to 4 in 450/49 BC (*IG* i^3 263.iv.21), reduced to 3 in 433/2 BC (*IG* i^3 279.i.74) and to 6 in 417/16 BC (*IG* i^3 288.i.10). They were assessed at 10 talents in 426/5 BC (*IG* i^3 71.i.69).

[106] Pi. *Pae.* 4.7; 52–3. Str. 10.5.6: 'It seems that there was a law ordering those over 60 to drink hemlock, so that there would be sufficient food for the rest.' Cf. Men. *PCG* 879; Val. Max. 2.6.8; Heracl. Lemb. Excerpt. Const. = Aristot. fr. 511 Rose; Ael. *VH* 3.37; Str. 11.517; St. Byz. s.v. *Ἰουλίς*.

[107] Islands are aware of the need for maritime connections to ensure survival, militarily and economically: see e.g. *Old Oligarch* 2.2 cited below in Ch. 5 on Rhodes. *Olympian 7* develops the opposite picture of an island rich in resources and maritime connections. Constantakopoulou (2005) discusses island networks.

Paros

Pindar's enigmatic and badly preserved fragment 140a is another song, quite possibly a paean, in which the known Cretan past is, as far as we can tell, similarly superseded. The wonderful little piece of song that survives from the latter part of the song has Herakles found the Delion of Paros, the precious temple complex, refurbished at the end of the sixth century and sublimely overlooking the bay of Paros' main harbour:[108]

***Π*]αρίοις [εἰς Ἀπόλλωνα (?)]**
φ[ι]λ̣[.]ν̣ μ̣ι̣[
τοὶ πρόϊδ[ο]ν αἶσαν α̣[
ζο̣ι̣ τ̣ότ᾽ ἀμφε̣.ο̣υτα̣τ̣ . [
Ἡρακλ̣έης· ἁλία̣ [δ᾽ ἐ]π̣ὶ̣[
ναΐ μολόντα σ[.]υ̣[. .] π̣[.] . [.] . σ̣ο̣εν̣
θο . . οι φύγον ον̣[. . . . . .] . [.] . . .
πάντων γὰρ ὑπ[έ]ρβιος ανα̣.σ̣ ἔφα[
ψυχὰν κενεῶ[ν] ἔμ̣᾽ ἔ[η̣]κ̣᾽ ἐ̣ρ̣υ̣κε̣ν̣ . . [
λαῶν ξενοδα[ΐ]κ̣τα βα̣σι̣λ̣ῆ-
ος ἀτασθαλία̣ κοτέω[ν] θαμά,
ἀρχαγέτα̣ τε [Δ]άλου
πίθετο παῦσέ̣ν̣ [τ᾽] ἔ̣ρ̣γ᾽ ἀ̣ναι̣δῆ̣· . . . .
γάρ σε λ̣[ι]γυσφα̣ρ̣ά̣γων̣ κ̣λ̣υ̣τ̣ᾶ̣ν̣ ἀ̣υ-
τά, Ἑκαβόλ̣ε̣, φορμίγγων,
μνάσθηθ᾽ ὅτι τ̣οι ζαθέας
Πάρου ἐν γυάλοις ἕσσατο ἄ[ν]ακτι
βωμὸν πατρί τε Κρονίῳ τιμάεν-
τι πέραν ἰσθμὸν διαβαίς,
ὅτε Λαομέδον-
b39 *τι πεπρωμένοι̣᾽ ἤ̣ρ̣χ̣ε̣τ̣ο̣*
μόροιο κάρυξ.
ep.b *ἦ̣ν̣ γάρ τι̣ παλαίφατον [. .] . . . ο̣ν̣*
ἷκε συγγό̣νους
τρεῖς π̣[. .] . ε̣ω[.]ν̣ κ̣ε̣φα̣λ̣ὰ̣ν̣ . . ρ . . τ̣αι̣ [
ἐπιδ[~ 10]αι̣μ̣α[. .] . [. . . .] . [

For the P]arians [to Apollo (?)]
(b21) They foresaw their fate . . . then . . . Heracles: . . . (someone) coming in a ship of the sea . . . they fled . . . superior to all in might . . . he said (?) . . . '(Apollo) sent me to suppress the spirit of the foolish people, often angry at the arrogance of the people's guest-killing king . . .'. And he obeyed the leader of Delos and stopped shameless deeds . . . Since, Far-shooter, the sound of bright-sounding famous lyres reaches (?) you, remember that he founded in the hollows of holy Paros an altar for the lord (Apollo) and the honoured Cronian father, striding over the neck of land, when he began the appointed doom for Laomedon, a herald of it. For it was something long proclaimed. He came to the three relatives . . . head . . . (Pindar fr. 140a = G8 Ruth, ll. b20–43, text and tr. Rutherford)

[108] Previous discussions of the song are Rutherford (2001) 377–82; Rubensohn (1962) 44 ff. D'Alessio (1997) argues for an attribution to Pindar's paeans. For the Delion on Paros see n. 41 above.

Herakles' adventures on Paros are well known to the mythical tradition, and recur in the paean (ll. 1–7/b20–9), but their link to Apollo Delios (ll. 7 ff./b30 ff.) is unique to this song. From Apollodorus we know that Herakles sailed there with his companions 'in a ship of the sea' (cf. ll. 2–3/b23–4: ἁλίᾳ [δ' ἐ]π̣ὶ̣[ναῒ) to find the belt for the Amazon Hippolyte at a time when the island was ruled by sons of Minos. By an unhappy accident, on landing, two of Herakles' cohort were killed by the Cretan rulers, prompting the siege of the island. Eventually the conflict was resolved diplomatically, and Herakles received two grandsons of Minos in replacement for his lost men.[109] In the paean, this story is told in an emphatically violent way, and closely linked to Delian Apollo and the establishment of the Delion on Paros: we hear of the brutality of the island's sovereign ('tearing apart his guests' ξενοδα[ΐ̣]κ̣τα l. 6/b28); on behalf of Delian Apollo Herakles gets rid of this king, and there is even an ambiguous reference to this actually freeing the Parian people from their tyrannical overlord, bringing to an end the lamentable current state of affairs (ἔ̣ρ̣γ' ἀ̣ναι̣δῆ̣ l. 8 / b31 is too uncertain to know what exactly is being stopped). The song then switches to a flash of performative mode where the ritual accompaniment of the sound of the lyre summons Apollo to remember that Herakles 'striding over the neck of land' set up an altar for him and for Zeus: might this picture Herakles' move a little west from the ancient city of Paros along the promontory sheltering Paroikia bay, towards the Delion?

As we saw above, the Delion on Paros was home to a whole set of Delian deities, and it is very likely that this song forms an aetiology for the shrine.[110] While, however, Herakles' dealings with Paros recur in the traditions, this is not the case for the cult foundation, which is only remembered here. It is tempting to surmise that the association was forged through this cult song, which imperceptibly links the end of Cretan despotism on the island with the worship of Delian Apollo in a fashion analogous to that of *Paean 4* for Keos' Cretan past. This is all the more appealing since Apollo Delios in the song suggestively oscillates between Delos and Paros: Delian Apollo is first the one on whose instruction Herakles acts, in order then to receive a cult on Paros.[111] That Apollo is called *arkhegetes* ('leader') of Delos (l. 30) strikes a colonial chord and conjures up an image of a well-connected island world linked through the figure of Apollo Delios. In this respect it is not so different from the *periplous* pictured in *Paean 5* for the Athenians, where Athenian settlers sail through Apollo Delios' insular catchment area (p. 83f).

A competing positive tradition of the Cretan domination suggests that the Parians underwent a process similar to that of the compliant Keans: I have already mentioned that Minos was an overlord cherished by the Parians, who joined him in celebrating the festival of the Graces on Paros mourning his son Androgeus killed by the Athenians: a ritual of lamentation 'without pipes and

[109] Apollod. 2.5.9; D.S. 5.79.2 knows that Rhadamanthys installed his general Alkaios on Paros.

[110] Rubensohn (1962) 44 ff. A cult of Zeus Hypatos bordering that of Eileithyia is known from the *horos*-stone *IG* xii.5 183 (5th cent.); it has been thought that this cult was referred to in the song: Rubensohn (1949) 1841.

[111] The oracle may come from Delian Apollo himself; an alleged oracle on Delos prophesied Athenian thalassocracy: Semos of Delos *FGrH* 396 F 12.

crowns' featuring in Callimachus' *aitia* that survived until the days of Apollodorus.[112] Androgeus' sons happen to be the two replacement men given to Herakles, further confirmation that these different episodes all belong to the same cluster fashioning a mythical geography in transition from one era, the Minoan, to another, the Athenian. Overcoming Cretans was certainly a theme that was very much *en vogue* in myth-ritual performances on, or in connection with, Delos. Like *Paean 4*, fr. 140a very likely operated in the context of choral *theoria* to Delos, and independently of whether it was performed on Paros, on Delos, or, as is most likely, in both localities, placed Paros firmly amongst the chorus of islands in the web of Delian myths and rituals.

Kos

The intriguing and unique tradition that Herakles founded the Delion on Paros develops yet further the larger island network operating through a number of shared and reinterpreted traditions. Herakles' doings in the Aegean in the service of Apollo would be a topic in itself,[113] but for the moment it suffices to point to his connection with one further Apolline cult, linking yet another island to the central Delian web, the Dorian island of Kos. The Koan theoric tie to Delos was in the ancient imagination among the most long-standing; Kos already in the *Homeric Hymn to Apollo* appears in the Delian orbit, in the fourth century marked by the very chorus of the Dorian Daliades.[114] Pindar's 'Hymn to Zeus', recently and convincingly reinterpreted as a 'Hymn to Apollo', a few lines before recounting at quite some length the Delian twin birth (fr. 33d), alludes to the story of Herakles' visit to the Dorian island of Kos.[115]

– ᴗ – σκᾶπ]τον χερί· τὰν δ' ἱεράν
– – ᴗ – –]. Κῶν, ἐπὶ δὲ στρατὸν ἄϊσ-
σ – ᴗ – ⏑̲ – ᴗ]ọς οὔτε θαλασ-
σ – – ᴗ ᴗ – ἀνέ]μοισιν
– – ᴗ –]ẹ.[– ᴗ ᴗ]τ̣η̣ρ̣

hand . . . holy Kos . . . army . . . fate . . . sea . . . winds

(Pindar fr. 33a, with D'Alessio's corrections (2005))[116]

[112] Apollod. 3.15.7. Call. *Aet.* frr. 3–7 Pf with Σ ad 3–7.

[113] Herakles is intriguingly related with many Apolline cults, often in connection with Herakleian conquest and representing not the Dorian, but a pre-Dorian tradition. Cf. Thessaly: Hes. *Sc.*; Asine: Bacch. fr. 4 (Ch. 3 below); the Pythion in Pheneos' territory, at the time of Herakles' conquest of Elis: Paus. 8.15.5 (cf. Plut. *De Sera Num. Vind.* 557c); Herakles and Apollo, often rivals, are co-founders at Gytheion: Paus. 3.21.8. Herakles sets up the oracle at Didyma 'from the blood of the sacrifical victims': Paus. 5.13.11. Cf. the struggle for the Delphic tripod between Herakles and Apollo (Ch. 3 below).

[114] Rutherford (forthcoming and n. 51 above); Kos has conspicuous long-standing links to Athens and the Kykladic island world, at least as old as certain parts of the *Ehoiai*: Rutherford (2005), esp. 111–14.

[115] D'Alessio (2005) and (forthcoming *a*), whose brilliant reconstruction shows that the 'Hymn to Zeus' is more than anything an editorial construction. On Herakles on Kos and fr. 33a see recently also Mingarelli (2003).

[116] Cf. Pi. test. fr. 33a: Str. 7 epit. Vat. = 2.91.9 KR = fr. 57 p. 380 Jones (= fr. 51) Quint. *Instit.* 8.6.71:

The poetic link between Kos and Delos was topical: apart from the *Homeric Hymn to Apollo*, Callimachus' *Hymn to Delos* makes the island Leto's last station before giving birth to Apollo on Delos itself, as so often echoing the Pindaric wording, all of which suggests that fr. 33a on Kos and 33c and d alluding to the Delian birth form part of the same mythic tale.[117] The old story of Herakles' visit to Kos is known from the *Iliad* and is alluded to several times by Pindar: Herakles fought against the Meropes, the indigenous population on Kos, and ended up marrying the king's daughter Khalkiope, yet another instance of dynastic change in an island's mythical past.[118] Herakles is closely linked in myth to Apollo Dalios on Kos, leading us to suspect that his stopover there was as aetiological as the episode on the Kykladic island of Paros. Though no Cretans feature in this tale, Herakles' visit falls into the same period of Minoan dominance. At least from the fourth century BC onwards, texts know of a wooden Kolossos of Apollo dedicated on Delos, according to Pseudo-Plutarch's *De Musica* (!) fashioned by the Meropes 'who lived at the time of Herakles', in other texts worked by two sculptors who were pupils of the archetypal sculptor Daidalos from Crete.[119] That the ancient statue existed in the Greeks' imagination as early as the classical period rules out a Hellenistic reinvention to strengthen the then-popular links between Delos and Kos. Rather, it conjures up the memory of a mythic geography centred on Delos, in which both Crete and Kos played a part; Herakles' intervention and cult foundation on Kos should thus be located at the same juncture of an older and a subsequent mythical network as the other two songs. While at present there is no evidence for a 'Koan' song, the Pindaric fragments in any case reveal a fifth-century Koan link to Delian performances; especially as a 'hymn to Apollo', the song of fr. 33 a–d places Kos, too, in whichever network our paeans tried to foster.[120]

'Pindar when [in his hymns] he describes Herakles' attack on the Meropes, who are said to have lived on the island of Kos, he speaks of the hero not like fire, wind or sea, but rather like a thunderbolt.'

[117] See D'Alessio (forthcoming *a*), who refers to several authors who seem to have had Pindar's whole text before them: Call. *Del.* (4) 160–1: *ὠγυγίην* (...) *Κόων Μεροπηΐδα νῆσον* (...) *Χαλκιόπης ἱερὸν μυχὸν ἡρωίνης*. 'the ancient ... Meropid island of the Koans ... sacred recess of the heroine Khalkiope'. Cf. Theocr. 17; Ael. Arist. *Or.* 38.11–12 Keil. Herzog (1895) 154–5, citing Herodas 2.98 and Tac. *Ann.* 12.61, argues that Leto's father Koios served to construe Kos' primary link to the cult at Delos.

[118] *Il.* 14.255; 15.28; Pi. *N.* 4.26; *I.* 6.31–2; Apollod. 2.7.1; *Σ Il.* 1.590; 14.255; Tz. *Chil.* 2.445; Ov. *Met.* 7.363–4; cf. *SH* 903a = pp. 133–5 Bernabé (the Meropis). In Plut *QG* 304c Herakles lands at Cape Laketer, near Halasarna, where there was a cult of Dalian Apollo (n. 51 above). This may be the sanctuary Apollo and Herakles shared: Sherwin-White (1978) 319–20; PH 367; 368; *SEG* xlv 1120 (3rd cent. BC); Parker and Obbink (2001) 257–9.

[119] [Plut.] *De Mus.* 1136a (quoting 4th–3rd-cent. BC Antikleides *FGrH* 334 F 35 and Istros' 3rd *Epiphaneiai FGrH* 140 F 14); Call. *Aet.* 3 fr. 114 Pf. Paus. 2.32.5; 9.35.3 names the sculptors Aggelion and Tektaios. Apollo's image holds the bow in one hand, the Graces with three different musical instruments in the other (cf. Jackson (1996)). The Graces are prominent cult figures in the Kyklades, see e.g. on Paros and Keos, nn. 95, 100, 112 above.

[120] D'Alessio (forthcoming *a*) rather thinks the song a Theban commission, possibly to accompany the rededication of the image of Apollo into the Boiotian Delion in the 470s BC. According to a

The chorus of islands thus paid rich musical tributes to the Delian triad. It is striking how many of Pindar's scrappiest little poems, only a slight improvement on the state of Simonides' two-line survivals, concern either the Delian gods or island-states or both. These are methodical instances of how this kind of study can be done, not by examining individual songs, but only by puzzling the fragmented pieces into a more or less coherent picture. No commissioners of these scraps can be identified, but protagonists and topical allusions are precisely the ones we know already. So-called *Paean 12* (a) has mention of the 'children of Leto', of a moment of giving birth, and of a *khoros* which is being sent somewhere.[121] So-called *Paean 16* is a prayer to Apollo; fr. 60(b) has a chorus-leader and features Mount Kynthos.[122] By contrast, *Paean 7* (a) seems to be another fragmentary mention of the birth of Apollo and Artemis and of an 'island with a narrow back', just as Keos was described above.[123] The performative parts of two more paeans for Apollo survive as part of the same group, though here the Delian connection is only a good guess, while a final one takes up again the island patriotism known from *Paean 4*: should these be another up to five samples of the choral offering to the gods on Delos?[124]

Of the altogether more than a dozen fragmentary songs for the Delian deities, all known commissioners are islands, a few more play on anonymous islands, but most importantly we have no evidence for a Delian song *not* from an island. Despite the paeans' extremely fragmentary nature, the group of Naxos, Keos, Paros, and indirectly Kos forms a picture consistent enough to establish the themes of this fifth-century insular song-culture. The chants retain a certain ambiguity about their place of performance on either Delos or the locality, which conveniently places them in the space in between. The blend of mythical past and ritual present in the songs allows locality and centre to fuse, so that this distinction too collapses and makes possible a reformulation of their relationship. Several tell local myths situated, mythically speaking, at the demise of Cretan thalassocracy and its replacement by a different mythical network, to which Apollo on Delos is central. In the case of Bacchylides' *Ode 17* the switch from Minoan to Athenian is clearly pronounced, perhaps because this song, though treated here first, comes last in the series. But in the Parian song (fr. 140a) the changeover is even expressed in alluringly fifth-century terms when the expulsion of royal Cretan despotism frees an oppressed native island population.

famous story the statue had been displaced during the Persian Wars (Hdt. 6.118). The Boiotians had an enigmatic, yet tight link to Delos through the Delion (see n. 158 below), and it is plausible that some of their conflict with Athens during the fifth century (Ch. 7 below) was expressed using the language of the Delian network of myth and ritual.

121 Pi. *Pae.* 12(a) (= G2 Ruth) l. 4]*Λατοΐδαιν*[; l. 8 *τέκε*; l. 10 *χορόν* ; l. 12 *π*]*έμπει* 'Leto's twins', 'gave birth', 'chorus', 'send'.

122 Pi. *Pae.* 16 (= G3 Ruth), without a local reference; fr. 60 (b) (= G4 Ruth) ll. 13–14.

123 Pi. *Pae.* 7(a) (= G5 Ruth) ll. 5–6 lines *λαχύν*[*ωτον νᾶσον* 'island with a long back'.

124 The two paeans are *Pae.* 8b (a) 1–4 (= G6 Ruth) and *Pae.* 8b (a) 5 ff. (= G7 Ruth). The patriotic song is fr. 215 (a) (= G10 Ruth).

The songs almost undetectably replace an older ruling network with a newly formulated web of cultic relations. The reinterpretation of existing practices and links in song actually masks a change of allegiance.

The prominence of locality and local concerns forms part of a wider pattern in the creation of local identities, intricately related to the functioning of the network as a whole. Fostering the notion of the poor yet proud island is one strategy in operation. Pindar's *Paean 4* shows well the correlation of island poverty and local pride, instilling a sense of locality on the one hand, while necessitating the link to the wider Athenian network on the other. It is no surprise that fifth-century Old Comedy—not that much later than the Delian songs—continues exactly that, the labouring of the image of impoverished islanders characterized by strained living conditions that sharply contrast with the luxury of Athenian—and, as we shall see, particularly Ionian—life. At least two plays with the title *Islanders* survive, evidence for the attention the insular chorus attracted on the Athenian stage. An alternative name *Greece* for Plato the Comedian's *Islands* draws the insular world into the contemporary debate of definitions of Greece in this period (on which see Chapter 4). An Isomakhos from Mykonos turns up in Kratinos' *Ploutoi* as an example of parsimony because of the poverty and infertility of this island. Islands are mocked because of their special diet; picking grapes for wine and plucking olives appear as typical islanders' pursuits, and (superior) farming is contrasted with (inferior) fishing, a set of attributes repeating exactly those praised in the Keans' *Paean 4*.[125]

The example of Andros discussed above has already made it clear that the wholly poor island is a handy cliché rather than a reality. In comedy even the Kykladic, the smallest and most barren, islands are occasionally pooled with their rich Ionian counterparts and become part of those Greeks hopelessly given over to the pleasures of the Ionian lifestyle. But it seems clear that a fifth-century, professedly frail yet patriotic, island cosmos is as much a creation of the world of song as it may have been of the rhetoric of Athenian imperialism. That the comic chorus is functional in this construction is, in part, to be attributed to the role of choral poetry in the island world. And this should also mean that we need to beware of falling into the trap of Athenian ideology: this was an assertive Aegean chorus, with enough pride and resources to make confident choices. The Aegean islands flourished in the archaic and classical periods, probably as they had never before and would never again.[126] Choices represented in the songs are unlikely to have been those of oppressed and fearful islanders, but rather of individual powerful pro-Athenian minorities or groups who felt that some advantage lay in joining, rather than rejecting, the Athenian catchment area.

125 Plato, *Islands* or *Greece*; Telekleides ?*Islanders*; Ar. *Islands PCG* 402: farming vs. fishing; insular diet; frr. 405; 406; 408 (harvesting grapes, plucking olives). Crat. *PCG* 365 features Isomakhos, the mean Mykonian.

126 Cf. Brun (1993), esp. 175–83, (1996). Islands capitalized on their often special natural resources: Horden–Purcell (2000) 346; Brun (1998).

Sixth- and early fifth-century Naxos, for example, the likely commissioner of *Paean 12* and itself in the shadow of its large, unfinished late sixth-century Delion, was immensely prosperous and so strong at sea that at the time of the Ionian Revolt in the early fifth century it was still said to rule over numerous adjacent islands; it later paid an enormous tribute to the league and continued to make extravagant dedications at major Greek sanctuaries. But it had, for this very reason probably, an unfortunate relationship to the Persians, who had brutally razed it to the ground in 490 BC; the Naxians' appearance among the theoric choruses on Delos at first sight is more plausible than surprising. Indeed, on this island, too, there are traces of Theseus' mythical *periplous* wiping out the Minoan thalassocracy in the Aegean. Ion of Chios, an interesting figure in the choral world, knows that Theseus stops off at Naxos to leave behind Ariadne, not, however, without changing the lineage of the local hero Oinopion: traditionally a product of Cretan Ariadne's union with Naxian Dionysos, he now turns into Theseus' own son.[127] On the other hand, throughout this period Naxos is a place of civic unrest (*stasis*), and if the island that so soon revolted from Athens had sent or would send in the future a *Paean 12* to Delos, this is symptomatic of the varying interpretations that the idea of an Athenian-led island network prompted, and that membership in it was contested.[128] Similarly, as already mentioned, an Andrian elite hub of its own colonial network probably had little to gain from Athenian imperialism, just as we shall discover below that Aiginetans found self-assured mythical formulations by which to parade their unwillingness to join.[129]

By contrast, on other islands singing the Delian chorus quite possibly was a—probably similarly elite-born—constituent of democratic ideology, as, incidentally, in Athens itself.[130] Few signs of this can be perceived on Keos or on Paros

[127] Oinopion becomes the first settler of Chios: Ion of Chios fr. eleg. 29 W = in Plut. *Thes.* 20.2–5. Note that the Naxians had a tradition of 'two Minoses', indicating that just as on Keos and on Paros, the interpretation of Cretan rule was ambiguous. That Oinopion settles Chios is one of a set of close allegiances to Athens which Ion's *Foundation of Chios* (*Χίου κτίσις*) was keen to cultivate. Whitby (1998) discusses Ion of Chios' oeuvre between philo-Lakonism and Atheno-centrism. Hornblower (2004) 145–56 intriguingly suggests the attribution of Pi. frr. 71–4 to a dithyramb composed for Chios, possibly theoric and sent to Delos (a (fated) chorus of boys travelled from Chios to Delphi in the 6th cent. (Hdt. 6.21)); Likymnios of Chios is a local dithyrambic poet (*PMG* 768–73) with Hordern (2002) 123. For dithyrambs sent to Delos see n. 5 above. I plan to examine the rather complex musical world on Chios in a separate treatment (for Ion of Chios see now Pelling (2007)).

[128] That Naxos had an important share in bringing about the 'Ionian Revolt' (and its failure) is similarly symptomatic of a powerful and pivotal island state. See Reger in *Inventory* 761–2 for the detailed references to Naxian history, the in-fighting, the relationship with Persia, and its naval and financial strength in this period.

[129] Andros' active links to its colonies in the north are listed in n. 82 above.

[130] It is interesting that Athenian-loyal Keos seems to have a *genos* link to Athenian-founded Miletus (Rutherford (2001) 291–2; first observed by G. Huxley (1965) 244). Euxantios' son Miletus founded the city of the same name (Aristokrates of Miletus *FGrH* 493 F 3 (= Σ A.R. 1.186, 23.16 Wendel)). Cf. Σ Pi. *Pae.* 4.61a Ὀνειτ̣[ής perhaps eponym of the Milesian Onitadai, a *genos* known from the Molpoi inscription.

where singing in the theoric chorus perhaps went alongside the formation of civic self-consciousness tied to 'democratic' rule and the expulsion of an unpopular king in myth. The theoric chorus—or a chorus that presupposes the practice of *theoria* to Delos—in these communities seems to have served to place an island within a system of values that also defined its relationship to Athens.

It is for this role in the phrasing of a civic identity, I believe, that male theoric choruses identifying with the female Deliades in the birth-shout of the myth-ritual nexus do not seem to pose a 'gender' problem. Athenian dramatic *khoroi*, arguably pivotal in fostering democratic ideology, were consistently composed of men, regardless of the gender of the mythical dancers they represented. Similarly, *theoroi* were usually men, even ephebes. If Delian songs played a vital role in forging the civic self-awareness of the *poleis* participating in fifth-century *theoria* as suggested here, a *khoros* of male citizens, or of young men about to become citizens, is a good candidate for taking on such a function—all the more so if bits and pieces of democratic rhetoric also made it into these songs. This interpretation squares curiously well with evidence for birth-shout singing choruses on Delos before and after the fifth century. In the *Homeric Hymn*, there is as yet no trace of foreign choruses; rather, the Deliades themselves take on the job of representing the communities in attendance, by graciously imitating the sounds of many dialects. Similarly, during the period of independence between the middle of the third century and 166 BC, the Delian inventories mention a local Delian chorus of Deliades performing. By contrast, when the island is under Athenian rule again, no more local women's *khoroi* appear; instead we get lists of ephebes.[131] This state of affairs supports the interpretation that Athenians liked to use Delos as a place, and *theoria* to Delos as a practice, where relations between them and the rest of the world were defined. It is in this way that fifth-century theoric song construed identity and hierarchy in the relations between Athens and 'tributary' cities.

Ionians dancing elsewhere

This is just as true for the most complicated group of the Aegean dance, the Ionians of Asia Minor—but in a different way. These are always thought to be part of the earliest Delian League; Thucydides says explicitly that the Ionians had asked the Athenians to take on the leadership of Hellas at the end of the Persian Wars.[132] However, on looking more closely, evidence in support of this claim is slight and ambiguous. The ambiguity over Ionian involvement is exacerbated when considered in the context of the Delian myth-ritual complex, showing once again the delicate interplay between political alignments and long-standing

[131] Bruneau (1970) 76–81.

[132] Th. 1.95.1 The Ionians are routinely considered to be part of the earliest league, not least because they had sparked off the Persian War in the first place; Hdt. 9.106 is also often cited here; see n. 146 below.

shared ritual practices. A series of pieces of evidence suggests that the cities of the Ionian mainland were not among the *poleis* sending choruses to Delos in the early fifth century.[133] The case of the Ionians reveals yet another facet of how myth, ritual, and song were productive in forging ties and releasing unwanted bonds; and that in the fifth century one best resisted conscription to Delos by responding in the language of *theoria*. The Ionians' non-attendance contributes just as much to the understanding of the myth-ritual dynamic on Delos as dutiful island performances.

The *Homeric Hymn to Apollo* clearly states that Ionians were prominent at the sixth-century Delian festival, but in the early fifth they are absent in both song and archaeology.[134] By contrast, they were highly visible elsewhere. Thucydides, in the same chapter from which we learn that Ionians at some point stopped going to Delos, compares the old Delian panegyris with the Ionian Ἐφέσια of his own times, thereby somehow implying that this is where the Ionians went instead, and that Ephesos had replaced Delos as the central Ionian cult site. The Panionian festival and the Panionion on the promontory of Mykale, prominent in the Ionian Revolt, had moved to Ephesos at some point before 373 BC, when they returned to their earlier setting.[135] The change of locale also entailed a change of deity from Poseidon to Artemis.[136] In this context, it is curious that by far the most interesting disruption of the Delian theoric landscape duly occurs at Ephesos. The city fashioned a powerful myth to rival the Delian, a kind of counter legend: Strabo, centuries later, tells the alternative birth-story for Artemis at Ephesos, displaying striking analogies with the Delian narrative. The Delian paeans had stressed the double birth of Apollo and Artemis on Delos. By contrast, here, the birth of Artemis alone occurs on an offshore island of Ephesos: the island's name was Ortygia, Delos' alternative name. There is a Mount Solmissos on which Zeus sits and watches the event, and a nymph-midwife just like Eileithyia, while an olive tree at the river Kenkhrios forms the natural ambience of the birth scene just like the palm and lake on Delos. Although the myth as a whole is attested so much later, it belabours the same myth-ritual nexus that we have worked out above.[137]

The legend is obviously crafted to imitate the Delian myth: are these traces of a myth-ritual complex rivalling the Delian? It is duly another cult song of Pindar's that makes appealing suggestions in this direction. Theseus, featuring frequently

[133] Note too that Dion. Per. 525–37 and Σ 525 separates the Kyklades (characterized by their dispatch of choruses to Delos) from the 'Ionian islands' of Samos, Chios, etc.

[134] *H. Ap.* 151–5.

[135] D.S. 15.49.1. See the debate n. 140 below. The Thucydides passage was 3.104 (pp. 69–70 above).

[136] The Ephesia are mentioned together with other festivals for Artemis of Ephesos: *IK Ephesos* iv. 1105; *BMI* iii no. 605 = *IK Ephesos* v. 1605; see also Pollux i.37 ἑορταὶ δὲ ἔντιμοι . . . Ἀρτέμιδος Ἀρτεμίσια καὶ Ἐφέσια 'festivals in honour of Artemis are the Artemisia and the Ephesia'. See also Hicks in *BMI* iii p. 79.

[137] Str. 14.1.20; Tac. *Ann.* 3.61. According to a 3rd-cent. legend, Leto and Zeus met in the precinct of Apollo at Didyma (Herzog, *SbBerlin* 1905, 979 ff.). A 6th-cent. statue of Leto and Zeus there seems to confirm the antiquity of this legend: Hahland (1964) 145–6 with n. 8 and 162.

in Bacchylides, is not an illustrious performer in surviving Pindaric poetry—except in connection with Artemis at Ephesos. According to Pausanias, Pindar was wrong in claiming that the 'Amazons had built her sanctuary when they went against Athens and Theseus'. Pindar here links the construction of the sanctuary of Ephesian Artemis with the war against the most important hero of Athenian thalassocracy centred on Delos.[138] The Theseion at Athens beautifully depicts the relevance of this tradition in a fifth-century context. If Pindar was rebuked for his claim with regard to the temple at Ephesos, the rebuke is proof of the short-lived, functional nature of the contention, one that evidently lost impact and hence its claim to veracity as cult communities at both Delos and Ephesos changed around once again not much later in response to changing political conditions. But for the early fifth century it airs the possibility that the Ionians at Ephesos kept a safe distance from the myth-ritual network surrounding Delos.[139]

An Ionian desire to stay away from the Delian worshipping group by constructing an alternative worshipping group around the migrated Panionion at Ephesos can indeed be traced. When and why the Panionion was relocated has provoked much debate, but the Ionian Ephesia were evidently taken for granted by the time Thucydides was writing.[140] Curiously, the possibility that the move of the Ionian festival might relate directly to matters of Ionian identity has never been seriously considered. Meanwhile, however, it seems that the festivals on Delos and at Ephesos were focal points in a process of competitive renegotiation and redefinition of what it meant to be Ionian in the early fifth century, intimately tied to developments in the Athenian Aegean.[141]

The festival's relocation is plausibly linked to the Ionians' changing relationship with Athens, and perhaps even directly with the end of the Ionian Revolt and the fall of Miletus in 494 BC. There are indications that Miletus' destruction was a watershed in the future relationship between Athens and the Ionians of Asia

[138] Pi. fr. 174 = Paus. 7.2.7: *Ἀμαζόνας τὸ ἱερὸν ἱδρύσασθαι στρατευομένας ἐπὶ Ἀθήνας τε καὶ Θησέα.* Note that Maehler by mistake attributes the claim to Apollo at Didyma. Frr. 173–6 may constitute a little 'Theseis'. von Wilamowitz-Moellendorff (1922) 320–1 discusses the poem, though it is unnecessary to suspect a unique 'Ionian' commission for Pindar.

[139] For Artemis and the Amazons see also Paus. 4.31.8; Call. *Dian.* (3) 237–9; Str. 14.1.20–3 sketches the history of the sanctuary. Artemis of Ephesos: Paus. 7.2.6–8 for the various foundation legends of the shrine. Kreophilos *FGrH* 417 F 1 = Ath. 8.361d is another cult myth. For the cult title 'Panionios' at Ephesos see n. 160 below. For the Theseion see n. 93 above.

[140] The conventional date is 440 BC: Hornblower (1982*b*) and on 3.104.3, quoting Andrewes ('It sounds as if the festival was very well established at the time Thucydides wrote 3.104 . . . and that might suggest a date even earlier [than 440]'). Cf. Stylianou's idea (1983) that Diodorus' passage might refer to the return of the festival from Ephesos to Priene where it is in Strabo 14.1.20. See Hommel, Kleiner, and Müller-Wiener (1967) for the history of the Panionion.

[141] The continuous reinterpretation of Ionian identity and changing perceptions of Ionian culture during the 5th cent. is perhaps under-researched: cf. Nilsson (1951) 59–64; Connor (1993); Wilson (2003*a*); Smarczyk (1990) is mainly interested in how imperial Athens cultivated its role as the Ionian metropolis. G. Huxley (1972) is still a very helpful study.

Minor. The Athenians took the fall of Miletus very seriously indeed, and it is just worth pointing out that some of the evidence for this comes from the world of choral song: Phrynikhos' *Capture of Miletus* caused floods of tears in the Athenian audience, the poet was fined, and the play banned forever.[142] Miletus was the one Ionian city that really had an unambiguous relationship to Athens as its mother city,[143] and the Milesians had asked repeatedly for help from the Athenians on the grounds of *syngeneia*, but in the event they were abandoned by their kin. Somehow 'kinship' was not a pressing enough reason any more for the Athenian assembly. The Athenians' extreme reaction to the play can only be understood in the context of a fierce dispute over the city's present and future relationship to Ionia. Reaching back at least as far as Solon, the liaison with Ionia was as long-standing as it was ambiguous. Certainly around 500 BC the Ionians were not much in Athenian favour. Kleisthenes' constitutional reforms explicitly severed the overseas ties, aiming at inner-Athenian cohesion rather than kinship-based contacts across the Aegean, accessible perhaps only to a privileged few. If Herodotus reports Athens'—and many other Greeks'—embarrassment at their Ionianness, this should probably be seen in a context in which the Athenians' internal affairs and the status and role of their kinship bonds abroad were inextricably related.[144] That the Athenians got so emotional over Phrynikhos' play shows on the one hand that a Milesian bond was felt and its abrogation not universally approved. On the other, the various manifestations of 'ethnicity', that network covering vast areas of the Mediterranean, were at times the democratic city's most hated enemy. Athens' relationship to Ionia was ambiguous and problematic, not least perhaps for this reason.

And similarly, despite the fact that the Persian Wars were notionally fought to liberate the Ionians from the oriental grasp, and the Delian League ostensibly set up to keep the Persians out of Greek territory in 'Asia', it is not clear that this was of much consequence in the future relationship between Athens and Ionia. The 'historical' evidence for the Delian League's establishment is for the most part thoroughly muddled up and full of inconsistencies, suggesting that, by the time

[142] Hdt. 5.67; 6.21 for the Μιλήτου Ἅλωσις, staged probably shortly after the event in 494 BC. Rosenbloom (1993) discusses the social and identity intricacies of the play. Phrynikhos put on another historical and anti-Persian play in 476 BC, *Phoenician Women*, dealing with the Persian defeat at Salamis as did, in 472 BC, Aeschylus' *Persians*. Themistokles was the *khoregos* of the *Phoenician Women*.

[143] Hdt. 5.97; 6.21; 9.97; all other Ionian cities were founded by bastard sons of Kodros.

[144] Solon: fr. 4a W; Hes. fr. 10a 20–3 for Ion's early association with Athens. Kleisthenes had abolished the four Ionian tribes and replaced them with ten tribes headed by autochthonous Attic heroes (Hdt. 5.67; *Ath. Pol.* 19–26). Allegedly he looked down upon the the Ionians (ὑπεριδεῖν); perhaps his competitor Isagoras, from a priestly family attending to Karian Zeus, is a representative of the kind of links between elite Athenians and Asia Minor that the reforms sought to deny or to reformulate. All Ionians shunned the name: Hdt. 1.143. Various attempts have been made to explain why this may be, most recently J. Hall (1997) 51–6. The Ionian Revolt seems to serve as a foil against which Athenian civic ideology is formulated. Murray (1988) is the fullest treatment of the events and the significance of the Ionian revolt.

of our sources, the truth had long been swallowed by traditions constantly reformulating themselves. We have of course learned to live with the idea of the 'Ionian' character of the early Delian League, but this vision is fraught with contradictions that can only be solved by turning a distinct Ionic identity into a contested concept, rather than one that was neatly defined throughout the fifth century. Incidentally, as we shall now also see, on numerous occasions islands and mainland Ionians were pitched against each other, and this will come to bear significance.[145]

The passages on the league's foundation in Herodotus and Thucydides and some later authors share too many incongruities for them not to record the same episode, or set of episodes. And Ionian *syngeneia* is a strident, but failed theme in both.[146] Despite the prominence of mainland Ionians in the narrative, no author gives evidence for any mainland Ionians actually joining the league in its nascent state. In Herodotus' account, the Athenians end up with leadership over the Greeks at the end of the Persian Wars in the context of a debate about what to do with their kin, the Ionian mainlanders, but then proceed to admit only the triad of Chios, Samos, and Lesbos, and 'the other islanders' to the League. As already mentioned above, those cities that the Athenians sought to conscript immediately prior to the end of the Persian Wars were islands: places such as Andros, Karystos, and Paros. The great promise to the Greeks in Herodotus' account is not, as one might expect, the domination of Asia Minor, but rather the 'prizes' are the islands and the Hellespont.[147] Thucydides is much vaguer on the issue of recruitment at that point and only mentions Athenians who together with 'those allies from Ionia and the Hellespont who had already revolted from Persia' go on a raiding expedition which does not demonstrably seek to liberate the rest, aiming rather for Sestos and Byzantion at the Hellespont. Only later does he report that the 'Ionians had asked the Athenians to lead them against the Persians'.[148] *Ath. Pol.* and Plutarch share the fixed phrase of the insular trinity of Chios, Samos, and Lesbos (at that point perhaps already a formula of oral history), but also the uncertainty about the Asian mainland. Rather, the tribute-assessor Aristeides 'encourages' the Ionians to break away from Persia, and is later 'popular with the Ionians', although no individual Ionian city is ever mentioned; by contrast,

[145] For the alleged Ionian character of the league see e.g. Meiggs (1972) 36–41.

[146] Hdt. 9.106; Th. 1.89 ff. Cf. D.S. 11.50, on 475 BC, which explains the Athenian takeover as Spartan disinterest in a sea-empire. Among the vast bibliography on this matter are Meiggs (1972) 36–41; Robertson (1980*a*); Seager and Tuplin (1980); M. Austin (1990); Whitby (1998); Hornblower (2002) 9–18 (9–12 on how the Spartans came to lose leadership), esp. 14–15.

[147] Chios, Samos, Lesbos: Hdt. 9.106; *Ath. Pol.* 23.5; previous island recruitment: Hdt. 8.111–12; 121; Hdt. 9.101.3: ὥς σφι καὶ αἱ νῆσοι καὶ ὁ Ἑλλήσποντος ἄεθλα προέκειτο 'that the islands and the Hellespont were lying before them as a prize'. Herodotus' curious remark immediately following these events, on a notional defection of Ionia after the battle of Mykale in 479 BC 'and so for the second time Ionia revolted' (9.104), can therefore not be directly related to the early Delian League. That should not, however, detract from the fact that the Ionians had a due share in the subsequent victory (9.103–4).

[148] Th. 1.89 ff.

Plutarch lets it be understood that the 'just' Aristeides may have made his own private deals with the Ionian mainlanders. Similarly when describing Kimon's journey up to the Hellespont after Mykale, he mysteriously refers to 'the Athenians and those Ionians who had already been freed', but does not supply any specifics.[149] All these reports seem more than anything coloured by the ideology, assumptions, and difficulties of the later Athenian empire. No individual Ionian city is ever mentioned as part of the league, let alone the Ionians as a whole, before the battle of Tanagra in 458 BC, where they fought, still unspecifically, with the Athenians against Sparta.[150]

Rather, one wonders whether some of the 'liberation' talk of the sources in the early phase is not part of a crude ideology that involves an element of laborious conquest which was in part itself ideological. There are few signs of Ionians considering joining the Greeks once the Persians were going to be defeated. The Athenians effectively secured alliance with very few of the states along the coastline of Asia Minor in the 470s and 460s BC, who rather continued to pay tribute to the Persians, and not necessarily reluctantly so. Sailing along the western Anatolian seaboard, there were pockets of anti-Athenian sentiment, places granted by the Persian king to those fallen Greeks who had successfully steered themselves into mischief with Athens.[151] More widely, it has long been noted that the so-called Ionian Revolt in the early years of the fifth century (*c.*499–494 BC) did little to alter the opportunism of Asia Minor's cities and, especially, its leaders.[152] How unproblematically many cities were two-faced is nicely illustrated by an anecdote about the Athenian conscription of the pro-Persian Phaselites all the way down in Lykia, who eventually agreed to join when their 'friends,' the pro-Athenian Chians, ensured them that this was to their benefit, which must largely have concerned naval matters.[153] For a later period, Thucydides makes it very clear that the most efficient way for islanders of rallying supporters for a

[149] *Ath. Pol.* 23–7; Plut. *Arist.* 23–5; 23.4 'the captains and generals of the Greeks, but particularly the Chians, Samians and Lesbians' are keen to get rid of the Spartan general Pausanias, eventually removed through a plot arranged by two men from Chios and Samos; 26.3 for Aristeides' bribery; the *Ath. Pol.* has the Ionians 'swear to the same friends and enemies' in a formula known from high-imperial treaties: Tod 68 (cited by Hornblower (2002) 14).

[150] ML 36 (date uncertain, *c.*458 BC?) reconstructed on the basis of Paus. 5.10.4. Very little is certain of this early period: the islands named can be considered plausible on the basis of literary evidence; the cities of the Chalkidike peninsula were in Th. 5.18.5 asked to revert to the 'tribute of Aristeides', indicating their likely membership early on. The ambiguity with regard to Ionia is perhaps the best indicator for badly defined membership. See Hornblower (2002) 14–15.

[151] The argument has recently been formulated in detail by Whitby (1998). The list of places he names is impressive and includes major coastal cities (220): Myrina, Gryneion, Gambreion, Palaigambreion, Magnesia, Myous, Lampsakos, Perkote, Palaiskepsis, Aigai, Kyme, Ephesos (note that Themistokles eventually flees here), Sigeion, Kolonai in the Hellespont. J. Cook (1962) 16 maintained that as maritime cities the Ionians were allies and subjects of Athens, but as communities of substantial landowners they paid their rent primarily to the King.

[152] M. Austin (1990).

[153] Plut. *Cim.* 12.3–4. How keen the Athenians were on the Phaselites' naval strength and excellent position on the trade routes towards the east also comes across through ML 31 (469–50 BC).

revolt was simply to look across the straits to the mainland of Asia Minor.[154] While the absence of any positive evidence for mainland Ionians does not definitely deny their presence in the league, it must be clear that whatever their status was, they were by no means a secure bet. Rather, they posed a constant threat to the stability and cohesion of the empire; and this may also be the reason why they are constantly at the very heart of Delian League propaganda, and myth-making is almost exclusively dedicated to them.[155] Ionians were *never* an unproblematic category of allies, and if, as we shall later see, it is their tribute that is the most difficult to get, it is not a surprise that their willingness to send *khoroi* to Delos became an issue.

Seen within this wider framework, the idea of competing worshipping groups at Delos and Ephesos in the early fifth century has some appeal. A shift of the Ionian *panegyris* to Ephesos in this context is a plausible scenario, not least because this is the city that denied all ties to Athens throughout the fifth century—quite apart from the fact that the Ephesians will have seized the opportunity to deprive their perennial rival of leadership among the Ionians, notably in the Ionian Revolt, by having the common cult on their territory.[156] Should we therefore not see two rival worshipping communities on Delos and at Ephesos, vying even for candidates for admission, quite possibly even for a definition of Ionianness at a time when this was a contested concept? It is tempting to suspect that the competing birth-legend at Ephesos grew out of this milieu, just as might, also, Pindar's little *Theseis* discussed above. More bits and pieces of a construed rivalry can indeed be identified. While, for example, celebrating Poseidon in the Panionion at Mykale did not pose a problem for dancing in honour of Apollo and Artemis on Delos, honouring Artemis at Ephesos might have: the Ephesians celebrated Artemis' birthday on 6 Thargelion, the same day as the Delians held it.[157] It is worth calling to mind once more how vigorously all our songs to Delos propagate the tale of a *double* birth of Artemis and Apollo on Delos itself: the *Homeric Hymn* of a century or so earlier made no such claim. Certainly others

[154] The Samian revolt was planned by oligarchs gone underground in Ionia: Th. 1.115–17; oligarchs chronically have sympathizers on the mainland; cf. the advice of the Ionian exiles to the Spartan Alkidas in Th. 3.31, paraphrased p. 112 below.

[155] As is exposed e.g. by Smarczyk (1990) 328–84. Not even Delos itself remains unaffected by the lack of commitment when the Spartans undisturbedly put in there every now and then on the way to help eastern Aegean states revolt, e.g. at Mytilene in 427 BC (Th. 3.29.1). Cf. the Spartans again on Delos in 411 BC (Th. 8.80.3). See Chankowski (2001) for the historical links between Sparta and Delos; Smarczyk (1990) 508–12 on Spartan ships in Delian waters, perhaps having prompted the removal of the treasury to Athens in the 450s BC.

[156] There comes to be a certain rivalry between Miletus and Ephesos over the Athenian ancestry descending from Kodros: Nele(i)us is founder of Miletus in Hdt. 9.97 and leader of the Ionian colonization in Hellanikos *FGrH* 4 F 125 while Pherekydes *FGrH* 3 F 155 makes Androklos, founder of Ephesos and bastard-son of Kodros, the *arkhegetes* ('leader in founding a colony'). The later Ephesians made the point particularly by celebrating a festival of Artemis called 'Neleis': Plut. *Mul. Virt.* 253f–54a; Polyaen. *Str.* 8.35; Aristainet. *Epist.* 1.15. Smarczyk (1990) 328–59, though not concerned with inner-Ionian rivalry, discusses and lists the evidence for Athenians settling Ionia.

[157] Nilsson (1906/95) 247.

in the fifth century had the same idea of appropriating the locality and story of the birth for their own cult when trying to rival the Athenian priority to the Delian gods, as for example the Boiotians when they happened to be in greatest conflict over their Delion with the Athenians.[158] And furthermore, while the *Homeric Hymn* has Artemis simply born on Ortygia (ll.14–16), Pindar makes sure that Asteria, Ortygia, and Delos all merge into the same island, indicating that the location of Artemis' birth was a matter of dispute.[159] It looks as if the Ionians chose to play Artemis as a trump card here: this must have been effective because this deity, as we shall see below (Section 4), was the older deity on Delos by a long way and had a catchment area among the Ionians and islanders that exceeded that of Delian Apollo into the unknowable past. Ephesos itself had a major role in this construction. Fifth-century Delian myth-ritual performances work with, and make use of, this obscure memory.[160]

Apollo and Artemis on Delos, and Artemis on Ephesos may have been something like competitive centres for Ionianness: this is an exaggerated formulation, but it brings across one important aspect, which is that theoric worshipping communities have the tendency to attribute to themselves a certain exclusivity, which in turn incites the desire for inclusion.[161] On this logic, being part of a worshipping group is not just an obligation, it is a privilege; as we saw above, in the case of island *theoria* to Delos it came with the 'special advantage' of participation in a prosperous and successful maritime network. We saw that islands were prominent dancers on Delos in this period, and their songs immensely busy forging a, probably novel, link integrating Athens, Delos, and the islands into a shared, and seemingly rather exclusive, tradition. That this was effectively a rephrasing of the traditional Delian catchment area of 'Ionians and islanders' into a community of 'Athenians and islanders' (as Thucydides has it) is plausible in the light of the island imagery that imperial Athens developed in application to itself, while the intimate link between islands, thalassocracy, and democracy has also been observed.[162] But in view of the contemporary conspicuousness of matters Ionian, it is even likely that the island fashion served a competitive

[158] In 424 BC the Boiotians had freed the Delion in Boiotia from Athenian rule and instituted a post-battle festival with an *agon*. Th. 4.76.4; 90–101; D.S. 12.69–70 notes that the festival (*τὴν τῶν Δηλίων πανήγυριν*) was financed by the spoils of the battle. Significantly, this occurs only shortly after the Athenians had restaked their claim to Delos (Ch. 7.2 below). Apollo's birth at Tegyra occurs in an oracle to the Delians in Plut. *De Def. Or.* 412c–d; Semos *FGrH* 396 F 20; Kallisthenes *FGrH* 124 F 11 = St. Byz. s.v. *Τέγυρα*; Plut. *Pelop.* 16. The Delion in Boiotia is closely linked to Delos in an enigmatic tradition: Hdt. 6.118 (cf. Paus. 10.28.6); Str. 9.2.7 (where it is *ἐκ Δήλου ἀφιδρυμένον* 'founded from Delos'); Artemis, Apollo, and Leto were worshipped here: *IG* vii 20.12; Paus. 9.22.1; 10.28.6; *Σ* Pi. *O.* 7.154a; see Schachter (1981–94) i. 44–7; Smarczyk (1990) 521–2 n. 67.

[159] Pi. *Pae.* 5.42; 7b.42 and 48; fr. 33c.

[160] Imperial Ephesos claimed an *Ἀπόλλων Πανιώνιος*: *JÖAI* 45 (1960) Beibl. 75–6 no. 2 = *I. Eph.* 814 (imperial); cf. at Athens: *IG* ii^2 4995 (1st cent. AD). Similarly Apollo Oulios n. 213 below.

[161] For example, the language the Panionion uses to keep its members in check—mostly taken from Pausanias, but also known from Herodotus—reveals precisely that when the talk is about 'pleading for admission': Hdt. 1.149; Paus. 7.2 ff.; Kowalzig (2005) 45–56.

[162] Ceccarelli (1993) and Constantakopoulou (2002).

reformulation of Ionianness itself: a new definition of who these Ionians were had been found in the myth of Athenian colonization of the islands. While, on the one hand, labouring to create a tight, exclusive, and cohesive theoric worshipping group, fifth-century *theoria* to Delos continued to play with, and exploit, its Ionian associations (and insisting on Artemis' role in the cult is part of this, too), perhaps with a view to making itself attractive. It is in this suggestive way that we may understand Bacchylides, *Ode 17*'s call upon the Ionian youth, the Ἰάωνες.[163] On the other hand, this is the only theoric song that makes an explicit connection between islands and Ionianness, and it may well have come late in the series. But even then, the chances are that it says explicitly what the earlier island choruses had long been suggesting, namely that every Ionian was invited to join in singing the birth-shout, and that promises of liberation from the Cretan tribute could easily be extended. Repetitive, reiterative performances sounding the same Ionian note might eventually result in recruitment.

If there is no proof that Ionians were in either league or on the island, this still does not mean that league and worshipping group were identical. Performances of myth and ritual on Delos feature right in the middle of a fierce conflict over identity and power spheres in the Aegean carried out simultaneously in multiple media. Delian *theoria* in the fifth century was one of several attempts to create a worshipping group identical with political groupings, conducted on the assumption, however, that the two were essentially different sets of people. Whether and when the people who participated in the Delian cult community described themselves as 'Ionians' is less clear than the fact that they were actually talking about the traditions of 'Ionians'. The point may well lie in how best to exploit the notion of an ancestral cult community on Delos, which in the past included Ionians and islanders: Athenians tried to lure the traditional worshipping group to Delos, while the Ionians at Ephesos might have attempted the same with their Panionion; and both of them were excluding as much as attracting the other on the same grounds, that their sanctuary was the original birth-place of deities whose worship was constitutive of Ionian identity. If we feel it impossible to come up with a firm conclusion about Ionian whereabouts and religious commitments, this shows the success of the phenomenon itself: who was at which cult centre, and for what reasons, remains ambiguous.

3. THE IMPERIAL *KHOROS* IN THE 420s BC

That such a view of ambiguously interacting political and religious communities with the capricious Ionians in the midst is not so far off the mark finally emerges from what Thucydides gives as the last stage in the development of choral *polis-theoria* to Delos. With the relocation of the Delian treasury to the Athenian

[163] Bacch. 17.3.

akropolis at the instigation of the Samians in the mid-fifth century, Delos disappears from the surface of historical (and quite possibly choral) narrative.[164] In 426/5 BC, in the heat of the Archidamian War, the Athenians suddenly remembered the cult's choral potential and fished Delos out of the sea once again. Thucydides in his fundamental passage (3.104, cited pp. 69–70 above) tells us explicitly that they reorganized and expanded the Delia on the model of the old Ionian festival, and even cites the relevant lines of the *Homeric Hymn to Apollo*. A pointed initiative especially if seen in the light of what we have learned about the Ionians and Delos. Surely he was not the only one to have this model in mind, and not only because the *Hymn*'s catalogue coincides, at least roughly, with the members of the late fifth-century league. No new *panegyris* on Delos could have failed to carry the old associations: this was an explicit attempt to exploit the island's potential as a religious centre for political purposes, to play with the fuzzy boundaries of religious and cult communities at a period when the empire could be regarded as entering a serious crisis.[165]

The time when the festival was reformed in the 420s BC was a period of turmoil for the Athenians, a period of getting into dire straits with their allies, and when the very nature and extent of the imperial community came into question. There are external signs of this crisis, such as Athenian manpower problems after the plague, tribute reassessments in 425 and 422 BC, and cases of failed payment. The health of 'imperial finances' is a notorious problem for this period,[166] but whether or not the empire was actually short of funds is independent of the perhaps observable crisis over the identity of the imperial 'community'. It is hardly a coincidence that this was also the period when Athenian 'theoric' strategies were most pronounced, in an attempt to redefine these obligations in an oblique yet powerful way. The Athenians themselves invested much in this first 'Ionian' *theoria* in 425 BC when sending as many as six *arkhitheoroi*, 'leaders of the *theoria*', and possibly leaving behind a new temple to the god as well. The *theoriai* led by the enormously rich and immensely ambitious Nikias and Kallias followed not long after, both setting up showpiece dedications.[167]

[164] Plut. *Arist.* 25.2 ff. (removal of the treasury). Nevertheless a temple of Delian Apollo was probably built at Phaleron in the 430s BC: Parker (1996) 150; 154 (with 125 n. 15): *IG* i^3 130 (*c.*432 BC) and the debate Lewis, *ABSA* 55 (1960) 190–4 versus Mattingly, *ZPE* 83 (1990) 112–13.

[165] Th. 3.104 with Hornblower on 'Ionianism'; for the reformed festival see Parker (1996) 87–8 (6th cent.); 149–51 (5th cent.); 222–5 (4th cent.); (2005) 80–2. Wilson (2007) 175 imagines that musical contests were revived on Delos at this time.

[166] Kallet-Marx (1993). The tribute reassessments are ML 69 = Fornara 136 (426/5 BC, the decree of Thoudippos, probably the son-in-law of the Athenian demagogue Kleon: Hornblower (2002) 146); on the inefficacy of this assessment see Kallet-Marx, ibid. 164–70; Hornblower (1991–6), vol. ii, 93–8.

[167] The six leaders of the 425 BC *theoria* left a dedication: *IG* i^3 1468 = *ID* 43. The small 'temple of the Athenians': Bruneau and Ducat (1983) 129–30; Boersma (1970) 171. Nikias: Plut. *Nic.* 3.5–8 (see above), with *IG* i^3 1474 and Hornblower on 3.104, p. 518 for the dispute over the date. Kallias: *ID* 104.115–16. Cf. other Athenian dedications: Coupry on *ID* 47; 48 (?) (end of 5th cent.); Smarczyk (1990) 519 n. 59. Is *ID* 49 a contemporary Naxian dedication?

There are some intriguing indications that the renewal of the festival in 426/5 BC was seen, and reflected upon, as a piece of choral strategy. The suggestive power of theoric choral song for community-building and the notion of *theoria* itself were exploited for the redefinition of what it meant to dance in an imperial chorus. The crisis was formulated as an issue of tribute, as if to imply that allied contributions—not exclusively financial—were fundamental to the cohesion of the empire. In this context, the malleability of theoric relations deploys its full powers, by blurring real and imagined tributes, thus redefining the notion of 'tribute' to the empire.

There are clues that the issue of 'tribute' was to a great extent tied up with the loyalty of the Ionian allies, and the tampering with the Delian choral levy must be seen in this context. Throughout the fifth century, Ionia sheltered many of those unconvinced by the attractions of the Athenian empire.[168] In the midst of the Mytilenean revolt in 427 BC we get an interesting self-assessment by such 'Ionian exiles' (and the Lesbian rebels) in their plea for Spartan support. The Ionian *phoros*, they claimed, was the 'greatest of Athens' sources of revenue' and cutting it off would severely hurt the Athenians—an idea that is found elsewhere in Thucydides. Ionia features as a promising target for rallying anti-Athenian bands: the Spartans should seize one of the Ionian cities or Kyme in Aiolia, and use it as a base for organizing a revolt in Ionia. This, they claimed, was a distinct possibility, 'since they would be welcomed everywhere'. Though the Spartan leader remained unconvinced, his fleet subsequently sailed apparently undisturbed up and down the coast of Asia Minor. What is striking in this episode (and similar ones could be adduced) is the clear view that Ionia was never a risk-free zone, always with split loyalties, and its tribute problematic.[169]

In fact, no other group within the empire was quite as abused by contemporary texts, and it is perhaps no surprise that much of this happens in another choral genre, namely, Old Comedy. The problems Athenians had with Ionian tribute and loyalty feature as a common theme, continuing the notorious stereotypes well known from Herodotus' portrayal of the Ionian Revolt, topoi recurring on the comic stage conspicuously during the 420s, but also before and after. Ionians, defeated by indulgence in luxury and wanton hedonism, are chronically corrupt villains looking exclusively to their individual profit, often derived from trade—useless warriors and notorious deserters, shield-throwers who lack a sense of community.[170] The epitome of the Ionian is the legendary Killikon, whose

[168] Cf. n. 154 above.

[169] Th. 3.29–33; esp. 3.31. Not much was put in the Spartans' way on their journey eastwards: they land unobserved on Delos, sail to Mykonos and Ikaria, set across to Embaton in Erythrai (3.29.1), and quietly proceed down the coast of Asia Minor (Myonessos, Teios; Ephesos, Klaros). The importance of the Ionian *prosodos* ('revenue'): 3.31; cf. 3.13.6–7. Th. 3.34 continues with an almost absurdly factional portrayal of the split city of Kolophon. Note the Chians loyal to Athens (nn. 171, 177, 185 below). Spartan prisoners: Th. 3.32. Ionian instability prompts the so-called Ionian war from 411 BC onwards.

[170] The stereotypes are old: e.g. in Archil. fr. 108 W; 124a W; Hdt. 5.67; 1.143 etc.; Th. 6.77 on unpopular, weak, and unreliable Ionians.

unfailing wickedness is variously attached to places of mainland and island Ionia; but other individuals too carry the burden of the 'ethnic' character. Even the Chians, otherwise steadfast Athenian allies all the way to 411 BC, appear as unremittingly iniquitous.[171] Effeminacy and obsession with lifestyle stands in the way of being good warriors. So, for instance, Dionysos the 'Ionian' soldier insists on the warm bath that only Ionians take before fighting, or on enjoying 'Naxian' almonds.[172] Ionians sit in exquisite attire at their overloaded tables enjoying their courses according to a specific Ionian dining order, while engaging in polite conversation (with its preference for 'female nouns') and relaxing to the oriental sounds of Ionia and Karia—and so on and so forth.[173]

It is no surprise to learn that these high-livers are the Athenian empire's worst tribute-payers, at least in comedy. The Athenian demagogue Kleon is immediately associated with the tribute by his two reassessments in 425 BC and 422 BC, the profit from which he greedily sucks up himself in *Knights*. If he is the personal beneficiary of his policy, as the constant claim goes, the Ionians in Old Comedy are its greatest 'sufferers', by implication confirming Thucydides' view of the importance of the *Ionikos phoros*. So, for example, Milesians appear chronically unwilling to pay, inducing Kleon in the *Knights* to play his lyre in the 'Dorian' mode (the tune always ready for bribery); and it is an Ionian spectator who curses him in Aristophanes' *Peace* of 421 BC, more than anything perhaps because Kleon, not unlike 'Ionian' Alkibiades, is a bit too much like the spectator himself.[174]

[171] Killikon's legendary badness is variously attached to places of mainland and island Ionia (*Pax* 363–4 and Σ; Samos, Miletus, Syros). Other such chronic evildoers are Phrynondas and Eurybatos, cf. Olson on *Pax* 362–3. Chians are loyal Athenian allies (Eup. *PCG* 246) turned into notorious villains (Ar. *Pax* 169–72; *Apoth. Lac.* 232f–3a; cf. Ael. *VH* 2.15 where the same story is about Klazomenai); Ar. *Triphales* (after 411 BC) *PCG* 556 gives a profile of Chios, Klazomenai, Ephesos, Abydos, a collection of cities quoted by Athenaios as examples of Ionian softness (Ath. 12.525a).

[172] Corrupt deserters: Crat. *Pytine* (wine-flask) (424 BC or later) *PCG* 211 (alluding to Archil. fr. 109 W, on the Ionians); Ar. *Daidalos* (*c.*415 BC or later) *PCG* 198 on the (!) Ephesian traitor Eurybatos who went over to the Persians in the 6th cent. Crat. *Arkhilokhoi* (449 BC) *PCG* 1 contrasts (?) Kimon 'best of the Panhellenes' with the *Arkhilokhoi*, the notorious shield-throwers (cf. n. 170 above); Eup. *Taxiarkhoi* (*c.*415 BC Storey (2003) 246–8) *PCG* 272 has Dionysos the future warrior starting his training with an 'Ionian' bath.

[173] Effeminacy and luxury: Crat. *PCG* 506 on preference for female nouns and below on *Peace* (cf. also Olson on 932); Crat. *PCG* 460: *Ἰωνόκυσθος* Ionian-tailed = effeminate; Kallias, *Kyklopes* (*c.*434 BC) *PCG* 8 Ionians' luxurious dinner tables (*c.*434 BC, ?repeated by Diokles in 393); Ar. *PCG* 930: *χιάζειν*, *σιφνιάζειν* to 'Chianize' or to 'Siphnianize' is to employ overwrought tunes (*περιέργοις μέλεσι χρᾶσθαι*). Plato, *Lakonians* (*c.*406 BC?) *PCG* 71 a dinner-order, with Karian and Ionian music; Ar. *Thesm.* 2 (*c.*406 BC) *PCG* 355 luxurious Ionian shoes for women. Ionian song is stigmatized with lewdness and sexual suggestion: Ar. *Thesm.* 159–70 (ridiculing Ionian poets); *Eccl.* 882–3; 918–20 (singing in an 'Ionian way' in order to attract sexual attention (cf. Sommerstein on 883)).

[174] Ar. *Equ.* 311 ff.; cf. 361 (Kleon); esp. 927–40: Milesians not wanting to pay, bribed by Kleon; 989–96: Kleon's 'Dorian' lyre-tunes (cf. 529); cf. *Nub.* 575 ff.; *Vesp.* 355 (note that 284 has philo-Athenian Samians). An Ionian arriving in a trade-ship from Naxos complains about the tribute in *Peace* 43–9, see n. 185 below.

Singing paeans on Delos as part of the renewal of the festival in 426/5 BC as reported in Thucydides 3.104 could have had an interesting, if ambiguous, function in these circumstances. Could choral contributions now symbolize something more than the happy gathering of singing crowds? It is not a coincidence that in comedy, too, Athenian choral strategy is unforgivingly targeted, and its 'Ionian' policies on Delos are stridently reflected. There is a cluster of at least four plays in the late 420s BC that make it clear how the Delian festival reform relates directly to the empire's shaken confidence: Eupolis' *Poleis*, Kratinos' *Deliades*, and Aristophanes' *Clouds* and *Peace* all allude to the choral complex. Athenian musical manoeuvring did not escape apprehension on the comic stage.

This at least is what a fragment of Eupolis' *Poleis* strongly suggests. In this play, of 422 BC, cities—an allied chorus of the chorus of allies—are paraded before a panel for assessment of their conduct.[175] Congratulating and defending themselves on the grounds of accurate timber deliveries, the provision of luxury goods, or the dutiful contribution of manpower, places such as Chios, Miletus, or Kyzikos, but also tribes in northern Greece, perform in front of a committee of *ἄνδρες λογισταὶ τῶν ὑπευθύνων χορῶν*: 'accountants of choruses under scrutiny'.[176] *Poleis* disguised as choruses are subjected to *euthyne*, the accountability test that every Athenian official had to undergo. But they imperceptibly blur with the notion of real, theoric choruses being made *ὑπεύθυνοι* ('accountable'). For while a chorus should be judged on the quality of its dance, or the sum and timely payment of its tribute, this one is assessed on the quality of the goods it brings to Athens! So, the slippery Tenians bring scorpions and sycophants; the Kyzikenes attractive lovers, the Amorgians expensive garments, and the famously loyal Chians unexciting manpower and ships 'as many as needed'.[177] Corruption and exploitation of the dubious tribute—both on the part of Athens and on that of Athenian individuals—also feature: some prominent politicians get married to cities, while unwanted suitors are sent off to found a colony; 'inspection' of a city's wine consumption reveals wine-guards feasting at public expense. An unnamed place is stripped of its most basic commodities; and Miletus loses its identity when stripped of all its wool.[178]

The comedy plays on the ambiguous nature of the tribute, choral and monetary, and even throws in a third (rather more elusive) dimension, the economic. The play transposes material obligation into the imagery of the tributary chorus. This is, incidentally, the play that gives away the precious piece of information that the allies' tribute was presented at the Dionysia each year.[179] The

[175] On Eupolis' fragments we now have the indispensable commentary and translation of the fragments by Storey (2003).

[176] Eup. *Poleis PCG* 239.

[177] Eup. *Poleis PCG* 245 Tenos; 246 Chios; 247 Kyzikos; 256 Amorgos.

[178] Eup. *Poleis PCG* 219 (wine inspectors), 223 (colony), 243 (marriage with a *polis*); 242 has a list of utensils of a city which is being held accountable for them; in 244 a *polis* is scrutinized for the quality of her land.

[179] Eup. *Poleis PCG* 254; *Σ* Ar. *Ach.* 504–7; Isocr. *De Pace* (8) 82, with Goldhill (1987/90).

image of the theoric chorus affords the confluence of three types of tributary relations that allies had to Athens, implying the identity of a religious, political, and economic community.[180] Eupolis' *Poleis* thus expresses a perceived reality of the Athenian empire, that a sacred tribute handily disguised crude imperial policy—as if the Athenians somehow managed their empire like a cult community: a system of mutual obligations between cities which is in reality, so the play suggests, a sinister way of controlling people who are given the illusion that those ties exist for their own benefit.

Pointed as it is, this is not the only direct comment on Athens' choral strategy. Kratinos' *Deliades*, performed in the same year, is yet another piece with choral content. Its few fragments barely allow for the plot's reconstruction beyond a nudge on the pageantry of the Delian festival procession; the generous investment in Delian *theoria* was already evident in Nikias' showpiece.[181] The *Clouds*, also performed in 422 BC, invokes Apollo on Delos, Artemis at Ephesos, together with Athenian Athena and Dionysos, in the quasi-hymnic *parabasis*, as if to invent a pantheon specially geared towards solving the paradox of empire and democracy: the Delian gods serving the former, Athena and Dionysos the latter. The Delian triad is incidentally called upon again in the comic presentation of the Ionian crisis in the last decade of the century, whenever the relationship between city and choral poet is at stake.[182]

A fourth and last comic *khoros* may be recalled in order to return more directly to the Ionian dimension of the Delia's renewal some years earlier, and the intertwined imperial, choral, but also Ionian policies. Aristophanes' *Peace* was performed in 421 BC, shortly after the conclusion of the 'Peace of Nikias'. Though the play is not as overflowing with choral imagery as others, this comic *khoros*, too, can be read as a sharp comment on Athenian theoric strategy on Delos. Here a further complication emerges: not only is the old Ionian elite the target of comic derision, but to the same extent a new, similarly spoiled, elite is targeted, namely, the Ionianized Athenian *demos* itself.[183]

Peace is pretty much a settlement in Ionian terms, but with a double spin: the plot has the two women Ὀπώρα ('Harvest') and Θεωρία given to the *boule* as fundamental to the construction of the meaning of 'peace'. It may or may not be a coincidence that Theoria's portrayal can easily be read in terms of the reformed Ionian Delia.[184] The 'penteteris' is the attribute of her attractive bottom and her

[180] For this idea cf. Eup. *Poleis PCG* 254; Th. 2.38.2; cf. also Hermippos *PCG* 23.

[181] Crat. *Deliades PCG* 32–3.

[182] Ar. *Nub.* 595–606. Cf. Ar. *Thesm.* 101–29.

[183] e.g. Trygaios becomes a typical Ionian (Alkibiades); leaders share their corrupt nature with Ionians (Kleon); effeminacy and softness (πραότης) characterize the slack *demos*, notably interested in the pleasures of the symposion now widely accessible. On the historical background see Olson's commentary.

[184] The character Θεωρία tends to be translated as 'festival' or 'holiday' (Olson on 523); Sommerstein chooses 'showtime' (on 523), which I think misses some of the ridicule of the play with its more direct allusion to to theoric practices. I have already briefly made these points in (2005) 60–1.

legs are 'drawn back' like those of the sacrificial animal on the 'Draw-back Day', the Anarrhysis, the second day of the Apatouria, Herodotus' quintessential Ionian festival. She signifies athletic contests followed by horse-races, features as the 'mistress of *khoroi*', and her sacrifice is an 'Ionian' lamb 'so that when in the future, in the assembly, someone says we ought to go to war, the audience will be terrified and go 'oi' (= Ionian for 'lamb', a pun on the exclamation)', and 'in other respects, too, we will be gentle like lambs . . . and we'll be much milder with our allies'.[185]

Once the play's version of *theoria* and 'harvest' are granted, the audience will change into soft Ionians; the episode ridicules the Athenians' refurbished Ionian identity by turning its negative characteristics (Ionian softness and reluctance to go to war) to the benefit of the city's *Peace*. In addition, the anti-elite dynamic of the ridicule is directed against the *demos* itself, further complicating the already intricate comic question of whether the people or its leaders won the prize for greatest corruption. Whatever the case may be, it is attractive to think of the passage as a gloss on Athens' theoric politics on Delos.[186]

The comic plays' chief jibe is to point out the paradox that lies in exploiting for war a cultural practice designed, as our texts postulate, to generate and keep the *Peace*! In handling the empire just like a theoric community, Athens had successfully tweaked the nature of *theoria* so that it now produced what it was supposed to prevent. These are biting remarks on the motivation behind the attempt to inculcate in the allies the wish to participate in the Delian festival. It is tempting to see Delian affairs as part of a wider Athenian strategy at exactly this time to build up a robust network of obligations fit to withstand the continuous challenges put to the system. Major religious obligations to the Athenian empire—at the Dionysia, the Panathenaia, the Eleusinia—were now reassessed or set out for the first time, almost as if to reformulate the set of ties that kept this community together, by a sort of redefinition of what it meant to be 'tributary'. So a decree of 425 BC making known a new tribute sum to be paid also pronounces that the four-yearly Panathenaia will in future be the occasion for new assessments, as if to give the evaluation exercise a divine patron and a ritual regularity.[187] The motivation of the so-called 'first-fruit decree', usually dated to *c.*422 BC, is unclear, except of course that it implicates the very 'essence' of the Athenian

185 The festival scene in Ar. *Pax* 871 ff. 876 πρωκτοπεντετηρίδα, 889–93 ἀνάρρυσιν; 894 f. contests; 929 ff. the peaceful (ἤπιοι) Ionian lamb turning the audience 'milder' (πρᾳότεροι) towards the allies; 976 Peace is the 'mistress of *khoroi*'. The play is full of unexplored Ionian satire. The plot is set off by an 'Ionian visitor' (43–9) who arrives in a 'Naxian ship' in Peiraieus (143), while the big Aegean islands also get their fair share: loyal Chiotians in 169–72 (cf. *Apoth. Lac.* 232f–3a; Eup. *PCG* 246; Ar. *Pax* 835 ff. features the poet Ion of Chios). There are also allusions to other festivals, such as the Brauronia (872).

186 See p. 81 f. above on the interrelated associations of *theoria* and peace (Kowalzig (2005) 57–60). The 'Peace of Nikias' itself was supposed to enable *theoria*: Th. 5.18.1–2.

187 Thoudippos: ML 69, esp. ll. 26 ff. Severe penalties are introduced, should the officiating prytany fail to reassess. The Panathenaia as an imperial festival is discussed in great detail by Smarczyk (1990) 549–69.

empire, corn: places in Attika were forced to contribute, and others were 'invited', but not compelled, to follow the Athenians in an ancestral practice, to offer annually the 'first-fruits' to the Eleusinian goddesses. But freedom of choice is more notional than real when the decree continues to wish that those who do offer first-fruits will enjoy 'much good and plentiful harvests, as long as they do not wrong either the Athenians or the city of the Athenians, or the two goddesses'.[188] And a minor contemporary incident perhaps, the Methonians up in the Chalkidike were granted exemption from the tribute itself, but were still asked to pay the tax (*tithe*) to Athena, suggesting that the 'religious' contribution was an important marker of participation in this group, even when the larger financial obligation could actually not be paid.[189] Three decrees of the 420s BC, all concerned with strengthening the bonds between Athens and the allies by working upon religious ties and obligations: this is unlikely to be a coincidence.

Considered together with Delian choral stipulations, we perceive the subtlety with which the imperial worshipping group kept itself together: each of these individual cult communities, while probably encompassing roughly one and the same group of cities, is defined through a slightly different set of obligations, all formulating the bond with different degrees of intensity and compulsion. As in the case of the tribute to the Eleusinian deities, there is of course no evidence that cities were under strict obligation to send choruses to Delos. The force of this lies elsewhere, in the powerful suggestions it makes about the nature of this worshipping community and the invocation of the island's ritual traditions. In renewing the festival, Athens made a conscious effort to put on stage its empire as a cult community that was identical in religious, ethnic, and political terms and interests—none of which, of course, was true. The choral ritual on Delos, where this may be perceived most clearly, at the time may have worked to conceal the crude reality: by making choral and monetary tribute indistinguishable, the associations of both became blurred; whether you went to Delos as a tribute to the god, or to please the Athenians is unclear. What the excerpts of Old Comedy suggest, then, is that contributing a chorus looked dangerously like paying tribute, and that by singing this particular chorus one signed up for much more. Through participation in the dance one also gave consent to the rules of its rhythm: *you cannot argue with a song*.[190]

Ritual has an amazing power to give the illusion that a freshly invented (or renewed) practice is a long-standing tradition: through the powerful invocation of the island's ritual past—at a time when this provided a more appropriate image than, for example, at the time of the early fifth-century songs—it must have felt as if neither Athens nor the allies over the past fifty years had been doing

[188] *IG* i^3 78, a (= ML 73, ?422 BC) ll. 44–7), with Parker (1996) 143–4, also alluding to the notion of 'tribute'. That contributing places are commemorated on a stele is part of the same strategy to inspire the will to participation.

[189] ML 65 (430 BC or later), esp. ll. 24 ff.

[190] Bloch (1974) 71: see pp. 49–51 above.

anything other than congratulating each other on a peaceful coexistence as politically, ethnically, and religiously homogeneous and equal Ionians with jolly choral festivals on Delos. How explicitly roles were, nevertheless, shared out in this cult community becomes clear from examples of actual festivals. Xenophon recalls that on these occasions, the Athenians always outstripped everyone else with their performance.[191] The pomp and circumstance of Nikias' chorus mentioned above confirms what Xenophon later described as the special εὐανδρία ('manliness') and εὐφωνία ('beautiful voices') of the Athenian paean-singing chorus. As mentioned before, Delian paean-singing is unlikely to have been carried out in competition. There is, however, no greater appeal to the competitive spirit than when there is no explicit contest. A deliberately non-competitive stance at the outset will have had precisely the opposite effect. This is why a glorious *theoria* to Delos could in fact make an impact. It would be blindingly obvious that the Athenians had gone to most trouble to please the Delian gods and were therefore worthiest of their favour.

It is interesting that all of this seems to work on the assumption that cult and political communities were perceived as essentially different from each other. What else could Eupolis' point in the *Cities* have been in playing on the ambiguity of the musical tribute? The Athenian reinvention of the festival seems to rely on the fact that the catchment area of a cult centre such as Delos may have been a form of grouping existing alongside other forms of social or political organization; they could, but need not, be made to overlap with each other. Through this ambiguity, Delos' myth-ritual performances became flexible types of social action whose meaning changed with the situation in which they were applied.

4. DIGGING UP THE THEORIC PAST

I have left it to the end to elaborate, in a sort of epilogue to the preceding argument, on an important and intriguing aspect in the history of Delian *theoria*, illuminating the specific dynamic operating in Delos' constantly changing catchment area: the role of Artemis and the 'Ionians and islanders', Thucydides' formula for the earlier cult community, in the continuous and competitive reformulation of the Delian worshipping community. This emerges when we consider what is preserved about the changes in the Delian catchment area over time. What we can extract from scattered pieces of evidence from within the Delian orbit shows that the cultic networks and religious communities involved reconstitute and reinvent themselves continually, probably in ways that reflect historical change in these areas not itself surviving in our sources. However, an awareness, even a real memory, of a different ritual past shapes the manner in

[191] Xen. *Mem.* 3.3.12.

which the different, partially overlapping, sets of religious spaces formulate their relations to each other, and how they enter into a kind of contest with each other.[192]

It is well known that Artemis had been residing on Delos long before Apollo; and there are clear indications that this goddess attracted people from the Ionian mainland and the island world. The eventual Apolline worshipping group built upon these older traditions, particularly through the way it seems to have manipulated the traditions of Delos' archetypal theoric worshippers, the Hyperboreans. There is a cluster of evidence related to Delos' religious past that we need to look at in order to understand why, in the fifth century, the birth-shout singing choruses on Delos can make the effective claims they do, particularly how they construe their relationship to the Ionian mainlanders. On a more general level, the situation on and around Delos makes clear how contemporary, often reformed, religious practices always work with, and exploit, the assumptions of preceding forms of worship at a traditional religious locality.

There is, then, first of all, the question of primacy. The very earliest mention of Delos as a cult place in a text that survives in some substance, the *Odyssey*, presupposes the triad of Artemis, Apollo, and Leto, situated perhaps at the moment when Apollo came to enjoy greater privilege over the rest of his immediate family.[193] A certain confusion also comes across in the *Certamen*, where Homer's hymn to Delian Apollo is put up as a dedication in Artemis' shrine and affords him citizenship in the Ionian *koinon*.[194] But this is not the oldest record associated with religious life on the island, which more explicitly suggests that Artemis got there first. Artemis or a female predecessor of hers was honoured on Delos with a proper sanctuary a considerable time before there was even a trace of worship of Apollo. Built upon Mycenaean foundations, her temple was one of the first archaic ones, boasting a fine sixth-century altar, while the first of Apollo's many temples was to follow much later.[195] If architectural monumentalization is not a safe indicator of a cult's chronology, the associated votives must be: the earliest statue dedications on Delos are marble *korai*, many of them found in Artemis' precinct and dating from the seventh century, of which Naxian Nikandra's dedication to Artemis, of around 650 BC, is the most famous.[196] Significant numbers of early inscribed votives are dedicated to Artemis or Hera

[192] Chaniotis (2002), esp. 38–43 exceptionally pinpoints the question of ritual diachrony in a more general way.

[193] *Od.* 6.162–5. There is a comparison to Artemis (cf. the preceding lines); the reason for mentioning Delos here is the miraculous nature of the palm tree, not to indicate that Apollo was more prominent than other deities.

[194] *Cert.* 315–21 . . . *διέπλευσεν εἰς Δῆλον εἰς τὴν πανήγυριν. καὶ σταθεὶς ἐπὶ τὸν κεράτινον βωμὸν λέγει ὕμνον εἰς Ἀπόλλωνος οὗ ἡ ἀρχή ̔μνήσομαι οὐδὲ λάθωμαι Ἀπόλλωνος ἑκάτοιο.̓ ῥηθέντος δὲ τοῦ ὕμνου οἱ μὲν Ἴωνες πολίτην αὐτὸν κοινὸν ἐποιήσαντο, Δήλιοι δὲ γράψαντες τὰ ἔπη εἰς λεύκωμα ἀνέθηκαν ἐν τῷ τῆς Ἀρτέμιδος ἱερῷ.* 'He sailed to the panegyris at Delos, and standing at the "horned altar" he sang the hymn to Apollo, the beginning of which goes "I shall sing of, and not pass over the far-shooting Apollo." Once the hymn was performed, the Ionians made him a citizen of their *koinon*, and the Delians wrote the words onto a piece of white wood and put it up in Artemis' sanctuary'.

[195] For the age of Apollo's possible 'temples' on Delos see n. 39 above.

[196] See especially Homolle (1885).

(the latter being a problem that cannot be discussed here).[197] It is perhaps also worth remembering that the main emphasis in the Delion on Paros seems to have lain on Artemis; her temple, not Apollo's, receives great elaboration towards the end of the sixth century.[198]

However, it is the Deliades, that *khoros* operative first and foremost in Delian myth and ritual in the archaic and later periods, whose portrayal in ancient literature reveals Artemis' prior prominence, surviving to the late days of tragedy. So, for example, the Deliades appear explicitly as Artemis' attendants in a passage of Euripides' *Hekabe*, which strangely mixes awareness of the twin-birth on the island with the Deliades' explicit commitment to Artemis.

> *ἢ νάσων ἁλιήρει*
> *κώπᾳ πεμπομέναν τάλαι-*
> *ναν, οἰκτρὰν βιοτὰν ἔχουσαν οἴκοις,*
> *ἔνθα πρωτόγονός τε φοῖ-*
> *νιξ δάφνα θ' ἱεροὺς ἀνέ-*
> *σχε πτόρθους Λατοῖ φίλον ὠ-*
> *δῖνος ἄγαλμα Δίας;*
> *σὺν Δηλιάσιν τε κού-*
> *ραισιν Ἀρτέμιδος θεᾶς*
> *χρυσέαν τ' ἄμπυκα τόξα τ' εὐλογήσω;*
>
> Or to an island home, sped on my way in grief
> by an oar plied in the brine, to spend a life of
> misery in the house, there where the date palm,
> first of all its line, and the laurel tree sent up
> their holy shoots as an adornment dear to
> Leto to grace the birth of her children by Zeus?
> Shall I with the maidens of Delos sing in praise
> of the golden headband and bow of the goddess
> Artemis?
>
> (Euripides, *Hekabe* 455–65, tr. D. Kovacs)

Similarly, the chorus of Iphigeneia at Tauris' attendants laments its *amousia* and dreams itself back to Artemis Lokhia on Delos and to the lake where 'the melodious swan served the Muses', which may well be a reference to Delian song.[199]

How intimately Artemisian and Apolline associations merge on Delos is, ironically, exposed by Apollo's own archetypal theoric worshippers on Delos, the

[197] For the temple of Artemis around 700 BC see Bruneau–Ducat (1983) 154–9; the altar: Étienne–Fraisse (1989); female 7th-century *korai*: e.g. A 4062; A 3996; others in Homolle (1885); the Nikandra *kore* and inscription *ID* 2: *Νικάνδρη μ' ἀνέθεκεν hεκήβολοι ἰοχεαίρηι κόρη κτλ.* 'the girl Nikandra dedicated me to the far-shooting and arrow-handed [goddess]'. For the terracotta votives: pre-archaic period: Laumonier (1956): 'Mycenaean and Geometric': female votives B 7121; A 632; A 1870; A 626; A 795; B 7243 out of a total of 20, of which the rest are animals; 'style primitif': A 335, A 872, A 309 out of 8 votives, of which the rest are animals.

[198] See n. 41 above.

[199] Eur. *IT* 1089–1105.

Hyperborean maidens. Herodotus has a long excursus on the mythical journeys of the Hyperborean maidens and their original offerings from somewhere far beyond northern Greece all the way to Delos in the central Aegean. The Hyperboreans had been firmly linked to Apollo since at least the time of Alkaios, are so throughout Pindar, and by the time of Herodotus had developed into something like the *aition* of *polis-theoria* to Delos.[200] Callimachus in his *Hymn to Delos* more explicitly portrays the birth of Apollo as an *aition* for why Delos receives first-fruit offerings (*ἀπαρχαί*). The first of these offerings are those of the Hyperborean maidens:

> *ἀλλά τοι ἀμφιετεῖς δεκατηφόροι αἰὲν ἀπαρχαί*
> *πέμπονται, πᾶσαι δὲ χοροὺς ἀνάγουσι πόληες.*
> *αἵ τε . . .,*
> *. . . καὶ οἳ καθύπερθε βορείης*
> *οἰκία θινὸς ἔχουσι, πολυχρονιώτατον αἷμα.*
> *οἵ μέν τοι καλάμην τε καὶ ἱερὰ δράγματα πρῶτοι*
> *ἀσταχύων φορέουσιν. ἃ Δωδώνηθε . . .*
> . . . .
> *πρῶταί τοι τάδ᾽ ἔνεικαν ἀπὸ ξανθῶν Ἀριμασπῶν*
> *Οὖπίς τε Λοξώ τε καὶ εὐαίων Ἑκαέργη,*
> *θυγατέρες Βορέαο, καὶ ἄρσενες οἵ τότ᾽ ἄριστοι*
> *ἠϊθέων.*
>
> instead the wheeling year bestows its offering of
> tithes of first-fruits to you, all the cities send their
> dancing troupes to do you honour . . .
> . . . and so do those that live beyond the strand of
> Boreas, famed for their longevity.
> From them begins the journey of stalks and sacred
> handfuls that come to you from Dodona . . .
> (. . . there follows the journey of the Hyperborean offerings . . .)
> Long ago the first to arrive were the gifts from the
> fair-haired Arimaspians, brought by Boreas'
> daughters Oupis and Loxo and Hekaerge the blest,
> And their entourage were youths . . .
>
> (Callimachus, *Hymn to Delos* (4) 278–94,
> tr. Nisetich, adapted)

This is an *aition* of choral *polis-theoria*, working on the assumption that all future worshippers would follow the model of the Hyperborean first-fruit tribute. Two inscriptions attesting Hyperborean offerings of the fourth century furnish proof that their tribute, if not real in itself, was certainly thought to be real.[201] So much prestige was attached to these archetypal *theoroi* that the Athenians famously intercepted the traditional route by which their offerings travelled in order to

[200] Cf. Alc. fr. 307 LP; Pi. *O.* 3.16; *P.* 10.34–6; Bacch. 3.58–62; Hdt. 4.32–5. See Seltman (1928).

[201] *BCH* 35 (1911) 5–11, no. 1, line 49 (= *ID* 100.49): *τὰ ἐξ] Ὑπερβορέων ἱερά*; *IG* ii² 1636 A, 8 (= *ID* 104(3) A 8): *εἰς ἱερὰ]τὰ ἐξ Ὑπερβορέων H* (?).

have their *theoria* arrive along with them: they redirected the journey via Prasiai in east Attika, from where the Athenian *theoria* itself set off—the Hyperborean *phoros* could not travel without due escort![202] *Theoria* to Delos is closely linked to the myth of the Hyperboreans, and association with them mattered in the dynamics of *theoria*.

But the process of how the girls reached this privileged position is rather more complicated. Artemis and the Ionians have a due share in it. Herodotus knew of two legends of how the Hyperborean tribute was first delivered, which also indicate multiple reworkings of the tradition. Both accounts of the Hyperboreans show signs of a theoric reality intertwined with elements of a different, possibly local, religious practice for the girls themselves, as well as their closeness to Artemis.[203] There are first of all their names, as they are transmitted in Herodotus but also in other texts. Of those, Oupis is an epithet of Artemis in a number of places, notably Ephesos, while Hekaerge is Artemis' epiklesis in Aristophanes' *Thesmophoriazousai*.[204] Herodotus himself locates the Hyperboreans' graves in or near Artemis' precinct, where in fact some prehistoric tombs have been identified; and he also knows that 'the manner in which they wrap their offerings (*hiera*)' derives from the practice in a cult for Artemis *Βασιλήια* in the northern Aegean.[205]

And finally, there are significant overlaps between the Hyperborean girls and the Deliades, suggesting that the local and the non-local came to merge, and did not do so through Apollo. One of the few surviving fragments of Kratinos' *Deliades*, the play of 422 BC already discussed above, contains a reference to 'Hyperborean' cult practice, suggesting an intriguing link between the different sets of mythical worshippers.[206] The Hyperborean girls had come to Delos 'to give to Eileithyia the tribute (*phoros*) that had been ordered in return for an easy birth' in the case of the first pair, Hyperokhe and Laodike, while the second pair,

[202] Paus. 1.31.2, with Parker (1996) 225 and *AD* 38 (1984), *Chron.* 45 for a tentative identification of the site of Apollo Delios. The cities Herodotus names (Dodona, the Malian gulf, Karystos, Tenos) are likely to have been part of the catchment area of the cult too, particularly in view of the fact that for some of them links with Apollo Delios are attested: Jessen, *RE* iv, 1901, 2443–6. See Romm (1989) for the place of the Hyperboreans in Herodotus' mythical geography.

[203] Hdt. 4.32–5. The first two girls are protected on their journey by five anonymous male companions, called *Περφαρέες*, explained as *θεωροί* by Hesykhios, while the girls are worshipped as heroines in a pre-marital ritual by the local youth. By contrast, the second pair of Hyperboreans is honoured in song by the local women, a custom that spread elsewhere.

[204] See *Der Kleine Pauly* s.v. Oupo. Ar. *Thesm.* 972; Arge too might be connected with Hekaerge: cf. Radermacher (1950) 325–9. Cf. V. *Aen.* 11.532–3; Cic. *Nat. Deor.* 3.58; *EM* ο 641.54–642.3 s.v. *Οὖπις*. Corcella on 4.35.4 relates even the sacrifice recounted in the passage to Artemis.

[205] Hdt. 4.33.5.

[206] Cratinus, *Δηλιάδες* *PCG* 24 = Hsych. α 1869 *αἴθρια· Κρατῖνος Δηλιάσιν· Ὑπερβορείους αἴθρια τιμῶντας στέφη. τὰ γαρ Ὑπερβορέων ἱερὰ κατά τινα πάτριον ἁγιστεῖαν οὐχ ὑπὸ στέγην ἀλλ' ὑπαίθρια διαφυλάττεται* 'under a clear sky: Kratinos in the "Deliades" says that the Hyperboreans conducted worship in the open air. For following an ancient custom the Hyperborean offerings are observed not under a roof but under a clear sky'.

Arge and Oupo had arrived 'together with the gods themselves'. The two sets of mythical girls overlap in their job as birth-helpers and in their shared relation to Eileithyia. Pausanias even makes Eileithyia arrive on Delos directly from the land of the Hyperboreans 'to assist Leto with her birth-pangs'; it is from there that her cult spread to the rest of Greece.[207]

Not even the Hyperborean girls and Eileithyia escape choral orchestration as befits the musical island, and in the process expose an aspect of the geographical reach of the Delian deities from an irretrievable past. Herodotus' second pair of Hyperboreans was honoured by the local Delian women with songs composed by Lykian Olen, a custom, Herodotus says, that spread to the 'Ionians and islanders'—that same geographical formula delineating Thucydides' early catchment area of Delos.[208] Lykian Olen's hymns, honouring the entire collection of Delian deities, circulated throughout antiquity as famous mythical songs from time immemorial, while their primary cultic context became more and more nebulous. The traditions surrounding them and their poet are nevertheless most valuable.[209] The oeuvre and its creator, eventually tied to the Hyperboreans and Apolline worship, are suspiciously caught between Artemisian and Apolline traditions and represent a Delian catchment area transposed rather further to the east. Olen's own putative homeland Lykia had associations (perhaps of long standing) with the Delian deities.[210] Apart from the hymns to Eileithyia and the Hyperborean maidens sung for 'Ionians and islanders', another of Olen's compositions, known from Pausanias, tells of a girl 'Akhaiia' who had gone to Delos via the Hyperboreans: this is interesting in the light of the Peloponnesian origins of the settlers of Ionian Asia Minor.[211] The same type of tradition is picked up once more in a cultic hymn by a certain Melanopous of Kyme, quoted subsequently by Pausanias, stating that Oupo and Hekaerge had already arrived on Delos prior to Akhaiia. The very attempt—evidently not entirely successful—to root theoric piety, modelled on the Hyperborean maidens, in a period when

[207] Hdt. 4.35; the twin birth on the island recurs in 6.97; Paus. 1.18.5. In Hekataios *FGrH* 264 F 7 Leto is born in the land of the Hyperboreans.

[208] Hdt. 4.35.3–4 for the hymn to Opis and Arge, spreading amongst Ionians and islanders.

[209] Olen's hymns: Paus. 1.18.5; 8.21.3; 9.27.2 (Eileithyia); 2.13.3 (to Hera); 5.7.8 (to Akhaiia; to Apollo, of whom Olen was the first prophet). Melanopous of Kyme sang a hymn to the Hyperboreans: Paus. 5.7.8.

[210] Lykia and Apollo (cf. Apollo Lykeios): Ov. *Met.* 6.317–81; Ant. Lib. *Met.* 35 after 4th-cent. Menekrates of Xanthos. Xanthos' Letoon was the chief place of worship for the Delian triad.

[211] The pious Akhaiia: Paus. 5.7.8. According to Athenian tradition, Ionians had formerly lived in Akhaia in the Peloponnese before settling at Athens and moving on to Ionia (e.g. Hdt. 1.145). Or does Akhaia here refer to the Ionian origins in Pylos, incidentally the region for which 8th-cent. Eumelos of Korinth composed the very first theoric song to Delos? Paus. 4.4.1; 33.2; 5.19.10, though the authenticity of this song needs to be questioned. Messenians intensely laboured their traditions after their liberation in 364 BC. See West (1995) 218; now D'Alessio (forthcoming *b*) suggestively places the song in the milieu of Messenian exiles at Naupaktos during the Peloponnesian War, and the paean to Delos allowing expression of their local identity within the Athenian empire; it is unclear how much there was of Messenian 'identity' at this period (Luraghi (2002); Alcock (2002)).

Ionians still lived in the Peloponnese (and Ionia was not even colonized) clearly shows how important it was to keep Ionia in the picture of *theoria*.

There are other, neglected, pieces of evidence suggesting that early in the archaic period Ionian mainlanders and islanders formed a kind of cultural *koine* that has only left stray documentation, nevertheless helping us to identify who was imagined to have been on Delos at some point in the distant past, and what linked these people together.[212] So it might not be a coincidence that a Hyperborean girl's name Oupis became the actual epithet of Artemis at Ephesos, and even the latecomer Apollo was called *Οὔλιος* at both Delos and Miletus, as well as on Rhodos and Kos.[213] Similarly, if Apollo at Ephesos attracted the name Panionios, late as it may be, this suggests some veracity for the city's Panionian claims.[214]

All these traditions, it is evident, went through many reinterpretations in antiquity. The whole set gives us an insight into who laid what kind of claims to Delos when the birth-shout singing choruses of the early fifth-century paeans appeared, and in what ways the traditional custom could have shaped contemporary relations between the participating cities. Delian cult figures at some stage seem to have embraced a different religious community. If Artemis even in later periods preserves a more special relationship with the worshippers designed to honour both deities, this is a remnant of a period when she was the recipient of a form of *theoria*; whether this was on Delos or elsewhere is impossible to say. The Ionian mainland seems to have been pivotal in this worshipping community, fashioning a cultic network possibly even centred on Artemis of Ephesos, and transposed significantly further east, to include the formulaic 'Ionians and islanders' characteristic of the Delian past for both Herodotus and Thucydides.

Unspecific in time as it may need to remain, the indication that there was cultic activity on Delos before it underwent such heavy Apolline influence gives weight to the idea of a possible classical rivalry between Ephesos and Delos as the pan-Ionian gathering place that I alluded to above. What survives into the fifth century, then, is a contemporary theoric reality intertwined with the memory of a previous catchment area and ritual customs revolving around Artemis, Eileithyia, and the Hyperborean maidens, possibly even with elements of a more local religious practice for the girls themselves. Choral *theoria* or its denial to Delos in the fifth century functioned by deploying the different pasts in a contemporary context, bringing to life and shaping anew, re-ritualizing, the memory of long-standing relations between participants.

212 It is interesting in this respect that the Greeks believed that the mysterious Karians and Lelegians, ancient inhabitants of Delos too, were their predecessors on the islands and in Ionia, notably holding a maritime empire. Polykrates was one of Delos' 'most generous patrons'; his thalassocracy also covered 'Ionians and islanders' (Hdt. 3.122.2).

213 Miletus and Delos: Str. 14.1.6; then in the wider island catchment area too: Rhodos: *Lindos II* 228.9, 282.20; Kos *SEG* xviii 328 (3rd cent. BC): therefore perhaps also in Athens: Pherec. *FGrH* 3 F 149 = Macrob. 1.17.21; *RE* xvii, col. 1999, s.v. Oulios. Cf. Masson (1988), citing Pherekydes; for Kimon and Oulios see Capodicasa (1997); Barron (1980).

214 n. 160 above.

TRIBUTE TO THE *KHOROS*

In 1996 the Greek sculptor Babis Kritikos, living and working on the island of Tenos, unveiled a fascinating manifestation of the continued life of the island *khoros*, his 'Dedication to the Kyklades for the year AD 2000' (*Αφιέρωμα στις Κυκλάδες για το* 2000 *μ.χ*). The artwork assembles a group of delicately fashioned 'fragments' of marble heads of women, representing the Kykladic islands, a head for each island sometimes standing by itself, sometimes two islands indelibly linked to one another—a dozen island personalities altogether. With their archaizing traits and gracious faces, turning heads and hair sometimes floating, sometimes neatly curled up, the islands inevitably invoke equally elusive ancient images of soft-paced dancing nymphs or mainads. Created over a period of several years, the *Kyklades* were first put together for the public in the artist's own integrated workplace and exhibition space, an elaborate architectural complex rather resembling a finely carved marble quarry. They were introduced in an open-air presentation, set to light and music, before the insular chorus started travelling and was made available—without its original performance context—to a larger public at Athens' Titanium Gallery of modern art.[215]

What is intriguing about this contemporary *Χορός Κυκλάδων* is the evocation of a cultural memory in which the chorus of islands is much more than a visual representation—it is the reworking of a set of mental images, practices, and spatial relations brought to life through a form of performance. It would be wrong to construe a more direct link to the world of early fifth-century song, but the work is still suggestive of an image that survives by configuring a set of recurrent elements, the islands, the *khoros*, the movement, and the space they construe between them.[216] Kritikos' elegant women's heads each somehow have their own character, but their identity also merges with that of the group as a whole. The tiniest islets—such as Donousa, Herakleia, Keros, the 'Small Kyklades' floating around the much bigger Naxos—have a place in this chorus as proud individuals, and as long as they dance in the *khoros* there is not the smallest suggestion that insular size and significance stand in any meaningful relation. Tenos and Delos are tied to each other in a double head like Siamese twins, a perception perhaps reflecting the sculptor's local perspective, as if an insular self-portrayal were always drawn in relation to Delos. And, in view of Tenos' later history as itself a place of *theoria* to Poseidon and later to the Christian shrine of the Panagia Evangelistria, it importantly joins the two islands conceptually, as places of pilgrimage, focal points in the Aegean.[217] The 'Tribute to the Kyklades' powerfully recreates a set of relations between the islands, reworking the floating

[215] Tenos, 7 Sept. 1996 (http://www.tinos.biz/culture/bkritikos.htm).

[216] But note that the catchment area has shifted: islands represented are Tenos–Delos, Amorgos, Donousa, Keros, Herakleia of those immediately around Delos, but also Siphnos–Ekaterini, Melos–Rheneia, Thera.

[217] On contemporary Christian pilgrimage to Tenos see Dubisch (1995). Tenos' sanctuary of Poseidon was a Hellenistic centre of *theoria* (Étienne–Braun (1986)).

and movable space that the island chorus encapsulates and continues to reformulate. Within this, relations between individual places remain fluid, are constantly recomposed, and always carry with them the entire array of previous configurations.

It is ultimately this very malleable space linking the Aegean island world together that our performances of Delian myth and ritual compose and recompose through the continued interaction of myth and ritual in theoric song, working in the multiple associations that this space has acquired over time. It is also this space that, we can postulate, Athens during the fifth century tried to delineate more sharply than its religious traditions would allow. The Delian songs build the fundamental case for how the creation of communal, sacred space through the interaction of myth and ritual comes to operate in actual social contexts. We can observe in the paeans how choral performance manages to break down the distinction between mythical past and ritual present, creating the illusion that the birth of Apollo and Artemis happens in the here and now of the performance and allowing every local chorus arriving at Delos to claim a share in the establishment of the cult. Theoric choruses—including those from minute places, such as one, we may imagine, from Despotiko, our youngest Delion!—thus have a fundamental share in the forging of a worshipping community and a communal religious space in which localities and centre are tied to each other through an interactive set of stories and practices.

It is this momentary collapse of the distinction between past and present that also allows mythical time and ritual place to be reconfigured, to be put together in a, as it were, 'new way'. This is perhaps most strikingly the case in Bacchylides' *Ode 17* where Keans unwittingly become part of the Athenian orbit through the interaction of Athenian myth and Delian ritual. But Pindar's *Paean 5*, which so nicely sketches out the problematic first ever Athenian *theoria* to Delos, is also an intriguing attempt at mythical rearrangements of Aegean ritual space. Similarly, the examples of Paros and Kos are striking if, as it seems, their songs seek the association of the local Delian cults to a mythico-ritual network bearing the stamp of Athenian ideology. So the theoric songs constantly set in motion the religious space in which *theoria* is enacted.

It is in this role that they come to operate in the highly dynamic context of the Delian League in the early fifth century. While one is at first sight inclined to identify religious communities with contemporary politico-military alliances, this does not seem to be the case in Greece, where religious communities tend to be autonomous communal bodies, groupings of *poleis* different from, and alternative to, political ones. That said, it is clear that in the fifth century, choral song to Delos explores the elusive boundaries between such groupings through a blurring of imagery, most explicitly that of the 'tribute'. Merging the tradition of the choral tribute to Delos and the financial obligation to Athens plays on an awareness of the force of the religious tribute to the island. Several conclusions emerge for early fifth-century historical dynamics. As in Kritikos' *khoros*, island size does not necessarily match the importance they attribute to themselves. Many of these islands, such as Andros, were rich in resources and fruitful maritime connections, and certainly in symbolic capital, accumulated during the sixth century; only in this way can a prosperous song-culture or the monumental Delia on minuscule islets be explained. The decision as to whether or not to dance to Athenian tunes does not seem to be up to the Athenians only; rather it appears that islands were divided about which and how many bits and pieces of Athenian ideology to embrace. And songs are very likely to have had an important function in pushing perhaps an entire wavering community into commitment to the Athenian empire. The choruses thus formulated local identities in a theoric context and are statements of a communal self-perception; but they reveal that joining the dance on Delos in the early days of Athenian imperial power came with a set of commitments to set identities—poverty if you happen to be an islander, abundance in the case of mainland Ionian origins, in need of Athenian help in the case of the one (e.g. Keos), obliged to loyal support in the case of the other (e.g. the loyal Chians). *Theoria* is thus a context in which the image of the poor and helpless island is made to work politically: through the creation of such 'conditioned' local identities, performances of myth and ritual on Delos have an active share in the definition of social and power relations in the early fifth-century Aegean.

The Ionian denial of the Athenian world of song and dance for much or all of the fifth century is, when barely any evidence for Ionian political inclinations survives for the early period, perhaps itself a sign of the importance of the musical alliance. Creating worshipping groups is a means of forging exclusivity and of inculcating the wish to participate, but also a means of maintaining independence. Athens' renewal of the festival on Delos in 425 BC deserves its detailed treatment in this chapter because the preposterous move brings together musical and political threads at the height of the empire but also at its most exposed. No actual songs of this period survive, but the fact that much of the Delian discourse seems to be carried out in Old Comedy suggests its controversial nature, and justifies a choral perspective on the Athenian empire as it is presented through this chapter, and perhaps even the comic suggestion of the Athenian empire *also* as a collection of theoric worshipping communities. With a view to the power of performance, perhaps it is indeed the precariousness of the historical situation that made Athens turn imperial politics into Showtime. We also learn that if in 425 BC the Delia were reformulated as the old Ionian Delia, this does not mean that mainland Ionians were actually there or indeed that they had ceased to be the troublemakers of the *khoros*, dancing against the rhythm; scathing jibes on Ionians and Ionian customs (as we said above, not unrelated to internal Athenian developments, but that remains a separate problem) reveal the fragility of Athens' pan-Ionian constructions.

These are the interactions of a large Aegean *khoros* and the set of performances of myth and ritual constituting it. Despite the overbearing presence of the Athenian rhythm, the phenomenon observed is not just an Athenian one. When we now shift to the Peloponnese, we shall meet another imperial power which similarly impinges on the scene of choral dance and ritual music in the attempt to reformulate social and power relations in a territorial sphere with strong local traditions. And, as in the island world, performances of myth and ritual and the religious community that they map out, are caught between the power of traditional ritual bonds and their own drive towards innovation. Let us change scene, then, moving over not, as one might think, to Sparta, but to Argos.

3

New Tunes in Musical Argos: Mapping out the Argolid in Cultic Song

At the time of Polykrates, the sixth-century tyrant of Samos, Herodotus writes, 'the Argives were reputedly front-runners amongst the Greeks in matters musical'. This is a strange contention, which bears no relation to what the preceding story about Polykrates relates, nor with anything else said about Argos in the *Histories*.[1] On digging a little further into the musicology of our antiquarian authors, however, one soon discovers that the Argives were part of a lively sixth-century scene of *mousike*, which goes beyond the framework of their *polis* to include a number of cities in the immediate proximity. The 'Dorian' Sakadas, a conspicuous Argive aulete, laid claim to Panhellenic fame as the inventor of the Pythian *nomos*, first performed, it seems, at the newly-instituted Pythia after the so-called Sacred War at the beginning of the sixth century. Aristonikos of Argos was a famous earlier kitharist; Argives were keen singers of Homeric epic, as we know from Kleisthenes of Sikyon's censure of these tunes at public performances in his city out of a hatred against the Argives. That competition is even expressed musically elsewhere: the Sikyonians had a serious competitor to Sakadas in the sixth century aulete Pythokritos and a set of virtuoso kitharists and innovative theorists, of which one was 'the first to surround himself with a *khoros*'. Choral issues are also exposed when one looks beyond Argos into the Argolid along the Argive *Akte*, the Argolid's seaboard, and the cities lining it. A city in this area is home to Lasos of Hermione, whom we know as the inventor of the circular dithyramb, the *kyklios khoros*. The local traditions of Argos and the Argolid reveal a vibrant world of ritual music, the importance of which reached well beyond the artistic: musical performance, inter-*polis* rivalry, and the formation of civic identity are closely interlinked. The sixth century is a period when the communal chorus seems to undergo important social changes, while musical innovation appears to go along with a redefinition of Argos that also has to do with its turning itself into a 'Dorian *polis*'.[2]

[1] Hdt. 3.131: *Ἀργεῖοι ἤκουον μουσικὴν εἶναι Ἑλλήνων πρῶτοι*. Note that the passage is sometimes considered spurious: How and Wells ad loc.

[2] Argos: Sakadas the aulete and victor of the three first Pythia: Paus. 2.22.8–9; 10.7.4; [Plut.] *De Mus.* 1134a–b; Poll. 4.78. Aristonikos of Argos: Menaech. *FGrH* 131 F 5=Ath. 14.637f. Sikyon: Kleisthenes of Sikyon: Hdt. 5.67, Epigonos invented the enigmatic *ἔναυλος κιθάρισις*; Lysander (around 500 BC or later?): Philoch. *FGrH* 328 F 23; Ath. 14.637f–38a. Pythokritos, son of Kallikratides (winner of the Pythia 574–554 BC): Paus. 6.14.10. Lasos of Hermione: Pi. fr. 70b; *Σ* Ar. *Av.* 1403 with D'Angour (1997). For Argos becoming Dorian in the 6th cent. see pp. 149–53 below.

The string of anecdotal evidence exposes a dynamic geographical milieu, within which interaction is expressed in a competitive music and performance culture tied to the consolidation of civic identities often founded in heroic myth. It is this legacy that forms an attractive background for the intriguing cycle of religious songs that survive for Argos and the Argolid from the fifth century. These are situated, as I shall argue, in the midst of a drawn-out process embracing the most lasting changes to occur in the Argolid for some time to come. Argos undergoes a social and political transformation that has left its scattered traces in historiography and archaeology at the end of which it heads not only the cities in the Argolid, but also its mythical traditions. A synoikism of the Argive Plain goes hand in hand with the establishment of democracy at Argos, at the same time as the city aspires to leadership over the cities of the eastern Argolid, notably in competition with Sparta. This chapter will demonstrate that surviving cult songs may well have had a full share in these contemporary historical processes: a drawing together of myths and rituals, a religious synoikism, reconfiguring the gods and heroes of the Plain, was part and parcel of the way Argos orchestrated internal social change and externally kept pace with the fifth-century developments in Greece. Two perspectives can be unfolded: that of the eastern Argolid, concerning the maritime cities placed along the coast, the Argive *Akte* (the first half of this chapter), and that of the Argive plain, the *Argeia*—whose *poleis*, especially Mykenai, were the figureheads of the all-Greek past, the Trojan War itself (the second half of this chapter).

The poet Bacchylides at some point in the first half of the fifth century BC composed a paean for Apollo Pythaieus at Asine, located just east of the Argive Plain on the Argolic Gulf (Bacch. fr. 4). Generally thought to be an Argive commission, the song recounts Apollo's aetiology whilst worshipping him in choral ritual.[3] With nearly 100 lines, the paean almost reaches the length of Bacchylides' victory odes and is certainly the best preserved among his hymns for gods. In the historical period, this cultic site was a place of worship for Argos and the maritime cities in the eastern Argolid, notably the so-called Dryopian *poleis* along the Argive *Akte*. Delos in the preceding chapter emerged as a centre of large-scale choral *polis-theoria* tying the surrounding communities into a wider network of worshippers. Apollo Pythaieus more obviously fits the idea of an 'amphiktyony': a gathering place for an assortment of literally neighbouring communities with a distinct role in a local and regional context.[4]

Apollo's aetiological myth, and the choral form it takes, presents an enthralling example of how performed aetiology reformulates already multiply reformulated

[3] The basic treatment to date of this song, performed in the cult of Asine rather than at Argos, is Barrett (1954). Cf. Villarrubia (1987–8); Maehler (1982–97), ii. 291–308; Irigoin *et al.* (1993) 216–18; Hornblower (2004) 124–5; Piérart (2004) 28–9; Angeli Bernardini (2004*b*) 135–8. Ratinaud-Lachkar (2004) 80 now suggests linking the paean to Hermione.

[4] Pindar makes the point best when lining up the victories of his subjects at a great number of local festivals, at some of which he explicitly has 'periktiones' or 'amphiktiones' assemble: Pi. *P.* 4.66; 10.8; *N.* 6.39–40; 11.19; *I.* 1.56–9; 4.8; 8.64–5. *O.* 7.81–7 offers an impressive circuit of local festivals.

pasts in the service of a redefinition of local social and power relations. The first half of this chapter will investigate the dynamics between cities participating in this cult over time, that is to say how worshipping the same god is quite a different matter from sharing the same battlefield. The placing of Apollo's myth-ritual ensemble within the local network of myths and rituals will reveal a cult whose worship was central in integrating the different *ethne* of the eastern Argolid. Glimpses of interacting memories, disclosing a history of ethnic diversity and constant attempts at integration, give the clue to the operation of the song in its contemporary fifth-century setting.

Having become sensitive to the religious dynamic in the eastern Argolid, the second half of this chapter will turn inland, to the Argive Plain. A series of songs was in part definitely, in part very plausibly, performed in an early to mid-fifth-century Argive context: Pindar's *Dithyrambs 1* and *4* for a Dionysos at Argos, so-called *Paeans 18* for Elektryon at Argos, *20* for a Herakles, *21* for a Hera, and *Nemean 10* honouring the victory of the Argive Theaios. Less evidence survives for each individual song and the local gods they honour, but taken together the set suggests an intriguing confluence of traditions, of an Argive Plain whose myths and rituals are being shuffled and recomposed during the first part of the fifth century. The process of reconfiguring the Argeia's gods and heroes emerges as fundamental to the way in which Argos ritualized internal social change and externally ensured for itself a place in the dynamics of Greece's fifth-century social and political transformation. The second part of this chapter suggests a role for the Argive song-cycle in these processes, which can be seen as complementary to those demonstrated in the first part.

1. APOLLO PYTHAIEUS AT ASINE AND ETHNIC INTEGRATION IN THE EASTERN ARGOLID

Ὁ βασιλιὰς τῆς Ἀσίνης ἕνα κενὸ κάτω ἀπ' τὴν προσωπίδα
παντοῦ μαζί μας παντοῦ μαζί μας, κάτω ἀπὸ ἕνα ὄνομα·
Ἀσίνην τε ... Ἀσίνην τε ...
καὶ τὰ παιδιά του ἀγάλματα
κι οἱ πόθοι του φτερουγίσματα πουλιῶν κι ὁ ἀγέρας
στὰ διαστήματα τῶν στοχασμῶν του καὶ τὰ καράβια του
ἀραγμένα σ' ἄφαντο λιμάνι·
κάτω ἀπ' τὴν προσωπίδα ἕνα κενό.

(G. Seferis, *The King of Asine*, 1938/40)[5]

Seferis' lines capture the distant memory of Asine's mysterious past, irretrievably lost, it seems, in the mists of time. One in a long list of names resounding in the *Catalogue of Ships* from a time immemorial, Asine to the present day retains the air of impenetrable sublimity. Asine is a very old settlement on the southern coast of the Argolid, in the bay of Tholon. The city, geographically belonging to the group of cities lining the coast along the eastern Argolid, was thought to have already vanished from the scene by the late eighth century. By then, it had had a lively history as a dynamic maritime entrepôt, linked into the entire Aegean from Sub-Mycenaean to Late Geometric times, leaving the shell, but little of the substance of this energy in the picturesque double harbour today. Yet the king's ships somehow remained anchored in the vanished port, invisibly, silently following the course of Greek history.[6]

The story of Asine's evanescence is known from Pausanias and is set in the context of one of those legendary long-term inter-*polis* rivalries: Argos in the late eighth century BC destroyed the city, taking revenge for Asine's help given to the Spartans in raiding Argive territory. Once Messenia was conquered, Sparta granted the Asinaians new homes in modern Koroni, near Pylos on the southern Peloponnesian coast, as part of Spartan strategy to fortify herself against the resilient Messenians by settling migrant peoples at their borders. Though this tale might at first sight look suspiciously like a foundation myth for Messenian Asine,

[5] The king of Asine a void under the mask.
Everywhere with us everywhere with us, under a name:
'*Asinen te . . . Asinen te . . .*'
and his children statues
and his desires the fluttering of birds, and the wind
in the gaps between his thoughts, and his ships
anchored in a vanished port:
under the mask a void.

(tr. Eur. Keelye, P. Steward).

The idea of the 'king of Asine' hiding behind his 'mask' evokes a Mycenaean clay mask, now in the museum of Nauplion.

[6] On Asine's past see Zangger (1994); on Geometric Asine see Morgan and Whitelaw (1991); Hägg (1965).

the Late Geometric fortification walls of Asine in the Argolid bear signs of violent, though as we now know not total, destruction dating to around 720 BC, a fact which for a long time has been thought roughly to confirm Pausanias' chronology and, perhaps, the core of the narrative. It is here that Apollo Pythaieus was at home: the Argives had left him standing, as if through this god to give continuity to a broken history (Fig. 3.1).[7]

Herakles, the Dryopians, and the Dorian conquest (Bacch. fr. 4)

The song fr. 4 for Apollo Pythaieus, with about a hundred lines Bacchylides' longest extant paean, gives an aetiology for the cult at Asine. Two sections survive: the fragmentary lines 21–5 present part of the story of Herakles' visit to the house of Keyx, king of Trakhis; the cult *aition* then extends from lines 39 to 56a followed by a long and lively description of an idealized ritual setting in lines 56b to 80.

The mythical narrative recounts the origins of the Asinaians in the Argolid, culminating in the establishment of the cult of Apollo Pythaieus. The surviving text reads as follows:

– ⏑ ⏑ – ⏑]τ̣α Πυθω[– ⏑ – –
– ⏑ – –   ]ε̣ι̣ τ̣ελευ̣τ̣[–
(.) . . . . . .] κ̣έλευσεν Φοῖβος [Ἀλ-
κμήνας] πολεμαίνετον υ̣[ἱόν
(.) . . . . . .] ἐκ ναοῦ τε καὶ παρ[– ⏑ –
ἀλλ' ὅ γε τᾶ]ιδ' ἐνὶ χώρα<ι>
(.) . . . .]χ̣ισεν ταν φυλλο .[–
(.) . . . . στ]ρ̣έ̣ψας ἐλαίας
(.) . . . .]φ' Ἀσινεῖς
(.) . . . .]λε . .᾽· ἐν δὲ χρόν[ωι
(.) . . . . . .]ες ἐξ Ἁλικῶν τε . [– ⏑ – –
μάντι]ς ἐξ Ἄργευς Μελάμ[πους
ἦλ]θ̣' Ἀμυθαονίδας
βω]μόν τε Πυθα<ι>εῖ κτίσε[– ⏑ ⏑ –
καὶ] τέμενος ζάθ̣ε̣ον
κείν]ας ἀπὸ ῥίζας. τὸ δὲ χρ[– – ⏑ – –
ἐξό]χως τίμασ' Ἀπόλλων
ἄλσο]ς, ἵν' ἀγλαΐαι

[7] Paus. 2.36.4–5; 3.7.4; 4.8.3; 14.3; 34.9. Ratinaud-Lachkar (2004) now radically challenges this tradition: the Spartano–Argive animosity is a *topos* in Pausanias, while historically it cannot be traced beyond the middle of the 6th cent. and the 'Battle of the Champions' (on which p. 156 below). See also Theopompos *FGrH* 115 F 383=Str. 8.6.11; Billot (1989–90) 37 interprets this as an ethnic rather than a territorial conflict (Kelly (1967) and (1976)). Carbon remains, indicative of destruction by fire, have been found at the walls on Barbouna Hill (Wells (1987–8) 351); Poulsen (1994) and Wells (2002*b*) strongly suggest that Asine continued to be inhabited after 720 BC, though perhaps on a smaller scale and as a less prosperous city than before. On Messenian Asine see Beloch (1912–27) i.33; Kelly (1967) and (1976) 64; Billot ibid. 38; J. Hall (1995) 582.

Figure 3.1 View over the harbour and the Barbouna hill from the akropolis of Asine

τ' ἀνθ]εῦσ[ι] καὶ μολπαὶ λίγ[ειαι
(.) . . . . . .] ονες, ὦ ἄνα, τ' . . [[8]

. . . Pytho . . . end . . . Phoibos ordered the battle-famed (son of Alkmena to convey them) from the temple and (the earth's navel?), (and he settled them?) in (this?) land . . . (leaf?) . . . when he had twisted olive-trees, (he called them) Asinaians; and in time . . . from the men of Halieis . . . (the seer) Melampous, son of Amythaon, (came) from Argos and founded an altar for Pythaieus and a holy sanctuary. From that root (came) this (precinct), and Apollo gave it exceptional honour, a place where festivities blossom and clear songs . . . (Bacch. fr. 4.39–58; tr. adapted from D. A. Campbell)

The paean is the aetiological myth's only, lamentably fragmented attestation, but the story of Herakles settling the Asinaians in the Argolid is preserved in many antiquarian accounts.[9] The future Asinaians belong to the larger *ethnos* of the Δρύοπες, a mysterious people who have attracted much scholarly attention, ancient and modern. They are reported to have lived near Delphi on Mount Parnassos in the area later to become Δωρίς. Herakles, on his conquering raid in Central Greece, chased the Dryopians out of their original homeland. From then onwards they were scattered all over maritime Greece, particularly on the islands: Euboia, the Kyklades, and even as far as Cyprus.[10] The greatest number of them were said to have gone to form the cities along the southern coast of the Argolid, considered Dryopian throughout antiquity. Their cities in historical times were Asine, Halieis, and Hermione;[11] a place called Eion appears as early as the *Catalogue of Ships* among the Dryopian cities in the Mykenaian realm of Agamemnon, as does the city of Mases in the *Catalogue of Women*.[12]

Pausanias' account helpfully provides the motivation for the Dryopians' expulsion from the Parnassos area. In the third generation after their founder Dryops, he says,

[8] Snell–Maehler's text (1968; repr. 1992) has not been substantially changed since Snell (1932) combined Ath. 5.5, p. 178b with *POxy.* 426 as Bacch. fr. 4. For some minor points see Heichelheim (1953) and Merkelbach (1973*b*).

[9] D.S. 4.37.1–2; Apollod. 2.7.7; Paus. 4.34.9–12. For a brief discussion of the Dryopians in the Argolid see Jameson, Runnels, and van Andel (1994) 62–5.

[10] Hdt. 8.46.4; D.S. 4.37.2. For the legendary and historical Dryopians see Fontenrose (1959) 335–44; Sakellariou (1977) 255–78; Jameson, Runnels, and van Andel (1994) 62–5; Fourgous (1989) discusses how the Dryopians were perceived by the Greeks. See now Strid (1999), who doubts the historical existence of the Dryopians altogether; his volume also contains a useful collection of sources. J. Hall (1997) 74–7 discusses the Dryopians with regard to ethnic differentiation in the Argolid.

[11] D.S. 4.37.2; Str. 8.6.12–13; Callimachus in a very similar mythical narrative names the Asinaians (*Aet.* fr. 24 and 25 Pf); Asine, Hermione, and Halieis (fr. 705 Pf = Call. *Hec.* fr. 174 = St. Byz. s.v. Ἅλυκος). Halieis is in historiography known as Ἁλία (Skyl. 50; Hsch. s.v) and Ἁλιεῖς (St. Byz. s.v. Ἁλιεῖς, Τίρυνς, Ἁλαί); Σ Ar. *Lys.* 403. There are different forms of the *ethnikon* Ἁλικός: Bacch. fr. 4.49; St. Byz. Ἁλύκιος and Ἁλιεύς.

[12] Eion: *Il.* 2.561; D.S. 4.37.2; Str. 8.6.13 mentions it as a Mycenaean port; Mases: *Il.* 2.562; Hes. fr. 204.47 MW; cf. Str. 8.6.17; Paus. 2.36.1–3. There is an interesting overlap in the realms of Diomedes and of Aias in the *Catalogue of Women* (Finkelberg (1988)). Cf. Nic. Dam. *FGrH* 90 F 30 for the Dryopian area.

The Asinaians originally lived around Parnassos next to Lykorea, and their name, which they preserved when they came to the Peloponnese, was the Dryopes, after their founder. Two generations after Dryops, in the reign of Phylas, the Dryopes were conquered in battle by Herakles and dedicated to Apollo at Delphi. When brought to the Peloponnese according to the god's instructions to Herakles, they first occupied Asine near Hermione. Then when the Argives expelled them from there, they settled in Messenia. This was the gift of the Lakedaimonians, and when in the course of time the Messenians were restored, their city was allowed to stay. (Pausanias 4.34.9)

Herakles' hostility, in other texts, is motivated by the Dryopians' putative impiety towards the god at Delphi and their violation of the sanctuary's rules when, in one instance, they are caught 'feasting in the temenos' (a violation that we shall meet again in a different form in the next chapter).[13] Their king is killed, the Dryopians dedicated to Apollo, but the god rejects the offer and instead orders them to be dispatched from Parnassos into the Peloponnese. Bacchylides' paean starts at this point. The song's events are located in the sanctuary at Delphi where Apollo pronounces an oracle (*κέλευσεν* l. 41), the recipient of which must be Herakles (*πολεμαίνετον* l. 42). *ἐκ ναοῦ* (l. 43) indicates the expulsion of the Dryopians from the sacred precinct, so that Barrett's supplement *παρ[' ὀμφάλου* reflects the idea of the passage. Lines 44–8 describe the settling of the Dryopians in a *χώρα* (l. 44). We are told of something to do with leaves, and of a twisted olive branch, recalling the Herakles we know fencing off the sacred precinct at Olympia, or marking territorial boundaries elsewhere in the Argolid.[14] The conjecture *σ]φ' Ἀσινεῖς ... κά]λεσσ'* in 47–8 is not out of place, implying an etymological *aition*: the deceitful Asinaians, through displacement, are literally made 'not-harming' (*ἀσινεῖς*).[15] The pun and the story of the hubristic Asinaians—who normally feature as *Ἀσιναῖοι*—must therefore recede to at least the time of the allusion to the story in Bacchylides.[16]

Finally, the seer Melampous appears in the aetiology's last lines and founds the oracle of Apollo Pythaieus (l. 50 ff.). Melampous, because of his strong Argive

[13] D.S. 4.37.1 Phylas 'seeming to have broken the rules at the Delphian shrine' (*δόξαντο ... εἰς τὸ ἐν Δελφοῖς ἱερὸν παρανενομηκέναι*); Apollod. 2.7.7: 'and he killed Laogoras king of the Dryopians and his children, whilst he was feasting in Apollo's temple, because he behaved in a hybristic manner and was an ally of the Lapiths' (*ἀπέκτεινε δὲ καὶ Λαογόραν μετὰ τῶν τέκνων, βασιλέα Δρυόπων, ἐν Ἀπόλλωνος τεμένει δαινύμενον, ὑβριστὴν ὄντα καὶ Λαπιθῶν σύμμαχον*).

[14] Pi. *O.* 3.17–35, esp. 33–4. Paus. 2.28.2 (see n. 52 below).

[15] Barrett (1954); cf. Lobel *οὔνομα δέ σ]φ' Ἀσινεῖς* with a similar sense.

[16] Cf. *HN*^{2} 432 [*Δ*]*ΡΥΟΨ ΑΣΙΝΑΙΩ*[*Ν*] (2nd cent. BC); Paus. *passim*; *EM* α 154.7–14 s.v. *Ἀσινεῖς· οἱ Δρύοπες οἱ τὴν Ἀσίνην κατοικοῦντες. Καλλίμαχος· "δειλαίοις Ἀσινεῦσιν ἐπὶ τριπτῆρος† ἅπάσας"* (Call. fr. 25 Pf). *εἴρηται γὰρ ὅτι Ἡρακλῆς τοὺς Δρύοπας ληστεύοντας ἀπὸ τῶν περὶ Πυθῶ χωρίων ἐν τῇ Πελοποννήσῳ μετῴκισεν, ἵνα διὰ τὴν πολυπληθίαν τῶν ἐνοικούντων εἴργοιντο τοῦ κακουργεῖν. καὶ διὰ τοῦτο Ἀσινεῖς αὐτοὺς ὠνομάσθαι ὡς μηκέτι κατὰ τὸ πρότερον σινομένους.* 'Asinaians: the Dryopians who inhabit Asine. Callimachus: "To the miserable Asinaians all on the ?mortar": for it has been said that Herakles resettled the plundering Dryopians away from the area around the Pytho in the Peloponnese, so that due to the large numbers of the inhabitants there they would be held back from committing outrages. And for this reason they are called "harmless ones", since they were no longer harmful as before.'

connections, has given scholars the key to the assumed commissioner. In mythology he is inextricably connected with Argos. Already in the *Odyssey* he reigns over this city. He is the ancestor of the seer family, which culminates in Amphiaraos, one of the *Seven Against Thebes*.[17] The myth is hence believed to represent the Argive view of things. Similarly, Herakles setting up the Dryopians has been interpreted as being part of a typically Argive story. His links in the area, for example the Perseid ancestry or his birth in Tiryns, would point in this direction. Many of his labours are also located in the Argolid, as if he had set to order on behalf of the Argives not only Asine but the entire wild east: both Troizen and Hermione claimed that Herakles dragged Kerberos out of their local entrances to the underworld; Troizen furthermore boasted the olive tree out of which Herakles had fashioned his club, and the eponymous well there was also his discovery.[18]

But Herakles is no Argive hero, and, as I shall argue below, was probably only in the process of becoming one at the time when Bacchylides composed his song. Moreover, to reduce Herakles to an Argive hero would make Melampous' arrival from Argos redundant. Herakles is not a local hero in this paean, but an ethnic one, specifically a Dorian. Herakles' activities in the context of this cult aetiology represent attempts at ethnic integration in the eastern Argolid. This in antiquity was an area inhabited by a remarkable number of different populations. Herakles' role in this myth (Section 1 of this half of the chapter) will give us the clue to what Apollo's worship at Asine is all about: it is a cult addressing such local ethnic diversity (Section 2). The social integration of this mixed group of people will then emerge as of particular relevance in the fifth-century eastern Argolid, and explains the commission and performance of this paean (Section 3).

The Dorian dimension emerges from a closer look at Herakles' conflict with the Dryopians. This lays open an exciting and rarely considered history of ethnic diversity in the Argolid, and how the Greeks dealt with the changes arising from the perceived arrival of the so-called Dorians. The stories related to this ethnic diversity give away much about how the Greeks conceived of cultural conflict and the social change arising from it. In the case of the Dryopians' expulsion from Delphi and arrival in the Argolid, some motifs are reminiscent of colonial stories which deal with a structurally similar problem of old and new populations meeting each other. The consultation of Apollo at Delphi before sending out an *apoikia*, the establishment of a cult of Apollo at the other end, and the consecration of an entire people to the god before dispatching it abroad are all familiar elements. The dedication of the nuisance group occurs at moments of crisis in the archaic community. In these situations, a scapegoat's collective 'guilt', disturbing, sometimes even polluting, the calm of the community, is brought before the oracle's court, and in fulfilling the order of the Pythia evildoers is

[17] *Od.* 15.223–55; esp. 238–47; cf. Stesich. *PMG* 228; Hes. fr. 37.13; 131 MW; Acus. *FGrH* 2 F 28; Apollod. 2.2.2; 3.6.2; Hyg. *Fab.* 70, 128; *Σ* Pi. *N.* 9.30b.

[18] Paus. 2.31.2, 10; 32.4; 34.1; 35.10.

purified.[19] In the case of the Asinaians this kind of structure deals with a period much further in the past, harking back to the time of the 'Dorian' conquest. Just as many 'colonial' accounts, the surviving story on the one hand reflects a conquering power seeking justification for its actions, covering up the violence that accompanies change. On the other, we shall see that traces of a memory of the defeated Dryopians survive, suggesting that the conquerors were never quite as sovereign as the plot might superficially lead one to believe. Herakles' conflict with the Dryopians expresses a process of major social change, as well as the particular Greek way of remembering such transformations.

The Dryopians are one of those many peoples whose stories preserve the memory of historical Greece's prehistory, difficult to pin down chronologically, but explicitly pre-Dorian. They numbered amongst the most ancient inhabitants of Greece, a privilege that comes with certain cultural stigmas. In a tradition going back to at least the Homeric epics, the mythical ancestors of the historical Dryopians routinely appear as a rowdy bunch dwelling in central Greek backwaters before they were 'fortunate' enough to be civilized by cultured later Greeks. Their past as noisy savages is contained in the Dryopians' *nom parlant*, in epic proverbs associated with δρῦς—the oak tree—and a particular sort of pre-historic primitivism.[20] In mythical genealogy, the Dryopians' eponymous ancestor Dryops is the son of Arkas, father of the Arkadians, themselves held to be the most backward of all the ἔθνη living in Greece.[21] By the fifth century and the time of the mythographer Pherekydes at the latest, the mythical Dryopians had become the notorious troublemakers and primordial temple robbers of the Parnassos neighbourhood; Dryopian criminal inclination was traditional as late as Apollonios of Rhodes' *Argonautica* where the same story of their expulsion is told since 'they lived with no regard to justice' (ἐπεὶ οὐ δίκης ἀλέγοντες ἔναιον 1.1219).[22]

This was going to change with the arrival of the Dorians. Migratory traditions make it clear how affected the Dryopians, specifically, were by the Dorians' movements in Central Greece. As if to pitch the two peoples against each other, these stories hold that the Dryopians once lived in the Dorians' most recent

[19] See Parke (1948). Such instances are Klaros, Magnesia (Arist./Theophr. *ap.* Ath. 4.173e–f = *FHG* ii 198a; Konon *FGrH* 26 F 1 (xxix); Tanagra (*Suda* δ 1395 s.v. δόρυ κηρύκειον; Zenob. 3.26; Eust. 408.4); cf. Arist. fr. 485 = Plut. *Thes.* 16.2; Plut. *QG* 298f–99a for the Macedonian Bottiaioi in Thrace. A δεκάτη dedication appears to be a form of collective punishment which purifies the community of its misdeeds: cf. the usage of δεκατεύειν/δεκάτη in Hdt. 7.132; D.S. 11.65.5; Eur. *Phoen.* 202–3 uses *akrothinia* in a similar sense. See Malkin (1987) 31–41 on the case of Rhegion in Italy.

[20] *Il.* 22.126–7; *Od.* 19.163; cf. Eust. 1262.23; Hes. *Th.* 35; cf. also Zenob. 2.40.

[21] Arist. fr. 99 Rose = Str. 8.6.13. A different genealogy locates Dryops in Thessaly: Pherec. *FGrH* 3 F 19. The Arkadians: Hdt. 8.73; Th. 1.2.3; A.R. 4.263–5; the Arkadians eating acorns: Hdt. 1.66 with How and Wells. The *Homeric Hymns* recount a marriage to Dryops' daughter of Hermes in Arkadia, from which union Pan, a god associated with wildness and nature, was born: *H. Pan* esp. 1–16; Dryops' grandson is significantly called Ὕλας: A.R. 1.1207–19 and Σ 1.1212–19a; Apollod. 1.9.19.

[22] Pherec. *FGrH* 3 F 19 who again calls them a ληστρικὸν ἔθνος 'pillaging people' sharing a border with the Malians (ὁμοροῦν τοῖς Μηλιεῦσιν). Cf. 3 F 8. Σ A.R. 1.1212–19a: this is a wonderful aetiology back-projecting the present state of affairs into mythical times (cf. Fourgous (1989)).

home in Central Greece and last station before the Peloponnese. According to Herodotus, they started from Phthiotis, went up into the Histiaiotis, the area between Ossa and Olympus, then arrived in the land between Malis and Phokis, the Dryopis, and only thence set off to the Peloponnese.[23] *Dryopis* and *Doris* were two names for the same area in Herodotus' times, the latter of which presumably derived from its having ex-post-facto been made the metropolis of the Dorians. The tradition of the Dryopians' expulsion from this territory was hence inherently related to how the Dorians pictured their own arrival in the Peloponnese.

Herakles is no doubt central here. His dealings with the Dryopians are part of the much larger mythical narrative in which his activities foreshadow the Dorians' perceived conquest of the Peloponnese.[24] Bacchylides' song, too, deals with the wider social impact of Herakles' whereabouts. The hero's visit to Keyx king of Trachis (ll. 21–5) appears, following which Herakles forms an alliance with the adjacent Malians, later rewarded with the Dryopians' conquered land.[25] This Heraklean–Malian collaboration is known to Herodotus,[26] where it is countered by an alliance between Dryopians and Lapiths, another people about to undergo conquest by Herakles in the same set of Heraklean myths. In Diodorus, this central Greek episode ends in Herakles fighting alongside the 'Dorians' under Aigimios, ancestor of the Spartan royal families, to whom the conquered land is entrusted until the return of Herakles' sons.[27] Herakles, therefore, in this Central Greek sweep, takes on more than one uneasy people on his way to secure the land to be bequeathed to his descendants. The Dryopians' and their troublesome neighbours' banishment from Parnassos was for the ancients part of a larger ethnic conflict between Dorians and pre-Dorians. This is also the view the paean seeks to convey.

The Dryopians' case is slightly more special, however, giving us an insight into how problematic this alleged Dorian conquest was. This people's own version of events survives and significantly adds to our ideas of how to evaluate this string of myths, and the Dryopians' own adopted tradition makes the 'Dorian' edifice crumble. Of those Asinaians who moved from Asine in the Argolid to Asine in Messenia, Pausanias gives the following report:

Ἀσιναῖοι δὲ αὐτοὶ περὶ σφῶν οὕτω λέγουσι· κρατηθῆναι μὲν ὑπὸ Ἡρακλέους μάχῃ συγχωροῦσιν ἁλῶναί τε τὴν ἐν τῷ Παρνασσῷ πόλιν, αἰχμάλωτοι δὲ γενέσθαι καὶ ἀχθῆναι παρὰ τὸν Ἀπόλλωνα οὔ φασι· ἀλλ' ὡς ἡλίσκετο ὑπὸ τοῦ Ἡρακλέους τὸ τεῖχος, ἐκλιπεῖν τὴν πόλιν καὶ ἀναφυγεῖν ἐς τὰ ἄκρα τοῦ Παρνασσοῦ, διαβάντες δὲ ὕστερον ναυσὶν ἐς

[23] Cf. Hdt. 8.31: ἥ [the Doris] *περ ἦν τὸ παλαιὸν Δρυοπίς· ἡ δὲ χώρη αὕτη ἐστὶ μητρόπολις Δωριέων τῶν ἐν Πελοποννήσῳ*. '[Doris] is the old Dryopis: this land is the mother-city of the Dorians from the Peloponnese'. Cf. 8.43: *ἐκ τῆς νῦν Δωρίδος καλεομένης χώρης* 'from the land now called Doris'. Cf. Hdt. 1.56. For the Doris as the alleged Dryopian core area see Prinz (1979) 259–76.

[24] Malkin (1994) Ch. 1.

[25] Keyx' land is also the place where the Herakleids dwell for some time before they eventually enter the Peloponnese: D.S. 4.57–8; Apollod. 2.8.1.

[26] Hdt. 8.43.

[27] D.S. 4.37.3–4.

Πελοπόννησον γενέσθαι φασὶν Εὐρυσθέως ἱκέται, καὶ σφίσιν Εὐρυσθέα ἅτε ἀπεχθανόμενον τῷ Ἡρακλεῖ δοῦναι τὴν ἐν τῇ Ἀργολίδι Ἀσίνην. μόνοι δὲ τοῦ γένους τοῦ Δρυόπων οἱ Ἀσιναῖοι σεμνύνονται καὶ ἐς ἡμᾶς ἔτι τῷ ὀνόματι, οὐδὲν ὁμοίως καὶ Εὐβοέων οἱ Στύρα ἔχοντες. . . ., Ἀσιναῖοι δὲ Δρύοπές τε τὰ μάλιστα χαίρουσι καλούμενοι καὶ τῶν ἱερῶν τὰ ἁγιώτατά εἰσι δῆλοι κατὰ μνήμην πεποιημένοι τῶν ποτε ἐν Παρνασσῷ σφισιν ἱδρυμένων. τοῦτο μὲν γὰρ Ἀπόλλωνός ἐστιν αὐτοῖς ναὸς, τοῦτο δὲ Δρύοπος ἱερὸν καὶ ἄγαλμα ἀρχαῖον· ἄγουσι καὶ παρὰ ἔτος αὐτῷ τελετήν, παῖδα τὸν Δρύοπα Ἀπόλλωνος εἶναι λέγοντες. κεῖται δὲ ἐπὶ θαλάσσῃ καὶ αὐτὴ κατὰ τὰ αὐτὰ τῇ ποτε ἐν μοίρᾳ τῇ Ἀργολίδι Ἀσίνῃ·

But the Asinaians tell their own story as follows. They admit having been conquered by Herakles and their city on Parnassos captured, but they deny that they were made prisoners and taken to Apollo. But when the walls were taken by Herakles, they deserted the town and fled to the heights of Parnassos, and afterwards crossed to the Peloponnese in their ships and appealed to Eurystheus. Being at feud with Herakles, he gave them Asine in the Argolid. [11] The men of Asine are the only people of the race of the Dryopes to pride themselves on the name to this day, quite unlike the Euboians of Styra . . . But the Asinaians take the greatest pleasure in being called Dryopes, and clearly have made the most holy of their sanctuaries in memory of those which they once had built on Parnassos. For they have both a temple of Apollo and again a temple and ancient statue of Dryops, whose mysteries they celebrate every year, saying that he is the son of Apollo. [12] Their city lies at the sea just as Asine in the Argolid. (Pausanias 4.34.10–12)

Though this tradition may well have been embellished in later times, it puts the finger on issues of concern to us here. For a start, the appearance of Eurystheus, Herakles' arch-enemy and main contender for power, confirms the Dryopians' involvement in Herakles' conquest of the Peloponnese. The decision to leave is the Dryopians' own, as it is elsewhere in Pausanias, too, when the conquered Dryopians packed up their families, took to their ships and left before Herakles could catch them. Above all, Dryopian *asebeia* ('impiety') against Apollo is a contradiction in terms; as a people of the Parnassos area, they profess a precious closeness to their ancestral god. Their inherited cults travel with them to the Peloponnese, and they specially honour their eponymous ancestor who is the son of Apollo himself.

This version of events makes it clear that the memory of the Dryopians' conquest was at least ambiguous, and possibly distorted in the process of transmission. While the prevalent story professes a religious fault as an excuse for expulsion from the territory, in their own tradition the Dryopians were the least likely to commit sacrilege. Herakles in the Dryopian version of things is not the civilizer any more, but the merciless vanquisher of this people's land. The Dryopian account is an interesting instance of a surviving anti-Herakleid tradition that makes it abundantly clear what the pro-Heraklean tradition achieves: Apollo's dutiful attendants in the one version become the god's greatest enemy in the other; their own perceived piety is turned against them. By inventing a religious pretext for the Dryopians' removal, neatly fitted into the texture of the familiar, and highly successful, colonization stories, the Dorian myth in which the god is conquered is turned into one of his defence.[28]

[28] Cf. similarly the way the amphiktyons took over Delphi (Ch. 4 below).

The fact that two fundamentally different versions of the same conflict have survived is striking. The set of traditions may well belong to the larger context of ethnic, and more widely social, clashes perceived as being a result of the alleged Dorian immigration and which were expressed as a religious conflict at Delphi. The reinterpretion of religious traditions often serves the representation of social change. Herakles' mysterious theft of the Delphic tripod is similarly a situation of the god being caught between old possessors and new lords.[29] Apollo is also the Herakleids' greatest opponent in the story of their long-drawn-out conquest of the Peloponnese (held back, first, by a(n Apollo-sent?) plague; then a misinterpreted oracle; and on their third, successful attempt, they find themselves killing a local seer sacred to Apollo himself).[30] It is as ironic as it is typical that the triumphing Dorians characteristically adopt among their principal deities the god—as Pythios and Karneios—who most opposed their pioneering ancestors.

The Dryopians' removal effected over a conflict at Apollo's sanctuary is also placed within this set of traditions, and the intermezzo at Delphi shows faint traces of the kinds of clashes that were thought to have shaken the ancient universe at the remote times of the Dorians' imagined arrival. The story that survives reflects an intruding power seeking justification for its actions as a way of covering up the brutality of change. It alerts us to the fact that, whatever transformations it expresses, social change in Greece is hardly ever total, incomplete enough at least to leave us with a tradition in which traces of resistance are preserved.

What reached the Bacchylidean paean was no doubt the product of a long series of reworked and contested ideas about this particular piece of past. The story presents a template for ways in which the 'civilizing'—the swallowing-up—of non-Doric ἔθνη was conceived of within the dominant Dorian framework of the Peloponnese. The myths of Herakles' activities, both in Central Greece and in the Argolid, arose in an attempt to supersede different ethnic backgrounds. It is important to note that Herakles himself is *not* associated with any particular city in these myths. Although the link between his descendants and a city's Dorian identity was, for example at Sparta, made as early as in seventh-century BC Tyrtaios, Herakles' association with the Dorians does not seem to be prompted by individual *poleis*; rather, he seems to head a less clearly identifiable wave of change of which the rise of cities such as Sparta may well have been a result.[31]

[29] The set of images accompanying this story are among the first visual representations in Geometric times, as if the myth were of great antiquity and relevant to Delphi's post Dark-Age history. The story then faded out of the fashionable repertoire of images until the late archaic period when we presume that further major changes at Delphi took place. See *LIMC* v (1991) 133–43 s.v. Herakles. References in Boardman and Parke (1957), Defradas (1972) 123–33; Brommer (1984) 7–10. It is in the period between 560 and 460 BC that the scene becomes popular again (esp. on the Siphnian treasury at Delphi), a phenomenon which may or may not be related to 6th-cent. changes. For the myth in literature see Hes. *Sc.* 477–80; Pi. *O.* 9.32–3; Apollod. 2.6.2; Paus. 10.13.8.

[30] Apollod. 2.8.1–5. For the seer see also Paus. 3.13.4; Konon *FGrH* 26 F 1 (xxvi); *Σ* Theocr. 5.83; for the Herakleidai's narrative cf. D.S. 4.57–8.

[31] The Herakleids and Sparta: Tyrt. fr. el. 2 W. In Ch. 2 we saw that Herakles himself was just as active for example on Aegean islands even when these are not Dorian (Paros, Pi. fr. 140a).

The Dorians came to be part of the tradition of 'Dorianization', a process of assimilation that Herodotus knew had occurred smoothly in Ionian Kynouria.[32] Most Dryopians were themselves symptomatic of this process, adapted perfectly and refused to be thought of as Dryopians, inventing for themselves a story of successful ethnic assimilation. Their ability to mix with non-Dryopians became almost proverbial, leading the scholiast to Apollonios to speculate on a special reason for Herakles' initiatives: 'so that through thorough mixing up with people they would cease their criminal ways' (*ἵνα τῇ πολλῇ τῶν ἀνθρώπων ἐπιμιξίᾳ τοῦ λῃστρικοῦ ἤθους ἀπόσχωνται*). If the myth claimed that the *polyplethia*, the great number of people living in the Peloponnnese, would keep the Asinaians from doing further harm, a vision of ethnic integration is thus built into the traditions about the Dryopians.[33]

The Dryopians in the Argolid, as we saw, were different. These Dryopians stubbornly preserved their identity; hence the survival of the myth of resistance. Dryopian identity in the Argolid remained strong: in the fifth century, for example, Dryopians were singled out from Ionians and Dorians when fighting in the Persian and Peloponnesian Wars.[34] So what has survived is a conflict, not, as the myth might try to persuade us, its solution. As we shall now see when examining Apollo Pythaieus in his cultic context, this tradition has left very few traces in the record of historical events, but it very much survived in religious practice. The ambiguity of the aetiology will also give us the key to the function of the cult. Although a possible concrete nature of the former ethnic problem may long have been forgotten, the cult's fifth-century workings can be seen to rely on, and operate within, a memory of this traditional conflict. The continued performance of this story is also one of a continued, laboured memory of the social upheavals thought to underlie it. Worship of this god offers a tantalizing example of the perceived origins of a cult transpiring in continuous religious practice over a long period of history; it is an instance of religious practice being itself about a perceived transmission of history.

Apollo Pythaieus, Argos, and their *ἀμφικτίονες*

Ethnic integration at Asine

Although in Pausanias' tale the Argives had razed the city of Asine to the ground, they had exempted the temple of Apollo Pythaieus, the subject of our song, and buried one of their most noble men in it:

[32] Hdt. 8.73.3 (*ἐκδεδωρίευνται*). For patterns of such a 'Dorianization', particularly in the Argolid, see Figueira (1981) 170–92, 176–9 on the Dryopians.

[33] Σ A.R. 1212–19a; D.S. 4.37.1–2: *τοῖς ἐγχωρίοις ἀναμιχθέντες* 'being mixed up with the locals' and *πολυπληθίαν* 'populousness' in *EM*.

[34] Hermione: Hdt. 8.43 (Salamis); 9.28.4 (Plataiai); Th. 1.27.2; 8.3.2; 33.1. Halieis: Th. 1.105.1; 2.56.5; 4.45.2. Cf. Hdt. 8.43; 46; 73.

For a time the Asinaians defended themselves from their wall, and killed among others Lysistratos, one of the most distinguished men of Argos. But when the wall was lost, the citizens put their wives and children into their ships and and left their homes (*εἰς τὰ πλοῖα ἐνθέμενοι καὶ ἐκλείπουσι τὴν αὑτῶν*); the Argives, while levelling Asine to the ground and annexing its territory, left standing (*ὑπελίποντο*) the sanctuary of Apollo Pythaeus, still visible, and buried Lysistratos beside it. (Paus. 2.36.5)

Archaeology interprets this note in an intriguing way. The city of Asine and the temple usually held to be Apollo's were excavated by Swedish archaeologists, first in the 1920s, then again in the 1970s, and intermittently since.[35] Though the temple's structure and associated finds still await final publication, preliminary reports reveal that on the upper terrace of Barbouna hill at Asine, opposite the ancient akropolis, there are traces of two different shrines. The older temple B is a small apsidal building that, judging by the pottery found in the temple, was erected around the middle of the eighth century at the earliest. The area further down the slope shows signs of violent destruction around 720 BC. Even though urban life at Asine had not developed again in the same measure as before, the building was replaced at the end of that same century by the slightly bigger squared temple A.[36]

Pausanias' account then is not literally true, but has a point in informing us of a temple that survives. The builders of the new house for the god sought to mark the cult's continuity at the same time as rephrasing its appeal. The related finds communicate a difference in the worshippers' behaviour after the destruction of the first temple. The older votive deposits yielded a series of gigantic geometric tripod amphoras, ritual equipment probably dedicated after the ceremony. These objects are so far unique in the ancient world, and of very high quality. The clay used indicates that their production was entirely local, just as there is no other imported material in this stratum of finds.[37] The later material, by contrast, is not so outstanding in quality, but, in its turn, is of more varied geographic origin. In the area around the more recent temple numerous Geometric and Korinthian sherds have been retrieved, as well as a fair amount of complete sixth-century miniature vessels and other votive pottery. There are also a series of idols from the archaic period, and a small lead *kouros* figurine appeared in the very first

[35] Frödin and Persson (1938); continued in the Asine series (Asine II–VI) appeared/appearing in *Skrifter utgivna av Svenska institutet i Athen*, 4, 24; 1–6. A late archaic candidate located closer to the plain at Lefkakia, between Nauplion and Asine has been suggested for Apollo's temple, or possibly its successor: Jameson, Runnels, and van Andel (1994) 63 n. 11; Piteros, *AΔ* 51 (1996), *B′* 1, 92.

[36] The publication is announced in Wells (2002*b*) 97 n. 6 as *Apollo Pythaeus at Asine*. For preliminary reports on the temple and its surroundings see Frödin and Persson (1938) 147–51; Wells (1987–8) on the 1985 season; (1990); (1988); the temple is related to early architecture in the Argolid: Foley (1988) 142–3, and Hägg (1992*a*) 18–19.

[37] Finds of the old excavations were given to Sweden in the 1930s and are now in the Asine Collection at Uppsala. Berit Wells very kindly allowed me to see the material associated with the cult still preserved in the Nauplion Museum in December 1998, and discussed it with me along the lines presented here. A tripod amphora from the entrance to the Akropolis of Asine was then exhibited in the museum.

excavation reports, but was subsequently lost.[38] The rich excavation diaries from the 1920s further note 'a great amount of Lakonian and Corinthian tile fragments', and the burnt remains of a wooden roof, suggesting that new work was done at the temple at some point in the archaic period.[39]

While we can safely infer from this a change in this god's customers from a local elite to a more integrated cult community in the earlier eighth century, Pausanias' indirect suggestion of a level of Argive control of the sanctuary from then onwards is supported only for a later period. An archaic terracotta sima, dating to *c.*500 BC and of the kind frequently found in the Peloponnese, is similar in type to ones crafted by Argive workshops, and could suggest a rebuilding of the temple under Argive auspices at around the turn of the century.[40]

So even if the temple's archaeology has not yet been studied in all its detail, it makes clear how Pausanias is right, and how he is not. There is, on the one hand, the romantic tale of the cult's continuity in solitary existence, with its city taken away; and with it its role in the midst of seaborne traffic. Even if there was a level of settlement continuity, Asine's favourable position with the two harbours either side of the akropolis, through which formerly a considerable amount of goods had travelled, was not exploited later. So had the Dryopians of Asine once again 'put their women and children into their ships and sailed off', leaving behind Seferis' 'vanished port', the *άφαντο λιμάνι*? Whatever the case may be, the cult did continue, with a new audience from the time of the rebuilding of the temple in the late eighth century well into the classical period. Apollo was not spared destruction together with the rest of Asine, but received a new shape and attracted a different clientele.[41]

What was Apollo doing in his new guise? Argive control, as Pausanias' destruction story suggests, cannot unambiguously be inferred from the archaeology, and definitely not from the earlier material. Argos did, however, have a conspicuous presence at this cult in the late fifth century, and Apollo's behaviour then also discloses something about his nature and function. The god is mentioned in a Thucydidean episode leading up to the events of the Argive–Epidaurian War in 419 BC. This war the Argives had long had in mind, and they were finally able to launch the attack

προφάσει μὲν . . . περὶ τοῦ θύματος τοῦ Ἀπόλλωνος τοῦ Πυθαέως, ὃ δέον ἀπαγαγεῖν οὐκ ἀπέπεμπον ὑπὲρ βοταμίων Ἐπιδαύριοι (κυριώτατοι δὲ τοῦ ἱεροῦ ἦσαν Ἀργεῖοι)

[38] Frödin and Persson (1938) 149 and 333–4; pl. 225.1.

[39] Cited in Wells (1990) 157.

[40] As 5382, Asine Collection Uppsala. See Wells (1990) 160, comparing its pictorial decoration with a fragment from Tiryns (Nauplion Museum inv. no. 17282).

[41] For this advantageous harbour at Asine cf. Zangger (1994). Asine, by contrast with the Argive Plain, had traded with Attika, Crete, and the Kyklades: J. Hall (1995) 582 and n. 37. All 'Dryopian' people had good harbours; their seafaring character is also suggested by the way they left the Parnassos area and later Asine in the Argolid 'sailing', as well as the stress on the homes 'by the sea': D.S. 4.37.2; Paus. 2.36.5; 4.34.9–12; 3.14.3.

under the pretext of the sacrifice to Apollo Pythaieus, which the Epidaurians were obliged to send ὑπὲρ βοταμίων ('for the pastures'?) but did not (the Argives had chief authority of the cult) (Thucydides 5.53)

So this Apollo demanded tribute. The Epidaurians had apparently not satisfied their sacrificial obligations to a god who was common to at least the Argives and the Epidaurians.[42] Diodorus appears to recount the same episode in slightly different terms, when Troizenians rather than Epidaurians are reluctant in their sacrificial duties, which then causes the Argive attack. Whatever the possible inaccuracy of Diodorus, the misattribution, by implying the possibility that the Troizenians could fall into similar disgrace with the god, turns the episode into a generic incident. We must infer that cities other than, but sharing some characteristics with, the Epidaurians, paid the cult tribute on a regular basis.[43]

A glance around the area gives us an idea of others who might have been involved in the worship of this god. Apollo Pythaieus, or just Apollo, was extremely popular with the cities sitting around the Argolic Gulf and the Argolid itself. The Argives cherished their own Pythaieus in a cult of respectable scale and expenditure.[44] Hermione, one of the Dryopian cities, worshipped three Apollos, one of which carried the precise epiklesis Pythaieus;[45] Dryopian Halieis and the area near Dryopian Mases have prominent cults of Apollo, though no epithet survives for these.[46] The places of sacrificial violation, Epidauros and Troizen, counted Apollo Maleatas and an Apollo Thearios among their more important deities.[47] Most interestingly, Apollo *Πυθαιεύς* had already been dwelling for a long time, apparently as a patron god, in the principal cities of Kynouria, the long stretch of land along the coast of the eastern Peloponnese separating Lakonia from the Argolid and for many centuries a bone of violent contention between Argos and Sparta. Two sixth-century inscriptions on bronze tablets come

[42] The connection between the paean, the cult, and the Thucydidean passage was first made by Barrett (1954). It has been suggested that the sanctuary Thucydides mentions was the sanctuary of Apollo Pythaieus in Argos itself, but then the reference to Argive authority would be superfluous. The definition τοῦ Ἀπόλλωνος τοῦ Πυθαέως presupposes that every reader of Thucydides' account would have known exactly to what he was referring. Cf. Gomme on Th. 5.53.

[43] D.S. 12.78: ὅτι τὰ θύματα οὐκ ἀπέδωσαν τῷ Ἀπόλλωνι τῷ Πυθαιεῖ 'because they were not paying the sacrifices to Apollo Pythaieus'; it is widely held that, as is often the case in Diodorus, the 'Lakedaimonians' mentioned in this passage are the allies of the Spartans and here the Troizenians in particular. Farnell (1896–1909) iv. 215 n. b and Barrett (1954) 442 n. 1 quote this passage as evidence for Asine's amphiktyonic role.

[44] Paus. 2.24.1. For the archaeology see n. 74 below.

[45] Paus. 2.35.2.

[46] Halieis: Foley (1988), 149–50 (with reference to the excavation reports); Cooper (1989) 33–47 and plates 10–14; a temple key from the 5th cent. identifies this building as a sanctuary of Apollo; there is another temple of his at the feet of Kokkygion between Halieis and Mases mentioned in Paus. 2.36.1–2; a further in Didymoi near Mases: Paus. 2.36.3; perhaps one in Mases itself, as indicated by J. Dengate, 'The Archaic Doric Temple at Mases', in *Abstracts of Papers*. 6th General Meeting of the Arch. Inst. of America, 1974, Section II A, 123; Cooper (1989), 64 and pl. 21.

[47] Epidauros: Apollon Maleatas Paus. 2.27.7; this, too, is, in Pausanias' words, an 'old' temple. Troizen: Apollon Thearios in Paus. 2.31.6; this is the oldest Apollo temple that Pausanias thought he saw.

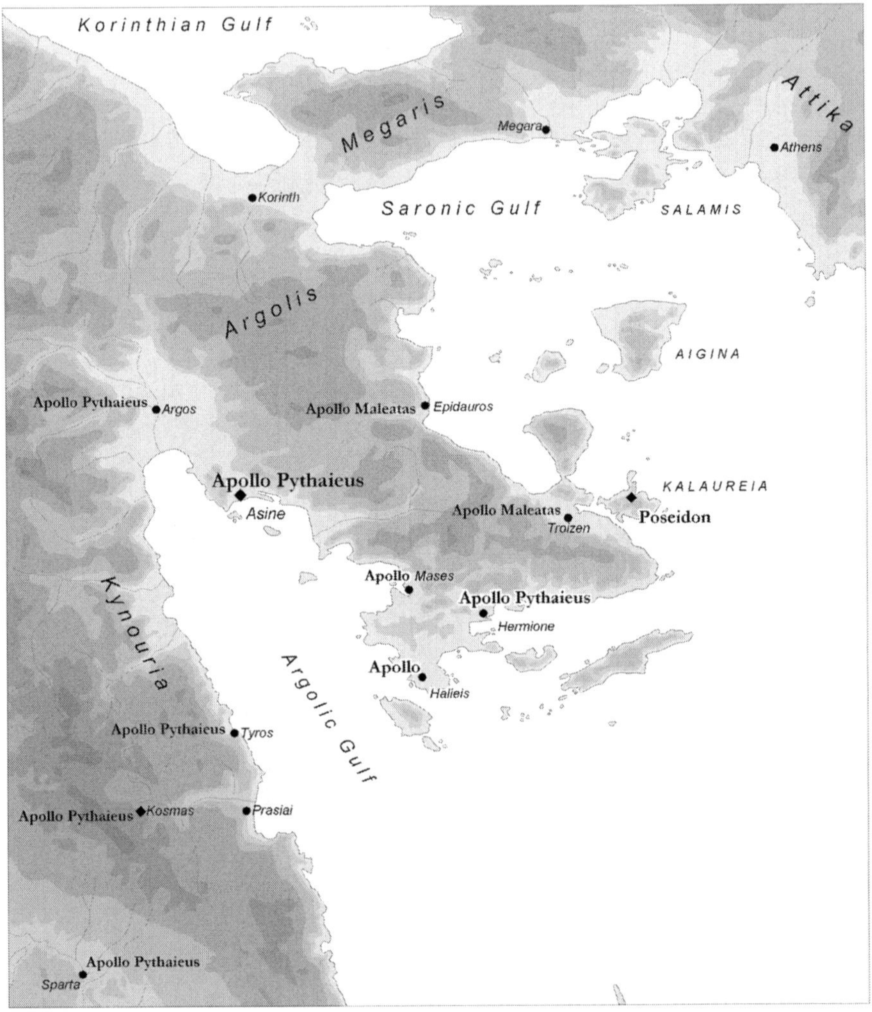

Map 3.1 Cults of Apollo Pythaieus on the Argolic Gulf and along the Argive *Akte*. Created from digital map data © Collins Bartholomew (2004) 2007

from Tyros and Kosmas, and the ancient foundations of the temple at Tyros survive to the present day (Map 3.1).[48]

Judging from the diffusion of Apollo Pythaieus in the area together with the

[48] *IG* v.1 928; *LSAG* 200 no. 36; 199 no. 14. For the cults see Phaklares (1990) 173–83. The Megarians had a festival *Πυθαιεία* in Roman times: *IG* vii 106, see Hanell (1934) 84 ff.; for the relationship between Megara and Argos especially ibid. 69–91. From the 4th cent. onwards we find the epiklesis in Rhodes, which claimed Argive origins, from the 1st cent. BC at the latest complemented by an oracular cult; see Morelli (1959) 108–10, with bibliography.

Thucydidean passage, it looks as if at the time of the historian's writing, and very possibly earlier, Apollo embraced a cult community of cities lining the eastern seaboard of the Peloponnese, including Kynouria and the Akte. Similarly but on a smaller scale than on Delos, these cities, one imagines, delineated their shared seaborne network in regular *theoria*—by ship—to Asine. This cult community did not in any way correspond to political allegiances around 420 BC, or indeed at any time in the Argive peninsula's history in the fifth century. Argos had no military or administrative control over Epidauros or any of the other cities in the eastern Argolid, let alone those in Kynouria. Rather, these places had a pronounced tradition of support for Sparta in the Peloponnesian League throughout the sixth century and the Persian Wars, and in the fifth wavered constantly between Sparta and Athens. The Argives, by contrast, were Sparta's greatest rivals for sovereignty in the Peloponnese and maintained a noticeable difference from the communities in their vicinity. They had distanced themselves from the league, and kept out of all the great Greek wars at the time.[49]

Still, the Argives could apparently exert a form of pressure on religious grounds that would eventually lead to war. What was the force of this gathering? Evidence is scarce but indicative once placed in context. Thucydides says that the Epidaurians' sacrificial tribute was ὑπὲρ βοταμίων. Because the meaning of βοταμίων is obscure the nature of the cult obligation has remained unidentified. A rite or festival involving bull-slaughter to which sacrificial victims were to be delivered has been suspected, but this hypothesis can be safely abandoned because of the morphological and grammatical problems it causes.[50] By contrast, the old interpretation 'pastures, grazing land' is less of an anomaly on both accounts. 'For pastures' might perhaps indicate that some form of negotiation over land was going on. If the meaning is territorial, then the Epidaurian tribute was paid to make up for 'pastures' whose ownership may have been problematic.[51]

This is interesting in so far as territorial boundaries particularly between the Dryopian and other cities were something of an issue that kept raising its ugly head in the course of the Argolid's history. Pausanias mentions the possibility that Herakles put up a named olive tree on Mount Koryphon, between the territory

[49] Hdt. 1.82 mentions Argos' 6th-cent. rule over Kynouria and 'the islands' in the past. Eastern Argolid supporting the Peloponnesian League: Hdt. 7.180; 8.1.2, 43, 72; 9.28.3; ML 27; Paus. 5.23.1–2 (Persian Wars); cf. e.g. Th. 1.27.2; 8.3.2; Xen. *Hell.* 4.2.16 (Troizen); Th. 1.27.3; 105.1; 5.57 (Epidauros). For the Dryopian cities see n. 34 above.

[50] E.g. Robertson (1980*b*) 19–21. If the word were to be dissected as deriving from a form of βοῦς ('ox') and τέμνειν ('cut'), one would expect a trace of the long vowel (as in βουσφαγία). Unexplained religious and/or hieratic terms in Thucydides occur e.g. 1.126.1; 5.11.1.

[51] See LSJ s.v. and Andrewes as in Gomme ad loc. This may be supported by βοταναί in some manuscripts. Bursian (1862–72) ii. 61, 77, suggested the reading παραποταμία, the 'land beyond the river' which he identifies with the plain of Iria several miles to the east of Asine. This reading is revived in Jameson, Runnels, and van Andel (1994) 63 n. 11. ὑπέρ in the sense of 'cause or motive' (LSJ II.4): for punishment, reward, e.g. *Leg. Gort.* 11.42; thanksgiving: Isocr. 9.57; 4.56; payment: *IG* i.2. 140.2 *et al.*

of Asine and Epidauros, marking the border between the two.[52] It would not be surprising if this were the same olive tree as the one fencing off the Dryopians in Bacchylides' paean (ll. 43–6). The fact that this border has an associated legend at all suggests that there is an issue here. In the plain of Iria, a few miles further along the Argive Akte beyond Asine, a late fifth-century *horos* stone has been found, marking the land of an Apollo as *Πυθῆιδος* as if the territory of the sanctuary reached up to here, or, more likely, the god held a revenue-earning *temenos* in this area.[53] Iria, strikingly, was still Epidaurian in post-classical times and we know that the Epidaurians had continuous and long-standing border conflicts with all the peoples dwelling around them; later Hermionean inscriptions try to resolve one such ancient problem.[54] One of the Hermioneans' three Apollos is *Ὅριος* ('of boundaries'), an unusual epiklesis for the god.[55] All of this could be suggestive: was Apollo in the Argolid the god through whom division of territory was ritually regulated and controlled? Was the cult originally instituted as a way to facilitate fierce negotiations over land?

An interpretation under which Apollo sorts out conflict stands in noticeable contrast to what is conventionally thought about this particular cult. It has been argued that it was established as a Dryopian religious centre when Asine was still important as a city.[56] Such an ethnic meeting point based on the cult of Apollo, if it ever existed, could not have lasted for very long, for the old temple on the Barbouna hill apparently did not function for more than about thirty years before it was supposedly destroyed—quite apart from the fact that the associated finds are more local than regional. Rather, one might want to integrate the ethnic component in a different fashion. The whole point of having such a cult centre lay precisely in that it was not ethnically exclusive but allowed a number of communities to communicate and negotiate as *amphiktiones* of diverse ethnic origin.

This could explain why the stories associated with this cult are not purely the traditions fostered by the winning party, but preserve a history of conflict. Worship of Apollo in the area may put this into religious practice. The point may well be the re-enactment of ethnic conflict, rather than its suppression. Shared worship would keep its memory alive, implying that neither is the conflict solved, nor is it necessarily desirable to suppress it, as if the cult kept functioning locally in the way the myth suggests. This phenomenon of a cult integrating ethnic diversity, rather than ethnic similarity, is not unique: the Panionion, for example,

[52] Paus. 2.28.2: *ἐς δὲ τὸ ὄρος ἀνιοῦσι τὸ Κόρυφον, ἔστι καθ' ὁδὸν Στρεπτῆς καλουμένης ἐλαίας φυτόν, αἰτίου τοῦ περιαγαγόντος τῇ χειρὶ Ἡρακλέους ἐς τοῦτο τὸ σχῆμα. εἰ δὲ καὶ Ἀσιναίοις τοῖς ἐν τῆι Ἀργολίδι ἔθηκεν ὅρον τοῦτον, οὐκ ἂν ἔγωγε εἰδείην, ἐπεὶ μηδὲ ἑτέρωθι ἀναστάτου γενομένης χώρας τὸ σαφὲς ἔτι οἷόν τε τῶν ὅρων ἐξευρεῖν.* 'As you go up to Mount Koryphon you see by the road an olive tree called Twisted. It was Herakles who gave it this shape by bending it round with his hand. Whether or not he put it there as a boundary mark to the Asinaians in the Argolid I cannot say, since it is no longer possible to identify clearly the boundaries in a land which has been depopulated.'

[53] Jeffery *ΑΔ* 21 (1966) 18–25; *SEG* xxiv 275 (4th/3rd cent).

[54] Hermione and Epidauros: *IG* iv^{2}1.74 (300–250 BC) and Jameson, Runnels, and van Andel (1994) app. F 596–606.

[55] Paus. 2.35.2.

[56] Tausend (1992) 9–12; Billot (1989–90) 50–1.

may well have had a similar function in Western Asia Minor, and our texts make much of the fact that at some point the group admitted Aiolian Smyrna to its members. Apollo Pythaieus at Asine will thus, if he did not solve, mediate the relations between various communities, whose lives in the Argolid probably had all begun at rather different moments of Greek history.[57]

Transforming long-term shared religious space

Strikingly, Apollo's worshipping group, the collection of maritime cities lining the Argolic Gulf and the Akte, had a long-term tradition of social integration and change. The power of tradition behind this particular configuration of cities perhaps allows for the particular dynamic that we see in operation in the fifth century. How instrumental Apollo Pythaieus must have been in joining this set of people together in a single *khoros*, or several *khoroi*, emerges when we look at the common traditions of Apollo's catchment area on the *Akte* and the coast of Kynouria. These reveal a group of cities tied together in a shared sacred space, and whose relations the Dorians' alleged arrival upset in a lasting way. I have discussed some aspects of the specifically Dryopian matters in the Argolid; but Epidaurians and Troizenians have similarly confused ethnic origins, and likewise face a complicated situation with the perceived arrival of the 'Dorians'.

The collection of cities making up Apollo's worshipping group emerges as a fascinating case study of perceived 'Dorian' and non-Dorian integration, and intriguingly so in the context of the apparent rise of Argos and Sparta as the two major epicentres in the Peloponnese. There are traces to suggest their traditional interaction not only as worshippers of Apollo Pythaieus. Apollo's catchment area is strikingly similar to that of the so-called Kalaureian amphiktyony, a semi-mythical institution centred around the cult of Poseidon on Kalaureia, modern Poros in the Saronic Gulf (Map 3.1). The participating cities were no doubt pooled here because of their shared maritime connections. Strabo names Epidauros, Troizen, Hermione, Nauplia, Prasiai, Aigina, and Boiotian Orkhomenos. 'Later', he says, 'Prasiai was substituted by Sparta and Nauplia by Argos'. Prasiai in the historical period was a dependency of Sparta; Nauplia had been destroyed by Argos in the late eighth century. So the changes in membership of this amphiktyony could be a reference to the changes brought about by the rise of Sparta and Argos: are these the perceived consequences of the Dorian migration?[58]

It is easy to be seduced into such an interpretation by another enigmatic episode involving the same Poseidon. Pausanias and Strabo quote an ancient oracle according to which Poseidon used to dwell on Delos and at Delphi, but swapped them with Apollo for Kalaureia and Tainaron in Lakonia. The story

[57] Kowalzig (2005) 46–56; the Panionion, too, seems to have been involved in territorial negotiations between *poleis*.

[58] Str. 8.6.14; Paus. 2.33.2. On the Kalaureian amphiktyony see Tausend (1992) 12–19; on the shrine Schumacher (1993) 74–6; 86 n. 39 for the earlier bibliography; for the latest excavations there see *AR* 47 (2000–1) 19; 50 (2003–4) 13–4.

makes suggestions about how the Greeks themselves conceived of interlocking religious and social change. It may indicate an awareness of Poseidon being relegated to the sideline in connection with the arrival of the 'Dorians' at Delphi, and the simultaneous development of Delos as a cult centre particularly for the islands and Asia Minor, the future 'Ionians'. If Apollo had taken over the realm of Kalaureian Poseidon in these two cases the striking overlap in Poseidon's semi-mythical catchment area and Apollo at Asine's historical one bears significance: Apollo's overwhelming presence, and travel, in the archaic Greek Mediterranean may well be the religious sign of contemporary social transformation, intimately linked to the so-called Dorians and Ionians, perpetrators of this change. The apparent 'migration' of Asine's worshipping community from Poseidon to Apollo quite possibly expresses this phenomenon.[59]

Whatever the wider, largely irretrievable, case of long-term intertwined social and religious change may be, Apollo and Poseidon were among those who tied the Akte's maritime communities together. Particularly when set against the religious landscape of the Argive Plain, Argos and the cities of the coast are noticeably different. While Hera dominates the Argeia, Apollo and Poseidon rule Argos and the seaboard. Apollo's spread along the *Akte* I have already discussed. Poseidon is especially prominent in these cities. That there is a tradition of Poseidon scuffling with Hera over guardianship of the Argive Plain, just as he does with Athena at Athens, may indicate the god's inherited standing at Argos. Poseidon has a similar experience at Troizen, and he is a conspicuous deity at Hermione.[60]

So Argos, the cities of the Akte, and to a less perceivable extent, Kynouria, were closely linked in a set of relations thought to go back a very long time, prior to the imagined arrival of the 'Dorians'. Intriguingly, there are vestiges revealing a change in the relationship between these cities with the coming of the 'Dorians' at Argos. This too is communicated through the gods and traditions tying them together. Demeter is the third in a trio of the *Akte*'s shared divinities. She was, according to Herodotus, brought to Greece by Danaos' daughters, yet her worship in the Peloponnese 'ended' when the Dorians arrived. Nevertheless, she had prominent sanctuaries both at Lerna and above all at Hermione, where Kerberos is supposed to have been dragged up by Herakles, as he was at Troizen. Pausanias similarly thinks of the foundation of the mysteries at Lerna as pre-dating the

[59] On the oracle see Sourvinou-Inwood (1987). Poseidon and Apollo certainly are in a somewhat tense relationship elsewhere in the Greek world, e.g. in the Dodekanese, where they share patronage of individual communities, such as on Karpathos or on Nisyros; Boiotia may be another case in point where Poseidon's old, Homeric centre at Onkhestos in the archaic period seems to compete for attention with the set of cults of Apollo placed around the Kopaïs (see Ch. 7 below).

[60] J. Hall (1997) 99–106 discusses the differences in divine landscape between the Plain and the eastern Argolid (see also below). Cf. Burkert (1998). Poseidon's interferences at Argos end in his eventual supersession by Hera: is this myth, analogous to the Athenian, a product of Argos' 5th-cent. religious reconfiguration (see below)? Poseidon: Paus. 2.20.6; 22.4 (Argos); 34.9–11 (Hermione); 32.8; 33.2 (Troizen), with Musti–Torelli (1986) on the archaeology; Burkert ibid. 50–1 thinks of the cult of Poseidon and the myths of Danaos as a Bronze Age continuity; Athena at Argos seems another such goddess connected to the Dorian migration.

arrival of the Dorians.[61] The *Akte* also shares a peculiar 'Lykian' connection, involving other areas of Asia Minor as well. The cities of the Argolid sent out *apoikiai* to Karia and the Dodekanese, in some traditions prompted by the 'Dorian' arrival, in others reinterpreted as 'Dorian' colonies. All traditions point to a shared maritime network amongst the cities of the *Akte*, reaching across to far places in the Eastern Mediterranean and in Greek imagination set before the advent of the Dorians.[62]

The 'Dorians' who arrive at Argos seem to have promoted these links on the one hand, but stirred up conflict on the *Akte* on the other.[63] Epidauros, Troizen, and Hermione all had Ionian or Dryopian legacies, but were thought to have been resettled by Dorians from Argos; actual institutions going back to the classical period reflect this being a reality to some extent and add Halieis to the collection.[64] Argos and Epidauros especially were linked through the myth of the Herakleidai, but not necessarily in a way that pleased the Epidaurians.[65] Theirs is a relationship characterized by a mixture of allegiance and conflict. The story-

[61] Demeter in the Argolid: Hdt. 2.171 (Danaids introducing Thesmophoria in Peloponnese); Paus. 2.37.1–3 (Lerna); 34.12 (Hermione); Demeter Khthonia at Hermione: Paus. 35.4–10; Lasos *PMG* 702 honoured her in a song; cf. Jameson, Runnels, and van Andel (1994) 592–3; Paus. 2.32.8 (Troizen); 34.6 (between Troizen and Hermione). Cf. J. Hall (1997) 109 crediting Müller (1830) 414 with the observation of Demeter's early prominence. The area between Mases and the Asinaia has three temples, one each of Poseidon, Apollo, and Demeter: Paus. 2.36.3. Note that the Argives also remoulded the later mysteries at Hermione, just as they came to dominate Pythaieus. Wells (2002*b*) 130–1 suspects a cult of Demeter on the akropolis of Asine. Fossey (1987) argues that cults of Artemis along the Akte differ substantially from those lining the western border of the Argive Plain.

[62] The tradition that the Argolid extended to the eastern Aegean, Karia, and Lykia cannot be late: Halikarnassos, Kos, Nisyros, Kalymnos, Myndos were all founded from Epidauros and Troizen: Hdt. 7.99; Paus. 2.30.9; 32.6; St. Byz. s.v. Ἁλικαρνασσός (cf. Vitr. 2.8.12; Pomp. Mela 1.16.3: founded from Argos). The 'Lykian' connection: Argos itself is full of Lykian landmarks—the city's divine patron is Apollo Lykeios (*IG* iv 557, 559, 658), but equally enigmatic are the admittedly later Letoon, the Pamphyliakon, or the cult of Demeter Mysia at Argos (Paus. 2.18.3), the Kyklopes' coming from Lykia to build Tiryns (Str. 8.6.11) or one tradition's exile for Proitos' to Lykia (Apollod. 2.2.1). Artemis Lykeia also existed at Troizen (Paus. 2.31.4), considered the metropolis of Halikarnassos in Karia (Paus. 2.32.6). Cf. Kytenion's appeal to Xanthos on the grounds of their 'Dorian' ancestry, that is to say their shared connection to Argos (206/5 BC): *SEG* xxxviii 1476. *BCH* (1992) 335–43 for Perseus' dedication to Apollo Lykeios from Kilikia.

[63] Musti (2004) discusses Argos' dynamism, not least expressed in myth.

[64] Dorians at Troizen and Epidauros: Hdt. 7.99; Paus. 2.30.10; at Hermione: Paus. 2.34.5. Institutions shared between Argos and Halieis: assembly (*haliaia*), boule, and magistrates, *synartyontes* and *tamiai*: *IG* iv 554 = *SEG* xi 315 = *Nomima* I 107; 'Ionian' tradition at Epidauros: Paus. 2.26.1–2; Str. 8.6.15; Troizen: Paus. 2.30.10 accepting Herakleids; 33.1 Athena Apatouria, the Apatouria being a typically Ionian festival (Hdt.1.146).

[65] The origins of the Herakleidai are very problematic indeed. They are often thought to be rooted in the early Argolid: J. Hall (1997) 61–2; (2002) 80 ff.; Piérart (1985*a*) 287 thinks the tradition formulated there but much later, in the 6th/5th centuries; cf. already Tigerstedt (1965–78) i. 33–5; *contra* Prinz (1979) 289 n. 122. Certainly Argos has the monopoly on Herakleid memorials: e.g. Pi. *O.* 7.20 ff.; Paus. 2.22.8 (Likymnios); 21.3 (Hegeleos); 23.5–6 (Deianeira); 23.3 (Hyrnetho); 36.6; 38.1–2 (Temenion). However, this squares badly with the lack of evidence for Herakles himself at Argos: see pp. 172–3 below. The first attestation of the Herakleid myth is in connection with Sparta: Tyrt. fr. 2 W. See J. Hall (2002) 82–9 for an early Dorian identity at Sparta; 80 ff. on non-unitary Dorian myth.

drama of the Herakleid-daughter Hyrnetho from Argos, whose love-marriage to the Epidaurian Deiphontes is against the will of her Herakleid brothers, ends in tragic deaths, but leaves behind Hyrnetho and Deiphontes as eponyms of fifth-century Argive *phatrai*. Tellingly, according to Nikolaos of Damaskos, the whole Dryopian Akte got involved in this conflict, featuring in a shared revolt against Argos.[66]

There are certain tip-offs that the sixth century was a period of particularly fervent activity to produce the (self-conscious) Dorianization of Argos and the *Akte* in its train. According to the Epidaurians, their eponym Epidauros was a son of Apollo, while the sixth-century *Megalai Ehoiai* make him a son of the hero Argos; there is a hint of conflict there.[67] But this is also the time when Doros marries the Argive king Phoroneus' daughter in the same poem, suggesting that new pasts were contemporarily dreamed up for the Argives themselves. It is important to note that the Argives themselves were thought to have 'originally' been no more Dorians than the cities in the *Akte*, but integrated—not unlike the Spartans—the Dorians into an existing line of ancestors. Pausanias maintains that the people of Argos spoke Ionian before the advent of the Herakleidai, just as some other Peloponnesians were 'formerly' Ionians, such as the people in Kynouria. Herodotus is aware of this, too, when he has Danaos arrive in the Peloponnese subsequently to the Ionians; and implies it when claiming that since Perseus the Danaid has come from Egypt, this proves that the leaders of the Dorians were actually Egyptians.[68] Behind this lies a perceived pre-Dorian past at Argos. This is borne out elsewhere in Argive tradition, for example when the Dorians at Argos are taught the tunes of Athena Salpinx' trumpet as if here an old tune was taught to newcomers. It is always worth remembering Herodotus' precious piece of information, that the sixth-century tyrant Kleisthenes of Sikyon disliked the 'Dorians' at Argos, who had come into his city, according to Pausanias, under Phalkes the Temenid and his 'Dorian army' just as at Epidauros, Hermione, and Troizen. Kleisthenes famously repealed this memory in abolishing at least for a while the Dorian tribes and forbidding Argive-sounding song, the recitation of the Homeric epics.[69] That the famous Argive piper Sakadas, the inventor of the Pythian *nomos*, is known as the 'Dorian piper' probably fits this context, too. In this company the range of musical activity cited at the beginning of this chapter makes it perhaps clear why the sixth-century Argives were cutting

[66] Deiphontes and Hyrnetho: Paus. 2.28.3 ff. Nic. Dam. *FGrH* 90 F 30 where he is king of Epidauros, alternative founder of the Dryopian cities in the Argolid, rallying them against Argos when threatened by the Herakleids; cf. D.S. 7.13.1; Apollod. 2.8.5. See Piérart (2004) on the relations between Argos and Epidauros.

[67] Hes. fr. 247 MW = Paus. 2.26.2.

[68] Phoroneus: Hes. fr. 10 (b) MW; Ionian Argos: Paus. 2.37.3; Danaos and Dorian Perseus: Hdt. 6.53–5; 7.94. The historical Argives do not celebrate the Karneia as other Dorians: Nilsson (1906/95) 120; cf. Th. 5.54.2; 75.2.

[69] Athena Salpinx: Paus. 2.21.2; Kleisthenes: Hdt. 5.67; Phalkes: Paus. 2.6.7. Note that the recitation of Homer at Argos at this time might itself have been part of Argos' reinvention: see n. 95 below on the relative lack of archaic epic traditions from the Homeric cycle.

edge in matters musical: this must have been a vibrant and creative scene for the forging of new identities, a period when things were happening at Argos, even if we cannot quite say what social changes this entailed.[70]

One could easily adduce more evidence on the same subject; the picture is, I think, appealing. Apollo Pythaieus' worshipping group, the Argives and the cities of the Akte, and to a lesser degree Kynouria, share a memory of many common things, mapped out in an intertwined network of myths, rituals, and also musical traditions: some ethnicity, their gods, and their maritime inclinations. Argos' self-Dorianization seems to have made these ties problematic; or, formulated otherwise, a problematic relationship between Argos and its neighbours was phrased as an issue of Dorianization. A powerful role for Apollo Pythaieus in this area makes good sense in this light. The cult at Asine as we can trace it is an expression of these controversial links in the way it pitches Dorians and the inhabitants of the eastern Argolid against each other. Apollo's *khoros* appears to be making use of traditional links between the cities of the Akte, but reinterprets them in the light of its Dorianization.[71]

So, we can conclude that ethnic integration was high on Apollo Pythaieus' agenda, but without therefore swallowing up all the local traditions concerned; rather, Apollo was good at keeping them alive. The way the aetiological myth of Bacchylides fr. 4 ties into ritual practice seems to offer two possible views of why this cult should be revered, neither denying nor privileging the element of change. For the 'winning' party, the 'Dorians', worshipping this god is a way of making up for having started the conflict with the Dryopians in the first place. Apollo's refusal of Herakles' initial intention to dedicate the Dryopians to him might suggest that this *anathema* was not quite the right offering: would he otherwise not have accepted the *dekate*? Founding a new cult for the Asinaians is a way of expiating the initial offence against Apollo, by granting him worship elsewhere. His worship at Asine on the part of the Dorians makes up for the injustice done to the Dryopians, 'people of Apollo'. By contrast, for Dryopian communities worshipping this god would have functioned as a powerful reminder of how they had arrived in the Argolid in the first place, pinpointing the 'injustice' they had suffered, and in this way allowing them to keep a distinct, non-Dorian identity, as expressed in the literary sources.

Whether this be enacted in a choral tribute by each city, or in a joint choral performance is in a way irrelevant from the point of view of what dancing for Pythaieus did for the worshipping group as a whole. Rather, the compensatory nature of the cult also accounts for the form of worship in *khoroi*. We will never know whether membership in the cult community entailed the obligation to both sacrificial and choral tribute as on Delos, but this is at least a reasonable

[70] Sakadas: Paus. 2.22.8–9; musical Argives: Hdt. 3.131.3. J. Hall (1997) 69–70 also thinks of 'Dorian' Argos as a 6th-cent. invention, partly on shared grounds.

[71] See pp. 132–42 above.

hypothesis. One imagines the cult to have had a similar role in affirming local identities whilst tying them into a larger, overarching network. Regular instalments of *khoroi* to gods are often conceived of as tributes paid to soothe a deity for a crime that a community has committed in myth. In such contexts, the actual *khoroi* members constitute real-life counterparts of the victims of the aetiological story, thus re-living the original crime. The stories tend to be set at moments of social and cultural change in a given community. For example, the Korinthians' annual choral tribute to Hera across the gulf at Perakhora, consisting of seven local boys and girls each, expiates the murder of Medea's children, in local Korinthian tradition committed not by the mother but by the Korinthians themselves. If one were to search at all for the social significance of Medea's myth in the local Korinthian context, the animosity towards the children represented that towards changes caused perhaps by the opening up of Korinthian–Black Sea communications picked up in the myth of the resident foreigner at Korinth.[72]

The survival of the aetiological myth and its associated ritual suggests then that an ethnic conflict thought to have underlain the establishment of the cult and the continued worship of this god, was renewed and resolved with every single performance in ritual. The ambiguity in both myth and ritual illustrates how the archaic world coped with elements of social change: it left the culprits ambiguous, and turned the parties into the god's tributaries. And this is what is interestingly different about this cult, or at least interestingly different in comparison to a routine interpretation by which this myth in performance does no more than bluntly state Argive superiority.

Apollo's fifth-century *Akte* between Argos and Sparta

How central such a mechanism of ethnic integration was becomes clear when we move closer in time to the contemporary historical context in which our paean was performed, the early fifth century. Argos may have held some sway over Apollo at Asine in the sixth century and earlier; but the Argive volume around this otherwise rather silent shrine is raised so considerably in the fifth century that one feels that Thucydides' note, that Argives had chief authority in the cult (κυριώτατοι τοῦ ἱεροῦ) in 418 BC, rather suggests that their influence could not be taken for granted.[73]

Argos at some point started to consider control of this cult important. The Argives put considerable effort into becoming the god's patrons, and this patronage is then extended to the cult's recurrences in the participating cities. As mentioned above, Argos had its own Pythaieus on Deiras, the hill below the akropolis he shared with Athena. This Pythaieus came into existence archaeologically when the Asine sanctuary was being ravaged, and is therefore, at least

[72] For Medea's children and the subsequent tribute to Hera at Perakhora see Brelich (1959).
[73] Th. 5.53. On the meaning of κυριώτατοι: Dignas (2002) 221 n. 515.

materially, younger than its Dryopian equivalent.[74] The cult's actual lesser age is opportunely turned into superiority in a myth of origin, however, quite possibly no earlier than the fifth century. The contemporary poetess Telesilla claimed that Argive Pythaieus was founded by a certain Pytheas, son of Apollo who had specially come to Argos from Delphi to institute the cult; the Argives were allegedly the first to whom this god appeared. To fashion an oracular cult along Delphic lines would imbue the Argive Pythaieus with dignity. It is interesting that the Asinaian one perhaps provided divination, too, but only according to a supplement in Bacchylides' paean.[75] Argive Pythaieus was also putatively superior to his corresponding cults along the *Akte*: Pausanias concludes from Telesilla's claim that the Hermioneans received their Apollo's epiklesis from the Argives. And two recently discovered fifth-century inscriptions from Epidauros mention Apollo Δειραδιώτης, Pythaieus' alternative epiklesis at Argos. Melampous' coming from Argos specially to establish Pythaieus in the paean makes a further claim to the cult's indebtedness to Argos (more about Melampous below). These Argive attempts to represent their cult as being as old and authoritative as possible and turn all others into derivatives show that it was important to override the simple truth that the cult at Asine was just older. But it is also clear that the Argives could ultimately not deny Asine's seniority. Introducing all these derivation theories is a contorted way of explaining Argive leadership while conceding that the cult's role was tied to its original locality.[76]

If the Argives were prepared to go to this much trouble to reformulate the traditions, it must mean that control over both the cult and the traditions associated with it were highly desirable. Why is winning this one so important to the Argives? To find out we must look in greater detail at both the wider traditions with which this god Pythaieus is associated, and the contemporary historical context in which this paean was performed.

Argos' relation to Sparta, according to tradition at the heart of Argos' capturing of Apollo for itself, is the key here. The Spartans, too, had a Pythaieus,

[74] See Vollgraff (1956) 33, whose monograph on the cult is indispensable; Morgan and Whitelaw (1991) 83; J. Hall (1995) 581; here (582) it is also suspected that the introduction of Apollo Pythaieus to Argos is a symbol for Argive dominion over Asine, or even over the Argolis: cf. Billot (1989–90) 35 and 97. An archaic *temenos* in Argos, though, can only be found for the 6th cent.: Hägg (1992*a*) 12 and n. 20. Cf. Roux (1957); Pouilloux (1958); Roux (1961) 65–82; Piérart (1990) 320–3; Kadletz (1978); Billot (1989–90) 52–97; Auffarth (1994) 113–14.

[75] No archaeological evidence for an oracle at Asine survives to confirm a supplement in terms of an oracle in Bacch. fr. 4.54 χρ-: cf. already Fränkel *apud* Barrett (1954) 434–5: χρ[ησμ- e.g. like χρησμωιδόν; he sees another possibility in χρησμοῖς or χρησμῶν referring to ἄλσος ('precinct'), or a conjecture similar to ὦ Ἄπολλον χρηστήριε in Hdt. 6.80. A composite of χρυσο- is rejected on metrical grounds: Barrett (1954) 434 and n. 4. For line 50 μάντις ('seer') has been conjectured by Snell in SM. For Telesilla's important role in the forging of Apollo's past see Hornblower (2004) 125 and n. 143; cf. Piérart (2003) on the role of Telesilla in Argive myth-making more widely.

[76] Paus. 2.24.1; 35.2; *SEG* xxxviii 320–1 (Epidauros). Apollo's epiklesis Deiradiotes (Paus. 2.24.1) is supposed to reflect *H.Ap.* 281. The analogy with Delphi is briefly discussed in Vollgraff (1956) 29; 38–40; Roux (1976) 21–3; 25–30; Piérart (1990) 327–8; Billot (1989–90) 54–5 and n. 60–4; Auffarth (1994) 113–14.

essentially associated with the most prominent symbol of the long-standing enmity between these two cities. Located in the Spartan agora, Apollo Pythaieus was the patron of the Gymnopaidiai, known for its ferocious tests of stamina and strength. At this festival, the armed youth sang and danced paeans in commemoration of the Spartan victory over the Argives in the most legendary of their conflicts. The so-called Battle of the Champions, in *c.*560 BC, was fought over possession of Kynouria, the stretch of land south of Argos between modern Astros and Leonidio along the easternmost of the three Peloponnesian promontories, separating Lakonia from the Argolid. The story goes that this battle saw two 300-strong elite squadrons confront each other with each side claiming victory for itself. The legend reflects an ever-lasting conflict over this contested border area; claims to victory on each side were still made as late as the Roman imperial period.[77]

Our Apollo Pythaieus, significantly, as we saw above, was the prevalent deity in Kynouria with at least two sixth-century attestations. Paying the Spartan version of this Apollo a tribute in an explicitly anti-Argive ritual, as if the victory over Argos had only just been won, indicates that the god's sympathies were as ambiguous as the outcome of the battle itself. Though the antiquity of the tradition linking the Gymnopaidiai and the Battle of the Champions cannot be ascertained, it is important that the association was made at all. Apollo Pythaieus stood for what separated Argives and Spartans, imbued with connotations of the Spartano-Argive conflict. The god seems to have meant similar things to both: he was closely associated with military affairs, territorial negotiation, and conquest.[78]

When thinking of Apollo Pythaieus in this way, one quickly realizes that the Asinaian Apollo's catchment area was where the Argives had a permanent problem with the Spartans. Spartans at all times were conspicuously present in the eastern Argolid, continuously undermining Argive ambitions in this area, but also providing for themselves access to the Saronic Gulf (particularly via the Halieis–Epidauros route). For a start, Asine had itself been deleted from the map

[77] Hdt. 1.82; Paus. 2.38.5; Str. 8.6.17; Plut. *Apophth. Lac.* 231e (fought under Polydoros, contemporary of Theopompos). The conflict over Kynouria was believed to have had its history then already: Paus. 3.2.2: Spartans invade Kynouria under Ekhestratos, son of Agis ancestor of the Spartan Agiadai; 3.7.2: battle under Prytanis, the first Eurypontid; 3.7.5: further battle under Theopompos (dated by Eusebius to 720 BC, by Solinus 7.9 to 736 BC); cf. the battle of Hysiai 669 BC (Paus. 2.24.7, Argive victory); Spartano-Argive conflict over their borders in Roman times: Paus. 7.11.1–2. Much later funerary epigrams indicate that into late antiquity both Spartans and Argives were concerned to prove their victory: e.g. *Anth. Pal.* 7.430, an epitaph of two Argives in which the Spartan victory features as *κῦδος . . . νόθον* 'vain glory'. See Brelich (1961) 25–6, esp. n. 30; for the moulding and remoulding of the traditions related to this battle, 22–34; Robertson (1992) 179–207; Dillery (1996) for a comparison of the narrative patterns to the account of the battle at Thermopylai.

[78] *Suda γ* 486 s.v. Gymnopaidia: 'Boys' choruses . . . who sang for the gods in honour of those Spartiates who had died in the Thyreatis' (*χοροὶ ἐκ παίδων . . . εἰς θεοὺς ὕμνους ᾄδοντες εἰς τιμὴν τῶν ἐν Θυραιαῖς ἀποθανόντων Σπαρτιατῶν*; *EM* s.v.; *Anecd. Bekk.* 32. Sosibios = Ath.15.678b–c: wreath of palm trees, called 'of feathers', worn as a 'reminder of the victory at Thyrea' (*ὑπόμνημα τῆς ἐν Θυρέᾳ γενομένης νίκης*) by the leaders (*προστάται*) of the festive boys' and men's choruses. On the nature of the Gymnopaidiai see now Pettersson (1992) 42–56.

in the context of their conflict, an act of revenge against its inhabitants for plotting with Spartans against the Argives. Beyond that, Pausanias lists a number of further clashes in the area between the Argives and Spartans in the eighth century. The destruction levels of the akropolis at Halieis revealed a pit full of Lakonian cups, such as were not usually exported from Sparta, suggesting Spartan presence at Halieis in the early sixth century. Even the earliest script in the eastern Argolid is Spartan and not Argive. Cities such as Epidauros and Troizen were traditionally members of the Spartan-led Peloponnesian League, from which Argos kept off as much as possible.[79]

The fifth century in particular, the time when our paean was performed, presents us with constant Spartan appearances in the Argolid. Much of the First Peloponnesian War and significant parts of the Peloponnesian War itself involves the Spartans stirring up the eastern Argolid, mostly directed against Athens in the first instance, but troubling the Argives not least in the wake of the Athenian–Argive alliance of the late 460s. The Dryopian city of Halieis, habitually a refuge for anti-Argive individuals (see below), was a particular hotbed of unrest: having resisted an Athenian attack around 460 BC, it was captured by a Spartan merchant ship full of troops some time before the mid-440s and the thirty-years peace in 446 BC.[80] In 424/3 BC Halieis accepts an Athenian garrison and promises to refuse access to the Spartans in the future. Nevertheless, more Spartan troops seem to have arrived via this route in Epidauros in 419 BC—incidentally to help the Epidaurians against Argos in the Thucydidean passage that also involves our god![81]

This may give us a clue to why fifth-century Argives in particular, but also those who made the earlier terracotta sima, might have been keen to make sure they had Apollo under control: the Spartans kept making trouble in the area that Apollo Pythaieus had been carefully watching ever since the Spartans were first chased out in the attempt to thwart Argive ambitions in the Akte. Sovereignty over the cult also meant sovereignty over the degree to which the Spartans could interfere in the Argolid. Both the long-term associative baggage of cult and the immediate historical circumstances suggest that a similar situation to that of the Spartans sitting just a few bays further on from Asine (as occurred just before 446 BC) might have provoked the composition and performance of the paean at a festival at Asine in the mid-fifth century.

How this whole set of correlated mythical and historical associations is made relevant in a fifth-century context is nowhere clearer than in Bacchylides' paean itself, which blends myth and ritual in an exemplary and detailed way, holding

[79] *LSAG* 174–5. For Halieis see Jameson, Runnels, and van Andel (1994) 70–1.

[80] Th. 1.105.1; D.S. 11.78.2 (Athenian attack on Halieis); Hdt. 7.137.2–3 (Spartans in Halieis). Tirynthians in exile at Halieis after the destruction of Tiryns by the Argives (464 or 462 BC): Hdt. 7.137.

[81] Athenian garrison: *IG* i^3 75 = i^2 87 (cf. Troizen Th. 4.118.4); Spartans arriving in Epidauros: Th. 5.56.1–2, possibly because the plain of Iria was Epidaurian? Hermione and Athens made a treaty in *c.*446 BC: *IG* i^3 31. For the most lucid understanding of the context within the First Peloponnesian War see Lewis (1981); helpful also Jameson, Runnels, and van Andel (1994) 76–7.

many suggestions about the power of such myth-ritual performances. For like the paeans sung by the Spartans in honour of their Apollo Pythaieus at the Gymnopaidiai, this too presents itself as a victory song. The mythical narrative leads into a long invocation of the festival's ritual present in a passage only rivalled by the *Iliad*'s description of Achilles' shield, contrasting the violence of war with an ideal of peace in which a community busies itself in cheerful religious activity:

ἄλσο]ς, ἵν' ἀγλαΐαι
τ' ἀνθ]εῦσ[ι] καὶ μολπαὶ λίγ[ειαι
(.) . . . . . .]ονẹς, ὦ ἄνα, τ. . [
(.) . . . . . .]τι σ̣ὺ δ' ὀλ[β
(.) . . . . . .] . α̣ιοισιν[
τίκτει δέ τε θνατοῖσιν εἰ-
ρήνα μεγαλάνορα πλοῦτον
καὶ μελιγλώσσων ἀοιδᾶν ἄνθεα
δαιδαλέων τ' ἐπὶ βωμῶν
θεοῖσιν αἴθεσθαι βοῶν ξανθᾶι φλογί
μηρί' εὐμάλ]λων τε μήλων
γυμνασίων τε νέοις
αὐλῶν τε καὶ κώμων μέλειν.
ἐν δὲ σιδαροδέτοις πόρπαξιν αἰθᾶν
ἀραχνᾶν ἱστοὶ πέλονται,
ἔγχεα τε λογχωτὰ ξίφεα
τ' ἀμφάκεα δάμναται εὐρώς.

(desunt 73–4)

χαλκεᾶν δ' οὐκ ἔστι σαλπίγγων κτύπος,
οὐδὲ συλᾶται μελίφρων
ὕπνος ἀπὸ βλεφάρων
ἀῷιος ὃς θάλπει κέαρ.
συμποσίων δ' ἐρατῶν βρίθοντ' ἀγυιαί,
παιδικοί θ' ὕμνοι φλέγονται.

[Apollo's sanctuary] where festivities blossom and clear songs; . . ., lord, . . .; grant prosperity . . . to . . . . Peace gives birth to noble wealth for mortals, to the flowers of honey-tongued songs, to the burning for gods of thighs of oxen and fleecy sheep in yellow flame on elaborate altars, to young men's concern with the gymnasium, with pipes and revelry. On iron-pinned shieldgrips are found the spinnings of red-brown spiders, and sharp-pointed spears and double-edged swords are subdued by rust.

(lines 73–4 are missing)

There is no din of bronze trumpets, and sleep, honey for the mind, still soothing the heart at daybreak is not pillaged from men's eyelids. The streets are laden with lovely feasts, and the songs of boys rise like flame. (Bacch. fr. 4.56–80, tr. adapted from D. A. Campbell)

Summoning the gods before, or expressing gratitude after, battle are among the most frequent occasions when paeans were sung, and they form an important item on the ritual agenda of war situations. Joy after victory prompts the informal singing of paeans, as if the paean cry expressed relief after the tension of the battle. 'Literary' paeans sometimes reflect such elements of spontaneity: Pindar's *Paean 2*, for example, integrates, in a more formal celebration at home, an established religious festival into the commemoration of a victory or a series of victories that have only just been won.[82]

In the song here, the aetiological myth for Apollo Pythaieus is delicately interwoven with the peace scene suggested by an imagined ritual present. Myth and ritual in the text coincide in the figure of the god. At the moment when the cult is founded, the narrative switches time levels, bringing the myth into the present: in ll. 56–7 both time levels come together in the *khoroi* of Apollo Pythaieus, whose precinct and altar are brought to life by the festive song. This is the moment when the reality of *khoros*-singing and imagination of the myth merge into aetiology's timeless continuity between the time of the foundation of the cult and the here and now the song is celebrating. The actual prayer becomes part of this blending in performance: lines 59–60 contain something like a wish for benediction for the celebratory community, which is subsequently sketched in the peace scene. Immediately connected with the cult of Apollo through the aition, the idealized depiction of the contemporary ritual is thus both part and object of the prayer, as if 'peace' was, is, or will be, granted by this Apollo Pythaieus.

But, as the *khoros* says, peace is preceded by war (ll. 75–80). The paean recreates a post-battle situation, exploiting its own generic conventions. The *khoroi* of young men (*neoi*) in the paean, busying themselves in physical exercise, revels (*komoi*) and pipe-playing, as well as the boys (*paides*) singing hymns, are given a quite particular slant to their activity: this is conspicuously close to what the Spartans engage in during their peace-time victory festival of the Gymnopaidiai, similarly characterized by the peaceful antonyms of wartime activity, music, and sport instead of war-cries and battle. Apollo Pythaieus as celebrated in this paean seems to be doing the same for the Argives as he would have done at the Gymnopaidiai for the Spartans.

The Apollo Pythaieus that now emerges is one, as it were, who symbolizes victory over the Spartans. What was remembered as a traditionally tightly knit worshipping community of cities around the Akte might have been reinterpreted as a bulwark against Spartan influence. The gentle tradition of the Argives piously sparing Apollo Pythaieus is really one of their appropriation of the cult, and its employment in their own interest. That this tradition had them even care to bury one of their war dead next to the god further suggests that Apollo was imbued with elements of the long-standing Spartano-Argive conflict in this area. The cult's legacy of ethnic integration becomes a tool for gathering together a group of cities whose perceived traditional communality had actually long been superseded by fragmentation. It is clear, then, why the Argives so enthusiastically promoted the cult. Sovereignty over Apollo meant also sovereignty over the

[82] For the latter see Rutherford (2001) 257–75 on Pi. *Pae.* 2; generally in military situations Käppel (1992) 45–6. The commemoration of military victory typically underlies festivals: see Brelich (1961); Robertson (1992).

degree to which the Spartans could interfere in the Argolid. If as seems apparent Spartans were constantly turning up in the eastern Argolid, a situation in the context of that of the Spartans sitting just a few bays further on from Asine as noted above, possibly in the context of the First Peloponnesian War during 461–446 BC, would be an alluring scenario in which such a performance would be mind-bogglingly calling up the bonds of traditional, ritual allegiance.

By means of the interaction of Apollo's aetiology and the contemporary choral ritual, the performance of the paean in effect constitutes a fifth-century recreation of the cult's foundation. The myth of origin, with the Argives setting up a cult integrating the Asinaians and other Dryopian cities as well as presumably the non-Dryopian cities of Troizen and Epidauros, delineates the worshipping community, invoking what is presented as a common binding tradition of all the worshippers gathered at the festival—as if the old ethnic issue suddenly became interesting again and it was worth remembering what the cult stood for. (The city of Halieis, that city out of all the other Dryopian cities that most recently stood for Lakonizing tendencies, is explicitly named in the mythical part of the poem (l. 49).) Assembling the *khoros* of the cities involved works with the cult's traditional associations as well as those emerging from the contemporary historical situation: the non-political nature of the cult possibly as a form of agreement over territory in the Argolid, ultimately designed to integrate ethnic diversity tied into the—probably more recently—alleged Argive origins of the cult. In merging the aetiological myth with the ritual of the victory celebrations, the dancing *khoros* evokes the taking possession of the cult by the Argives. The performance thus marks the cult's role as a landmark balancing the ethnic diversity the Spartans had sought to exploit.

Gathering all the communities of the eastern Argolid together in song makes forceful statements about social realities in the area. Apollo Pythaieus at Asine emerges as a god whose worship was essential to the configuration of inter-*polis* relations in the eastern Argolid. This gathering provides another instance of a different network of obligations alongside political and military federations, and one that operated differently from a *symmakhia*, an alliance ('shared battle'). Membership in such a cult community counted just as much as membership in a more strictly political organization; indeed the participants in the cult seem to make a point of not sharing political allegiances, leaving cultic and political communities as conspicuously different from each other. The local cult centre existed as an alternative network of social relations and social obligations, possibly based on a somewhat shadowy traditional consensus regarding territorial divisions or boundary marking within the area. If holding this cult community together effectively emerges as a form of Argive control over the Argolid, this was possible because of the traditional role played by the cult at Asine, as a local cult centre that integrated the surrounding communities in the choral worship of a common god and kept their relations in careful balance against outsiders.

2. SIX SYNOIKIZING SONGS AND SOCIAL TRANSFORMATION OF THE ARGIVE PLAIN

Bacchylides' paean for Apollo Pythaieus functions within the continuous Spartano-Argive conflict, keeping together a fragile worshipping community through the power of tradition. If Thucydides thinks it worth mentioning the Epidaurians' one-time failure to contribute to the cult, this indicates that Apollo was successful to a point. This paean's particular instance is, because of the wealth of surviving evidence in its connection, indicative, and exemplary, of a much wider strategy through which Argos in the first half of the fifth century dealt with its neighbours in the Argolid. The Bacchylidean performance is the most accessible of a series of similar myth-ritual scenarios, seemingly all operating in a delicate phase in Argive history, and in the service of significant changes in the local social and power configurations in the Argolid, which in the larger Peloponnesian picture are intimately tied to the relationship between Argos and Sparta. I shall now develop this wider picture through cultic song commissioned in an Argive context.

Understanding the *Argeia*

We need to turn our eye away from the seaboard, inland to that other arena of Argive interest, the vast and fertile Argive Plain (Map 3.2, Fig. 3.2). Argos in the course of the fifth century is embroiled in the difficult and long-drawn-out process of an integrated synoikism and democratization of the Argeia, not dissimilar to that of Athens and Attika in the late sixth century. These changes were in part aimed at escaping Spartan pressure, but just as much at developing the Argives' own *hegemonia* in the Peloponnese and to some extent, by implication, in Greece.[83] Pausanias' comments in particular put the synoikism into such a wider Peloponnesian framework: the Argives had been in almost daily danger of being overrun by Sparta, but then synoikized, incorporating the people of Tiryns, Hysiai, Mykenai, Midea, and 'every other insignificant town in the Argolid'. At once Lakonian pressure decreased and the Argives were able to deal more strongly 'with the provincials'. The passage, told in connection with the Arkadian League, smacks of a long history of successful federalism, but it offers an important hint of Argos' fifth-century concerns, where the synoikism, democracy, and Argos' standing in the Peloponnese are intimately linked.[84]

[83] On Argos in the 5th cent. generally see Lewis (1992*a*) 101–2; Hornblower (2002) 75–88; and now Piérart in *Inventory* s.v.; J. Hall (1995); an older account is Kelly (1974).

[84] Paus. 8.27.1. The synoikism: Moggi (1974); Kritzas (1992); Piérart (1997). For the tribal reform see n. 99 below. Argos was certainly a democracy by the late 5th cent: Th. 5.27–8; 44; 82 mentioning a variety of democratic institutions (assembly, council, *artynai*), discussed by Wörrle (1964) and recently Leppin (1999). At 5.82 Argives build long walls as if to become another Athens. Argos'

Competition between Argos and Sparta over hegemony in the Peloponnese we tend to associate with the sixth century and not with the *Pentekontaetia*. Contemporary democratization and synoikism at Argos have not been studied much in conjunction, not least because of the nature of the evidence, though the newly discovered archive of Athena Pallas will no doubt reveal some tantalizing new insights.[85] As will emerge, whatever Argos' actual resources to implement its pretence to leadership, the perseverance with which they pursue the issue of leadership within the Peloponnese is intriguing and might well be the justification for Argos' internal restructuring.

Fifth-century cultic song integrates these three mainstays of classical Argive history, *hegemonia*, synoikism, and democratization, into a suggestive sequence of performances. Their creative power ties Argive aspirations to leadership in the Peloponnese into social reforms at home. As many as six contemporary songs other than the Bacchylidean paean may encompass the contemporary world of the Argolid, hardly exploited for an understanding of the enigmatic Argive fifth century. Among these feature Pindar's *Dithyrambs 1* and *4* which I have discussed elsewhere and will treat here only superficially. Pindar's so-called *Paeans 18* (Elektryon), *20* (Herakles), and *21* (Hera) have recently and attractively been identified as set in an Argive context.[86] Pindar's *Nemean 10* was an ode for an Argive victory, possibly at the reformed games of Hera at Prosymna, the important goddess dwelling on the Argeia's edges. What follows aims at full discussion of the broader historical function of these songs in the Argives' contemporary attempt at the Plain's interlocking social and religious reformulation (Map 3.2).

Our narrative sources frame these Argive aspirations by two pronouncements: in 481 BC the Argives graciously declare their satisfaction with 'half' the leadership (τὸ ἥμισυ τῆς ἡγεμονίας) if they are to support the Greeks against Persia, when really they deserve to have it all. This might strike one simply as overly self-important, but there is evidence in the later fifth century to suggest that headship within the Peloponnese and even more, of Greece, was what others at times had in mind for them and certainly the Argives thought themselves to deserve. Korinthians knew well that flattery in these terms easily made Argos hostage to its own ambitions. So when after the Peace of Nikias (421 BC) Korinth talks them into entering into an alliance with 'whichever Hellenic state would want to' (τὴν βουλομένην πόλιν Ἑλλήνων) which would allow the Argives to see 'that the Peloponnese may be preserved' (ὅπως σωθήσεται ἡ Πελοπόννησος) from enslavement by Lakedaimon (καταδούλωσις), the Argives take this on motivated

democratization may go back to the early 5th cent.: cf. *SEG* xiii 239, recently reattributed to Argos (Brandt (1992) *contra* Jameson (1974) 71 f.; cf. the architrave block found on which the bronze tablets were affixed: *BCH* 105 (1981) 607 ff.). On Themistokles and Argos' democratization in the 460s BC e.g. Forrest (1960). 'The people' came to hold a sway over Argos' past: Paus. 2.19.2; 21.8; ostrakismos: Arist. *Pol.* 1302^{b}18–19; oligarchic–democratic opposition: 1304^{a}25–7; Aesch. *Hiketidai* (set in 'democratic' Argos according to Bakewell (1997), see below).

85 Some foretaste of this in *AR* 50 (2003–4) 19–20, announcing future publications.

86 D'Alessio (2004); Kowalzig (2007) 226–32.

by their characteristic mix of fear and ambition: 'on the one hand their 30-years peace was about to expire, but . . . they also hoped to gain leadership in the Peloponnese'. The same factors stimulate their moves towards a renewal of the treaty with Sparta not much later. The most intriguing case of apparent Argive self-delusion is how they are spurred on to fight at Mantineia, in 418–17 BC, 'for their old supremacy in the Peloponnese' ὑπὲρ τῆς παλαιᾶς ἡγεμονίας, almost as if the memory of such ancestral leadership was something that not only the Argives believed in.[87]

The textual sources stop here, as if they formed the two chronological pillars enclosing the evidence from myth-ritual performances in the intervening decades between the Persian Wars and the brief spell of Argos' appearances on the Hellenic stage of the Peloponnesian War in 421–418 BC. Similarly, on the theme of democratization and synoikism, the texts are elusive yet link it firmly to the Spartan problem. Argos' internal reinvention starts with the catastrophic defeat by Sparta at Sepeia in 494 BC. Much discussed in the ancient sources, as if tradition were aware of a pivotal moment in Argive history, this sets off the—mutually dependent—processes of synoikism, democratization, and increase in military strength. This legendary battle depleted the Argive citizenry by 6,000 casualties, leading to a mass enfranchisement, but no text is quite clear about who these newly enrolled people were:[88] they are interchangeably called 'slaves', 'perioikoi', and also sometimes thought to be the people of Tiryns; Argives also had a large number of dependent cities in the archaic period, and a significant helot-type population, called *gymnetes*. The ancient tradition is generally sceptical with regard to the Herodotean 'slaves', and the one attempt to explain the unusual move makes it quite clear that what is at stake in the enfranchisement is the quality of the men, not their social class: Diodorus says that the remaining Argives thought it better to give freedom to their 'slaves' than share government with the 'rabble', suggesting new citizens taken from the neighbouring cities rather than the Argive *demos*.[89]

While the problem of this emerging new citizenry just cannot be solved, it seems pretty clear that the battle of Sepeia set off both the enfranchisement of people of the Plain and the likely incorporation of their land into the Argive *polis*. This is certainly the implication of the legends that the battle itself

[87] Hdt. 7.148–53 (on early 5th-cent. claims to leadership of Greece); Th. 5.27–8 (Korinth and Argos); 40–1 (attempts at renewal of the treaty); 69 (Mantineia); D.S. 12.75, discussed most recently in Hornblower (2002) 80–7. What is the *palaia hegemonia*? Perhaps a retrojection of Homeric power relations onto Argos; perhaps a reference to Pheidon's semi-mythical reign, for which see recently Tausend (1995*b*).

[88] According to Aristotle, ancient cities quite normally behave in this way during times of crisis, so the sudden growth of the citizen body should not per se astonish: Arist. *Pol.* 1303^a3–13.

[89] Hdt. 6.77–83; Arist. *Pol.* 1303^a3–13; D.S. 12.75.7; Paus. 2.20.8–10; Plut. *Mul. Virt.* 245d–f; *Apophth. Lac.* 223b–c; Poll. 3.83 (*gymnetes*), on the dependent cities particularly Piérart (1997); *Inventory* s.v. For a discussion of Argive post-Sepeia turmoils see Forrest (1960) 221–9; Lotze (1971); Zambelli (1971; 1974); Lewis (1981).

produced. Famously, the women of Argos, rallied by the poetess Telesilla (who as we learned above also fiddled with Argive Pythaieus' mythology), seeing their men slaughtered one by one, got up in arms onto the city wall 'together with their slaves' to ward off the Spartan attack. The episode, at least as old as Herodotus, was considered important; it gave rise to, and was remembered, in the Hybristika, an annual Argive cross-dressing festival. So-called marginal groups—women and 'slaves'—appear as the antithesis to the male citizenry, as if the story served to delineate and socially integrate this group into a new Argive civic community in the same way as many think happened in democratic Athens. The legend pointedly gives away the intertwined nature of the changes at Argos. Overlapping *douloi*, *oiketai*, and perioikic populations appear interchangeably as defenders of Argos and its future citizens. This suggests the memory of simultaneous enfranchisement and synoikism; the two are definitely blended in the admittedly later note from Plutarch whereby Argive women, holding in such little esteem the 'dwellers around' (*perioikoi*) to whom they were married, put on fake beards as if their higher social status outweighed their inferior gender.[90]

The following period in Argive history, misleadingly termed *interregnum servile*, ended when the sons of the killed warriors were old enough to take up their fathers' legacy. Although the 'slaves' flee, to Tiryns, we have no evidence that this also entailed a return to oligarchy. Quite the contrary, whoever was in charge at Argos from the 470s or so onwards capitalized on what in 494 BC might have seemed the bad fortune of having to empower the dwellers-around. For this generation also spans the period when the Argives systematically get to grips with the Argive Plain by wiping out one by one Mykenai, Tiryns, and Midea during the 460s BC.[91] How fully these cities were destroyed, however, is at least in the case of Tiryns open to debate: we have epigraphic notice of people fleeing, significantly, to the cities on the *Akte*, to Epidauros and to Halieis. Pausanias mentions—without giving an idea of the time frame—that the Argives incorporated the Tirynthians as *synoikoi* 'because they wanted to enlarge their city' (τὴν πόλιν ἐπαυξῆσαι ἠθέλησαν); and he also knows of the eponymous hero Tiryns turned into Argos' son. Below we shall come across more such indications that the integration into Argos of Tiryns' inhabitants together with their traditions was at least as prominent as was their expulsion. So while the supposed flattening of the three cities may have meant exile for some members of the local elites of the

[90] Hdt. 6.77; Paus. 2.20.8–10; Plut. *Mul. Virt.* 245e–f. *Suda* τ 260 s.v. Τελέσιλλα. Cf. Musti–Torelli ad loc.; the best account of the festival is still Nilsson (1906/95) 371; cf. Halliday (1909–10). On the story see now Piérart (2003); previously Stadter (1965) 45–53; Jacoby on *FGrH* 310 F 6. Valiant Argive women became a topos of Argive history, cf. the treatment of Pyrrhus: Paus. 1.13.7–9, quoting Hieronymos of Kardia (*FGrH* 154 F 15); and Lykeas (*FGrH* 312 F 1); Plut. *Pyrrh.* 34 (= Phylarkhos? See Jacoby on *FGrH* 154 F 15); Polyaen. 8.68.

[91] D.S. 11.65; cf. Paus. 2.16.5; 8.33.2 (Mykenai); Hdt. 7.137; Ephor. *FGrH* 70 F 56; Str. 8.6.11 (Tiryns); Str. 8.6.11; *Σ* Theocr. 13.20; Paus. 2.25.9; St. Byz. s.v. *Μίδεια* (Midea); Paus. 5.23.3; 7.25.5–6; 8.27.1; 33.2 refer to the destruction of the cities of the Plain in general. Cf. Moggi (1974). On the precise dates (between 468 and 462 BC) of these destructions see Forrest (1960) 231–2; Tomlinson (1972) 104–8; Adshead (1986), esp. 86–103.

Plain, for others it entailed being synoikized into the socially restructured Argive *polis*.[92]

It is facets of these social processes in the Plain, designed to bolster Argos against Sparta, that can be elucidated through myth-ritual performances. All six songs taken together attest a reconfiguration of the Plain's myths and rituals in relation to their inherited localities, a transformation of a set of places into a shared religious space. While narrative history is patchy and inconclusive for this period, myth-ritual performances restructure the relations between gods, heroes, and their worshippers in the Argive Plain. What in narrative accounts features as the violent destruction of feeble neighbours, re-emerges in cultic performances as integration of the area's heroic past into the synoikized Argive *polis*; what features as a temporary enslavement of the 'dwellers around' and a marginal episode seemingly fast overturned by the grown-up old elites, becomes a lasting Argive identity. We can trace in some detail a new identity, plausibly a new community, being crafted in the Argeia.

While with modern hindsight a redirection of the Plain's religious traditions towards Argos may not appear spectacular, from an early fifth-century perspective the Argive appropriation and reinterpretation of the Plain's rich traditions is baffling. We need to dig a little further into the utterly confusing pasts of the Plain, into a complexity that suggests the area's great dynamism over a long period of time (Map 3.2). As discussed above, Argos overwhelmingly shares traditions with the Akte, much less with the rest of the Plain. On the other hand, Argives no doubt have a constant eye on the Plain, creating a rather irregular web of cults and associated mythical figures. Jonathan Hall has recently suggested some sort of system behind the dense grid of mythology covering the Plain, arguing for competitive traditions rooted at Argos and in the Eastern Plain respectively, each with an unfulfilled claim to control of the entire area. On that reading, Argos would be the hub of the descendants of King Proitos who culminate in the personnel of the *Seven against Thebes*. By contrast, the family of Perseus, producing Herakles and eventually the Atreids and Trojan warriors, are located in the Eastern Plain, particularly Mykenai.[93] This division cannot be fully supported; but the tentative separation does account for the respective geographical clustering of traditions and, what is perhaps worth more, their monumentalization at Argos. The *Seven*, often neglected in favour of the greater warriors of Troy, are endowed with a sixth-century heroon in the centre of the Argive *polis*. Pausanias'

[92] Tirynthians at Halieis: Hdt. 7.137.2; Str. 8.6.11; some Argives appear as exiles at Epidauros: *SEG* xxvi 449 = *Nomima* II 28 (475–450 BC). Incorporated into Argos: Paus. 2.25.8; 8.27.1. *Douloi* fleeing to Tiryns, eventually evicted: Hdt. 6.83. Tiryns and Epidauros, sons of Argos: Paus. 2.25.8; 26.2. Cf. Piérart (1997) for the history of Argos' relationship to the cities of the Plain until the late classical period.

[93] J. Hall (1997) 93–9; (2002) 54–5; Ch. 3 and *passim*. The Proitids' close connection with Tiryns and the Eastern Plain, rather than Argos: Bacch. 11; Pherec. *FGrH* 3 F 114; their monuments near Tiryns: Paus. 2.25.9; 16.2 (Proitos reigning over the Heraion, Midea, Tiryns); 9.8 mentions a series of bronze statues near the temple of Apollo Lykeios at Sikyon called 'the Proitids'; 12.2 a statue dedicated by Proitos in the temple of Hera; 7.8 a temple of Apollo built by Proitos. Dorati (2004) is a recent discussion on the Proitid myth and Argos.

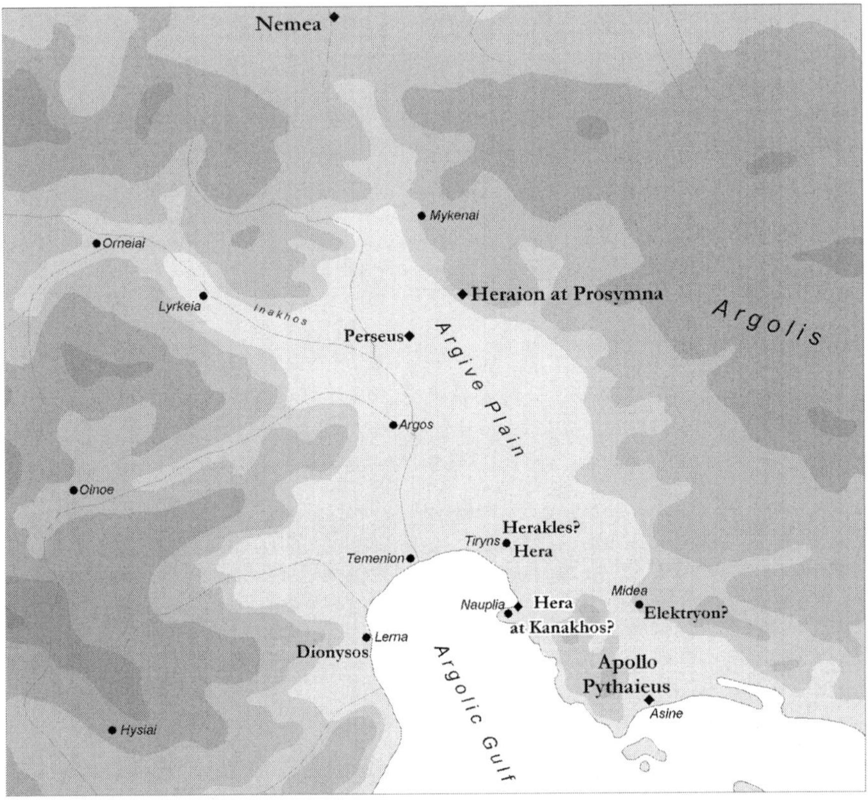

Map 3.2 Destinations of cult song in the Argive Plain. Created from digital map data © Collins Bartholomew (2004) 2007

downtown Argos fully commemorates this set of heroes.[94] By contrast, monuments to the Trojan War cycle are oblique and references certainly in Pausanias very general. This is so conspicuous that one starts wondering whether Herodotus' important notice, that the warriors of Troy were the targets of Kleisthenes of Sikyon's hatred against Argives, refers, rather than to a well-established presence of the Trojan cycle warriors at Argos, to Argive sixth-century myth-making rather than long-standing cultic reality. In the Eastern Plain, this situation is reversed; the heroes of Troy receive a full showing whilst the *Seven* are virtually absent.[95]

[94] For the heroon of the *Seven* (Paus. 2.19.8) see Pariente (1992); other monuments to the *Seven* at Argos: Paus. 2.20.5; 21.2; 23.2.

[95] Argos—not unlike Athens—seems to forge a secondary relation to the Trojan War: Diomedes's ancestry is north-western Greek/Aitolian, and his association to Athena at Argos connected to the Dorian migration (Plut. *QG* 302c–d; at Argos: Paus. 2.24.2); cf. Burkert (1998) 51–3. Trojan War monuments are conspicuously general, dedicated by/for 'those Argives who fought at Troy': 2.20.6; 22.3. Cingano's (2004) discussion of the epic traditions also suggests this. Kleisthenes of Sikyon: Hdt. 5.67. More on Argos and the Atreids p. 174–7 below.

Similarly, the current view that Hera dominates the cities of the Eastern Plain, but cedes precedence to Apollo and Athena as patrons of Argos itself is extreme, but in essence probably right. Argos, none the less, always had a keen eye to the Heraion in the Eastern Plain which symbolized control of the entire *Argeia* and, more importantly, its traditions. If the Spartan king Kleomenes chooses the Heraion for a sacrifice marking the end of his campaign against Argos after Sepeia, this should be taken seriously, symbolizing Argive claims perhaps more than Argive realities in the early fifth century.[96] However, archaeology warns that a privileged relationship of Argos to the Heraion is difficult to prove prior to the mid-fifth century; rather, it is Mykenai that cultivates this goddess; and Hera guards the cities of the Eastern Plain, whilst at Argos she is less prominent.[97]

Fifth-century Argive flattening of the Eastern Plain and subsequent synoikism inverses the distribution of these figures of myth and cult when the *Seven* march into the Plain, and the inhabitants of the Plain, the Heraion, Herakles, and the warriors of Troy, take an Argive direction. The Heraion at Prosymna in the course of the fifth century came under Argive auspices; a new temple was built in the 460s, the festival restructured, and the Heraia, games in honour of Hera, were either introduced from scratch, or elevated to Panhellenic status.[98] The synoikism has a good chance of running parallel to a nearly contemporary tribal reform, by which a fourth tribe is added to the three traditional Dorian ones (the Dymanes, Hylleis, Pamphyloi). Several of the twelve subdivisions (*phatrai*) of this 'new' tribe Hyrnathioi bear the names of localities or heroes associated with the Eastern Plain and one even with the *Akte*: the Ἡρα(ι)έες, Ναυπλιάδαι, and the Δαιφοντέες.[99]

[96] Hdt. 6.81; early myths concerning Argos' connection to the Heraion include those of Io, Phoroneus, the Proitids (see below, Ch. 6; Burkert (1998) 53–4, *contra* J. Hall (1995)). Inakhos sacrifices to Hera: Paus. 2.15.4; Hera and Io (daughter of Inakhos) are depicted on the throne of Amyklai: 3.18.13. Hera is the guardian of the entire plain, not of Argos: *Il.* 4.8, 51–2; 5.908; Phoronis fr. 4 Bernabé; Hes. *Th.* 12; cf. Eur. *Troad.* 23–6 versus Aesch. *Suppl.* 291 ff. (Hera Argos' protective deity).

[97] The Mykenaian claim to the Heraion is mentioned in D.S. 11.65; Str. 8.6.10; Diktys of Crete *Belli Troiani* 1.16. Cf. Billot (1997); J. Hall (1995); and from an archaeological point of view, Strøm (1988); (1995, 1998). It would be wrong to deny Argos Hera's presence altogether, but her two cults at Argos, as Hera Akraia (Paus. 2.24.1 (cf. Vollgraff, *BCH* 31 (1907), 155–6)) and as Hera Antheia (Paus. 2.22.1 (Foley (1988) 141)) bear little archaeological material to suggest early Argive control of the Heraion. The old view: Nilsson (1967–74) i. 428; Farnell (1921) 188–9; Kelly (1976) 60–1. De Polignac revised his original position (1995; Fr. 1984) to understanding the Heraion as a place mediating between the different communities in the Argolid (1994).

[98] For Argive 5th-cent. control and refurbishment of the Heraion and the restructuring of the festival see J. Hall (1995) 611–13; Amandry (1980). Pi. *N.* 10.22–4 is the first attestation of Heraia, at which *hydriai* could be won; two bronze vessels of the 460s do indeed survive: Amandry ibid. 212–17; Robinson (1942). The old temple famously burnt down in 423 BC: Th. 4.133.2–3; Paus. 2.17.7.

[99] For a discussion of the tribal reform and a list of the known *phatrai* see Piérart (2000), esp. 299; previous studies include Kritzas (1992); Piérart (1985*b*); the earlier literature is listed in Musti–Torelli on 2.28.20–54. For Deiphontes king of Epidauros with a heroon at Argos see p. 151–2 above. Euripides' plays *Temenos* and *Temenidai*, featuring the story of Daiphontes, might well be about Argos' ambitions in the Argolid after 421 BC, on which see below. In adding a non-Dorian tribe, Argos behaves like other Peloponnesian cities: Sikyon (Hdt. 5.67); Epidauros has only two Dorian tribes and two 'local' ones: *IG* iv^2 1.106 C 37–40.

Myth-ritual performances have a considerable share in orchestrating the reorientation of these divine and heroic figures. Argos' predilection for choral performances in this period helps restructure the mythical past in myth and ritual. The surviving songs that can certainly or probably be attributed to Argive commission embrace those divine and heroic figures whose attachment to Argos is loose, contested, or non-existent. They are thus a good example of the creative force of myth-ritual performances, and their lasting effect: these figures would forever remain part of the Argive legacy. The movements of the Seven are less conspicuous than those by the Eastern Plain into the West, suggesting that the *Seven* were a less good strategy to reach out to the Plain than the Atreids were a catch for Argos. Nor are the *Seven* an explicit target of song-culture, suggesting their rootedness at Argos did not need stressing in ritual, or at least did not need eminent poets forging a link in myth through public ritual. The set of performances of myth and ritual integrate the traditions of Argos and those of the Eastern Plain into a shared religious framework.

Six synoikizing songs (Pi. *Diths.* 1, 4; *Pae.* 18, 20, 21; *N.* 10)

With that in mind, let us look at the actual songs. I shall not start with the fascinating new interpretation of so-called *Paeans 18*, *20* and *21*, but with two Pindaric dithyrambs, which make intriguing suggestions about the role of myth-ritual performances in the process of integrating new citizens, and hence to some extent of democratization. *Dithyrambs 1* and *4* (frr. 70a and d) are good candidates for Argive commission; the πτόλις Argos itself is named in *Dithyramb 1* (l. 6).[100] Both songs feature the myth of Perseus fetching the head of Gorgo. This is a story that in Argive tradition is associated with the aetiological myth for the local cult of Dionysos. According to this tale, which shapes Pausanias' portrayal of everything Dionysiac in his second-century Argos, Dionysos came to Argos from the sea, accompanied by a swarm of maritime mainads (ἅλιαι), and encountered Perseus in a great battle fought with Gorgo Medusa's head and the accoutrements of Dionysiac mystery cult. Dionysos had mysteries at nearby Lerna, where at least since the third century the god was celebrated in secret nocturnal rituals at the Lernaean Lake (Map 3.2). The two dithyrambs can, I think, be placed in the context of the god's mysteries there, just as some other contemporary Pindaric dithyrambs seem to have been performed in a mystic setting. Aetiological myth and ritual can be seen to merge once again in the timelessness of choral ritual: Perseus' story of his war against Dionysos is patterned on a typical resistance myth, characteristically leading to the establishment of Dionysos' mystery cult featuring choruses in a given Greek city. In all these cases, Dionysos' dancing rites are at first rejected and then accepted; Dionysos is first repelled and then

[100] For the Argive context of *Diths.* 1 and 4 cf. Lavecchia (2000) 93–105; D'Alessio (1995) 271; (2004); Zimmermann (1992) 41–3; 51–2.

re-emerges in choral form. The communal choral dithyramb functions simultaneously as the rejection and acceptance of the rites, the aetiological myth is re-enacted, and the introduction of the god's cult into the city reaffirmed.[101]

Two elements are of interest to us here, of which the 'mystic' aspect is the first. It is very difficult indeed to be clear about what is 'mystic' about Dionysiac mystery cult in this period, other than to note that the cultic attributes (ivy, thyrsos, etc.) and certain ritual elements (bacchic dance, the god's epiphany) featuring in the dithyrambs are those associated with Dionysos' mystic side.[102] However, the specific practice of 'mystery' worship has great potential for creating new religious communities, something that both the Hellenistic and Roman world knew how to exploit. The significance of this observation may actually be greater in the context of the social transformation in archaic and classical Greece-from aristocracy to democracy. Mystery worship categorically distinguishes between those who are initiated and those who are not. In a world where religious participation is highly exclusive, determined by either family relations or at best citizenship, mystery worship lends itself well to the formation of, paradoxically, a new exclusivity. It can help create a cult community that is characterized not by shared ancestry but by shared mystic experience and the 'criterion' of initiation. In this way it can be instrumental in the creation of civic identities.[103]

Secondly, Dionysiac resistance myths tend to hover between 'private' and public worship and thus themselves contain elements of a social reconfiguration of Dionysos' worshippers over time. At Argos, Perseus is not alone in his initial dislike of Dionysos: those facing the god are in some myths the Proitids, daughters of the local king, but in others the anonymous collective body of the Women of Argos.[104] The ambiguity in the aetiological myth over its protagonists and hence future worshippers suggests that the 'mystic' (that is to say the resistance-myth) aspect of the god thus has something to do with, and is exploited for, the creation of a new—different—cult community and is linked to social change. *Dithyrambs 1* and *4* might well have had a share in this process at Argos and perhaps Dionysiac ritual in its 'mystic form' a significant role in the

[101] This issue is discussed in greater detail in Kowalzig (2007) 226–32. Monuments at Argos associated with this Perseus-Dionysos episode: Paus. 2.22.1, 20.4, 21.5.7; cf. 23.7–8; the cult foundation after the spectacular battle occurs in Nonnos 25.728–41; for Dionysos at Argos, including this legend and his mysteries with nighttime rites at Lerna, see Piérart (1996); Casadio (1994). 4th-cent. Sokrates of Argos knows of a nocturnal ceremony by which Dionysos was called up from the Lernaian Lake using trumpets (*salpinges*) wrapped in *thyrsoi*: *FGrH* 310 F 2 = Plut. *De Is. Os.* 364f; cf. Σ T *Il.* 14.319 (180–150 BC). For the performance of Pi. *Dith.* 3 (fr. 70c) in a mystery context see Wilson (2003*b*).

[102] Cole (1980) has a list of relevant vocabulary.

[103] These features of mystery cult have to my knowledge not been explored. See, however, Burkert (1987) 30–53 on the 'exclusiveness' of mystery cult.

[104] The Proitids at Argos (Hsych. s.v. *Ἀγριάνια*; Bacch. 11) and the Minyads at Orkhomenos (Plut. *QG* 299e–300a) are examples of the first; the 'Women of Elis' and the 'Women of Tanagra' of the latter (Plut. *QG* 299b; Paus. 9.20.4–5). The Proitids in Hdt. 9.34; D.S. 4.68.4–5; Apollod. 3.5.2; Paus. 2.18.4 have turned into the 'Women of Argos' maddened by Dionysos.

developing *polis* of the late archaic period. The re-enactment of Dionysiac myths in choral ritual, presumably 'officially' in publicly performed dithyramb, supports the definition, constant reconstitution, and affirmation of a citizenry which is swiftly priding itself on its new exclusivity, celebrating the god in the shared choral experience of the dithyramb.

On this interpretation, the Argive dithyramb(s) may have had a very specific function in the contemporary *polis*, to do with the creation of a citizen body. It is just as interesting that the hero Perseus should turn up in this context. On the one hand, it is probably fair to see him as a 'king' in the sense of Pentheus whose inherited privileges, for example in the *Bacchae*, are threatened by the advent of Dionysos. His appearance in an early fifth-century dithyramb also relates to the social recomposition of Dionysos' worshippers that the Dionysiac resistance myths embrace.[105] But king of which city? Perseus in later tradition is indelibly linked to Argos, and numerous monuments commemorate him there, but in the archaic period his allegiance is ambiguous. Though as son of Danae and perhaps through the myth of the Gorgones he might seem tied to Argos, Perseus is more explicitly linked to Mykenai, where he has a fountain; and a sixth-century heroon, featuring a curious collegium of cult officials, is a roadside shrine between these two cities (Map 3.2). Unlike Herakles who, as we shall see, was never a hero at Argos in the archaic period, Perseus quite likely moved in and out of the picture depending on whose interests in the city prevailed. If he firmly returns to Argos in this dithyramb, this choral performance is a suggestive representation of his final establishment in the city, but in a changed social context. Might Perseus have undergone what the hero Adrastos had experienced a century earlier at Sikyon? Adrastos' *tragikoi khoroi*, the choruses recounting his life's tales, were 'given' to Dionysos in the broader context of a more 'democratic' tribal reform—an intriguing analogy to the situation at Argos in the fifth century.[106]

So-called *Paeans 18*, *20*, and *21* are songs in praise of Elektryon, Herakles, and Hera respectively. All three more likely featuring among Pindar's *prosodia* rather than *paianes* have recently been interpreted as Argive commissions. This we know for *Paean 18*, composed 'for the Argives' (Ἀ]ργείοις . . .]ς Ἠλεκτρύω̣[ν), and can appealingly suggest for the other two. A fifth-century Argive song-cycle makes best sense in view of the order of the songs as they appear on the papyrus. It is tantalizing that a later, Hellenistic inscription speaks of a ἱερὰ καὶ δημοσία

105 Seaford goes much further in such an interpretation when he sees King Pentheus in Euripides' *Bacchae* having to yield to the power of initiation as a metaphor for a transition to democracy: e.g. (1996).

106 Perseus son of Danae linked to Argos through the Gorgones: Acus. *FGrH* 2 F 24; Pherec. *FGrH* 3 F 10; 11. Perseus was destined to become king at Argos but exchanged his reign for Mykenai and Midea, which he supplied with city walls: Paus. 2.15.4; 16.3; Apollod. 2.4.4; Arrigoni (1999) esp. 56–9 argues for his presence in the city at least from the 6th cent. (Paus. 2.23.7). For his cult rather at Mykenai see Jameson (1990). His fountain there: Paus. 2.16.6; his heroon on the road to Argos: 2.18.1; *IG* iv 493 (=*SEG* xi 298; xxii 260). Adrastos: Hdt. 5.67 (on which Kowalzig (2007)).

γῆ ('sacred and public land') belonging to a quartet of the deities addressed in fifth-century song: Elektryon, Hera, Herakles, and Apollo Pythaieus. The coincidence must not be overrated, but should not be underrated either: did these deities have special status at Argos, acquired perhaps in the context of fifth-century Argive imperialism in the Argeia?[107]

Of Pindar's so-called *Paean 18* too little survives to pin down how myth relates to ritual, but it is an especially good example of how cult-song performances for Argos were concerned with non-Argive characters. Elektryon belonged to the Eastern Plain and was king of Tiryns, and sometimes Midea (Map 3.2). The song is the one and only sign of his worship in connection with Argos prior to the attestation of his territory in the Hellenistic inscription, more probably referring to territory located in the Plain. Tellingly, in our song he is just a guest at Argos: Pindar seems to imply a *temenos* shared with the Dioskouroi (ll. 1 ff.). It is plausible that this was the twins' shrine on the road to Tiryns, which they temporarily lent to this foreign hero. But even from the scraps hinting at the celebration it is clear that this was not a cheap ritual. Rather, we face the interesting paradox that Elektryon's 'secret nocturnal ritual' (l. 10 [ἐ]ννύχιον κρυφα[) was propped up by, we must assume, the public performance of a song commissioned by a poet of Panhellenic fame.[108]

Elektryon we know because of his sons, all but one of whom perished in the war against the Teleboiai. The surviving son Likymnios is also the one who preserves Elektryon's memory. Born to the concubine and eponymous nymph Midea, Likymnios, in a tradition going back to at least the *Catalogue of Ships*, was killed by the Herakleid Tlepolemos. Likymnios' grave could be seen at Argos in Pausanias' times. Both Elektryon and Likymnios are therefore representative of the tradition that eventually was superseded by the Herakleids.[109] Their lasting presence at Argos could indicate the usual survival of a conflict in contemporary religious practice, and this is possible in the case of Likymnios. Elektryon, however, is never mentioned again with a cult at Argos itself. Rather, the song looks as if it is celebrating something like the hero's temporary appropriation by Argos perhaps in the context of the destruction of whichever city hosted his cult in the first place, Tiryns or Midea, both plausible candidates. A suggestive Tirynthian component lies in the Dioskouroi, whose shrine at Argos there is reason to believe

[107] D'Alessio (2004) suggests the identification of these songs as Argive commissions and mentions the inscription, on which see Kritzas (1992) 237–8. On Athenian imperial confiscation of allied land, turned sacred to Athenian gods see Parker (1996) 144–5. Quite possibly all three songs were prosodia: D'Alessio (1997) 35–9; 41–3.

[108] D'Alessio (2004) 109–13 on this song. Elektryon at Midea (but no grave): Paus. 2.25.9; Str. 8.6.11 (for Midea); cf. Pi. *O.* 10.65–6; at Tiryns: Hes. *Sc.* 82; Eur. *Alc.* 839; Paus. 9.11.1. Mykenai is also attested: Apollod. 2.4.6; Σ Lyc. 932 bis.

[109] Elektryon against the Teleboiai: Apollod. 2.4.5–6, cf. J. Scherf, *DNP* 12.1 (2002) 88 s.v.; Likymnios' death: *Il.* 2.653–70; Pi. *O.* 7.24–31; cf. D.S. 4.58.7; Apollod. 2.8.2. His grave at Argos: Paus. 2.22.8.

was run by a Tirynthian family, suggesting intimate links between Argive and Tirynthian elites beyond *polis* boundaries.[110]

Elektryon's song, particularly if performed in a Tirynthian-run shrine, hints at the possibility that the supporters—or beneficiaries—of the breaking-up of the Plain's territorial divisions in the 460s BC were not necessarily just the Argives just as Pausanias had implied (pp. 163–5 above). On this reading, the song merges Argive claims and non-Argive ties to the land that this hero watched as in the case of Perseus. Even amongst the incredibly fragmentary pieces of Elektryon's song, a blending of the traditions of the Eastern and Western Plain is apparent: the few fragmented references to mythical events include one to Troy and one to Thebes, as if to make a point of marrying the Trojan and the Theban cycle. In honouring this hero of the anti-Herakleid tradition in a public festival—paid for, one could imagine, by the hero's accustomed sponsors, from Tiryns (or possibly Midea)—the song carefully integrates the traditions and associated claims of powerful non-Argive families with those of the city of Argos itself.[111]

It is worth speculating along these lines for a new role of old Tirynthians in a reinvented Argos because *Paeans 20* and *21* also have curiously Tirynthian slants. Both songs similarly belong to Pindar's book of *prosodia*, processional songs, as to the paeans.[112] *Paean 20*, for Herakles, is the more problematic performance, with no reference to a locality, so that its destination cannot be definitely proven. But even beyond the appeal of a possible Pindaric series on the Argolid, there are good reasons to believe that Herakles, too, was bound to be conscribed into what emerges as the Plain's restructured web of traditions. A detailed myth survives in this *Paean 20*, recounting the story of baby Herakles' first feat, when right after his birth he warded off a pair of snakes sent by Hera, a story known well from *Nemean* 1.38 ff.[113] *Nemean 10* confidently advertises Herakles as Argive offspring, but just like Elektryon, Herakles is not present at Argos in myth and decidedly a latecomer in cult.[114] By contrast, Mykenai, Tiryns, and Midea have close associations with Herakles serving and eventually superseding the king of Mykenai, Eurystheus.[115] But Herakles' clearest association in the Argolid is with Tiryns, the

[110] We know from Pi. *N.* 10 that the victor's maternal uncle Pamphaes had proved his commitment to the twins in a pageant Theoxenia: Pi. *N.* 10.49–50. It is generally assumed that this uncle was a Tirynthian: Pamphaes' home is the 'city of Proitos' (l. 39–42), which in the ancient tradition is always Tiryns. Cf., however, Pherekydes *Σ Od.* 15.225; *Σ* Eur. *Phoen.* 1109, where Proitos' city is Argos. On the Dioskouroi at Argos see Moretti (1998) 237–9, with all known evidence. Already Farnell (1896–1909) 316–17 connected the issue of the Dioskouroi cult with the incorporation of Tirynthians into Argos. Is the point the ambiguity and/or deliberate elusiveness of Proitos' and Pamphaes' 5th-cent. homes?

[111] Pi. *Pae.* 18.7–8 has]αρ̣δανίᾳ̣ and Θήβᾳ̣. See p. 167 above on the marrying of these traditions in the Argolid in this period.

[112] D'Alessio (1997) 35–9; (2004) 113–21 argues for the Argive performance context.

[113] The parallels in the telling of the myth are explicated by D'Alessio (2004), but already observed by Rutherford (2001) 401.

[114] Herakles at Argos: Pi. *N.* 10.16–17. The first unambiguous attestation of Herakles at Argos is a late 5th-cent. graffito found in or near the theatre (*c.*425–400 BC): Moretti (1998) 240; *BCH* 113 (1989) 721 fig. 30.

[115] Herakles' mother Alkmene is linked to Midea: Theoc. 13.20; 24.1–2; Paus. 2.25.9; Apollod. 2.4.6.

city he firmly belongs to in myth; and a sixth-century inscription confirms his existence in cult there at an early stage. If our song is bound for the Argolid, this cult is the most plausible candidate (Map 3.2).[116]

Herakles' absence from Argos is puzzling, not least since Herakles is a prominent hero everywhere else, including Lakonia, Messenia, and the rest of the Argolid.[117] How spectacularly un-Argive he was is clear perhaps from Bacchylides' *Ode 9*. Here Herakles' exploits are recounted with much verve by a locality that seemingly could afford to distance itself from Argos: Phlious in 418 BC hosted exiles from the Argive democracy, and apparently had not bought into the new system of the synoikized Plain. A recent careful reading of this ode for a Phliasian victor reveals how the story of Herakles' defeat of the Nemean lion outdoes the aetiology of the Nemean Games that favoured the Argives—in this version Adrastos founded the games when the *Seven* were on their way to Thebes. In this context, *Paean 20* an Argive *prosodion* to or from a shrine of Tirynthian Herakles singing of his feats from the cradle might have done well in redefining his lordship of the Plain to include, and to be headed by, the city of Argos.[118]

A Tirynthian theme may also be argued for the last piece of song, the so-called *Paean 21*. Again a *prosodion* rather than a paean, it accompanied a ritual for Hera. Little survives other than the intriguing refrain 'Ie Ie [praise], the Queen of the Olympians, the bride with the best husband', which was tediously repeated at least three times (ll. 3f., 11f., 19f.). A *kranion* ('well' l. 10) suggests ritual washing, a typical local ritual for Hera. While alternative interpretations cannot be ruled out, D'Alessio suggests for this *prosodion* the bathing of Hera's statue at the spring Kanathos located by Pausanias in the area of today's Nauplion (cf. *ναῦται* l. 16), which he tentatively identifies with a well at the medieval church Hagia Moni, on a hilltop overlooking the Argolic Gulf just outside the modern city (Map 3.2). At this spring Kanathos, Pausanias says, 'the Argives say Hera washes every year to renew her virginity', suggestive in the context of a cult song where the goddess is addressed as *νύμφα ἀριστόποσις* ('bride with the best husband'), as if to reiterate the fact of a pre-marriage ritual in the *invocatio*. One could imagine a traditional procession in which nearby Tirynthian Hera would have been paraded to the Kanathos fountain at Nauplia. Interestingly, Hera's image at Tiryns was at some point stolen by the Argives and put up in the Heraion at Prosymna, presumably in the context of the fifth-century developments. The old tradition of the procession from Tiryns to Nauplia would have been continued from the Heraion once Hera's *xoanon* had migrated there: did the song accompany such a pageant to the sea? It would be a powerful example of

[116] Herakles at Tiryns: Hes. *Th.* 292; Eur. *Telephos TrGF* 696; Soph. *Trach.* 1151–2; Eur. *Alc.* 838; cf. Call. *Dian.* (3) 146. For the cult see N. Verdelis, M. Jameson, and I. Papachristodoulou, *AE* 1975, 182–3, no. 15 [105–205], late 7th cent. BC. Herakles features as guardian of the entire plain in the epic poems: *Il.* 19.117 ff., with Wathelet (1992) 99–101.

[117] See Piérart (1992a) for a baffled account of the comparative lack of evidence on Herakles at Argos, including tables on Herakles' presence elsewhere in the Peloponnese; for the 5th-cent. developments see also Vannicelli (2004).

[118] For Bacchylides' *Ode 9* see Fearn (2003); cf. Th. 5.83.3.

how the Argives were busy reconfiguring the myths and rituals of the Argive Plain, by rerouting existing rituals, rather than inventing new ones.[119]

Ναῦται feature in the song (l. 16), as if to make a pun on the ritual's locality, good support for a Nauplian identification. But an *asty* and something *poli-* also occurs (ll. 15, 17). If this did refer to Nauplia, it referred to a non-existent city, long razed to the ground by the Argives themselves.[120] The Argive phratry of the *Naupliadai* appearing in the fifth century suggests that the city was somehow resuscitated in religious imagination at the time. Nauplia's reappearance in mythical and ritual consciousness may push us towards some fundamental issues in the processes of the Plain's mythical reformulation. Tragic plays of the later fifth century make it very clear that in myth Nauplia is the harbour not of Argos, but of Mykenai, the seat of the Heraion in myth. It is here, for example, that the Greek warriors landed on their return from Troy, or that Menelaos came from Sparta on his way to Mykenai.[121] Retracing this 'epic' sacred way from the recently appropriated Heraion in a *prosodion* such as *Paean 21* would mean no less than at once cultivating and rephrasing the most prestigious of mythical pasts, that constructed around the Atreid tradition and the Trojan War.

The precious point arising from a rather scrappy song hints at the wider agenda behind the Argive appropriation of the Eastern Plain's myths and cults. The Plain was home to the Akhaian past, the gateway to anyone's ambitions to leadership in the Peloponnese as much as to wider Panhellenic claims, both, as we saw above, fifth-century Argive aspirations. The acquisition of the Heraion on the part of the Argives was essential to any such pretence, because it offered unrestricted access to the Akhaian past. As noted above already, Mykenai had the more intimate relationship to the Heraion, tied to it by a Bronze Age sacred way and thence commanding the entire Atreid cast of the Trojan warriors in graves and monuments relating to the epic cycle.[122] Greek Mykenai, too soon flattened to have left much of an impression in the antiquarian record (*c.*464 BC), nevertheless has a record of conflicts with Argos set in the mid-fifth century revealing that the scuffle here was over prestigious memories rather than territorial possessions. Diodorus says that Mykenai was destroyed for its claim to control both the Nemean Games and the Heraion, the latter according to Strabo a sanctuary common (*κοινόν*) to both Argives and Mykenaians. Fame in Hellas was an issue: Pausanias perceptively contends that Argos struck down Mykenai 'out of jealousy' (*ὑπὸ ζηλοτυπίας*) because the Mykenaians had fought at Thermopylai in

[119] D'Alessio (2004) 115–21 for the argument in relation to the Kanathos fountain. The Tirynthian *xoanon* at the Heraion: Paus. 2.17.5; cf. 8.46.3, a Tirynthian *xoanon* in the shrine of Apollo Lykeios at Argos.

[120] Paus. 4.24.4; 27.8; 35.2; Str. 8.6.11 = Theopompos *FGrH* 115 F 383, though see J. Hall (1995) 583–4 for a sceptical view on Nauplia's 8th-cent. destruction.

[121] Eur. *El.* 169 ff.; for the Hera-festival in the play (at 169 ff.) see Pötscher (1996–7).

[122] For Akhaian *lieux de mémoire* at Mykenai see Paus. 2.16.6; at the Heraion 2.17. Str. 8.6.10 on epic personnel connected with Mykenai. Worship of the Atreids here postdates that at Sparta: J. Hall (1997) 91–3.

Figure 3.2 The *Argeia* seen from the Heraion at Prosymna, looking towards the sea; Larissa, the akropolis of Argos, can be perceived in the background to the right

the Persian Wars, an opportunity famously passed over by the Argives. The new temple at the Heraion at Prosymna built in the 460s by the Argive Eupolemos was decorated with scenes from the Trojan War.[123] Further powerful suggestions for Argos' keen adoption of the Atreid past comes from tragedy of the later fifth century. Not all plays set in the Plain deal with this issue in the same way; but it is overwhelmingly clear that the Heraion is a setting for tragic plots located in a city that is interchangeably called Argos or Mykenai.[124] Argos' desire to hijack the Mykenaian past during the fifth century cannot and should not be ignored.

The Atreid legacy emerges as extremely important to fifth-century Argos, though it is only one of many ways in which managing the traditions related to Hera's shrine supplied a web of connections steering diverse local traditions into the Argive hub, including Aeschylus' *Suppliant Women* and the lists of priestesses put together by the historian Akousilaos of Argos.[125] The culmination of the attempt to merge a number of these traditions in the command of *Argive* Hera over the Plain can be seen in Pindar's *Nemean 10*, possibly commissioned in the context of the inauguration of the new Heraion and the games of Hera, perhaps in the 460s BC.[126] This ode ruthlessly amalgamates the Argeia's heroic landscape, but this does not push the actual claims any closer to reality. Argos here is confidently Hera's 'house' (δῶμα l. 2), which assembles in it the heroic gallery of the synoikized Argeia. Danaos and his daughters head the procession, followed by the ambiguous Perseus and his adventures with the Gorgo, the Danaid Epaphos in Egypt, and Danaos' successor to the throne at Argos, Lynkeus; there follow Diomedes and Amphiaraos. The line continues in a female strand, with Alkmene (of Tiryns or Midea) and Danae, and turns to Adrastos and Amphitryon of the *Seven*. Pindar's mouth 'spills over' with all these heroic deeds, which he says 'the Argeion τέμενος' holds: this 'territory' is the area the Heraion guarded, the entire Plain, religiously recomposed and turned into the sacred precinct of Hera (Fig. 3.2).[127] That this ode expresses aspiration rather than reality is perhaps suggested by the fact that at around the same time a monumental dedication of the *Seven Against Thebes* still marked the Argive victory at the battle of Oinoe at

[123] D.S. 11.65; Paus. 2.17.3.

[124] See Saïd (1993) for a detailed account in plays set in the Argive Plain (Aesch. *Orest.*; *Suppl.*; Soph. *El.*; Eur. *El.*, *Or.*). These plays merge Argive religious traditions with those of the Eastern Plain; Apollo Lykeios strikingly occurs in those plays in which Apollo's share in driving Orestes mad is particularly pronounced, e.g. in the *Electra*. For the Heraion cf. Soph. *El.* 674. Euripides' *Temenidai* may also have had a role here. The issues are worth further exploration; see now Avezzù (2004). On the continuous ambiguity in later texts over whether Agamemnon and the Atreids lived in Mykenai or in Argos see e.g. Sinatra (1994) 94–5, who argues that Argos emerges with leadership at the collapse of the Mycenaean world, but Mykenai still boasts the better traditions.

[125] Aeschylus' *Supplices* of the 460s BC, where the Heraion also features, ties King Pelasgos' immigration policy into contemporary Argive concerns: see Bakewell (1997) on the *Supplices*' metic politics. The Argive historian Akousilaos's catalogue of priestesses must have pooled the shrine's past personnel into something local to Argos: *FGrH* 4 F 28; Pherec. *FGrH* 3 F 114 (cf. Calame (2004) on the catalogue and its role in local history).

[126] For the date of this ode see von Wilamowitz-Moellendorff (1922) 426; Bowra (1964) 411; 147–8.

[127] Pi. *N.* 10.1–20.

around 460 BC, fought between Argives and Athenians on one side and Sparta on the other. By the fourth century, *Nemean 10*'s set of heroes and heroines, adding Elektryon and a few other holders of the Argive *khora*, had taken on that role when they were erected facing the *Seven* on the other side of Delphi's sacred road.[128]

What can we conclude from these apparent reformulations of the Argeia through myth and ritual in song and dance? I have argued above how Apollo Pythaieus tied the cities in the eastern Argolid to Argos and into a religious community by appealing to a long-standing, multi-layered, and shared tradition designed to keep out the Spartans (pp. 154–60). The case is similar in the Plain, though not identical. Though the Plain's history is all too short and its past eradicated by the lasting Argive synoikism, there are intriguing traces indicating that what the Eastern Plain did not share with Argos, it shared with Sparta. Unlike Argos, Mykenai and Tiryns side with the Peloponnesian League during the Persian Wars. Some have attributed their enthusiasm for the Greek cause to the weakness of Argos' elites after Sepeia, and this may well be true. But more relevantly, like their later destruction and/or incorporation into Argos, a participation in the Persian Wars implies animosities between them and Argos which were certainly not mitigated by the Spartans.[129]

The world of cult again suggests that there may have been more to this sympathy than historical narrative reveals, leading us to suspect that Sparta and the Eastern Plain were closely linked. This concerns the three of the religious figureheads singled out for cult song above: Herakles, invisible at Argos until the mid-fifth century, is conspicuous elsewhere in the Peloponnese, and notably of course in Lakonia. Hera Argeia, too, is in evidence at Sparta at least in Pausanias' times, with a shrine related to Akrisios, the Tirynthian. The seventh-century throne at Amyklai depicts the goddess's issue with the heroine Io who later became Hera's first priestess.[130] Perseus is intriguingly present in Lakonia and Messenia. An obscure character Sparton, father of Mykenos, had his grave at Mykenai and was interesting enough to be mentioned by Akousilaos of Argos, the fifth-century logographer who also in other respects meshed the Plain's mythical figures.[131] Then, the Dioskouroi. Widespread in the Greek world, in the Peloponnese the Spartan Tyndarids seem to have eliminated the traditions of all other Peloponnesian twins, except that the Argives preserved their own mythology for them. But *Nemean 10* recounts their Spartan aetiology in the context of the Heraion's fantastical heroic produce. Presenting them as guest-friends of

[128] Paus. 10.10.3–5; see Bommelaer (1991) nos. 112 and 113 for the two monuments.

[129] On Argive control (or not) of the cities in the Plain in the archaic period see Piérart (1997); cf. Koerner (1987). Tiryns and Mykenai in the Persian Wars: Hdt. 7.202; Paus. 2.16.5 (Thermopylai); Hdt. 9.28 (Plataiai); their names on the serpent column: *Syll.*[3] 31 = ML 27.6, 7.

[130] Paus. 3.13.8; 18.3. Cf. Orestes at Troizen: 2.31.4, 8.

[131] A tradition not much liked by the Spartans, as this figure was also brother, son, or nephew to Phoroneus: Akousilaos *apud* Paus. 2.16.4; Herodian *De Pros. Cath.* 36.17 Lentz; *Σ* Eur. *Or.* 1246; St. Byz. s.v. *Μυκῆναι*; Eust. *Il.* 446.28–30.

Tirynthian Pamphaes could be seen to postulate their move from the Akhaian-Lakonian Plain to Dorian Argos.[132]

And finally, there is the conspicuously bolstered Akhaian/Atreid tradition, not all that visible at Argos prior to the fifth century. It has recently been suggested that the reworking of this myth might have been initiated not in the Argolid, but in Lakonia, where worship at the Agamemnoneion occurs exceptionally early. But it is perhaps less relevant in our context to establish where the roots of this tradition lay than to point out the apparent impossibility of placing it locally at all. However, a shared leadership of Lakonian Menelaos and Mykenaian Agamemnon suggests Sparta had more in common with Mykenai and Tiryns than these cities had with Argos. The fact that Orestes cannot be located with exactitude, meandering as he does between Mykenai, Arkadia, and Sparta, perhaps indicates a common, rather than competitive, relationship between these Peloponnesian places prior to the appearance of the Argives on the scene—at which point a claim to Orestes' Argive identity also occurs.[133]

Dorian Sparta, as is well known, invests heavily in an Akhaian heritage in the course of the sixth century at the latest to justify its leadership in the Peloponnese.[134] As already mentioned, at this time Argives visibly invested in the memory of the *Seven against Thebes*. It is difficult to say whether these were mutually prompted strategies, each designed to use the past to establish a set of power relations in the present. But it is without a doubt that the Spartans' strategy in adopting the—more recent—warriors at Troy was ultimately more successful in bolstering their position in the Peloponnese. Would it be too bold to suggest that Argive song-dance in the fifth century is aimed at cultivating those myth-ritual traditions that Argos, the maritime hub traditionally orientated towards the *Akte*, Egypt, and perhaps even Asia Minor, had either previously disregarded, or had not been very successful at appropriating? That it chose to counter Sparta, as it were, in the terms that Sparta had adopted, rather than the ones it had invented for itself, that is to say, the *Seven*? This certainly squares nicely with the peculiarities that we have observed at Argos, with regard to their differently construed past; and takes much further the view that an *Argive* plain cannot really be taken for granted in the early period.[135]

[132] For the Argive aetiology see Paus. 2.22.6, mentioning their sons and the wives of these; Plut. *QG* 296e–f, where Kastor is 'half a founder' (mixarchegetes) of Argos. For the cult see n. 110 above.

[133] J. Hall (1997) 91–2 on a supposed Lakonian origin of the Akhaian myth, n. 126 on the Lakonian Agamemnoneion. The Spartans (and some lyric authors) place the Atreids, esp. Orestes, at Amyklai: Stesich. *PMG* 216; Pi. *P.* 11.15–37; *N.* 11.34–5; *Σ* Eur. *Or.* 46; Paus. 3.19.6; cf. 2.16.6, where he received cultic honours after his bones had been brought from Tegea: Hdt. 1.65–7.

[134] The literature on this subject is vast. I quote selectively: Cartledge (1979) 139; Osborne (1996) 287–91; very detailed Giangiulio (1989) 205 n. 140; cf. Boedeker (1993); Malkin (1994) 26–34 specifically on the transferral of the bones of Orestes; Parker (1998*a*) for Spartan split identity between Dorians and Akhaians. For 'Argive' Orestes see e.g. Eur. *Or. passim.*

[135] Which is a view propounded by J. Hall (1995); Piérart (1997) maintains the view of an Argeia largely dependent on Argos.

A RECONFIGURED SACRED LANDSCAPE

When in 418 BC the ephemeral, Spartan-supported oligarchy at Argos is overthrown and the Argives return to democracy, Sparta is busy celebrating the Gymnopaidiai at home. The news of the anti-Spartan rebellion arrives on Apollo Pythaieus' Spartan Dancing Floor, the *Khoros*, and the festival is put on hold. But the envoys sent to Argos come too late, democracy is already back on track, and the pro-Spartan oligarchs have fled to Phleious, that place favouring Herakles' claim to have founded the Nemean Games over Argive Adrastos'. The Spartans resume their dancing for Apollo Pythaieus at the Gymnopaidiai, as if... the Battle of the Champions had only just been won.[136]

There may well be little to this coincidence of a loaded festival at a tense moment of the Spartano-Argive relationship. But it nicely illustrates the unifying Spartan factor in Argos' fifth-century dealings with both the *Argeia* and the *Akte*, and that, rather than being seen in isolation, these dealings must be understood in the light of the competition over leadership in the Peloponnese. At the same time, the episode pointedly illustrates the relationship between the Spartan issue and Argos' internal democratic reforms, just as Pausanias had commented, while all of this is neatly situated in a context of religious song and dance.

But the flowing together of Argos' fifth-century whereabouts in this affair also makes clear how intricately interlinked the matters of the *Argeia* and *Akte* were. Singing for Apollo Pythaieus against such a complex and highly charged background in an early or mid-fifth-century performance must inevitably have been an audacious and confident move on the part of the Argives. When set against the activities in the Plain, a case for Bacchylides' paean's *khoros* assuming an important role in the delicate relationship between Argos and the cities in the *Akte* in this period, as suggested above, acquires yet more force. Argives took their standing amongst their neighbours in the eastern Argolid very seriously indeed and in no way dissociated it from their undertakings in the Plain. Tying Argeia and Akte into a shared set of traditions—offsetting the eastern Argolid's different past—might have been an Argive concern that Apollo Pythaieus' *khoros* helped to formulate. If Melampous comes to Asine to found the cult, this is one of the few instances in which the line of the future *Seven against Thebes* intrudes into the Dryopian world. Akousilaos, the Argive mythographer, saw fit to turn Dryops—formerly a descendant of Arkadian Arkas—into Danaos' son, relegating Dryopian antiquity to the junior position. Had Argives finally been successful in joining the different pasts that surrounded them?[137]

The massive orchestration of Apollo Pythaieus' festival, celebrated in Bacchylides' song for a cult whose only other literary attestation is Thucydides, suggests that the scrappy chants investigated here are probably just the loft of a

[136] Th. 5.82.2–3. Above I associate this festival with Spartano-Argive rivalry carried out through the cult of Apollo Pythaieus.

[137] Acus. *FGrH* 2 F 24 = Paus. 2.16.3.

monumental musical edifice through which whole new landscapes kept being construed and reconstrued. When we embed the less well-preserved cult songs of this chapter's second half into the wider myth-ritual framework of the Argolid, glimpses are caught of what must have been an intense interrelation between song-dance and contemporary local history—political, social, and cultural. Although only in the case of the two dithyrambs can we pin down another myth-ritual nexus in its specifically choral detail, even the songs for which that relationship cannot be clearly established contribute to the overall picture. The performances flesh out Argos' patchy and enigmatic political narrative, clustering around a few central episodes, and reveal a lively and complicated local scene changing gradually rather than radically over the whole course of the fifth century. Performances of myth and ritual, with their ability to suggest new social realities for traditional worshipping groups, may well have embraced these developments. If as many as six songs were indeed to have survived for Argos in this period, this is as much a testimony to the effectiveness of this kind of religious event as to the quantity of change it delineates.

If all these reconstructions are at least correct in essence, the Plain was synoikized by pooling its myths and rituals, Apollo Pythaieus forged the Akte's cities back into a long-standing community by parading difference rather than denying it. If Pausanias said much later that at this time in their history the Argives synoikized in order to enlarge their city to withstand the Spartans, certainly the apparatus of ancestors escorting them now became larger than Spartan life! Perhaps it is for this reason that, when negotiating the renewal of the Spartan–Argive truce in 421 BC, the Argives mark their unswerving aspirations to leadership in the Peloponnese by suggesting what the Spartans then consider a foolish idea: a rerun of the event that Apollo Pythaieus had won for both Spartans and Argives, the Battle of the Champions, landmark of the eternal rivalry between these two Dorian cities.[138]

[138] Th. 5.41; for the Spartans this is *μωρία* ('nonsense'; 41.3).

4

Locality and Panhellenism: Aiginetan Myth and Delphic Ritual

καὶ ἐὰν ἐν Αἰγίνῃ ἐπὶ τοῦ Διὸς τοῦ Ἑλλανίου νεφέλη καθίζηται, ὡς τὰ πολλὰ ὕδωρ γίνεται.[1]

(Theophr. *Sign.* 1.24)

To the present day the cloud on Aigina's Mount Oros is used as an indicator of rain, desperately sought during certain periods of the year. One would be hard-pressed to consider this a subtle piece of weather forecasting, and yet it is the rain from these clouds that has made this Zeus an active god. The ancient cult-site, today occupied by the little chapel *Η Όμορφη Εκκλησία* and commanding a splendid view across the entire Saronic Gulf, has always been a place of worship tightly linked to the geography in which it dwells: the mountain-top position, on the highest of Aigina's rocky summits, has rendered Zeus Hellanios an obvious port of call when rain was desired, but the thundering god's powers also empowered his worshippers, the Aiginetans. Its ancient aetiological legend, linking the cult to the whereabouts of the island's most prominent local hero, Aiakos, son of Zeus, makes the first known case for this continuity:

τοῦτο μὲν γὰρ Αἰακὸς ὁ Διὸς μὲν ἔκγονος, τοῦ δὲ γένους Τευκριδῶν πρόγονος, τοσοῦτον διήνεγκεν ὥστε γενομένων αὐχμῶν ἐν τοῖς Ἕλλησιν καὶ πολλῶν ἀνθρώπων διαφθαρέντων ἐπειδὴ τὸ μέγεθος τῆς συμφορᾶς ὑπερέβαλλεν, ἦλθον οἱ προεστῶτες τῶν πόλεων ἱκετεύοντες αὐτὸν, νομίζοντες διὰ τῆς συγγενείας καὶ τῆς εὐσεβείας τῆς ἐκείνου τάχιστ' ἂν εὑρέσθαι παρὰ τῶν θεῶν τῶν παρόντων κακῶν ἀπαλλαγήν. σωθέντες δὲ καὶ τυχόντες ἁπάντων ὧν ἐδεήθησαν, ἱερὸν ἐν Αἰγίνῃ κατεστήσαντο κοινὸν τῶν Ἑλλήνων, οὗπερ ἐκεῖνος ἐποιήσατο τὴν εὐχήν.

In the first place Aiakos, son of Zeus and ancestor of the family of the Teukridai, was so distinguished that when a drought visited the Greeks and many people had perished, and when the magnitude of the calamity had passed all bounds, the leaders of the cities came as suppliants to him; for they thought that, by reason of his kinship with Zeus and his piety, they would most quickly obtain from the gods relief from the woes that afflicted them. Having gained their desire, they were saved and built in Aigina a temple to be shared by all the Greeks on the very spot where he had offered his prayer. (Isocrates 9.14–15, tr. Norlin)

[1] 'And when on Aigina a cloud sits on Zeus Hellanios, generally there is rain.' Cf. such weather deities on Mount Lykaion in Arkadia, or on Hymettos above Athens: Langdon (1976); A. Cook (1964–5) i. 63–99; ii.2 894 n. 3; Burkert (1983) 84–93; (1985) 130; 266.

The cult of Zeus Hellanios, the god with whose help Aiakos rescued Greece from famine, was, despite the epithet's suggestion, no great Panhellenic gathering place along the lines of Delos, Delphi, or Olympia. Aiakos, born of Zeus' union with the island-nymph Aigina, was viewed as the ancestor of the historical Aiginetans. That a hero who is intimately tied to one particular locality should found a local cult is not surprising; that he should set about establishing a cult centre whose 'Hellenic' character is not attested outside this legend is somewhat more unusual. The myth, exceptionally, shows little or no variation in the many texts attesting it. Pausanias, for instance, adds that the Greek mission to Aiakos had been motivated by an oracle; he interestingly delineates the area concerned as the Peloponnese and the 'land outside the Isthmos' (τὴν ἐκτὸς ἰσθμοῦ χώραν), and that this god was *Pan*Hellenios, but for the rest does little to cause controversy. Aiakos' cult foundation on behalf of the Greeks to lift a drought is curiously uncontested, as if for once all Greeks agreed. All Greeks? Not quite: Diodorus knows that the drought continued at Athens even after the supposed establishment of the cult, and this will be significant.[2]

This interesting aetiological configuration of the Aiginetan local hero who acts to the benefit of a fictitious Panhellenic worshipping community will be the topic of this chapter. The myth of Aiakos the Aiginetan drought-lifter, with the implied aetiology of Zeus Hellanios, recurs frequently in early fifth-century Aiginetan songs. In *Nemean 8* Aiakos appears as adviser for the 'best of the neighbouring leaders' (ἡρώων ἄωτοι περιναιεταόντων) who regularly came to see him—and these are then qualified as the Athenians and Spartans. In *Nemean 5* Aiakos' sons are standing at Zeus' altar praying for the island to become a land of 'brave men and famous for its sailings' (εὔανδρόν τε καὶ ναυσικλυτάν).[3] Above all, the cult and its founder feature in Pindar's *Paean 6*. This is a song—undated like all the others—composed 'for the Delphians in honour of Apollo' (Δελφοῖς εἰς Πυθώ), and was, the paean implies while the scholia tell us explicitly, performed at the Delphic Theoxenia. So the ritual performance context is Panhellenic. But the greater part of the paean is devoted to recounting the deeds of Aiakos and his sons. In particular, in the last triad Aigina is invoked as the 'splendid star of Zeus Hellanios', as if the island and its god were the addressee of the cult song (l. 123–61, see Section 2 below for the text).

Zeus Hellanios' appearance in the paean has been taken as a hint on how to fill a gap in the text likely to have contained the aetiological myth explaining the nature of the festival at which the paean was performed. A lengthy beginning (ll.1–61) revolving around poet and performance context leads into a passage smoothly connecting ritual present with mythical past (ll. 62–73).

[2] Paus. 2.29.7–8; cf. 1.44.9, explaining the Panhellenic Greek mission to Aiakos decorating the Aiakeion and not alluding to the end of the aetiological myth until later, at 2.30.4; Σ Pi. *N.* 5.17b; *N.* 8.19a; *Pae.* 6.125; Apollod. 3.12.6; Clem. Al. *Strom.* 6.3.28.4–6 p. 753; Σ Ar. *Equ.* 1253a, b and next note. Athens: D.S. 4.61.

[3] Pi. *N.* 8.9–12; *N.* 5.9–13.

ἔρα[ται] δέ μο[ι]
γλῶσσα μέλιτος ἄῳτον γλυκὺν [⏑ ⏑ – –
ἀγῶνα Λοξίᾳ καταβάντ' εὐρὺν
  ἐν θεῶν ξενίᾳ.
θύεται γὰρ ἀγλαᾶς ὑπὲρ Πανελ-
  λάδος, ἅν τε Δελφῶν
ἔθ[ν]ος εὔξατο λι-
  μοῦ θ̣[⏑ – ⏑ – ⏑ – –
ἐκδι̣[⏑ – ⏑ – – ⏑ –
φιλει[⏑ – – ⏑ ⏑ – ⏑ ⏑ ⏑ –
Κρόν[ιε ⏑ ⏑ ⏑ – ⏑ ⏑ –
  πρύτα̣[νι ⏑ – – ⏑ ⏑ –
τοὶ πα[⏑ – – ⏑ – ⏑ ⏑ ⏑ ⏑ –
χρησ[τ]η̣[ρι – ⏑ ⏑ – ⏑ – –
  Πυ]θωνόθ[εν – ⏑ – –
καί ποτε [⏑ ⏑ – – ⏑ ⏑ – ⏑ ⏑ – –

My tongue longs (to sing?) the sweet essence of honey . . . having come to the broad gathering for Loxias in the guest-feast of the gods.
For sacrifice is made on behalf of splendid Pan-Hellas, which the race of the Delphians prayed (to be relieved?) of famine . . . son of Kronos . . . ruler . . . they who . . . oracle . . . from Pytho. And once . . . (Pindar, *Paean* 6.58–73 = D6 Ruth, tr. Race)

The lines reveal the ritual setting: *ἐν θεῶν ξενίᾳ* gives away the festival of the Theoxenia. In typically cult-aetiological manner (pp. 29–31 above), the text glides from depicting the present ritual context into the past mythical narrative through a relative clause (ll. 63–5). A reference to the aetiological myth for Zeus Hellanios in this missing *aition* is attractive and plausible. A *λιμός* (ll. 64–5), it was hoped, would be warded off by the word that followed. Zeus is involved, and is possibly invoked in a prayer as *Κρόνιε* (l. 68); *πρύτανις* (l. 69) is used for Zeus by Pindar in other places in combination with his Kronid ancestry.[4] Then there is mention of an oracle *χρησ[τ]η̣[ρι* (l. 71) that someone seems to have received from Delphi *Πυ]θωνόθ[εν*.[5] The supplement *τοὶ πα[ν* suggested for line 70 may refer to the assembled Greeks beseeching Aiakos, and is as sensible as any other attempt to reconstruct the passage.[6] Discontinuous narrative, distorting the myth's chronology, is a recurrent feature of Pindaric myth-telling and should not worry us here. It has sometimes been pointed out that the Delphian *ἔθνος* has no role in the antiquarian tradition of the myth. This may, but need not, be a valid argument: in involving the Delphians, the song may pick up the Pausanian detail by which the leaders of the Greeks consulted Aiakos on oracular advice. A part for them to play in a song performed at Delphi 'for the Delphians' is likely.

[4] Pi. *P.* 6.23–5.
[5] Cf. *P.* 5.105–7.
[6] The grounds given in their support do not make the more conservative readings *Πάνθοο[ς* or *πᾶν θο[ός* as an epithet for Achilles preferable (Radt (1958) 134–8).

Though a reconstruction along these lines is plausible, there is ultimately no way of telling what filled the lacuna in the text. What is more interesting is that, independently of whether the myth featured, the paean deliberately forges an association of the ritual of the Theoxenia with the aetiological myth of Zeus Hellanios, not least suggested by generous quotation from Aiginetan myth in the rest of the song. In what follows, I shall disentangle the intricacies of a choral performance which can be seen to fuse the Panhellenic ritual and the local Aiginetan myth. This association gives us an important key to understanding the song and the role played by its performance in the historical context of early fifth-century Greece, where locality and Panhellenism were constantly charted against each other.

Of Pindar's cult poetry, *Paean 6* has received fuller attention than any other, and this is due to the perceived problem of the treatment of the hero Neoptolemos, amongst the descendants of Aiakos.[7] Who performed it is another much-debated question; many scholars have thought that this poem could not, despite the explicit reference to the Delphians in the title, have been performed by anyone other than the Aiginetans themselves. Similarly, the discovery that the paean's last triad praising Aigina, circulated at some point independently as a *prosodion* to Aiakos, stresses the importance of the Aiginetan angle of the paean, and has instantly prompted new treatments of the song's circumstances of performance. But the flurry of scholarship is still grappling with the paradox described, the juxtaposition of locality and Panhellenism in myth and ritual, and its historical implications.[8]

How exactly the problem is configured emerges when one looks in greater detail at what the paean itself tells us about the relation between ritual setting and mythical narrative. The Theoxenia had a prominent place in the Delphic festival calendar, indicated among other things by the existence of a Delphic month *Theoxenios* (March/April), but although the event is reasonably well attested, its role in the Delphic religious cycle is not much illuminated.[9] Pindar himself, in the passage quoted above, tells us that in this festival 'sacrifice was made for all of Greece' (*θύεται . . . ὑπὲρ Πανελλάδος*, ll. 62–3). A Panhellenic character also transpires in Philodamos' paean, composed for the same festival in around

[7] See nn. 35 and 36 below.

[8] Radt (1958); Käppel (1992); Burnett (1998); Rutherford (2001) 298–338; Kurke (2005); Currie (2005) 322–5. The discussion over who sang the paean illustrates well the extent of the 'Aiginetan' problem: von Wilamowitz-Moellendorff (1922) 134–5 thinks of an Aiginetan chorus, as do Wüst (1967) 134 and Hoekstra (1962), who surmises that Aigina had a traditional claim for performing the chorus at the Theoxenia but was prevented on this occasion because of Athenian–Aiginetan conflicts in the mid-460s BC. Fogelmark (1972) 132 hoped for 'a contemporary text that will show beyond doubt that not only the Aiginetans but other communities as well were entitled to order Paeans to be performed at the Delphic Theoxenia'. For the last triad as a *prosodion* to Aiakos see Rutherford (1997); (2001) 323–31, and the use made of this by Kurke (2005), thinking of a double *khoros* performing the paean.

[9] Samuel (1972) 73–4; for the Delphic calendar see Pomtow, *RE* iv (1901) 2532, s.v. 'Delphoi'. For studies of the Theoxenia see n. 20 below.

340/339 BC and possibly inaugurating Philip of Makedon's new temple of Apollo at Delphi. This invokes the god with 'universal prayers of a blessed Greece' (*σὺν Ἑλλάδος ὀλβίας πανδήμοις ἱκετείαις*).[10] From Pindar's scholiast we gather what *Ἑλλὰς ὀλβία* was expecting from the god. The annual Panhellenic efforts were performed *περὶ εὐετηρίας*.[11] *Εὐετηρία* means 'good season' or 'rich crop', as if the springtime Delphic Theoxenia were a festival aimed at a good harvest later in the year.[12] Incidentally, the Roman version of the rite, the so-called Lectisternia, always followed a pan-Roman agricultural crisis—plague or famine—perhaps complementing Pindar's scholiast for the motives of the Greek festival.[13] Apollo is therefore worshipped with a paean, so that he may avert natural catastrophe from his devotees. Paeans had a marked role at the Theoxenia, and only the Delia can boast more surviving cult songs composed for one single festival. Pindar's paean is the earliest piece, followed by a host of others, of which Philodamos, was one. Poets such as Kleokhares, Limenios, and an anonymous Athenian are all known to have put up good paean shows in Hellenistic times. The poets were rewarded with a striking number of privileges, suggesting that their songs did something for the gathered cult community of Greeks.[14]

Despite this Panhellenic context, in what follows after the notional cult aetiology the paean only talks about Aiakos and the Aiakids as the mythical ancestors of the Aiginetans, as if this were a victory song for a local athlete and not one for a god in his all-Greek cult centre (ll. 79–183). This is intriguing because, for a start, the Aiakids' Aiginetan allegiance cannot necessarily be taken for granted; they had ties equally to Central Greece, especially Thessaly.[15]

[10] Philod. Scarph. 113–14, with Stewart (1982).

[11] *Σ* Pi. *Pae.* 6.62 ff.: [< 15] . [. . . .]ητ . τὴ̣ν Ἑλλάδα [< 20]περὶ ε[ὐ]ετηρίας [< 20]α̣ν̣, ἃ̣ς̣ καὶ μέχρι [τοῦ νῦν < 7] ἑκάστ[ο]υ ἔτους [~ ?] 'Hellas . . . about "good harvest" . . . which to [this day they perform] every year'. For the sense of the relative clause see e.g. Snell: *θυσίας ἔθυσαν ἃς καὶ μέχρι νῦν θύουσιν ἑκάστου ἔτους* 'they offered sacrifices which they perform annually to this day'. Cf. Philodamos 149: *πᾶσαν [Ἑλ]λάδ' ἀν' ὀ[λβί]αν* 'for all of blessed Greece'.

[12] See LSJ s.v. The word can be used in a strict agricultural sense, often contrasted with *limos* (e.g. Arist. *HA* 601^{b}; Theophr. *HP* 6.24.9; 8.8.2; Poll. 1.51–3), with the meaning of 'good season' (Hsch. *E* 6810 s.v.), but also to denote ensuing social welfare (*Suda* σ 3447 s.v. *εὐετηρία· εὐθηνία, εὐνομία, εἰρήνη, τὸ καλῶς διακεῖσθαι* 'blossom, good law, peace, to be in a good state'); and moreover referring to a functioning local economy, often faciliated by euergetism, e.g. D. 4.49; 69; D.H. 7.20.1; 9.26.9; Philo, *De Spec. Leg.* 203 etc.

[13] The Roman Lectisternia seem to be one-off apotropaic occasions: Liv. 7.2.2 (*c.*364 BC); 7.27.1 (*c.*348 BC); 8.25.1 (*c.*326 BC); 22.10.9. See Deneken (1881) 1 f.; Wissowa (1912 (1902)) 421–3; Latte (1960) 242–4; Muth (1988) 264–7.

[14] Philodamos' paean (*CA* 165–71, the most recent text (B. L. Rainer, Ph.D. Illinois 1975)): Marchetti (1977); Stewart (1982); Calame (forthcoming); Kleokhares (230–225 BC): *Syll.*[3] 450 = *FD* iii.2 78.4–6 = *SEG* xxxii 540; Limenios: *Syll.*[3] 698C = *CA* 149–59 = *FD* iii.2 138 (129 BC); anonymous Athenian: *Syll.*[3] 698B = *FD* iii.2 137 = *CA* 141–8. The most careful analysis of the hymns on stone is by Bélis in *CID* iii; see Käppel (1992) 327–8; 355–6; 89–91 for short general discussions.

[15] The Aiakids are Aiakos' descendants and for the best part migrant heroes, all having also a home other than Aigina. The descendants of Peleus, Achilles and Neoptolemos are Thessalians, Telamon and his son Aias live on Salamis, and Phokos by virtue of his name does not remain a local. See p. 203 below. See Zunker (1988) and now Burnett (2005) 13–28.

However, the last triad of *Paean* 6 in particular is an ode to the island and contains extensive praise for these heroes in their Aiginetan guise, making it clear that the Aiakids here are, or are primarily, Aiginetans, hence also this part's existence as an independent poem. Such disproportionate devotion to the Aiakids in a cult song for Apollo seems even odder considering the fact that the Aiakids were the god's traditional enemies, due to their many misdeeds in the Trojan War, another Panhellenic mainstay. Apollo is praised here through the heroes who most of all undermined his power, and nowhere does the song miss the opportunity to point out Apolline–Aiakid enmity. Achilles, the main warrior of the Greeks at Troy, is killed by Apollo in the guise of Paris (*c.* ll. 78–91);[16] Neoptolemos incites the god's lasting hostility through sacrilege: he slew Priam at the altar of Zeus Herkeios. Promptly praise is showered upon Apollo for having killed Neoptolemos at Delphi (ll. 88 to 122). Aiakos, the ancestor of the race, famously helped Poseidon and Herakles build Troy's first walls but built them thinly; his piece of wall proved permeable to snakes, anticipating his descendants' destruction of the later city. Somewhere in the lacunose but lengthy story of Aiakos (*c.*ll. 140–56) this problem may well also have featured.[17]

Paradoxically, in the concluding lines, the tables are turned and the paean ends, after all this slandering of heroes, by lavishly praising the Aiakids and their *polis* Aigina.

]ι̣ μυρία[ ]ό̣γοι
τῶν γε δο̣[ρικτ]ύπων[. . .]ειν ἀπείρονας ἀρετὰς
Αἰακ]ι̣δᾶν· φ[ιλεῖ]τ̣ε
. . .]ι̣ πόλιν πατρίαν, φί-
λεῖτε] δ̣' εὔφ[ρον]α̣ λαὸν
τόνδ̣ε̣ καὶ στεφάνοισί νιν
πανθαλέος ὑγιε[ίας] σκιάζετε· Μοισᾶν
ἐ̣παβολέ̣οντ̣[α] πολλάκι, Παιάν, δέ-
ξ'] ἐννόμων ἐ̣[νοπ]ᾶν.

Spear-clashing, boundless virtues of the Aiakidai. Love . . . your home city, love this kind people . . . and shade them over with garlands of all-blooming health. Receive Paian, one often having the harmonious tunes of the Muses. (Pindar, *Paean* 6.175–83 =D6 Ruth cf. D'Alessio and Ferrari (1988))

A Panhellenic ritual featuring near-exclusively local Aiginetan myth in which abusing the Aiakids culminates in their excessive praise: it is hard to think that this could make sense. By quoting extensively from Aiginetan myth, the song suggests that the Aiakidai had an important role in the Panhellenic Theoxenia.[18]

[16] Apollo's arrow kills, or is prophesied to kill, Achilles in *Il.* 21.277–8; Aesch. fr. 350; Soph. *Phil.* 334–5; Eur. *Andr.* 52–3; Paris kills him together with Apollo in *Il.* 22.358–60; *Aith.* arg. 15–16 Bernabé; Apollod. *Epit.* 5.3; Hyg. 107, 113; cf. *LIMC* i.1/2 (1981), s.v. no. 851 (an Apolline Paris and Apollo).

[17] Cf. Aiakos in Pi. *O.* 8.31–46; cf. *I.* 5.34–8.

[18] Currie (2005) 331–40 develops the attested links between Aigina and Delphi among other things through *Pae.* 6, to argue for a performance of *N.* 7 in the Aiginetan *thearion*. The ode's victor's father Thearion may have been involved in the administration of Aiginetan *theoria* to Delphi: 333–8.

Why should that be the case? The riddle may be solved by examining the dynamic produced by the interaction of myth and ritual in this paean. We need to take seriously the paean's own suggestion: as we have seen, religious choral song regularly features narrative either strictly aetiological, or immediately pertinent to its ritual setting. So either *Paean 6* is a tantalizing exception to the general rule, or myth and ritual in this song do cooperate, but do so in a different way. And this is what I shall proceed to argue.

In unfolding the relationship between the Panhellenic festival and local Aiginetan myths I shall demonstrate how *Paean 6* construes a claim of Aiakid importance for the festival and its worshipping community. This it does firstly by exploring the Theoxenia's pretensions as a Panhellenic festival, particularly through its presentation of the story of Neoptolemos' relationship with Apollo. Secondly, the paean exploits the aetiological myth of Zeus Hellanios' cult on Aiginetan Oros for the ritual context of the Theoxenia through their shared associations—notably the Panhellenic soundings and the common goal of *eueteria* 'good crop'. It merges Aiginetan myth and Theoxenic ritual in choral performance and turns Zeus' aetiology into that of the Theoxenia. Aiakos the drought-lifter will be one crucial hinge in forging that association, providing a 'good crop' by lifting the 'pan-Greek' famine.

The intriguing implication in an actual early fifth-century situation is that Aiginetans had a significant part to play in what the Theoxenia aimed for: the 'good crop' for 'all of Greece'. This is an extraordinary assertion which as I shall argue seeks to establish a role for Aigina in a post-Persian War world led, increasingly, by imperial Athenians who might have thought this role be better given to them. In a Panhellenic performance context at Delphi, for which this paean was composed, this is a powerful claim to make: such a vision for the celebrative community of the Theoxenia, as the assembled Greeks, as we shall see, is itself a combative and questionable assertion.

As it will turn out, *Paean 6* stands right at the centre of a heated contemporary debate on the nature of Panhellenism, and what its consequences are for Greece's *eueteria*. This debate contrasts different social and economic visions for Greece, and sets out the role of individual localities within them. It forms part of a much broader contemporary controversy amongst the Greek cities on what their world should look like in the early fifth century, glimpses of which, on local identity and citizenship in the context of the Delian League, we have already been able to perceive in Chapter 2 on Delian performances. *Paean 6* thereby challenges views which argue for a geographically, socially, and culturally unified sense of Greekness developing in the context, and aftermath, of the Persian Wars, and corrects the (ancient and modern) Athenocentrism underlying such interpretations. The paean provides an impressive example of the interaction of local myth and Panhellenic ritual, and the *communitas* created through their association. Through the blending of myth and ritual in performance this *khoros* expresses claims of which on a first view few traces survive in historical narrative; but, on a second, Greek local traditions are full of details suggesting that the paean's visions were deeply rooted in reality, building the case for *why you cannot argue with this song.*[19]

1. HELLENICITY AND THE DELPHIC THEOXENIA

The Delphic Theoxenia

What else is known about the Theoxenia, the Panhellenic gathering to do with *eueteria*? The Delphic festival seems to be the large-scale extension of a ritual type of the simple description ἡ ξενία or its derivations that has only recently received the attention it deserves.[20] Traditionally held to be a rite, marginal as well as inferior to the standard Greek ritual practice revolving around *thysia*, burnt animal sacrifice, *xenia* is really a different form of sacrifice and has its own special dynamics. What *thysia* and *xenia* share is ritual commensality, a salient feature of Greek religion and central to the way in which ritual shapes worshipping communities; however, the two types of sacrificial ritual seem to achieve this in different ways.

In traditional *thysia* rites, certain parts of the sacrifice are burnt on the altar for the gods; the choicer bits, according to Prometheus' most significant of religious aetiologies, are roasted for consumption by humans; preferred parts are often divided up among the cult personnel or selected participants in the procession, rarely among others. Characteristically, in many of these rituals involving burnt animal sacrifice, the world full of gods is kept well apart from that of men; it is human feasting that this is really about, confirming the often-claimed imbalance of reciprocity between gods and humans in ritual. He who ate was amongst those—sometimes a select few—whom the cult embraced; human feasting could be a privilege and highly exclusive; not infrequently those who ate were also those in power.[21]

The theoxenic rite professed different attitudes, both to the gods and to the humans it sought to involve. It entailed offering ξενία to the gods by inviting

[19] Bloch (1974) pp. 49–51 above, 36–7 for Turner, 39–40 for the creative *communitas*. For recent views on (Pan)Hellenism see, among many others, J. Hall (2002) esp. Ch. 6, preceded by Harrison (2000); E. Hall (1989); Georges (1994). For the older views on Greek identity in connection with the Persian Wars see J. Hall ibid. 175 n. 10. See below, Sect. 2 for the full discussion.

[20] Jameson (1994); Kearns in *OCD* s.v. Older studies include Deneken (1881); Nilsson (1906/95) 160–2, 418–20; more recently Burkert (1985) 107, 213; Bruit (1984) 358–67; (1989); (1990) 170–2; Bruit-Zaidman (2005); see also Muth (1988) 265 n. 673; cf. Radt (1958) 83–4 (on Pi. *Pae.* 6) and based on that Käppel (1992) 55–6, 209–11.

[21] The inclusive Panathenaia are the exception to the general rule that public banqueting occurred only occasionally in the archaic and early classical periods, but still suggests that ritual commensality is exclusive, here including the Athenian democratic citizenry only (cf. *Σ* Pi. *O.* 7.152d for the distribution of meat at the Heraia at Argos); cf. Schmitt Pantel (1992). For the apparent relation to the Theoxenia, as exemplified in e.g. *IG* xii.5 129, 56–61 (Paros), see Bruit (1984) 358–61. On reciprocity in ritual see Parker (1998*b*).

them to a feast among humans. The language of furniture and hospitality in text and image, mentioning τράπεζαι and κλῖναι, suggests that gods attending were expected to behave just like any other dinner guest, to recline on duly covered 'couches' in order to eat from well-laid 'tables' placed beside them.[22] Normally a τράπεζα ('table') provided the space where the priest's or other officials' shares of the animal sacrifice ended up alongside lesser offerings, fruit and vegetables, cakes and cheeses.[23] 'Tables' are typically put up for minor deities who could thus be honoured in addition to the main god without proportionally raising the expenditure. Hence *xeniai* in their own right are generally thought of as minor religious occasions associated with heroes, especially the Dioskouroi and Herakles, as if lesser deities were more inclined to reside among humans than the Olympians.[24]

This is not the entire truth however. *Xenia* rites are attested in the context of large public festivals, and are often a central aspect of the ceremonies of major city gods such as Apollo or Dionysos. Apollo Theoxenios at Akhaian Pellene, for example, was honoured in a Theoxenia or Philoxenia, which involved contests at which χλαῖναι ('woollen garments') could be gained.[25] It follows that the rite was probably much more normal, and honoured a much wider spectrum of deities, than has previously been thought.[26] So the presence of a table need not indicate a moderate feast at all; quite the contrary: it seems that the best you can get as a god is combined *thysia*-and-table-offerings.

This at any rate appears to be the case with our Delphic Θεοξένια.[27] From a much-quoted passage of Polemon cited by Athenaios we know that the meat from that sacrifice ended up on the sacrificial table: whoever, at the *thysia*, brought the biggest onion (γηθυλλίς) to Apollo's mother Leto, was allowed to take a portion of meat from this table (μοῖρα).[28] But more importantly, this piece of

[22] Jameson (1994) 39–41. See Pi. *Σ O.* 3. inscr.

[23] Gill (1974), incorporated in the monograph (1991). On the division of meat see references in Jameson (1994) 56 n. 83.

[24] Jameson (1994) 44; Bruit (1990) 172. Collective ἡρωξένια '*xenia* of heroes' were yet another mode: Thasos (*LSS* 69 (late 3rd cent. BC)). Cf. Hsch. η 824 s.v. ἡρόχια; *Σ* Pi. *N.* 7.68 (see n. 106 below). *Xeniai* used to be believed to be less conspicuous, often enacted within private religious associations or individual families: Diomedon of Kos; *Lex Sacra* from Selinous (for which see Jameson (1994) 42–5); Kastor and Pollux at Akragas (Pi. *O.* 3.1–4; 38–41).

[25] Paus. 7.27.4; the same festival is known as Hermaia at Pellene: *Σ* Pi. *O.* 7.156c. Cf. *Σ O.* 9.146h; *Σ N.* 10.82a and b; *Σ O.* 13.155 names the festival Φιλοξένια.

[26] Known examples include feasts for Apollo, Dionysos, Zeus Soter and Athena Soteira, Athena on her own, the Twelve Gods, Asklepios, and others: Jameson (1994) 39–42. See also on Paros (2nd cent. BC): *IG* xii.5 129.57–8 for the Dioskouroi; Keos *IG* xii.5 544 B1, 2–3 (4th–3rd cent. BC); Tenos *IG* xii.5 872.117 (3rd cent. BC) mentions an association of Θεοξενιασταί.

[27] A *thysia* is attested in all passages relating to the Delphic Theoxenia: Pi. *Pae.* 6.62 (θύεται γάρ . . .); Philodamos e.g. line 112 θυ[σ]ίαν; Kleokhares *Syll.*[3] 450=*SEG* xxxii 540.3: αἴδωντι οἱ παῖδες τᾶι θυσίαι τῶν Θεοξενίων 'the boys sing at the sacrifice of the Theoxenia' and following note.

[28] Polemon, *Περὶ Σαμοθράκης* fr. 36 Preller = Ath. 9.372a: διατέτακται παρὰ Δελφοῖς τῇ θυσίᾳ τῶν Θεοξενίων, ὃς ἂν κομίσῃ γηθυλλίδα μεγίστην τῇ Λητοῖ λαμβάνειν μοῖραν ἀπὸ τῆς τραπέζης. The passage also suggests that all gods were involved in Apollo's *Theoxenia* at Delphi; cf. *Σ* Pi. *O.* 3 p. 105, 14–16 Dr.

antiquarianism indicates that the feasting community at the Delphic Theoxenia was carefully controlled. The suggestion is that there was competition for the *moira*, as if this was what allowed you to become part of the select few whom the god protected. By the same token, the competition, in which the prize could theoretically go to anyone, suggests that who belonged to this group was negotiable and not fixed, inclusive on the one hand, exclusive on the other.

Gaining access to Apollo at Delphi does in fact seem to lie at the heart of the Theoxenia festival. Certainly the shares from the table lent special status to those who obtained them, presumably marking their membership of the worshipping community. In an unusual attestation of phratry religion, the Delphic *Λαβυάδαι* partook of the theoxenic experience by being granted a place at the *θοίνη* ('banquet'). More relevantly, however, sacrificial shares in the feast were offered to the *theoroi*, the worshippers coming from all over Greece. The Delphians granted to the island of Skiathos' regular delegation the provision of standard equipment for a *θεωρία* on tour: salt, oil, vinegar, wood, and a *hestiatorion* but also, specifically, *μοῖραι* at the Theoxenia.[29] Pindar himself was believed to have taken part in ritual meals (though his portion remains unspecified), and his descendants were thought to have received a publicly announced share in a sacrifice (*ἡ καλὴ μερίς*), though the festival context is not explicit.[30]

Sacrificial shares are a topos in the traditions of Delphic ritual more generally, and culinary pleasure and having the god on your side seem to have been considered one and the same thing. The practice of *theoria*—in the loose sense of pilgrimage by either indviduals or state delegations—is likely to be the source of these traditions. The Delphians were proverbially fussy about who should have a *moira* and who should not, as is suggested by anecdotes about their greed when it came to the distribution of the sacrifice. These stories claim that whoever came to make a sacrifice at Delphi could be sure that the officiating priest would be surrounded by locals carrying *μάχαιραι*, sacrificial knives, with which they snatched the meat as soon as the entrails (*σπλάγχα*) of the victim were roasted (the signal that the holy part of the *thysia* was finished). The proverbial consequence was *Δελφοῖσι θύσας αὐτὸς ὀψωνεῖ κρέας* ('whoever sacrifices at Delphi will end up 'buying his own meat' or even 'eating fish'): whoever made their way to Delphi to sacrifice regularly came out of it without a share (*ἄμοιρον*) because of the great number of those dining at the ritual (*ἑστιώμενοι*), of which the most famous victim in the anecdotal tradition was Aesop. While superficially the caricature of the greedy Delphians perhaps addresses the economics of the sanctuary, the story also gives away that access to the god, membership in the

[29] Labyadai: *CID* i 9 = Osborne–Rhodes no. 1 D1 ff. Skiathos: *LSCGS* no. 41 esp. 26–34; see Amandry (1939) 192–214, esp. 209. Such arrangements were probably mutual: the Delphians when arriving on Delos also received salt, vinegar, oil, wood, and blankets; whenever Delphians arrived at their apoikia at Magnesia, they were hosted with a shelter, salt, oil, vinegar, lamps, beds, blankets, and tables (Semos of Delos *FGrH* 396 F 7; Arist. fr. 392 Rose = Ath. 4.173e–f). The supplement 31 *μοίρ]αν* is widely accepted.

[30] Plut. *De Ser. Num.* 557f–58a. Note the use of *ἀφαιροῦντες*. *Vit. Pind.* 15–16.

feasting community, could not just be taken for granted. The sanctuary was quite particular about who was an acceptable participant in its rites—an interesting observation for a cult centre that claims to be 'Panhellenic'.[31]

The problem addressed here is one of theoric reciprocity, whereby sanctuary and worshippers establish a working relationship with each other. That meat distribution is at the heart of their relationship is illustrated nicely by the concluding lines of the Delphian part of the *Homeric Hymn to Apollo*. The god himself prophesies his own cult's future as a theoric centre and firmly establishes an association between *theoria* specifically and the Delphian priest's sacrificial *μάχαιρα*.

> *δεξιτερῇ μάλ᾽ ἕκαστος ἔχων ἐν χειρὶ μάχαιραν*
> *σφάζειν αἰεὶ μῆλα· τὰ δ᾽ ἄφθονα πάντα παρέσται,*
> *ὅσσα κ᾽ ἐμοί ἀγάγωσι περικλυτὰ φῦλ᾽ ἀνθρώπων·*
> *νηὸν δὲ προφύλαχθε, δέδεχθε δὲ φῦλ᾽ ἀνθρώπων*
> *ἐνθάδ᾽ ἀγειρομένων κατ᾽ ἐμὴν ἰθύν τε μάλιστα*

Each of you must just keep a knife in this right hand and keep slaughtering sheep: they will be available in abundance, as many as the thronging peoples bring for me. Watch over my temple, and welcome the peoples as they gather here, and ⟨regard⟩ my will above all . . . (*Homeric Hymn to Apollo* 535–9, tr. West)

Addressed to Apollo's pristine Cretan priests, these lines suggest that Delphi's material survival depends entirely on its visitors from outside and their meat contributions, while it is the job of the locals to give hospitality to the incoming worshippers. The discrepancy between the stipulated reciprocity between sanctuary and the *theoroi* and the Delphians' actual or perceived behaviour in the anecdotal tradition is striking: as if who the Delphians chose as shareholders and who they did not were something of a constant issue in the sanctuary's life. Who was allowed to join the community of diners was not straightforward. Arrangements in the context of *theoria*, such as that between the Delphians and the Skiathians cited above, were not redundant, but an intrinsic part of the way in which a festival was made meaningful to those who attended; it was a way to regulate participation.

It is plausible, then, that the distribution of shares, as well as its associated tales, played a role in establishing a worshipping community where it was not

[31] Plut. *Quaest. Conv.* 709a; cf. Kock, Adesp. 460 = App. prov. 1.95: *ἐπὶ τῶν πολλὰ μὲν δαπανώντων, μηδενὸς δὲ ἀπολαυόντων. Παρόσον τοὺς ἐν Δελφοῖς θύοντας συνέβαινε διὰ τὸ πλῆθος τῶν ἑστιωμένων αὐτοὺς μηδενὸς γεύεσθαι* 'this is about those who go to much expense, and get nothing out of it, as happened to those sacrificing at Delphi who because of the great number of dining guests did not get to taste anything themselves'. Aesopus: *POxy.* 1800, fr. 2.33–46 = Aesop. *Test.* 25: *ἐπὰν [εἰσέ]λ̣θῃ τις τῷ θεῷ θυσιάσ̣[ων οἱ Δελφοὶ̣ περ[ι]εστήκασιν τὸν βωμ[ὸ]ν ὑφ᾽ ἑαυτοῖς μαχαίρας κ[ο]μίζοντες, σφαγιασαμένου δὲ τοῦ ἱερέως καὶ δείραντος τὸ ἱερεῖον καὶ τὰ σπλάγχα περιεξελομένου, οἱ περιεστῶτες ἕκαστος ἣν ἂν ἰσχύσῃ μοῖραν ἀποτεμνόμενος ἄπεισιν, ὡς πολλάκις τὸν θυσιάσαντα αὐτὸν ἄμοιρ[ο]ν ἀπιέναι* 'whenever anybody comes [to Delphi] to sacrifice to the god, the Delphians stand around the altar keeping their knives ready, and as soon as the priest has slaughtered the victim, torn off the skin and taken out the entrails, everyone standing around cuts off the share he manages and leaves, so that very often the one who makes the sacrifice goes off himself without a share'.

necessarily very clear who that worshipping community was. This practice of defining, and limiting, the cult group interestingly contrasts with that found in, for example, civic cults, where the criterion for participation would on the whole be citizenship. The observation may well have consequences for the manner in which we should imagine a 'Panhellenic' worshipping community constituted itself—not as a loosely defined gathering of Greeks, but following its own rules on who has what kind of access to the god.

While anecdotal Delphic meanness is of course not all specific to the Delphic Theoxenia, there is clearly a significant overlap in the traditions regarding the shares; perhaps the Theoxenia were even an occasion where this 'problem' was particularly pronounced. The Theoxenia thus emerge as a festival to which delegations and perhaps individuals from all over Greece came, ideally to share the table with the gods.[32] The cultic table was laid and the food consumed by the *theoroi* themselves. But participation does not seem to have been universal, or was at least stratified and controversial. The banqueters were those who had managed to grasp a *moira* —less likely by pure physical force than careful negotiation with the sanctuary itself.[33] That the *moira* could be won in an agon implies competition for access to the god, and a certain exclusivity. Hence this particular theoxenic rite is intrinsically bound up with the creation of a worshipping community, enacted by shared feasting at the god's table. It is in this sense that one could say that the god's presence was essential for the human—feasting—cult community, almost as if the god ratified this carefully chosen community.[34] It will emerge in what follows that the Theoxenia exploited typically Delphic dining practices for the formation of the worshipping community, turning the festival into one of many arenas for the perennial discussion of who had the right to be admitted to that most exclusive of groups, the Greeks themselves.

Neoptolemos

It is at this point that Neoptolemos joins the feast. We shall see that this hero epitomizes the access issue so relevant for the Theoxenia and at the same time gives the festival a role in the definition of what it meant to be a Greek. There is striking evidence relating Neoptolemos both to the Delphic practice that caused so much offence, and to the 'Hellenic' aspect of the Theoxenia.[35]

[32] Bruit (1990), esp. 170–2 for the integration of 'difference' through *xenia*-rites.

[33] That participation was indeed a major issue is suggested by Kurke (2003), interpreting the anecdotal evidence for Aesop as a matter of elite versus non-elite access at Delphi.

[34] So one could develop Bruit's notion for the theoric context ((1989) 21): 'la présence du dieu a pour fonction de sanctionner la commensalité entre les hommes, la commensalité civique, qui fait, à l'époque classique, des compagnons de banquet, des concitoyens liés par le partage de la nourriture issue du sacrifice'.

[35] That there is a relationship between Delphic sacrifice and Neoptolemos' myth of some sort has long been recognized: e.g. Fontenrose (1960) 191–266; Burkert (1983) 119–20; Nagy (1979) 118–41, esp. 123–7; Suarez de la Torre (1997) 161–3; the link to the Theoxenia has recently received fresh and detailed attention: Kurke (2005); Currie (2005) 301–3.

Neoptolemos was famously killed in Apollo's precinct when he came to visit Delphi shortly after the Trojan War. The circumstances of his death feature in *Paean 6* and in *Nemean 7* and have provoked probably the greatest flurry of scholarly discussion on any Pindaric issue. The argument revolves around whether Neoptolemos was deliberately assassinated by one of Apollo's attendants, as the god's retaliation for murdering Priam at the altar of Zeus Herkeios at Troy, as some infer from the relevant passage in *Paean 6*:

> ⌊ἀ⌋μφιπόλοις δὲ
> μ]υριᾶν περὶ τιμᾶν
> δηρι]αζόμενον κτάνεν
> ⟨ἐν⟩ τεμέ]νεϊ φίλῳ γᾶς παρ' ὀμφαλὸν εὐρύν.

He slew him as he was quarreling with attendants over countless honours in his own sanctuary at the broad navel of the earth (Pindar, *Paean* 6.117–20, tr. Race)

or whether he died by accident, as some read into the following lines of *Nemean 7*:

> ἵνα κρεῶν νιν ὕπερ μάχας
> ἔλασεν ἀντιτυχόντ' ἀνὴρ μαχαίρᾳ.

There, when he became involved in a quarrel over sacrificial meats, a man struck him with a sword (Pindar, *Nemean* 7.42–3, tr. Race)

Initiated by one of Pindar's scholiasts, fierce discussion has arisen about whether Pindar meant to condemn Neoptolemos for *asebeia* against the god in one poem, and acquit him of it in the other.[36] As we shall see, however, the question of how Neoptolemos died is irrelevant to Pindar's presentation of the story. What matters is the fact that he does die, and why.

The straightforward reading of these passages is, I believe, also the correct one: both poems refer to the peculiar Delphic sacrifice. The 'countless honours' (μ]υριᾶν περὶ τιμᾶν l. 118) are not some abstract concept, but very concretely the

[36] The theory goes back to the Alexandrian scholars Aristarkhos and his pupil Aristodemos: *Σ* Pi. *N.* 7.70; 94a (Aristarkhos); *Σ* Pi. *N.* 7.150a: ὁ δὲ Ἀριστόδημος ὅτι μεμφθεὶς ὑπὸ Αἰγινητῶν ἐπὶ τῷ δοκεῖν ἐν Παιᾶσιν εἰπεῖν τὸν Νεοπτόλεμον ἐπὶ ἱεροσυλίᾳ ἐληλυθέναι εἰς Δελφούς, νῦν ὥσπερ ὑπεραπολογεῖται, εἰπὼν ὅτι οὐχ ἱεροσυλῶν ἐτελεύτησε, ἀλλ' ὑπὲρ κρεῶν φιλοτιμηθεὶς ἀνῃρέθη. 'Aristodemos says that Pindar, having apparently been reproached by the Aiginetans for having said that Neoptolemos had come to Delphi in order to despoil the sanctuary, now virtually defends himself by saying that Neoptolemos was not killed because he sacked the sanctuary, but because he was arguing over sacrificial meat.' Pindar's self-justification is normally read into *N.* 7.48–50, 64–5, 102–4. The orthodoxy used to be credulous towards the scholiasts' portrayal of the affair (e.g. Lloyd-Jones 1973, still Arrighetti (1987)). The most recent discussion on the subject is Currie (2005) 321–31. Views either deny any relation between the two pieces on poetic grounds: Bundy (1986) 4 and n. 14, 29 n. 70; Lefkowitz (1991) 137–8; or make the two poems complementary: Tugendhat (1960); C. Segal (1967); Gentili (1981); Most (1985); or do not relate them for different reasons: Burnett (1998); Rutherford (2001) 306–38 argues that it is the Aiginetans' (not Neoptolemos') bad relations with Apollo as depicted in *Pae.* 6 that they complain about in *Nemean* 7, similar to Radt (1958) 85–8. Evidence from tragedy is very helpful here: see Allan (2000) Ch. 1. A quarrel over priority in receiving sacrifical meat also occurs at Th. 1.25.4, with Hornblower.

sacrificial shares; and this is also the most likely interpretation of the 'scuffle over the meat'.[37] The fifth-century mythographer Pherekydes and the Pindaric scholiasts after him, though giving various reasons for Neoptolemos' death, know of the tradition suggesting that both passages of Pindar relate to an argument over sacrificial meat between Neoptolemos and the Delphians: when Neoptolemos saw 'the Delphians tearing apart the meat, he took it from them, and was himself killed. Makhaireus, their priest, stabbed him at the entry of the temple'.[38] The scholiasts add that he was so aggrieved by the sight that he went on to prevent it, and this was how he found his death.[39]

Neoptolemos, then, seems to have been just such a person who came to make a sacrifice at Delphi and received no seat at the dining table. He impersonates in myth the traditions that have developed around the Delphic sacrifice and theoric reciprocity at the shrine. The Delphic personnel conspiring to murder him reveal this through their names. *Μαχαιρεύς*, 'the Knifer' and priest of Apollo, is Neoptolemos' murderer in Pherekydes and in Sophokles' *Hermione*, simply featuring as *ἀνὴρ Δελφός* in Euripides' *Andromache*. The much-feared sacrificial knife, itself with its own anecdotal tradition,[40] is the due attribute of the *ἀνὴρ μαχαίρᾳ* ('a man with a knife') in Pindar's version. The father *Δαῖτας* ('The Feaster') invented for this man makes it clear that the murderer is a hypostasis of the typical Delphic sacrifice, and his alternative name *Φιλοξενίδης* ('Friend of Strangers') says what is really at stake: Neoptolemos' hosts violate the *Homeric Hymn to Apollo*'s recommendation of theoric reciprocity, and prevent the hero

[37] The very first treatments of this matter already realized that sacrificial meat was at issue here, and not, as some argue, a more symbolic form of 'honours' (*τιμαί*): Radt (1958) (cf. Burkert (1983) 119; Nagy (1979) 124 ff.), later denied e.g. by Braswell on *Pyth.* 4.260. Rutherford (2001) 308, 313–15 takes on the old interpretation but does not develop it. For *timai* meaning 'sacrificial shares' see LSJ s.v.

[38] Pherec. *FGrH* 3 F 64a (=Σ Eur. *Or.* 1655 (cf. Σ Eur. *Andr.* 52): *καὶ ὡς ὁρᾷ κατὰ τὸ χρηστήριον κρέα διαρπάζοντας τοὺς Δελφοὺς ἀφαιρεῖται τὰ κρέα αὐτοὺς, ἑαυτὸν δὲ κτεῖναι. Μαχαιρεὺς ὁ δὲ τούτων ἱερεὺς αὐτὸν κατορύσσει ὑπὸ τὸν οὐδὸν τοῦ νεώ.* For the problems in reconstructing the text see Jacoby ad loc. and Fowler (2002) app. crit.

[39] Σ *Pae.* 6.117 ff.: *ἤτοι τῶν κ[ρ]εῶν ἃ διαρπαζόντων συνήθως τῶν Δ[ελφ]ῶν ἐδυσχέραινε καὶ ἐκώλυε, διὸ καὶ ἀνήρηται, ἢ τῶν χρημάτων ἃ διαρπάζων εἰς ἐκδικίαν τοῦ πατρὸς ἀνηρέθη* 'It is said that Neoptolemos was killed either because he was disgusted at how the Delphians as usual tore the meat to pieces and tried to prevent them, or because of the money that he took from them for the revindication of his father.' Cf. Σ N. 7.62a: *φασὶ τοῦ Νεοπτολέμου θύοντος τοὺς Δελφοὺς ἁρπάζειν τὰ θύματα ὡς ἔθος αὐτοῖς· τὸν δὲ Νεοπτόλεμον δυσανασχέτως ἔχοντα διακωλύειν. αὐτοὺς δὲ διαχρήσασθαι αὐτὸν ξίφη ἔχοντας* 'They say that when he sacrificed the Delphians as was their custom snatched the victims. Neoptolemos finding this unbearable prevented them, and they ran him through with their swords.' Neoptolemos here comes to Delphi to inquire as to the reasons why he has remained childless by his then wife Hermione.

[40] The *Δελφικὸν ξίφος*/*Δελφικὴ μάχαιρα* was feared: Hsch. δ 603 s.v. *Δελφικὴ μάχαιρα*; App. Prov. 94 s.v. 1.393: *ἐπὶ τῶν φιλοκερδῶν καὶ ἀπὸ παντὸς λαμβάνειν προαιρουμένων παρόσον οἱ Δελφοὶ τὸ μέν τι τῶν ἱερείων ἐλάμβανον, τὸ δέ τι ὑπὲρ τῆς μαχαίρας ἐπράττοντο* 'meaning the greedy and those wanting to have a share of everything, as the Delphians on the one hand took something from the victim, on the other they demanded something on behalf of their knives'. For the topos of the sacrificial knife see also *H. Ap.* 535–6.

from performing a *theoros*' sacrifice, in other words, from participating in the cult and/or festival.[41]

We can conclude that Neoptolemos essentially seems to be a *theoros* whose visit to Delphi went badly wrong, and he was not permitted into the god's closer circle. If we let him speak for himself, this was far from obvious: he is puzzled by his treatment, for example, when in Euripides' *Andromache* he is about to make the sacrifice, and officious temple police instantly appear whom he naively confronts with the question 'why are you killing me when I am coming for pious purposes?'[42] Why deny him the customary reciprocity? We shall see that just as in the case of the Asinaians above, there are two combative traditions about Neoptolemos in circulation, one by which he was Apollo's enemy, and one by which he was so 'close' to him that he was eventually buried in Apollo's very shrine. His problem can be seen to revolve around a definition of the established rules of reciprocity between local cult personnel and theoric guests arriving from elsewhere: when comparing Neoptolemos' story with that of the sanctuary itself, it emerges that a long-standing issue lurks behind this problematic figure, concerning Delphi's position in the early Greek world.

The Sacred War Traditions

Neoptolemos' conflict with Delphic 'hospitality' goes, I think, to the heart of Delphi's role as a Panhellenic centre of *theoria*. His myth encapsulates Delphi's change from a local shrine to a theoric cult, expressed through the perceived arrival of what is later known as the so-called amphiktyons at Delphi from their alleged former seat at Anthela in Thessaly. Neoptolemos has a special relation to these amphiktyons since his home, as theirs, was Central Greece, and Thessaly in particular. The amphiktyony was precisely there to regulate cultic matters of the shrine, but also came to be at the centre of inter-state relations throughout Greek history. Neoptolemos' myth is therefore also intricately linked to Delphi's Panhellenic status and the sanctuary's role as a mediator between the different Greeks.[43]

The amphiktyons are mostly held to have come to Delphi as a consequence of a series of events that circulate under the name of the 'Sacred War'. This semi-mythical event, supposed to have happened in the first decade of the sixth century, brings to light exactly Neoptolemos' problems of granted and withheld

[41] *Μαχαιρεύς*: Pherec. *FGrH* 3 F 64a; Soph. *Hermione* arg. *TrGF* iv.192 = Eusth. *Od.* 14.124–9 and Σ EHQRT *Od.* 4.6f.; Apollod. 6.14: *ὑπὸ Μαχαιρέως τοῦ Φωκέως*; Str. 9.3.9; Σ Eur. *Andr.* 53 (Makhaireus). Cf. Eur. *Andr.* 1149–52: *Δελφοῦ πρὸς ἀνδρός* 'by a man from Delphi'; Σ *Or.* 1655: *ὑπὸ τῶν Δελφῶν*. Ascl. Trag. *FGrH* 12 F 15 = Σ Pi. *N.* 7.62b (*Δαῖτας*). Σ Eur. *Andr.* 53 = *Suda* s.v. *Φιλοξενίδης*. *Μαχαιρεύς* has a descendant *Βράγχος* who is the overseer (*προστάτης*) at Apollo's sanctuary at Didyma in Strabo's times (loc. cit.). Cf. Pi. *N.* 7.42: 'a man with a knife'; Eur. *Or.* 1654: *θανεῖν γὰρ αὐτῷ Δελφικῷ ξίφει* 'to die by the Delphic sword'.

[42] Eur. *Andr.* 1125: *Τίνος μ' ἕκατι κτείνετ' εὐσεβεῖς ὁδούς;*

[43] Cf. recently Sanchez (2001) for the historical role of the amphiktyony and now *CID* iv for the important decrees.

theoric reciprocity. The Sacred War traditions make up a story in which the winner had a good hold on what was later believed to be the truth about its motivation; they are therefore sometimes difficult to decode. In this context Neoptolemos' story suggests that this victory by the amphiktyons is much more contested than most ancient texts lead one to believe. Just as in the case of the Asinaians, discussed in the preceding chapter, stories have developed around an event precisely because its outcome was ambiguous or problematic.

What was really expressed through the legend of this war is unclear. The most popular reconstruction suggests that the war led to the long-lasting control of Delphi by the amphiktyony, a group of cities that arrived at Delphi possibly from their supposed previous seat at Anthela, near Thermopylai in Thessaly. The Sacred War therefore marks the end of a locally controlled sanctuary in favour of collectively regulated cult-activity. The institution of the first Pythian Games around 582 BC might be connected with these changes, celebrating the new order of the place; more widely, the sixth century sees a particularly intense phase of Panhellenism when not much later the games at Nemea and Isthmia are also established. The 'Sacred War' also needs to be seen in this wider Greek context.[44]

Fourth-century assumptions, taking for granted amphiktyonic rule at Delphi, characterize this 'story of the winner' and what it claims about the origins of the war. The narrative suffers from the kind of anachronism that characterizes every aetiological story and starts from the idea that the amphiktyons already controlled Delphi at the time of the war whereas the 'Sacred War' really introduced them in the first place.[45] According to these stories, the war arose over a conflict with Krisa (Kirrha in historical times), situated in the Pleistos valley just below the sanctuary and presumably at the time in control of Delphi.[46] The amphiktyons thought it right to march into Krisa when, according to Aiskhines, its inhabitants, 'most unlawful peoples' (*γένη παρανομώτατα*), committed sacrilege (*ἀσέβεια*) against the dedications (*ἀναθήματα*) in the shrine.[47] They were also

[44] The most recent discussions of the Sacred War are Fowler (1998) 13–14; McInerney (1999) 167–72. See Davies (1994) and Tausend (1992) on the sources and their problems; also Morgan (1990) 135–6. Forrest (1956) is still a standard treatment; Robertson (1978) denies its historicity altogether. Anthelian amphiktyony based on the sanctuary of Demeter at Thermopylai: Hdt. 7.200; *Marm. Par.* 5, Str. 9.3.7. Woodbury (1979) alone has thought about Neoptolemos' relationship to the Sacred War, though with different conclusions from those presented here. Nemea and Isthmia: n. 53 below.

[45] Such anachronisms in the Sacred War traditions confirm the supposed establishment of the amphiktyony at Delphi from Thessaly: the leading general was the Thessalian Eurylokhos (Str. 9.3.4); the first person to manage the amphiktyony was a certain 'Akrisios', slotting the 'Krisaian' regime into the amphiktyony's history. The possible changes mentioned in *H. Ap.* 540–4 have also long been acknowledged as such anachronisms.

[46] The location of either of these places in the more remote periods is unknown (Morgan (1990) 135). In all earlier texts Krisa is the name for Delphi: *Od.*, *H. Ap. passim*: *Il.* 2.520 (Krisa); Alc. fr. 7.9 *PLF* (Kirsa). Krisa in Hellenistic times was Delphi's harbour under the name Kirrha.

[47] Aeschin. 3.107–12: *εἰς τὸ ἱερὸν περὶ τὰ ἀναθήματα ἠσέβουν, ἐξημάρτανον δὲ καὶ εἰς τοὺς Ἀμφικτύονας* 'they committed sacrilege against the dedications in the shrine, and behaved badly against the amphiktyons'. Plut. *Sol.* 11: *ὑβρίζοντας εἰς τὸ μαντεῖον* 'committing sacrilege against the oracle'. Paus. 10.37.5: *ἠσέβησαν ἐς τὸν Ἀπόλλωνα καὶ ἀπέτεμνον τοῦ θεοῦ τῆς χώρας* 'they acted impiously towards Apollo and took some of his land'.

misbehaving against the amphiktyons, and according to the antiquarian tradition generally treated their visitors badly in making extortionate profits from the taxes levied for both harbour and sanctuary.[48] The charges reveal that reciprocity between the sanctuary and its visitors is at stake again; and the definition of what constituted *asebeia* was most likely construed after the Krisaians' transgressions had been successfully punished. In other words, the Krisaians are violating rules that are about to be established in the first place, under the pretence of coming to 'help the god and his land' (βοηθήσειν τῷ θεῷ καὶ τῇ γῇ).[49]

The story of the Sacred War seems to reflect a sanctuary embroiled in a difficult process of change from a local to a non-local shrine, or else, in the process of becoming a place of more institutionalized *theoria*, quite possibly under amphiktyonic control. Presumably this would also have entailed defining the set of rules pertaining to this change, potentially including those concerning 'theoric reciprocity'. In other words, this is a legend setting up the amphiktyons' rule at Delphi, but that it could preserve all these elements of a resistance suggests that their establishment was a highly contested and difficult process, and the problems and violence it entailed never quite forgotten. In a more extreme interpretation, it also suggests that the amphiktyony's control of Delphi was not as absolute as we might think, that Delphi never quite ceased to be a local sanctuary.[50]

The alleged Sacred War thus altered the sanctuary's running and significantly reconfigured Delphi's role within archaic Greece, which in turn impinged on the Greek world at large. The Sacred War is increasingly considered to be the context for the pseudo-Hesiodic *Catalogue of Women* and its genealogical constructions. These reflect a world-view where Thessalians shape the stemmata of the Greeks, supporting the claim to Thessalian domination of Delphi through the amphiktyony. Together with that, however, the poem advertises a notion of 'Hellas' as extended from a small part of Thessaly, a region called Ἑλλάς, into something that strikingly coincides with the boundaries of the sixth-century amphiktyony. A figure Ἕλλην emerges for the first time as the common ancestor of all amphiktyons, while at the same time leaving no doubt about the Thessalian core. The group of cities around the amphiktyony thus staked a claim to Hellenicity.[51]

[48] Str. 9.3.4: the Krisaians levied harsh taxes (πικρῶς ἐτελώνουν) on the visitors to the shrine and in archaic times prospered because of the harbour tax they imposed for goods coming in from Italy and Sicily. People from Amphissa later on were 'even worse about the strangers' (χείρους περὶ τοὺς ξένους).

[49] Aeschin. 3.107–9. In other versions, the Kirrhaians carried away Megisto, daughter of the Phokian Pelagon, and an Argive woman, on their way home from the Delphic shrine: Kallisthenes *FGrH* 124 F 1 *ap.* Ath. 13.560c. The Κραγ(υ)αλίδαι are their fellow-criminals, an obscure local tribe (Harpocr. s.v.), interestingly associated with the Dryopes (Hyg. *Fab.* 14) perhaps with a view to the split of Phokis: n. 66 below.

[50] A recently published sacred law suggests the interest of the amphiktyons in Delphic *theoria*: *CID* iv 2, esp. 49–55, but how far their powers interfered or overlapped with those of the Delphians themselves is unclear.

[51] As was already argued by Grote (1846–56) i. 89 and other 19th-cent. scholars: Fowler (1998) 12 n. 27. More recently see Lévy (1991) and Lazenby in *OCD*^{3} s.v. Hellenes; Vannicelli (1989) discusses 'Dorians' and 'Hellenes' in the Homeric epics. For the connection between Hesiod's catalogues and the 'Sacred War' see Fowler (1998): J. Hall (2002) 134 ff.

This is a bold claim, but one that must be taken seriously, for it creates a pretence in which the amphiktyony at Delphi purported to be an institution that looked after the Hellenes: in other words, the amphiktyony carefully guarded who was allowed to be a Greek and who was not. That this was quite possibly a stipulation is suggested by a votive inscription set up, according to Pausanias, by the victor of the first Pythian Games, those contests that are likely to have been celebrated at the taking over of Delphi by the amphiktyony. It daringly equates *ἀμφικτίονες* and *Ἕλληνες*. Additionally, some ancient texts make the movements of the early Delphic amphiktyony central to the process by which the name 'Hellenes' eventually came to mean all Greeks.[52] It is controversial to think of 'the Greeks' as an invention of as late as the early sixth century and by the Thessalians. But seen in a larger sixth-century context, the small region Hellas might have come in usefully in a competitively circulating definition of Hellenicity. There are other suggestions that who the Hellenes were was seemingly a hotly debated issue at the time: the roughly contemporary Hellenion at Naukratis, including northern Ionian cities and the Dorian Pentapolis, surely had a different definition to hand. I have already mentioned that the formalization of the three Panhellenic games at Delphi, Nemea, and Isthmia within a few decades suggests an interest in formulations of 'Greekness'.[53]

It is striking that Neoptolemos manages to be implicated in all the problems posed by the Sacred War as just analysed. The similarities between the complaints launched against the Krisaians' bad treatment of theoric visitors, the laments about the insatiable *makhaireis* hanging about in the sanctuary, and Neoptolemos' personal fate are already too conspicuously striking to be overlooked. But what is more, Neoptolemos' ancestry is wholly Thessalian and stems from the land of the intruding amphiktyony. Neoptolemos' homeland is Achilles' Phthia.[54] Phthia is closely associated with the very 'Hellas' of the amphiktyony, reigned over by Peleus and later by Neoptolemos in the Homeric Epics. That the region Hellas is sometimes located not in Thessaly but in Neoptolemos' place of exile Molossia also indicates a close relationship between the hero and things 'Hellenic'.[55]

In taking all the threads together one might be inclined to think that Neoptolemos personalized the problems arising over the administration of Delphi, assumed by the Thessalian-dominated amphiktyons. He embodied their

[52] Paus. 10.7.6; cf. D.H. *Ant. Rom.* 4.25.3. The role of the amphiktyony is stressed by J. Hall (2002) 134–54.

[53] Hdt 2.178; the Nemean Games were reorganized in 573 BC; those at Isthmia in 582 BC.

[54] Only in the *Little Iliad* does he arrive back there after Troy; all other traditions deny him the return. Leskh. *Il. Parv.* 21 Bernabé (Pharsalia, part of Phthiotis).

[55] Independent Thessalian Hellas: *Il.* 9.447; 478; with Phthia: 2.683–4; 9.363; 16.595; *Od.* 11.495–6; cf. St. Byz. s.v. *Πανέλληνες*. Some texts place a region Hellas at Dodona, doubtless because of the Aiakids' Molossian ancestry: Arist. *Meteor.* 352^{a}33 f.; *Σ* Townsl *Il.* 21.194. Cf J. Miller, *RE* viii. 1 (1912) 158 f. s.v. Hellas; Hammond (1967) 370–3. The Homeric *Σελλοί*, priests at Dodona (*Il.* 16.234; St. Byz. s.v. *Σελλοί*, see (Ch. 7 below)), and *Ἑλλοπίη* (Hes. fr. 240.1 MW; cf. Str. 7.7.10; *EM* σ 709.30 s.v. *Σελλοί*; St. Byz. s.v. *Ἑλλοπία*) are possibly, but not certainly, related to *Ἑλλάς*: F. Bölte, *RE* viii.1 (1912) 194–6, s.v. Helloi.

not entirely justified rule. Hence Neoptolemos himself remained forever an alien at Delphi: as even a small selection of episodes from his future life in myth and cult suggests, the hero's presence at the shrine never ceased to be ambiguous and subject to interpretation. No version of the myth is able to disguise that Neoptolemos came to Delphi as Apollo's greatest enemy, suggesting that the fight over his *moira* at the sacrificial table was symptomatic of a much larger issue.[56] The texts, despite floating various ideas about why Neoptolemos came to Delphi,[57] make it overwhelmingly clear that his real motivation was to sack the place, for example Strabo saying that he paid the visit to Delphi 'maybe in order to seek redress from Apollo', and continuing 'but, what is more probable, he came to attack the sanctuary'.[58] Neoptolemos evidently did not have the remotest chance of superseding his own myth and achieving rehabilitation before the god however 'sincere' his professed interests—perhaps an interesting insight into how limited the potential for poetic rearrangement of myth might have been in some cases.[59] Neoptolemos' story and the story of the sanctuary at Delphi were intrinsically interlinked, and would forever remain so.

Despite the amphiktyony's unquestioned presence at Delphi in later history, the traditions keep their curiously anti-Neoptolemean slant, as if the issue was never really resolved. This is well reflected in the truly disconcerting development in Neoptolemos' career, that despite everything he was buried at Delphi, within Apollo's temenos. Pindar's formulation leaves little doubt that his grave was there in the early fifth century; he certainly dwelled beneath the Knidian Leskhe—which held his picture—in the fifth.[60] But this shrine remained full of contra-

[56] The mythical justification for his death remained the episode at Priam's altar, although Apollo's hostility might itself have been evoked only once the Sacred War had changed mythical truths at Delphi: Arktinos' version: *Ilioup.* arg. 13–14 Bernabé: ἐπὶ τὸν τοῦ Διὸς τοῦ Ἑρκείου βωμὸν καταφυγόντα 'having fled to the altar of Zeus Herkeios'; cf. Eur. *Hec.* 23–4; *Troad.* 15–17; 481–3; Paus. 4.17.4; Apollod. 5.21; V. *Aen.* 2.501–2; Heliod. *Aeth.* 2.34. See Kullmann (1960) 216–17. Priamos dragged from the altar and slaughtered at the gates (of his house?), not at the altar: Leskhes *Il. Parv.* 16 Bernabé; Paus. 10.27.2.

[57] Neoptolemos comes to ask about his childlessness, to make Apollo pay compensation for murdering his father Achilles, or to make amends for when he first summoned the god to court: Soph. *Herm.* arg. Eusth.; Pherec. *FGrH* 3 F 64a = Σ Eur. *Or.* 1655; Σ Eur. *Andr.* 53; *Or.* 1655 and others.

[58] Str. 9.3.9: ὡς δὲ εἰκός, ἐπιθέμενον τῷ ἱερῷ. Apollod. 6.14 pools all three motives, saying that he came to seek redress, to burgle and to burn Delphi (ἀπαιτεῖν ὑπὲρ τοῦ πατρὸς τὸν Ἀπόλλωνα δίκας καὶ συλᾶν τὰ ἀναθήματα καὶ τὸν νεὼν ἐμπιμπράναι). Pausanias puts him in the catalogue of the shrine's sackers: the others are a son of a certain Euboian Krios, Xerxes, the Phokians (presumably in the Third Sacred War), the Gauls, Nero (Paus. 10.7.1). In the *Andromache*, Delphic security is always ready to intervene: Eur. *Andr.* 1085–1165; esp. 1092–9.

[59] On this problem in relation to Neoptolemos see most recently e.g. Allan (2000) 16 and Ch. 1 *passim.*

[60] *N.* 7.34–5: ἐν Πυθίοισι δὲ δαπέδοις / κεῖται Πριάμου πόλιν Νεοπτόλεμος ἐπεὶ πράθεν, 'in the glens of Pytho lies Neoptolemos after he burned the city of Priamos'; 44–7, cited n. 104 below. His tomb in the sanctuary recurs in Pherec. *FGrH* 3 F 64a; Paus. 10.24.6; Str. 9.3.9; Σ *N.* 7.62b. His grave is closely associated with his death at the altar, and he is buried by his murderers: Paus. 10.24.4 (ἑστία); 6 his grave (τάφος); 4.17.4 (killed 'at the altar' πρὸς τῷ βωμῷ). Several possibilities for the location of his shrine have been raised: a 4th-cent. structure see Pouilloux, *FD* ii.9 49–60; Bommelaer (1991) 190–5. Currie (2005) 296–307 is the most recent treatment of the cult. The Leskhe: Paus. 10.25.1–31.12.

dictions: Andromache's label *ὄνειδος Δελφοῖς* ('shame to the Delphians' Eur. *Andr.* 1239–42) for the tomb emphasizes a perceived memory of the locals' evil treatment of the hero. There is even a tradition that Menelaos removed Neoptolemos from too close contact with Apollo, digging up his grave at the temple's threshold and reinstating it outside.[61] According to Pausanias, the Delphians had held Neoptolemos in *atimia* 'since he was an enemy of theirs' until he warded off the Galatians in 278 BC, as if this were finally proof of his benevolence. If the Molossian tribe of the Ainianes, supposed members of the early amphiktyony who share with Neoptolemos their homeland, grandly worshipped Neoptolemos in the imperial period, this fosters a further link between the hero, the amphiktyony, and the practices of *theoria*. Neoptolemos might have been specifically worshipped by those who brought him there, but denied cult by the locals in a way that symbolically marks their resistance to the change once upon a time brought about by the amphiktyons.[62]

Neoptolemos thus forms a link between the peculiar Delphic sacrifice and the festival's Panhellenic pretensions, almost as if his myth —not ostensibly a cult-foundation legend—were the aetiology of the Theoxenia, perhaps first celebrated after the 'First Sacred War'. All of this leaves us with a detailed picture of the long-term religious context in which *Paean 6* was performed, and its cultural associations. The Theoxenia were a festival supposedly for 'all of Greece', but the issues surrounding the distribution of sacrificial meat rather suggest that who was part of this 'all of Greece' was tightly controlled and membership in this select group of worshippers highly contested. Ritual dining was at the centre of the festival, and instrumental in shaping the cult community. The figure of the archetypal, but rejected diner Neoptolemos suggests that worship at Delphi was, or could be made, exclusive. It also suggests that practices at the Theoxenia were linked to changes introduced to Delphi by whatever it is that the Sacred War expresses and the establishment of the collective body of the amphiktyons at Delphi. The link is provided by Neoptolemos' connection to the Thessalian region Hellas, which associates the dining issue with the Hellenicity of the festival.

If the amphiktyons introduced the notion of 'Hellas' to Delphi, there is a strong suggestion that the Theoxenia, a festival in which they were presumably crucially involved, had symbolic control of who was part of this exclusive group of Hellenes. While the reality of policing at Delphi must have been much more blurred, we do know that individual states could be barred from participation in the Panhellenic circuit when they were considered to break the rules of Greek

[61] Asklepiades *FGrH* 12 F 15 = *Σ N.* 7.62b: 'he was buried first at the threshold of the temple, then Menelaos arrived and dug him up from there, and built a grave in the temenos' (*ταφῆναι δὲ τὸ μὲν πρῶτον ὑπὸ τὸν οὐδόν τοῦ νεώ, μετὰ δὲ ταῦτα Μενέλαον ἐλθόντα ἀνελεῖν, καὶ τὸν τάφον ποιῆσαι ἐν τῷ τεμένει*).

[62] Paus. 1.4.4; Heliod. *Aeth.* 2.34. The Ainianes are one of the obscure migrant tribal groups in central Greece, harking back to Neoptolemos presumably because of his stay in Molossia. Later on the Ainianes moved to Thessaly and were part of the Anthelian amphiktyony: see Sakellariou (1990) 190–200; also (1984).

inter-state relations, as if their 'Greekness' was temporarily in doubt: such happened to the Spartans during the Peloponnesian War, who were excluded from the Olympic Games as if their behaviour was not what one would expect from true Greeks. The close link between Theoxenia and Hellenicity might also be suggested by Philodamos' paean, which if composed for the inauguration of Philip's temple at Delphi was performed perhaps with a view to fostering his public image as a Hellene. In its most extreme formulation, the claim is that a dinner invitation to the Delphic banquet is a testimony to one's Greekness. An intriguing conclusion follows for the Delphic Theoxenia: the *eueteria*, the 'good crop' and prosperity that the festival is supposed to bestow, is also granted selectively: that is to say to a restricted and carefully chosen group who called themselves 'Greeks'—and that this included all Greeks is not entirely taken for granted!

2. ZEUS HELLANIOS OF AIGINA: GREEKNESS AND 'GOOD CROP'

The appearance of a local god Zeus Hellanios in a supposedly Panhellenic performance context of our song at Delphi is all the more perplexing if set against the heavily loaded background just explored. It is this ritual claim of the Greeks assembled and sharing the privilege of a 'good crop' that matters for *Paean 6*. Let us therefore return to the specifically Aiginetan issue. Zeus Hellanios heads the paean's last triad, the part of the song that carries the Aiginetan flag in particular, the 'hymn to Aigina' and the hero Aiakos. The idea that this triad may have circulated as a separate *prosodion* for the Aiginetans further deepens the local colour of *Paean 6* as a whole.[63] The 'hymn' puts under the protection of Aiginetan Zeus Hellanios all that is Aiginetan when its beginning invokes the island as the 'shining star of Zeus Hellanios':

ὀνομακλύτα γάρ ἐσσι Δωριεῖ
  μ[ε]δέοισα [πό]ντῳ
νᾶσος, [ὦ] Διὸς Ἑλ-
  λανίου φαεννὸν ἄστρον
οὕνεκεν οὔ σε παιηόνων
ἄδορπον εὐνάξομεν, ἀλλ' ἀοιδᾶν
ῥόθια δεκομένα κατερεῖς,
  πόθεν ἔλαβες ναυπρύτανιν
δαίμονα καὶ τὰν θεμίξενον ἀρετ[άν.
ὁ πάντα τοι τά τε καὶ τὰ τεύχων
  σὸν ἐγγυάλιξεν ὄλβον
εὐρύο[πα] Κρόνου παῖς, . . .

Island whose name is famous indeed, you live and rule in the Dorian sea, O shining star of Zeus Hellanios. Therefore we shall not put you to bed without a banquet of paeans; rather,

[63] Rutherford (1997), see p. 184 above.

as you receive waves of songs you will recount where you got your ship-ruling fortune and that virtue of just regard for strangers. Truly, the far-seeing son of Kronos who accomplishes all things, both this and that, has bestowed prosperity on you, . . . (Pindar, *Paean* 6.123–34 = D6 Ruth, tr. Race)

The featuring of Zeus Hellanios here is crucial, and the invocation of Aigina as his home seems to put the rest of the song under his guardianship. Not only the rest of the song: the Aiginetans' characteristics here and elsewhere seem intrinsically linked with this god. The self-attributed virtues of 'nauprytany' ('leading in ships') and *themixenia* ('justice to strangers'), two in a whole set of recurring Aiginetan characteristics, are more than once connected with this god.[64] It is through the cult of Zeus Hellanios, closely tied as he is to the Aiginetan self-portrayal, that the song seeks to establish a special role for Aiginetans amongst the Hellenes of the Theoxenia. The paean can be seen to forge a link between the ritual of the Theoxenia and the aetiological myth for the cult of Zeus Hellanios, the Aiginetan god. For the aetiological myth whereby Aiakos brings to an end a Panhellenic drought in a curious way reflects the issue of Greece's 'good crop' and links the two chief concerns of the Theoxenia festival, Panhellenism and *eueteria*, yet turns Zeus Hellanios rather than Apollo into their source. In the context of the Theoxenia, therefore, the evocation of Zeus Hellanios' aetiology suggests a pivotal role for Aiginetans in the festival's Panhellenic worshipping group, somehow linked to *eueteria*. (If Aigina receives a banquet of paeans for supper (ll. 125–6), she clearly presides over the Delphic Theoxenia concerned with food provisions.)

In the early fifth century any claim along such lines must have been highly problematic: this is a time when both what it meant to be a 'Hellene' and the *eueteria* of Greece were much debated. However, as we shall see, the contention that Aiginetans were a good thing for Greece's 'good crop' goes right to the heart of a heated contemporary discussion on both these issues, what it means to be a Greek, and how to ensure that Greece is well fed. Just as the Delian songs could be seen to illuminate the nature of early Athenian imperialism, *Paean 6* forms part of a broader discourse about the shape of post-Persian War Greece, intrinsically related to the nature and function of the Delian League. The song sits in the midst of a fascinating cluster of evidence suggesting that many broader issues are epitomized, perhaps even borne out, in the example of contemporary Aigina.[65]

[64] *N.* 5 and 8 (as n. 3 above). On Aiginetan ideology in these terms see Figueira (1981) 521–30; Gzella (1981); De Ste. Croix (2004*b*); Hornblower (2004) 208–16; (2007). Aiginetans and ships: *I.* 9.1–2 (κλεινὰ δὲ καὶ ναυσικλυτὸς Αἴγινα 'renowned Aigina, famous for its ships'); *O.* 8.20; *I.* 9.6–7 (Aiginetans as dolphins). See n. 76 below for the fierce scholarly discussion of whether this maritime imagery refers to Aiginetans' commercial or military prowess. Aiginetans praised for their *themixenia* 'justice to strangers' and hospitality: *N.* 3.2–3; 4.12–13, 23; 5.8; *I.* 9.4–6. In *O.* 8.21–3 Aigina is seat of Themis and Zeus Xenios, possibly our Hellanios. *P.* 8.22 (δικαιόπολις 'just city'); *O.* 8.25–30. Aiginetans were thought to be the first builders of ships: Hes. fr. 205.6–7 MW: οἳ δή τοι πρῶτοι ζεῦξαν νέας ἀμφιελίσσας, πρῶτοι δ' ἱστί' ἔθεν νηὸς πτερὰ ποντοπόροιο 'they were the first to equip ships curved on both sides, the first to put up the sails as wings of the sea-going ship'.

[65] On 5th-cent. Panhellenism in particular see, in addition to n. 19 above, Flower (2000); Jacquemin (2001); Green (1996).

This section, then, will firstly examine the suggestion of Aigina's special commitment to Greece, followed by its link to the 'good crop'. Let us therefore scrutinize the Aiginetans themselves and look in greater detail at their fifth-century portrayal, both by themselves and by the world around them. But before I proceed with that, there is yet another issue to be sorted out to make the stipulation for Aigina's role in a Panhellenic context ritually plausible. For the Aiginetans too boast a link to the special Delphic, that is Thessalian-shaped, Hellenicity which goes back to the early sixth century. This is necessary to establish because in the early fifth century we can then see this medium-term link operate productively in a Panhellenic setting, revamping an existing religious tradition in a new historical milieu; another of those instances where the fifth-century world is indelibly linked to its partly real, partly perceived religious past.

Aigina and Zeus Hellanios in the sixth century

Aiginetans already in the sixth century seem to have sought a share in the particular Hellenicity construed in the greater orbit of the Thessalians, and Zeus Hellanios clearly helped them in that endeavour. The islanders have a curious but important bond with that same Thessalian region Hellas and in the sixth century started to lay claim to its heroes, who were then to become their ancestors, the 'Aiakids', beginning with Aiakos and culminating in Achilles and his son Neoptolemos. Aiakos in the epic tradition is a hero without home or family and his island just one of many parts of Agamemnon's reign. By the time of the Hesiodic poems, the *Catalogue of Women*, the *Ehoiai*, and the *Megalai Ehoiai*, however, Aiakos probably found himself on Aigina, and certainly Peleus already featured as an 'Aiakid'; by the time of Pindar at the latest, Aiakos had three sons, Peleus and Telamon by one woman, Phokos, later eponym of the region Phokis, by another. Peleus and Telamon accidentally killed their half-brother whilst practising discus-throwing; as a consequence, one went to Phthia in Thessaly to become father of Achilles (and grandfather of Neoptolemos); the other to Salamis to produce Telamonian Aias. Phokos, whose death is mentioned as early as the sixth-century *Alkmaionis*, remained on Aigina, where he had a shrine in the centre of town. That the Aiginetans hung on to Phokos, but sent the other two back to the places of their mythical origin, could suggest Aiginetan involvement in what may have been competing claims to Delphi during the 'Sacred War'.[66]

[66] Aiakos: Hes. fr. 205 MW; Peleus: Hes. fr. 211 MW. Phokos' murder by Peleus and/or Telamon: Pi. *N.* 5.14–16 (cf. Hes. *Theog.* 1003–7); D.S. 4.72.6; Apollod. 3.12.6; Paus. 2.29.9 (his grave at Aigina). *Σ* Eur. *Andr.* 687 *et al.* Aigina and Phthiotis: Furtwängler (1906) 437–8; A. Cook (1964–5) ii.1 894 n. 1; both see in Aiakos' Myrmidons a real Thessalian tribe who brought the god to Aigina; cf. now Burnett (2005) 13–28. According to Hes. fr. 58.10–15 MW, Phokos' two children Krisos and Panopeus squabbled already in their mother's womb, and historically are considered possible contenders for the running of the shrine at Delphi, with local traditions suggesting that the Panopeians eventually summoned the amphiktyony for help. The story of the Phlegyans seeking help at Panope after their attack on Apollo (Paus. 9.36) may also be part of the complex of legends associated with the Sacred War (see Fowler (1998) 14, and esp. n. 32). Is *stasis* in Phokis the context for the Aiginetan adoption of Phokos? Neoptolemos'murderer, it may be noted, is a Phokian in Apollod. 6.14.

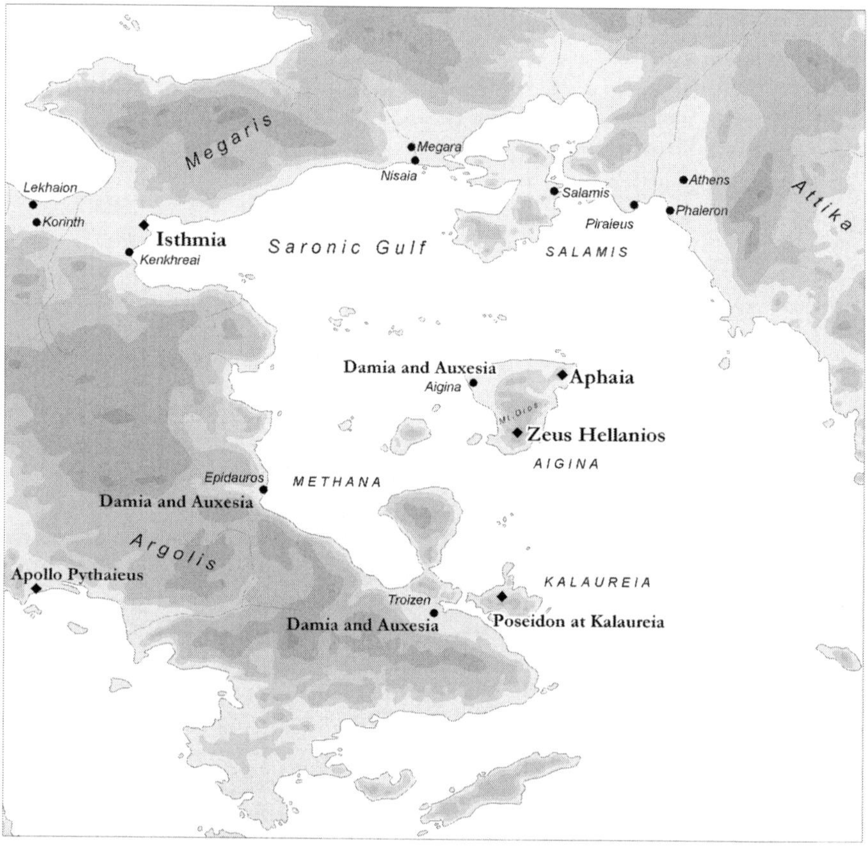

MAP 4.1 Aigina and Zeus Hellanios in the Saronic Gulf. Created from digital map data © Collins Bartholomew (2004) 2007

That the link between Aigina and Thessaly was forged during the sixth century, and quite possibly in the wider context of the Sacred War 'events', can for the moment be no more than a guess, but it may be a good one. For our Zeus Hellanios seems to represent the Aiginetans' link in cult to this same Thessalian world. *Ἑλλάνιος* is believed to be the *ethnikon* of the region *Ἑλλάς*, the Aiakids' home in Thessaly. Not long ago, Zeus Hellanios on Aigina still had little history, but very recent excavations have reshaped the life of this god and identified an archaic floruit at least since the later sixth century. The cult was located on modern Oros, the highest and steepest of Aigina's rocky summits (Fig. 4.1). First excavated in the late nineteenth and early twentieth centuries, the precinct comprised a small temple on the mountain top itself, foundations of which underlie the tiny modern chapel, and a large structure on its slopes. It is now clear that the sanctuary was in existence from Geometric to Roman times. The lower remains were long thought to be a Pergamene extension of the sanctuary by a large

Figure 4.1 Mount Oros, on top of which stand the foundations of the archaic temple for Zeus Hellanios; the lower sanctuary and *hestiatorion* (?) are at the foot of the mountain to the left, perhaps linked to the top by a sacred way

terrace, but in fact both building and terrace have beautiful archaic predecessors, clearly visible under the surviving Hellenistic structures (Fig. 4.2). Sixth-century architectural remains are scattered along the slope. The great numbers of mainly archaic drinking vessels as well as bones and ashes have led to the identification of this structure as a *hestiatorion*. On the day of the festival, one imagines, the festive community would have made its way between the lower ceremonial building and the mountain-top shrine in a procession which ended in feasting and drinking.[67] That the god was highly active into the early fifth century and frequented by an affluent clientele is clear from two fine inscribed bronze dedications of 480–460 BC, one of which is a well-preserved hydria in Athens' National Museum.[68]

[67] The excavations of 1997 and 1998; see *AR* 44 (1997–8) 18–19; *AR* 45 (1998–9) 19–20, and now *AR* 47 (2000–1) 18–19. I am grateful to H.-R. Götte for informing me of the excavation's results prior to their final publication. Further new finds include bits of both a Hellenistic and a classical Dorian capital, and a statue base of unknown date. The foundations of the archaic temple are at the top of the mountain to the north of the terrace, but a recent cementing of the whole chapel terrace (to accommodate the annual procession and festival to the chapel) has covered these. Mycenaean traces have long been known, including a prehistoric settlement at the foot of the hill: cf. recently Pilafidis-Williams (1995). For the earlier excavations see Furtwängler (1906) 473–4; Welter (1938*a*) 26–7; 91–2; 102; (1938*b*) 8–15.

[68] J. B. Harlan, *AJA* 29 (1925), 76–8, here 77 and fig. 1f; Welter (1938*b*) 8–10 figs. 3 and 4: *Πλάθων Ἐκεσθένης ἀνέθεν | hυιοὶ Προκλέους hΕλλανίοι Διί* 'Platon and Ekesthenes sons of Prokles dedicated to Zeus Hellanios'.

Figure 4.2 The lower sanctuary of Zeus Hellanios. Recent excavations have revealed its sixth-century monumentalization

Zeus Hellanios, then, received particular attention from the Aiginetans from the sixth century onwards. While the epithet Hellanios creates a link to Thessaly on the one hand, it also addresses the issue of 'Hellenism'. There are curious traces in Herodotus to confirm what we have just learnt from the *Catalogue*, that 'Hellenism', and how to define, or indeed confine, it, was as much debated prior to Herodotus' time of writing as in his own era. We may remember from Chapter 3 that Herodotus maintains that Phthiotis was the area from which the Dorians first set out, calling them, somewhat disconcertingly, *τὸ Ἑλληνικὸν ἔθνος* (as opposed to the Ionians, *τὸ Πελασγικὸν ἔθνος*); he then continues to refer to 'Hellenioi theoi' only in Spartan contexts as if to forge a link between whoever it was who came from Thessalian Phthiotis and the Dorians as a whole.[69] As I have already suggested, a rather different notion of Hellenism was implicit in the

[69] Hdt. 1.56–8, with Sourvinou-Inwood (2003*b*) 121–31. Aristagoras asks Kleomenes to swear by the *Ἑλλήνιοι θεοί* 5.49.3; and these are the gods the Korinthians call upon when appealing for the deposal of Hippias at 92η5: both of these are probably reinterpreted by Herodotus as 'Greek', whilst they might have entered the traditions as 'Dorian', gods; similar perhaps 9.7.2. Cf. LSJ s.v. *Ἑλλήνιος* and Paus. 3.12.6; cf. the *Ἑλλανοδίκαι* in Xen. *Lac.* 13.11 invoked to arbitrate between the Spartans and their allies. The identification of Dorians and Hellenes in Herodotus might suggest that the Spartans/Peloponnesians 'bought into' the amphiktyonic ideology. What exactly is going on is a complicated, interesting issue, which I cannot explore further here. See also next note.

creation of a Hellenion at Naukratis by the northern Ionian states assembling together with the Dorian Pentapolis. Significantly, the Aiginetans had a separate shrine—albeit without the epithet of Hellanios—apart from the other 'Greeks'. All of this is, I think, worth mentioning because it proves that the Thessalian region Hellas and its associated adjective Hellanios, epithet of our god, had an input into the process of multiple versions of Hellenicity, and these were relevant in the run-up to the early fifth-century Theoxenia celebrated by *Paean* 6.[70] The Aiginetans thus can be seen to overhaul their cult—and quite possibly turn Zeus Hellanios from a local god into one with 'Hellenic' pretensions. The excursus into the sixth century and the traditions surrounding the Thessalian associations of Zeus' epithet suggests that Aiginetans sought a share in the processes of definition over 'Hellenicity' revolving around Delphi. The cult's appearance in the fifth-century paean performed at the Panhellenic Theoxenia then sets itself into an inherited context of competing notions over 'what it means to be a Hellene', and who this exclusive group should be.

Aiginetans, the good Panhellenists

Aiginetans as dedicated Greeks, pivotal in a Panhellenic setting here at the Theoxenia—this is hardly what many of our fifth-century historical sources seem to think. If we are to believe them, Hellenism is everything other than an Aiginetan trademark. Commitment to the Greek cause was at this time manifested in one's role in the Persian Wars, and in the case of Aigina it is, according to Herodotus, half-hearted and purely motivated by animosities against Athens. The Aiginetans had previously given 'earth and water' to the Persian King, and this legacy of medism is held against them throughout in Herodotus' version of events. Aiginetans appear first among the long list of medizers, branded as 'betrayers' of Greece. Indeed, how friendly some Aiginetans were with Persia comes out when looking at Herodotus' colourful Aiginetan prosopography.[71] Nevertheless, the Aiginetans eventually became the Athenians' greatest rivals for the title of the best performers on behalf of Greece in the crucial battle of Salamis,

[70] Naukratis: Hdt. 2.178. Just as the Dorians of the Peloponnese, the Dorians of Aigina were imagined to have arrived under the 'reign of Hyllos and Aigimios'. The pooling of Dorians and 'Hellenes' is therefore not a surprise (Pi. *I.* 9.1–4). The 'Doric island' in *N.* 3.1–3: Ὦ πότνια Μοῖσα . . . ἵκεο Δωρίδα νᾶσον Αἴγιναν 'O Lady Muse, come to the Dorian island of Aigina'. The island is often thought to have been settled from the Peloponnese: Hdt. 8.46; Str. 8.6.16; Paus. 2.29.5; Σ Pi. *O.* 8.39, reflected in the myths and cults of Damia and Auxesia in the Saronic Gulf area (Hdt. 5.82–8). Euripides calls Athena Aphaia Ἑλλανία: Eur. *Hipp.* 1123.

[71] Hdt. 6.49 for Aigina's medism, which the Athenians interpret as directed against them. This prompts the calling in of the Spartans, who take until 6.73 to imprison the culpable pro-Persian Aiginetans, notably Krios and Kasambos (who are among ten hostages, 'taken from the richest'). Examples of Aiginetan individuals: Krios the ram: Hdt. 6.50; 73; cf. Simonides' *epinikion PMG* 507; his son Polykritos mocks Themistokles on Aiginetan medism: 8.92; Lampon's 'barbarian' taste 9.78–9; Pytheas, son of Iskhenoos, was captured and butchered by a Persian crew at Skiathos: 7.181, but put together again by them 'because of his valour'. Aiginetans join the Hellenic League as late as 7.145. Wolski (1973); Gillis (1979) discuss Aiginetan medism.

or at least some liked to think they did. A considerable amount of fifth-century material survives on this topic, confirming attitudes just as forcefully reiterated by later authors; whether this means that the Aiginetans were *de facto* Athens' fiercest competitors for this title, or whether Athenian–Aiginetan competition was just one of many and happened to survive in media that withstood the censorship of tradition, we are unable to say.

Let us explore the traditions of Aigina's attitude to Greece in greater detail. Herodotus' description of the battle of Salamis suggests how much Aigina's exemplary commitment or the lack thereof was an issue of concern. This ritual moment of Greek history is not only characterized by a staggering concentration on Aiginetan–Athenian rivalry, but so much of an Aiginetan Panhellenic devotion now transpires that one starts to wonder what the true story was: Aiginetans receive the *aristeia* ('reward for prowess') of the battle despite having provided only the second greatest number of ships after the Athenians, who in fact deliver six times as many; the top individual fighter is an Athenian, *proxime accessit* an Aiginetan; Aiginetans have good strategic plans, and their local knowledge ensures that Persians who managed to escape the Athenians are inevitably drowned by them. Aiginetans sink as many ships as the Athenians; Aiginetans rescue Athenian ships from sinking. Aiginetans also lend their local gods to the Greeks: when the Greek ships have gathered to begin the battle, an earthquake prompts the invocation of the local Salaminian heroes Aias and his father Telamon, whilst 'a ship was sent to Aigina to get Aiakos and the other Aiakids'. Note however, that once the ship arrives, whether it was an Aiginetan or an Athenian ship that opened the battle is again contested.[72]

That Aigina's former medism is at stake here throughout is suggested by a last anecdote of the island's high-powered performance: while Aiginetans rescue an Athenian ship, Themistokles happens to be sailing by, prompting the Aiginetan captain to shout out loud at him, 'mocking Themistokles for charging the Aiginetans with medism'. The suggestion is that in this story, Aiginetans battle well to prove their commitment to the Greek cause. However, while Herodotus' version of events will not believably establish Athenian superiority at the battle of Salamis—as it was later portrayed, for example in an Athenian speech by Thucydides or implied by Aeschylus' *Persians*—Aiginetans, too, are just too perfect for them to come out of this as credibly devoted Panhellenists.[73]

[72] Hdt. 8.40 ff. Number of Aiginetan ships: 8.46; good strategy and local knowledge: 74; 91; Aiginetans sinking as many ships as the Athenians: 86; Aristeides bonding with Themistokles despite long-standing personal enmities: 79–81; *aristeia* for the Aiginetans, Athenians in second place: 93; 122; local Aiakids in support of Greeks: 64; 83–4. The Aiakids were sent in support of Thebans against Athenians in 5.79–81; but what the nature of these venerable talismans was is unclear: see Thiersch (1928); Woodbury (1979) 124; Zunker (1988) 71–2; von Wilamowitz-Moellendorff (1922) 64 n. 3, and now Burnett (2005) 26–8, esp. 73 (cf. D.S. 8.32: Spartan Tyndaridai sent in support of Lokroi at the battle at the Sagras against the Krotoniates).

[73] Polykritos vs. Themistokles: Hdt. 8.92. Themistokles himself was going to become a medizer, which tradition records in connection with this battle: Paus. 10.14.5–6. Athenians were exceptionally keen to propagate their contribution to the victory: Th. 1.73.4–74; the Korinthians certainly had an ambiguous role in the battle: contrast Hdt. 8.94; Plut. *De Her. Mal.* 870b–f and ML 24 (480 BC).

Rather, whether and how engaged the Aiginetans were in Hellenic affairs is clearly a debated matter at the time. It is one thing that Pausanias still knows of Aiginetan prowess at Salamis. But more contemporarily, Pindar's Aiginetan odes reveal not only how wonderfully the Aiginetans fought in the struggle against Persia, but also how great their loyalty to Hellas was and always had been. Pindar's *Isthmians 5* and *8* refer to Aigina's role in the battle of Salamis, and make an explicit reference to the end of the Persian Wars. As mentioned above, the aetiology of Zeus Hellanios is alluded to in two of Pindar's *Nemean Odes*, and both passages make it clear how indebted to the Aiginetans the rest of Greece should feel. But the islanders' love for Hellas is particularly obvious from the way in which the Aiakids are turned into the Greeks' greatest asset at Troy, that other war against 'Asia' that traditionally helped the case for one's Panhellenic commitment. The regular appearance in all the Aiginetan odes of Neoptolemos, Achilles, Aias, as well as all the older generation that produced this set of virtuous warriors (Peleus, Telamon) cannot suggest anything else, carefully woven as it is into the fabric of the odes, with references to contemporary Aiginetans. This forms too meticulously stitched and repetitive a set of associations in Pindar's odes to be just a standard gallery of local heroes through which to praise a victor. Aiginetan bravery at Troy justifies their attribute of good Panhellenists.[74]

Finally, there is the intriguing tradition that Aiakos himself was the cornerstone of the Greeks' first capture of Troy, pre-empting and anticipating his descendants' legacy to come. This is suggestively depicted in Pindar's odes, where, incidentally, the myth first appears in literature. It is also presupposed when the Aiakid Telamon's sack of Troy with Herakles replaces an earlier scene of Aiakos' birth on the east pediment of Aphaia's splendid temple in the gentle valleys of Aigina. The west pediment then turned to the later, main expedition, glorifying the deeds of Aias son of Telamon and Achilles, again suggesting the link between the Aiginetans' ancestors and the heroes who destroyed Troy. The dating of these early fifth-century sculptures remains contested, but it is clear that the Aiakids had a big part to play on pre- and post-Persian War Aigina. The answer to why the Knidian Leskhe at Delphi, built shortly after 480 BC, should feature Neoptolemos as the last remaining Greek fighter, certainly also has a share in this context. All this Trojan talk is peculiar and certainly a novelty: Aigina epically speaking was rather inconspicuous in Homeric Troy, forming part of the Argive contingent in the *Catalogue*, and with no great heroes on show.[75]

Aiginetan commitment to the Greeks was debated, and quite vociferously so. We can conclude that if an early fifth-century Panhellenic festival featured Aiakos

[74] Zeus Hellanios: *N.* 5.8–13; 8.9–12. Allusions to the Persian Wars: *I.* 5.34–8 (stressing a double Aiakid victory at Troy); 48–50 (Salamis); *I.* 8.5–12; Aiakids and Troy: *N.* 6.44–end; 7.17–20; 5.

[75] Aiakos and Troy: Pi. *O.* 8.31–46; cf. *I.* 5.34–8 (Figueira (1993*a*) 207 thinks of the role of Aiakos in *O.* 8 as 'consolatory' to Aiginetans recently defeated by Athens); Aphaia pediments: Furtwängler (1906); Ohly (1976–2001); Gill (1993) for a recent attempt at their dating. Knidian Leskhe at Delphi: Paus. 10.25–31; catalogue: *Il.* 2.562. Both temple and odes incidentally raise a claim on Aias for Aigina rather than Athens: Kowalzig (2006) 89 and n. 44.

and his Aiginetans, this would immediately have prompted a string of associations, referring to what it meant to be a good Greek at a time when Greece was under the threat of Persian conquest. While Aiginetans were much maligned in some traditions for their medism, those Aiginetans who commissioned public monuments—including the victory odes—were unreservedly keen to point out their devotion to the Greek cause. Why did they care? A straightforward answer would be that this is what everyone did at the time, and that is partly right. But there is also a more complex response, one that involves Aiginetans and Athenians embroiled in a definition of Panhellenism and Panhellenic commitment, a debate which formed a crucial part in the pervading question of what should be the political and, by association, economic consequences of the Persian Wars. Or, more briefly, in giving shape to post-Persian War Greece.

Eueteria

This is where I turn to *eueteria*—'good crop, good harvest', the second element shared between the Theoxenia and the myth of Aiakos the Aiginetan, who by extracting rain from his father Zeus once made sure that the Greeks did not have to starve. The point of cult legends is not to portray something that really happened at a distant time in the past, but something of contemporary relevance. This is obviously not to say, that, if this myth was summoned in connection with the Theoxenia in *Paean 6*, there was a drought in the early fifth century. Rather I propose that the legend's prominence more widely in Pindar, and the character of Aiakos in particular, reveals Aigina's awareness of the economic potential of its position in the Saronic Gulf, as if this were enabling it, and had enabled it in the past, to 'ward off a drought'. I am inclined to see an economic dimension in this myth: the motif of 'rain' in the Aiakos legend implies claims going beyond the natural phenomenon. Its absence in the myth is a metaphor for the disruption and reconstitution of a disturbed cycle of redistribution of agricultural goods, in which Aigina somehow had a role. For Aiakos' story is only one of a number of local oral traditions revealing that Aiginetan identity was tied up with its advantageous geographical location at a nodal point of communication in the Saronic Gulf (Map 4.1). This allowed them to become pivotal not in agriculture, but in trading agricultural goods, and visibly the grain-supply. Aiginetans (or rather: some Aiginetans, see below) picture themselves mythically in terms of their economic independence, and the degree to which others depended on them. These traditions, some of which resurface in Pindar, suggest among other things that the Aiginetan elite commissioning his songs was, even if not an outright commercial aristocracy, at least deeply embedded in economic activities. In the end, local Aiginetan benefits from trade might have been at the heart of the *eueteria* that *Paean 6* was meant to invoke at the Panhellenic Theoxenia.[76]

[76] I shall not at this point rehearse the long-standing discussion on the topic of Aigina's commercialism, most recently illuminated by Hornblower (2004) 207–35; (2007); Parker (2004*a*). Suggestions from myth have as far as I am aware not been taken into account for this question. The interpretation of Pindar's maritime metaphors has unduly dominated this debate, e.g. *N* 5.2–3, 21;

A fascinating cluster of evidence implies that the Aiginetan economic self is embedded in the local, and perhaps even not-so-local grain chain. The convoluted story of the παλαιὴ ἔχθρη, the long-standing enmity between Athens and Aigina, recounted over six or seven chapters in Herodotus, gives one key to this view.[77] The legend is narrated here with a view to explaining why renewed hostilities between Athens and Aigina broke out around 506 BC. In it, we learn that Aigina was once tributary to the Epidaurians, themselves tributary to the Athenians; and we learn how the Aiginetans manage to break away from the Epidaurian tie, and by implication from the Athenian one as well. This they do by, as is typical for stories communicating patterns of social change, committing sacrilege against the divine figures symbolic of this bond. They steal the statues of the heroines Damia and Auxesia. To ward off a drought, the Epidaurians had once been advised by Delphi to build statues of the heroines of olive wood. Athens being then the 'only place where the olive grew' allowed access to their stock in return for an annual sacred tribute to Athena and Erekhtheus. (This in itself is an interesting story forging dependence construed around basic agricultural goods.) It is these two girls that the Aiginetans snatched when they felt fit to break free from Epidauros.[78] When challenging the Epidaurians for the tribute, the Athenians were referred to the Aiginetans, who flatly refused to pay. And so war broke out between Athens and Aigina, in which the statues, supported by thunder and earthquake (the standard messengers of imminent injustice and sacrilege), refused to be taken to Athens, as if to justify the Aiginetan case.[79]

The cultural consequence of this episode is interesting: angry Athenian women stabbed to death with their dress pins their one returning warrior; from this point onward the women of Athens were reduced to wearing Ionian garments, which could do with smaller pins. Aiginetans (and, incidentally, Argives) introduced pins twice as big, and these monumental accessories became the standard

5.50–1; 6.32: for the minimalist view see the recent publication of de Ste. Croix' 1960s manuscript (2004*b*), and the afterword by Parker (2004*a*). De Ste. Croix is promptly answered by Hornblower (2004) 211–17, accepting the denial of primary Aiginetan commercialism in the odes, while not excluding involvement in commercial activity in principle. The 'modernist' view is old: e.g. Hegyi's Marxist interpretation (1969), but above all Figueira's (1981), esp. 230–98; (1993*a*) *passim*; Gehrke (1986) 172–4. More generally see Nixon and Price (1990) or Horden and Purcell (2000) 119–20.

[77] Hdt. 5.82–9, discussed by Figueira (1993*d*; cf. *c* and *e*) 35 ff., without bringing out the 'economic' dimension quite as much as one might. Paus. 2.30.4 gives the short version, right after discussing the cult of Zeus Hellanios (note the agricultural link!). Kratinos fr. 165 Kock speaks of an ancient life when everyone eats Aiginetan bread: what could that mean?

[78] The Aiginetans started to celebrate their independence in choral ritual, as if this marked their civic identity; and in a ritual known for the mystery cult of Demeter at Eleusis: Paus. 2.30.4; cf. Hdt. 5.83.3 on the 'secret rites' at Epidauros. Damia and Auxesia are shared by cities of the Saronic Gulf: Troizen: Paus. 2.32.2; Zenob. 4.20; see Nilsson (1906/95) 415–16. Their names varied locally: Epidauros: *IG* iv^2.1 386; 398; 410; Aigina: *IG* iv 1588. A relation between Aiginetan independence and the island's 'commercialism' à la Figueira, esp. (1993*c*) 10–11, is a possibility.

[79] Though in the Athenian version the images 'fell to their knees, in which position they are visible to the present day': Hdt. 5.86. In the Aiginetan version the island was helped by Argives, who took a route via Epidauros, in their successful attempt to ward off the Athenian threat.

dedication to Damia and Auxesia, who would from now on no more accept Athenian pottery: an interesting attempt to separate ideologically what seems like deeply intertwined cultural and economic spheres.[80] This is a myth talking about local crops and local products on the one hand, but tied into an economic network and rivalry in the Saronic Gulf on the other. The Aiginetans manage to settle this set of affairs to their advantage then, whilst paying for their independence with a lasting hatred by the Athenians that would eventually thwart their autarky in the fifth century. The story results in the construction of ethnic differentiation within the different people inhabiting the Saronic Gulf tied to distinct social set-ups and economic choices. It is indeed the nature of this network and how it would ensure a 'good crop' for its shareholders, that would characterize this conflict again in the future.

There are reasons to believe that Aiginetans were actually involved in the grain trade in the Aegean and Eastern Mediterreanean, even though pieces of literary evidence are disparate, and archaeology for the moment cannot help either. Their involvement at Naukratis, where Aiginetans had a shrine of Zeus as on their own Oros, suggests as much. Xerxes at Abydos in the Hellespont in 480 BC patiently watches corn-ships plying their way from the Black Sea to Aigina and to the Peloponnese, and fourth-century Aiginetan pirates raiding Attika contribute to Athens' exhaustion, leading not just to the peace of 375 BC but also to a tax on grain from its island cleruchies.[81]

But myth again makes the stronger case: on close inspection the figure of Aiakos, the Aiginetan ancestor himself, emerges as a hero of the grain-supply. This must be related to his role as drought-lifter for the common good in the myth of Zeus Hellanios. It is the Athenian appropriation of this hero that accompanies an attempt to subdue Aigina in 506 BC, the conflict that prompts the telling of the story of the ancestral hatred, which was all about Aigina's economic independence from Athens. Athenians build their own shrine of Aiakos at Athens, and move against the Aiginetans in the local war that built Themistokles' anti-Persian fleet that won at Salamis. Having Aiakos in their city was supposed to support the Athenians in this continued maritime conflict. But this is the shrine in which, as we now know from the new, fourth-century grain-tax law, the Athenians stored their grain! In addition, in fourth-century vase-painting that presumably picks up on dramatic plots, Aiakos appears in connection with Triptolemos, the hero of the imperial crop, also someone who travelled around to

[80] The pottery ban has been subject to much discussion, but there is little material evidence, suggesting its aetiological, rather than historical value: cf. Ath. 11.502c and Figueira (1993*d*) 37–40; on the pins and dress 41–4, arguing for a 5th-cent. invention. Sacred bans implicating the 'economy' perhaps deserve further consideration: *LSCG* no. 110; but also of course the Megarian decree: Th. 1.139.1–2; Plut. *Per.* 29.4; 30.3; D.S. 12.39.4–5.

[81] Naukratis: Hdt. 2.178, where the Aiginetans have a temple apart from the other Greeks; Xerxes: 7.147.2; 4th-cent. Aiginetan pirates: X. *Hell.* 6.2.1; the grain-tax law: Shear (1987). For a discussion of Hdt. 7.147.2 and the possibility of 6th-cent. Aiginetan involvement in the Pontic grain trade see Figueira (1981) 272–5; (1993*e*) 148, but the question is not solved at present; on Aigina and Naukratis see Figueira (1981) 258–61.

give the Greeks the benefit of 'a good crop'. And finally, as mentioned above, there is the splendid early fifth-century tradition of Aiakos prompting Troy's first destruction. In so far as the Trojan War may have been fought not least over the exit from the Hellespont, that Aiakos should be the first Greek hero to have ensured access to the Pontus not only puts Aigina into close rapport with the Black Sea trade just as Xerxes had observed, but also adds to Aiakos' privileged connection to the grain-supply.[82]

Aiakos thus emerges as a hero somehow concerned with the routes that the grain took before coming to mainland Greece, and to Athens in particular. In wrangling over Aiakos, from the late sixth century onwards, Athenians and Aiginetans may well be competing over some aspect of the grain trade, perhaps even the corn route to the Euxine. While the extent of actual Aiginetan involvement in this enterprise cannot be ascertained, the minimum conclusion must be that Aigina was in the way of lucrative Athenian business as long as merchant-ships put in at the island rather than Piraeus. This is the 'independent' island that the myth of Aiakos invokes, and that of Damia and Auxesia also supports, not as an agriculturally self-sufficient place, but as watching over what comes in and goes out of the harbour. Is this what is meant when famous Athenian politicians stigmatized Aigina as the *λήμη τοῦ Πειραιῶς*, the 'pus in the eye of the Piraeus', causing 'lack of vision'? The ubiquitous myth of Aiakos the drought-lifter certainly makes a case for Aigina to continue playing that role.[83]

Panhellenism and the grain-chain

Panhellenic commitment and *eueteria* for Greece thus seem to converge in the figure of Aiginetan Aiakos, destroyer of Troy and averter of famine. One extraordinary implication is that Aiginetans are the linchpin in an all-Greek grain chain, in that set of connections that guarantees the Greeks a reliable food-supply. In the context of the Panhellenic ceremony at the Theoxenia where one sang for 'the good crop' in all of Greece, this is a pretty strong claim to parade. Quite apart from the actual extent of Aiginetan involvement in the grain-trade, as we have seen whether or not the Aiginetans were committed Greeks was highly contested at the time. This brings us to the issue of why the Aiginetans' medism or its absence is a recurrent topic in the traditions, or else why someone was interested

[82] Aiakos' shrine: Hdt. 5.89 with Zunker (1988); Parker (1996) 157 and n. 18 for the debated chronology; Stroud (1998) thinks of Athenian mimesis of the Aiginetan shrine (Paus. 2.29.6–7). Aiakos as an underworld judge, often together with Triptolemos: *Ran.* 414–78; Pl. *Apol.* 41a; *Gorg.* 523e–24a; Isocr. 9.15; *LIMC* i (1981) 311–12 s.v., nos. 1–3. For Troy as a trading centre see Korfmann (1986); (1995).

[83] D.H. *De Th.* 15; Plut. *Per.* 8.7 with Stadter: *λῆμα* or *λήμη* is often translated as the 'eyesore of the Piraeus', but rather invokes a more forceful image: 'conjunctivitis was a common ancient disease, marked by a purulent discharge of the eye, sticking the eyelids together and impairing or blocking vision. The offending matter needed to be cleaned out.' Cf. LSJ 'the humour that gathers round the eye', 'rheum': Arist. *Rhet.* 3.10.7, 1411^{a}15–16; Plut. *Dem.* 1.2; *Reg. et Imp. Apoth.* 186c; *Praec. Ger. Rei Publ.* 803a; Ath. 3.99d; in Str. 9.1.14 it is the island of Psyttalia.

in maligning them so much that Aiginetans were so very keen to prove their Panhellenic persuasion in cultic song.

The answer lies, I think, in the different models of Panhellenism in circulation immediately after the Persian Wars, and the social and economic set-ups in their train. To put it simply, the divide essentially lies between a vision of Panhellenism based on international elite connectivity and one characterized by Athenocentrism embedded in popular politics, and both of them bound up with specific economic concerns, or perhaps just aspirations. The dilemma tends to be writ large at Athens, but it is likely to be an issue relevant to many places in Greece. There is no question that one's Panhellenic commitment became an important political bargaining tool after the Persian Wars both within and between cities; the best proof of this is that any politician or general who fell out of favour was instantly turned into a Persian sympathizer. But that also leaves room for different interpretations of what it means to be committed to the Greeks. In particular, much of the fragmented politics of the early Delian League, ostensibly founded to ward off a continued Persian threat, seems to hover between these two extremes.[84]

The Delian League's oscillation between two such views of what early fifth-century Greece should look like—crudely speaking Athens-focused or internationalist—is also the context in which Aiginetans' Panhellenic commitment and its denial need to be seen. The island's history at this time is a continuous redefinition of its relationship to Athens, giving us an insight into how difficult and socially complex life in post-Salamis Greece was. The case of Aigina is special in some respects, since its proximity to Athens meant that Aiginetan and Athenian affairs were very closely intertwined. The island's image is bizarrely shaped by Athenian public discourse. Aigina seems to have floated in and out of the Athenian orbit depending on whose interest in either proximity or distance prevailed in either place at any one time, and not only because both liked to send political exiles to the other as if to keep them at a distance yet close by.[85]

But in other respects, Aigina's fate might well present a paradigm for the factors that shaped relations between Athens and candidates for—willing or enforced—inclusion in the league, in other words the advantages and disadvantages of alliance and independence, and who within a particular society would benefit

[84] Panhellenism is often studied from an Athenian point of view, particularly as part of the Greek–Persian antithesis, including also a debate on democracy (e.g. E. Hall (1989); J. Hall (2002) Ch. 6; T. Harrison (2000*b*); Flower (2000)), less often in the context of competing economic choices. Traditional views on the (un)popularity of the Athenian empire (e.g. Meiggs (1972); de Ste. Croix (1954); Finley (1978)) tend to isolate political factors. Chapter 2 has already shown that allies were facing more complex choices. Politicians turned into medizers: e.g. Pausanias: Th. 1.128.3–7; Aristeides: Plut. *Arist.* 8.1; Themistokles: Plut. *Them.* 25 ff.

[85] In the Athenian imagination Aigina seems to have become the refuge for all anti-democrats, notably comic poets: Eupolis died in Aigina according to Ael. *Nat. An.* 10.41; at Sikyon, Paus. 2.7.3. Aristophanes was also thought a resident: Ar. *Ach.* 652–5 (a reason for the Spartans to recover Aigina); *Σ* 654b; Theogenes *FGrH* 300 F 2. Exiled Athenians on Aigina had become proverbial and tended to gather around a bronze bull to gossip: Kock, *Adesp.* 40; cf. Plin. *NH* 34.5.10; Hdt. 8.79.1. Cf. e.g. Aristeid. ([Dem.] 26.6; *Suda* α 3903, δ 72); Thoukydides son of Melesias: Figueira (1993*a*) 187–8). See Figueira ibid. 182 ff. for further details.

from either. Perhaps precisely because Aigina was so close to Athens, more differentiation is possible here than on other islands. For despite the impression we get from Pindar, it would be wrong to think that early fifth-century Aiginetans were a closely knit community of self-appointed nobles with a strong and shared mythical identity and a collective hatred for Athens.[86] On the contrary, they were an extremely argumentative group of people with a number of Athenian sympathizers and, more importantly, Aiginetan individuals had many and varied long-standing Athenian connections. Stasis at the time gives away that not all leading Aiginetans were automatically anti-Athenian, and a certain Nikodromos' attempted democratic revolution in the 490s BC leads to a contingent of 700 democrats being settled at Sounion. These then keep raiding the territory of their former homes and are plausibly the profiteers of the Athenian cleruchy established in 431 BC, when Aigina was eventually incorporated into the empire.[87]

Above all, Athens and Aigina were tied to each other by cross-continental family bonds. It is in these that the problems of the Athenian–Aiginetan relationship tantalizingly converge, implicating some of Athens' most prominent politicians. My somewhat simplistic opposition between elite connectivity versus populist Athenocentrism also comes to the fore here. Here we launch straight into matters of elite initiatives and their social and economic consequences for the Athenians, and these are conspicuously related to Panhellenism and the grain-supply, and also involve Aigina. A striking illustration is given by the Athenian Philaids, a family that moulded the history of their city like no other. Herodotus attributes an Aiginetan origin to Miltiades the Elder, a descendant of Aiakos himself, who had been an Athenian northward pioneer in settling the Chersonese, ever-contested for its fertile and extensive land. His nephew, heir, and star of Marathon in 490 BC, the younger Miltiades, rather than declaring himself tyrant and pocketing all the profit, was the first allegedly to turn his conquests into benefits for the Athenian people when 'having taken the island of Lemnos . . . he gave it to the Athenians'.[88] The pertinent 'Aiginetan' legacy is his son Kimon who

[86] This is taken for granted, with varied differentiation, by most scholars studying the island's history: e.g. Figueira (1981) Ch. 5; Gehrke (1986) 172–4; but also de Ste. Croix (2004*b*); it tends to characterize Pindaric studies, e.g. Hubbard (2001; thinking of a 'problematised elite'); Pfeijffer (1999); Kurke (1991); Burnett (2005). Contrast Hornblower (2004) 207–17; see also n. 87.

[87] Hdt. 6.87–93 (*c.*491–487 BC) on Nikodromos' attempted revolt which also develops a tradition of the cruelty of the Aiginetan elite; 6.90 for the fugitives at Sounion from where they regularly raided Aigina. Aiginetans hold off the league in 477 BC, 459/8 is their first entry (rather than earlier): D.S. 11.78; Th. 1.105.2; 108.4; Lewis (1992*b*) 500–1; in 446 BC possibly autonomy is granted to Aigina (cf. Th. 1.67.2): Lewis (1992*a*) 130 and 137 n. 45; *IG* i^3 38. Repatriated democrats: Figueira (1993*a*) 278; (1981) 115–20. Aigina's complicated 5th-cent. fate is conveniently set out by Hornblower (2004) 221–3; cf. Gehrke (1986) 172–4. Aiginetan prosopography is a fascinating subject: see now the long chapter in Hornblower (2004) 218–35 and (2007); cf. Figueira (1981) 299–313, and n. 71 above.

[88] Miltiades the Elder, a descendant from Aiakos: Hdt. 6.35. Figueira (1993*a*) 78 n. 58; 211–12 thinks this is a claim by the 5th-cent. Philaids *against* the Aiginetan elite while I believe it rather suggests their interaction, as does their connection to the Aiakid Philaos, son of Aias: Marcell. *Vit. Th.* 3; Pherec. *FGrH* 3 F 2; Hell. *FGrH* 4 F 22. Miltiades the Younger and Lemnos: Hdt. 6.136.2–140. His (failed) expedition to Paros had also promised to make the Athenians rich (καταπλουτεῖν): 6.132.

famously used not only his personal estate's produce, but also his talent for conquest, as Plutarch says, in order to make the Athenians rich—and turn them into his supporters.[89]

The counter image to the life of the farming and conquering benefactor is of course found in the less glamorous aristocrats who were not rich but all the more avid Athenians, such as Themistokles, and, later, Perikles. To gain the popular support they could not afford to buy, they turned to distributing public wealth—that accrued by, for example, Kimon's raiding expeditions mentioned above.[90] The differences between Philaid-Kimonian and Themistoklean or later Periklean visions of what the post-Persian War world should look like are often reduced to that of sole Athenian leadership versus a dual hegemony shared between Athens and Sparta. But certainly in Athens, these visions have complex social and, by implication, economic realities behind them even if both are designed to make the people 'rich': either to maintain a travelling and conquering elite, tied into a broader Mediterranean network of viable harbours, and happy to pour its constantly augmented riches into the entertainment of the poor; or to empower the same *demos* through accumulated state funds and public distribution of conquered, often allied, land. The two associated economic set-ups are presumably a wider network of flourishing commercial centres, as opposed to investment into Athens where, as eventually occurred, Piraeus would (not least through harbour tax) greatly benefit the Athenian state and the democracy.[91]

That visions along these lines were phrased as competing versions of Panhellenism becomes clear through both the contemporary, as well as Plutarchian, portrayal of two of these famous Athenian leaders. Kimon and Themistokles compete not least through their shared aspiration for title of 'best Hellene'. Kimon the great Greek is of course a theme in Plutarch, but seemingly already part of fifth-century tradition when Kratinos calls him the 'best of the Panhellenes', and his biography overflows with references to all-Greek appreciation. Plutarch's account also emphasizes how well Kimon treated the

[89] Kimon's proverbial wealth is lavished on the Athenians in return for honour: *Ath. Pol.* 27.2–3; Kratinos, *Arkhilokhoi PCG* 1 (Cf. Plut. *Cim.* 10.3–4); making the city rich through expeditions: *Cim.* 9.6; 13.5–7; 14.2–4; conquered land given to Athenians: *Cim.* 7.3; 8.2 ff. See Thomas (1989) 203–5 for the difficulty in reconstructing Kimon's career due to the whims of Athenian democratic tradition. On the Philaids see recently Culasso Gastaldi (1996). Incidentally, Kimon's political heir Thucydides (for whom see Figueira (1993*a*) Ch. 8) was the son of a certain Melesias, a coach of Aiginetan boys and antagonist to Perikles (201 ff.): *Ath. Pol.* 28.2; Plut. *Per.* 8.5; 11 (on this milieu see now Burnett (2005)); possible relation to Kimon: Plut. *Per.* 11.1; *Ath. Pol.* 28.2; *Σ* Aristid. 3.446 Dind. This was a family that put wrestling first: *N.* 4.93–6; 6.66–9; Pl. *Men.* 94c. Figueira, ibid., discusses some aspects of mutual support between Athenian and Aiginetan elites.

[90] For Themistokles' obscure birth, poverty, and wealth accrued through politics see Plut. *Them.* 1; 5; 25. Perikles: Plut. *Per.*; *Ath. Pol.* 27–28.2.

[91] Generally on ancient cities hovering, as well as mediating, between euergetism and imperialism to ensure basic food-supply ('a network of institutions . . . monitored by governments') see Garnsey (1988) *passim*; (1999) esp. 32–3, also on the role of Piraeus during the Athenian empire, including examples of Athenians redirecting traffic. On the importance of harbour tax for a connected *polis* world see now thought-provokingly Purcell (2005).

non-Athenian Greeks, whilst stressing his connection to the great and the good of Hellas.[92] Themistokles' *Life* is similarly full of references to Panhellenism but cherishes the opposite values: while Themistokles is popular with the people, he is disliked by the allies and particularly unsympathetic to leading Greek aristocrats who also happen to be those of vibrant economic centres. If Timokreon of Rhodes or the Aiginetan Krios both manifested their antipathy in surviving contemporary elegiac song, this suggests that Plutarch's contrived narrative of the Second Sophistic might after all have conveyed some fifth-century truths.[93]

However blurred this artificial distinction was in reality, it is likely that the early Delian League, committed as it was to the Panhellenic cause, oscillated between elite and demotic policies not only at Athens but across all its members. And that also entailed that Panhellenism, while a shared ideology and slogan, could be interpreted in different ways by different people, carrying among other things distinct economic interpretations. 'Corn supply'—in real benefits, or in the form of land—emerges as a constant theme in these discussions, almost as if your quality as a Panhellene depended on how well you did in this area.

The portrayal of the Aiginetans is caught between these two poles. For the myth of Aiakos and Zeus Hellanios suggests exactly this: that being key in food supply makes you a good Greek. The overemphasis on Aiginetan Panhellenic commitment as well as the tendency to turn them into Greece's greatest enemy are the outcome of these competing versions of Panhellenism. Aiginetan medism then is, among other things, a product of a growing Athenian imperialism, a tradition not so keen for Aigina to remain 'independent' in Aiakos' terms: it cannot be a coincidence that those two Athenian politicians, Themistokles and Perikles, who pronounced themselves forcefully on the economic power of Aigina—the 'λήμη of the Piraeus', an expression for something truly repulsive—also happened to be the democrats with an Athens-centred league in mind.[94] Attached to Themistokles' career in particular is a series of anti-Aiginetan pronouncements. To turn the (rich) Aiginetans into medizers, that is to say take away

[92] Kimon the great Greek: Crat. *Arch. PCG* 1: *σὺν . . . πάντ' ἀρίστῳ τῶν Πανελλήνων †πρώτῳ Κίμωνι* 'with in every way the best of all the Greek men'; Plut. *Cim.* 3; 10.4 ff. (compared to Likhas, famous among the Hellenes); 6.2 (Kimon the supreme general against the Persians); 7.4 ff. (honorary epigrams); 8.1; 12; 16.3; 18; 19.5 (Kitians on Cyprus paying honours at Kimon's tomb, *Ἑλληνικὸς ἡγεμών* 'the Greek leader'). Kimon good with the rest of the Greeks: *Cim.* 11.2; 16.3 ('mild with the *symmakhoi*'); 16.9 (double hegemony in the name of Hellas); 18: seeking policies in order that 'Athens may not trouble the Hellenes'. Kimon's connectedness with the Hellenic elite: 4; 14.4; 16.1. Philolakonism: Ar. *Lys.* 1143 f.; Plut. *Cim.* 10.7; 14.4; 16.1; Eupolis *PCG* 221 *ap. Cim.* 15.4).

[93] Themistokles the Hellene: Plut. *Them.* 1.1; 3.5; 6.4; 17.4 (the pride of Hellas against the Barbarian); his merits in Persian Wars: 7. Liked by the people and not susceptible to bribes: 5.6; choregic victory with Phrynikhos: 5.5; disliked by the allies: 21; hated by leading Greek aristocrats, e.g Krios the ram: Sim. *PMG* 507; Timokreon of Rhodes: *PMG* 727 (Themistokles' meanness). His rivalry with Kimon: Plut. *Cim.* 5; 9.1; *Them.* 5.4. See pp. 254–6 below.

[94] Cf. n. 83 above. Aigina's military and economic vantage positions are not mutually exclusive: rallying place in the Persian Wars: Hdt. 8.131.1; 132.1–2; D.S. 11.34.2; calling point esp. for troops in the 5th cent.: Th. 2.31.3; 5.53; 6.32.2; 7.20.3 (Athenians); Ar. *Ach.* 652–4 (Spartans); in the Korinthian War: see Figueira (1990).

their appeal for the Greeks, was a way to belittle them in front of the the Athenian *demos*, and eventually expel them all together.[95] Such a strategy might well have had supporters amongst some Aiginetans who fared much better once their island had become part of the Athenian empire, not least because of the immediate advantages that would result when former 'democrats' might be resettled on the island. There are faint traces of a 'democratic' tradition on Aigina when the elite's behaviour during *stasis* is depicted as shamefully dishonouring the communal gods. We should also note that the triremes dedicated after Salamis bypassed Aigina and went straight to Sounion, almost as if only exiled Aiginetans were credited with prowess in the battle![96]

On the other hand, there was clearly a sizeable number of Aiginetans who were happier in a 'Kimonian' model of the world which would not alienate some of the wealthy elites in the allied states as the Athenian empire eventually did. The rhetoric of Panhellenism in the Aiginetan odes thus gives testimony to that other story probably in circulation until the Athenian democracy took full credit for having evicted the barbarian: that by which individual city-states advertised their perceived role in that war and which, more importantly, may be the story on which the Kimonian vision of empire was built. For individual cities' commitment to the Panhellenic cause also meant a role for them in a post-Persian War world not only ideologically but also practically.[97] Such a role for Aigina may have entailed the island being a hub in the wider Mediterranean world, and quite probably the maintenance of a viable smaller-scale regional network in the Saronic Gulf—rather than one where Piraeus sucked in whatever came in its direction. Something of the sort is curiously suggested by Aigina's athletic connections locally: Aiginetan victories at Nemea, Isthmia, Sikyon, Epidauros, at Megara and Argos, point towards their ties, prominence, and interests amongst the aristocracies of the Saronic Gulf.[98] We might recall that after all the vantage point of Zeus Hellanios on Aiginetan Oros commands the panorama of a maritime set of connections seemingly overseen by this god. In this kind of experience, the Aiginetans might not have been different from other eventually subjected places, whose elites similarly struggled to maintain a local identity that was indissolubly linked to their position in a wider network of exchange. Facets of this have already been illuminated by the discussion above on paean-singing island states and Ionians, in which we also learned that their (apparently commercial) elites were similarly victims of Athenian calumny.[99] Specifically in

[95] Themistokles' problematic relationship with the Aiginetans: Plut. *Them.* 4.1; 19.1 Aiginetans opposing the building of the long walls; cf. Hdt.'s Aiakidai episode surviving into 15.2. Aigina's favourable geographical position is almost proverbial: cf. Th. 2.27.1 and Plut. *Per.* 8.7; Arist. *Rhet.* 1411^{a}15–16; Cic. *Off.* 3.11.46.

[96] Hdt. 6.87–93 and the elite's misdeeds in the Thesmophorion at Aigina (6.91); 6.90 exiles at Sounion who might have returned to Aigina; the trireme dedications are at 8.121.

[97] But cf. Cawkwell (2005).

[98] Pi. *P.* 8.78; 9.90–1; *N.* 3.84; 5.45–6 (Megara); *N.* 3.84; 5.52–3; *I.* 8.68 (Epidauros); *P.* 8.79–80 (Marathon, Argos).

[99] pp. 100, 112–13 above.

the wake of the Delian League, all this talk about the Aiginetans' Panhellenic devotion constitutes the sturdy self-perception of those, but certainly not all, Aiginetans who were favouring, and trying to maintain independence, and this independence was not only political.

3. JOINING IN THE PAN-GREEK *KHOROS*

We conclude that if Aiakos the drought-lifter and founder of the cult of Zeus Hellanios appears at the Panhellenic Theoxenia aimed at Greece's 'good crop', this was not only controversial, but also raises issues reaching beyond the little island plunged into the midst of the Saronic Gulf. *Paean 6* seems to merge the overlapping associations of the ritual of the Theoxenia and the myth of Zeus Hellanios for the orchestration of a much wider contemporary historical claim. The performance seeks to imply that Aiginetan commitment to the Panhellenic worshipping community through their pivotal role in Greece's *eueteria*. This is a startling assertion, which hits right at the heart of the contemporary pre-occupation with different forms of Panhellenism and its economic consequences.

We can go one step further, though, in examining now certain points of detail about the interaction of myth and ritual through the medium of choral performance. For through merging, as it were, the wrong myth with the wrong ritual, *Paean 6* turns itself into a re-enactment of Zeus' aetiology in the ritual context of the Apolline Theoxenia. While Zeus Hellanios is a local Aiginetan god, the illusion of his myth's re-enactment in an actual all-Greek context not only virtually converts Hellanios into a Panhellenic god, but more relevantly it also delineates the Panhellenic cult community at Delphi in the very terms of this aetiology. This is a bold move, considering that the Theoxenia were themselves the festival which I argued above claimed a hold over who was allowed access to the group who called themselves Hellenes. How this broader claim is orchestrated can, finally, be pinned down in vocabulary, the mode of performance, and yet again the figure of Neoptolemos.

The Theoxenia address Apollo in his known functions as averter (*ἀλεξίκακος*) of misfortunes such as famine and plague. Zeus' aetiology as it survives in Isokrates or Pausanias is packed with Apolline idioms when it talks about the 'relief of evil' (*λύσις τῶν κακῶν*), or its 'aversion' (*ἀπαλλαγὴ τῶν κακῶν*). The Greeks are portrayed as 'saved' (*σωθέντες*) just as Apollo is invoked as *σωτήρ* for example in Philodamos' song. The myth of Zeus Hellanios therefore provides a suitable semantic framework for projection onto Apollo. But there might also be more specific reference to the Theoxenia implicit for example in the emphasis on abundance of goods following Zeus' lifting of the drought, when the Greeks proceeded to have 'everything they desired' (*τυχόντες ἁπάντων ὧν ἐδεήθησαν*).[100]

[100] Isocr. 9.14–15; Paus. 2.29.7–8; Philod. Scarph. refrain: *ἴθι σωτήρ*; for Apollo *σωτήρ* in paeans see Käppel (1992) 32–3; 44–9.

But Apollo's festival and Zeus' myth also coincide in their ritual form. Zeus' aetiology is formulated in the way that typically leads to worship in choral ritual. Choral aetiological myths often demonstrate the inevitability of the communal cult foundation by implying that a community's crisis is simply the result of failed worship: it was a neglected Zeus who sent the famine, just as, according to another myth, he sent *stasis* to the Peloponnese when his worship at Olympia was temporarily discontinued. In the case of Zeus Hellanios, both Isokrates and Pausanias use the words ἱλάσκεσθαι and ἱκετεύω, which typically indicate the 'soothing' of an insulted god and regularly prompt choral ritual. We have no idea, of course, whether Zeus on Aigina was actually worshipped in the *khoros*. But this is perhaps not of chief relevance here. What is significant is that the one known ritual situation in which this cult aetiology was active makes use of those features of the myth that lead one to expect a choral performance.[101]

The effect is quite special: the worshipping community implied in Zeus' aetiological myth blends with that of the contemporary ritual at Delphi's Theoxenia. The situation is well known already from the last two chapters: those who are involved in the myth also perform the choral ritual; mythical claims and present ritual merge in the choral performance. The tricks of time that aetiology affords through the performance produce a remarkable illusion. When the Greeks came to ask for rain, this was the first time an Aiginetan restored *eueteria* on behalf of all of Greece, and the same group of people is suggested for the here and now of the early fifth-century Delphic Theoxenia. The 'ambassadors of the Greek cities' appear to re-enact Zeus' myth in an Apolline context, and those who came to pray to Aiakos and Zeus now turn into Apollo's *khoros*.

A *communitas* is created that gives Aiginetans a deserved place in this Panhellenic worshipping community, almost as if rehabilitating them from malign Athenian claims to the contrary. It is quite possible that the song celebrated the Aiginetans' reinstatement into the Panhellenic community from which medizers had been excluded. More importantly, however, the myth-ritual effect here goes beyond the case of the Aiginetans. Rather, it forges a link between locality and Panhellenic centre, between local and Panhellenic concerns. The Theoxenia, as we saw above, were a festival concerned with the definition and delineation of what it meant to be a Greek; the paean therefore also perpetuates the vision of Panhellenism so paradigmatically represented by the Aiginetans, that is to say one in which the Greek cities, or probably more precisely some of their elites, resisted a developing orientation towards Athens that quite possibly also curtailed their inherited privileges accompanying the control of local and wider maritime networks. Quite to what extent the traditional archaic elites in maritime communities suffered economically from the advent of the Delian League no doubt deserves further research, and the context of contemporary Rhodes (Chapter 5) will attempt this in part. What we can definitely conclude, however, is that just as the island choruses had their own visions about what it meant to be an island, *Paean 6* testifies to an assertive set of Greeks who, at least in song, were confident

[101] I discuss such choral myths in (2004). Olympia: Phlegon of Tralles *FGrH* 257 F 1.

enough to resist whichever definition of Panhellenism was current at Athens at the time, and retain in theirs a place for individual localities.

Delphi was no doubt intensely involved in creating visions of early fifth-century Panhellenism, and these were not so dissimilar from that of our song. What sources we have suggest that the sanctuary used the same tropes as the Aiginetan islanders themselves, likewise showing little support for Athens' predominant role in Greece. It is at Delphi that the Greeks gathered after Salamis as mentioned by Herodotus, and a *dekate* of medizers' possessions were to have been offered at the shrine. But despite his feats for the Greeks, Apollo—who incidentally formerly medized himself—strongly disliked Themistokles, the man who had reinterpreted the god's oracle prior to Salamis in a manner that in the future would bolster the Athenians. Pausanias still knows that Delphi rejected Themistokles' post-Salamis offerings—on the charge of the general's later medism. Apollo had obviously switched sides and was now supporting the Greeks, but certainly not the Athenians. The god also picks up on the Aiginetans' role at Salamis: at this same gathering of victorious Hellas, he laments Aiginetan parsimony when he demands the extra reward of the 'three stars' from their successful ships. If Aiakids, the summoned Aiginetan helpers at Salamis, appeared in our paean as the main mythical protagonists whose story culminates in the praise of their 'countless virtues' (ἀπείρονας ἀρετὰς Αἰακ]ιδᾶν ll. 176–7), this is yet another hint that the god passed judgement over who was a good Greek and who was not.[102]

But it is again Neoptolemos (*qua* Aiginetan?) who clinches the issue of Panhellenism, particularly with a view to the celebration of our early fifth-century Theoxenia. There are several indications that his animosities against Apollo were at least temporarily turned into close proximity at this time, and that from a notorious villain Neoptolemos was turned into a good thing for the Greeks. The story of Pindar's *Nemean 7* differs from other known versions of Neoptolemos' appearance at Delphi in one crucial detail when here the hero comes to offer the ἀκροθίνια of the Trojan War (ll. 40–1). Could this respond to the historical situation mentioned above, when Aiginetans were asked to present proudly their special spoils as a sign of their Hellenism?[103] In fact, one could argue that Pindar's apparent fatalism in that ode is a pithy reformulation of Neoptolemos' fate: there was no way round his death, one of the Aiakids just *had* to lie in Apollo's precinct.[104] Neoptolemos' 'accidental' death is paradoxically 'mourned much' by the Delphians here explicitly called ξεναγέται: this takes up the idea proposed

[102] Hdt. 7.143–4; Paus. 10.14.3; Hdt. 8.122.

[103] Hdt. 8.122. For these ἀκροθίνια (first-fruits) see Gauer (1968) 32–4 and n. 112 for the possible difference between ἀκροθίνια and δεκάτη (Hdt. 9.81.1) offered after Plataiai; also Burkert (1985) 69. Cf. Paus. 10.14.5.

[104] *N.* 7.44–7: ἐχρῆν δέ τιν' ἔνδον ἄλσει παλαιτάτῳ / Αἰακιδᾶν κρεόντων τὸ λοιπὸν ἔμμεναι / θεοῦ παρ' εὐτειχέα δόμον ἡροΐαις δὲ πομπαῖς / θεμισκόπον οἰκεῖν ἐόντα πολυθύτοις 'for it was necessary that within that most ancient precinct / one of the royal Aiakidai remain ever after / beside the god's well-walled temple to dwell there / as a rightful overseer of processions honouring heroes with many sacrifices' (tr. Race). Cf. *Σ N.* 7.62c.

above, that his murder was a violation of theoric *xenia* in the first place.[105] Neoptolemos then becomes one of the βοάθοοι of the shrine, a challenging role for the hero who is normally the precinct's greatest sacker: during the Persian attack on Delphi mentioned by Herodotus—prior to Salamis—Neoptolemos did certainly not feature as a protective hero. The most intriguing development in his career, however, is that he is put in charge (θεμίσκοπος ('overseer'?)) of rather enigmatic 'processions for heroes carrying many sacrifices'. This could be a ritual for the whole array of Delphi's local protective heroes, as known in other communities, now led by Neoptolemos. Whatever this office entails, there is certainly a point in the fact that Neoptolemos, himself a victim of unjust sacrificial shares, ends up supervising the ritual order (*themis*). Ironically, while Neoptolemos' Hellenicity had formerly made his life difficult, he now guards the smooth running of the Hellenic community.[106]

Neoptolemos' temporary popularity within the Panhellenic community is further suggested by Polygnotos' painting in the Leskhe of the Knidians, thought to date to immediately after the Persian Wars. This depicted Neoptolemos alone among all the Greek warriors still fighting. This Leskhe, incidentally, lay opposite the entrance to the temple at Delphi, thus forming a foil to Neoptolemos' own tomb at Apollo's threshold.[107] *Paean 6* and *Nemean 7*, then, are clearly doing the same thing, rehabilitating the hero in the Delphic setting, which was itself very specific to the early fifth century and the time immediately following the Persian Wars. The ambiguous treatment Neoptolemos receives in the course of the fifth century, especially from Euripides, indicates that this laboriously developed position at Delphi continued to be full of problems. Or shall we say, at that time the Athenians had long reshaped the mythical paradigms of Panhellenism once again?[108]

[105] Pi. *N.* 7.43: βάρυνθεν δὲ περισσὰ Δελφοὶ ξεναγέται 'the Delphian "leaders of guests" were exceedingly grieved'.

[106] The enigmatic phrase suggests Neoptolemos as an 'overseer of heroic sacrifice' (*Σ N.* 7.62c, *Σ N.* 7.68a, b), or himself receiving heroic honours (ἡρωΐαις δὲ πομπαῖς=ἡρωικαὶ τιμαί, as e.g. in A.R. 1.1048 etc.), of which the latter is preferable: Currie (2005) 299–301 (with the entire bibliography). Later sources grant him elaborate cult: Paus. 10.24.6 (*enagismata*); Heliod. *Aeth.* 2.34; 3.1 ff. (*pompe* and hecatomb). It may seem artificial to think of βοαθόων τεθνακότων (Pi. *N.* 7.32–3) as referring to the immortality of Pindar's praise for Delphi, as implied in Race's Loeb translation, or, similarly, in Rutherford (2001) 309 and n. 11. For the language of hero-cult at Delphi cf. Köhnken (1971) 67 n. 144, and Lo Scalzo (1998). Cf. the calendars of Marathon *IG* ii^2 1358 B4; 52–3 tables for the 'hero and the heroine' and the 'Tritopatores', and at Thorikos: *SEG* xxxiii 147 for local hero(in)es e.g. 30; 44–5. For the possible coincidence of *heroxenia*, (*Σ* Pi. *N.* 7.68a), and the Theoxenia see Currie (2005) 303. Hdt. 8.35–9 for the Persian attack on Delphi in 480 BC (cf. Paus. 10.8.7).

[107] Paus. 10.25.1–31.12. On Polygnotos' depiction being honorific rather than unfavourable to Neoptolemos see Currie (2005) 305, with the previous bibliography.

[108] For the sustained ambiguity over his attitude to Delphi see pp. 198–200 above and cf. Eur. *Andr.* 54–5: εἴ πως τὰ πρόσθε σφάλματ' ἐξαιτούμενος / θεὸν παράσχοιτ' ἐς τὸ λοιπὸν εὐμενῆ '[he asked Apollo] . . . in the hope that by begging forgiveness for his previous sin he might win the god's favor for the future'; 1106–7: Φοίβῳ τῆς πάροιθ' ἁμαρτίας / δίκας παρασχεῖν βουλόμεσθ' 'I want to give satisfaction to Phoebus for my earlier sin' (tr. D. Kovacs). *Nemean 7*'s last sentence, which gave rise to much discussion in the secondary literature (n. 36), should also refer to Neoptolemos' problematic relationship to Apollo.

It is in this way that the paean becomes operative as a re-enactment of the Greeks' *khoros* of ambassadors to Aiakos the Aiginetan, as a formulation of what the Greek world should or could look like at this time. The song emerges as an interesting instance in which relations between the Greeks are expressed through their ritualization in myth-ritual performance. Common worship of the same cult ties people to each other who previously had no reason to socialize, or in fact kept themselves deliberately distinct. We have of course no way of telling who witnessed these Theoxenia, and one cannot exclude the possibility that the paean actually preached to the converted. But particularly in view of what I suggested above as the Delphic Theoxenia's claim to a (notional) control of Hellenicity, it is likely that the festival assembled all contemporary aspirants to 'Greekness', and that must include the Athenians. What may therefore appear as a politically delicate situation is in the paean integrated into an evocative ritual through which pretty audacious claims on Panhellenism could be made. Those in relation to Aigina were certainly not short-lived: this is proved by the survival of the anti-Athenian traditions for the battle of Salamis, as well as that of Zeus Hellanios as a 'Panhellenic' god; and, as mentioned above, the Greek mission to Aiakos was eternalized in stone on Aigina itself. It is striking that the Kean hero Aristaios postulates a Panhellenic Zeus on his own island, as if the Aiginetans had established the paradigm for local Panhellenic merit.[109] But independently of whether the paean effectively introduced a long-standing tradition, what mattered was the effect the song would have had on a Panhellenic worshipping community at the time of its performance. Of course the views on the nature of Panhellenism communicated might have remained no more than a claim. But I suspect that just as we have already seen, and will see again, the paean bears testimony to a thriving Greek *polis* world which felt it had the resources, and certainly the confidence, to question an emerging imperial power. It must be clear that this is a world which could have taken numerous paths, and it was by no means clear from the beginning which one it would choose. *Paean 6* is an intriguing example of how conflicting relations are reconfigured by projecting them into a ritual that turns delicate relationships into traditional bonds.

[109] See esp. D.S. 4.82 for the 'Panhellenic' role of Aristaios. Cf. Burkert (1983) 110–11, who collects all the sources.

5

Returning to the Beginning: Towards Insular Identity on Fifth-Century Rhodes

Ταύτην τὴν ᾠδὴν ἀνακεῖσθαί φησι Γόργων
ἐν τῷ τῆς Λινδίας Ἀθηναίας ἱερῷ χρυσοῖς γράμμασιν.

(Gorgon *FGrH* 515 F 18)[1]

Pindar's *Olympian 7*, glittering from Athena's temple at Lindos, was chosen out of all the imaginable expressions of cultural identity to decorate Rhodes' religious showpiece, provoking one of the most evocative images of antiquity. Spectacularly situated at the utmost edge of a steep cliff, Athena's Lindian precinct is to the present day the second most visited place in Greece after the akropolis of Athens, boasting a constant stream of visitors in continuation of the cult's long-standing claim that Athena was not just all about Athens. Rhodian identity was deeply intertwined with the worship of Athena at Lindos, at least if we believe the goddess's impressive guest-book, the *Lindian Chronicle*: composed in 99 BC almost a century after the sanctuary had gone up in flames, this lists a splendid array of dedicants from all periods of myth and history. The collection of stories of Athena and her devotees functioned as a kind of receptacle of Rhodian collective identity.[2]

The tradition of *Olympian 7* greeting Athena's visitors to the temple is profoundly tied to local Rhodian identity and pride. It intriguingly assumes that *Olympian 7* was uniquely appropriate to represent what was dear to all the Rhodians, that it communicated a sort of pan-Rhodianism matching that of the island's most conspicuous deity. However, at the time when *Olympian 7* was actually performed the notion of an all-island identity was far from obvious. The song celebrates Diagoras of Rhodes for his boxing victory at the Olympic Games of 464 BC (the ode is entitled *Διαγόραι Ῥοδίωι Πύκτηι*). At this time, Rhodes was not a unified island; it had three independent cities Ialysos, Kameiros, and Lindos, who were members of the Athenian empire, paying separate tributes assessed individually for each *polis*. It was not until 411 BC that the Rhodians collectively broke away from the Athenians, and formed a synoikism in about 408/7 BC. Physically the unification was expressed in the foundation of the island's 'capital' Rhodes, at the northernmost tip of the island, three-harboured, and destined to

[1] 'Gorgon says this ode was dedicated in the temple of Athena Lindia in gold letters' = *Σ* Pi. *O.* 7 p. 195 Dr.

[2] For the wider cultural context of the *Chronicle* see Higbie (2003).

become a maritime hub of the Hellenistic world; religiously unity featured in a number of pan-Rhodian cults assumed by the new city, notably the cult of Helios the sun-god. But as early as 464 BC pan-Rhodianism of the sort presupposed by the story of the song beaming off the temple was a good half century away.[3]

Olympian 7's splendid preservation indicates that later times took the song to communicate things that were still in the future at the time of its composition and performance, as a monument to Rhodian collective identity. This presents a remarkable coincidence regarding performance and reception of an *epinikion*, as far as I am aware unique in the history of religious song. Those who put up the ode on the temple unwittingly gauged what matter it addressed: this chapter will suggest that *Olympian 7* formulated a pan-Rhodianism of which many elements were going to be adopted by the unified island in the future; the victory song for Diagoras may have been part of the process by which the synoikism was brought about.

The ode, often quoted as an exemplar of the perennially indefinable genre of victory songs, presents us with an unusually simple structure consisting of priamel (ll. 1–12), portrait of victor and victory (ll. 13–19), a long and continuous mythical section (ll. 20–76), followed by further praise of the victor, and a concluding *gnome* (ll. 77–94). The song also has a series of intercalated *gnomai*, nicely positioned between the myths so as to give the ode the requisite unity.[4] Three religious aetiologies form the mythical part, offering a selective survey of the history of cults on Rhodes associated with several phases in the island's history. The tale is told backwards, starting with the most recent event, the settlement of Rhodes by the Herakleid Tlepolemos (ll. 20–33). The centrepiece of the narrative is the birth of Athena and the establishment of her rites on Rhodes (ll. 34–53), followed by a story recounting the genesis of the island itself and Helios' patronage of it (ll. 54–76).

The ritual frame of the mythical section suggests that the song was performed as part of the Tlepolemeia, an occasion that stands a good chance of having been a foundation festival for Rhodes in honour of its mythical ancestor, its *oikist*—a suitable context for the telling of beginnings. Yet the aetiological nature of these three myths, has attracted little attention from commentators, anxious rather to unite the three tales through a common, quintessentially human moral, foreshadowed in the atmosphere of 'gift and grace' between the protagonists of the initial priamel.[5] Rather, these three tales of origins, intricately tied to each

[3] For the synoikism see pp. 250 ff. below, esp. Gabrielsen (2000*a*), also arguing that the synoikism did not extinguish the three old cities; cf. now id. and Nielsen in *Inventory* s.v.; Parker (forthcoming) on pan-Rhodian cults established by the synoikism.

[4] ll. 30b–31a, 53; see e.g. Willcock on l. 111 for the role of these *gnomai*.

[5] e.g. the idea—of rather Christian colouring—that all the myths contain an element of human error, which is then mercifully not punished by the gods, but releases their particular favour; this is thought to be in sharp contrast to the ὀρθαὶ φρένες 'upright mind' of Diagoras, and, metaphorically, the poet: e.g. Gildersleeve on 183: 'In each of the three cases we have a good beginning followed by misfortune, and yet a good ending crowns all'; Norwood (1945) 138–45, esp. 142: 'bloom beside sunshine, joy following pain'; Young (1968) 79–81; Barkhuisen (1968) 34: 'success granted by the gods

other, directly address the all-important issue in the history of Rhodes, the relationship between the three *poleis* and the island as a whole. We shall see here that in linking a set of aetiological myths and rituals to each other for one and the same festive occasion, the song puts to use aetiology's local dimension for a restructuring of the entire island's diverse religious traditions. The performance thereby evokes a religious community unified through a monolithic Rhodian past. It overwrites a memory and an awareness of great diversity, of traditions representing different localities and social groups over various periods of time, with an island-wide 'time of origins', an *illud tempus* whose religious settings and their social implications are presented as lasting to the present-day performance.[6]

In this way, *Olympian 7* prematurely develops a kind of civic ideology for the whole island. It also provokingly devises a City-of-Rhodes in anti-Athenian terms in tackling a number of issues dear to Athenian democratic and imperial ideology. These include the integration, and politicization, of elite and non-elite interests. It is no coincidence that *Olympian 7* honours a member of the Diagorids: these were not only the most famous sporting family in antiquity, but also heavily involved in stirring up revolt against Athens and, we think, creating the unified island-state in the late fifth century.[7] The ode's appeals to pan-Rhodianism are also directed against Athens' claims to superiority over other Greek cities (often expressed in myth); against the Athenian tendency to break up relationships between allies (in this case between the three Rhodian cities in relation to their island as a whole); and even air aspects of economic dependencies. The Rhodians who emerge from *Olympian 7* are also a community aloof from the attractions and drawbacks of the Athenian alliance.[8] The ode's formulation of pan-Rhodianism would, at the height of the island's dividedness towards the middle of the fifth century (464 BC), present a powerful alternative to membership in the Athenian empire, which may well have been a matter of debate at the time. In what follows I shall first look at the three aetiological myths and their individual ritual contexts, before turning to their method of operating in the contemporary performance, and the demonstration of how *Olympian 7* may well have been instrumental in unifying the island through a compelling suggestion of a new reality expressed in myth and ritual.

in spite of mistakes made', which he believes is reflected in the structure of the ode; Hooker (1985) 64: 'Pindar's gods bestow or withhold benefits without considering the merits of beneficiaries'. Other readings are O. Smith (1967) 180–1; S. Sullivan (1982) 221; Rubin (1980–1). On the priamel see e.g. Brown (1984).

6 Athanassaki (2003) has recently discussed Pindaric strategies for the smoothing out of a rocky colonial past and the construction of a homogeneous mythical history, particularly for *apoikiai*, Greek settlements abroad (108–13 on *O.* 7).

7 See n. 78 below for the Diagorid involvement in the synoikism. Diagoras the famous athlete: e.g. Cic. *Tusc.* 1.111; Paus. 6.7.3. Diagoras' descendants were singularly successful sportsmen (Paus. 6.7.1–7); see Pouilloux (1970) for the family tree. The family had a shared monument at Olympia: Paus. loc. cit.; *Olympia V*, nos. 151–2, 159.

8 For a political context of the ode see Hornblower (2004) 131–4; F. Cairns (2005). Sfyoeras (1993) already suggested competition with Athens in this ode implied in the myth of the fireless sacrifice (see Sect. 1).

1. ATHENA'S ἄπυρα ἱερά

The song's mythical and ritual hub, the aetiology recounting the origins of the 'fireless sacrifices' offered to the goddess Athena on Rhodes, also presents the starting point for these considerations.[9] Pindar's text is the main, and certainly the earliest, literary evidence for both cult and customs associated with Rhodian Athena all over the island, not just at Lindos:

ἔνθα ποτὲ βρέχε θεῶν βασιλεὺς ὁ μέγας
χρυσέαις νιφάδεσσι πόλιν,
ἀνίχ᾽ Ἁφαίστου τέχναισιν
χαλκελάτῳ πελέκει πα-
τέρος Ἀθαναία κορυφὰν κατ᾽ ἄκραν
ἀνορούσαισ᾽ ἀλάλαξεν ὑπερμάκει βοᾷ.
Οὐρανὸς δ᾽ ἔφριξέ νιν καὶ Γαῖα μάτηρ.
τότε καὶ φαυσίμβροτος δαίμων Ὑπεριονίδας
μέλλον ἔντειλεν φυλάξασθαι χρέος
παισὶν φίλοις,
ὡς ἂν θεᾷ πρῶτοι κτίσαιεν
βωμὸν ἐναργέα, καὶ σεμνὰν θυσίαν θέμενοι
πατρί τε θυμὸν ἰάναι-
εν κόρᾳ τ᾽ ἐγχειβρόμῳ. ἐν δ᾽ ἀρετάν
ἔβαλεν καὶ χάρματ᾽ ἀνθρώποισι προμαθέος αἰδώς·
ἐπὶ μὰν βαίνει τι καὶ λάθας ἀτέκμαρτα νέφος,
καὶ παρέλκει πραγμάτων ὀρθὰν ὁδόν
ἔξω φρενῶν.
καὶ τοὶ γὰρ αἰθοίσας ἔχοντες
σπέρμ᾽ ἀνέβαν φλογὸς οὔ. τεῦξαν δ᾽ ἀπύροις ἱεροῖς
ἄλσος ἐν ἀκροπόλει. κεί-
νοις ὁ μὲν ξανθὰν ἀγαγὼν νεφέλαν (Ζεύς)
πολὺν ὗσε χρυσόν· αὐτὰ δέ σφισιν ὤπασε τέχναν
πᾶσαν ἐπιχθονίων Γλαυκ-
ῶπις ἀριστοπόνοις χερσὶ κρατεῖν.
ἔργα δὲ ζωοῖσιν ἑρπόν-
τεσσί θ᾽ ὁμοῖα κέλευθοι φέρον·
ἦν δὲ κλέος βαθύ.

[on Rhodes] where once the great king of gods showered
the city with snows of gold,
when, by the skills of Hephaistos
with the stroke of a bronze-forged axe,
Athena sprang forth on the top of her father's head
and shouted a prodigious battle cry,
and Heaven shuddered at her, and mother Earth.
at that time Hyperion's son, divine bringer of light

[9] On this aetiology cf. esp. Sfyoeras (1993).

to mortals, charged his dear children
to observe the obligation that was to come,
that they might be the first to build for the goddess
  an altar in full view, and by making
a sacred sacrifice might cheer the hearts of the father
  and his daughter of the thundering spear. Reverence
for one who has foresight plants excellence and its joys in humans
but without warning some cloud of forgetfulness comes upon them
and wrests the straight path of affairs
from their minds.
Thus it was that they made their ascent without taking
  the seed of blazing flame, and with fireless sacrifices
they made a sanctuary on the acropolis.
  He brought in a yellow cloud and upon them
rained gold in abundance; but the gray-eyed goddess
herself gave them every kind of skill to surpass mortals
  with their superlative handiwork.
Their streets bore works of art in the likeness of beings
  that lived and moved,
and great was their fame.

(Pindar, *Olympian* 7.34–53, tr. Race)

In this central myth, Athena's birth stirs up competition for her possession amongst her future worshippers. Athena is born in full martial equipment out of Zeus' head, with only a little hammering help from Hephaistos. Eager to ensure a prime spot in the goddess' favour, Helios urges on his seven sons to get together a sacrifice as soon as possible. In their hurry the over-zealous Heliadai forget to bring that element crucial for the sacrificial procedure, fire. So they build an *ἄλσος* ('precinct') for Athena on the akropolis offering her *ἄπυρα ἱερά* ('fireless sacrifices') instead. Zeus and Athena applaud this initiative by showering golden rain and miraculous gifts of craftsmanship onto the Heliadai, thereby ensuring the prosperity of the island. Pindar omits the aetiological conclusion, but it is clear that we may infer what Diodorus states at the end of his narrative of the same episode:

διόπερ φασὶ διαμένειν μέχρι τοῦ νῦν τὸ κατὰ τὴν θυσίαν ἴδιον ἐν τῇ Ῥόδῳ, καὶ τὴν θεὸν ἐν αὐτῇ καθιδρῦσθαι.

This is the reason, men say, why the peculiar practice as regards the manner of sacrificing persists on Rhodes to this day, and why the goddess settled on the island. (Diodorus 5.56.7)

Athena's *apyra hiera*, attested in a number of antiquarian texts,[10] are normally interpreted as a sacrifice of unburnt fruit and vegetables, as opposed to the more

[10] Cf. Apollonios fr. 11 (Michael, diss. Hal. 1875) = *Σ O.* 7.86b: 'ever since those beginnings the Rhodians sacrifice to Athena without fire' (*ἄπυρα δὲ [ὅτι] μέχρι νῦν οἱ Ῥόδιοι θύουσιν ἀπ' ἐκείνης τῆς ἀρχῆς τῇ Ἀθηνᾷ*); *Σ* Pi. *O.* 7.71b. A 'fireless' sacrifice comes to mean 'mean' service to the gods, notably by poets: Ath. 1.8e; *Anth. Pal.* 6.321.

common burnt animal sacrifice.[11] The reason for this is perhaps simply the formulaic character which ἄπυρα ἱερά seem to have adopted by classical times, and to hold firmly by the time of Diodorus, that is that of fireless sacrifice of fruit, vegetables, or bread. The notion probably developed in deliberate contrast to burnt meat θυσία, the core rite of Greek sacrificial practice. An equation of fireless and meatless sacrifice can indeed be supported by various pieces of evidence. According to Euripides, Zeus Hades receives a 'fireless *thysia* of different types of fruit' (θυσία ἄπυρος καὶ παγκαρπείας). Arkadian Demeter, another 'khthonian' deity, is offered grapes, honeycomb, and wool in oil. Apollo Genetor on Delos, the only god whose worship was compatible with the strict Pythagorean diet, is given mostly cereals.[12]

A close look at even just some classical evidence, however, reveals that the use of vegetarian materials in sacrifice is not necessarily identical with sacrifice where fire is absent. Though οὐδὲν ἔμψυχον ('nothing alive') is offered, for instance, to Zeus Hypatos on the Akropolis, a vegetable holocaust is performed on his altar in front of the Erekhtheion. Similarly, in the Athenian *Diasia* the god received pastry animal substitutes, which were probably burnt on his altar. Meatless offerings such as these, therefore, can be performed with or without fire. In real life then, there is no simple dichotomy between burnt meat offerings and non-burnt non-meat offerings as is often suggested. We may conclude that the mere qualification 'fireless' does not tell us anything about the sacrificed products.[13]

More intriguing, however, the widespread belief in Rhodian Athena's alleged vegetarian preferences can also be corrected by examining the aetiology's actual narrative—which beautifully illustrates how aetiology works by evoking images of a tangible ritual reality. The Heliadai aimed to be 'the first' (πρῶτοι) to found a clearly visible altar for Athena (βωμὸν ἐναργέα) on the akropolis, on which the σεμνὰ θυσία was to take place (l. 42). The narrative implies a sacrificial procession ascending to the akropolis where the promised rite was to be performed (ἀνέβαν (l. 48)); only on arrival did the Heliadai discover what was lacking in their solemn enterprise. As a result, indispensably to the plot, they perform their rites without fire.

The imagery in this myth suggests that everything in preparation of the sacrifice proceeds as expected, except for the use of fire. This is even clearer from Diodorus' and Philostratos' later accounts of the same episode. While in Pindar competition is implied, other sources actually name the competitor—perhaps a pointer towards the interpretation that Athens was somehow addressed in this aetiology even if this was nowhere actually said.[14] In either versions Athenians

[11] See e.g. *Lindos I* 10–11.

[12] Zeus Hades: Eur. *TrGF* 912.4; Demeter at Phigaleia: Paus. 8.42.11–13; Apollo Genetor on Delos: Arist. fr. 489 Rose = D.L. 8.13 (Iambl. *VP* 25; 35; Porph. *Abst.* 2.28; Macr. 3.6.2).

[13] Zeus Hypatos in front of the Erekhtheion: Paus. 8.2.3 ('local baked goods which they call pelanoi'); cf. Paus. 1.26.5. Diasia: Th. 1.126.6–7 + Σ Th. Bruit-Zaidman (2005) now also addresses this issue.

[14] As first argued by Sfyoeras (1993).

under Kekrops' reign enter the trial for the possession of Athena. The whole plot is only relevant if we assume that both parties are trying to conform to the same pattern. So in Diodorus, the Heliadai forgot 'in their haste to put fire beneath the victims, but nevertheless laid them on the altars (ἐπιθεῖναι τότε τὰ θύματα)', whereas 'Kekrops ... performed the sacrifice over fire, but later than the Heliadai'. Similarly, Philostratos contrasts the two parties as οἱ μὲν ἄπυρα ἱερὰ καὶ ἀτελῆ, ὁ δὲ Ἀθήνησι δῆμος πῦρ ἐκεῖ καὶ κνῖσαν ἱερῶν ('the Rhodians offer fireless and "incomplete" sacrifices, while the Athenian people offer as you can see fire and the savour of burnt meat'). The special reference to the characteristic smoke arising from the Athenian victim, elaborated on in its pictorial representation in the following sentence, brings out even more that the Heliadai's sacrifice followed normal Greek rules, up to the moment when the meat was burnt.[15]

These variants of the aetiological story are of course ultimately designed to tell us why Athena resides both on Rhodes and at Athens and are suitably set at a primordial time when religious institutions were only about to be founded.[16] But two different logics produce this outcome. Winner and loser in this competition are not clearly defined: the Rhodians were first to perform the sacrifice, the Athenians did it 'correctly'. The Heliadai won the race, but Kekrops won according to the notional rules of Greek sacrifice. If the Heliadai nevertheless gloriously receive the deity on the island, they must have carried out a valid sacrifice. The contrast between the two appears not to be predicated of two different types, such as fruit or animal sacrifice; rather, while Athena on the akropolis at Athens was certainly worshipped with burnt animal sacrifice, the implication is that Athena on Rhodes receives animal sacrifice without fire. In this sense, the Heliadai's sacrifice was perceived as normal, but, as Philostratos says, 'incomplete'.[17]

How can non-burnt animal sacrifice be a valid sacrifice, when, as is nowhere clearer than in Aristophanes' *Birds*, on the whole it is the fire that enables a city's communication with the gods? A comparative and an archaeological line of inquiry might lead further here. Non-burnt animal sacrifice, strange as it might seem to the Greek eye, is not an entirely unknown practice. It was the dominant pattern in the prehistoric Mediterranean East, that is, in Bronze Age Anatolia, the Near East, and in Egypt, where it continued to prevail into historic times. Similarly, whereas fire occurs regularly in Greek sacrificial iconography, Minoan depictions, although offering abundant evidence for animal sacrifice, provide none for the use of fire. Minoan seals, the repertory for such imagery, feature

[15] D.S. 5.56.5–7; Philostr. *Im.* 2.27; see also *Σ* Pi. *O.* 7.71b.

[16] Sfyoeras (1993) 9 notes that the contest mythically pre-dates the invention of the Panathenaia at Athens.

[17] Sfyoeras (1993) esp. 6–15 interestingly reads Pindar's *aition* as a deliberate inversion of the *aition* and the rules for the torch-race at the Athenian Panathenaia, where loss of fire leads to loss of victory (as in Paus. 1.30.2), listing a series of allusions to the Athenian ritual in *O.* 7 (5–7). On this interpretation the Heliadai had not 'forgotten' (l. 45 λάθας) the fire, but had not 'taken heed' to keep it going (7, 10–11). In the remainder of the poem, Pindar implicitly transforms and reverses the rules of the Panathenaia (12 ff.).

slaughtered animals on tables, sometimes with a jar placed underneath, suggesting a role for blood in the ritual, similar to the smearing of the altar in Greece. Fire, however, does not feature; what happens to the dead animal is unclear: an animal appears once in a libation scene, and elsewhere one is carried away on a woman's shoulder.[18] In this respect, it is suggestive that, for example, no Minoan altar structures have been revealed, nor have traces of burnt bones been found in connection with the possible candidates. All there is presents evidence for the cooking and consumption of ritual meals.[19]

It makes sense to understand such practices within the larger context of these Bronze Age Aegean sacrificial traditions where fireless animal sacrifice was more usual; the Minoans were a culture at the fringes of the Near Eastern world. Seen from this angle, a place like Rhodes, itself with thick layers of Minoan settlement and mythology as well as connections to the Near East, was a good deal more central to this world than the rest of Greece.[20] Rhodes generally offers greater historical continuity from the Late Bronze Age than its mainland counterparts when historic settlement traces pre-date most of their equivalents on the Greek mainland by almost a century. The situation is similar on Cyprus even further east where, incidentally, Aphrodite at Amathous' divinatory rituals supply another prominent instance of unburnt animal sacrifice in the Graeco-Roman world. Both Cyprus and Rhodes, as indeed the rest of the eastern Mediterranean, experienced less of a cultural break in the 'Dark Ages' than the remainder of Greece, perhaps with lasting consequences for religious practices.[21]

A survey of sacrificial customs in this geographical milieu confirms the impression. A continuous tradition of unburnt animal sacrifice reaching into the Iron Age is known notably from Egypt, though it is also attested elsewhere, particularly Mesopotamia.[22] From Egypt we also get an idea of what one did at such a fireless event. In the so-called opening of the mouth ceremony, for example, designated parts of the slaughtered animal, in this case its left foreleg, had to touch the face of the cult statue in order to establish contact with the god. Once it had fulfilled this function, the piece was simply discarded.[23]

[18] See the Hagia Triada sarcophagus (Bergquist (1988) 29 fig. 8). Cf. a ceremonial procession leading towards a wooden table on Minoan seals: Marinatos (1988) fig. 8. For Greek depictions see van Straten (1995).

[19] See Bergquist (1988) and esp. (1993). The same used to be thought for Mycenaean religion, e.g. Hägg (1998); this has recently been revised: Isaakidou *et al.* (2002); Hamilakis and Konsolaki (2004); Halstead and Isaakidou (2004).

[20] On prehistoric Rhodes see Benzi (1992) 3–6, with bibliography; on Mycenaean Rhodes see also Mee (1982); Benzi (1988), (1992); Marketou (1998). Mycenaean finds especially stem from several nekropoleis and a few settlement structures near Ialysos at Trianda, Kattavia, Apsaktiras (Vati), and Lindos; contacts with the Greek mainland are attested in pottery of the Argolid especially at Ialysos (LH IIIA:2).

[21] Tac. *Hist.* 2.3 (cf. *Ann.* 3.62). For Rhodes' and Cyprus' Dark Age archaeology see generally Osborne (1996) 19–28 with earlier, detailed bibliography 357–8; on Rhodes recently I. Morris (2000) 243–4; on Cyprus Snodgrass (1988), esp. 14 ff.

[22] Bergquist (1988) 32–3.

[23] Cf. H. Altenmüller, *Lexikon der Ägyptologie* iv (1982) 579–84 s.v. 'Opfer'; A. Eggebrecht, ibid. vol. i (1975) s.v. 'Brandopfer'. R. Grieshammer, ibid. vol. i (1975) s.v. 'Mundopferritual'.

Egypt is also the place with which Rhodes seems to have enjoyed lasting contact. Egyptian or Egyptianizing artisanship dominated many places in the Greek east, but Rhodes in particular is credited with the manufacture, regional distribution, and circulation of Greek faiences in the early archaic period. The number of Egyptian and Egyptianizing small finds at all three cults of Athena is overwhelming.[24] Rhodians themselves certainly travelled around Egypt: mercenary soldiers from Greece, specifically Ionia and Karia, were going to battle as early as the era of Psammetikhos I (664–610 BC); the inscriptions at Abu Simbel attest the presence of Ialysians serving Psammetikhos II during the first decade of the sixth century.[25] Votive dedications for Athena at Ialysos point towards the same world: five pieces of faience bear a regal inscription by the earlier Egyptian pharaoh Nekho II (610–595 BC), elsewhere known as bringer of offerings to the Apollonion in Miletus.[26] The fourth pharaoh in line, Apries (589–70 BC), was believed by Herodotus to have recruited some 30, 000 soldiers from Greece. At Lindos somewhat later Amasis (570–526 BC) offered various objects to Athena during a votive tour through the Aegean. He dedicated as many as two statues of Athena herself, but also brought her a linen thorax (*θώρηκα λίνεον*), suggesting that his Aegean *theoria* related to negotiations over mercenary forces. According to Herodotus it was not *ξενία* that motivated this journey, but Amasis was on the tracks of Danaos' daughters who on their way to Argos founded Athena's sanctuary at Lindos. *Xenia*, such as that between Amasis and Polykrates of Samos, is contrasted with a more important link, a genealogical relationship to the island. The case for cultural continuities is well embedded in Rhodian connectivity with the Mediterranean east, and fireless sacrifices may be one such continuity.[27]

However, does this square with what Rhodian Athena's archaeology has to say on the issue? This is the moment to draw attention to Athenas' triple presence on Rhodes. Pindar does not associate the ritual with Lindos but *Olympian 7* is nevertheless often thought to recount a custom performed exclusively for the Athena of Lindos—in a tradition that probably reaches back at least to Gorgon, quoted at the beginning. Because of her rich, highly orientalizing votive complex, in modern scholarship Lindian Athena has traditionally been believed to come 'from the east', and therefore could perhaps tolerate fireless, that is (on the

[24] *Lindos I* 336–55; Martelli (1988) 109–10; *Clara Rhodos* vi-vii (1932–3), 303 ff.; esp. the inscribed scarabs 321–2.

[25] Psammetikhos I (664–610 BC): Hdt. 2.151 ff.; Psammetikhos II (595–589 BC): *LSAG* 348; 356 (no. 4; 48a–c). Nubian campaign 591 BC: *LSAG* 348; 356, 358; ML 7; Boardman (1980) 115–16, fig. 134.

[26] Five intarsian elements of faience: Martelli (1988) 109–10 and fig. 7; cf. Martelli (1996); N. Skon, at the 79th AIA conference (27–30 Dec. 1977): *AJA* 82 (1978), 249; A. DeVita, *ASAA* 55 (1977/1980), 349; Hdt. 2.159.

[27] Apries: Hdt. 2.163, 169: Amasis: Hdt. 2.182. Danaos and his daughters at Lindos also feature in Call. fr. 100 Pf; D.S. 5.58.1; 14.2.11; Apollod. 2.1.4; D.L. 1.89. Hdt. 3.47 mentions the votive gifts again; Plin. *NH* 19.12; Ael. *NA* 9.17. For Amasis' relation to Lindos see Francis and Vickers (1985–88 iii. 29), for Rhodes and Egypt Momigliano (1936*a*) 553; Lloyd (1975–88) iii. 239.

Figure 5.1 One of the three steep seats of Athena and her 'fireless sacrifices', here at Lindos. The *Boukopion* inscriptions have been found in the bedrock by the sea, on the other side of the Akropolis

traditional view) fruit-based, sacrifice.[28] But in reality there is no evidence that fireless cult was perceived as a characteristic of this specific Athena. Athena was the poliadic deity of all three Rhodian cities, Lindos, Ialysos, and Kameiros (Map 5.1). Remarkably, topography and archaeology of these three cults are almost interchangeable. Pindar himself gives all the criteria: despite the admittedly spectacular location of the Lindian cult (Fig. 5.1), the ascent to which is essential for the effect of the story, his βωμὸς ἐναργής on top of the akropolis could be imagined not less attractively on steep Ialysian Mount Philerimos, or overlooking the classical town from the high akropolis at Kameiros. Although Pindar customarily uses ἄλσος in a rather unspecific sense, it is worth noting that cult of all three took place within a sacred enclosure distinctly marked by the temenos walls.[29]

The three cults' history is very similar too. The shrines can be traced back as early as the ninth century BC and reach their peak in late geometric and early archaic times. Archaic predecessors are assumed for all three temples, traces remain for none. Rather, the shrines survive in their Hellenistic reshaping after a substantial monumentalization; a fountain house, the ritual function of which is obscure, seems to be attached to at least two of the three cults. During the same period, the three deities become associated with Zeus Polieus and seem to work as θεοὶ πολιοῦχοι (protectors of the city) within the local religious system. Nothing in the cultic topography suggests that fireless sacrifice suited one locality better than another. All fit surprisingly well into the mythical story; any

[28] e.g. Blinkenberg in *Lindos I* 10–11; but also the Pindar commentaries: e.g. Verdenius on 40 and 48; Kirkwood 95. The first excavators assumed for Athena at Lindos an *alsos* with aniconic cult statue: Blinkenberg (1917); in *Lindos I* 14–15; cf. Call. fr. 100.4: λεῖον ἕδος on which see Pugliese Carratelli (1953); Cazzaniga (1953).

[29] For chronology of the architecture of the sanctuary at Lindos cf. Lippolis (1988–9) 97–103 and (1996); for Ialysos: Livadiotti (1996); Rocco (1996) 43–5, complementing *Lindos III* 81–154. Kameiros: *Clara Rhodos* vi–vii (1932–3) 223–65. No altars have been discovered, though some traces at Lindos point to ritual meals: Blinkenberg in *Lindos I* 15–16.

akropolis could quite happily have served the Heliadai for the first performance of their rites.[30]

Finds unearthed in association with the three goddesses confirm this picture; the three votive complexes are almost indistiguishable in quality and quantity. Though the dedicatory material of Lindos is seductively well presented to the public, the essentially unedited archaic votive complex of Ialysos appears to be equally, if not more, impressive. Kameiros, where fewer pre-classical finds were made, has still produced a fair amount of archaic material too.[31] The frequency of limestone statuettes of Cypriot style, ivories, fibulae of various geographical origins, and faiences occurring at all sites suggests relations with places such as Cyprus, Naukratis, Samos and other islands, and the Near East (Syria, Phoenicia, Egypt) from at least the Geometric era. They confirm the island's location in the centre of the economically and culturally extremely mobile archaic Mediterranean east, and the goods that this brought spread evenly amongst the three local patronesses.

Items that should be considered special gifts to Rhodian Athena are also identical in all three cults. Two of the deity's iconographical depictions are particularly worth mentioning. Cypriot limestone figurines portray a goddess seated on a throne and sometimes accompanied by a ram-headed seated deity.[32] This statuette type, often considered Egyptian, is on Rhodes dedicated to Athena alone and elsewhere has been found only in connection with the goddess worshipped at Amathous on Cyprus.[33] Another unusual feature of Athena is her representation as a *kourotrophos*, that pictorial formula responsible for a range of vague hypotheses on an alleged oriental origin for the deity.[34] By contrast, the link may be one to the world of *parthenoi* and choral dance: the three cults of Athena on Rhodes yield a respectable number of figurines representing *auletai*, lyre players,

[30] Lindos: Lippolis (1988–9) 107. Until *c.*295 BC there was only a priest of Athena (*ἱερεὺς Ἀθαναίας Λινδίας*); the 'priest of Athana and Zeus' *ἱερεὺς* [or *ἱερατεύσας*] *Ἀθαναίας* or *Ἀθάνας Λινδίας καὶ Διὸς Πολιέως* occurs as late as 266 BC: *Lindos II* 104, no. 70; 106a; Zeus is thought to have come into the cult in 300–275 BC (Blinkenberg, ibid. 103), which is not, however, confirmed by the *ex-voto*: van Gelder (1900) 313–14; Morelli (1959) 80; 11–12 on his advent in the other two cities.

[31] The preliminary study for Ialysos was made by Martelli (1988) and, including further finds, (1996). I was fortunate to be able to see the votive material mentioned in the preliminary publications at the Museum of Rhodes in March 1998, for which I thank Dr I. Papachristodoulou, Mrs A. Giannikouri, and Prof A. De Vita. For Kameiros see *Clara Rhodos* vi–vii (1932–3).

[32] *Lindos I* 400–1 pl. 74, nos. 1793–5; Ialysos: Martelli (1988) 107 and 117 n. 37, and among the not fully published votives. Kameiros has a whole series of Cypriot limestone figurines with 'Egyptian subject': *BMC Sculptures* i.1 (1928) 158 ff.; B 364–7, 384–7, 390, 334 and Egyptian influences in others. B 390 is another ram-headed seated deity from Lardos, near Lindos; see also *MDAI(A)* (1886) 155–6. nos. 7959, 7960, 7963.

[33] See Buchholz (1991) on these statuettes in Cyprus, on the Lindian figures 119. Cypriot limestone figures have nowhere else (other than Cyprus) been discovered in such great quantities (Blinkenberg in *Lindos I* 400–5), manifesting close contacts between the two islands. The other findspots of Naukratis and Knidos may also be related.

[34] Hadzisteliou-Price (1978) 154–6. *Lindos I* 538 ff. e.g. nos. 2226, 2242, 2243, 2257 (mid-5th cent.); Kameiros: *Clara Rhodos* vi–vii (1932–3) 281–2 no. 5 (14330). Cf. the curious statuettes of a woman with girl: Martelli (1988) 107 fig. 3.

and entire groups of musicians. Should this allude to an Athena that attracts marriageable girls and boys in choral performances? It would certainly fit with her myth being the centrepiece in a chorally performed *Olympian 7*.[35]

Why these three cults look just so alike is an intriguing question, which I shall briefly consider below (p. 264). To return to the nature of the sacrifices with or without fire, it is interesting that all three cults systematically yield archaic *kriophoros* figurines, little male images carrying a ram. This pictorial formula, which derives its name from the famous statue in Athens, appears to show the young male offering-bearer on his way to perform an animal sacrifice. Boiotian Tanagra, for instance, invents a divine prototype for this image: in the same way as Hermes once carried the ram on his shoulders around the city walls, so does the city's most beautiful young man at an annual festival with a lamb. Others of Athena's male figurines carry goats. Moreover, the votive material includes a large group of limestone and terracotta bulls, as well as several rams of the same manufacture.[36]

None of these are of course likely offerings if vegetables in oil largely nourish one's deity. Little token sacrificial animals occur in votive contexts throughout Greece. There is obviously no way of telling whether such items were dedicated precisely because their real equivalents were not, or could not be, offered; but in many cases in mainland Greece both symbol and real object were given.[37] Substitute offerings of this kind seem to have a certain tradition on Rhodes itself: the cult of Zeus Atabyrios, eponym of the mountain of south-western Rhodes, has produced dozens of little bronze bulls, and clay versions are known from the so-called *Boukopion* below the Lindian akropolis.[38]

So, animals were more likely in the cult than not, but does that mean we can make a case for unburnt animal sacrifice? This is difficult territory. The interpretation implies a continuity of, or a conscious return to, a sacrificial practice from prehistoric, that is, 'pre-Greek' times. Clearly Rhodian Athena did acquire gifts local to her character at Rhodes. However, the *kriophoroi* figurines and animal substitutes occur just as they do anywhere else in Greece. Too little is understood about the role of such votives in Greek cult to exclude with certainty the possibility that their pictorial formulae are flexible enough to denote two

[35] Musicians: Blinkenberg in *Lindos I*: 425–8, nos. 1703–20 (mid-6th cent.); nos. 222, 2224, 2247–8 (mid-5th cent.): double pipe-players, lyre-players, and tambourine-players, which accompany choral dance on a patera from Idalion: Perrot (1882–1914) iii. 673, fig. 482. Ialysos: mentioned by Martelli (1988) 107, among which a standing trio on a seal: 110; Kameiros: *Clara Rhodos* vi–vii (1932–3) 281 no. 4 (14329) and 282 fig. 5.

[36] Tanagra: Paus. 9.22.1. Kriophoroi: *Lindos I* 429–30, nos. 1721–38; goats: 1739–63. Ialysos: Martelli (1988) 107 (all unpublished); Kameiros: *Clara Rhodos* vi–vii (1932–3) 280 nos. 2 and 3, fig. 2.

[37] Lindos: individual bulls: *Lindos I* nos. 1897, 1899; 1902; 2405; 2407; bull statuettes at Ialysos: Martelli (1988) 107. Often enough both symbol and the real object were dedicated. Cake substitutes for sacrificial animals were a frequent and spectacular part of Greek sacrifice: Kearns (1994).

[38] Cf. Σ Pi. *O.* 7.160c: 'there are also bronze bulls (*βόες χαλκοῖ*) on the mountain on Rhodes, who bellow (*μυκῶνται*) whenever something bad is about to happen to the *polis*'. The bronze bulls of Zeus Atabyrios fill a drawer in the Museum of Rhodes. For the Boukopion bulls see n. 40.

diametrically opposite modes of sacrifice. The generic nature of small votives across the Greek world on the whole serves to stress similarity of religious custom rather than difference, one of the ways in which 'Greek religion' is expressed universally. Seen from this angle, the more reasonable interpretation of these figurines is that Athena's archaic, that is to say seventh- and early sixth-century sacrifices were done in the normal Greek way, that is with animal pieces set on fire.

So we remain with a myth of fireless, an archaeological context of animal sacrifice with fire. But the (comparatively small) body of fifth- and fourth-century votive material unearthed at all three cults throws strikingly different light on the issue. It offers insight into some remarkable changes in Athena's cult that apparently occurred during the fifth century. It is this change that may provide a key to the understanding of the fireless sacrifices. The first part of the argument can be made for Lindos only and not fully, while the second concerns again all three Rhodian Athenas. Below the Lindian akropolis there is an outcrop of bedrock, a very peculiar feature in the landscape, the so-called Boukopion. Sheltered by a series of major rocks, a further small religious area and associated votive material was discovered here, dating back to the ninth century BC.[39] The deity worshipped has not been identified. The shrine has, however, become known for a substantial number of rupestral sacrificial inscriptions which start to appear in great quantities in the natural wall surrounding the plateau from about the mid-fifth century onwards. Many of them are family dedications, set up on behalf of a whole clan. A typical inscription would be that 'a *pro(s)kharaios thysia* by x and his descendants at the festival of Boukopia/together with the rite of *boukopia*' and now also '(?)outside the festival of/without Boukopia'.[40]

The traditional interpretation of these inscriptions is that 'Boukopion' was the place where Lindians performed proper 'Dorian' burnt animal sacrifice,[41] 'bull-slaughter' which was not allowed on the akropolis, and so was held *πρὸ ἐσχάρας*, 'before the *eskhara*'. This interpretation, however, cannot be supported linguistically: there are no parallel cases in which the vowels behave in similar

[39] It is not known whether this feature was shared by its sister cults on the island.

[40] e.g. *IG* xii.1 798: *θυσία | προσχάρα-|ιος Βουκ-|οπία Ἀγησίπ(π)ου | καὶ ἐγγό-|νων* ('a *proskharaios thysia* at the Boukopia (together with the *boukopia*?) by Hegesippos and his descendants') and *Προ-(σ)χάραιο(ς) Πρατάρχου θυσία οὐ βοκοπία* ('a *proskharaios thysia* of Pratarkhos ?without *boukopia*'), discussed by Kostomitsopoulou (1988) 125–6. A number of fine bronze bulls have also been found: *Lindos III* ii. 464.

[41] Blinkenberg in *Lindos I* 10–11; *Lindos II* i. 791–804; ii. 904–10 and the inscriptions nos. 580–619 and in *IG* xii.1 791–804; cf. Morelli (1959) 86–8. The deity is not named, except as Athena Phratria in *Lindos II* 615. These inscriptions are extremely interesting and would warrant more detailed research in the light of late 5th-cent. Rhodian history as family dedications, perhaps connected to a liturgy (?); some prominent names identified by Blinkenberg in *Lindos II* 581; *θεοδαίσια* occurring in about half the samples instead of *boukopia* are often identified with *xenia* (on which Ch. 4 above) and are popular in aristocratic settings; cf. e.g. *Suda* α 4266 s.v. *Ἀστυδρόμια* for *γενέθλια* and *θεοδαίσια* in the same context.

fashion, though there is no strong evidence against it either.[42] More plausibly, the double appearance in the inscriptions of the word qualifying *thysia* as προ(σ)χάραιος may derive from a compound with a stem χαρ-, in which the alternation προ-/προσ- is frequent. A possible parallel can be found in a name for the Athenian festival called interchangeably Προ(σ)χαριστήρια and Προ(σ)χαιρετήρια. This festival, in honour of Athena or perhaps Demeter, is concerned with the reappearance and growing of the crops (καρποί) in spring.[43] A προ(σ)χάραιος θυσία could well be a rite in which the offering of fruit was involved. At Lindos this could then happen with or without a slaughter of a bull, the nature of which has to remain, for yet a bit longer, obscure.

This custom could be related to a rite attested for all three of Athena's akropolis cults on Rhodes, but ignored in the attempts to think of her cult as a whole. The greatest quantity of any specific type of dedication for Athena, so far unique in the Greek world, consists of large quantities of ceramic sherds, mainly shattered bottoms of vessels with inscribed graffiti dating from *c*.450 BC to the end of the fourth century, that is roughly contemporary with the Boukopion inscriptions, and with *Olympian 7*. These sherds have never been fully published but it is known that some two hundred were found at Ialysos, several dozen at Lindos, and at least a dozen appear in the Kameiros publication.[44] They are inscribed with various configurations of a standard votive formula, which in its most complex form reads Ἀθαναίαι ἀπαρχὴν (δεκάτην/ἄπαργμα) ὁ δεῖνος ἀνέθηκε ('[someone] dedicated an aparkhe/dekate/apargma to Athena') as if commenting on a frequent ritual act: private persons offer 'a part of something' to the deity, a share of a shareable commodity. *Aparkhai* ('first-fruits') typically occur in agricultural contexts, for example as first-fruits of harvest, both burnt and unburnt, and meatless. They are mostly, though not exclusively, related to springtime festivals.[45] The aparkhic vessels, tantalizing and plentiful attestation of Athena's fifth-century worship, might constitute evidence that Athena's offerings had eventually

[42] This was communicated to me in a letter by A. Morpurgo Davies in March 1998. Ekroth (2002) 25–59 discusses the meaning of *eskhara*.

[43] *Suda* π 2928 s.v. Προχαριστήρια: 'this is the day when at the end of the winter the crops start to grow, everyone sacrifices to Athena. The name of the sacrifice is "Prokharisteria". Lykourgos in his "On priesthood" talks about it, saying that this very old sacrifice happened because of the rising of the goddess, and that it was called Prokharisteria because of the appearance of the growing crops.' Cf. *DNP* s.v.

[44] *Lindos I* 662–9, nos. 2795–2852. Ialysos: Martelli (1988) 113–14 (some of these are offerings by public bodies); Kameiros: *Clara Rhodos* vi–vii (1932–3) 363 no. xiii and fig. 107.

[45] West (1997) 39 thinks that *aparkhai* are always offerings of fruit and vegetables, but this is not confirmed by the occasional wider use for other commodities (and the term appears to have been quite flexible: *kore* statues regularly describe themselves as an ἀπαρχή to e.g. Apollo or Artemis): see Parker (2004*b*). First-fruits of harvest: Xen. *Oec.* 5.10. Ἀπαρχαί in springtime festivals: e.g. the first-fruit decree *IG* i^3 78. R. Stengel, *RE* i (1898) 2666–8 s.v. ἀπαρχαί, quotes a number of agricultural *aparkhai*: Th. 3.58; Soph. *Trach.* 761; Eur. *Phoen.* 857, and some epigraphical evidence. Δεκάτη is altogether more widely used (Parker ibid.) and can therefore not help the identification of the dedicated product.

turned into ἄπυρα ἱερά of the kind that accorded with the common Greek distinction between burnt animal sacrifice and fireless sacrifice of fruit, vegetables, and cakes. These pieces could well be connected with the *boukopion* inscriptions, attesting meatless offerings for Athena at a springtime sacrifice for Athena, the closest equivalent of which are the Athenian *Prokharisteria*.

This is as far as Athena's fireless sacrifice can be tracked down: the simple equation of fireless and meatless offerings is old, but does not correspond to actual cultic practice. *Olympian 7*'s aetiology actually suggests that the tradition associated with Athena was not one of fruit and vegetable offerings, but of fireless animal sacrifice. Fireless animal sacrifice was the prevailing practice in the Bronze Age Near East, and it is likely that the tradition of Athena's fireless sacrifices is either really rooted in that milieu, or presents a conscious evocation of it, a point to which I shall return below. Evidence for Athena's real-life worship, however, suggests that in the archaic period, animals, burnt or unburnt, were sacrificed in her honour. But by the mid-fifth century an overwhelming number of dedicants made a point of offering her what look like the first-fruits of agricultural produce, and without fire. If the interpretation of the votive vessels is correct, the fifth-century rite perhaps presents one of the earlier instances of the erroneous yet common identification of *apyra hiera* with meatless offerings. They form the fifth-century and later ritual interpretation of 'fireless sacrifices'. As we shall see, a key point may well be that the rite was so popular, as if to extend to a wider clientele a custom that had been reserved for the privileged few, for example those who dedicated, and continued to dedicate, the Boukopion inscriptions, individual families as we saw above. These fireless *hiera* were by no means a feature of any particular one of the three Athenas specifically, but rather are a remarkable testimony to shared religious practice within the Rhodian *tripolis* in the mid-fifth century, and I shall discuss this matter below.

So these meatless *apyra hiera* in the mid-fifth century, imagined to originate in a mythical *aition* for meat sacrifice *without fire*, may well constitute a peculiar change in ritual behaviour in Rhodian Athena's cult. Perhaps this was a conscious adoption of a practice associated with the geographical milieu of the island—a Greek gateway to the Eastern Mediterranean—or with an ancient practice, or with both. As I shall demonstrate in the remainder of this chapter, the performance of this ode does indeed evoke a special continuity from a pre-Greek past and is interested in Rhodes' geographical position in the eastern Mediterranean. The island's imagined prehistory is brought into the present through the interaction of religious aetiology with ritual occasion. For this to become apparent, we need to look at the song's other two religious aetiologies, also concerned with foundational moments in the island's past, before turning to how all three stories work in a fifth-century performance setting.

2. TWO STORIES OF ORIGIN: TLEPOLEMOS AND HELIOS

The first of Pindar's three aetiologies recounts the settling of Rhodes from Argos. According to this story, the Herakleid Tlepolemos murdered his uncle Likymnios because of the latter's unseemly desires for his own mother Midea, and subsequently was exiled and went off to found Rhodes (ll. 20–32). Commentators, in somewhat convoluted constructions not dissimilar to those developed for the exculpation of Neoptolemos (Chapter 4), struggle to discern Pindar's programmatic 'correction' (*διορθῶσαι* l. 21) in releasing Tlepolemos from any 'blood guilt' as it is implied in a passage of the *Iliad* on the same episode, generally on the assumption that this would stain the spotless curriculum of a founder hero. By contrast, I think, the distancing from the oral tradition concerns the type of foundation that the ode attributes to Tlepolemos, that of an archaic colony rather than a pre-Trojan War Mycenaean outpost. The principal passage used for comparison is the Rhodian section in the *Catalogue of Ships*, which includes the episode:

Τληπόλεμος δ' ἐπεὶ οὖν τράφ' ἐνὶ μεγάρῳ εὐπήκτῳ,
αὐτίκα πατρὸς ἑοῖο φίλον μήτρωα κατέκτα
ἤδη γηράσκοντα Λικύμνιον, ὄζον Ἄρηος·
αἶψα δὲ νῆας ἔπηξε, πολὺν δ' ὅ γε λαὸν ἀγείρας
βῆ φεύγων ἐπὶ πόντον· ἀπείλησαν γάρ οἱ ἄλλοι
υἱέες υἱωνοί τε βίης Ἡρακληείης.
αὐτὰρ ὅ γ' ἐς Ῥόδον ἷξεν ἀλώμενος ἄλγεα πάσχων·
τριχθὰ δὲ ᾤκηθεν καταφυλαδόν, ἠδ' ἐφίληθεν
ἐκ Διός, ὅς τε θεοῖσι καὶ ἀνθρώποισιν ἀνάσσει,
καί σφιν θεσπέσιον πλοῦτον κατέχευε Κρονίων.

Now when Tlepolemos was grown in the strong-built mansion,
He struck to death his own father's beloved uncle,
Likymnios, scion of Ares, a man already ageing,
At once he put ships together and assembled a host of people
And went fugitive over the sea, since the others threatened,
The rest of the sons and the grandsons of the strength of Herakles.
And he came to Rhodes a wanderer, a man of misfortune,
And they settled there in triple division by tribes, beloved
Of Zeus himself, who is lord over all gods and all men,
Kronos' son, who showered the wonder of wealth upon them.
(*Iliad* 2.661–70, tr. Lattimore)

A closer look at this passage reveals that epic and lyric narratives are almost pedantically similar, except perhaps for Tlepolemos' mother's name.[46] The conflict between Likymnios, half-brother of Herakles' mother Alkmene, and

[46] Tlepolemos' mother, Astyokheia in the *Iliad* (2.558), is more often Astydameia: Hes. fr. 190.4,6; *Σ* Pi. *O.* 7.42a quotes the genealogy of an anonymous 'Akhaian' historian (*FHG* iv 286) as Pindar's source; cf. Pherec. *FGrH* 3 F 80: *Ἀστυγένεια*. Midea is a Phrygian in Apollod. 2.4.5; *Σ* Pi. *O.* 7.49a; b.

Herakles' son Tlepolemos seems to be one of royal succession, which typically precedes the foundation of cities.[47] It is possible that Tlepolemos killed his uncle unintentionally, and is consequently exculpated as 'enraged' (*χολωθείς*) by Pindar. The problem of Tlepolemos' guilt, however, exists well beyond Pindar and in itself causes much discussion, which rather indicates an ambiguous tradition, of which Pindar was aware, too.[48]

By contrast, the crucial difference between *Olympian 7* and the epic version lies in the introduction of a foundation oracle. This is a typical element of archaic colonial stories.[49] The three Rhodian cities, however, are not colonial settlements of the archaic period, but a rare example of settlements believed to have been set up in the period preceding the Trojan War. Most places founded by the heroes of Troy occur as part of the *Nostoi* tradition where returning heroes build their new cities *en route*. Delphic authority is not desired, and only seldom received, for such 'Akhaian' foundations.[50]

The Tlepolemos of the ode is an exception to this general rule. In addition, social convention and colonial experience overlap in the motif of the murderer-founder who is equally a common feature of such archaic legends.[51] Tlepolemos' heroic honours mentioned towards the end of the ode are those typically offered to an archaic oikist, and I shall say something about this cult further below.[52] That is to say, although referring to a different type of foundation perceived as dating

[47] Likymnios is the eponym of Tiryns' akropolis *Λικύμνια* (Str. 8.6.11). *Σ O.* 7.54: 'Pindar follows the view of those who say that Tlepolemos committed the murder because of some honours and power positions' (*διὰ τιμάς τινας καὶ ἀρχάς*); cf. *Σ* Pi. *O.* 7.49a. Conflicts of this kind resulting in emigration: Proitos and Akrisios (Argos: Bacch. 11.59–84); Medon and Neileus (Athens: e.g. Paus. 7.2.1); the motif of the bastard's colonizing is similar: Battos of Kyrene (Hdt. 4.150 ff.); Dorieus is the son of one of his father, king of Sparta's concubines (Hdt. 5.41). The epic version has Tlepolemos flee in fear of the other first-generation Herakleids (*Il.* 2.665–6).

[48] Cf. D.S. 5.59.5, according to whom Tlepolemos, who had 'involuntarily killed [Likymnios], went voluntarily into exile from Argos' (*ὃν ἀκουσίως ἦν ἀνῃρηκώς, ἔφυγεν ἑκουσίως ἐξ Ἄργους*); Apollod. 2.8.2: 'Tlepolemus had killed Likymnios inadvertently before they [the Herakleids] left the Peloponnese; for while he was beating a servant with his stick Likymnios ran in between (*τῇ βακτηρίᾳ γὰρ αὐτοῦ θεράποντα πλήσσοντος ὑπέδραμε*); so he fled with not a few, and came to Rhodes, and dwelt there (*φεύγων μετ' οὐκ ὀλίγων ἧκεν εἰς Ῥόδον, κἀκεῖ κατῴκει*)'; Paus. 2.22.8.

[49] The oracle is taken up by D.S. 5.59.5: 'having received an oracle about an apoikia he sailed to Rhodes with some people, and he was welcomed by the locals and settled there (*χρησμὸν δὲ λαβὼν ὑπὲρ ἀποικίας μετά τινων λαῶν κατέπλευσεν ἐς τὴν Ῥόδον, καὶ προσδεχθεὶς ὑπὸ τῶν ἐγχωρίων αὐτοῦ κατῴκησε*). See Malkin (1987) 17–91 and Leschhorn (1984) esp. 105–9 for the role of oracles in archaic *apoikia*, and generally Pl. *Leg.* 738b ff.; Cic. *Div.* 1.3; Vitr. 4.1.4; Plut. *De Pyth. Or.* 398d; 407f–408a.

[50] *Nostoi* foundations occur mostly in Southern Italy: see Bérard (1957) 323–83 and Fabre (1981); Malkin (1998*b*); see Ch. 6 below.

[51] First characterized thus by Dougherty (1993) 31–44 but see already Malkin (1987). A 'historical' murderer-founder is e.g Arkhias of Syracuse (Plut. *Am. Narr.* 772e–73b); Alkmaion of Arkanania: Th. 2.102.5–6; cf. the foundation of Athamantia by Athamas: Apollod. 1.9.2; of Mykenai by Perseus: Paus. 2.16.3. Orestes' purification programme (Eur. *Or.* 1643b–7; cf. *El.* 1250–75) includes his exile in Arkadia at *Ὀρέστειον* (Argos Orestikon *ap.* Str. 7.7.8). See Parker (1983) 375–92; 386–8; app. 7. Orestes is the leader in the Aiolian colonization: Pi. *N.* 11.35; Hellan. *FGrH* 4 F 32.

[52] On oikist cult see Malkin (1987) 189–260. Tlepolemos' death at Troy: *Il.* 5.655–6. Cf. D.S. 5.59.6.

much further back, our story has the narrative form of colonial legends of the archaic period. If the myth adopts topoi otherwise unknown for the pre- or post-Trojan War story type, the content borne by these elements must have travelled with them: Apollo's oracle and the other features give the settling enterprise the air of an archaic *apoikia*. The narrative implies that the Rhodians were immigrants to the island, and considerably more recent ones than their presumed Argive forefathers, of the generation of the Herakleids, would imply.

Historically speaking, this makes no sense. As was mentioned above, the Rhodians tend to be archaeologically rather older than their mainland Greek counterparts, and so also much older than most so-called colonial foundations. Indeed, the Rhodian *poleis* distribute population through colonies all over the Mediterranean: Gela in Sicily (itself mother city of Akragas), Phaselis, and Soloi on the coast of Anatolia, all belong to the first generation of any Greek settlements abroad.[53] It is therefore not immediately evident why the Rhodians should think themselves more recent than their mainland Greek equivalents. That said, Rhodes was densely settled in the Mycenaean period, and its alleged foundation from 'Mycenaean' Argos may well constitute a memory of its being a Bronze Age mainstay in the Aegean. *Olympian 7* seems to mix 'colonial' experience and the Rhodians' own long-standing perception of having themselves once arrived from mainland Greece. What is of interest to us is the evocation of a sense that Rhodes' Greek history started peculiarly late; the Tlepolemos myth stresses the fact that the Rhodians were not the island's original inhabitants, but just its secondary settlers. And the myth claims an awareness of marginality, of not being quite part of Greece. Why should *Olympian 7* construe this view that the Rhodians were to any degree younger than their equivalents dwelling in what is arguably thought the historic homeland of all the Greeks?

By contrast, the third of the aetiological myths of this ode (ll. 54–76) gives the opposite picture. Pindar here goes back to the times of Rhodes' emergence from the sea, that is to the time of the island's very earliest beginnings. When Zeus, Poseidon, and Hades divided up the *kosmos*, the sun-god Ἅλιος accidentally remained without his portion. Just as Zeus set about reshuffling thc lots, Helios spotted a flourishing Ῥόδος emerging in great splendour from the sea. Taking his chance, he claimed the island from the assembled gods, and once it was fully arisen made the island his. Seven Ἁλιάδαι were then born from the relationship of Helios with the local nymph Rhodes. One of them, Kerkaphos, fathers Helios' grandchildren Kameiros, Ialysos, and Lindos. These three divide up the island in equal parts and become the eponyms of its *tripolis*.

Here we are at the very origins of civilization on Rhodes. This is not a story of immigration, but one of autochthony, told through an aetiology of the cult of Helios on the island. But just as the song builds up the problematic image of Tlepolemos' settling the island rather too late in mythical chronology, so is this

[53] Th. 6.4.3; Hdt. 7.153; Str. 14.5.8.

claim about Helios' Ur-patronage of the island neither straightforward nor uncontested. This myth in the first place aligns itself with a type of story characteristic of the island world, a set of traditions designed to cope with historical change rather than unbroken continuities. The myth of Helios contains a number of topoi typical of island self-imagery. Flooding and population change are frequent such motifs; floating and becoming fixed indicate an island's change of status. Recurrent rebirths accompany repeated re-namings: Delos, for example, became Delos 'the visible' when it stopped floating about as *Ἀστερία*, and Aigina's former name was *Οἰνώνη*.[54] The traditions no doubt are interpretations of maritime vicissitudes and the difficult natural conditions in which island life seeks to subsist. But the other, important dimension of these island lives is that of constant change, also embedded in natural conditions, but in a different way: islands, sitting as they do right in the midst of seaborne traffic and often defenceless, are singularly exposed to, and often the first and last to feel, all the greater or smaller waves of change hitting the Mediterranean in its long history. By the same token, however, islands rarely undergo full and radical change, and a perception of this too comes across in the traditions of insularity.[55]

Rhodes' antiquarian record is no exception to this wider rule. The island was flooded and reborn at least twice before Helios appeared. According to Strabo, Rhodes' pristine names were Ophioussa and Stadia, the first of which arose, according to a different source, because of the many snakes dwelling there. The *Τελχῖνες*, wizards active on many Aegean islands, killed the snakes and settled Rhodes, which took its name *Τελχινίς* from these first 'human' inhabitants.[56] The island sank, the Telkhines spread widely in the Mediterranean. This is

[54] Delos' name Asteria is sometimes identical with, sometimes different from, Ortygia (above, Ch. 2): Hes. *Th.* 409; Pi. *Pae.* 7b.42–9; *Pae.* 5.42; fr. 33d; a different etymology in fr. 33c; Call. *Del.* (4) 36–54; *Σ Lyc.* 401. The onomastic aetiology is much used, e.g. Call. *Del.* (4) 53 'no longer invisible' (*οὐκέτ' ἄδηλος*); cf. St. Byz. s.v. *Δῆλος* (Kynthos and Asteria alternative names for Delos); Apollod. 1.4.1; Plin. *NH* 4.66; Ant. Lib. 35. *H. Ap.* 16; Str. 10.5.5 have Ortygia as a different island, often Rheneia, the small rocky place just opposite Delos. Aigina was *Οἰνώνα* in Pi. *N.* 4.46; 5.16; 8.7; *I.* 5.34 (*Οἰνοπία* in Pi. *I.* 8.21 and Ov. *Met.* 7.471–4); Sicily was first called Trinakria, then Sikania, then Sikelia (D.S. 5.2.1); Keos had at least two settlement phases (see esp. Call. fr. 75.54–77; cf. Plin. *NH* 4.62). Samothrace was initially named *Σάμος* or *Σαόννησος* (D.S. 5.47.1–2); Naxos was *Στρογγύλη* (50.1) and *Δία* (51.2); Lesbos was *Ἴσσα* and *Πελασγία* (81.2); Tenedos was called *Λεύκοφρυς* (83.2). Floating islands: Aiolian islands in *Od.* 10.1–4; the Ploades: A.R. 2.288 ff. Much island history can be found in Diodorus' fifth book 'On Islands'.

[55] On the topic of fast and frequent change on islands see e.g. Brun (1996); it is often implied in Horden and Purcell (2000) *passim* (see index s.v. 'islands'). A history of Greece could easily be written through one of Delos. The theme of islands being the first and the last to feel change, but never completely so, is exemplified for antiquity e.g. by insular behaviour in the Persian Wars (cf. Ch. 2, Sect. 2). The anthropological case study by Just (2000) often makes the point of islands being at once backwaters and highly progressive.

[56] Str. 14.2.7. Cf. Heracl. Lemb. fr. 65 Dilts: 'They say that the island of Rhodes was formerly hidden by the sea, but dried up and emerged later. It was called "The Snaky One" because of the many snakes dwelling there' (*Ῥόδον τὴν νῆσον τὸ παλαιὸν κεκρύφθαι λέγουσιν ὑπὸ τῆς θαλάσσης, ἀναφανῆναι δὲ ὕστερον ξηρανθεῖσαν. ἐκαλεῖτο δὲ Ὀφιοῦσσα διὰ τὸ πλῆθος τῶν ἐνόντων ὄφεων*). Eust. *Il.* 789.17 also has *Τελχινία* as the island's first name.

when Helios arrived on the eastern Aegean scene, presumably drying Rhodes the island with his 'sharp' (*ὀξειᾶν* *O.* 7.70) beams, and then lying with Rhodes the nymph who gave the island its new and lasting name. Henceforth their sons, the Heliadai, lived on the island.[57]

This long history of the island, often dismissed as Hellenistic, conforms surprisingly well to the tradition alluded to in *Olympian 7* but at the same time undermines it. The song evidently knew of a pristine sub-marine existence of Rhodes, but here no phase precedes it. This need not mean that stories of repeated drowning did not, or did not yet, exist in 464 BC. Rather, it represents a choice geared to a crucial rhetorical effect: telling the origins of the island as 'birth' suggests, in a mild *damnatio memoriae*, that the ultimate, solely relevant history of the island starts with this last emergence, and that it continues uninterruptedly to the present. Pindar makes this remarkably clear through allusion to the *Iliad* at the time when the world was first divided among the gods.[58] The division (*δέδασται* 189—*δατέοντο* 55) of earth is performed by mixing (*παλλομένων* 191—*ἄμπαλον* 61) and drawing lots (*ἔλαχον*/*ἔλαχε*/*ἔλαχ'* 190/1/2—*ἔνδειξεν λάχος* 58); this is why Helios can remain 'without lot' (*ἀκλάρωτον* 59).

The island's lasting existence in the song is hence intrinsically bound up with Helios' presence. The birth of the island is really an aetiology for Helios as Rhodes' divine patron, expressed in all texts narrating or implying the story. A scholion to Pindar claims that by taking the island under his wing he dedicated it to himself.[59] Diodorus, too, says that following this most recent flood, the drying up of the island's moist soil and its repopulation by the Heliadai, 'the island was thought sacred to Helios' (*ἀκολούθως δὲ τούτοις νομισθῆναι τὴν νῆσον ἱερὰν Ἡλίου*).[60] Most explicit is Pindar himself when finishing his emergence story with a direct reference to Helios' patronage:

[57] See D.S. 5.55 for the spread of the Telkhines. The nymph Rhodes herself is, according to Diodorus, daughter of the Telkhines' sister Halia by Poseidon: 5.56.4. Heliadai on Rhodes: 5.56.

[58] *Il.* 15.189–93 (speaks Poseidon):

> *τριχθὰ δὲ πάντα δέδασται, ἕκαστος δ' ἔμμορε τιμῆς*
> *ἦ τοι ἐγὼν ἔλαχον πολιὴν ἅλα ναιέμεν αἰεὶ*
> *παλλομένων, Ἀίδης δ' ἔλαχε ζόφον ἠερόεντα,*
> *Ζεὺς δ' ἔλαχ' οὐρανὸν εὐρὺν ἐν αἰθέρι καὶ νεφέλῃσι·*
> *γαῖα δ' ἔτι ξυνὴ πάντων καὶ μακρὸς Ὄλυμπος.*
>
> All was divided among us three ways, each given his domain.
> I when the lots were shaken drew the grey sea to live in
> forever; Hades drew the lot of the mists and the darkness,
> and Zeus was allotted the wide sky, in the cold and the bright air.
> But earth and high Olympos are common to all three. (tr. Lattimore)

It is unlikely that Helios' participation in this division goes back to an epic model since Helios' stipulation *γῆ* should remain common to all: *ὅτε χθόνα δατέοντο* 55; *χώρας ἀκλάρωτον* 59. See Bresson (1979) 18–21; *contra* Verdenius ad loc.

[59] *Σ* Pi. *O.* 7.100a *ἀκλάρωτος μείνας ὁ θεὸς ταύτην εἵλετο τὴν μερίδα, ἱερὰν αὑτῷ τὴν νῆσον ἐπιτρεψάμενος* 'having remained without a lot the god seized this portion, and made the island his own'. Cf. Rubin (1980–1) 76 ff. on the Pindaric tale.

[60] D.S. 5.56.4.

βλάστε μὲν ἐξ ἁλὸς ὑγρᾶς
νᾶσος, ἔχει τέ νιν ὀξει-
ᾶν ὁ γενέθλιος ἀκτίνων πατήρ,
πῦρ πνεόντων ἀρχὸς ἵππων·

The island grew from the watery sea
and belongs to the father who engenders the piercing sunbeams,
the master of fire-breathing horses.

(Pindar, *Olympian* 7.69–71, tr. Race)

ἔχει—present tense—refers to the narrator's time, expressing in a typical way the lasting relationship between the patron deity and the land it protects.[61]

Olympian 7's unambiguous declaration of Helios as Rhodes' patron god squares badly with the modern idea that the sun-god only came to prominence on the island as late as the late fifth century, as patron deity after the synoikism of 408/7 BC.[62] The archaic cult of Helios on Rhodes is a perennial *enfant terrible*, and will remain so in the near future. But his presence and the importance of his legends on Rhodes at an early time, even if we do not know whether and in what form he was worshipped, are undeniable. For a long time, there were no material traces of his cult preceding the synoikism at all, generating the idea that the god was altogether either a later invention, or existed quietly as a gentile cult.[63] This situation, however, has changed lately with a superb discovery. In the territory of Ialysos, near the plain of Trianda and close to the north-eastern border of the prehistoric settlement, an archaic cult place has been discovered. Among the great number of sixth-century BC *olpai* vase fragments at least two have been found bearing the inscription *ΚΕΡΚΑΦΟ*. This is an exceptional find, about which one would like to know more: Kerkaphos, one remembers, is one of the seven Heliadai and father of the three eponymous heroes of the Rhodian tripolis, Kameiros, Ialysos, and Lindos.[64]

Indeed, despite the paucity of evidence, Helios and the Heliadai were certainly not unknown figures before the synoikism in 408/7 BC. Later texts inform us that, after a little family scandal, Helios' sons dispersed from Rhodes into the eastern Aegean: they move towards eponymous ancestorship on Kos, at the Triopion, on

[61] Cf. e.g. Th. 2.74.2, the invocation of the Plataian local gods as θεοὶ ὅσοι γῆν τὴν Πλαταιΐδα ἔχετε καὶ ἥρωες ('You gods and heroes who hold the Plataian territory'). Cf. Verdenius on Pi. *O.* 7.70 for this meaning of ἔχει, mentioning also Xen. *Cyr.* 8.3.24. See also Burkert (1985) 205 and 430 n. 26; Th. 4.87.2; *Syll.*[3] 360.

[62] Morelli (1959) s.v. Ἅλιος. See also Malkin (1987) 245, 248.

[63] Cf. von Wilamowitz-Moellendorff (1931–2) i. 84; Pugliese Carratelli (1951) 81–2; Morelli (1959) 95–6.

[64] Papachristodoulou (1992) 260 without any detail having followed. Cf. *SEG* xxvii 481 with Johnston (1977); *Inventory* (2004) 1197 on a disc testifying games for Helios, which may already date to the second half of the 5th cent. BC.

Lesbos, in Karia, and in Helioupolis in Egypt.[65] This is reflected in the contemporary distribution of Helios' cult in this area: on Lesbos, Helios was worshipped during Hellenistic times. Kos had an altar to Helios and *θεοὶ σύμβωμοι* ('gods sharing the altar').[66] Helios also spreads widely in the Rhodian Peraia and Knidos. Thera and Arkesine on Amorgos, not part of this tradition, but geographically in the Rhodian orbit, both provide scattered fourth-century rupestral inscriptions.[67] What lends all these pieces an antiquity preceding the god's prominent position in Rhodes' powerful economic network in the Hellenistic period is that Pindar already presupposes the tradition of the spread. We remember that all seven sons who are still on the island perform the service to Athena. But then Kerkaphos' sons—Helios' grandsons—the very same three eponymous ancestors Ialysos, Lindos and Kameiros, divided up the island in three parts among themselves only. The other Heliadai, uncles of the three eponymous heroes, must have been gone by then. Indeed, fifth-century Hellanikos lists the names of the Heliadai, suggesting the sons were known, and, more importantly, that who they were attracted the interest of those seeking to tidy up Greece's mythical past at the time. An idea that Helios' descendancy covered a good part of the eastern Aegean and reached as far as Egypt was certainly currency by the mid-fifth century (Map 5.1).[68]

So Helios and the Heliadai had radiated by the time the song sang this myth. Rhodes was quite possibly the hub of a local Heliadic tradition that spread with the political and economic movements of the people disseminating it, little chance though there is that we will ever know who these people were. The island was sufficiently well connected in the eastern Mediterranean before the synoikism to produce a set of traditions linking all these places together.[69] The ode invokes this cult and its spread, and thus the image of a well-connected island. Moreover, the song's suggestion is that the Heliadic tradition was 'old' and original, and in mythical chronology came prior to the Akhaian settlements from the Peloponnese. These two traditions, the one telling of Tlepolemos and

[65] D.S. 5.56.3–57.8; St. Byz. s.v. *Ἡλιούπολις* (founded by Aktis); *Σ* *O.* 7.131 mentions Khrysippos' foundation Khrysippa in Kilikia. von Wilamowitz-Moellendorff (1931–2) i. 84; (1883).

[66] Lesbos: in *IG* xii.2 526 C20; xii, suppl. 24 (3rd cent.); Kos: PH 64 (*c.*200 BC), mentioning Helios and a group of deities, possibly that occurring in *HG* p. 48 *Ἀλίο Ἀμέρας Μαχάονος Ἑκάτας* (on which Sherwin-White (1978) 334), a late 4th-cent. stone from the Asklepieion. Cf. the altar with four groups of *σύμβωμοι* ibid. 362–3.

[67] Fraser and Bean (1954) 130–2 on evidence for the worship of Helios in the Peraia (in Karia, including Knidos, Lagina, Panamara, Alabanda), though this more likely reflects the state of affairs after the synoikism. *Σ* Pi. *O.* 7.35b mentions a border temple at Embolos near Arykanda in Lykia just opposite Rhodes. Lykian coins show Helios from the 4th century onwards. Knidos has a priest of Helios: *CIG* 2653.4–6 = *IK Knidos* 91.1 (2nd cent. AD). Thera: *IG* xii.3 407 (4th cent. BC); Arkesine *IG* xii.7 87 (no date).

[68] Pi. *O.* 7.71–6. Hellan. *FGrH* 4 F 137 = *Σ* Pi. *O.* 7.132a names Okhimos, Kerkaphos, Aktis, Makaras, Kandalos, Triopes, Phaethon or Tenages; cf. *Σ* Pi. *O.* 7.131; Nonn. 14.44 ff. See St. Byz. s.v. *Λίνδος* (where Okhimos is Helios' father-in-law), *Κάμειρος*; Plut. *QG* 297c–d.

[69] Cf. pp. 253–4 below.

Map 5.1 Rhodes in its cultic-economic network: attestations of 1. cults of Athena, sometimes as 'Lindia'; 2. cults and traditions of Helios and sons in the eastern Aegean island world. Created from digital map data © Collins Bartholomew (2004) 2007

the Rhodians having migrated to Rhodes from the Greek mainland, the other, of Helios, one of autochthony and a people well-connected in the eastern Mediterranean, are set up against each other in the actual performance of *Olympian 7* in 464 BC. It is this historical setting to which I shall now turn.

3. A NEW PATRON FOR THE ISLAND

Helios rather than Tlepolemos

It has been suspected that the ode was performed in the context of a cult for Tlepolemos, at a kind of foundation festival for the island's oikist. This is a likely hypothesis, and is certainly what the song itself wants us to believe. Tlepolemos' myth forms the aetiological framework of the ode, and commands the song's moves between myth and ritual. In typical aetiological manner, Tlepolemos' story engenders the transition between performative and narrative parts of the song, both at the narrative's entry and exit. The long beginning (ll. 1–19), introduced by the famous priamel featuring a wedding *phiale*, continues by talking about athletic occasions past and present; it ends with a reference to the victor, the island, and the 'Argive spear' (*Ἀργεία αἰχμή*) which brought the Akhaians to Rhodes, only to launch straight into the details of Tlepolemos' expedition. The relative *τοῖσι* (l. 20) blends Akhaians of both the ritual present and mythical past. The exit from the string of myths is similar: when eventually the narrative arrives at the current state of affairs with the three cities of Kameiros, Ialysos, and Lindos (ll. 63–4),

> *τόθι λύτρον συμφορᾶς οἰκτρᾶς γλυκὺ Τλαπολέμῳ*
> *ἵσταται Τιρυνθίων ἀρχαγέτᾳ*
> *ὥσπερ θεῷ,*
> *μήλων τε κνισάεσσα πομπὰ*
> *καὶ κρίσις ἀμφ' ἀέθλοις. τῶν ἄνθεσιν Διαγόρας*
> *ἐστεφανώσατο δίς, . . .*
>
> There in sweet recompense for his bitter troubles,
> is established for Tlapolemos, the Tirynthians' colony-founder,
> as if for a god,
> a procession steaming of burnt sheep sacrifice and the judging
> of athletic contests, with whose flowers Diagoras
> has twice crowned himself, . . .
>
> (Pindar *Olympian* 7.77–81, tr. Race, adapted)

τόθι (l. 77) functions as the local reference to create a continuity from the mythical past, so elaborately told, into the ritual present, and the narrative seems to glide into a ritual celebration at this point. The transition from ritual to myth and myth to ritual in this song establishes the worship of Tlepolemos as the link between the two time spheres of myth and ritual in the performance.[70]

A coincidence of victory celebration and ritual for the oikist sits attractively with the nature of the ode's myths, all suitably talking about origins. What we know about the historical Tlepolemeia at first sight does not undermine this idea. The Tlepolemeia have a good chance of having been a significant public occasion, quite possibly with a pretence, but not necessarily with a reality, of mustering the

[70] See pp. 29–31 above.

whole island. Described as an *agon epitaphios* by the scholia, the festival involved a procession 'steaming with burnt sheep sacrifice' (l. 80) and a sporting contest, a sumptuous formula implying that Tlepolemos' honours were no less than those of Pelops at Olympia, Melikertes-Palaimon at Isthmia, and Opheltes-Archemoros at Nemea, all heroes whose funerary games turn into athletic festivals. In Pindar's times the games at the Tlepolemeia were what a Rhodian athlete regularly went through on a local level before embarking on the Panhellenic stage: Diagoras certainly had won them twice before his victory at Olympia celebrated in *Olympian 7* (ll. 80b–1).[71]

That the scholia speak of Tlepolemos' honours as an *agon epitaphios* has led to the plausible hypothesis that this is the festival known as the unified island's Epitaphia, attested in Hellenistic inscriptions. Here Rhodes' three *phylai*, consisting of the three old cities, came together to celebrate, as it seems, their unity in ritualized competition. The Epitaphia are often thought the equivalent to the festival of the war dead so powerfully utilized to glue together the citizenry of democratic Athens. *Olympian 7*'s Tlepolemeia, by contrast, rather seem a celebration in honour of an aristocratic founder-warrior, a Herakleid whose direct line descended to the victorious Diagorids.[72] If the Tlepolemeia were to have *become* the Epitaphia in the synoikized state, that is to say the Epitaphia are the Tlepolemeia under new cover, this would suggest that Tlepolemos' cult gained in public appeal and the hero was turned into someone the entire citizenry of Rhodes eventually came to identify with. Are these the traces of a cult changing from aristocratic worshipping group to a wider clientele? This interpretation may raise some objections, but at the very least we can conclude that at various points in the history of Rhodes it was a matter of debate who it was that Tlepolemos looked after, both geographically and socially.[73]

The claim that the fifth-century Tlepolemeia were a 'foundation festival' may therefore not have been straightforward—and what we have just learnt about the diverse models of the island's past that the two myths of origin offer sits right at the heart of this issue. For the song seems to construe an extraordinary claim: that Helios replaces Tlepolemos as the island's patron and mythical ancestor of the Rhodians. It is the scholia to *Olympian 7* that give the important hint that the perceived contradiction in the recounting of the origins is not a modern worry.

[71] On more general aspects of hero-cult new perspectives are opened up in Currie (2005) 31–88.

[72] Pi. *O.* 7.22 for the Herakleid descent of the Diagorids.

[73] *Σ* Pi. *O.* 7.36c (see next note) mentions a shrine, a grave, and funerary games for Tlepolemos in the city of Rhodes (Ekroth (2002) esp. 210). For the later Epitaphia featuring tribal competitions, see Pugliese Carratelli (1952–4) nos. 18, 19 (2nd cent. BC); Maiuri, *Nuova Silloge* 18; *Lindos II* 222 and 707. Their proximity to the festival of the Athenian war-dead (for the importance of which in the formation of civic identity see Loraux (1986)): see the note to *Lindos II* 222. So-called Tlepolemeia exist in the Rhodian Peraia, at 2nd cent. BC Kedreai: *Syll.*^{3}1067 = *IK Per.* 555, but the importance of the festival there might have lain in Tlepolemos being a hero shared between Rhodes and the Karian/Lykian coast: see Bresson (1999) 99–100 on Tlepolemos' Anatolian credentials. The inscription is therefore not perfect evidence to support the existence of a festival named Tlepolemeia on Rhodes itself. On the cult see also *Σ* Pi. *Ol.* 7.141c; 146a; 147c; Tz. Lyc. 911. *Σ* *O.* 7.145: thinks of the agon as the Herakleia. Cf. Morelli (1959) 69–70; 175–6; Moggi (1976*a*) 223 n. 2; Bresson (1979) 30–1; (1986) 414.

They suitably discuss the Tlepolemeia at either the entry to, or the exit from, the myth; but they are not at all clear about the identity of the actual festival: one claims that the Rhodians hold funerary games for Tlepolemos, 'but according to others this agon was sacred to Helios'.[74] Another suggests that Pindar lied, for the contest was not established for Tlepolemos, but for Helios, 'for which reason it is also called *ἡλιορόδιον*'. And a third thinks that Pindar did really mean the *Ἁλίεια*, the games for Helios which were the island's most significant festival after the synoikism, but that the poet 'encomiastically' terms them Tlepolemeia.[75]

The scholiasts' uncertainty is significant: the reason for their confusion lies in the fact that both occasions were a form of foundation festival celebrating the mythical origins of Rhodes, and, more significantly, that it was ambiguous to whom the foundation should be attributed. The scholiasts are obviously thinking in post-synoikism terms, when Helios *was* the island's patron god. However, we remember, Helios was not the island's patron in 464 BC. He had to wait to rise to this status until he was finally made the synoikized Rhodians' divine ancestor no earlier than 408/7 BC. In casually postulating an agon for Helios where the song tells us one for Tlepolemos was going on, the scholia may unwittingly have hit the nail on the head for the understanding of the ode. Trapped by the song's strategies, they read into *Olympian 7* what at the point of the song's performance lies yet in the future: that Helios had superseded Tlepolemos as the island's patron and ancestor of the Rhodians, and that the Halieia had replaced the Tlepolemeia as Rhodes' chief foundation festival.

I shall in the remainder of this chapter demonstrate how *Olympian 7* orchestrates precisely that claim and realizes it in performance. In the ritual context of the Tlepolemeia, the festival for the ancestor from Argos, the song tells an alternative story of origins, a different past, in which Helios and the Heliadic tradition overwrite Tlepolemos as Rhodes' mythical ancestor. The ode exploits the ritual associations of the Akhaian founder's festival with the times of beginnings for the formulation of a new collective identity for the island revolving around the cult of Helios: an identity that was autochthonous and pan-Rhodian, as opposed to immigrant and separatist, and one that placed Rhodes at the centre of maritime connectivity in the south-eastern Aegean and the Mediterranean east rather than at the supposed edges of the Greek world—just as Helios spread his (son-) beams from Rhodes. And in dragging in the aetiological myth of Athena's fireless

[74] *Σ* Pi. *O.* 7.36c: *ἔστι δὲ αὐτοῦ* [sc. Tlepolemos'] *ἱερὸν καὶ τάφος ἐν Ῥόδῳ· οἱ γὰρ συστρατευσάμενοι αὐτῷ διήγαγον τὰ ὀστᾶ ἀπὸ τῆς Ἰλίου εἰς τὴν Ῥόδον, οὐκ εὖ ἔχειν κρίναντες τὸ ἄνευ τοῦ βασιλέως ἐπινοστῆσαι τῇ πατρίδι. τελεῖται δὲ καὶ ἀγὼν ἐπιτάφιος ἐν τῇ πόλει Τληπολέμου, κατὰ δὲ ἑτέρους ἱερὸς Ἡλίῳ· ἀγωνίζονται δὲ παίδων ἡλικίαι καὶ στέφονται ἐκ λεύκης.* 'There is a shrine and his grave on Rhodes: those who went to war with him brought back his bones from Ilion to Rhodes, thinking it not a good idea to return to their homeland without the king. They hold funerary games for Tlepolemos in the *polis*; according to others, however, the agon is sacred to Helios; age-groups of boys enter the contest and are given crowns made of white poplar'. Angeli Bernardini (1977) dismisses these scholia.

[75] *Σ* Pi. *O.* 7.146a and b; 147c: *ἐγκωμιαστικῶς δὲ ὁ Πίνδαρος τὸν ἀγῶνα, Ἡλίῳ τελούμενον, εἰς τὸν Τληπόλεμον μετήγαγε* 'for encomiastic reasons Pindar transferred the contest held for Helios to Tlepolemos'.

sacrifices, performed as we remember by the sons of Helios who would then leave the island, this new past is tied to (worship of) what appears to be the island's most conspicuous deity.

In this world-view, the song strikingly anticipates elements of Rhodian identity that still belonged to the future, those representative of the synoikized Rhodian state after 408/7 BC. *Olympian 7* might therefore have had an extremely important role preparing, even supporting, the coming about of the synoikism through its forceful construction of a worshipping community that had a pan-Rhodian past to share instead of mythical diversity to separate them. In a mid-fifth-century context, the simultaneous forging of and appeal to local pride and identity must have presented an impressive counter-image to what we might imagine accompanied membership in the growing Athenian empire, facets of which we have already touched upon in Chapters 2 and 4. The image was attractive not least by setting up a competitive relationship with Athens, through the aetiology of the sacrifice for Athena as much as through the Heliadic myth of maritime connectivity.

Motivating the synoikism

To argue this view we need to leap into the island's synoikized future: this was that of a vibrant maritime hub and economic centre, a naval democracy, a resourceful and by Greek standards sizeable state, whose fate was subtly but unswervingly steered by a powerful elite intensely engaged in maritime commerce. According to a recently argued view, the island's eventual synoikism at the end of the fifth century completed a long-existing tendency to unification. Such a case for 'federal action' in the strict sense of the word—a communal body of decision-making—cannot be maintained unproblematically, but there is no doubt that Rhodes had always oscillated between unity and separation into different *poleis*.[76] Sometimes seen as a primarily political phenomenon, the late fifth-century process of synoikizing already had a strong commercial aspect, and the breaking from the Athenian empire in 411 BC with Spartan help and the presumed synoikism in 408/7 BC are intimately linked by the sources.[77] Similarly, elite involvement in the synoikism and their economic interests in all probability can and should not be separated. This is interesting for us since our victor Diagoras' descendants, above all the then exiled Dorieus, were amongst the

[76] Gabrielsen (2000*a*); Nielsen and Gabrielsen in *Inventory* s.v. (cf. Reger (1997) 476–7); Gabrielsen 180–7 gives a detailed and useful list of Rhodes' unified vs. separate actions until 411 BC; the problem has been bothering scholars for decades: Pugliese Carratelli (1951); Moggi (1976*a*) 220–2; Gehrke (1986) 125–8. For island synoikism in particular see now Constantakopoulou (2005).

[77] Th. 8.44; 60; Xen. *Hell.* 1.1.2; D.S. 13.38.5 (411 BC); on the synoikism D.S. 13.75.1; Str. 14.2.9; 11; Konon *FGrH* 26 F 1 xlvii; Plin. *NH* 5.132; Ael. Arist. *Or.* 25.50ff Keil. The basic study is now Gabrielsen (2000*a*), esp. 187–96; Nielsen and Gabrielsen in *Inventory* s.v.; earlier accounts include Moggi (1976*a*) 214–20; Gehrke (1985) 134–6. Demand (1990) 89–94, taking up Meiggs (1972) 210, sees the synoikism as a purely military phenomenon responding to Athenian pressures. See below, n. 96, on intertwined agricultural and commercial interests of the Rhodian elites.

island's *dynatotatoi* keen to revolt from Athens and implicated in the city's synoikism. They definitely had maritime concerns: Dorieus appeared on the scene of the revolt 'with his own ships', ten altogether, implying a family with maritime connections.[78]

That unity and investment in Rhodes' maritime character go together is suggested by the odd piece of information revealing the island floating between the poles of unity and separation. For Rhodian pre-synoikism concerted action continually concerns their strength at sea. The Rhodians are strong at sea, and their joint appearances before 408/7 BC often involve them colonizing, trading, and especially fighting at sea. So in the *Catalogue of Ships* or in the Persian Wars, when they seem to side with Dareios. Rhodes' naval prowess is also what the Spartans hope to win for themselves when they stir up secession from Athens in 411 BC, 'because of the island's manpower on sea and land, and since it would help them finance their fleet without having to have recourse to the Persians'. The Thucydidean passage clearly revolves around matters maritime, linking as it does the revolt on Rhodes to Rhodian ships and the financing of the Peloponnesian fleet—whether this be an allusion to the 38 talents later extracted from the Rhodians by the Spartans, but then not used, or to actual ship supply remains unclear.[79]

It is no news that Rhodes' selling point in post-synoikism times is naval superiority, militarily and commercially, which should not be distinguished. This is what made the island an attractive ally from the fourth century onward for any of the major powers in the area and a major player itself.[80] But it is somewhat more controversial to stipulate Rhodes' maritime nature as a sticking point in the questions of insular unity in the fifth century, and vital to the patterns of economic activity accompanying it.

However, holding Rhodes' archaic world and its post-synoikism revival against its fifth-century existence leads one to suspect exactly that. Strength at sea is indelibly linked to all-Rhodian *eudaimonia* in post-synoikism times. But the old motif of the wealthy island was topical ever since the first mention of a 'shower of wealth' in the *Catalogue of Ships* (discussed in detail below), proverbial fortune quite probably deriving from the riches the sea brought to the island thanks to a favourable geographical position linking the Aegean and the eastern

[78] Dorieus (and his ships): Th. 3.8.1; 8.35.1; Xen. *Hell.* 1.5.19; Paus. 6.7.1, 4–7 (= Androtion *FGrH* 324 F 46 *ναυσὶν οἰκείαις* 'in his own ships'); *Anth. Gr.* 13.11; most recently discussed by Hornblower (2004) 136–42. For the Diagorids' involvement in the synoikism, inferred from both Dorieus' prominence towards the end of the 5th cent. and the family's role in local Rhodian affairs immediately after, see notably van Gelder (1900); it is presupposed by Gehrke (1985) 134–40, with earlier bibliography.

[79] Maritime Rhodes: *Il.* 2.653–6; Aesch. *Pers.* 852–95; Th. 8.44; D.S. 11.3.8; cf. *Chronicle* D1–59. Rhodians 'strong at sea' (*ἰσχυσάντων κατὰ θάλατταν*) becomes a topos: implied in Pindar (n. 101 below); Th. 8.44.1; Arist. *Pol.* 1304^{b}27 ff.; D. 15 (*Rhod.*); *Σ* D. 13 (8), 166, 5–6 Dilts; D.S. 20.81.2.

[80] Cf. D.S. 20.81.2–4, including a comment on Alexander's admiration for Rhodes. Cf. already Mausolus (Hornblower (1982*a*) 104–5; 124–30); Alexander (Hauben (1977)); the Hellenistic kings (e.g. D.S. 20.93) and Rome (on Perseus and Rhodes e.g. Plb. 27.4).

Mediterranean, particularly Egypt.[81] Archaic Rhodes was tied into an intense network of cross-Mediterranean communications, a Rhodian Mediterreanean which linked the three Rhodian cities regionally in the Hexapolis, a group of cities involved in the Greek trading post at the Hellenion at Naukratis in Egypt. The island, not unsurprisingly, forms part of Chapter 3's Argive milieu linking the Argolid to the Eastern Mediterranean and Egypt; Althaimenes the Cretan features as the alternative founder of Kameiros.[82] Mythical Rhodian *ktistai* were feverishly active in founding later Lykian cities,[83] have a share in Kyrene's origins,[84] and are busy in the West, particularly Gela in Sicily, and, more enigmatically, Greek Spain.[85] Rhodians were no doubt well travelled in archaic times.

It is significant for the understanding of what motivated the late fifth-century synoikism that the two vaguely contemporary documents concern the resurgence of exactly this extensive network. Two decrees declare *proxenoi*, of 'all the Rhodians' the one, 'of the Lindians' the other, two inhabitants of Naukratis, the important trading port (*emporion*) in Egypt. That alone cannot be a coincidence, but the case for the revival of an elite-born maritime network of trade is strengthened by the fact that one of the individuals is a descendant of none other than an Aiginetan Pytheas. Could this be a Pytheas of the family for whom Pindar and Bacchylides had composed several odes, and who had probably been amongst the chief medizers? Both decrees bestow among other privileges that of free sailing into and out of the port(s).[86]

[81] 6th-cent. Ialysos and Lindos minted on the Phoenician standard, attesting 'a commercial relation to the east': Berthold (1984) 48. Cf. Str. 14.2.10 speculating on pre-synoikism Rhodian wealth through travel by sea (cited n. 109 below).

[82] *Il.* 2.668–70; Hdt. 1.144; 2.178; Althaimenes: Str. 14.2.6; Konon *FGrH* 26 F 1 (xlvii).

[83] Lykia: Phaselis: Ath. 7.297e–f; cf. *Chronicle* xxiv; Korydalla: St. Byz. s.v. (= Hecat. *FGrH* 1 F 246); Ptol. 5.3.3; Gagai: *EM* 219.6, s.v., all this notwithstanding traditional animosities going back a long time: Bresson (1999) 99–102, also raising the issue of contacts between Rhodian individuals and Lykian coastal cities. The Lindian tyrant Kleoboulos undertook a campaign in this area: *Chronicle* xxiii. Phaselis kept good relations with its mother city: *Chronicle* xxiv and Blinkenberg's comm. 170–1. Soloi: Str. 14.5.8.

[84] Kyrene is an interesting case and a lasting relation, which also includes Samos: HN^2 867: 5th-cent. coins showing Ialysos'/Lindos' symbols jointly with Kyrene's; cf. Hdt. 2.182: Amasis' votive tour to Rhodes, Kyrene, Samos (involved in Kyrene's foundation: Hdt. 4.152). *Chronicle* xvii names Pankis of Rhodes co-settler at Kyrene; his descendants appear in *IG* xii.1 773 (= *Lindos II* 44 (4th cent.)); *Clara Rhodos* vi–vii (1932–3) no. 1 (4th cent.) refers to interactions between Kyrene and Rhodes before the synoikism, cf. Momigliano (1936*b*) 49–51. Rhodes was part of Polykrates' 'sea-empire': Anacr. *PMG* 146.

[85] Gela and Akragas: Hdt. 7.153; Th. 6.4.3; Plb. 9.27.7–8. Southern Italy Str. 6.1.14; Rhodes in Iberia and the Baleares: Str. 3.4.8; 14.2.10. The literary evidence for all alleged Rhodian foundations abroad is surveyed by van Gelder (1900) 65–70.

[86] *Lindos II* 16 (= *Syll.*^{3} 110) makes an 'interpreter' called *—ας Πυθέω Αἰγ[ινάταν proxenos* 'of all the Rhodians' (*Ῥοδίων πάντων*), and grants him 'free entry and exit' [into/from the harbour] (*ἔσπλ[ο]ν καὶ ἔκπλον* ll. 8–9). In *Lindos II* 16 app. Damoxenos is made *proxenos* of the Lindians on a stele to be set up in the Hellenion (at Naukratis; ll. 17–18), and he is granted 'exemption from entry and exit tax' (*ἀτέλεια εἰς ἐσαγωγὰν καὶ ἐξαγωγάν*, ll. 13–14). These two late 5th-cent. decrees (cf. also

I choose to single out these two decrees because of the inherent suggestion that membership in the Athenian empire might well have meant for the Rhodian naval elite (not dissimilar to Chapter 4's seafaring Aiginetans) the breaking up of a network of maritime connections, both regional and long-distance. The *Old Oligarch* revealingly comments on precisely this aspect of insular synoikism, in a slightly oblique way: 'subject people at sea cannot join their cities together into the same unit. For the sea is in the way, and those now in power are thalassocrats. If it is possible for islanders to combine unnoticed on a single island, they will die of starvation.' The implication is that island synoikism is futile unless it is accompanied by a seaborne network of supply and the power of the 'thalassocrat' is broken.[87] If a unified island is hopeless without a set of links [sc. by sea], we need not wonder why the Rhodians with the synoikism started recultivating their old relations. Certainly the new state was relatively quick to reincorporate those nearby islands of the Dodecanese and parts of the mainland *peraia* which there is reason to believe had in archaic times already been dependent on Rhodes,[88] such as Syme, Chalke, Megiste (modern Kastellorizo), and quite possibly Karpathos.[89]

Lindos II 15) have been dated variously to before, during, or after the synoikism on the basis of identity of the issuing body, but given the lack of knowledge of Rhodes' institutions at the time all that can really be stated is their near contemporary date to the synoikism: Gabrielsen (2000*a*) 179 f.; 185–7. Hornblower (2004) 220 uses *Lindos II* 16 to support 5th-cent. elite mobility, in this case in the Dorian island world. Hellenistic proxenies were clearly often issued in commercial contexts: Ziebarth (1932) and Rostovtzeff (1937); now briefly Gabrielsen (1997), *contra* Reger (1994). On elite networks in the Mediterreanean see n. 96 below; for Aiginetan medism p. 207 n. 71.

[87] [Xen.] *Ath. Pol.* 2.2. The passage also makes similar comments on the necessity of import and export by sea in the case of mainland cities (2.3), with Osborne (2004). Cf. Hsch. α 462, s.v. ἀγέρωχοι.

[88] The quick reincorporation itself has often been commented on as a form of territorial aggression, but less attention has been given to what economic benefits it brought to whom: Fraser and Bean (1954) 94–117 (*peraia*); 138–54 (islands); now Bresson (1999) for Lykia. The evidence does not allow certainty on either pre-synoikism incorporation (Moggi (1976*a*) 226 n. 38; van Gelder (1900)) or independence (e.g. Robert (1934)), but links were in any case intense. Gabrielsen (2000*b*) (cf. also Papachristodoulou (1989) 242) has started to unfold the great complexity of Rhodian regional relations (3rd/2nd cent. BC), which at all times went beyond Fraser and Bean's categories of 'incorporated' and 'subject' *peraia*. The history of Rhodes, its surrounding islands, and the *peraia* is far from definite.

[89] Religious evidence and mythical links are rarely taken into account in this matter. *Ktoinai*, a pre-synoikism division peculiar to Rhodes, have been taken as indicative for early dependence: Fraser and Bean (1954) 95–6; Gabrielsen (1997) 141–54 on their social function. I quote only the sources for *ktoinai* and evidence not normally cited in support of these islands' close connections to Rhodes. For all three lack of 4th-cent. coinage and other signs of independence are taken to indicate their early (re-)-incorporation into Rhodes. Karpathos (later a deme of Lindos): Hsch. κ 3967: νῆσος Ῥόδου; *IG* xii.1 1033 = *Syll.*[3] 570 (*ktoina* of Potidaion, late 3rd cent. BC); Athana Lindia: *IG* xii.1 997–8 (at Brykous; *BCH* 4 (1880) 279 mentions another unpublished text attesting a cult of Athena Lindia (Map 5.1)); 1033 (Potidaion); *Historia* 7 (1933) 577–9; an area Thoanteion on Rhodes and Karpathos: Ptol. 5.2.19 M; Str. 14.2.12. Chalke (later a deme of Kameiros): *Syll.*[3] 339 *ktoinai* (early 3rd cent.?); cf. Theophr. *HP* 8.2.9. Syme: *IG* xii.3 6 (*ktoinai*); D.S. 5.53: colonized by Lakedaimonians, Argives, Rhodians, and Knidians, its earliest kings lived on Syme and the Knidian peninsula. Syme is the daughter of Ialysos: St. Byz. s.v. Σύμη. Daidala and Megiste were incorporated by the mid-4th cent.: [Skyl.] 100, but cf. Holleaux (1883), Bresson (1999) 104–6, who think that Megiste had long-term connections with Rhodes, possibly dating back to the archaic period.

The same is true of some of the Rhodian *peraia*.[90] Other islands or southern Anatolian cities, such as Telos, Nisyros, or three-harboured Phaselis did not end up as part of actual Rhodian territory until Hellenistic times.[91] But these had always been meandering between the three bigger maritime centres, Kos, Knidos, and Rhodes, attesting a dynamic between all the places in this region quite independently of political allegiances.[92]

All the places that previously and later clung to Rhodes feature with individual entries in the Athenian Tribute Lists, just as each of the three Rhodian cities pays separately.[93] This is a good indication that the Athenians were keen to disrupt existing links, and prevent the development of new ones, on sea just as much as they prevented synoikism on land. That such Athenian strategies could hit particularly the islands' maritime elite is not unlikely. That aspects of the Athenian empire stood in the way of a Rhodian sea-bound aristocracy is nicely illustrated by the fate of the Rhodian noble and poet Timokreon. Timokreon like our Diagorids was from Ialysos, quite possibly home to commercially particularly active Rhodians. Notorious for his boundless wealth, indulgence in food and drink, and a sharp tongue, his jibes against Themistokles give away much about the allied elites' alienation in this early phase of the Athenian empire in the 470s BC, such as in this fragment:

[90] The dekadrachm hoard of 465–460 BC indicates links between Rhodes and Lykia in the mid-5th cent. (cf. Bresson (1999) 103). The *peraia*: the *kherronesioi*, on the peninsula south of Physkos, were probably incorporated before the 5th cent. (*ktoinai* at Tymnos: Fraser and Bean (1954) no. 26; Phoinix: *SGDI* 4264); cf. Livy 32.33.6; Hsch. s.v. α 462 ἀγέρωχοι. The area adjoining east is more problematic: Physkos is a Lindian *deme* in the times of Alexander (*Lindos II* 51); Erine, Kryassos, and Euthana of Ialysos and Kameiros in the Hellenistic period (*Clara Rhodos* ii (1932) 238–9 nos. 151.5 ff.; 150.14); Kedreai belonged to Rhodes after 404 BC (Xen. *Hell.* 2.1.15).

[91] Telos, Nisyros, and Kasos are incorporated as late as *c.*200 BC (Fraser and Bean (1954) 145–54 for the data), but older, religious links to Rhodes do exist: Telos: 4th-cent. bronze coins, though affiliated with Kos: cf. *HG* p. 45; from *c.*200 BC it was probably part of Kameiros; cf. Athena Polias, Zeus Polieus (*IG* xii.3 40.9; *SEG* iii 715 (2nd cent. BC); 4th-cent. cult of Poseidon: *IG* xii.3 37); a Telian colonized Gela together with the Lindian Antiphemos: Hdt. 7.153.1. Nisyros: D.S. 5.54 cites colonists from Kos and Rhodes at points of crisis; but in myth the island was always closer to Kos: *Il.* 2.676; Str. 10.5.16; Paus. 1.2.4 (cf. the Nisyridai on Kos: PH 368 vi ll. 38–9); Str. 10.5.17 knows of Nisyros (?Saros) on Karpathos. Kasos: probably incorporated in *c.* early 2nd cent. BC, though Kasos was always close to Karpathos.

[92] The literary testimonia on the whole group of islands are partly helpful: *Il.* 2.676–7: Nisyros, Karpathos, Kasos, Kos, Kalymnos led by two 'Thessalian' Herakleids. Hdt. 7.99: Artemisia, queen of Halikarnassos, commands Kos, Nisyros, Kalymnos (three islands closely linked in modern sea-routes). In 411 BC Astyokhos wins at Syme over Athens, puts up a *tropaion*, and the Spartans move on to Rhodes: Ar. *Thesm.* 804; Th. 8.41 ff. D.S. 14.84.3–4 lists Kos, Nisyros, Teos going over to the Athenians after Konon's victory in the battle of Knidos in 394 BC, taken to indicate independence at that time. Late 4th-cent. Scyl. 99–100: κατὰ δὲ τὴν Ῥόδον αἵδε νῆσοί εἰσιν οἰκούμεναι· Χάλκεια, Τῆλος, Κάσος, Κάρπαθος· αὕτη τρίπολις. 'The following islands belong to Rhodes: Chalke, Telos, Kasos, Karpathos, which is an island of three cities.' Cf. Plin. *NH* 5.133 (Karpathos, Kasos, Nisyros, Knidos, Syme to Rhodes); Ael. Arist. *Or.* 25.31 Keil (Kasos, Karpathos, and other islands). Note that Rhodes, Syme, and Karpathos all allege Argive origins.

[93] Smaller Rhodian units also appear: cf. *ATL* 454 BC (communities probably belonging to Lindos); *ATL* 438 ff. BC (Ialysos). Cf. van Gelder (1900) 74–5.

ἀλλ' εἰ τύ γε Παυσανίαν ἢ καὶ τύ γε Ξάνθιππον αἰνεῖς,
ἢ τύ γε Λευτυχίδαν, ἐγὼ δ' Ἀριστείδαν ἐπαινέω
ἄνδρ' ἱερᾶν ἀπ' Ἀθανᾶν
ἐλθεῖν ἕνα λῷστον, ἐπεὶ Θεμιστοκλῆν ἤχθαρε Λατώ,
ψεύσταν ἄδικον προδόταν, ὃς Τιμοκρέοντα ξεῖνον ἐόντα
ἀργυρίοισι, κοβαλικοῖσι πεισθεὶς οὐ κατᾶγεν
πατρίδ' Ἰαλυσὸν εἴσ <*ω*>,
λαβὼν δὲ τρί' ἀργυρίου τάλαντ' ἔβα πλέων εἰς ὄλεθρον,
τοὺς μὲν κατάγων ἀδίκως, τοὺς δ' ἐκδιώκων, τοὺς δὲ καίνων·
ἀργυρίων δ' ὑπόπλεως Ἰσθμοῖ γελοίως πανδόκευε
ψυχρὰ <*τὰ*> *κρεῖα παρίσχων·*
οἱ δ' ἤσθιον κηὔχοντο μὴ ὥραν Θεμιστοκλέος γενέσθαι.

Well, you may approve of Pausanias or of Xanthippos
or Leotykhidas, but I approve
of Aristeides as the one best man
to come from Athens, since Themistokles
forfeits the favour of Leto:
the criminal liar and traitor, who, bribed by the silver
of knaves, refused to help Timokreon
his friend back to his home, Ialysos,
but took three silver talents and sailed off
into the sunset, to blazes,
restoring some wrongfully, killing or exiling others;
and at the Isthmus, loaded up to here
with cash, he made a comical Mine Host
and served the meat cold. So they ate, and prayed
God for Themistokles' ruin.

(Timokreon *PMG* 727, tr. West)

Timokreon here laments Themistokles' failure to recall him from exile, where he was sent presumably in the context of the Rhodian cities' change to democracy after the Persian Wars. The piece must come from the 470s, before Themistokles was himself exiled on the grounds of medism, something also commented on by Timokreon.[94] Leto here has been taken as a reference to Delos and the Delian League; the comparison with Aristeides hints at the allied elite's sympathy for the 'fair' setter of tributes as well as at the allies' hatred for Themistokles as emphasized in Chapters 2 and 4.[95] Presumably the idea is that Themistokles' concentration on Athens prevented a 'Delian' League which, as we may postulate,

[94] *PMG* 729; Plut. *Them.* 21.3 ff.; on Timokreon see Fornara (1966) 257–61; Meiggs (1972) 414–15; Robertson (1980*a*); Scodel (1983); McMullin (2001–2). Timokreon was known enough at Athens to appear in comedy: *Σ* Ar. *Ach.* 532 (*PMG* 731); *Vesp.* 1060–70 (*PMG* 733), not least as a counter-figure to the 'community poet' Simonides: *Anth. Pal.* 13.31, 30; 7.34, on which rivalry see e.g. McMullin ibid. The evidence for democracy on Rhodes after 478 BC is *Lindos II* 16 app. = *DGE* 278 = Accame (1938) 221; also see 211 f.

[95] In this reading I go along with Bowra (1961) 349–54, followed by nearly everyone except Scodel (1983), who thinks that 'Leto' refers to the Greeks' meeting, directed by Themistokles, at Isthmia near Korinth, where there was also a cult of Leto.

was the more allied-centred version (perhaps in the internationalist sense as discussed in Chapter 4 above) and which Timokreon sees as beneficial to people like him.[96]

Membership in the Athenian empire as it eventually developed was, in this earlier period as much as at the end of the fifth century, perceived as countering the interests of a local elite well connected in a maritime world, be they situated on Rhodes, on Aigina, or even Andros (Chapter 2 above). The synoikism restored Rhodes' privileged regional and wider connections and made that elite rich, laying the foundation for the thriving economic centre of the fourth and later centuries, and for the phenomenon now described as 'naval aristocracy'.[97] That it took much of the fourth century only for a small group of neighbouring islands and mainland cities to become part of the Rhodian sphere suggests that the late fifth-century Athenian empire had had some impact on the shape of communications in the Aegean, as much as the politicization of these communications: continuous fourth-century stasis on Rhodes and the islands around it suggests a long-standing argument over which part of society was to benefit from these maritime links.[98] The eventual outcome may well have been what caught Strabo's imagination: 'the Rhodians care for the people in general (*δημοκηδεῖς*), though they are not democratic (*οὐ δημοκρατούμενοι*). Still, they wish to take care of the multitude of people. And so the *demos* is provided with food and the wealthy support those in need according to an old tradition'. This passage also forbids a simple equation between synoikizing oligarchs and separatist democrats as one might read into Thucydides' story of the Rhodian defection from Athens. Rather it suggests as so often that it was the *demos*' role that required most careful consideration, and what Strabo describes sounds like a carefully wrought balance between elite and non-elite concerns in the synoikized state.[99]

Olympian 7's 464 BC performance turns, I shall now propose, some of these crucial issues in the making of the synoikism into long-standing mythical truths, into something like an inherited reality long before the island actually unified. In the invention of a pan-Rhodian tradition it seems to invest in Rhodes as a maritime place, blend island-wide concerns with the interests of a maritime elite

[96] 'Elite networks' in the archaic and classical Aegean might deserve further scrutiny. Moreno (2003) addresses some aspects of this problem. For individual Hellenistic *Rhodioi* creating such webs see e.g. Gabrielsen (1997) 62–3, pointing not least to the necessity of finding safe anchorage (41); here (Ch. 2) also the staggering amount of naval facilities on Rhodes; 105–8 give tantalizing new evidence for at least the Hellenistic elite combining shipownership, possession of farms, and maritime trade.

[97] Gabrielsen (1997).

[98] 4th-cent. Rhodes: *c.*398–395 BC revolt from Sparta, democratic revolution and the Diagorids' expulsion (*Hell. Oxy.* 10; D.S. 14.79.6–8; Androt. *FGrH* 324 F 46 = Paus. 6.7.6), countered by oligarchs soon after (*c.*391–388 BC; Arist. *Pol.* 1302^{b}21 ff.; 1304^{b}27 ff.; Xen. *Hell.* 4.8.20 ff.; D.S. 14.97 ff.). After the King's Peace (386 BC) until the end of the Social War (357–355 BC) it was probably a democracy, definitely after Issos (333 BC): Str. 14.2.5. Discussions of Rhodes' internal affairs, incl. the uncertain chronology, in Bruce (1961); Berthold (1980); Hauben (1977); O'Neil (1981); David (1984); the overview in Gehrke (1985) 134–40.

[99] Str. 14.2.5; Plb. 27.4.7; D.S. 20.93.6–7 on the Hellenistic democracy.

in the figure of Diagoras, merge the mythical associations of the island as a whole with those of individual cities, and tackles Rhodes' relationship to Athens. This it does through the rewriting of the Rhodian mythical past as a continuous and unified history, validated in performance by tying Rhodes' different myths into the ritual context of a 'foundation'.[100] An imperceptible mutation of the cult community of Tlepolemos into one of Helios forms the performative framework within which these claims can be made.

4. TURNING INTO A *KHOROS* OF HELIADAI

Merging elite and civic interests on sea-bound Rhodes

For a start, I observed above that pre-synoikism concerted action of the islanders is sea-bound, and it is striking how intensely the song appeals to Rhodes' floating in the midst of the sea, as if to bring across the point that this was what brought the place together, that it was a locality where the sea mattered most. Pindar proposes to hymn *τὰν ποντίαν . . . Ῥόδον* (ll. 13–14); Tlepolemos embarks on a naval future when ordered to 'sail away from the coast of Lerna' straight to the 'meadow in the midst of the sea' (*εὐθὺν ἐς ἀμφιθάλασσαν νόμον*, ll. 32–3). Rhodes' resting at the bottom of the sea is pictured in vividly watery terms with many redundancies, and the baroque story of Rhodes' emergence from amidst all the salty froth leaves no doubt about the island's closest associate.[101] If the Diagorids live on this three-citied island with their 'Argive spear' 'neighbour to the *embolon* ('promontory') of broad Asia', this steers the attention to Rhodes' favourable position in the area and the potential that that holds; it may also be a direct hint at Rhodian possessions in the mainland *peraia*, temporarily lost to the Athenians.[102]

But also Diagoras himself belabours pan-Rhodianism by playing with an ambiguity over for whom his victory has actually been gained. This is first of all expressed in the way the ode links Diagoras to public affairs on Rhodes as a whole. Victory odes tend to shed as much praise on the victor's city as on the victor himself, manifesting the degree to which victors saw themselves as part of their civic framework.[103] In the case of *Olympian 7*, however, Diagoras' allegiance is not clearly expressed. The Diagorids were from Ialysos, but nowhere in the

[100] Cf. Athanassaki (2003) (as n. 6 above).

[101] Pi. *Ol.* 7.54 ff.; esp. 56–7 on Rhodes' pristine underwater life: *οὔπω φανερὰν ἐν πελάγει Ῥόδον ἔμμεν ποντίῳ, ἁλμυροῖς δ' ἐν βένθεσιν νᾶσον κεκρύφθαι* ('Rhodes had not yet appeared in the expanse of the sea, but the island lay hidden in the salty depths'); spotted by Helios *πολιᾶς . . . ἔνδον θαλάσσας αὐξομέναν* ('as it rose out of the gray sea', ll. 61–2) and eventually *βλάστε . . . ἐξ ἁλὸς ὑγρᾶς νᾶσος* ('the island grew from the watery sea', ll. 69–70) (tr. Race).

[102] ll. 17–18, first interpreted by Fraser and Bean (1954) 131 as referring to the *peraia.*

[103] The debate on the degree and motivation of elite integration into the archaic *polis*, involving the role of epinician song, is heated and interesting: cf. Kurke (1991) 86–90, 135–47; (1993); (1999) 19–23; I. Morris (2000) 187–90 and recently Thomas (2007).

ode is that actually said. Diagoras' alignment is with Rhodes the island whenever one would expect the victor's city to appear: Pindar announces a hymn to Rhodes (l. 13); the Diagorids' home is referred to as the 'island of three cities' (*τρίπολιν νᾶσον*, l. 18), as may seem normal for victory odes. That said, the *polis* is not therefore absent. Rather, for example, the golden shower prompted by the birth of Athena pours down on an unnamed *polis* while nowhere in the ancient sources is there an indication that the wealth-bringing rain was anything other than all-inclusive of the island (l. 39). Through this ambiguity over Diagoras' origins, maintained over the course of the ode, Rhodes imperceptibly becomes a *polis*, and one whose affairs are very much tied to the victor himself. Towards the end of the song, the pan-Rhodian god Zeus Atabyrios is invoked to grant Diagoras 'suitable favour from both citizens and strangers' (*αἰδοίαν χάριν καὶ ποτ' ἀστῶν καὶ ποτὶ ξείνων*, ll. 89–90).[104] The use of such highly political terms in this context is hardly coincidental and lends Diagoras' victory social significance. Neither *ἀστοί* nor *ξένοι* are unequivocal; they could refer to citizens of Diagoras' own city and the rest of the Rhodians, or, much more provocatively, to all the 'citizens' of Rhodes and non-Rhodian *xenoi*. And the final lines take up the elusive Rhodian 'city' again when good wishes for the family are tied to the well-being of the *polis*: *μὴ κρύπτε κοινὸν σπέρμ' ἀπὸ Καλλιάνακτος· Ἐρατιδᾶν τοι σὺν χαρίτεσσιν ἔχει θαλίας καὶ πόλις* ('Do not conceal the lineage from the time of Kallianaktos: for at the celebrations of (for?) the Eratids, the *polis*, too, has its festivals', ll. 92–4). Throughout the ode, then, the choice of political terms is extremely careful and ambiguous, linking Diagoras' personal achievements with those of the island and *polis*.[105] Rhodian and Diagorean affairs come together in the *polis* for which this Olympian victory had been won.

The evocation of Helios as a pan-Rhodian god and the bolstering of the Heliadic tradition, too, are fundamentally motivated by such attempts at forging an identity of insular and elite interests. We remember that the spread of the myth and cult of Helios and his sons arguably manifests an intertwined maritime network in the eastern Aegean and Egypt that precedes Hellenistic times. The ode quite possibly construes a bold link between Helios *qua* ancestor of the historical Rhodians and a unified island cultivating its commercial possibilities, through meshing elite concerns and Rhodian civic ('insular') identity in a spectacular way. Hints in this direction come from evidence surrounding Ialysos, home to the family of the Diagorids, future promoters of the synoikism, and to Timokreon, who above gave us some idea of elite attitudes towards Athenian imperial arrangements. Ialysos was either really home to the most commercially active

104 On Zeus Atabyrios see D.S. 5.59.1–2; Apollod. 3.2.1; Bresson (1986) for a comparison of these different versions. Cf. van Gelder (1900) 301 f.; Morelli (1959) 140 (138–41, the only existing documentation of the cult); Papachristodoulou (1992) 252–4. See n. 38 above for the spectacular bronze bulls found at the site.

105 All of this is quite Pindaric: cf. Pi. *P.* 1.60–6: where Deinomenes of Aitna's effective despotic position is veiled by pointing to Spartan mythical ancestry anchored in a constitution; similarly *P.* 10: cf. Luraghi (1994) 358–60.

Rhodians, as some believe, or was turned into this by the sources after the synoikism just as the Heliadai might have arrived there in a secondary way.[106] According to Diodorus the Heliadai had settled at Ialysos to found 'Akhaian Ialysos', a tradition that could of course have been invented later to bolster the position of the Diagorids, themselves descendants of Herakles and therefore Akhaian. But in the light of Kerkaphos' sixth-century presence there (p. 244 above), a privileged relationship of the Ialysians to Helios and his family is now more thinkable (though less fashionable) than it was ever before. There is, for example, a connection to the stereotypical traders, the Phoenicians: Tlepolemos encountered these when landing at Ialysos, and they successfully mingled, summoning up the image of a mixed community with shared interests in maritime commerce. This is not purely a piece of antiquarianism, since it is at Ialysos that a well-known Phoenician workshop of Rhodian pottery has been located. Ialysian Athena's not fully published votive complex, at least as impressive as that of Athena Lindia, attests stunning contacts with the entire genealogy of Egyptian pharaohs from the seventh century onwards. Finds from the local seventh/late sixth-century cemetery give away a set of geographic links quite different from that of Kameiros' necropolis. It is therefore not implausible to attach Helios and his sons first to Ialysos, and secondly within Ialysos to a family, or a set of families, particularly active in seaborne trade. Such evidence, fragmented though it is, supports the suggestion that leading Ialysians engaged in maritime commerce heavily determined the history, and the commercial success, of synoikized Rhodes. The Heliadic traditions could well have in the first place represented, or have been adopted to represent, this particular social group.[107]

If this comes near to the historical reality, however, the song carefully avoids any suggestion that Helios may be closer to some than to others and this may not be accidental. Quite the contrary, his sons are unambiguously evoked as the ancestors of all the contemporary Rhodians, not just the privileged few. *Olympian 7*'s Helios is the god shared between all the islanders, the implication being that what he stands for is also being shared. This comes out particularly towards the end of Helios' aetiology, where much is made of the fact that Helios' grandsons were the eponyms of the three contemporary Rhodian cities. Later sources, too, are very clear about Helios, the 'founder of the race' (ἀρχηγὸς τοῦ γένους [sc. of the Rhodians]), who was there for all the Rhodians and did not care about social

[106] Moggi (1976*a*) 221; Pugliese Carratelli (1951) 80 n. 3; Morelli (1959) 96; Gehrke (1986) 125–8; all presuppose the Ialysian trading mentality, though no evidence is cited.

[107] Phoenicians meeting Tlepolemos at Ialysos: D.S. 5.58.2 (incidentally, Kadmos founded here a shrine of Poseidon, god of maritime travellers, and also dedicated to Athena); Coldstream (1969) (the workshop thought to have forged Nestor's Cup found on Pithekoussai); Athena Ialysia: Martelli (1988) and pp. 232–4 above; burials: Gates (1983); Heliadai at Ialysos: D.S. 5.57.6; Diekhidas *FHG* iv 389 fr. 7 = Ath. 6.262e; cf. *IG* xii.1 677 (cult of Alektryona, late 4th cent.). Note also an early similarity in coin type between Ialysos and several Lykian coinages, possible also Cyprus and Rhodes: Asyut hoard, *c.*475 BC (!), nos. 98–104, pls. xxvii–xxviii; nos. 783–6; 818–20, Bresson (1999) 102–3.

status. Lindian priests of a later period see themselves as 'priests of their ancestor Helios' (*ἱερεῖς τοῦ προπάτ[ορος Ἁλίου*).[108]

So Helios may have started out as socially and geographically limited, but his cult came to have a full part in Rhodian civic and democratic ideology in post-synoikism times. While quite possibly having emerged from a limited group of elite families with an interest in maritime connections, he turned into the symbol of what all Rhodians were about. This vision is anticipated in *Olympian 7*, and suggested by the song's myth-ritual nexus as it emerges in the actual choral performance. It is one of the song's strategies to establish the Heliadai as intimately bound up with everything Rhodian and eventually to turn the performing Rhodians themselves into the *khoros* of Heliadai.

Unifying the different pasts in ritual practice

The song labours the Heliadai's significance for the whole island, above all in the way it blurs the tradition of the god's sons with that of Athena's fireless sacrifice. On the way it takes in a couple of independent Rhodian myths, which are turned into lasting effects resulting from Athena's fireless sacrifice offered by the very same Heliadai. According to *Olympian 7*'s aetiological myth, the Heliadai not just ensured Athena's presence on the island, the sacrificial success also brought with it elements of what we know are two pieces of independent pan-Rhodian tradition. Athena is thus turned into the hub in which all Rhodian pasts converge. And the performers of her sacrifice, the song suggestively argues, are none other than the descendants of the Heliadai themselves, the contemporary Rhodians.

First, there is the myth of the golden shower Zeus poured onto the island in the times of mythical beginnings (ll. 34; 49–50). The episode pervades accounts of the island's past in the antiquarians, but its chronology is indeterminate. Wealth inundating the island is a fixed element in the tradition, but no one knew exactly how, why, and when it had occurred. In the *Catalogue* the rain is tied to the Akhaian settlement. *Εὐδαιμονία*, *εὐτυχία*, and wealth remained proverbial from the Dark Ages to Late Antiquity.[109] Pindar, by contrast, links it to the birth of Athena and her worship by the Heliadai, expressing in a metaphor consisting of a typical Zeus-epiphany what in the *Catalogue* is a shower of 'wealth' onto the

[108] D.S. 5.56.4. Later cult associations (*Ἡλιασταί*, *Ἡλιάδες*) exist in all three cities. A *κοινὸν τῶν Ἁλιαστῶν καὶ Ἁλιαδᾶν* issued honorific decrees: *IG* xii.1 155. The priests feature in *Tit.Cam. Suppl.* 42; *Lindos II* 465h and 482 (2nd cent. BC).

[109] From Strabo it becomes clear that Hellenistic Rhodes must have done a great deal for the dissemination and preservation of this particular myth. Str. 14.2.10: *Ἱστοροῦσιν δὲ καὶ ταῦτα περὶ τῶν Ῥοδίων, ὅτι οὐ μόνον ἀφ' οὗ χρόνου συνῴκισαν τὴν νῦν πόλιν εὐτύχουν κατὰ θάλατταν, ἀλλὰ καὶ πρὸ τῆς Ὀλυμπικῆς θέσεως συχνοῖς ἔτεσιν ἔπλεον πόρρω τῆς οἰκείας ἐπὶ σωτηρίᾳ τῶν ἀνθρώπων*. 'It is also related of the Rhodians not only that they were successful at sea since the time when they founded the present city, but even that many years before the establishment of the Olympian Games they used to sail far away from their homeland to ensure the safety of their people.' Cf. the proverbial *εὐπορία* ('prosperity') related to the golden shower: Lib. *Ep.* 348 = X p. 330.13–19 Foerster. Eust. *Il.* 317.7–12. Cf. Torr (1885) 31–52. Cf. *Σ* Pi. *O.* 7.71b: 'Zeus gave them wealth and good fortune' (*ὁ Ζεὺς πλοῦτον καὶ εὐδαιμονίαν παρέσχε*).

island.[110] For the first time perhaps, the ode attaches this particular piece of divine favour to a specific mythical episode: in *Olympian 7*, the mythical but lasting prosperity of the island is an effect of worshipping Athena, attributed to the initiative of the Heliadai.

Similarly, in the same myth the Heliadai are credited with a further cultural achievement in the island's prehistory in exchange for the establishment of Athena's rites. Once the sacrifice was completed, Athena and Hephaistos rewarded the Heliadai with the art of moulding wondrous statues which 'the streets carried as if they were walking creatures': *ἔργα δὲ ζωοῖσιν ἑρπόντεσσί θ' ὁμοῖα κέλευθοι φέρον* (l. 52). Pindar confounds the tradition of the Heliadai with that of their predecessors, the Telkhines. The Telkhines, the first inhabitants of the island in myth, circulate on those Aegean islands well furnished with pre-Greek, often Bronze Age traces: Crete, Cyprus, Rhodes, and Keos. They have all sorts of magic talents: especially as artisans forging bronze into statues which looked almost lifelike.[111] It is very suggestive that the Telkhines are not mentioned here themselves, but instead their special gifts are attributed to the mythically younger Heliadai. Placing them in the period after Helios had taken possession of the island and in the context of Athena's worship ties existing island traditions specifically into the aetiology of the fireless sacrifices.[112]

The two episodes share their chronological indeterminacy; pieces of memory are known to belong to *a* Rhodian past, but it is not quite clear which past that was. *Olympian 7* creates a temporal framework for them, the times of the very first origins of the island when Helios the island's patron was still alive and all his seven sons still on the island. It thus places them at the time when the island was unified by the Heliadic family. In particular, it uses Athena's fireless sacrifices to concentrate all these different traditions. If she had indeed once been a deity worshipped in the Near Eastern tradition of fireless meat sacrifice, this is perhaps what allows her to perform this role: because of her own oscillation between a Bronze Age tradition and an unmistakeably historic-Greek aspect, she can fit the unrelated memories into a Greek temporal and perceptual frame and gloss over the island's diverse pasts and peoples (Minoans, Egyptians, Greeks) and the

110 Soph. *Ant.* 950: *Ζηνὸς ταμιεύεσκε γονὰς χρυσορύτους* ('[Danae] looked after the gold-flowing seed of Zeus'); cf. Pi. *I.* 7.5–7.

111 Telkhines first people on Rhodes: D.S. 5.55; Str. 14.2.7; cf. Ov. *Met.* 7.365–7; Nic. Dam. *FGrH* 90 F 114; Hsch. ι 150 s.v. *Ἰγνητες*; Eust. *Il.* 789.1–20; Nonn. 14.36–48; Hdn. 2.622.1; 626.25 f.. On other Aegean islands: Keos: Call. fr. 75.64 ff. (= Xenomedes of Keos *FGrH* 442 F 1); Crete: St. Byz. s.v. *Τελχίς*; *Et. Gen.* s.v. *Τελχῖνος*; *EM* 751.32 s.v. *Τελχίν*; Cyprus: Nic. Dam. loc. cit. Paus. 9.19.1. Artisans, craftsmen, and wizards: D.S. 5.55.2; Str. 14.2.7; Nic. Dam., Eust. loc. cit.; Hsch. τ 448 s.v. *Τελχῖνες*. Moving statues: esp. D.S. 4.76.2–3 (Daidalos); living metallurgy: e.g. Hephaistos' tripods: *Σ IL.* 18.327; Alkinoos' dogs: *Od.* 6.91–4; Talos on Crete: A.R. 2.1051; Apollod. 1.9.26. See Frontisi-Ducroux (1975) on this type of artists' traditions. Zeus Atabyrios's bulls: *Σ* Pi. *O.* 7.160c. The archaic bronze figurines from the three cults of Athena are extremely noteworthy. From a poetic point of view the passage perhaps brings out the qualities of song over those of statuary: O'Sullivan (2005).

112 This 'reward' by contrast Sfyoeras (1993) 12–15 sees as matching the 'fireless sacrifices' for Athena with 'fireless *tekhne*' bestowed by Athena, while at Athens *tekhne* would normally require the fire supplied by Hephaistos.

various groups on the island cherishing traditions of Cretans, Telkhines, Heliadai, Akhaians. We know that in Hellenistic times, the island keenly capitalized on its geographical position for the creation of an 'oriental' identity in the context of the cultural melting-pot of the post-Alexandrian Mediterranean.[113] So the fact that Athena demands *apyra hiera* is crucial here: her 'oriental' nature is invoked as part of the goddess' new old image.

The upshot of all this is how the song roots the bundle of traditions in what it claims to be actual cultic reality of the fireless sacrifice. We remember, the archaeological evidence suggests that this claim might have involved a conscious archaizing of historical cult-practice starting in the middle of the fifth century, which until then is more likely to have been just the normal Greek burnt meat sacrifice. Could the contemporary appearances of the *aparkhai* for Athena constitute proof of the relevance, even success, of the ode's suggestions, while at the same time ritual is 'myth misunderstood'?[114] On this view, *Olympian 7* presents a delicate call to arms for resuming what masquerades as the continuation of the old rite of *apyra hiera*, uninterruptedly conducted 'since times mythical'. That dedicating the humble vessels of *aparkhai* was quite so widespread a practice might in addition strengthen the idea that Athena's sacrifices without fire were turned into something of wider appeal. The song would thus be a particularly striking example of the way in which religious song orchestrates innovation through traditionalizing: it employs the notion of long-term continuity assumed for any ritual to establish something that in reality constitutes a radical change.[115] The implication is that there had never been a break in the ritual customs for Rhodian Athena. The archaism then causes its own distortions: in a fifth-century world, 'fireless sacrifice' on the whole meant vegetarian sacrifice, hence the offerings of the *aparkhai* in vessels whose shattered bottoms survive. This is an interesting insight into the nature of archaizing in ritual—it is neither old nor literally archaizing, a ritual past is simply made up of current ritual patterns. In the big picture of the ode, however, we can conclude that the stipulated interaction between actual, but not therefore traditional, cult practice and the aetiological myth is what manages to draw together the different episodes and claims in the island's mythical history into a past beginning with the god Helios and his sons and reaching down in seamless continuity, to the Rhodians in the contemporary performance.

The link to real-life cult practice is also what ultimately seems to provide the song's myth-ritual nexus in the actual choral performance, through which all these things can be projected into the mythical past, and a continuity to the present can be claimed. For the inevitable implication of all this jumbling of

[113] This important but under-studied observation is made by Jackson (1999).

[114] The allusion is to Jane Harrison's early 20th-cent. ideas of 'myth is ritual misunderstood'. Above I argued that the myth implies fireless animal sacrifice while the archaeological evidence suggests fireless fruit sacrifice, according to the standard terminology in the 5th cent.

[115] Chapter 1, pp. 41–3, 52–3.

myths and rituals is that the performers of the fireless sacrifice are none other than the *khoros* that performs the ode, the contemporary Rhodians, themselves turned into the *khoros* of Heliadai. The song itself construes this claim: the performing *khoros* begins as that for an Akhaian (Dorian) warrior who had settled the island from mainland Greece and who, like Adrastos at Sikyon, might have been worshipped in choral performances. Through the interacting associations of narrated myth and contemporary ritual produced in the ode, it imperceptibly changes into a *khoros* of the autochthonous descendants of Helios the sun-god. The metamorphosis emerges when we follow the story of Helios' aetiology to its very end, the birth of Helios' sons and his grandsons, Ialysos, Kameiros, and Lindos (in this order). The three eponyms 'each held their ancestral land, dividing it up into three to parcel out to the citizens, and gave their names to their seats' (ll. 74–6). Starting with 'here' (*τόθι*), the following sentence picks up with Tlepolemos again, forging through the canonic aetiological boundary formula an uninterrupted continuity from the island's patron to Tlepolemos, and we are suddenly thrown back into the ritual in progress, the choral performance at the Tlepolemeia, as if nothing had happened to the *khoros*' identity (ll. 76–80). The product of the song's performance is a form of synaesthetic confusion by which Tlepolemos seems worshipped in a *khoros* of Heliadai, prompting ambiguity over the ode's divine honorand and, ultimately, over the island's actual mythical ancestry.

In this manner a new worshipping community, for Helios rather than for Tlepolemos, is established during the course of the ode. Athena, however, remains central: through her worship, the *khoros* of Heliadai has the pivotal task of relating the Heliadic phase of the island to the Greek present; regular cult of Athena in the fireless sacrifice fostered exactly that continuity. The Heliadai certainly kept a special relationship to Athena, as is attested by mythical dedications by the hero Lindos to her.[116] The idea of *Olympian 7* is that worshippers of Rhodian Athena continue to assemble in such a *khoros*, so that every sacrifice is a renewal of the original one and reiterates its embedded meanings: the claim to autochthony and the confidence gained through a long and successful past, outdating that of the Greek mainland. It is through this myth-ritual nexus that the ode rewrites Rhodian history as a history of autochthony, of continuity rather than change, and as a pan-Rhodian one.

[116] Lindos (*Lindos II* 477 (though this is from the 3rd cent. AD): *[Κερκαφί]δην ἥρωα Λίν[δον] Ἀθηναίης νηὸν ὃς ἠγλάϊσεν* ('the hero Lindos son of Kerkaphos who embellished the temple of Athena'). It recalls a passage of the Lindian chronicle (B 1–3, with Blinkenberg's (1915*a*) comments); cf. the earlier nos. 57A (313 BC) and 274 (100 BC).

TOWARDS INSULAR UNITY

In this way, *Olympian 7* construes an identity for the islanders straightening a tumultuous history of diversity and change into one seamless progression from origins in a pan-Rhodian *illud tempus* of the god Helios and his descendants. It invents a common past for the whole island. At the same time, despite all this pan-Rhodian talk, there is intriguingly no attempt at getting rid of the traditional tripartition of the island, leaving long-laboured local civic identities intact yet firmly anchored in a new insular ideology. The point seems to be harmonization of local *polis* and insular identity. Rhodes is comfortably called τρίπολις νᾶσος before Tlepolemos has even started on his expedition (l. 18), but more pointed is Helios' role as grandfather and common ancestor of the three eponymous heroes Ialysos, Kameiros, and Lindos who markedly receive and name their three cities (ll. 74–6, quoted above). That it is impossible to identify whether the myth of Athena's fireless sacrifices referred to one Athena more than others is particularly good proof that pan-Rhodianism by no means swallowed local religious identities. If Athena Lindia was a more pan-Rhodian deity in the archaic period (as might be suggested by Amasis' dedications), the ode thoroughly exploits her pan-Rhodian nature in order to reconfigure the three cities' relation to each other. By glossing over any particular Athena's prominence, the song anticipates the situation after the synoikism: then, paradoxically, Athena Lindia became less pan-Rhodian than she had been before, just as other candidates for pan-Rhodian worship such as Zeus Atabyrios near Kameiros and Apollo Erethimios at Ialysos.[117] So the people of Lindos would dedicate to Athena Lindia, and Athena at Ialysos was known as Ἀθάνα Ἰαλυσία. In fact, the similarity in the three cults' archaeological history—from the Geometric era to the spectacular archaic material to the rebuilding in the Hellenistic period—suggests that Athena on Rhodes epitomized the relationship between individual locality and the island as a whole. Her cult showed what the cities shared, while each had its own local poliadic goddess. *Olympian 7* confirms for a much earlier period what has not long ago been shown for the Hellenistic island world, that local *polis* and island identity develop alongside, rather than in antagonism; the stronger the sense of insularity, the more pronounced an awareness of locality.[118]

To conclude, through the interaction of aetiological myths and rituals the performance of *Olympian 7* forges a pan-Rhodian worshipping group, a religious community of islanders. It unifies the island through an invocation of the ritual past in a performance of the present, strikingly anticipating what would become reality at the end of the fifth century: Rhodes in 464 BC was a member of the

[117] Parker (forthcoming). Constantakopoulou (2005) 15–16 discusses the possibility of pan-Rhodian significance of Athena Lindia. Dignas (2003) examines priesthoods after the synoikism.

[118] Reger (1997). Athena Ialysia/Kameiras are attested in *IG* xii.1 786 = *Tit. Cam.* app. 38 (Roman period); cf. also a (Roman) priest 'of the Tripolis': *Tit. Cam.* 4b–d.

Athenian empire, and we think a democracy. In 411 BC it broke off the alliance with Athens and synoikized into a unified state not much later. *Olympian 7* is surprisingly premature in creating the later trademarks of the unified island by working its mythical traditions and customs into the performance's suggestions of an identical religious and insular community. In this process it chooses to highlight those elements that would determine the success of the later unified island-state: notably the linking of elite interests into the language of collective identity, the cult of Helios and his lineage, representative of maritime connectedness, and the integration of *polis* and insular identity by emphasizing Athena as simultaneously local and pan-Rhodian. The song thus ties locally and socially diverse forms of religious behaviour into a shared framework and creates a common set of references.

Olympian 7 suggests ideals important in the run-up to the eventual political realization of this community in the synoikism, which cannot be separated from the island's relationship to imperial Athens. In fact, the building blocks of this unified Rhodes pointedly shake the pillars of the carefully constructed edifice of Athenian imperial ideology, questioning its pretences over, and perceptions of, the allied states. So stipulating autochthony for the Rhodians means unbalancing a cornerstone of alleged Athenian superiority over everyone who was not earthborn.[119] Although *Olympian 7* does not name the competitor in the Heliadai's race, the Athenians are certainly implied. The warlike Athena bursting out of Zeus' head is no doubt what we know as the later Athena Parthenos of the Athenian akropolis. The assimilation was familiar at the time, as is suggested, among other things, by mid-fifth-century red-figure vase depictions from Lindos, featuring Athena in this attire.[120] The song's aetiology is a charter myth for Athena on Rhodes, even for Athena on Rhodes rather than at Athens. This was not an Athena 'looking after the affairs of Athens', but one exclusively caring for the Rhodians.[121] And finally, the ode's pan-Rhodianism addresses at once two important issues that are part and parcel of the imperial agenda. An island whose cities think alike squares badly with the Athenian attempt to dispel links between individual *poleis* and keep localities discrete, and instead cultivate their attachment to Athens. But *Olympian 7* also counters the strategy of vilifying local identities, of keeping cities' self-esteem deliberately low, as we could observe it in Chapters 2 and 4.

Olympian 7 then must have been questioning any allegiances with Athens that Rhodes might have had in 464 BC, and perhaps this is one of the points of the song. Is Rhodes not itself a worthy sea power, actually thalassocrat? Why pay

[119] Sfyoeras (1993) 12–15 goes so far as to say that certain parts of the ode actually undermine Athenian autochthony. For autochthony construed as superiority see e.g. Loraux (1986).

[120] e.g. *Lindos I* nos. 2332a and b (early 5th cent.); 2334–5 (mid-5th cent.). Sfyoeras (1993) discusses the cultic rivalry between Athens and Rhodes in the myth of the *apyra hiera*.

[121] The allusion is to the formula typically used for sacred land of Athenian Athena abroad, where Athena is Ἀθηνῶν μεδέουσα 'who rules Athens': *IG* i^3 1481–99; 1502, with Barron (1964), with Parker (1996) 144–5.

tribute for protection at sea if the sea is your closest associate and your most characteristic feature is strength at sea? Why pay honours to Athena at Athens, eventually with a panoply and a cow, when really the Rhodians are Athena's favourites, served as she was by the sons of Helios? And what about Helios himself, who ensures that Rhodes, not Athens, is the *kosmopolis* commanding an eastern Mediterranean maritime *réseau*?

Not least through the implied competition with Athens the ideas linked to a unified Rhodes in the ode proposed an alluring alternative to membership in the Athenian empire or if this was a disputed matter at the time, set up a strong position for Rhodian independence; the song appealed to, as much as it shaped, local island pride, a hitherto unarticulated 'civic' identity of the Rhodians. On an island whose unity in the past had been expressed through its maritime potential, evoking Rhodes' strength at sea is not a bad strategy. Nor is it to bring up the idea of all-island wealth (a bargain Athenians offered to their allies) and tie it to the local and autochthonous mythical figures, the Heliadai, who epitomized movement by sea from Rhodes. Does *Olympian 7* prefigure later history here, which from the fourth century onwards features Rhodes challenging Athenian naval superiority? I exaggerate a little, but it must be clear that the song thoroughly scrutinizes what contemporary Rhodes was all about, developing a sense of, and the sensitivity for, the Rhodian locality, through reconfiguring some of the island's most important, identity-giving aetiological myths and rituals.

The actual defection from Athens as much as the synoikism shortly afterwards are, at least in the sources, thoroughly unremarkable events when they eventually happen. Should this be considered proof of how the island's formal unification was the product, not at the origins, of changed attitudes amongst the Rhodians towards the possibilities of their island? That pomp and circumstances such as those coming with the performance of this ode managed to inculcate values and shaped attitudes towards the future model of Rhodes' social and economic set-up? *Olympian 7* might have helped to unify the island; it might well have been the cornerstone in building up a Rhodian civic ideology. At the very least it gives testimony to the existence and perpetration of such ideas long before the actual events. Their powerful pretences single out the high potential unity has for the island's future. The song introduces into a schematic distinction between an anti-Athenian elite and a pro-Athenian *demos* local and civic pride as providing a forum of social integration based on a shared religious tradition. *Olympian 7* illustrates well how ritual performances can embrace processes of social change: in returning to the very beginnings and redefining the chronology of Rhodes' mythical past, did Pindar eventually fulfil the promise made at the beginning of the ode that he would 'set right the shared tale'?[122]

[122] Pi. *O.* 7.21: ξυνὸν . . . διορθῶσαι λόγον. NB the 'shared tale'; 'to start from Tlepolemos' (ἐκ Τληπολέμου) is then the traditional way to begin a mythical account of Rhodes, which the song seeks to 'correct'.

6

Aetiology Overseas: From Epic to Ethnic Identity in Megale Hellas

In the mid-1990s an extraordinary find was made in the territory of Metapontion in southern Italy. Eight large ancient wine jars in clay, so-called *pithoi*, were unearthed in a remote spot of a farmer's field, each of them, so the story goes, filled to the brim with archaic and classical Greek coins. The spectacular hoard, having attracted much attention locally, vanished as quickly and as mysteriously as it had emerged, into the possession of a handful of private dealers, for the trivial sum of L. 2,000,000 (then worth around £800).[1]

What truth lies behind this story will never be known. Despite its recent origin it has firmly established for itself a place in the locality's oral tradition. And, as with many such traditions, this one too contains genuine elements of interest. Metapontion and the two other major places in the area, Sybaris and Kroton, were the first in southern Italy to mint silver coins. The appearance of these coins is sometimes related to the victory that a supposed 'Akhaian' collective of these three cities gained in the mid-sixth century BC over the troublemaker of the area, the 'Ionian' city of Siris. In the light of the alleged ethnic dimension of Siris' destruction it is an odd coincidence that such an enormous quantity of coins was discovered at Metapontion: it is at Metapontion that important evidence clusters for the birth of the concept and of the reality of 'Akhaia' in southern Italy as a whole.[2]

The common output of silver coins could be seen as just a novel way of confirming long-standing relations between the cities of shared 'Akhaian' origin. While the literary tradition is indeed quick to group these cities into a uniform collection of Greeks from mainland Akhaia in the Peloponnese, the gods that Greek settlers took with them to the west, together with an array of myth-ritual ensembles and songs in their honour, tell of their diversity. It belongs to the commonplaces of the study of Greeks going overseas[3] to suppose that people also

[1] I was told this story in 1998 by a local business-owner, who also casually dropped that his most recent dentist bill had been paid in the currency of a (presumably Lukanian) red-figure krater.

[2] According to Stazio (1983) 112–13 the coins were produced 'to cover the financial needs arising in connection with [the Akhaian coalition], or the victory resulting from the coalition with all the plunder gained furnished the opportunity to start monetary issues in our three cities'. On coinage and identity in Akhaia see now Papadopoulos (2002).

[3] I shall not consistently avoid the term 'colony' and its derivatives in this chapter dealing with many Greeks overseas. Thanks to Osborne (1998) much attention has been drawn to the conceptual differences between Greek colonization in the Mediterranean and the colonial movement of modern European states, and the term should by now be free of any culturally specific baggage.

settled their old cults in their new homes. Settlers of an *apoikia* ('a home away from home') replicate and faithfully continue ancestral festivals on virgin soil, as if to maintain metropolitan identities abroad. Pindar's *Pythian 5*, telling of Spartan Apollo Karneios' arrival at Kyrene, is perhaps the best literary example of a practice attested in the antiquarian tradition as a widespread motif.[4] Carrying along one's traditional cults served a number of social functions in 'colonial' situations, drawing settlers together through a shared tradition, maintaining ties with their place of origin, and allowing the invocation of these ties when needed.

Put like this, however, such statements show little regard for the complicated social reality of apoikic Greece. As more evidence emerges, it becomes increasingly apparent that the Greeks in southern Italy were far from being a specific group of settlers founding specific cities, but a much looser bunch of people from various parts of Greece whose new homes experienced substantial teething problems, instability, and social crises. The adventures of old gods in new lands illustrate these situations well. Rather than manifesting continuity, the southern Italian pantheons are a product of the vicissitudes of rapidly changing settlements and continuously reshuffled local and regional power relations. The myths and rituals of cults are media in which these changes find expression, and looking at the manner in which this occurs sheds some light on the extreme cultural fluidity of these localities.

That is not to say that the traditions of such migrant cults are of no historical value. On the contrary, such myths belaboured a fiction of religious continuity, which comes in handy in contested or volatile situations, allowing the invocation of a religious tie that need not in fact be traditional. In the multi-cultural context of southern Italy this comes into play intensely—and some of this is acted out in cult song. Bacchylides' *Ode 11* is a remarkable performance addressing precisely these issues. It recounts the foundation of a cult of Artemis at Metapontion in southern Italy, presenting us with one of the most elaborate cult aetiologies religious poetry has to offer. The ode is written for a certain Alexidamos, a boys' wrestling victor at the Pythian Games at an unknown date, and stands a good chance of having been performed at a festival of Artemis at Metapontion.[5] The poem starts with extensive personal praise for the victor extending over some thirty-five lines, before the present victory is credited to the local Artemis, as if only this deity could bestow victory:

> *ν̣ῦν δ' Ἄρτεμις ἀγροτέρα*
> *χ̣ρυσαλάκατος λιπαράν*
> *Ἡ̣μ]ἑ̣ρα τοξόκλυτος νίκαν ἔδωκε.*

[4] On Pi. *P.* 5 in a colonial context see Krummen (1990); Calame (1996*b*). Ancient examples for the transferral of gods are close at hand: Graham (1964) 14–15; but cf. e.g. Hdt. 1.147 for the Apatouria as markers of Ionian descent, the faultiness of which belief is given by the source itself: Ephesos and Kolophon do not celebrate the festival.

[5] Among the readings of the ode note Burnett (1985) 100–13; C. Segal (1976) 122–8; Seaford (1988); Maehler (1982–97) i. 195–242; Calame (1999); Giacometti (1999); Cairns (2005) most recently argued for performance of the ode in a public festival.

τ]ᾶι ποτ' Ἀβαντιάδας
β]ωμὸν κατένασσε πολύλ-
λ[ι]στον εὔπεπλοί τε κοῦραι·

But now Artemis *agrotera*, of the golden distaff, Artemis Hemera, famed for her bow, has given him splendid victory. For her the son of Abas, together with his fair-robed daughters, once established an altar full of prayers. (Bacchylides 11.37–42)

What follows is a long aetiological myth culminating in the establishment of Artemis' cult at Metapontion. The narrative ranges far afield: this Artemis comes from deep in the Peloponnese; it is from her former dwellings at Lousoi in mountainous northern Arkadia that 'the Akhaians' brought the goddess when they dispersed to southern Italy on their return from the feats at Troy. Most of the mythical narrative (ll. 40–123) is actually taken up with an account of the origin of the Arkadian cult and relates to a well-known story complex from the Peloponnese: the daughters of Proitos, the king of Tiryns, aroused Hera's wrath when claiming that their father's *megaron* ('palace') was greater and more magnificent than hers. The offended goddess strikes the girls with *μανίαι ἄθεοι* ('godless madness'), and they flee in frenzy from Tiryns into the rugged interior of the Peloponnese. Proitos follows them into the wilderness of inner Arkadia, takes a bath at the stream *Λοῦσος* and, with the promise of great sacrifices, appeals to Artemis to placate Hera's anger. Artemis does as asked, and when liberated from their *maniai* the girls pay the due reward: a sacred precinct, sheep sacrifice, and women's *khoroi* for the goddess:

ταὶ δ' αὐτίκα οἱ τέμενος βωμόν τε τεῦχον,
χραῖνόν τέ μιν αἵματι μήλων
καὶ χοροὺς ἵσταν γυναικῶν.

and they at once built a sanctuary and an altar for her, sprinkled it with sheeps' blood and established women's *khoroi*. (Bacchylides 11.110–12)

From there, so the myth continues, 'the war-loving Akhaians' returning from Troy and moving on to the west took Artemis to Metapontion, and established her near the local river Kasas (the modern Basento):

ἔνθεν καὶ ἀρηϊφίλοις
ἄνδρεσσιν ⟨ἐς⟩ ἱπποτρόφον πόλιν Ἀχαιοῖς
ἕσπεο· σὺν δὲ τύχαι
ναίεις Μεταπόντιον, ὦ
χρυσέα δέσποινα λαῶν·
ἄλσος τέ τοι ἱμερόεν
Κάσαν παρ' εὔυδρον †πρόγο-
νοι ἑσσάμενοι† Πριάμοι' ἐπεὶ χρόνωι
βουλαῖσι θεῶν μακάρων
πέρσαν πόλιν εὐκτιμέναν
χαλκοθωράκων μετ' Ἀτρειδᾶν. δικαίας
ὅστις ἔχει φρένας, εὑ-
ρήσει σὺν ἅπαντι χρόνωι
μυρίας ἀλκὰς Ἀχαιῶν.

From there you, Artemis, followed the war-loving men of Akhaia to the horse-rearing city, and with happy fortune you now dwell at Metapontion, O golden mistress of the people: a charming grove (they built . . .) for you by the river Kasas with its fair waters when finally by the plans of the blessed gods they had destroyed the well-built city of Priamos with the Atreids in their bronzen corselets. He whose mind is just will always throughout time find countless deeds of the Akhaians. (Bacchylides 11.113–26)

Formally, this is a beautiful cult aetiology, actually a double aetiology with two layers of mythical past. It adheres to the 'rules' of this type of myth almost to the letter (Introduction, pp. 29–31): towards the end of a description of an ongoing ritual, the victory celebration at Metapontion, the song makes mention of Artemis; and using a relative clause in the aorist shifts the narrative into the goddess's mythical past (ll. 37 ff.). Some sixty verses later after the story has been meandering around in the northern Peloponnese, Artemis reappears, as an actor at the end of her own tale. The girls build her precinct and altar and establish sacrifice and their *khoroi* in her honour, referred to in a relative sentence which then projects the whole sanctuary westwards and back into the performative present of the ode at Metapontion (ll. 110 ff.; compare the present tense at 1.115 ff.).

But *Ode 11* is everything but a straightforward myth-ritual scenario acted out in performance. Artemis did have cults in both Lousoi and Metapontion, and the myth is regularly quoted as the founding account of each. Looking more closely, it is highly complex, if not impossible, to sort out what in this song 'belongs' to which cult. I shall suggest that the interaction between myth and ritual in the performance of this song plays on the dynamic created by the ode's most challenging claim: that this Artemis participated in the *Nostoi*, the *Returns* of the Akhaian heroes of Troy which would carry them not back to mainland Greece but further west to the Adriatic coast and the Italian peninsula.

The claim to Akhaian origins for Metapontian Artemis is contentious in the early fifth century because of the ambiguity it carries. 'Akhaians' can be at once the epic heroes and those colonists who at some point in history came to assert origins from mainland Akhaia, the region in the northern Peloponnese. It is far from clear when and under what circumstances the Metapontians, and the Akhaians of southern Italy as a whole, came to think of themselves in such ethnic terms and used epic ancestry in support. What follows will propose that Bacchylides' *Ode 11* operates in the middle of a debate over Akhaian identity in early to mid-fifth-century southern Italy. 'Akhaia', I maintain, was by no means a fixed concept at the time of the song's performance. Rather, being Akhaian competed with several other possible allegiances that 'Akhaian' cities paraded: Ionian, Dorian, or even Italian.

The cult of Artemis of Metapontion is caught up in these complicated processes of self-definition, involving changing populations all referring to this deity. As seen in previous chapters, the gods' problem, and their opportunity, lies in the fact that they are always there: gods are not erased, nor are the religious practices performed in their honour. While the nature of a divinity does not easily change, the arrival of new settlers causes the associated mythical traditions to supersede each other. The problem in dealing with the gods abroad, then, is not that they have no pasts, but that they have too many of them. The performance of the ode, and the interaction between myth and ritual therein, plays upon a variety of existing mythical pasts for Artemis, for the Metapontians, and for the 'Akhaians' of Italy, activating and exploiting them for a powerful evocation of an Akhaian identity in the complex and volatile social milieu of fifth-century Italy. Here, too, localities invoked mythical pasts, often summoned in religious song, to formulate identities, placing them in relation to others and notably in confrontation with the ubiquitous Athenians. But this situation is additionally spiced with a rather remarkable self-awareness of mixed origins on the part of these places, allowing easy and profitable manipulation of such mythical references.[6]

1. DANCING IN ARTEMIS' SACRED HERD

Artemis *Ἡμέρα* ('the gentle') at first sight corresponds to the bucolic image proffered by the ode. Artemis had a real cult at Lousoi in northern Arkadia, in a valley bordering Akhaia in the Peloponnese, between Kynaitha and Kleitor on a high plateau about 700 m beneath the Khelmos mountain range, a popular skiing area for modern Greeks (Map 6.1, p. 287 below). From the slopes separating the Lousian from the neighbouring valley to the east, Artemis' *temenos* overlooked a plain of pastures and the barely surviving ancient city. Dwelling high up in the mountains away from everything at the fringes of civilization, she has often been thought a *Πότνια θηρῶν* ('Mistress of animals'), guardian and huntress of the animal world. Two literary occurrences incidentally name a 'sacred herd' (*τὰ θρέμματα τῆς θεοῦ*), a real flock of animals belonging to the goddess.[7] The spring Lousos serving Proitos for his bath in Bacchylides' ode, as well as the etymological play on *λούειν* ('to wash'), have led Artemis to be understood at the heart of a 'typical Arkadian' *Quellkult* ('spring cult') overseeing the world of nature, protecting man's hunting activities and offering him refreshment on a stroll. Local girls would chance upon this deity while frolicking with their peers in the pastures or on the way to the well. Girls' *khoroi* passed their days of maidenhood here in a privileged *locus amoenus* of rural Arkadia.[8]

The cult's archaeology superficially also suggests a divinity along such Arcadian lines, though Artemis was not a simple deity. Artemis was active from at least

[6] Identities in and of the West continue to fascinate current scholarship, as the recent flurry of collective volumes suggests: e.g. E. Greco (2002); Moscati Castelnuovo (2002); Lomas (2004). For the role of *syngeneia* in inter-state relations in the 5th cent., esp. in the Peloponnesian War, see Hornblower (1991–6) ii, 61–80.

[7] Plb. 4.18.10–12; 4.19.4–5 (other mentions of the sanctuary are 4.25.4; 9.34.10; Paus. 8.18.7–8). Sacred herds are an underresearched phenomenon. I can merely refer to Amandry (1939) 195, adducing evidence from Delphi; Sinn (1992); Isager (1992). The goddess is identified by inscribed dedications to Artemis *Ἡμέραι* or *τᾶι Λουσιάτι*: *IG* v.2 397–403.

[8] Muthmann (1975) 238–9; Stiglitz (1967) 100–5; also Chirassi Colombo (1964) *passim*; Jost (1992).

Figure 6.1 The fourth-century BC foundations of the temple of Artemis at Lousoi, looking down the southern end of the valley, situated on a high plateau. The 'bouleuterion' is located just below the temple; individual Hellenistic houses and the ancient city have been found a little further down the slope. The ninth–sixth century foundation layer is situated at the far end of the terrace

the late ninth century BC until the first century AD. Remains of cult buildings survive from as early as the sixth century, while what the visitor sees today are the foundations of a late fourth-century structure (Fig. 6.1). Some of the most accomplished early bronze figurines of all Greek antiquity are amongst the votives. These, together with the rest of the rich dedicatory material, indicate that the cult flourished in the geometric to classical periods. A series of unique anthropomorphic bronze idols thought to represent the cult image have become known as a type 'Artemis of Lousoi', distinctive for a particular helmet-like hair-cut (Fig. 6.2). Fine-quality bronze and terracotta animals from the geometric and early archaic periods, small birds and little bronze horses in particular, complement the picture of a much frequented cult whose worshippers did not shun expense to please the goddess.[9]

[9] See Reichel and Wilhelm (1901) for the archaeology of the sanctuary, and the reports on recent excavations *JÖAI* 1981/2 onwards. Summary accounts can be found in Jost (1985) 47–51; Sinn (1980) and (1992); Mitsopoulos-Leon (1992) and (2001*b*) for the latest discoveries. For a summary of the topography of the area see Tausend (1995*a*); (1999). The finds are discussed in great detail in Voyatzis (1990) 35–7, 91–2, 133–8, 143–4, 155–6, 175–218, 242–4. 'Artemis of Lousoi' (note the hairstyle): *LIMC* ii.1/2 (1984) s.v. Artemis, nos. 104–9.

Figure 6.2 Bronze votive statuette type 'Artemis of Lousoi' (2nd quarter of the fifth century BC); from Tegea. Artemis holds a phiale in one hand, a lost object in the other. The statuette is similar to those found at Lousoi itself and normally attributed to this group despite long hair running over its back; it may also hint at the distribution of similar cults of Artemis in this part of the Peloponnese

Female worshippers left the majority of the material traces: of the many terracotta statuettes, dating from the late seventh century onwards, most show the standard type of a female dedicant, that is to say a standing woman, with or without a 'feminine' attribute, little flowers or animals, sometimes little children. Very recent excavations have yielded a remarkable late sixth-century foundation deposit in a levelling stratum at the north side of the extant temple foundations. The late ninth-century layers have produced a fair number of well-forged fibulae and other jewellery. The seventh-century stratum also unveiled, together with some ritual equipment, around thirty closed pyxides, that is to say pyxides with the body and the lid formed into one, produced explicitly for use in cult ('Kult-pyxiden'). These objects are of local workmanship and unique to this sanctuary, a special votive gift to this Artemis. Spectacularly, a series of little inscribed bronze boxes also emerged, one example of which had been known from the old excavations of the beginning of the twentieth century. Both pyxides and the delicate (jewellery?) boxes regularly occur in wedding contexts and suggest dedications made as part of marriage rituals.[10]

The alluring ensemble of rural surroundings, sacred animals, mythical springs, and dancing maidens has often influenced the interpretation of this cult. Closer inspection of its functioning in the Arkadian religious landscape, however, reveals that the Arcadian surface of myth, ritual, and votive imagery is misleading. The idea of a deity dwelling peacefully in a remote valley amongst gracious animal votives and bubbling streams of thirst-quenching water can be replaced with that of a goddess central to the religious dynamic in the valley and beyond. The suggestions of a vibrant social ambience come in the first place from the very same myth that engendered the picture of the relaxed mountain deity: the interaction of myth and ritual, notably in the Bacchylidean song, is one source of such an interpretation (the remainder of Section 1); Artemis' role in the religious system of the northern Peloponnese another (Section 2). I shall consider those in turn.

The myth of the Proitids presented in Bacchylides' *Ode 11* has established a number of orthodoxies closely linked with the bucolic images, only some of which are justified. Often considered the 'authoritative' version of the story of the Proitids, Bacchylides' song has, for example, supplied the regular pattern for girls' initiation, if not the model from which the Greek pattern is itself derived. Van Gennep's three stages of 'séparation'—'marge'—'aggrégation' are thought to be paradigmatically realized by the Proitids' exile from home, their temporary roaming in the woods, and their reintegration into society through marriage as depicted by the 'women's choruses'.[11]

While an element of transition from girls to married women is indeed implicit in cult and aetiology Bacchylides' myth-telling is highly complex and cannot be reduced to a single local or ritual context. As we shall see, the text merges discrete

[10] Cf. already Reichel and Wilhelm (1901) nos. 114, 158; the new excavations and the foundation deposit are reported in *JÖAI* 58 (1988) 14–18; *JÖAI* 1996 and 1997; Mitsopoulos-Leon (2001*b*). The pyxides are both life-size and miniature and include plates with holes on one side, indicating their votive character: Schauer (1998), (2001). I am indebted to Dr Mitsopoulos-Leon and Dr Schauer from the Österreichisches Archäologisches Institut at Athens for showing me photographs of the recent finds and discussing them with me in 1998.

[11] Van Gennep (1909) 14 introduces the terms. On the transition from virginity to marriage in ritual see ibid. 165–207. For Bacchylides 11 see Burnett (1985) 100–13; Seaford (1988); Dowden (1989) 71–95; Suarez de la Torre (1992) 3–6; Calame (1997) 116–20; 135–7; Cairns (2005) 47.

mythical traditions.[12] One of these is the story of the Proitids who more commonly belong to Hera, specifically the Heraion of Argos; in these versions, the Proitids are healed by the seer Melampous in a myth that goes back to Hesiod.[13] Onto this tradition is grafted the episode involving Artemis at Lousoi, curiously moving the girls away from their original patroness. Artemis' involvement in the myth is practically unique to Bacchylides' ode.[14] The myth of the Proitids as represented here, because of the particular religious context to which it belonged, is a curious bricolage of several myth-ritual complexes put together in such a way as to link a cult in mainland Greece with one in southern Italy. The association of Hera and Artemis, which is unusual in any case, has, notably, a more pertinent role in Metapontion than in Peloponnesian Arkadia. The Heraion in the Argolid plays a large part in the fabrication of Akhaian identity (epic as much as ethnic), and it is for this reason that the ode takes up the habitual link of the Proitids to the goddess at Prosymna. Also often observed is a Dionysiac side to the myth-ritual complex which probably has its own specific role in a fifth-century climate. The beauty and the challenge of Bacchylides' performance lie in the interplay of these different traditions, which all belong to individual local contexts, each with its own intricate history and dynamic. What follows is one attempt to undo some of these entanglements.

The Proitids are among the key representatives of female worshippers of Hera at the Heraion at Prosymna. The Heraion seems to have several distinct aetiological myths, for example the epic poem *Phoronis* duly establishes the Proitid Kallithoe as priestess of the Heraion (*κλειδοῦχος*, literally the 'key-holder', i.e. the custodian), according to a common pattern by which actors in aetiological myths turn into attendants of the deity with whom they have been at odds.[15] The great wealth of aetiological myths for this goddess is quite possibly a result of constantly shifting power relations in the Argolid's distant and not so distant past, many of which notoriously revolve around the Heraion. The longish excursion into local dynastic struggles in Bacchylides' ode (ll. 59–82) clearly places the Proitids' story in the world of the Argive plain. The usual end of the myth suggests the same when not Artemis, but the seer Melampous arrives at Argos

[12] Dowden (1989) 71–95 gives a full account of all the different traditions of the Proitids; see Burkert (1983) 168–76; Cairns (2005) 40–6 is a recent discussion.

[13] Hes. fr. 37 MW (esp. 14–15); 129–33 MW = *Suda* μ 307 s.v. *μαχλοσύνη*. It used to be thought that some of these passages belong to the Melampodia: Loeffler (1963); Henrichs (1974), whilst they belong to the *Catalogue of Women*: Dowden (1989) 218 n. 12.

[14] Cf. Call. *Dian.* (3) 233–6, though this very likely harks back to the choral poem; Paus. 8.18.7–8.

[15] Cf. *Phoronis* 4 Bernabé; Clem. Al. *Str.* 1.24.164: *γράφει γοῦν ὁ τὴν Φορωνίδα ποιήσας· Καλλιθόη κλειδοῦχος Ὀλυμπιάδος βασιλείης / Ἥρης Ἀργείης ἣ στέμμασι καὶ θυσάνοισι / πρώτη ἐκόσμησεν περὶ κίονα μακρὸν ἀνάσσης*. 'The poet of the Phoronis says: 'Kallithoe the key-holder of the Queen of Olympus, Argive Hera, who was the first to ornament the great pillar of the mistress with crowns and tassel'. Cf. Aesch. *Suppl.* 291; Eur. *IT* 131. Io is another such primordial worshipper. For the phenomenon of mythical personnel becoming cultic attendants cf. Iphigenia, who becomes priestess of Artemis at Brauron (Eur. *IT.* 1462–3): *σὲ δ'. . . δεῖ τῇδε κλῃδουχεῖν θεᾷ* 'and you . . . must serve this goddess as a temple-warder'.

from Pylos in Messenia, offering his healing services in return for shares of the Argive kingdom.[16]

The ode sings of the Proitids' contempt for Hera's temple residence, probably also expressing such competing claims to the Argive plain.

> παρθενίαι γὰρ ἔτι
> ψυχᾶι κίον ἐς τέμενος
> πορφυροζώνοιο θεᾶς·
> φάσκον δὲ πολὺ σφέτερον
> πλούτωι προφέρειν πατέρα ξανθᾶς παρέδρου
> σεμνοῦ Διὸς εὐρυβία.

for when they still had the spirit of young girls (*parthenoi*), they went into the sanctuary of the purple-belted goddess and claimed that their father's wealth by far exceeded that of the fair-haired consort of the august and wide-powered Zeus. (Bacchylides 11.47–52)

The girls' belittling of Hera forms part of a long-standing tradition. Hesiod's piecemeal narrative already involved the palace of Proitos. Akousilaos turns the conflict over the kingdoms into one over Hera's divine authority when claiming that her *xoanon* was too poorly crafted to impress Proitos' proud daughters.[17] The myth is an early example of so-called resistance myths: myths which lead to the establishment of the rejected god's rituals, often containing an element of initiation or transition on the 'human' level, and an element of religious change in a civic or other social context. The offended deity imposes a punishment that can only be lifted through the performance of the unwelcome rites themselves. Dionysos most specially attracts this type of myth, which canonically forms the narrative framework and myth-ritual nexus of his arrival in places of future worship.[18] The structural similarities between the myth of the Proitids and Hera, and the generic Dionysiac resistance myth, seem to be one of the reasons why the girls occasionally interfere with the so-called Women of Argos who resist the frenzied god and with whom the Proitids are often confused. Indeed, not least because of their shared inclination for ὀρειβασία ('roaming on the mountains'), the Proitids' *mania* in various traditions attracts a fair amount of what one might call 'Dionysiac language'.[19] More fundamentally, the resemblances stand a good

[16] Both he and his brother Bias would receive portions of the kingdom of Argos: Hes. fr. 37 MW. On the interesting figure of Melampous and his relation to the Proitids see Vian (1965); Kouretas (1977); Suarez de la Torre (1992); Jost (1992); Dorati (2004). On the Bacchylidean excursus into the dynastic history of the Argolid cf. esp. Cairns (2005) 38–9; Angeli Bernardini (2004*b*) 135–8.

[17] Hes. fr. 129.25 MW: δώματα πατρός; Acus. *FGrH* 2 F 28 διότι τὸ τῆς Ἥρας ξόανον ἐξηυτέλισαν 'because they disparaged the "xoanon" of Hera'. The word *xoanon* here means merely 'cult image', since the idea of primitive wooden *xoana* is a modern misconception derived in part from Pausanias (Donohue (1988)). Rather, the Greeks thought of *xoana* as 'unworked' cult images.

[18] On such 'resistance myths' see e.g. Sourvinou-Inwood (1994) and Seaford (1996) 45. In the case of Dionysos, the punishment is *mania*, the Dionysiac frenzy, which in actual ritual turns into Dionysiac *khoroi* (Kowalzig (2007)).

[19] Picked up by modern critics: Seaford's interpretation plays with the absence and the presence of Dionysos for an interpretation that ultimately sees the ode as an aetiological myth for the cult of Dionysos (1988). Cairns (2005) 43 speaks of 'mutual attraction between myths in which the wildness

chance of being the result of shifting emphases in intertwining religious and social structures at Argos, part of the political changes in the Argive Plain towards democratization, and, possibly, a newly formulated civic ideology, which also bring about a new role for Dionysos.[20]

Until well into the fifth century, however, the two groups and the language tying them to their deities remain distinct. Herodotus, for example, quotes Melampous' cure of the Women of Argos, here acting on behalf of Dionysos, but does not make the connection when telling of the Proitids elsewhere in the *Histories.* Apollodorus reads the two groups as identical in the *Catalogue of Women*, but none of the actual quotations from Hesiod (or pseudo-Hesiod) confirm that the two *thiasoi* coincide this early.[21] Rather, when scrutinized in detail, the Proitids have little in common with Dionysiac maenadism to start with, a futher indication that the girls acquired Dionysiac language once the two legends mixed in a fifth-century context. The Proitids' earliest *mania* comes from Hesiod and is quite particular, showing the different facets that the process of 'girls' transition' can take. 'Girlish behaviour' gets the maidens into trouble in the first place, as remarked upon by several authors, first of all the ode itself, quoted above: παρθενίαι γὰρ ἔτι ψυχᾶι (l. 47–8). Carefree youthfulness reappears in the fifth-century mythographer Pherekydes' analysis of the Proitids' lack of piety: 'they insulted [the goddess] out of youthful foolishness'.[22] What we know of the subsequent *nosos* from its oldest source, Hesiod, quite literally tells us what girls' transition is all about: the Proitids take issue with their appearance—they undergo a period of aesthetic disfigurement and restoration, but rather than resisting sexuality[23] they develop it to an excessive degree. We hear of gross μαχλοσύνη, lasciviousness, and of ἠλοσύνη, a form of childish silliness, taking away the 'tender flower' of maidenhood (τέρεν ἄνθος) and turning it into a disease: the girls suffer from 'leprosy' (ἄλφος), a skin problem that makes them incessantly scratch their heads and eventually lose their hair altogether.[24]

of virgins is tamed before marriage and those in which married women renew their virginal wildness in the worship of Dionysos'.

[20] Ch. 3, pp. 168–70 above and Kowalzig (2007) 226–32. That so many 5th-cent. authors talk about the girls (Bacchylides, Pherekydes, Akousilaos, Herodotus) should be indicative of the importance that their divine affiliation held at the time.

[21] Hes. frr. 131–3 MW; Hdt. 9.34; cf. Apollod. 1.9.12, *contra* 2.2.2, inconsistent in naming both παρθένοι and γυναῖκες among the maddened; the latter rip apart their children and thus quite probably belong to Dionysos. Cf. D.S. 4.68.4; Paus. 2.18.4 (γυναῖκες). Cf. Cairns (2005) 44.

[22] Pherec. *FGrH* 3 F 114 τῶν γὰρ Προίτου θυγατέρων . . . διὰ τὴν ἐκ νεότητος ἀνεπιλογιστίαν ἁμαρτουσῶν εἰς Ἥραν—παραγενόμεναι γὰρ εἰς τὸν τῆς θεοῦ νεὼν ἔσκωπτον αὐτὸν λέγουσαι πλουσιώτερον μᾶλλον εἶναι τὸν τοῦ πατρὸς οἶκον . . . 'Proitos' daughters . . . erred against Hera because of youthful unreasonableness—for as they came to the goddess's shrine they belittled it saying that their father's house was much richer.'

[23] As has been widely argued: Seaford (1988); cf. Dowden (1989) 71–95; (1992) 108 f.

[24] This is a typically sacred disease. For ἄλφος caused by sacred offence see Parker (1983) 208–9: the Delians caught this when infringing the prohibition of burial on the island (Aesch. *Ep.* 1.2); Orestes' expectation, had he not been able to avenge his father, would have been ἄλφος: Aesch. *Cho.* 278–82. No doubt the borders between physical and mental illness were very fluid, as were the respective pollutions causing it: Parker (1983) 208–9, 212–13, 218.

Fourth-century vase paintings, possibly picking up on tragic reproductions, show the Proitids in utter mental and physical distress. The girls' loose hair is floating, and they seem to be taking off their clothes one by one. Two seventh-century depictions of a pair of girls lead one to suspect that loose hair and partial nudity may have been the customary *Bildformel* for the Proitids, the pictorial expression of the Proitids' temporarily overdeveloped sexuality (Fig. 6.3 (a) and (b)).[25] The erotic aspect of their disorder tends to be played down in later texts (possibly as a consequence of their relation with Dionysos). But Aelian in the second century still speaks of them as 'mad nudes' (γυμναὶ μαινόμεναι) and duly makes Aphrodite responsible for this kind of behaviour. Similarly, in Apollodorus they appear 'entirely disorderly' (μετ' ἀκοσμίας ἁπάσης).[26] This 'madness' bears little resemblance to the comparatively controlled maenadic behaviour inspired by Dionysos, whose maddened companions tend to be on the whole rather orderly—at least in Athenian fantasy.[27]

Girls' transitions are certainly an aspect of this myth, but it would be unwise to lump them into the same old category of girls running away from sexual harassment: the Proitids just express the issue of transition in a different way. However, the characteristic skin-disease does not seem to survive Hesiod even if, as we shall see, the fifth-century representations of the myth—when Dionysos was definitely part of the *imaginaire* surrounding the girls—retain the one or the other element. That said, much in the ode recalls the imagery usually found in the train of myths of resistance to marriage, better known, however, for Artemis than for Hera. As we shall now see, it is also Artemis who shapes the *mania* of Hera's attendants in the Bacchylidean song.

Unlike anything else in the Proitids' mythical baggage, the song also reveals a pervasive 'bestial imagery', which refers to their premarital status. Their conversion from 'untamed daughters' (ἄδματοι θύγατρες, l. 84) into performers of civilized choral dancers (χοροὺς γυναικῶν, l. 112) prefigures the real girls' imminent change of status. Such imagery is canonically used for the transition from *parthenos* to married woman and is the best indicator that at least some aspect of puberty rites is implied here.[28] But what is so interesting is that Bacchylides' ode takes this 'animal' imagery very far indeed. The girls' bestiality, inducing them to roam restlessly through the northern Peloponnese and especially Arkadia, is their chief characteristic, a wildness reflected perhaps in Callimachus' θυμὸν ἄγριον ('savage spirit') in his portrayal of the upset daughters.

[25] *LIMC* vii (1994) s.v. nos. 1 (*c*.625 BC) and 3 (*c*.660 BC); nos. 4 and 5 for the 4th-cent. southern Italian depictions, possibly going back to tragic plots. Note with Cairns (2005) 43 the presence of Dionysos on the vases. He takes these representations as indications for the myth's spread in Italy. See also n. 36 below

[26] Ael. *VH* 3.42, mentioning that the girls roamed (ἔδραμον, ἐξεφοίτησαν) the Peloponnese, and then the rest of Greece; Apollod. 2.2.2.

[27] On which see e.g. Osborne (1997); Bravo and Frontisi-Ducroux (1997).

[28] The expression 'bestial imagery' for the girls in Bacch. 11 was first used by Stern (1965); cf. Burnett (1985); C. Segal (1976). Seaford (1988) develops this point, discussing in particular the image of the 'yoke' for marriage, unmarried girls as unyoked (119–20); Cairns (2005) 44–5.

Figure 6.3 (a) A seventh-century ivory relief from Taras, showing two girls whose dresses have dropped, revealing their bare breasts, held to represent the Proitids

Figure 6.3 (b) Lukanian Nestoris, 390–370 BC, showing the Proitids' purification in a temple of Artemis, refuge to the roaming girls, here with loose hair and half naked. Melampous is also present. The image may be inspired by a tragic plot; note the similarity to scenes of Orestes' *hikesia*.

Animal noises resound from the ode when the Proitids 'sent forth dreadful howls' (σμερδαλέαν φωνὰν ἱεῖσαι, l. 56). This detail is, incidentally, picked up by Virgil and his commentators, claiming that the girls, believed to have changed into cows, were let loose into the countryside and filled the air with ear-piercing lowing.[29] This 'bestial imagery' is in the first instance linked to Argive Hera too: one of the few attested details regarding the nature of ritual activity at the Heraion is that some variety of cattle, probably white cattle, featured grandly in the sacrifice in all periods of antiquity. And Hera's Argive *kleidoukhos* Io, on the same model as the Proitids, is changed into a cow and was unleashed onto the plain in the shape of a white cow before being wedded to Zeus. The Proitids (just

[29] Call. *Dian.* (3) 236. V. *Ecl.* 6.48–51; Serv.: 'se putantes vaccas in saltus abirent . . . crederunt se boves factas' 'thinking themselves cows they ran away jumping . . . they believed that they had changed into cattle'; Prob. *App. Serv.* 'quos Iuno in vaccas convertit insania conpulsae crediderunt se boves esse et altos montes petierunt. falsis mugitibus quia transfiguratae erant', 'whom Iuno changed into cows. Impelled by madness they thought themselves to be cattle and sought the high mountains. For they were transfigured by false lowing.' Lact. Plac. in St. *Theb.* 3.453: 'in iuvencas vertit puellas et cupiditatem iniecit silvas petendi ⟨adeo ut plerumque mugirent et collo iuga timerent⟩, credentes se formam induxisse vaccarum'. 'she turned the girls into yoke-cows, had thrown into them a desire to strive for woods ⟨so much so that they mooed most of the time and feared the yoke around their neck⟩, thinking they had put on the shape of cows'.

like Hera's other mythical priestesses) then were known for shifting imperceptibly between girl and a form of cow in the process of establishing their ritual identity as Hera's attendants.[30]

But the punch line is that the girls are not just Hera's. In their stormiest phase there enters Lousian Artemis. Artemis' epiklesis *Hemera* ('the gentle', 'the tame') is unique to Lousoi; the ancient etymologists claim that she was so called because she tamed the Proitids.[31] Though Artemis first of all engages in soothing Hera, the story develops her as the divine force eventually calming the savage teenagers. Artemis the 'hunting goddess' discloses herself now, but in a way quite different from what is usually imagined of a *Potnia theron*. The myth is actually staged as a hunt representing the process of domestication expressed in the resulting choral dance. The daughters behave like chased animals, fleeing from place to place as if pursued by huntsmen; the notion of the turbulent pursuit and flight pervades the story as if the poor girls were nowhere safe from their *κυνηγέτις*, their huntress: 'they fled into the leafy mountains' (*φεῦγον δ' ὄρος ἐς τανίφυλλον*, l. 55); 'rushing off from there . . . ran the unfettered daughters' (*ἔνθεν ἀπεσσύμεναι . . . φεῦγον ἄδματοι θύγατρες*, ll. 82–4); 'they wandered distraught in the dark woods and fled into Arkadia' (*κατὰ δάσκιον ἠλύκταζον ὕλαν φεῦγόν τε κατ' Ἀρκαδίαν*, ll. 93–4).

Then, at the end of story, there features the change from wild to docile animals (ll. 104–12). The jumble of Heraian and Artemisian imagery continues into this part of the narrative. Proitos promises Artemis a sacrifice of twenty 'unyoked oxen' (*ἄζυγας βοῦς*, ll. 104–5) as a reward for halting the hunt and freeing his unbroken daughters from Hera's wrath. That Proitos invokes Artemis with Hera's epithet *βοῶπις* ('ox-eyed', l. 99), as if Hera's myth were also subliminally recounted here, confirms the view that an aetiology for the great goddess of the Argolid merges with a local tradition without tidying up the ensuing inconsistencies. With his suggestion Proitos prompts a familiar process in cults starring young maidens, marking the transition from aetiological myth to ritual: at the height of the story the 'human' sacrifice of a girl or girls is turned into that of an animal—just as Iphigenia was snatched away by Artemis and only just escaped being slaughtered in her honour. Similarly, the Proitids, victims of the goddess's power, are eventually substituted by sacrificial animals, oxen in the promise, replaced by typically Artemisian 'blood of sheep' in the actual ritual according to the ode.[32]

While the notion itself of a 'human' sacrifice to the god does not lead any further, it seems clear that this kind of story pattern seems to lead up to the ritual

[30] Aesch. *Suppl.* 290–308, note Io's *οἶστρος*. Apollod. 2.1.3; Ov. *Met.* 1.651–60; Plin. *NH* 16.239. *Παρθένοι* at the festival of Hera at Argos: Eur. *El.* 173–4, 178–80, dressed in white: Ov. *Am.* 3.27. Note Sen. *Ag.* 356–66.

[31] *Σ* Call. *Dian.* (3) 236: *διὰ τῆς Ἀρτέμιδος ἡμερώθησαν*: '[the Proitids] were softened by Artemis'; also *Ἡμέρης διότι τὰς κόρας ἡμέρωσεν* 'of Hemera because she softened the maidens'; see Stiglitz (1967) 103 ff.

[32] Interestingly, a number of terracotta bulls, patiently dwelling in archaeological store-rooms, are reported in association with this cult, waiting to be identified as the votive expression of the customary sacrifice in honour of Lousian Artemis.

moment of the aetiology, the transition from myth to ritual and the validation of myth in ritual. It marks quite literally the girls' 'dedication' to the goddess. That something like this is going on here is clear from the orchestration of the transitory ritual moment: here it is time for the girls to cease their existence as a troupe of wild animals and change into a cast of choral dancers. Artemis' part in this hunt is to put the libertine maidens into a well-ordered choral formation—to change the beasts into the sacred herd belonging to the goddess. The wild daughters are caught and put under Artemis' protection into this herd of chorus girls, become part of the flock of animals, τὰ θρέμματα τῆς θεοῦ in the words of Polybius. And indeed, the goddess emerges from all this just as much as 'overlord' and as 'guardian of animals', as θηροσκόπος (l. 107).

The choral dance has the desired cleansing effect on the girls' disturbed disposition, which has entered the tradition as a form of purification from the divine disease (*nosos*). Once again Dionysiac ritual language intrudes—his *khoroi* often have a 'kathartic' aspect.[33] Apollodorus, confusing the Dionysiac and the Heraian aspects of the Proitid myth-ritual ensemble, literally calls the process 'purification' (καθαρμοί), which in this case entails Melampous and a set of ephebes chasing the Proitids in a wild pursuit over the mountains down to Sikyon 'with loud howling and some divinely inspired *khoreia*'. The *khoroi* for Artemis replace what in other texts takes the shape of ritual therapy exercised by the seer Melampous and not by Artemis, often involving a purificatory bath that only survives in later tradition but quite possibly goes back to the time of Hesiod. The river Anigros in Elis, for example, cured the Proitids' *alphos* by conveniently 'washing it away' and itself took on the illness, and this is why the river remained muddy forever after.[34] Despite the absence of a full immersion rite in the ode, a puzzling trace of literal cleansing is still there: when the Proitids' father Proitos bathes himself in the 'stream at Lousos', he suspiciously washes his skin (χρόα νιψάμενος, l. 97) in a wording too close to Hesiod's not to recall the Proitidean skin-disease.[35]

[33] Cf. Wilson (2003*b*).

[34] Str. 8.3.19: the river is smelly and produces uneatable fish, which is attributed, according to some ἀπὸ τοῦ Μελάμποδα τοῖς ὕδασι τούτοις καθαρσίοις χρήσασθαι πρὸς τὸν τῶν Προιτίδων καθαρμόν· ἀλφοὺς δὲ καὶ λεύκας καὶ λειχῆνας ἰᾶται τὸ ἐντεῦθεν λουτρόν; 'to the fact that Melampous used these cleansing waters for the purification of the Proitids. The bathing-water from here cures leprosy, elephantiasis, and scabies' (tr. Jones). Cf. Paus. 5.5.10. Bdelykleon's court disease was expected to be purified in this way: Ar. *Vesp.* 118: ἀπέλου κἀκάθαιρ'. Healing springs: Ginouvès (1962) 361–73; cf. Croon (1967) 225–46. Dionysiac features infringe when a purifying spring in or near Lousoi's neighbour Kleitor made its drinkers resistant to wine, the same fountain perhaps explaining itself in an epigram cited by Vitruvius as μισάμπελος ('wine-hating'), adding that its water was not suitable for having a bath because Melampous had bathed the Proitids here: Eudoxos of Knidos *ap.* St. Byz. s.v. Ἀζανία; cf. Plin. *NH* 31.13; Phylarkhos (3rd cent. BC) *ap.* Ath. 2.43f = *FGrH* 81 F 63. Ov. *Met.* 15.322–8. Cf. Vitr. 8.3.21, a well: sacrificiis purgavisset Melampus rabiem 'Melampous cleansed the rage through sacrifices'. Cf. [Plut]. *Fluv.* 21.4. Ael. *VH* 3.42 quotes the girls' wanderings in the Peloponnese in the context of Dionysiac *khoroi.*

[35] Hes. fr. 133 MW: . . . ἀπείρονα γαῖαν καὶ γάρ σφιν κεφαλῇισι κατὰ κνύος αἰνὸν ἔχευεν· ἀλφὸς γὰρ χρόα πάντα κατέσχεθεν, αἱ δέ νυ χαῖται ἔρρεον ἐκ κεφαλέων, ψίλωτο δὲ καλὰ κάρηνα '. . . the boundless earth; and she poured down on them a terrible itch on their heads: *alphos* took hold of their entire skin, their hair fell off and their beautiful heads became bald'.

This is not a 'hunter's bath'; rather Proitos' lustral immersion points again to tangled mythical traditions in the ode. The purificatory bath only makes sense as long as there is a skin-disease to be washed off, but it has no place in the *nosos* the Proitids incur here. The purificatory bath also supplies a perfect pun, playing on the name of the toponym *Lousoi*, from *louein*, 'to wash', etymological riddling that is characteristic of aetiology. Rich sources of water in the modern village, appearing as *Λοῦσος καλλιρόη*, 'Lousos flowing beautifully', confirm the association of name and locality. But no actual spring has been found in the sanctuary itself, making the possibility of water purification unlikely. The goddess's locality seems to have attracted a cleansing imagery which, however, in the rituals for Artemis is represented in the choral dance.

So the Proitids' disease in the victory song was not washed away in the springs but danced off in the communal chorus for the goddess Artemis.[36] The conclusion that we need to draw is that singing in a ritual *khoros* at Lousoi meant becoming part of Artemis' sacred herd in the same way as the Proitids were once tamed into a *khoros* by Artemis. The *khoros* assumes the role of a tribute paid to Artemis in lieu of the maidens, while presumably the real sacrificial victim is chosen from the goddess's actual herd of animals. What appears in the ritual is a chorus of tamed animals, while the untamed past of the girls is given for the deity's consumption. The offering of a *khoros* following the mythical substitution is a familiar pattern, known for example for the cults of Artemis at Brauron or Mounikhia, whose *arktoi*, the title of the girls dancing there as if they were little 'bears', share the animalesque resonances of the Proitids. Animal blood flowing at the end of the story symbolizes the Burkertian 'Jungfrauenblut' typical of Artemis' sacrificial demands in public festivals. The regular choral performance in the cult ensures the constant renewal of Proitos' promised offerings. That is to say it engenders the continuous reconstitution of the sacred herd of Artemis, in other words, the worshipping community for this cult. On the surface, the choral performers at the sanctuary re-enact the cult myth in performance; myth and ritual merge in the same way as we have observed for other rituals involving the *khoros*, when myth-protagonists and myth-tellers imperceptibly blend, summoning the mythical past as a validation of the present.[37]

2. ARTEMIS TWICE BETWEEN *AGROTERA* AND *HEMERA*

To explain the jumbling of myths and rituals of the two goddesses Hera and Artemis we shall need to wait until we discuss the southern Italian performance

[36] If vase depictions inspired by tragedy (Fig. 6.3(b)) show the distressed Proitids seeking refuge at an altar in a formula known for (tragic) Orestes, this gives support to a 'choral' *katharsis*: *LIMC* vii (1994) s.v. Orestes nos. 7–54.

[37] Burkert (1983) 63–9 on 'maidens' blood'. A number of 4th-cent. terracotta figurines of masks and actors among the votives at Lousoi suggests that some form of mimetic choral performances may have been held in Artemis' honour: Reichel and Wilhelm (1901) 42–3.

context of the ode. For the moment let us keep in mind that Artemis at Lousoi does appear in this myth as a *Πότνια θηρῶν*, 'Mistress of Animals', yet she is a mistress not of actual wildlife, but of girls who imagine themselves to be wild animals whom the goddess Artemis the huntress chases down and puts in orderly choral shape: this is the Artemis that appears in terracotta, with a bow in one hand, a deer in the other.

But what is this rallying into a *khoros* all about? Choral dancing is certainly an image for a community that boasts a level of social integration—just as, for example, Athenian girls had to undergo the rituals at Brauron in order to become the wife of an Athenian citizen.[38] But what community is being celebrated here, what identity being constructed in the women's *khoroi*? This is the point at which to consider Artemis' role in the religious landscape of the northern Peloponnese. Artemis in studies of Greek religion has the status of a deity profoundly tied to *polis* life, that is to say that her myths and rituals are representative of a society whose imagination revolves around the city-state. Within this perceptual framework, she features as a goddess integrating margins and centre, managing the transitions between savagery and civilization. Thus, for example, she oversees adolescents' entry into adult life, but also the demarcation between Greeks and non-Greeks, even democracy and tyranny. Such an Artemis is typically located at the *eskhatiai* of cities, in areas that are themselves considered marginal and borderline—most notoriously the many Artemises *en limnais*, 'in the marshes'.[39] The general idea of Artemisian myths and rituals embracing a perception of change of status of worshippers from the outside to the inside of a given community can be attractively taken further in the case of Artemis at Lousoi. The observation that a memory of social change is represented in Artemisian myths by images or narrative involving an antagonism between savage and socially integrated wild life will also prove helpful. By contrast, in the case of Lousoi, Artemis' tie to the *polis* needs to be released and rebound in a new way.

One motivation behind this latter claim is that our understanding of Greek history beyond the *polis*, to include *ethne* ('ethnic groupings') and *koina* ('federations'), has changed considerably, and the consequences for religious life

[38] *Suda* α 3958 s.v. *Ἄρκτος ἢ Βραυρωνίοις*; *Σ* Ar. *Lys.* 645. On the fiction of widespread participation see Parker (2005) 232–48. As so often, the *arktoi* may have been elite girls representing their community through the blending of elite religious practice and Athenian public ideology. Ar. *Lys.* 638 ff. suggests that the ritual was of some importance to the *polis* when the female *khoros* reserves the right to advise the city. Cairns (2005) 45–6 notes that the Proitids are not individualized in the ode, as if to stress their generic role in the community; this is different from the mythographic tradition, where they all have names.

[39] Frontisi-Ducroux (1981) in a central and subtle article identifying this Artemis, a view taken further by Vernant (1991), esp. 195–206; cf. also the collection of articles in *Recherches sur les cultes grecs et l'Occident 2*. Cahiers du Centre Jean Bérard IX (Naples, 1984). The more general points of interpretation have since gained broad acceptance: e.g. Bruit-Zaidman and Schmitt Pantel (1992), index s.v. Artemis; Ellinger (1993). For the centrality of the *polis* in Greek religion see the seminal article by Sourvinou-Inwood (1990).

are yet to be explored.[40] Traces of urbanization, notably in so-called *ethnos*-states such as Akhaia, Arkadia, or Thessaly, are poor until well into the classical period. Recent archaeological exploration in the northern Peloponnese, less concerned with the workings of polytheism than with individual sanctuaries' functioning in a local religious landscape, has suggested that early archaic communities developed around (communal expression in) a sanctuary in the first place. Lousoi may well be such a case—no archaic city has been traced in the valley, but there is evidence for a lively classical *polis*, remains of which are located a little downhill from the temple.[41] Unlike many other cults of Artemis often situated at the ἐσχατιαί, of cities, this one was not marginal, rather Artemis was the central sacred authority in Lousiatan affairs. Decrees were erected in her shrine, and the city's proxenies, including arrangements about *theorodokia*, were accurately incised on delicate little bronze tablets left with the goddess. A public Hellenistic structure, perhaps somewhat rashly called a *bouleuterion*, is located adjacent to the temple. Artemis, dwelling in the heart of the community from the late fifth century onwards, may well have provided the focus of such urbanisation.[42]

But the earlier life of the sanctuary suggests that even Artemis's classical clientele may not have been primarily the *polis* that had developed about her. While the goddess clearly organized a set of people around herself in the archaic period, it is much less clear who this community was. The fine archaic dedications suggest that Artemis did look after the introduction of girls into a community sufficiently integrated for its members to invest in costly jewellery boxes as a marker of status, but it is doubtful whether this community was confined to the valley, let alone what would later constitute the city of Lousoi. Indeed, when one looks at Artemis' material belongings over time, the impression is that bronzen proxeny and *theorodokia* decrees, issued for citizens of other nearby cities, took the place of the gracious animal bronzes that the earlier worshipping community had conveyed across the Peloponnese as a gift to the goddess. We have to look further afield and for other forms of social groupings to make sense of Artemis' worshippers certainly in the archaic period, which must also be the time to which Bacchylides' ode refers.[43]

[40] I am thinking of studies such as Morgan (1997), (2001), introducing her approach in (2003), and the work of the *Copenhagen Polis Centre*, for the conceptual underpinnings of which see the introduction to *Inventory* by M. H. Hansen. Specifically for Akhaia and Arkadia see Morgan (1991); (1999); (2000) 205–11.

[41] Voyatzis (1999), and 148 on Lousoi. Nielsen (2002) esp. 165, 195–6, 564–5 on Lousoi's status as a *polis*.

[42] The so-called *bouleuterion* is of 4th or 3rd-cent. date: Reichel–Wilhelm (1901) 20–2. The goddess appears whenever Lousoi is mentioned in the literary sources. There is at present no account relating centres of public display to urban religious topography. Smaller places seem to have had only one or at most two places where decrees were put up for viewing. One of the motives for using extra-urban or suburban sanctuaries for that purpose may have been frequency of visitation, as, for instance, is true of Artemis Amarynthia in Euboia, and of the Asklepieion in Kos. The phrase ἐν τῷ ἐπιφανεστάτῳ τόπῳ 'in the most conspicuous place' used sometimes seems to support that hypothesis.

[43] *IG* v.2 387–96 has proxenies from the 5th cent. onwards (see Perlman (2000) 158–60; older dedications are nos. 397–410).

It appears that Artemis did provide a social order, yet beyond the local and in a community that escapes precise definition and probably derives its power from this elusiveness. To anticipate the line of reasoning to be unfolded, it will emerge that the open texture of her worshipping group in this period is also what makes possible her interpretation as a 'goddess of the Akhaians'. For it is becoming an increasingly serious possibility that this Artemis had a catchment area consisting of a number of places scattered through the locality's extended neighbourhood, and that the cult marked both a meeting point for communities from what we identify as Akhaia on the one hand, Arkadia and the Argolid on the other.[44] Artemis is located at the boundary of the later regions on an important route leading into the inner Peloponnese.[45] It is along this route that we have to assume that some of the Argive and Lakonian pottery travelled on its way to the Akhaian coast. Arkadian and Akhaian dialect mix in the later epigraphic record, suggesting that Artemis brought together the interior and the coast.[46] Of the few early inscriptions pertaining to the cult, two seem to come from neighbouring Kynaitha (Kalavryta), and one presumably found near the shrine regulates a kind of border conflict probably between the early fifth-century sanctuary and a city at the Akhaian coast, also indicating a wider range of people honouring the goddess and anticipating the series of international decrees.[47] The high quality of the dedications, coming from a variety of artistic environments, makes better sense in this light—these are traces of prestigious visitors who thought carefully about what to give to Artemis at what expense. Likewise, if the shrine became an *asylon* of international reputation in Hellenistic times, this perhaps responds to her being a traditional focus for a cult community that went beyond the valley (Map 6.1).[48]

A positioning in such a wider geographical dynamic is attractive in the light of another Artemisian cult also sitting right in the midst of the rocky stretch of

[44] Early graves at Kalavryta and Manesi (*c*.700 BC) indicate previously unknown communities in the area: Morgan (1997) 189–91; (1999) 418–20 and notes. De Polignac (1995) 37–8 already suspected (without citing material evidence) that inhabitants of nearby Kleitor and Pheneos were regulars at Lousoi, though traces of urbanization here are just as scarce. For the idea of a wider catchment area of Lousoi (albeit perhaps too wide) see already Tausend (1993) 23–6 and Nielsen–Roy (1998) 23–7. There is also some evidence for the site being frequented by the whole valley, but these testimonies are too sparse to build on. I am told that very recent archaeological findings add to the growing popularity of this idea.

[45] For the road system in this part of the Peloponnese see Tausend (1999); for the idea of cult places of Artemis as stops on the way (1995*a*) and below.

[46] For the epigraphic evidence: Jeffery, *JHS* 68 (1949) 30–1, quoting also *IG* v.2 360 (Pheneos) and Paus. 6.12.8–9. The travelling Peloponnesian pottery: Morgan (1997) 190.

[47] Inscriptions supposed to have been found near Kalavryta: *IG* v.2 397, 401. On the possible border conflict (*IG* v.2 410 = *SEG* xi 1121) see *LSAG* 224, Akhaia no. 8 (*c*.500–475 BC); Morpurgo Davies, *PP* 19 (1964) 351 on the curious combination of Arkadian dialect and Akhaian script. Neighbouring Kleitor is associated with the Proitids: n. 34 above.

[48] Particularly close links appear with the cities of later Akhaia: the 4th-cent. and later Hemerasia festival's first victor was someone from Aigion (*IG* v.1 1387). A citizen of Pharai was made *proxenos* and *theorodokos* at Lousoi (*IG* v.2 392 with Perlman (2000) 157–60, 242). For the proxenies see n. 43 above.

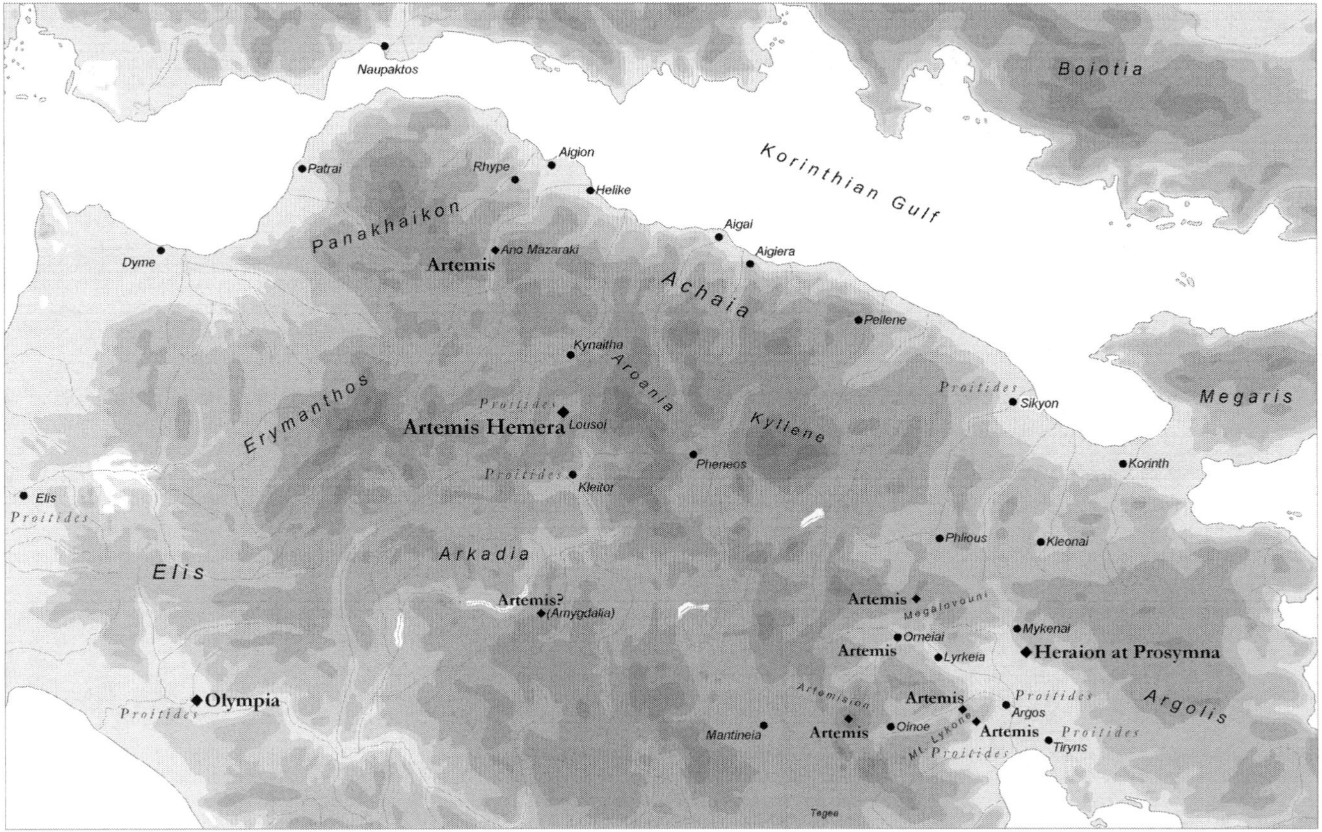

Map 6.1 The northern Peloponnese, revealing a 'network' of cults of Artemis through the mountains, and the journeys of the Proitids. Created from digital map data © Collins Bartholomew (2004) 2007

the Korinthian Gulf's hinterland. The spectacular eighth-century temple site at Ano Mazaraki (Rakita) stands 1,150 m high up on Mount Panakhaikos in the most rugged part of the Peloponnese, some 35 km south of Patras and two valleys to the west from Lousoi.[49] An impressive votive deposit, which shares some features with that at Lousoi, intimates that this was not the marginal cult its modern inaccessibility suggests, but rather a busy place in contact with Korinth, Argos, and the northern Peloponnese and a world that was mobile enough to carry exotica up into the mountains as a gift to Artemis.[50] This sanctuary, too, lay on major routes linking the coast with the interior, on the road leading from Aigion into the inner Peloponnese and watching over the north–south transportation route along the Selinous river corridor; it has even been suspected that this road continued all the way to Lousoi so that one could easily move between the two mountainous regions guarded by Artemis.[51] Perhaps, therefore, the two mountainous shrines of Artemis belonged to the same religious system; on this interpretation, Lousoi and Ano Mazaraki functioned as places of interaction between the people in this mountainous region and those who travelled with their goods from the coastal plains to the interior.[52] Indeed, this is exactly what Artemis in this part of the world seems to have been doing more generally: Lousoi and Ano Mazaraki are the identified and excavated larger sites, but shrines of Artemis, significantly, were also calling points on other central routes in the inner Peloponnese.[53] In particular, at all road entries and passes connecting the Argive plain with the Peloponnesian interior, on the route to Tegea, to Mantineia, and further north to Lyrkeia towards Sikyon and Phleious, Artemis sat on top of

[49] The site, now the oldest monumental sacred building in Akhaia, had been known since 1972 but, having been excavated much later, has only recently entered scholarly discussion. See Petropoulos (2002) for a summary discussion. The temple was first excavated in 1979, 1982, and 1984 (Papapostolou (1982); Petropoulos (1987–8)), then again in 1989–90 (Petropoulos 1992–3)); and in 1996 (Petropoulos (1997)). Petropoulos (1997) and (2001) for *Artemis Aontia* ('who blows'?). The significance of Ano Mazaraki was first noticed by Osanna (1996) 303; Morgan (1997) 190–1; cf. Morgan (1999) 416–20; Hall and Morgan (1996) 177–9; Voyatzis (1999) 135–6; Morgan (2000) 206–7; Mazarakis Ainian (1997) 120. The temple was destroyed in the 4th cent. though dedications continue; material traces reach to the 4th cent. AD. For the finds' close similarities with those of Lousoi see Schauer (1998); (2001).

[50] Cf. most recently Petropoulos (2002); 148 on scarabs. Hall and Morgan (1996) 178, with nn. 70, 71 cite local wares close to that found at Aigion, Lousoi, and Delphi; orthodox and Thapsos Korinthian imports; and Argive ware, probably travelling north from Arkadia. Voyatzis (1990) Ch. 3 suspects that Argive ware would have arrived from Argos on the inland route between the mountains rather than from the coast, where no Argive finds have been made so far.

[51] Petropoulos (2002) 156–7 and (1997) 172–5 for the road. Mackil (2003) 264 reckons that 'from the southernmost part of the Selinous river corridor it is a relatively straight shot across high planes to Kynaitha'.

[52] Morgan (1997) 190–1 discusses the proximity of the two shrines. This interpretation does not necessarily exclude strong links to Aigion: Petropoulos (2002); Hall and Morgan (1996) 179.

[53] A further possible cult of Artemis in an Arkadian mountain valley is that at Glanitsa, modern (A)Mygdalia: Metzger (1940–1); Jost (1985) 217–19. I owe this reference to Scott Scullion.

mountains or at the side of roads, a divine reference in an interconnected landscape (Map 6.1).[54]

The question of how a shrine such as that at Lousoi was run, gathering as it did a relatively mobile and presumably constantly changing worshipping community, must for the moment remain obscure. In any case, as the working of the sanctuary was perturbed, this caused great apprehension. It is here that Artemis' sacred flock trots back into the picture, as if worshipping community and divine herd were intrinsically interlinked (as I already suggested is expressed in the myth of the Proitids). This sacred herd was the Aitolians' target in the valley on their raiding tour through this part of the Peloponnese in the mid-third century BC. They even made a detour to Lousoi, having destroyed Kynaitha and aiming for Kleitor. In the first instance, some of the temple's sacred furniture was sold to the vandals and the herd preserved; but not much later the Aitolians vented on the animals their rage for having failed to capture neighbouring Kleitor. If this carnage still upset the Greeks decades later as a particularly savage crime that only the barbarous Aitolians could commit, this indicates that more was at stake at this sanctuary than the killing of animals alone: quite probably the Aitolians had destroyed the hallmark of a much wider social network protected by the goddess. The 'sacred herd' represented a flock of people or communities who saw themselves jointly guarded by Artemis.[55]

The bucolic imagery, Artemis 'Mistress of Animals' and huntress gathering worshippers in a 'sacred herd' around her, should therefore be looked at seriously. Pastoral imagery is not unique to Lousoi's Artemis: aetiologies for the folk-genre of the *βουκολικά*, the cattle-herd song for Artemis, attribute to actual performances (often exercised in competition) the role of assimilating herdsmen into a community, and associate the practice with the transition from nomadism and transhumance to settled life and agriculture, a more integrated form of 'community'.[56] The aetiologies with their implicit *Kulturtheorie* should not be taken literally: they conceive of a change of economic and possibly political status of these herdsmen, in a process intimately linked to worship of the goddess and

[54] This is an interesting, as yet underexplored phenomenon: cf. Fossey (1987); Tausend (1995*a*). Artemis links the Argolid with Arkadia in at least five attested cults: Paus. 2.24.5: a mountain-top shrine on Mt Lykone and one at the foot of the mountain on the road between Argos and Tegea (Kophiniotes, *AJA* 4 (1888) 360; 5 (1889) 101–2; Fraser on 210 with bibliography and synopsis of findings). 2.25.1–3: the route leading west to Mantineia, passing through Oinoa, above which was Mt Artemision, which derived its name from a mountain-top shrine of Artemis (possibly to be identified, or at least linked, with a precinct found on the upper south-west slopes of this range: *JHS* 10 (1889) 273). 2.25.4–6: the route to the north west, passing Lyrkeia, to Orneiai, where Artemis had a shrine and a *xoanon*. Artemis Oraia dwelled on the west side of Megalovouni, in a badly researched shrine with 6th–3rd-cent. sculptures, confirmed in a Hellenistic inscription: Mitsos (1949).

[55] Plb. 4.18.9 ff. Sinn (1992) discusses the passage.

[56] These aetiologies of song are beautifully discussed in Frontisi-Ducroux (1981), who sees them as documenting a change of economic, and possibly political, status of flock-herds (from 'alterité' to 'identité', i.e. civic identity, esp. 35–6), a kind of social metaphor.

itself a kind of metaphor for a level of social organization and integration in her catchment area. Three spectacular early archaic granary models unearthed not at the Lousoi temple, but at Artemis' shrine in Ano Mazaraki, are perhaps an impressive illustration of this issue. If in general Artemis' gifts are often baked goods in the shape of animals, this too merges in the votive object the transition from one social state to another.[57] Bestiality and civic order are indeed close associates in Arkadia: intriguingly, an often-cited passage in Polybius reprimands the Kynaithians, neighbours of Lousoi in the adjacent valley, for their degradation into savagery because of a neglect of *mousike*: the practice so characteristic of the Arkadians, who needed it to achieve some form of civilization amongst the inhabitants of a difficult landscape which favoured individualism and 'bestiality'.[58] To single out one city like this suggests that coordination between the different people of mountainous Arkadia was an important concern; animal-like savagery was in deeply felt opposition to social integration.

Mobile flocks from Khelmos and elsewhere promenading through the Lousoi valley might well have provided the specific imagery for our Artemis Hemera turning her clientele from 'savages' to 'gentle'.[59] That said, it is unlikely that it was literally herdsmen who dedicated to Artemis her well-forged likeness of the Prince Iron-Heart coiffure (Fig. 6.2 above), which rather points to a worshipping group that was itinerant in a more complex way. The sanctuary's mediatory role, between people in the coastal and mountainous areas as well as further into the Peloponnese, makes it likely that Artemis surveyed a network of social relations in a wider, relatively loosely defined catchment area. Her complementary epithets of *agrotera* and *hemera* symbolize the fluidity as much as the natural instability of a worshipping group going beyond the *polis*, but also beyond other forms of social organization: while we can be fairly sure that no such regional definitions existed much before the classical period, Lousoi's (like Ano Mazaraki's) location in between the later regions of Akhaia and Arkadia (Akhaia and Elis) even in later times lends it an ethnic indeterminacy, even ambiguity. It is not a coincidence, therefore, that the cult attracts the myth of the Proitids wandering across the northern Peloponnese in an aetiology that delineates a worshipping community cutting across boundaries and curiously overlapping with the set of geographical connections established by the archaeological material found at Lousoi (Map 6.1).

[57] The 8th-cent. granaries: Petropoulos (1987–8) 88–90; (2002) 150 and pl. 3.4. The *patisserie* is normally thought to represent substitutes for animal victims—which does not contradict the idea put forward here: the point of offerings is precisely that they are polyvalent and have no clearly defined meaning. The community of Ano Mazaraki to the present day retains a tradition of (ordered) transhumance, moving to Kato Mazaraki in the plain south of Patras during winter.

[58] Plb. 4.20–1. The word used for the Kynaithians' decadence (21.6) is ἀπεθηριώθησαν ('turned into beasts'); the observation belongs to Frontisi-Ducroux (1981).

[59] Sinn (1992) presupposes the use of the valley for pasturage.

Artemis at Metapontion

The idea of Artemis *Potnia theron* gathering the surrounding *eskhatiai* into her *khoros* and cutting across the boundaries of a territory and of what was to become an ethnic identity also enables us to forge the link between the goddess of the Arkadian highlands and Artemis at Metapontion dwelling gently between the agricultural plains and the low hills in Metapontine territory. Like her Lousian counterpart, this Artemis, too, has suffered from bucolic associations suggested by her 'Arkadian' surroundings, though the atmosphere at San Biagio could not be more different from that at the deity's home in the mountains. And, as in the case of Artemis at Lousoi, the romanticizing interpretation cannot be maintained. Hunting imagery at Metapontion, too, expresses Artemis' activity. But again this imagery does not literally represent her competences. Rather, it keeps together a fluid worshipping group which, similar to that at Lousoi, retains a certain ethnic indeterminacy.

The late archaic and classical *polis* of Metapontion is the furthest east of the 'Akhaian' cities lining the inner coast of Italy's foot. The city lay a little inland from the Ionian Sea, between the two rivers of the Basento (ancient Casuentus) and Bradano. The precinct of Artemis has been identified with a complex of buildings at San Biagio della Venella, located about seven kilometres inland from the coast and the ancient city. Artemis dwelled here on the river's left bank on a low elevation, overlooking the flow of the river. Her ἄλσος ('precinct') was a marshy area with a number of springs, to the present day the only local source of water. The archaic sanctuary literally stood submerged in this swamp, and the main temple was erected over a central well. A small seventh-century building was enlarged in the sixth century, and three disproportionately wide basins lay in front of the temple and caught the water from the springs nearby (Fig. 6.4).[60]

With one exception to be discussed below (pp. 308–10), there is no non-archaeological evidence for Artemis' cult at Metapontion other than Bacchylides' song. The bulk of votives dates to the middle of the seventh century BC and later. Several thousand terracotta statuettes seem to depict the deity herself, though their décor is peculiar: often winged, attired with a group of little round discs spherically enveloping the statuettes' head, the principal template is unique bar a few exemplars elsewhere in and around Metapontion (Fig. 6.5). A series of monumental figures of this type—unusually magnificent large statuettes—readily identify this goddess as a πότνια θηρῶν.[61] The iconographic formula of the 'Mistress of Animals' occurs all over the Mediterranean and persists from Minoan art to the Roman imperial period: a winged divinity holding, or accompanied by,

[60] The principal reports on the site are Adamesteanu (1974) 55–64; *AttTar* 1964, 127–72; Osanna (1992) 48–52. A black-figure vase with a graffito Ἀρτέμιδι (Naples, Coll. Santangelo 99) confirms the existence of a cult of hers at Metapontion (quoted by Maehler (1982–97) i. 195).

[61] See Olbrich (1979) for the statuettes, esp. 150–60, pls. 24–32 for the best impression of the *potnia* figures; a summary account in (1976).

Figure 6.4 Remains of Artemis' shrine at S. Biagio plunged into a swamp amidst gentle hills and agricultural plains 11 km north of Metapontion; the sixth-century refurbishment included enclosing the water sources in three large basins

Figure 6.5 Sample from several hundred terracotta votive figurines of the type 'Potnia Theron' (here 550–500 BC and later) from S. Biagio della Venella: female busts of 'Ionian' type with vase-shaped high polos, crowned; wings decorated with disks or serpent on the shoulders, sometimes accompanied by an animal

two beasts (most often lions or birds).[62] Though in the rest of the Mediterranean the *potnia* is matched with various goddesses, mainland Greece almost unanimously identifies her as Artemis, as is the case already in the *Iliad.* A softened version of the type survives at Metapontion in the many later wingless figurines whose hands still have a secure grip on two animals' necks; still later figurines come merely to hold tamed Artemisian animals in their laps—encapsulating at once the 'wild' and the 'civilized' in the sense described for Artemis of Lousoi.[63]

The cult of S. Biagio della Venella used to be cited amongst several extra-urban shrines in the city's territory, the most conspicuous of which are the *Tavole Palatine*, the temple of Hera to the east of the classical city. Indeed, Metapontion's territory (the *khora*) served as a showcase for the idea that 'border' sanctuaries functioned as territorial signposts for colonial settlers, that is to say investment in, and representations of, the space that had become a city's territory.[64] Local surveys in the hinterland of Metapontion conducted in the meantime, however, have seen more and more rural shrines popping up at regular intervals of about three kilometres along the valleys of the Basento and Bradano rivers. An array of individual farmsteads dividing the territory in the sixth century and intriguingly changing into regularly sized allotments around 500 BC, at first sight suggests that the scattered 'rural' shrines served these social units, possibly larger family groups with shared social and economic interests.[65] The hypothesis of the shrines' generic function in the rural countryside reflects their almost identical appearance: they are all of the same size, spatial arrangements prove similar, and their almost indistinguishable votive material, often including dedications for a range of female deities, suggest that they satisfied a variety of needs on the part of their worshippers.[66]

Such an interpretation takes careful account of the settlement structures in sixth-century and later Metapontion, but it leaves the very early history of the city out of the picture. This early history can be reconstructed, visibly shaping as it does the changing worshipping communities of Metapontian Artemis. For the *polis* of Metapontion as we have come to picture it—its fine *agora* spreading out from which is the neat grid-pattern of the classical *polis*—is a late creation, dating to no earlier than the mid-sixth century. The more recent finds beneath the late

[62] Andersen (1992–3). In Italy in particular, a πότνια occurs at Pyrge (Astarte-Aphrodite (architectural terracottas)), Francavilla (Athena), and certain places in Campania. See now the volume by Hägg–Laffineur (2001).

[63] *Il.* 21.470–1. See *LIMC* viii suppl. (1997) 1021–2 s.v. Potnia. Spartan Orthia's iconography is very comparable and remains difficult to explain. Lead figurines similar to the famous Spartan ones have also been disovered at S. Biagio: Olbrich (1976) 403; cf. *AttTar* 1964 tav. iv.1. Note Artemis *agrotera* near Taras: F. G. Lo Porto, *AttTar* 11 (1971), 500–2; 12 (1972) 375 and Lo Porto (1987).

[64] De Polignac (1995) Ch. 3, esp. 100, 106–18; orig. (1984) Ch. 3, esp. 103, 108–18. The theory has its forerunners in Vallet (1968).

[65] Carter (1994) esp. 180–3, with a helpful map; Osanna (1992) 56–72; between these allotments are a number of smaller shrines inland. A gradual expansion of territory indicated by the establishment of cults is ruled out by the non-sequential foundation dates of the cult places.

[66] It has been suggested that the cult at S. Biagio combines aspects of Artemis, Athena, Aphrodite, and Demeter: Olbrich (1979) 86–92.

archaic city suggest that the splendid 'colonial' sixth-century city is preceded by what is cautiously termed 'pre-colonial' settlements going back to as early as the ninth century ('villages'). These include the often-discussed early eighth-century site at Incoronata Greca, located at a distance of about seven kilometres west of the later urban centre, on a high cliff on the right bank of the Basento river and in direct line of sight from San Biagio. Since its discovery, the interpretation of the site has mirrored the ever-changing interpretations of the relationship between Greeks and non-Greeks, and whether Greeks, local people, or both lived here is impossible to say. In the more recent history of the excavations, similar contemporary settlements have been uncovered, under the colonial agora in the so-called Località Andrisani, as well as just beneath Incoronata Greca itself, at a yet earlier site, so-called Incoronata Indigena. Building structures here closely resemble those of Incoronata Greca, and the associated material, both Greek and local, suggests that all three sites were in close contact with each other. Surveys have also yielded considerable amounts of Greek and indigenous ware scattered in the surrounding countryside. Though fresh discoveries in this highly active field of archaeological exploration could alter the picture again, one relevant new insight is that all these 'pre-colonial' sites, the Località Andrisani beneath the later Greek city and the two sites at Incoronata Greca and Indigena, were settlements in one way or another aligned to each other.[67]

Artemis' lifetime coincides with that of these villages; her worship starts earlier than the evidence for the later 'colonial' city. She joins up with Apollo Lykeios in the city and the earliest traces beneath the divinity owning so-called Temple C as the first shrines in the entire area, built at some time around 650 BC—a whole century earlier than the gridded city of Metapontion. All these cults yield the same kind of early votive figurines contemporary with, and similar to, the material of the three villages. The existing shrines therefore can be seen to have attracted the same, or at least very similar, groups of 'pre-colonial' visitors.[68]

While the other two shrines are located near one of the uncovered settlements, our Artemis at S. Biagio does not seem to have been closer to one of the villages than to another. Her situation is thus not so very different from that of Artemis Hemera at Lousoi. Artemis at S. Biagio may also have served as the focal point for

[67] Incoronata Greca: Orlandini (1992); (1986); (1998); Adamesteanu (1974) 57 (mixed settlement, at most a Greek component). The earliest material is local (early 9th to late 8th cent.), the village was rebuilt on the older structures towards the end of the 8th cent., with prevailingly, but not exclusively, east Greek material between 700 and 625 BC. Incoronata Indigena: De Siena (1990) esp. 72 (cf. De Siena 1986*a*, *b*); the finds here are more local than Greek. Località Andrisani: De Siena (1986*a* and *b*); also (1990) 87, similarly, with indigenous material besides the prevailing Greek. According to De Siena (1990), there was a turning point in the life of the villages at around 700 BC when a road was built to make later Metapontion the centre of the group, but this remains uncertain. The literature on the subject is vast; among the surveys of the archaeology of Metapontion I have found helpful, Osanna (1992) 39–55 (40–3 on the three villages) and Carter (1994); De Siena (1998) for the layout of the colonial city.

[68] For Artemis's figurines see p. 291–4 above. The earliest Daedalic figurines for Apollo are dated to just after 640 BC. See Carter (1994) 168–71 and table 7.1.

a worshipping community dispersed in villages or small groups of houses in the countryside. Stray finds of the same nature as this early material suggesting more such dispersed settlements in the area make this idea even more likely.[69] One should also note that Metapontian Artemis too was situated on a river and a major communication route with the interior and, beyond, the Tyrrhenian coast.[70] Though the level of coordination beyond the common features of the different groups of settlements must remain obscure, it seems that the shrine of our *Πότνια θηρῶν* was a place of interaction for at least three (and probably more) hamlets, drawing together the dispersed villages in common worship, so as to rescue also this 'Mistress of animals and nature' from a remorselessly bucolic interpretation. Artemis at Metapontion, too, seems to have gathered her sacred herd into her shrine, perhaps even a mixed worshipping community in an environment of mixed Greek and non-Greek culture: in such a way is expressed what in the case of the mainland Greek cult integrates regional diversity and maintains a certain ethnic indeterminacy.[71]

Now this is the story of Artemis in the pre-colonial settlement. Bacchylides' myth, however, relates this Artemis to the archaic city of Metapontion. The sites of Incoronata Greca, Incoronata Indigena, and (presumably also) the Andrisani complex were razed to the ground in around 640/30 BC. Whether, and in what measure, they were immediately replaced is a matter of debate: charred remains have been discovered under some of the public buildings of the later colonial so-called Akhaian city, but we must wait until the middle of the sixth century for substantial investment in public structures and urbanization. So while the newcomers might well have had a share in destroying the pre-colonial settlements, they took some time before emerging as the impressively organized archaic Metapontion.[72]

Artemis at S. Biagio, however, survives all these events; in fact, she is a striking element of continuity in the constantly self-renewing settlement story of Metapontion. Though she is eventually moved from her role as focal point for the scattered communities to the margins of the new city, she is still not a rural deity. The sheer quantity of sixth-century votive material found at her cult site suggests that she went on to fulfil a major function in the archaic *polis* too. Great investment in her shrine occurs in the sixth century, at the same time as the new city comes to life. A high-quality roller-stamp frieze of epic scenes links her to

[69] Carter (1994) 174 n. 25: at Pantanello (c.3 km east of S. Biagio), and near Cozzo Presepe.

[70] Lepore (1977) on the importance of such routes between the Ionian and Tyrrhenian Seas.

[71] Carter (2004) puts renewed emphasis on the mixed environment of the pre-colonial Metapontine *khora*. Figurines of the S. Biagio type have also been discovered at an early to mid-6th cent. deposit at Incoronata 'Greca' (382). Note that the tradition of singing 'boukolika' is particularly pronounced in neighbouring Sicily: *Σ* Theocr. *prol.* pp. 2–3 Wendel (quoted in Frontisi-Ducroux (1981) 30–1).

[72] See Carter (1994) for the debate over the 'gap' in between the pre-colonial settlements and the colonial city. The more orthodox view is that the pre-colonial settlements were destroyed by arriving 'Akhaians' (widely assumed after De Siena's (1986) discoveries). Cf. Bottini and Guzzo (1986); Osanna (1992); Bottini (1986) 101 for the chronology.

Metapontion and other places in southern Italy.[73] Perhaps it is her accepted role as a gathering force in the pre-colonial settlements that turns her into a divinity of continued importance? Indeed, in now turning to the 'Akhaian' dimension of her cult, we shall see that Bacchylides' song suggests that Artemis was central to the formation of the sixth-century settlers' identity and took part in the most significant and lasting transformation in the history of Metapontion and southern Italy. Paradoxically, the cult's continuity is our best evidence for change in the area, functioning as the hub around which political developments gather and their story is rewritten. The goddess' life story gives striking insights into the role cults played in shaping the continually changing identities of Greek settlements abroad. That she turns into an 'Akhaian' goddess is a result of this process.

3. TOWARDS EPIC IDENTITY IN SOUTHERN ITALY

Bacchylides' myth claims that it was the 'Akhaians dear-to-Ares' (*ἀρηΐφιλοι Ἀχαιοί*) who brought Artemis to Metapontion, that she voyaged to Italy with the Greek heroes returning from Troy. The cult aetiology forms part of the *Nostoi* traditions, the set of myths telling of the Akhaian warriors' travels after the completed feat. Many heroes never made it back to their home cities, or found these in great disorder after ten years of absence. So they continued further west, settling many places especially in Italy.

Bacchylides' ode forms the first piece of evidence for 'Akhaian origins' of Metapontion, indeed for any 'Akhaians' in southern Italy. By this name ancient and modern scholars understand the series of large cities along the Ionian coast in the inlet of Italy's foot, a crescent extending from Kaulonia in the south via Kroton and Sybaris to Metapontion in the north, and framed by the two 'Dorian' bulwarks of Lokroi and Taras. 'Akhaia' also includes Poseidonia (Paestum) and other cities on the Tyrrhenian seaboard. All these cities would come to claim origins in the region of Akhaia in the Peloponnese. Evoking their namesake, the epic Akhaians, to bolster a shared ancestry therefore might not at first sight seem a great surprise. Their alleged relations in the Peloponnese did just the same at around the same time, with a pompous collective dedication at Olympia in the early fifth century, claiming the whole cast of Akhaian heroes as their own (Maps 6.2 and 6.3).[74]

But things are not that straightforward. An Artemis landing in Metapontion as a result of the Akhaian *nostos* touches on contested territory. The concept of 'Akhaian settlements' and 'Akhaianness' was and is problematic for the ancients just as it continues to puzzle the moderns. When, why, and whether in concert

[73] Mertens-Horn (1992) for the frieze with epic imagery; cf. also the richly decorated louteria: Ugolini (1983).

[74] For the geographical confines of Italian Akhaia see Str. 6.1.10–15; cf. Plin. *NH* 3.95 (Magna Graecia). The Akhaian statue group at Olympia, dated between 469 and 456 BC: Paus. 5.25.8–10.

either the southern Italians or the northern Peloponnesians began to give themselves the ethnic label 'Akhaian' is unclear; and whether there is any precise, historically verifiable relationship between the two Akhaians at all remains a question one would like to give a final answer to. While cities and groups of cities established in the archaic period, from the eighth century onwards, conceive of themselves as foundations of other cities, such a relation is not usually expressed in ethnico-regional terms, that is to say referring to future *ethnos*-states: we do not know of 'Boiotian', 'Aitolian', or 'Thessalian' foundations. The fact that there is no evidence for any region defined as 'Akhaia' in the Peloponnese until well into the fifth century does not make this problem easier.[75]

What follows will suggest that playing on the ambiguity of 'Akhaia' in mid-fifth-century Metapontion in the song goes to the heart of the delicate issue of competing ethnic identities in southern Italy. This issue had involved many places through the sixth century, and continued to an equal extent in the fifth. It was then called upon in the contemporary political situation when the southern Italian Greek cities faced, among other things, the Athenians' keen interest in the area. Bacchylides' *Ode 11*'s invocation of an Akhaian goddess participates in a long and contested process of the formation of an Akhaian identity in southern Italy, by no means completed by the time of the song's performance somewhere in the first half of the fifth century. The ode operates in a historical climate where being Akhaian was only one of the many possible identities one could assume. What stance it implied was deeply intertwined with the relations between the *poleis* in southern Italy and their complicated settlement history. Metapontion probably had a key position in this process because of its proximity to Dorian Taras, and Artemis herself was arguably central. But there is good reason to believe that what evidence clusters around this city is merely symptomatic of the wider issues enveloping southern Italy as a whole. I shall first sketch out the problems involved in the orthodoxy of an assumption of 'Akhaian' origins for these cities before embarking on the more complicated task of situating the ode's claims in the vibrant fifth-century Italian context.

Two Akhaias

The evidence for a historical relationship between Akhaia in the West and Akhaia in the Peloponnese at an early period is slim. Very recent research has started to look beyond the immediate borders of the later region of Akhaia into the wider patterns of activity in the Korinthian Gulf for an understanding of the connections between southern Italy and mainland Greece. Some of this can be fruitfully

[75] The literature on this subject is immense and no attempt can be made here to cite even just a fraction of what has been written. Some standard treatments are Mazzarino (1964); Goegebeur (1985); Guzzo (1987); Giangiulio (1989) 161–82; Mele (1995); Moscati Castelnuovo (1989); Hall and Morgan (1996) is fundamental for the archaeology; E. Greco (2002); *Inventory* s.v.; still very useful is Bérard (1957) 323–83. Cf. now Papadopoulos (2001), (2005). La Torre (2002) 35–47, 355–86 provides an excellent up-to-date discussion of archaeology and history.

developed for the debate over Akhaian identity in Italy. But let us first lay out briefly the problem.

The literary traditions cited in support of Akhaian origins in the cities dotted along the narrow coastal strip of the southern Korinthian Gulf are late and ambiguous, offering only tenuous indications for why the Akhaian element should be privileged over a number of rivalling claims from other areas of Greece. Indeed, the pattern of co-settling in Italian Akhaia is extremely intricate and points to a variety of Greeks having come from all over the eastern half of the Mediterranean eager to find new homes in the West. For example, Troizenians had a share in the foundation of Sybaris but were later expelled, notably by 'Akhaians'.[76] Spartans are said to have intermingled at Kroton,[77] Rhodians to have helped at Sybaris and Siris, and Phokaians at Metapontion.[78] 'Dorians' tended to Poseidonia, a *khoros* of settlers joined by central Greek Lokrians, and so on and so forth.[79]

It is fitting that the Akhaian hero-founders are just as obscure, and only Myskellos of Rhype possesses an elaborate tale of errands to and from oracles and the city to be founded before landing at Kroton; for the rest, Sybaris' founder is known merely by his name *Ἶς* of Helike (and even this passage is corrupt and scholars argue about a more likely name for the inconspicuous oikist); a certain Typhon of Aigion is supposed to have founded Kaulonia.[80] Metapontion, incidentally, had no 'Akhaian' oikist at all, offering instead a plethora of competing founders. This confirms the problematic settlement story that I have started to uncover: we know of Metabos (no origins are named), of a certain Daulis of Krisa, a Phokian, and a certain Leukippos from Taras, himself a colonial. Even if we optimistically take obscurity of tradition as the best proof of the veracity of some of these cities' actual origins in Akhaia in the Peloponnese, one cannot avoid concluding that alleging Akhaian ancestry was at no time an easy claim to maintain amongst so many competing bids for a city's origins.[81]

Recent archaeological research and much survey work in Peloponnesian Akhaia has enormously enlightened the history of this neglected region, but it has not directly brought the two Akhaias closer to each other. Material culture does not permit the identification of a privileged relationship. Urbanization did not

76 Arist. *Pol.* 1303^{a}29; cf. Solin. 2.10; Str. 6.1.13; cf. [Scymn.] 340. *Σ* Theocr. 5.1 knows of a founder *Σύβαρις*.

77 Str. 6.1.11–12; Paus. 3.3.1: preliminaries of the battle at the Sagras between Lokroi und Kroton, the mythical rhetoric of which requires the Spartan relation (cf. Giangiulio (1989) 182–212, 238–59 and Malkin (1994) 62–4); see D.S. 8.32; Iust. 20.2.10–14. Herakles is also frequent founder of Kroton: D.S. 4.24.7; cf. Ov. *Met.* 15.12–59. Hall and Morgan (1996) 208 air the possibility that the Spartan origins date to Roman times when Taras was the only city still existing.

78 Str. 6.1.14–15.

79 [Scymn.] 249; Sol. 2.10; Nikandros *ap.* Ant. Lib. 8.

80 Kroton: Antiokhos *FGrH* 555 F 10 = Str. 6.1.12; Hippys of Rhegion *FGrH* 554 F 1; D.S. 8.17; Str. 6.2.4; 8.7.5; D.H. 2.59.3; Solin. 2.10; Zen. 3.42; [Scymn.] 325. On Myskellos and Battos of Kyrene see Giangiulio (1981); Sybaris: n. 76 above; Kaulonia: Str. 6.1.10; Paus. 6.3.12.

81 Metapontion: Antiokhos *FGrH* 555 F 12 = Str. 6.1.15 *contra* Ephor. *FGrH* 70 F 141 = Str. 6.1.15. Metabos in certain traditions counts as an Aiolian/Boiotian: pp. 317 ff. and n.130 below.

start in Peloponnesian Akhaia until at least the fifth century or even later, excluding the (anyway contested) possibility of settlements abroad resulting from individual *poleis*' collective decision-making. But there are also few traces of attempts at regionalization, territorially or institutionally, difficult though they would be to detect in the 'age of colonization'. That there was already from the eighth century BC onwards a concept of a region 'Akhaia' covering roughly the geography of classical Akhaia, let alone bearing an ethnico-regional dimension, is extremely difficult to prove, and so is, therefore, the early claim to shared ethnic origins in Peloponnesian Akhaia on the part of the Greek settlers in Italy.[82]

However, as some scant evidence suggests, Akhaia in the Peloponnese was not isolated even in pre-colonial times, boasting contacts with Italy and the Adriatic since the Late Bronze Age. More importantly, Akhaian activity in the western Korinthian Gulf circuit, notably the Ionian islands and Adriatic coast, stepping stones on the route to the West, seems to develop in parallel with the Korinthian. This is interesting, since Korinthian material spreads particularly in the eastern Gulf, including eastern Akhaia, which happens to include those localities who also boast what there is of the Akhaian founding traditions. Lately, continuity of Bronze Age trading networks has tentatively been postulated for the distribution of so-called early Iron Age 'Grey Akhaian' ware, found in the entire northern Peloponnese.[83] That Metapontion particularly should retain the memory of a Phokian founder (among other possibilities) hints that the personnel for the southern Italian settlements may well be found amongst the perpetrators of the overlapping Akhaian–Korinthian spheres of mobility, emanating from the Korinthian Gulf. One could therefore speculate that the claim of Akhaian origins for the cities in Italy worked in a memory of long-standing connections to this area (eventually projected on the historical region). But it remains unlikely that Akhaia in the sense of the later Peloponnesian region, the *ethnos*, let alone the *koinon*, was a known entity in the period when these *poleis* are supposed to have been founded.

[82] Hall and Morgan (1996), preceded and complemented by Morgan (1991); (2000) 205–11; (2002); Rizakis (2002); new directions are taken in Papadopoulos (2001), (2002). Recent updates on individual cities are Katsonopoulou (2002; Helike); Vordos (2002; Rhype); Bammer (2002; Aigeira, Hyperesia). The association of ethnic Akhaians with the region in the Peloponnese is widely thought to date to the middle of the 6th cent., though even this date rests on the hypothetic correlation of the Spartan set of 'repatriations' of heroic bones, of Orestes from Tegea, mentioned in Herodotus, and of his son from Helike in Akhaia, known from Pausanias. Morgan and Hall (1996); Giangiulio (1989) 208. Orestes: Hdt. 1.67–8; Paus. 3.3.6–7; 11.10; 8.54.4. Teisamenos: Paus. 2.18.6–8; 7.1.3 and 7–8; cf. Plb. 2.41.4–5 and Apollod. 2.8.3. The link was established by the fifth century: n. 74 above (statue group in Olympia); 6.17.6–7 calls the athlete Oibotas Ἀχαιός. *IG* i^3 174 (late 5th cent.) mentions the Akhaian shipowner Lykon. Morgan and Hall (1996) maintain that the term at this time has an ethnic but not (yet) a political dimension, i.e. of the later *koinon*.

[83] Cf. Morgan (2002); (2003) Ch. 5 for the overlap between Bronze Age and early Korinthian and Akhaian networks; Papadopoulos (2001) for the distribution of 'Grey Akhaian' ware in the entire northern Peloponnese and in Italy particularly in the Siritis. Th. 2.66.1 knows of the colonization of Zakynthos from Akhaia (Vermeule (1960) 20). Already Hall and Morgan (1996) note that Korinthian material spreads in eastern Akhaia at the same time as the Italian cities supposedly came into being.

So trying to establish the link between Peloponnesian and Italian Akhaia by the traditional means used to elucidate the relationship between 'mother' and 'daughter city' only drives the two further apart. In addition, while the Akhaians in the Peloponnese dwelled in—admittedly rather complex, and continually changing forms of—rural assortments until well into the classical period,[84] the new *poleis* in southern Italy were amongst the earliest in Greece to boast a complex organization of urban and collective space. And while the western Greeks maintained strong relations with old Greece, ostentatiously manifested at Olympia where Metapontion even had a treasury, Akhaia does not seem to have been amongst their customary Peloponnesian stop-offs. Indeed, one might argue that the splendour of the Italian cities lies in their cultural hybridity, famously pooling artistic traditions from all over Greece.[85] The religious topography of south Italy, finally, makes the lack of an intimate link to Peloponnesian Akhaia yet more evident, hitting the core of the problems investigated here. Often taken as a secure index of either a real or a laboured relation, the cultic landscape yields no such connection. The deities caring patently for public affairs in the northern Peloponnese seem to have been Artemis and Poseidon, followed by Zeus and Dionysos;[86] the western Akhaians prefer Hera over all the Olympians, but also cultivate Apollo and, probably, Athena.[87]

An epic pantheon

While Akhaians from the Peloponnese are hardly noticeable figures in southern Italy, the Akhaians who were supposed to have brought Artemis to Metapontion are rather more conspicuous. The *Nostoi* myths give epic Akhaians a strong presence in this area, as indeed in the whole of southern Italy. Because of their principally late and specifically Hellenistic and Roman attestation scholars until recently have tended either to dismiss these traditions as later invention, or to see them as entirely and truthfully pre-historic, transmitting the memory of a

[84] Hall and Morgan (1996) *passim*, esp. 214–15; Morgan (2000) 205–11.

[85] Urban Italy: e.g. Vallet (1968); De Polignac (1995); (1984); note e.g. the monumental gathering place in Metapontion, the *ekklesiasterion* dating to *c.*550 BC. Olympia was extremely popular with the western Greeks: Philipp (1994); Metapontion's treasury: Paus. 6.19.11. Much has been written on the southern Italian 'Mischkultur', cf. recently Mertens (2002) with all the earlier bibliography. The local script in southern Italy bears little resemblance to what we know of later Peloponnesian, if anything pointing rather towards Arkadia: *LSAG* 148–50.

[86] See Giangiulio (1989) 174–82; Osanna (1996); Giangiulio (2002). The main literary references are to cults of Poseidon Helikonios: Hdt. 1.148 (cf. *Il.* 8.203); Paus. 7.24.5 ff.; Zeus Homagyrios: Paus. 7.24.2, and Homarios: Plb. 2.39.6; 5.93.10; Liv. 38.30.2 etc.; variants of the epithet occur in Str. 8.7.3; 7.5. For Artemis see Osanna (1996) esp. 303–4 index.

[87] Giangiulio (1989) 175; cf. Graf (1982). For cults of Athena see Mertens-Horn (1992) 59–73; for Francavilla Marittima Papadopoulos (2003). On Hera and Apollo see below. The cult of Zeus Homarios, so important for the later Akhaian League, was established in Italy only after 450 BC (Italiot league between Kroton, Kaulonia, Sybaris at the Traeis: Plb. 2.39.6), allegedly on the model of Akhaia (Giangiulio (1989) 76–7 and n. 52).

Mycenaean presence in the area.[88] Bacchylides' fifth-century testimony, however, should long have made it clear that the tradition is pre-Hellenistic without necessarily being as old as Mycenaean. Dazzling finds of an archaic hero shrine for Diomedes on a set of islands off the Kroatian coast, to be identified with the 'Islands of Diomedes' long searched for elsewhere, confirm the antiquity of what Ibykos already knew about the 'odyssey' of this particular hero. In Italy, Diomedes proceeded from his islands to a spectacular career in Daunia, today's Apulia, where his steps can be traced at a temple of Athena *Ἀχαία* hosting his bronzen axes (*pelekeis*) and the weapons of his companions. The parallel with the island of Achilles in the Black Sea, frequented by Greeks of all sorts, perhaps even with the Ithaka cave, suggests that the Akhaian warriors' travels constituted a reference framework for many Greeks on tour from at least as early as the seventh century.[89]

While the *Nostoi* cover large chunks of the Greek West, they cluster in what was to become western Akhaia, and it seems that this area knew how to capitalize on the set of heroes for a shared identity (Map 6.2). Many epic warriors travel to Italy, featuring as prolific cult and city founders, and recipients of cult there. Philoktetes associates himself with both Sybaris and Kroton, where he placed Herakles' bow and arrows in the nearby temple of Apollo Alaios. Epeios, the maker of the Trojan Horse, left his building tools at a temple of Athena *Ἑλληνία* (!) in Lagaria, near Metapontion, a city which claimed a cult 'of the Neleids', that is to say of the sons of Nestor's father Neleus.[90] Diomedes moved on from Daunia to the Ionian coast and had cults at Metapontion and Thurioi. Strabo explains how the Greek warriors chanced upon the splendid beaches of Calabria: the captive Trojan women, so the story goes, burnt the ships in order to stop their nauseating travel, and so the heroes stayed. Later a number of Akhaians followed *κατὰ τὸ ὁμόφυλον* 'since they belonged to the same tribe', implying an ethnic

[88] Bérard (1957) 323–83 is still an excellent overall account of the literary traditions; cf. also Giannelli (1963) s.v. the individual heroes. For Philoktetes and Epeios see the volume by De la Genière (1991). Malkin (1998*b*) esp. Chs. 7 and 8 suggests how these myths work in very varied and individual historical contexts.

[89] Diomedes: Kirigin and Cace (1998); [Arist.] *Mir. Ausc.* 109 840b (Daunia); Ibykos *PMG* 294 = *Σ* Pi. *N.* 10.12 (Islands, Metapontion and Thurioi); Mimn. fr. 22 W; Lyc. 592–632 and *Σ*. Island of Achilles: Pi. *N.* 4.49–50; Eur. *Andr.* 1262; *IT* 436; Arrian, *Peripl.* p. E. 21; cf. Achilleion with the tumulus at the entrance to the Black Sea: Str. 13.1.32; Plin. *NH* 5.125; cf. Hdt. 5.94; the dromos of Achilles: Plin. *NH* 4.83. Ithaka: Malkin (1998*b*) Ch. 3.

[90] Str. 6.1.14–15. Philoktetes is worshipped in Sybaris (where he also died: [Arist.] *Mir.* 107 840^{a}); he settles the area of Cape Krimissa, where there is the temple of Apollo Alaios, and the city of Khone in the hinterland (Apollod. *FGrH* 244 F 167), Petelia (metropolis of the Khones: Str. 6.1.3; Sol. 2.10), and Makala, in Krotoniate territory. The Krotoniates appropriated him after Sybaris' destruction ([Arist.] loc. cit. = Thurioi in Iust. 20.1.16). For his death, tomb, and worship by the locals see Lyc. 911–13, 919–29. Epeios: founds Lagaria, located in the Siritis (Str. 6.1.14); Athena's temple at Gargeria/Lagaria, housing the horse-building equipment: Lyc. 930; Iust. 20.2.1; [Arist.] *Mir. Ausc.* 108 840^{a}; in *Σ Il.* 23.665 Epeios' mother is called Lagaria. On the reading of Athena's cult title see Malkin (1998*b*) 214. To later 'Dorian' myth-making seem to belong Menelaos at Siris (later Herakleia) and Lakinia (Lyc. 856–8), while at Kroton there are late cults of Achilles and Helen: Giannelli (1963) 148–51.

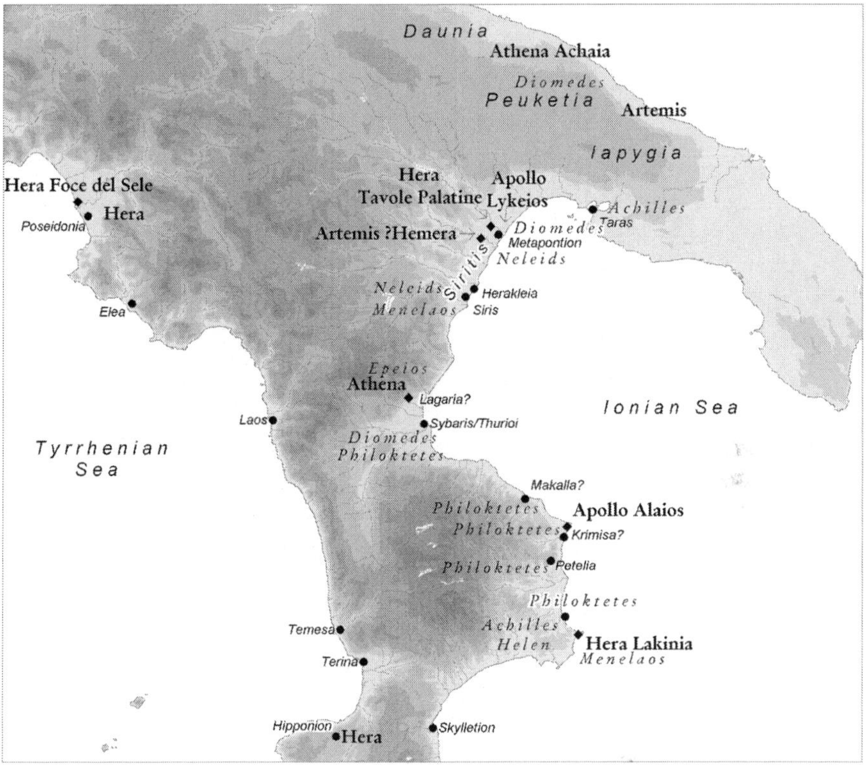

Map 6.2 Destinations of *Nostoi* heroes in southern Italy (selection). Created from digital map data © Collins Bartholomew (2004) 2007

aspect in this set of traditions, to which we shall return. This story, he says in a different passage, is told of many places in Italy.[91]

So Homeric heroes had been leaving signs of their presence for a while by Bacchylides' time, even if for the most part their itinerary and early chronology escapes us. Epic Akhaians in a sense also fashioned the local religious topography. The choices the southern Italian cities made for their gods reveal that the Argolid was perceived as the heartland of the epic Akhaians, and the western pantheon came to be modelled on this cultic landscape. As discussed in Chapter 3, Hera and Apollo enjoyed particular prominence back in what for later generations was the

[91] Str. 6.1.12, the etymological *aition* for the river Νέαιθος. All the cities in the area were 'named after the cities of mainland Greece'. Malkin's recent studies (1998*b*) 210–33; (1998*a*) have shown new ways of how these 'Akhaian' traditions should be seen as points of contact rather than conflict between Greeks and non-Greeks in the first instance; his paradigmatic case of Philoktetes then suggested that at a later stage these border-zone cults and figures were competed for amongst Greek cities themselves and bear accurate witness to their intra-Greek conflicts. Cf. with a similar line already Fusillo on Lyc. 984–92. For Diomedes see n. 89.

arena from within which the expedition to Troy was mounted. In the same way, southern Italians manifestly hark back to the Argolid in their investment in these deities (Map 6.3). Hera is altogether the most prominent divinity in Italian Akhaia, both as a poliadic and extra-urban deity. Similarities have long been observed between the rituals practised at the Argive Heraion and Akhaia's Hera Lakinia, about eleven kilometres south of Kroton, Akhaia's most conspicuous sanctuary and port of call for the whole area.[92] Hera has extra-urban shrines at Foce del Sele outside Poseidonia where she is Ἀργωνία (see below for the ambiguity of the epithet, alluding to both the Argive Hera and the Hera of the Argonauts), and at the *Tavole Palatine* at Metapontion, while inner-city temples stand out at Poseidonia, Metapontion, and Elea. In Roman times, the ritual for Hera at Phalerii was also modelled on that of the Heraion at Argos. A military character—a goddess supervising issues of war and battle just like the epic deity—is perhaps the most striking and pertinent feature of all Hera's cults, attested from archaic to Roman times.[93] Apollo's presence is slightly less pronounced, but nevertheless Philoktetes' Apollo Alaios dwelled in an archaic temple near Kroton. The god professed himself Lykeios at Metapontion as if he had been directly transplanted there from his shrine at Argos, about which we unfortunately know so little. Incidentally, this epithet for Apollo recurs at Sikyon in the eastern Korinthian Gulf.[94]

No doubt epic warriors had more gods than these. But the key point for us is that the cities of southern Italy construed an 'Akhaian' pantheon on the model of the historical distribution of cults in the Argolid in a way that was faithful to the phenomenon we have already aired in Chapter 3, that the prestigious ancestors who fought at Troy came to be entrenched in this part of Old Greece. Never mind that this was highly contested, as revealed by Sparta's sixth-century attempts to tie the Atreid family geographically to Lakonia. Even if this was a temporarily successful policy in the inner-Peloponnesian wrangle over leadership, the *onus probandi* lay on those who claimed that Agamemnon's story did *not* take place at

[92] The most thorough discussion of the cult is Giangiulio (1982), see also (1989) 178–81; (2002) 284–6; Camassa (1993) 573–83. Graf (1982) 165–71 makes the comparison with the Heraia at Prosymna (the 'Argive Heraion') and Samos. For Hera Lakinia's impressive gold treasury see Spadea (1996). For the Heraion at Prosymna in the Argolid see pp. 167, 174–7 above, cf. J. Hall (1995); Billot (1997). Often enough Hera Ἀργεία functions as an Akhaian or all-Greek patron goddess in the epics and elsewhere: e.g. *Il.* 4.8 (cf. 51–2); 5.908 (together with Athena Alalkomeneis). Cf. Eur. *Troad.* 23–5; in Hes. *Th.* 11–12 Ἀργεία is Hera's Olympic epithet; cf. *Phoronis* fr. 4 Bernabé: the Argive Kallithoe is κλειδοῦχος Ὀλυμπιάδος βασιλείης ('the priestess of the Queen of Olympus').

[93] Hera's dossier as a warrior is impressive: at Foce del Sele the goddess figures in a statuette type throwing the spear (23 pieces: G. Greco (1998) 50); the same type is found in Poseidonia-city: Cipriani (1997) 217–18 (cf. an inscribed disc: Guarducci, *Arch. Class.* 4 (1952), 150–2); at Metapontion: Olbrich (1979) 158, pl. 30 type A 124. At Lakinia Hera is Ὁπλοσμία: Lyc. 856–8; a recent discussion on the 'structural analogies' of Hera at Lakinia and the urban Hera shrine at Poseidonia is Giangiulio (2002) 294–6. The same deity rescues Diomedes in Daunia: Lyc. 614. Numerous weapon dedications occur at all shrines. At Argos the armed youth marched in the procession, and cavaliers competed in the *aspis* agon: Σ Pi. *O.* 7.152 (note the emphasis on weapon prizes).

[94] Apollo Alaios: n. 90 above; Apollo Lykeios: *IGASMG* iv 56 (= *IG* xiv 647), 57, 58, 60, 6th cent. BC; the *argoi lithoi* at Metapontion: Graf (1982) 171–4; Giangiulio (2002) 298–9. Sikyon's Apollo Lykeios: Paus. 2.9.7.

Map 6.3 Cities of 'Akhaia' in southern Italy and their 'epic' Pantheon. Created from digital map data © Collins Barholomew (2004) 2007

Mykenai.[95] By creating a past involving Akhaian heroes returning from Troy and adopting the cultic geography of their perceived core territory, Italy's Greeks crafted for themselves a valuable reference system of gods who would serve them just as they had served their ancestors, the Akhaians of the epics whose *nostos*, whose return journey, brought them to the West.[96]

[95] Ch. 3, 174–7 above.

[96] Papadopoulos (2002) argues in an interesting way that harking back to Bronze Age values is a feature of 'Akhaian' coinage of the time, featuring prestige items connected to the heroic world, i.e. tripods, cattle, barley, and the 'smiting god'.

Akhaian Proitids

How does Artemis' aetiology fit into all this? The Proitids' appearance at Metapontion intriguingly supports the idea that the southern Italians relied on the religious topography of the Homeric Akhaians for the creation of their mythical past. Fascinatingly, it also gives some details of how this link can be imagined to have come about. Proitos and his daughters are evidently not Homeric heroes; they precede the latter by several generations. But they are firmly rooted in the Argolid and are, as was argued above, attached to the Argive Heraion. Their wanderings into Akhaia and Arkadia allow an important insight into what this perceived Akhaian heartland comprised. We remember the Proitids' *parcours*, which in an approximate delineation of the cult's catchment area takes them in the direction of Sikyon (where the chase results in a local cult for one of their kind, Iphinoe, who died in the process). We have learnt of the various cult places linked to the Proitids in what we know as northern Arkadia, Kleitor and Lousoi of Bacchylides' ode, reaching as far as Elis. Bacchylides' story of the Proitids maps out in myth a territorial configuration tying parts of the Argolid and the later region of Akhaia into one and the same sphere of influence (see Map 6.1).

It is striking in this context that the roaming daughters roughly outline the geographical divisions sketched in the *Catalogue of Ships*. For the domain of the Greek chiefs based in the Argolid, Diomedes and Agamemnon, does not coincide with what is later perceived either as the Argolid or as Akhaia. Diomedes' sphere of influence covers Argos and the Akte, the group of maritime cities which are the subject of Chapter 3. By contrast, Agamemnon's, that is the Atreids', realm at Mykenai includes the Korinthias, Sikyon and its dependencies, and all the important cities in what was later to become Akhaia: Aigeira (Hyperesia), Pellene, Aigion, and Helike.[97] Lousoi does not figure in the *Catalogue*, but above we saw that Artemis dwelled in a locality along major routes leading into the Argolid in the south, and identified her vital role in communication with the coastal cities of later Akhaia in the north. Lousoi and its aetiological myth thus make good sense within Agamemnon's realm and what constituted 'Akhaia' in the sense of the most vigorous Homeric warrior's home. That said, the boundaries of the two kingdoms even in the epic poems were themselves elusive, as if power configurations and the mythical baggage justifying them were constantly changing and disputed. The epic rivalry between Diomedes and Agamemnon may well have marked even there some conflict over Akhaianness. So Diomedes, in the *Catalogue* deprived of access to the Korinthian Gulf, already in the *Iliad* has a personal tie to later Akhaia's female eponym Aigialeia;[98] later Akhaians of the

[97] *Il.* 2.559–80. Such problems are not addressed in recent studies on the *Catalogue*: e.g. Visser (1997) 151–238; 147–50 for his methodological principles; but cf. Finkelberg (1988).

[98] Diomedes' aunt or wife *Αἰγιάλεια* (= the old name *Αἰγιαλός* of the region): *Il.* 5.412; 2.569–79; for the old name cf. Hdt. 7.94; Str. 8.7.1: *Αἰγιάλεια*; *Αἰγιαλεῖς*; Paus. 7.1.1. See esp. Sinatra (1994) on the continuous ambiguity in later texts over whether Agamemnon and the Atreids lived in Mykenai or in Argos.

Peloponnese were keen to allege roots in Argos, and not in Mykenai.[99] The legend of the Proitids itself suggests the uncomfortable intimacy between all these different centres of power: though their father Proitos originates from Diomedean Argos, his daughters' journey in the northern Peloponnese rather corresponds to Agamemnon's 'Akhaian' realm in the *Catalogue*. (Indeed Pausanias thinks that Korinth was once a dependency of Proitos.)[100]

Bacchylides' myth then summons a memory of a time when a concept of Akhaia in the Peloponnesian sense did not exist, while the link between Akhaians and the Argolid (especially, but not only, Mykenai) was well established. The ode's insistence on *Nostoi* heroes conveying Artemis of Lousoi to Italy is actually good proof of the relative antiquity of the tradition: because Artemis' myth presupposes the notion of an epic Akhaia that comprises the cities of eastern Akhaia and the Korinthian Gulf, it is curiously more credibly old (and more credibly 'Akhaian') than the *Nostoi* myths per se. Artemis at Lousoi and the Proitids would have lost their claim to this epic Akhaianness in the process by which this part of the Peloponnese became a more closely delineated (though still not fixed) region 'Akhaia' or 'Arkadia', and, in mythical terms, had left the realm of Atreid Agamemnon. Had Bacchylides' 'war-loving Akhaians' founded the cult of Hera at Lakinia on the model of the Heraion at Prosymna, such a tradition would be undatable even in relative terms since the shrine in the Argolid continued to determine who was 'Akhaian' and who was not (see Ch. 3, Sect. 2). The importance of the Argive Hera for the fabrication of Akhaianness then also hints perhaps at why Hera is such a prominent deity in the aetiological myth for Akhaian Artemis at Metapontion. As being Akhaian entailed harking back to cults within this imagined power sphere in the northern Peloponnese, Proitos and his daughters outlining a large geographical area present plausible personnel for the claim of Akhaian identity, themselves furthermore transgressing the dividing lines drawn between Mykenaian Agamemnon and Argive Diomedes.[101]

It seems, then, that early on the links to epic Akhaia were more developed and the voyages of epic Akhaians provided a more elaborate framework of mythical references than those of the Akhaians in the Peloponnese. Meanwhile, *Nostoi* heroes were tending divinities whose shrines in the Argolid provided a tangible claim to epic Akhaianness. The Proitids and Artemis of Lousoi owe their appearance in this Akhaian sphere of operation to a wider conception of the epic 'heartland' in myth, comprising eastern Akhaia and parts of the Korinthian Gulf,

99 Pellene's eponymous founder is from Argos and the city's sanctuary of Demeter Mysia was founded by the Argive Mysios: Paus. 7.27.9. In St. Byz. s.v. *Αἰγιαλός* is the name of a place close to Sikyon, and the name derives from Aigialos, son of Inakhos. Cf. Hdt. 5.68.

100 This is Pausanias' interpretation of the *Catalogue of Ships* (2.4.2). For the Proitids in the Argolid see Ch. 3, n. 93 above.

101 Giacometti (1999) attributes Hera's prominence in the ode to the cult of Hera of the Palatine at Metapontion itself, which ties in well with the idea that all southern Italian cults are relations of the goddess in the Argolid.

as well as to Lousoi's historical role in a fluid north-eastern Peloponnesian dynamic. The recently emerging possibility that Peloponnesian Akhaia eventually became the mother-*ethnos* as a result of a memory of real contacts between people in the eastern Korinthian Gulf fits this idea marvellously—this area comprises eastern Akhaia, Korinthias, and parts of the Argolid, forming a significant overlap with the configuration of cities in the *Catalogue of Ships*.

4. TURNING AKHAIAN IN SONG

A rival myth for Metapontian Artemis

By contrast, by the fifth century the cities of southern Italy can be seen to hark back to ancestors in Peloponnesian Akhaia. Herodotus for example knows of the Krotoniates as Akhaians in that sense. Polybius in a much-cited passage associates the formation of the Italiotic league with the *politeia* of the Akhaians at a period in the middle of the fifth century.[102] But it appears that not even then does 'Akhaia' form a very fixed (consolidated) frame of reference in southern Italy (or for the Akhaians in the Peloponnese, a discussion that cannot be broached here). Rather, cities' identities remain flexible, are the product of competing mythical networks derived from the area's complicated past, of which the 'Akhaian' is only one. Bacchylides' victory song for Alexidamos of Metapontion comes to place itself in such a contemporary context, in which the summoning of Akhaian identity assumes important rhetorical power. The myth-ritual complex of Artemis at Metapontion operates in the midst of these competing claims.

Artemis at Metapontion is associated with another myth, and this shows clearly that she had a role, certainly a fair amount of religious baggage, in the shaping of changing ethnic alignments of cities expressed in myth. In a tradition that might already have been known by seventh-century Asios, Metapontion is the scene of some versions of the tragic legend of Melanippe, a story recounted alternatively as Euripides' *Wise Melanippe* (Μελανίππη ἡ σοφή) and as *Captive Melanippe* (Μελανίππη Δεσμῶτις). These fragmentary plays date to the last quarter of the fifth century and at least the latter is traditionally seen as having a share in the enigmatic nature of Athenian politics and imperial interests in southern Italy (of which we know considerably less than of neighbouring Sicily). The myth ties into the dynamic produced by parallel mythical claims and alliances in southern Italy,

[102] Hdt. 8.47 (Kroton); Plb. 2.39.5–6. Note that for Herodotus, 'Akhaia' means many different things: Homeric heroes (2.120), the circumscribed area in Thessaly (7.132; 173; 185; 196), occasionally Akhaia in the Peloponnese (7.94; 8.36), once Akhaia in southern Italy (loc. cit.; implicitly 1.145), while the Akhaians' migrations within the Peloponnese feature often: 1.145; 5.72; 7.94; 8.73 claims that the Akhaians came from outside the Peloponnese.

which are more complex, and reach back much further, than has hitherto been perceived.[103]

The myth of Melanippe provides the one other literary reference to Artemis' Metapontian cult besides Bacchylides' *aition*, and has a good chance of being an alternative aetiology. While little of what survives of the *Wise Melanippe* can be assembled into a meaningful whole, the plot of *Captive Melanippe* can be partially reconstructed with the help of one of Hyginus' *fabulae*, complemented by citations in antiquarians and scholiasts. Melanippe, daughter of either a certain Desmontes or of Aiolos, has twins by the god Poseidon, called Aiolos the younger and Boiotos. Melanippe's father, incredulous of the divine birth, blinds his daughter and throws her into prison, hence the title of the play *Δεσμῶτις*. The babies are abandoned in the countryside. Fed by a cow and raised by shepherds, they are later adopted by Metapontos, the childless king of Metapontion (alternatively of Italia, even Ikaria). According to Hyginus, Metapontos' own wife eventually also produces twins, and the two pairs end up fighting over Metapontos' kingdom in a wild pursuit through the city's countryside. In the Euripidean drama, the hunt leaves Melanippe's twins alive; Metapontos' wife commits suicide, and Aiolos and Boiotos kill Desmontes, set free their imprisoned mother and marry her to Metapontos. Note that in a different tradition Aiolos and Boiotos lose the battle and are sent into exile.[104]

The story somehow takes place in Artemis' sacred territory: there came the day when the king had decided to 'go out to the temple of Metapontian Artemis for a sacrifice' (*ut exiret ad Dianam Metapontinam ad sacrum faciendum*), thought a good opportunity by Metapontion's original wife for the planned murder. The fierce pursuit between the two sets of twins should be imagined to take place in Artemis' *khora*, perhaps the sacred land, certainly the realm of the goddess. The myth's motifs and language in both Hyginus and what survives of the tragedy are so similar to those found in the Bacchylidean story of the Proitids that an association is tempting: Melanippe's sons go out hunting, embarking on a sort of *oreibasia* ('going on the mountains'), rehearsing the 'Dionysian' element (*cum . . . in venatione exirent, in montem exissent* 'when they went out hunting', 'had gone to the mountain'). They are shadowed by the other set of twins armed with a *culter*, the Roman term for a hunting and sacrificial knife. A *culter venatorius* ('hunting knife') is also what Metapontos' original wife stabs herself with on

[103] Eur. *Mel. Soph. TrGF* 480–8; *Mel. Des. TrGF* *489–514. The two plays are easily accessible in *SFP* 240 ff. with previous bibliography; 243 on the southern Italian setting. Giacometti (1990–1) discusses the political context; see also Nafissi (1997). In the English-speaking world Hornblower (2004) 119–20 and 189 is the only, very recent, discussion of Bacch. 11 vis-à-vis the *Melanippe Desmotis*. The *terminus ante quem* for the play is given by references in Old Comedy: Ar. *Thesm.* 547 (411 BC); Eupolis' *Demoi* (412 BC) *PCG* 99. 102 = *TrGF* 507. The traditional venue for this myth is in Boiotia: D.S. 4.67.4–6; 5.7.6; cf. 19.53.6; perhaps Korinna *PMG* 658; Paus. 9.1.1.

[104] Hyg. *Fab.* 186 (Metapontus rex Italiae [Icariae]); D.S. 4.67; Str. 6.1.15; Σ Dion. Per. 461; Eur. *TrGF Mel. Des.* test. iib = *SFP* 496 = Ath. 12.523d = Tim. *FGrH* 566 F 52. The protagonists' names are changeable: Metabos for Metapontos; Siris also bears the name Theano. In Euripides' play the competing pairs are the stepbrothers of Melanippe and the twins.

hearing of her sons' death. Ambush and pursuit, central to the messenger's report in the best-preserved passage of Euripides' *Captive Melanippe*, are pictured in great detail, presumably with a view to hunting down the sacrificial victims—who we remember in Bacchylides' myth were beasts pursued and turned into civilized dancing girls. Overlapping hunting and bestial imagery, of flight and fear, killing and sacrificial slaughter prevails just as in the myth of the Proitids.[105] We cannot get as close to the possible ritual nature and the relationship between hunters, hunted, and future worshippers of Artemis as in the myth of the Proitids. But the degree to which the only other piece of myth associated with Artemis at Metapontion takes up the myth-ritual nexus in Bacchylides for the same cult is intriguing.

The idea that the two myths are versions, competing versions to be precise, of the same cult furnishes the key to understanding the significance of invoking a worshipping community tracing itself back to the Akhaians in Bacchylides' fifth-century song. It will shed light on the regional dynamics and the different ethnic alignments floated at the time of the Metapontian performance. That Metapontion has so many different founding accounts is itself an index of competing formulations of the city's past and their continuous reinterpretation in the light of Metapontion's turbulent history. But on a closer view, all the southern Italian cities have an issue with their origins, and were in a constant identity crisis in which manipulating their mixed pasts in one or another direction, highlighting one 'ethnic' aspect or another, was a favourite and frequent sport. This ethnic ambiguity can be seen to play particularly in the fifth century, when questions of commitment—to each other, to the ensemble of Italian cities, to Athens—were very much at stake.[106]

Akhaian identity emerging from the Ionian

Bacchylides' ode and Euripides' drama(s) each seem to evoke two oppositional ethno-mythical identities, symptomatic of how cities orchestrate allegiance or dissociation, with each other and, notably, the Athenians. The political dimension of *Captive Melanippe* has often and rightly been seen in Athenian late fifth-century interests in the West, particularly Metapontion's seemingly pro-Athenian

[105] Esp. *TrGF* 495 l. 4–5 where one of the twins 'eager to take the beast, shouted out' (θῆρ' ἑλεῖν πρόθυμος ὤν, βοᾶι δέ); cf. l. 8.ff. invitation to the hunt; in l. 29 death follows from a 'boar-spcar' (συοφόνωι); ll. 32 ff. has a marvellous description of the flight of the slaves, who are driven by fear and *not* killed with a φάσγανον like a sacrificial animal.

[106] This does not exclude the committed 'Dorians' of the area, such as Taras: in the archaic period, the city entertained close, though not uproblematic, relationships with various Italian cities independent of the alleged ethnicity: e.g. 3.136 ff. Persians are (not unanimously in a friendly way) received at Taras, then at Kroton; 7.170: Rhegion and Taras fight jointly against the Iapygians, while later Rhegion is Athens' most loyal ally. Kroton had tight links to Sparta: Hdt. 5.44; note that Kroton and Lokroi compete for Sparta's favour in the early 6th cent., resulting in Kroton's adoption of the cult of Herakles, probably towards the end of the 6th cent. (cf. Malkin (1998*b*) 217–18). The poet Ibykos, from 'Ionian' Rhegion or Messana 'tuned his lyre in the Dorian style' (Σ Pi. i 10 Dr = test. fr. 2 Campbell). See n. 111 below for Lokroi.

stance at the height of the Sicilian expedition in 413 BC. The myth of Melanippe is obviously not 'Akhaian', but belongs to a group of Aiolian myths rooted in central Greece, notably Boiotia and Thessaly.[107] Many scholars have linked the 'Aiolian' mythology of the play to a cult of the Neleids, the descendants of the hero Neleus, attested at Metapontion. Neleus, son of Poseidon and Tyro, is one of the oldest figures in surviving Greek mythology: he was Pelias' twin brother, with whom he squabbled over the kingship of Iolkos in Thessaly and eventually had to leave for the Peloponnese and founded Pylos.[108] The Neleids are the founders of the Ionian cities in Asia Minor. As we know from Mimnermos, they originally depart from Pylos in the Peloponnese, but in the fifth century at the latest their journey to the East goes via Athens, and the Neleids become crucial figures in Athens' Ionian policies in the Aegean. The play would thus invoke a kinship relation in support of an alliance between Metapontion and Athens. Neleids at Metapontion provide an Aiolian link shared with Athens to Ionian Asia Minor and give Metapontion a sort of Ionian slant.[109]

The idea of unmediated resonances of contemporary politics in Euripides, that the drama constitutes an Athenian appeal to the Metapontians for a specific alliance, should be treated with caution. By contrast, the idea that the play invokes an Ionian Mediterranean populated by 'Aiolian' figures is attractive and can be taken further. The phenomenon of Aiolian figures (re-)interpreted in Ionian terms, very visible in Asia Minor, is crucial also in southern Italy, as we shall see further below. But first of all let us look at the 'Ionians' in southern Italy. Although rarely noted, there is a whole flurry of evidence providing an Ionian past for the cities of southern Italy, in material culture on the one hand, and mythical and antiquarian traditions on the other. This milieu creates the dynamic from within which Akhaianness emerges not as anything like an ethnicity based on shared geographical origins, let alone blood, but rather a new configuration of cities to each other, perhaps tied to an (elusive) new social structure.

Let me start by briefly surveying the Ionian world of south Italy. A set of 'Ionian', that is east Greek, connections encompasses and implicates all of the southern Italian cities from Rhegion to Metapontion. To a degree this is unsurprising: after all we know well the stories of the Phokaians in the far Mediterreanean west, in Spain and southern France, notably Massilia. In Italy, mythical and material relations to the eastern Aegean can be traced for Rhegion, Lokroi, Kroton, Sybaris, and most prominently Siris, the one city for which an

[107] The testimonia for the localization of Melanippe's myth in Boiotia are assembled and discussed by Nafissi (1997) 340–5.

[108] *Od.* 11.235–53; cf. Hes. fr. 30–1 MW (in Iolkos); *Od.* 11.254–9; Hes. fr. 33a.5; D. S. 4.68.3, 6 (fleeing to the Peloponnese and founding Pylos). For the details of Neleus' career and that of his sons, the Neleids, see *DNP* s.v.

[109] Mimn. fr. 9; 10 W. Cf. the fine analysis by Giacometti (1990–1). On Siris, the name of Metapontos' wife in Euripides, and a Metapontian-Siritan-Athenian Ionian triangle see below. It is also supposed to reflect Athenian sympathy for Metapontion's claims to the Siritis. Discussions: Beloch (1894); Cozzoli (1968); Musti (1994*b*) 138 n. 2. I discuss the 'Aiolian' ancestry of the Ionians in Asia Minor in (2005) 45–54.

actual 'Ionian' foundation legend and stories related to its specifically Ionian history survive, as I shall discuss in detail below. Puzzling bonds to east Greek material culture, long known, have especially in recent years fostered the idea that the Greek West was well connected with the Ionian East.[110] The Lokrians, for example, always claim to be profoundly Dorian, even 'Spartan', and are by Thucydides' time a faithful ally of Dorian Syracuse. In the sixth century, by contrast, Lokroi is noticeably shaped by Ionian, east Greek culture, quite possibly the milieu in which featured Lokroi's most famous musician Xenokritos, apparently harshly criticized by Pindar for his Ionian tunes.[111] Lokroi also supported Ionian Siris in its fatal conflict with the Akhaian cities, and was the first city to receive refugees from Samos trekking westwards after the capture of Miletus in 494 BC. Samos' two Pythagorai, the philosopher and the sculptor, went not to Lokroi, but to its neighbours Kroton and Rhegion, while the poet Ibykos of Rhegion went in the opposite direction.[112] Even Sybaris has its Ionian credentials. Herodotus' notorious chapter on the *Capture of Miletus*, discussed already in Chapter 2, makes an intriguing remark about the Sybarites:

But when the Milesians had suffered these misfortunes from the Persians (494 BC) the Sybarites did not acknowledge the Milesian hardship in the same way (οὐκ ἀπέδοσαν τὴν ὁμοίην). For when Kroton razed Sybaris to the ground (in 510 BC), all the Milesians shaved their hair and displayed greatly their lamentations. For of all cities of the time that we knew, these two were most tied to each other by friendship (ἐξεινώθησαν). (Herodotus 6.21)

Though the tie here is *xenia* and not *syngeneia*, the passage is suggestive enough to allow us to comprehend phenomena such as Milesian Hekataios' interest in Italy. Incidentally, Herodotus proceeds by comparing favourably the Athenian outcry at Phrynikhos' drama, only one of the many ways in which the Athenians showed their grief at the οἰκεῖα κακά, the sufferings closer to home. Herodotus seeks to evoke the image of a well-connected Ionian world, otherwise the competitive grief behaviour of Sybarites and Athenians would make no sense. I shall

[110] Cf. e.g. Moscati Castelnuovo (1989); Osanna (1992) 40 (Metapontion); De Siena (1990). La Torre (2002); Papadopoulos (2003). For the notion of a cultural *koine* especially in the Siritis see e.g. Papadopoulos (2001).

[111] Lokroi's Ionian character is most recently discussed by Redfield (2003) 215–16. Pi. fr. 140b with Rutherford (2001) 382–7; Xenokritos, inventor of the 'Lokrian' mode: Call. fr. 669 Pf; Σ Pi. *O.* 10.18b; Ath. 14.625e; Poll. 4.65 (with West (1992) 184 n. 95); Fileni (1987). The 'Lokrian mode' was equated with 'Hypodorian' in the Aristoxenian tradition just as was the Aiolian (West (1992) 184). In the late 4th cent. songs known in the 5th as 'Ionian' were termed 'Lokrian' (Klearkhos fr. 33; *PMG* 853). Lokroi's ancestry in central Greece (on which relation Pi. *O.* 9, 10, 11 with Hornblower (2004) 168–70) is relevant with a view of the hypothesis of southern Italians hailing from the Korinthian Gulf area (p. 298 ff. above).

[112] Samians at Lokroi: Hdt. 6.23. The Samians are well known for their extravagant expeditions beyond Gibraltar: Hdt. 4.152. Demokedes the doctor from Kroton went to Polykrates' court (Hdt. 3.131). The list of cultural exchanges between Asia Minor and south Italy is long and to my knowledge not researched as a whole. Redfield (as preceding note); Pythagorids: Riedweg (2002) 67–8; Ibykos: *Suda* ι 80 s.v.

later return to Athenian involvement, but for the moment let us record that the southern Italians were firmly tied into the 'Ionian' world of the eastern Aegean islands and Asia Minor.[113]

It is from within the dynamic in this multifarious world that the notion of an Akhaia in southern Italy developed from within, and in a struggle against, the 'Ionian' milieu just outlined. Evidence projected by ancient authors onto earlier periods distinctly suggests that the formation of 'Akhaianness' came about vis-à-vis a sort of sixth-century and earlier 'Ionian' heritage. 'Akhaians' did a good job of reinterpreting existing traditions and integrating them into an 'Akhaian' mythical framework. It is unlikely, or at least unprovable, that a battle was fought involving the later ethnic nomenclature; but cultural links and differences, construed on the basis of religious custom, certainly seem to have been felt.

The story of Metapontion's relationship to a last Italian city, Siris, reveals this phenomenon in an exemplary way. The two cities have a long and entwined relation that encapsulates many of the bigger issues concerning ethnicity, identity, and the political alignments in southern Italy. Their entangled histories can therefore illustrate the more important matter at stake here, how 'Akhaian' identity developed as part of an inner-Greek dynamic in Italy and in interaction with a perceived 'Ionian' inheritance.

Again, Euripides' tragic chorus, the *Captive Melanippe*, set in Artemis' hunting grounds at Metapontion, can be our starting point, noteworthy perhaps in the light of the claim that the *Melanippe* and Bacchylides' song belong to the same religious and political context. Metapontos' original wife, and stepmother to the twins Aiolos and Boiotos, is the initiating figure here. This woman is called Siris in Euripides, representing the city of this name to the west of Metapontion.[114] The marriage bond is no accident but a very well-known association. The myth formulates union and disunion between the two cities; and indeed there is a notable emphasis on marriage in the drama's surviving fragments.[115] The divorce of the eponymous couple in the Euripidean tradition, their stubborn partnership in the other, may suggest that Metapontines and Siritans had a delicate relationship—common affairs which were at some point sundered, but not unproblematically so.

Such intimacy is confirmed by material connections. Siris surfaces in later tradition as conspicuously different from its fellow *poleis* in the area: this was not an Akhaian city, but one that traced its origins back to Ionian Asia Minor. 'Ionians from Kolophon' were thought to have taken this city from its 'Trojan'

[113] For the interwoven fates of Miletus and Sybaris cities see Hornblower (2004) 305–6, and esp. n. 55.

[114] Eur. *TrGF* T iib = *SFP* 496 = Ath. 12.523d = Timaios *FGrH* 566 F 52: *ὠνομάσθη δ' ἡ Σῖρις, ὡς μὲν Τιμαιός φησιν καὶ Εὐριπίδης ἐν Δεσμώτιδι Μελανίππῃ, ἀπὸ γυναικός τινος Σίριδος, ὡς δ' Ἀρχίλοχος ἀπὸ ποταμοῦ* 'Siris was named after a woman Siris, as confirm Timaios and Euripides in the *Melanippe Desmotis*, while Arkhilokhos (fr. 22 W) says after a river'. Cf. D.S. 4.67; *EM* 714.11 s.v. *Σῖρις*; *Σ* D. Per. 461 *GGM* ii. 449a, 23; *Anth. Pal.* 3.16. The woman's alternative name Theano, the same as that of the priestess of Athena Ilias at Troy, reflects Siris' Trojan past (Str. 6.1.14; Hyg. *Fab.* 196).

[115] Eur. *TrGF* 501, 502, 503. See also p. 317 below.

inhabitants.[116] The site of Siris has in fact yielded perhaps the most significant range of material attesting real-world contacts with the eastern Aegean and Asia Minor, among the more striking of which are figurative relief *pithoi* as they are widely found on the Kyklades (not least in connection with the cult of Apollo and Artemis on Delos), and faience and elephantine ware which occur in significant quantities in east Greek cults.[117] This set of finds bears strong similarities with that unearthed at the two sites of Incoronata and the Andrisani complex at Metapontion, discussed above together with Artemis's 'pre-colonial' clientele. The observation is old and long ago gave rise to the hypothesis that Incoronata was therefore a Siritan *emporion*, a trading post of mixed populations that served the channels to the Greek east and mediated with the hinterland.[118] More recent research has abandoned this particular theory, but the similarity in material in any case suggests close affiliation of these two localities in early times. The latest research claims a certain homogeneity, even hegemony, of material culture in the whole Siritis, that is to say the entire stretch of land from Siris to Metapontion.[119] So Siris and the early sixth-century Metapontian villages were part of the same social sphere, and it may well be that the myth of Melanippe at Metapontion represents a perceived former Metapontian–Siritan intimacy.

Siris' 'Ionian' nature is given much attention in the later antiquarian texts, suggesting that this difference from its 'Akhaian' surroundings was of some importance in the fabrication of the cities' traditions. The claim is substantiated when we look at how later historians connect the formation of an Akhaian identity in southern Italy on the one hand with the foundation of Metapontion, on the other with the fate of the Ionian city Siris. The most elaborate of Metapontian *ktiseis* signals the close link to Siris together with Metapontion's own ethnic indeterminacy. Antiokhos, who writes in the second half of the fifth century, is said to have portrayed the foundation in this way:

Antiokhos says that once abandoned the place [i.e. Metapontion] was resettled by some Akhaians who had been summoned by the Akhaians in Sybaris. They were called upon because of the hatred that the Akhaians who had been expelled from Lakonia had for the Tarentines, in order that the neighbouring Tarentines would not pounce upon the place. There were two cities, but since of the two Metapontion was closer to Taras, the Sybarites had persuaded the new arrivals to take hold of Metapontion: if they held this, they would also have the control of the Siritis; whereas if they turned to the Siritis, they would add Metapontion to the Tarentines, who sat right on the flanks of Metapontion. Later on, however, when the Metanpontians fought against the Tarantines and the Oinotrians of the

[116] Str. 6.1.14; Archil. fr. 22 W holding Siris' riches against the poverty of Aegean island life. Cf. Timaios *FGrH* 566 F 51; Arist. fr. 584 Rose.

[117] A summary account is in Moscati Castelnuovo (1989) 73–5, and 58 n. 4 for a full record of the excavations; cf. Panzeri-Pozetti (1986) 144–6.

[118] This is the thesis of Orlandini, e.g. (1986) 29–39 ('centro di raccolta di merci' which had contact with the 'indigeni').

[119] Papadopoulos (2001).

interior, a reconciliation was effected with regard to the portion of land which at that time marked the border of Italy and Iapygia. (Antiokhos *FGrH* 555 F 12 = Str. 6.1.15)[120]

The extract could easily be regarded as the foundation myth of Akhaian identity in southern Italy, but not without first disentangling a series of anachronisms, notably the Akhaian' relationship to Taras. We know from Herodotus that the Akhaians had at some stage in the past lived in Lakonia and were expelled to the northern Peloponnese by the penetrating Dorians.[121] By referring to bits of 'mainland Greek' history, Antiokhos here brings an ethnic dimension into what was later to become a rather hard-fought squabble between neighbours. Relations between Metapontion and Taras did become tense during the course of the fifth century, presumably for the reason Antiokhos implies, that is the domination of the Siritis. But such animosity is unlikely to pre-date 471/70 BC, when the Tarentines had finally evicted the Iapygians to their north and henceforth began to look south towards the Greek cities. That archaic Metapontion was founded as an ethnically motivated buffer against Taras is therefore not very credible.[122]

Nevertheless, the report implies that issues of ethnicity were relevant at Metapontion's foundation, or were at least regarded as relevant in retrospect; and the new city also entailed a novel 'Akhaian' sovereignty over the Siritis, motivated by Sybaris. Sybarites were also alleged settlers of Poseidonia, historically founded at around the same time (the traditional date is *c.*630 BC), as well as other, more obscure, cities in the area. Meanwhile, Kroton, the other leading city of later Akhaia, was understood to have done the same southwards, founding Kaulonia, and Terina on the Tyrrhenian coast.[123]

The memory of such an Akhaian expansion happening in one fell swoop is intriguing (and has often been related to the notion of a 'Sybarite empire'[124]), as is the idea that the supposed (re-) foundation of Metapontion meant at once appropriating Siris and the Siritis. For the same set of issues is formulated, a little

[120] This passage is one of the most discussed in southern Italian history: Musti (1994*b*).

[121] Hdt. 8.73; cf. Paus. 2.18.8–9; 38.1; 5.1.1; 7.1.7; 6.1–2; 18.5. This tradition lies at the bottom of the Spartan kings' claim to Akhaianness, most notoriously cited by Kleomenes on the Akropolis (Hdt. 5.72) with Parker (1998*a*).

[122] Cf. Malkin (1994) 138–9. The Iapygians inflicted upon Taras, helped by Rhegion, the 'biggest Greek slaughter' in 473 BC, as a consequence of which democracy was instituted (Hdt. 7.170; D.S. 11.52; Arist. *Pol.* 5.3.7). Pausanias (10.10.6; 13.10) knows of monuments of a Tarentine victory against the Messapians and the Peuketians, to be dated in the first half of the 5th cent. BC. Taras is definitely present in Akhaia from the time of the war over the Siritis (444/3–433/2 BC), which ends in the foundation of Herakleia on top of ancient Siris, claiming to be a Tarentine colony (followed by a war against the Messapians: Str. 6.3.4). See De Juliis (2000) for an up-to-date treatment of Taras' social and political history and material and religious culture. Generally it is not at all clear that the Tarentines were quite as isolated as we tend to think.

[123] Foundations from Sybaris: Poseidonia: Str. 6.1.1; [Scymn.] 249; Laos: Str. 6.1.1; Kaulonia: [Scymn.] 318–19; Solin. 2.10; St. Byz. s.v. *Αὐλών*. According to [Scymn.] 326–9 Pandosia and Thurioi are founded from Kroton, as is Terina on the Tyrrhenian coast: [Scymn.] 306–8; St. Byz. s.v. *Τέρινα*.

[124] The 'Sybarite empire': Str. 6.1.13; *ML* 10 (*c.*550–525 BC) for the friendship between Sybarites and a people *Σερδαῖοι*, lending some veracity to the 'Sybarite empire' and its legendary domination of 4 *ethne* and 25 cities: M. Greco (1990); Giangiulio (1992).

differently, in the tale of the destruction of Ionian Siris, which also implies that 'Akhaians' appeared on the scene all at once. Trogus puts Siris' fall at the dawn of history, right after expounding on the epic Akhaian heroes and their cult and city foundations in Italy, 'for which reason that whole part of Italy is called Graecia maior ("greater Greece")'. He continues 'but at the very first beginning the Metapontines together with the Sybarites and the Krotoniates resolved to expel the remaining Greeks from Italy'.[125] He then proceeds to tell the story of how Siris was taken by the three Akhaian cities in a great butchery at the temple of Athena Ilias, where fifty youths and the priest were holding onto the cult image. A plague befell the Akhaian cities in consequence, only to be lifted if the deity and the souls (*manes*) of the killed could be placated, and so the Krotoniates built statues 'appropriate in size' (*iustae magnitudinis*) for the dead and the goddess; the Metapontians did the same but chose 'moderate stone images and placated the deity with baked goods (*panificiis*)'.[126]

Siris was indeed destroyed, not at the beginning of history, but as late as around 550 BC. In setting the episode right after the epic phase of Magna Graecia this text ties the destruction of Siris into an Akhaian identity visibly based on the shared ancestry of Homeric heroes. It confirms the notion that epic forefathers were somewhat more important than ethnic origins. Moreover, the formation of this Akhaian sphere sets Greeks against Greeks, and not without repercussions: the Akhaian evildoers get into a good deal of trouble for the carnage, as if to suffer punishment for their bad behaviour towards Ionian Siris. The tale thus draws attention to competition between—basically very similar—Greeks in this area imagined to take place around the middle of the sixth century. Tradition indeed preserves instances of rivalry, notably between the two prosperous cities of Sybaris and Siris, the inhabitants of the latter known for their extravagant 'flowery tunics' (ἀνθίνους χιτῶνας) belted with costly sashes, giving them the nickname 'sash-tunics' (μιτροχιτῶνες). As we have seen, however, not only were the Siritans other Greeks, but manifestly even more closely related, and we might infer that those whom we know as Akhaians were a collection of people successful in imposing their ways (and an identity) on the fragmented people of southern Italy. An 'ethnic' identity thus emerges from a conflict between Greeks. Antiokhos and Trogus taken together make it clear that Akhaians arise in confrontation with, and quite possibly even from within, the Ionian milieu, and that epic warriors played their part in the process.[127]

[125] Iust. 20.1.1–2.2 (on the epic heroes in Italy): 2.3: sed principio originum Metapontini cum Sybaritanis et Crotoniensibus pellere ceteros Graecos Italia statuerunt.

[126] Iust. 20.2.3–8. Athena Ilias at Siris had already been witness to a similar slaughter once before. She had famously closed her eyes when 'Ionians' destroyed Trojan Siris—the other great sacrilege she suffered—never to open them again: Str. 6.1.14. Virtually all we know of Siris' turbulent histories is associated with this curious deity who survived them all.

[127] Note Antiokhos (*FGrH* 555 F12=Str. 6.1.15) claiming that 'the Akhaians from Sybaris' called upon the Peloponnesian Akhaians, implying that not only Akhaians live in Sybaris. For the extravagant Siritan attire see Ath. 12.523c–d.

Reinterpreting Aiolians in Ionian or Akhaian terms

It is for this reason that the reinterpretation, or reconfiguration, of existing mythical networks plays such an important role, and in this light we can understand the competitive relationship between Bacchylides' *khoros* of Proitids and that of the 'Aiolian' huntsmen in Euripides' *Melanippe.* The phenomenon underscores the degree to which continuity and change were intertwined in the process of identity formation. As already mentioned, the story of Metapontos, Melanippe, and their (step-)sons Aiolos and Boiotos belongs to an Aiolian cycle of myths. It is actually only one set of figures linking Siris and Metapontion in a shared 'Aiolian' reference framework. This 'Aiolian' framework could be turned 'Ionian' and be tied into a larger Ionian Mediterranean, but was also reinterpreted in 'Akhaian' terms. We remember Siris being founded from Kolophon in Asia Minor, itself settled by the mythical Neleids from Messenian Pylos, in turn founded from central Greece. Metapontion too claimed to be a Pylian foundation (κτίσμα Πυλίων) and worshipped the Neleids, in the untranslatable ἐναγισμός. Various historical explanations have been suggested to account for this mythical link between the two cities.[128] What matters is rather that the Neleids carry an ambiguity locating them exactly at the juncture of destruction and refoundation of both cities. For the Siritans, Neleids are what links them to the Ionian world of Asia Minor. In the case of Metapontion, the same Neleids are cited to bolster the city's *Nostoi*-shaped past and imperceptibly mutate into the 'followers of Nestor' in one and the same passage. For a cult for the 'sons of Neleus'—who were long dead before the heroes of Troy were even born—makes no sense in a *Nostoi* topography.[129] The cult at Metapontion integrates two differently charged traditions about one and the same epic family. Confirmation of a phenomenal reinterpretation of long-standing figures who had performed at Metapontion in changing roles comes from other local myths: Epeios the horse-builder, whom we already met above as a *Nostoi*-generated founder of Metapontion, also has a credible ancestry linking him to Neleid Pylos; he has a father who was allowed his ivory image at Olympia, and furthermore a grandfather Aiolos.[130]

[128] E.g. Metapontion could, like Siris, have been a Kolophonian foundation and the cult gives genuine testimony of the city's Ionian credentials. Alternatively, was the tradition lifted from Siris at the latter's destruction to mark Metapontian sovereignty over the Siritis? See Nafissi (1997) for these and other possibilities; esp. 349–52 for the cult of the Neleids.

[129] Str. 6.1.15; cf. Sol. 2.10; Vell. Pat. 1.1 where Epeios is separated from Nestor by a storm as if he were a contemporary.

[130] Epeios is the eponymous ancestor of the Epeioi (Arist. fr. 639 Rose; *Il.* 2.619 and *passim*; Hes. fr. 12 MW), in close contact with the Pylians (*Il.* 11.688 ff.; 23.629 ff.). On his very complicated mythography (including his double Phokian and Elean past), see Mele (1998) 77–9. Bérard (1957) 334–7; the 'Phokian' ancestry in Strabo might well really be 'Phokaian', as was already maintained by Bérard (337, 341). Metapontion's eponymous-indigenous founder Metabos was another grandchild in the Aiolian stemma: St. Byz. s.v. Μεταπόντιον· . . . ἀπὸ Μετάβου τοῦ Σισύφου τοῦ Αἰόλου 'Metapontion: . . . from Metabos, son of Sisyphos, son of Aiolos'.

Nestor (Neleus) and Epeios on this evidence were heroes of an 'Aiolian' tradition recalibrated in Akhaian terms at Metapontion. Epic Akhaians came to prevail as the eventually victorious line, but the 'Aiolian' was never extinguished. On closer inspection, the phenomenon is widespread in this part of the Greek West; the figures of Nestor and Epeios, just like that of Melanippe, are joints in an extended system of Aiolian myths many of which turn 'Akhaian'. Aiolian lore abounds especially at Poseidonia, another of those 'belated' Akhaian settlements with a similarly complicated chronology to Metapontion. The odd switch here from one to the other mythical framework can be pinpointed when, for example, the epithet of Hera at Foce del Sele near Poseidonia is in some texts *Ἀργωνία* from Jason's *Argo*, a set of myths placed in Aiolian Thessaly, and *Argiva*, recalling the homeland of the Akhaian warriors of Troy.[131] To give just a hint of the real world, Hera Lakinia near Kroton, close as she is to Hera at the Argive Heraion, has often been linked to the great Heraion of Samos: a cult of the Ionian–Aiolian milieu fleshing out Italy's Ionian character; but we remember that ultimately, Hera Lakinia came to be associated intimately with the Argive Heraion of the epic Akhaians.[132]

The possibility of two alternative aetiological stories for Artemis in S. Biagio's cult aetiology, the story of the Proitids and that of Melanippe's twins, can attractively be placed within this dynamic of a reinterpretation of Aiolian ancestors in Ionian or epic Akhaian terms. The chances are that this belongs to a sixth-century context of the formation of an Akhaian identity in southern Italy, developing in and around the destruction of Siris. Artemis, as we remember, already functioned for the pre-colonial population of Metapontion in the late seventh century, and in any case arrived before the settlers of the 'Akhaian' refoundation, fully set up by the middle of the sixth century. That Aiolian legends were popular lore everywhere in Italy makes this turning-point a plausible scenario for the reformulation of Artemis' legend in 'Akhaian' terms. On the other hand, we do not know whether Melanippe's myth was ever set at Metapontion before the times of Euripides' play. Does her localization there—during the Peloponnesian War—reflect the knowledge of an existing Aiolian network?[133] It may ultimately be unnecessary to engage in piecing together a precise history of when and in what relation to each other the two cult myths first appeared. What matters is that the two mythical frameworks they represent, the Akhaian and the Aiolian/Ionian,

[131] Poseidonia's local mythology is full of Aiolos' descendancy: Poseidon Enipeus (Lyc. 722–5 and *Σ*) produced Pelias and Neleus with Tyro, the grand-daughter of Aiolos (Soph. *TrGF* 657; for Tyro's Thessalian origins see *Od.* 11.235 ff.; Hes. fr. 30.24 ff. MW). The siren Leukosia on an off-shore island from Poseidonia (Lyc. 722–5; Str. 6.1.1) should be identified with Ino-Leukothea, daughter-in-law of Aiolos. Cf. also Iambl. *Vit. Pyth.* 267. The Aiolian myths in southern Italy are collected by Mele (1995) 430–3; (1998) 75–84; 75 quotes a 'hunting' Artemis at Poseidonia: D.S. 4.22.3–4. Hera Argonia/Argiva: Str. 5.1.1; Plin. *NH* 3.5.70; Sol. 2.10.

[132] Giangiulio (1989) and (1982) discusses some of the analogies between Hera at Samos and at Cape Lakinia.

[133] Nafissi (1997) defends the idea that Melanippe's location at Metapontion is a late phenomenon, citing Antiokhos' version recalling Asios fr. 2 Bernabé, which roots Melanippe in central Greece.

carry on vying well into the fifth century, incessantly redefining the Akhaian cities' allegiances. It is in this context that Bacchylides' song, as much as the Euripidean drama, will need to be placed.

So a number of conclusions emerge for the making of 'historical' Akhaian identity: Akhaianness in southern Italy presents itself as something arising from intra-Greek conflict and in opposition to previous and/or coexisting mythical identities, notably that based on an undeniable tie to the Ionian world of the eastern Aegean and Asia Minor. This is expressed in a network of figures for whose 'ethnic' affiliation the chronology of Greek mythology allows a certain ambiguity, hence the imperceptible mutation of Aiolian into Akhaian epic ancestors. Artemis at Metapontion seems to be caught between these different traditions. More generally, it seems that Greek religion expresses change as a reinterpretation, or reintegration, of old figures into a new mythical landscape. A question that arises is the relative authority of either of these mythical systems: are Aiolians necessarily more commanding forefathers than the younger Akhaians who fought for Greece at Troy? What social values are implied by the different mythical cycles must play a pivotal role in these considerations, but is impossible to establish due to our lacunose knowledge about the social matrix of southern Italy's cities. With a view to the association made between the enigmatic *Μεγάλη Ἑλλάς* ('Greater Greece') and the epic Akhaian heroes one could fruitfully speculate that degrees of perceived Greekness were also negotiated through these myths, just as they were elsewhere at this time (see Chapter 4).

Akhaians and Ionians in the fifth century

Either way, the fifth century sees a continued juxtaposition of these vibrant networks of identity, enlivened yet further by Athens' intrusion into the ethnic interface. Southern Italy is an excellent example of how tying and untying oneself from competing webs of myth and (less well articulated) ritual constitute highly political acts in immediate historical contexts. The evidence for this is a little scattered, but it is sufficient to suggest that questions of identity and belonging were a chief preoccupation of Italian cities at this time. To give a foretaste, Antiokhos of Syracuse heavily polemicizes against the localization of Melanippe in Metapontion, insisting on a Central Greek home instead; he thus denies 'Aiolian'–Ionian links in Italy. This is the same author who wrote a *Περὶ Ἰταλίας* ('On Italy') in the 420s, a choice of title suggesting a significant interest in definitions of locality and region.[134]

Indeed, several different groupings of the cities in southern Italy are around during the fifth century, none of them very focused. *Italia* and *Italiotai* are

[134] See Giacometti (1990–1) for an excellent treatment of the rivalry between Euripides and Antiokhos *FGrH* 555 F 12 in the late 5th-cent. climate; cf. Nafissi (1997). Antiokhos' use of Ionian Greek should be noted, though as Simon Hornblower points out to me this might well be a gesture to ethnographic idiom.

notions with vague and changing borders.[135] 'Akhaia' remains a blurred concept at the time: Herodotus' single mention of Kroton as 'Akhaian', cited above, stands alone amongst a flurry of tales in the *Histories* involving southern Italian cities without that *ethnikon*, as indeed Thucydides does not once apply the term in the ethnic sense. A well-connected 'Ionian' world is put to work by Herodotus, while Thucydides plays up the contrast with the Dorians in his construction of Athenian ambitions in the west. Their fluidity makes these notions instrumental in political discourse—just as in historiographical rhetoric—creating a dynamic of which Bacchylides' ode and Euripides' play also form a part.

The sketch of the sixth-century Ionian Mediterranean attempted above already indicated that the mapping out of fifth-century Greece in ethnic terms is not merely supportive rhetoric for the growing Athenian empire, nor is it fully a historiographical invention. Rather, it is an already highly volatile system of relations into which the Athenians, not associated with sixth-century southern Italy by the Greeks themselves, eventually slotted themselves when imperial interests steered them through the fluctuating Ionian sea, claiming kinship relations to a host of Italian cities quite probably as early as the Persian Wars or shortly after.[136] The intriguing Ionian triangle of Miletus, Sybaris, and Athens, brought up by Herodotus on the occasion of the destruction of Miletus in 494 BC, has already been discussed. When, before the battle of Salamis in 480 BC, the Spartans are tempted to withdraw to the Peloponnese, Themistokles reveals a threatening Athenian alternative:

> 'for if you will not [sc. abide by the proposition to fight at sea] we can simply dissolve households and move to Siris in Italy, which has been ours of old, and the oracles say that we will [re-?] found the city there'. (Herodotus 8.62.2)[137]

The passage is often thought anachronistic, an allusion to Athenian ambitions in the Siritis manifested in the rebuilding of Thurioi on the ruins of Sybaris and the refoundation of Siris, not by Athenians, but jointly by Thurioi and Taras after the middle of the fifth century. Contemporary flashes of Athenian strategies in the west in the *Histories* of the 430s BC are a possibility, but instead of inventing

[135] e.g. Th. 7.57.11 (the listing of the forces of the Athenians against Syracuse). For Herodotus, Italia seems to reach from Rhegion to Taras along the Ionian seaboard, but it is unclear how much it went up the Tyrrhenian coast (1.167.3 locates Velia in Oinotria; 1.24.2, 7; 3.136, 138 include Taras; 1.145; 4.15; 5.43; 6.127; 8.62.2 speak of various Akhaian cities in Italy). Ameruoso (1996) esp. 157–67 thinks that Herodotus' notions depend on Antiokhos; Ronconi (1997) understands Herodotus' vision of Italia as an Ionian–Akhaian continuity construed by the Athenians to bolster Italy as a mythical Ionian possession. Cf. Lepore (1980). For competing ethnicities in southern Italy, especially Sicily, I have found Antonaccio (2001) useful.

[136] Athenian interest in the West is normally not thought to date prior to the middle of the 5th cent. BC. Lepore (1980) 1333–40 discusses earlier Athenian–Ionian elements in the western Mediterranean; (1990) puts this in a pan-Mediterranean context.

[137] *εἰ δὲ ταῦτα μὴ ποιήσῃς, ἡμεῖς μὲν ὡς ἔχομεν ἀναλαβόντες τοὺς οἰκέτας κομιεύμεθα εἰς Σῖριν τὴν ἐν Ἰταλίῃ, ἥ περ ἡμετέρη τέ ἐστι ἐκ παλαιοῦ ἔτι, καὶ τὰ λόγια λέγει ὑπ' ἡμέων αὐτὴν δεῖν κτισθῆναι.*

a projection into the past we can rather understand them as part of a constantly evolving imperial discourse about the Athenian shape of the Ionian Mediterranean, traces of which we already tackled in Chapter 2.[138] Plutarch's intriguing citation of two daughters of Themistokles bearing the names Sybaris and Italia provides a further instance in which the Athenian general conjures up the Italian peninsula.[139] The *Life of Themistokles* is full of indications of this man's hopes and ambitions westwards, which makes it altogether unlikely that these names are merely an extrapolation from Herodotus.[140] That this was intertwined with Athenian imperialism is clear from what survives of Sophokles' *Triptolemos*, performed in 468 BC with Kimon as *khoregos*, where the hero's mission is to distribute Demeter's gift of corn along the coast of the Ionian Sea and up the Tyrrhenian, the land of Italia.[141] It is well known that Leontinoi and Rhegion already in 443 BC had concluded an alliance with Athens, ostensibly on the grounds of kinship and, according to Thucydides, to prevent the Triptolemean corn from entering the Peloponnese.[142] That Triptolemos did not deal with the unconverted is finally suggested by an independent note, also from Herodotus. The Krotonian Phayllos, commander of the one Akhaian contingent to participate at Salamis during the Persian Wars, had a statue on the Athenian Akropolis and was familiar enough to the Athenians to boast several appearances in fifth-century Old Comedy: certainly rich individuals from Akhaia frequented Athens throughout the Pentekontaetia and later.[143]

That 'Akhaian' and 'Ionian' were indeed notions competing for the cities of southern Italy becomes especially clear in the late fifth century, notably during the

[138] See Moscati Castelnuovo (1989) 27–41 for a good discussion of these passages. They tend to be linked to Athenians grumbling over their loss of control of the Siritis and ancestry of Thurioi, founded in 446/5 BC, as a result of the Thurioi–Tarentine war 444/3–434/3 BC. Herakleia, a joint *apoikia* by Thurioi and Taras in 434/3 BC, ended up declaring itself of Tarentine origin. Cf. Antiokhos *FGrH* 555 F 11 = Str. 6.1.14; D.S. 12.23.2; 35.1–3; 36.4.

[139] Plut. *Them.* 32.2. Note that during Themistokles' lifetime there was no city of Sybaris that could have felt honoured by being the namesakes of an Athenian leader's daughters. Sybaris had been destroyed in 510 BC, and was refounded once in 453 BC, and once in 446 BC and eventually became Thurioi in 444 BC: see *Inventory* s.v.

[140] Themistokles' history in the West reveals a good *philia* network: 'friends' on Kerkyra and Leukas for whom he acts as an arbitrator in their favour in 483/2 BC in an argument over Leukas with the Korinthians (24.1–3); a failed proposition to Hieron's daughter (24.7); Themistokles' flight also leads him to Kerkyra: Th. 1.136.1; Plut. *Them.* 23–4; and to Sicily: Stesimbrotos of Thasos *FGrH* 107 F 3 (cf. Meiggs (1972) 81). Doubts about the veracity of his journey to Sicily have been expressed since antiquity: Plut. *Them.* 24.7; Themist. *Ep.* 20. Apparently it was Hieron's lack of hospitality that drove him to Asia. See Moscati Castelnuovo (1989) 27–41. Nevertheless, it is not clear that Athens had already claimed motherhood of Ionia in the early 5th cent., as maintained e.g. by Meiggs (1972), 294 ff.

[141] Soph. *TrGF* 598 = D.H. 1.12.2 and Plut. *Cim.* 8.8–9; Vanotti (1979) esp. 95, 97–103. The notions of Italia and Ionians in the west are partly coextensive, a link often attributed to Hekataios: Lepore (1980). Sophokles is often thought to portray an 'Ionian' vision of southern Italy, but nothing says so in the text (Vanotti ibid.).

[142] ML 63–4 (443–442 BC, recarved 433–432 BC); Th. 3.86.3–5.

[143] Hdt. 8.47; Paus. 10.9.2 (statue at Delphi); *IG* i^2 655 (Tod i. 21); Ar. *Ach.* 215; *Vesp.* 1206; *Suda* υ 363 s.v. ὑπὲρ τὰ ἐσκαμμένα. Cf. Maddoli (1984) 332–3.

Sicilian expedition 415–413 BC, also suggestive of the role of the Bacchylidean song in this sort of setting some time earlier. It is clear by now that the cities of Italy all had contested ancestries and allegiances, expressed in incessantly reformulated (ethnic and other) identities. In the face of Athenian ambition at the time, all the cities there, not only the Akhaians, were continuously torn between local or external commitment, and their ethnic indeterminacy operates dynamically in this context. Paradoxically, it can also be observed that 'Akhaia' in southern Italy becomes more clearly circumscribed in the process. An unnamed Akhaia crystallizes unnoticeably, that is to say a map of Athenian sympathies and antipathies curiously frames a sort of Akhaian space. So, for example, Taras and Lokroi, the notional borders of Akhaia, are two unswerving anti-Athenian pillars enclosing a much more changeable area in between.[144] Pindar's surely earlier fr. 140b invoking Apollo and rejecting Xenokritos' of Lokroi's 'Ionian' tunes might well belong to this context. The song links into a wonderful story to explain why Italy was the land of Apolline paeans rather than, it seems, Dionysiac dithyrambs. These bits and pieces in the tradition suggest that something was created that tied the later 'Akhaian' cities together and to which the two outposts did not belong.[145]

But the more important information comes from the area in between the Dorian frame. The Athenian recruitment tours along the coast of Italy shortly before their much-orchestrated defeat at Syracuse are crucial sources for this argument. Cities throughout oscillated in their sympathies, and shared ethnicity is one but by no means the only tie summoned.[146] Internal *stasis* is at the root of these waverings and the frequent citation of that in our historical sources indicates that whichever ethnic identity was adopted was closely linked with a city's internal social structure. The Athenians sail twice along the sole of Italy, once on their way to Sicily in 415 BC, and once two years later, recruiting again before the actual fighting.[147] Cities' unpredictable moods emerge clearly during the two

[144] Anti-Athenian Tarentines: D.S. 13.3.4–5; Th. 6.34; 7.1.1; at 8.91.2 (after the Sicilian expedition), ships from Taras and Lokroi are amongst the Spartan fleet. In Th. 7.1.1 Gylippos sails from Taras to Lokroi. Athens and Lokroi have an especially problematic relationship, fighting each other in 425 BC: Th. 3.99; 4.1; 5.5. During the Sicilian expedition Athenians also recruited the Iapygians, arch-enemies of the Tarentines (Th. 7.33.3–4).

[145] Pi. fr. 140b, with n. 111 above. Apollonius Hist. *Mir.* 40 tells a wonder-story which implies a rejection of dithyrambic song/worship; 'the women were seized by such distractions that sometimes when seated at supper they would answer as if someone were calling and then dash out uncontrollably and run outside the city. When the Lokrians and Rhegines consulted the oracle about relief from the condition, the god told them to sing spring paians for sixty days. That, he says, is why there were many paian-writers in Italy.' Is this a version of a Dionysiac rejection myth? Choral poets, be it lyric or tragic, feature in southern Italy and Sicily, pointing to the importance of choral performances in the local communities.

[146] See Hornblower (2002) 167–8 for the entirety of Athens' 'western friends' by the time of the expedition. For the internal history of the cities in southern Italy and Sicily see Berger (1992); for Athenian influence on their institutions (1989); for democracy Lombardo (1998).

[147] Some of the Athenian ships had returned to the promontory of Iapygia in order to fetch further troops from mainland Greece (Th. 7.33.3–6), collecting at once also more forces amongst the Iapygians and Messapians.

periploi, described with some variety by Thucydides and Diodorus. Thucydides seems to rejoice in telling us that in 415 BC the Italian cities were unanimous in not granting the Athenian naval *pompe* 'a market', let alone entry into the city, though they did supply water and anchorage.[148] Diodorus elaborates that the Athenian file sails straight past Metapontion and the rebuilt city of Siris, Herakleia; Thurioi treats them 'with courtesy' (ἔτυχον τῶν φιλανθρώπων), while the Krotoniates granted 'a market' (λαβόντες ἀγοράν).[149] The journey continues via the sanctuary of Hera Lakinia, Lokroi, and Skylletion to Rhegion.

By the time of the second itinerary in 413 BC, both Metapontion and Thurioi were caught in *stasis* and therefore 'compelled' to join the Athenians.[150] Anti-Athenians had been expelled in Thurioi, and in both cities the Athenians managed to 'persuade' the people into an alliance and to give troops—not exactly convincing commitment, but laying open the quandary in which these cities found themselves. At Metapontion even an 'alliance' is now invoked, which curiously had no effect on matters in 415 BC.[151] Kroton, with its general Phayllos' likeness sculpted on the Akropolis and the earlier provision of 'a market', now refused the Athenian army permission to march through their territory, and so the troops sailed away to camp at Petra near, and not in, Rhegion. Rhegion itself, although not part of the Akhaian crescent, revealingly gives away the cities' volatility: its citizens, some twenty years earlier (433 BC), had renewed an existing alliance with Athens (of *c.*443 BC) on the basis of *syngeneia* but in the meantime the place had undergone severe *stasis*, and in 415 BC seems to need convincing to rejoin the Athenians. What the Rhegians do then is to declare that they would be neutral, 'but would do whatever the rest of the Italiots should decide': a bold statement that was deemed significant enough to be cited almost literally by both Thucydides and Diodorus.[152]

Whether or not one supported the Athenians was evidently a matter of debate, entangled with internal issues, and we have to assume that 'identities' were

148 Th. 6.44.2. The notion of the 'market' that can be granted or refused during military expeditions is interesting and intriguing: Thucydides himself says that along with the warships there sailed an escort of merchant ships 'for the sake of trade' (ἐμπορίας ἕνεκα). The link between commercial and military enterprise would deserve closer scrutiny.

149 D.S. 13.3.4.

150 Th. 7.57.11: ἐν τοιαύταις ἀνάγκαις τότε στασιωτικῶν καιρῶν κατειλημμένοι [sc. the Metapontines and Thurians] 'caught then in such pressures of times of revolt'.

151 Th. 7.33.5–6; 35; 57.11. Bonacci (2002) focuses on Metapontion and maintains that invading Lukanians distracted Italian Greeks from Athenian imperialism. Metapontion's institutional history is not well known, though settlement pattern (pp. 294–7 above) and the *ekklesiasterion* suggest a level of popular participation. A 6th-cent. tyranny is attested by Arist. *Eth. Eud.* 3.1, 1229^{a}23; Plut. *Amat.* 760c (on this see Lombardo (1982)). In Th. 6.61.6–7 Thurioi receives Alkibiades and the sacred warship of the Salaminia. In Th. 8.35.1 Thurian ships are under the Rhodian Dorieus' command (cf. 8.61.2).

152 Th. 6.44.3: ὅτι ἂν καὶ τοῖς ἄλλοις Ἰταλιώταις ξυνδοκῇ, τοῦτο ποιήσειν. Cf. D.S. 13.3.5: 'they would like to consult with the other Italians' (συμβουλεύεσθαι). Presumably for this reason the Athenians in 413 BC do not land at Rhegion itself. Constant *stasis* in Rhegion: Th. 4.1.

reformulated accordingly.[153] Italian, Ionian, or Akhaian, the latter hardly mentioned in the historical sources: it is clear that the cities of Megale Hellas were both none and all of these things. What had featured as strong kinship ties at some point during the fifth century could easily be reformulated into a different sort of tie with a different partner. The idea of 'Italy', just like the idea of Sicily, cutting across city, ethnic, and Greek–non-Greek boundaries was apparently one of the sets of connections that could be called upon. Akhaia, Ionia, and the Dorian element I have slightly neglected here[154] are other such reference systems. Singling out and emphasizing, in myth and ritual, one of the competing links, or sets of links, that each of these cities had both within Italy and to the rest of Greece could seemingly paint any one of them in different colours. The mix of populations and traditions is one reason why local identities are open-textured, manipulable and quickly changing; and why many of these identity constructs coexist at any one time and are competitive frames of cultural reference.

In view of Athens' remarkable incursion on the traditional Ionian web, the idea of cities swaying between Ionian and Akhaian becomes attractive, especially when one uses the Italian cities' later fifth-century unpredictability as indicators of the structural problem. What makes this yet more delicate, Ionian and Akhaian traditions were anyway uncomfortably close: in a myth well preserved throughout antiquity, the Ionians had once lived in Peloponnesian Akhaia, while Akhaians populated Lakonia. When the arriving Dorians pushed the Akhaians northwards, the Ionians sailed to Asia Minor and founded the Ionian Dodekapolis and a sanctuary of Poseidon, the later Panionion, in imitation of his cult at Helike in Akhaia. Opposing Akhaian and Ionian networks in southern Italy working with the same mythical personnel—we remember the reinterpretation of the Neleids of the 'Ionian' tradition as the Nestorids of the epic 'Akhaian' tradition—should therefore not surprise. It is yet another formulation of what we have found out already, that the Akhaian identity in southern Italy is the product of inter-*polis* confrontation—not too dissimilarly, incidentally, from Ionian identity in Asia Minor.[155]

[153] Cf. Leontinoi which also underwent *stasis* (Th. 5.4). Kaulonia seems to be among those providing supply ships and timber for Athens (7.25.3); Skylletion is a foundation of the Athenian Menestheus (Str. 6.1.10; V. *Aen.* 3.552).

[154] A close link between Taras and Metapontion definitely emerges in the last third of the 5th cent., after the foundation of Herakleia in 433 BC: e.g. [Scyl.] 14 classifies Taras, Metapontion, and Herakleia all as 'Iapygia'. The story of Leukippos, another possible founder of Metapontion, hints at an eventually entwined relationship (Str. 6.1.15) though not totally new: an Aiolian figure of this name occurs in Stesich. *PMG* 227; cf. Apollod. 1.9.5; 3.10.4; the figure in D.H. 19.3 settling Taras from Sparta is likely to be identical with the 'Aiolian' Leukippos: Apollod. 3.10.3; Paus. 4.2.2; 4. Mele (1998) 71–4 discusses some of this evidence. Leukippos has been analysed in different terms by Musti (1994*b*) 147–9.

[155] Hdt. 1.145; 5.72; 7.94; 8.73; Str. 8.7.2; Paus. 7.24.5. In Th. 3.92.5 Akhaians and Ionians are excluded from settling the Spartan colony of Herakleia. Cf. e.g. Timotheos, who features 'Ionians' of Asia Minor as 'the best of the Akhaians'. For 'Akhaia'–'Troia' from the Strabonian perspective see Musti (1994*c*) 120–2; cf. also Lombardo (1986) 70 nn. 60, 62. It is perhaps significant that e.g. [Arist.] *Mir. Ausc.* 106–8 840^{a-b} knows of 'Trojans' in Taras and Daunia too.

KEEPING TOGETHER ARTEMIS' AKHAIAN HERD

Viewed in this context, the performance of Bacchylides' victory ode with its claim of an Akhaian identity for the Metapontians touches on sensitive ground, striking at the heart of the processes of definition that the southern Italian cities were caught up in during much of the fifth century. That Bacchylides' *epinikion* was functional in formulating a stance against Athens' intruding Ionianism, an appeal to the wider Akhaian network is an almost inevitable conclusion. But it is set in a volatile context just as the city of Metapontion itself during the fifth century irregularly wavered between compliance with and defiance of Athens. Evoking the Akhaian origins of Artemis is anything other than a clear-cut claim; it unleashes a whole array of issues and memories, many associated with the history of the *longue durée* of this deity herself. The notion of 'Akhaia', though not entirely absent, was highly unstable, certainly erratic enough to prompt precisely nothing in terms of shared initiative for example during the Persian or Peloponnesian Wars. Calling up Akhaian origins for Metapontion in this victory song should therefore not be seen as confirming an identity that was long established, but rather as operating in a changeable historical milieu where forging Akhaian *syngeneia* bore great potential.

The image conjured up here is that of an epic Akhaia, and it is relevant to the ode's working in a lived myth-ritual setting. I have discussed above how the Proitids' journey approximately delineates both Artemis' catchment area and epic Akhaia. It is the effect of interacting myth and ritual in the song that projects an epic notion of Akhaia onto the virgin soil of Italy. Crucially, the ode's merging of myth and ritual, the transition from choral myth to the ritual *khoros*, happens in two clearly distinct stages, first at Artemis' shrine at Lousoi, and then at Metapontion. Having gathered her sacred herd at Lousoi, that is to say configured the worshipping community of this cult extending from the Argolid and the Korinthian Gulf into the inner Peloponnese, the whole construction of epic Akhaia is propelled towards southern Italy. This construction is therefore in part spatial, but equally bound to conceptions of the Akhaian past rooted in actual cult, notably that of the Heraion: the presence of the Hera of the 'Argive Heraion' in the aetiological myth is vital for the validity of a concept of epic Akhaia.

The jumbling of myths in the Bacchylidean lyrics, discussed in detail above, is perhaps particularly illustrative of how ritual performance, and choral performance in particular, fuse myth and ritual, past and present, time and space in order to recompose them as a communal identity seemingly rooted in long-standing religious practice. The fluidity of Artemis' mainland Greek and southern Italian worshipping communities is a pivotal factor; it allows the goddess to gather a mixed clientele into her lap, while a tradition of ethnic indeterminacy is easily bent into one of ethnic exclusivity. In the same vein, that Artemis was set up collectively by Akhaians rather than by an individual epic warrior in the first instance reminds us of the imprecise notions that the Metapontians had about their origins; but more importantly it situates the city of Metapontion amongst a broader Akhaian collective. If Alexidamos attributes his victory to an Akhaian Artemis, he puts himself, the goddess, and his city into this larger

Akhaian framework: Metapontine civic pride is put to the service of the broader Akhaian community, which was still in the making.

Polybius in the second century BC tells a story of how towards the middle of the fifth century the cities of Italian Akhaia revolted against the 'philosophical' rule of the Pythagoreans. The *stasis* was arbitrated by 'Akhaians from the Peloponnese', whose *politeia* the Italians eventually adopted to stop warring against each other and to ensure a peaceful future for Megale Hellas.[156] The tale curiously integrates a number of elements that have accompanied this chapter's meandering through the history of this complex ancient Greek cityscape: incessant conflicts internally and externally, preventing the unity that was nevertheless somehow felt; the curious yet secondary tie with the mainland Akhaians in the northern Peloponnese; and the awareness of Greekness, even 'greater' Greekness, somehow associated with the name 'Akhaia' and in Trogus even directly related to the epic Akhaians.[157]

Polybius no doubt builds on a set of associations firmly linked to the history of Akhaia. Pythagoras himself on arrival in the second half of the sixth century—notably from Ionian Samos—allegedly 'freed' the Italian cities who had been enslaving each other. Pythagoras' own life story, unfolding as it does in all major cities of the area, fascinatingly maps out the Akhaia of southern Italy. A concrete involvement of the Pythagoreans in the formation of Italian Akhaia, hazily linked to the notion of Megale Hellas, characterizes the later sources and has often been discussed but remains unprovable.[158] Rather, what is of interest here are the recurring motifs in the long process of the formation of Akhaianness and the notion that this extended over the long period from the middle of the sixth century to some point in the fifth.

Pythagoras dying as a *hiketes* at the temple of the Muses at Metapontion, his last stopping place, not only nicely underscores his entwined musical and political activity, but also reminds us of how much of these definitory processes was presumably carried out in religious song. It is suggestive that the Pythagoreans engaged in musical theories, as if to relate politics and music in the same way as many other Greek musicians.[159] Pindar's notional polemic against Ionian music at Lokroi may be adduced once again to suggest that rival musical conceptions

[156] Plb. 2.39 with Walbank's commentary.

[157] Iust. 20.1–20.2.2. I also recall the cults of Athena Hellenia established by Epeios at Metapontion, of Athena Akhaia established by Diomedes in Daunia, and Strabo's idea that the Greeks who settled in southern Italy did so on the model of the *Nostoi* heroes 'since they belonged to the same tribe' (Str. 6.1.12; Ibykos *PMG* 294; Str. 6.1.14).

[158] e.g. Porph. *VP* 20 ff; Iambl. *VP* 29.166; 32.214; 35.255; Dicaearch. frr. 34; 35 Wehrli; Aristox. fr. 18 Wehrli; Arist. fr. 75 Rose; Cic. *De Orat.* 2.154; *Lael.* 13; *Tusc.* 4.2; 5.10; Val. Max. 8.7. ext. 2. Cf. Nikomakhos of Gerasa *FGrH* 1063 F 1–3. Thrown out of Kroton, Pythagoras stops at Kaulonia, Lokroi, even Taras, and ends up at Metapontion. See Riedweg (2002) for the biography. On Pythagoras and Megale Hellas, von Fritz (1940), Mele (1982).

[159] The intertwining of politics and music in Pythagorean activity in Akhaia might warrant further research. The musical theorist Aristoxenos of Taras (*c.*370–322 BC) counts the Lawgivers Kharondas and Zaleukos amongst the Pythagoreans (fr. 43 Wehrli).

and the construction of regional identities are part of the same social phenomenon. Is it going too far to think of Bacchylides' ode performing in the same sort of process? That it may be a further instantiation of what the contemporary Pythagorean tradition also expressed as a search of Akhaianness? Either way, it must be clear that dancing in the *khoros* for Artemis were Akhaians whose epic baggage came to determine crucially the notion of what was eventually remembered as an Akhaia originating from the Peloponnese.[160] How much this in turn contributed to that notion of Megale Hellas, so often closely associated with the rich heroic lore in southern Italy, is yet another complex question.[161]

[160] That epic Akhaianness continued to play a role in immediate political circumstances is importantly suggested by the way in which 4th cent. Taras attired itself with all important heroes of the epic tradition: [Arist.] *Mir. Ausc.* 106 840^{a}, which names Atreids, Aiakids, Tydidai, Laertids while singling out the Agamemnonidai in a special rite from which the women were barred; there is also a cult of Achilles. These groups of heroes have widely been alleged to be (merely) 'literary', but see Malkin (1994) 60 and n. 49. Indeed, Taras soon became the head of the Akhaia-shaped Italiotic League.

[161] For the enigmatic concept of Megale Hellas see most recently Ameruoso (1996); earlier studies include Momigliano (1929/75); Maddoli (1982); Musti (1994*d*). Neither Herodotus nor Thucydides use the term. Ameruoso (1996) thinks the idea existed by the 5th cent. but was not applied by these historians, keen to maintain the West's colonial status and a wider vision of the Greek world (174–83); cf. Hdt. 7.170.3, where the defeat of Taras and Rhegion by the Iapygians is called 'the biggest slaughter of Greeks' (*φόνος Ἑλληνικὸς μέγιστος*). The term *Μεγάλη Ἑλλάς* possibly first occurs in Timaios *FGrH* 566 F 13a. It comprised Italy's coastal cities (Liv. 31.7), in a smaller version (Plin. *NH* 3.95; Ptolem. 3.1.10 (Lokroi to Taras)), or a bigger one ([Skymn.] 303 ff. (Terina to Taras); Serv. *Aen.* 1.569 (Kumai to Taras)). Str. 6.1.1 includes Sicily. Plin. *NH* 3.42; Ath. 12.523d–e think this part of Hellas 'grand' because of its wealth and prosperity. In Euripides Greece itself is Megale Hellas: *Med.* 439 ff.; *Troad.* 1115; *IA* 1378; for Italy as part of Hellas cf. Pi. *P.* 1.75; Cic. *Tusc.* 5.4.10. When the association with the Pythagoreans was made is not clear (Val. Max. 8.7). Cf. Weiss, *RE* s.v. Graecia Magna, cols. 1690–1.

7

Who were the Boiotians? Myths of Migration in Ritual

The traditions about the migrations of the various Greek sub-groups have appeared occasionally in previous chapters as having a share in producing and shaping religious change. On closer examination, peoples' wanderings are immensely productive of cultic aetiology. Aetiologies and the religious practices associated with them here serve to preserve the memory of alleged movements by motivating ritual tied to the localities left behind. Unlike the many myths keen to stress autochthony, myths of migrations emphasize the fact of a people's arrival in a given area and the re-enactment of a myth in cult continuously reaffirms and reinvents their arrival. Because they involve the elaboration of at least two mythical time levels, these cult aetiologies are an extreme instance of how present religious experience influences the nature of an imagined past, providing an excellent illustration of aetiology's propensity to anachronism.[1]

The Boiotians are among those Greeks who understood their past in terms of wanderings, which we can trace in a complicated set of traditions well established by the time of Thucydides and presumably reaching back much further. The Boiotians are imagined to have arrived in Boiotia from Thessaly around the time of the Trojan War, specifically from the unlocated city of Arne (*Ἄρνή*). Thessaly's historical Thessalians, in turn, were thought to have then been living in Epeiros. When the Thessalians pushed towards their new land the Boiotians were forced into Boiotia. Awaiting them were 'Thracians' and 'Pelasgians', not all that keen to be expelled but eventually dispersing into the Boiotian mountains and Attika respectively.[2]

What truth lies behind the memories of the fitful progress of these four populations is unclear but not uninteresting. We hit here more forcefully perhaps than elsewhere the problem signalled in the Introduction, whether genuine memories survive through these cults, or whether what is preserved is a nest of

[1] For collective memories being forged and sustained through ritual see Ch. 1 nn. 51, 54; and p. 53 n. 135.

[2] The main texts for the Boiotian wanderings are Th. 1.12.3: 'Sixty years after the fall of Troy, the Boiotians of today were driven out of Arne by the Thessalians and settled in what is now Boiotia, but used to be called Kadmeis. Part of the race had settled in Boiotia before this time, and some of these joined in the expedition to Troy'; Str. 9.2; D.S. 4.67.2–7. References to specific episodes are given later in this chapter (see esp. n. 67). Thessalians in Epeiros are known in Hdt. 7.176.4. For the basic stages of the Boiotian migrations see Sakellariou (1990) 180–9.

interconnected stories turned real through incessantly reiterated performance in cult.[3] While we shall never know the answer to this question, we can securely state that 'migration' forms a narrative framework for perceived social and historical change, and it is in this function that the migratory myths are put to work in cultic song. With that in mind, the stories of the wanderings probably do allow us to infer that Boiotia early on must have been a place of fantastic social variety, and have experienced a good deal of transformation. The vast number of diverse and contradicting mythical traditions attest this much—that this was a place where many different people had many different views of the region's past.[4] If one were to try to identify more specific historical realities, the conclusion must be that whatever changes the myths attest, they were not straightforward. If they entailed territorial acquisitions, these were highly conflictual. Neither the arrival of the Boiotians in Boiotia or that of the Thessalians in Thessaly, nor indeed the temporary dwelling of the one in the eventual homeland of the other, was ever uncontested. This leads one to suspect that the answer to the questions 'who were the Boiotians?' and 'who were the Thessalians?' formulated itself in a long and complicated process of exchange between these two groups, expressed in a shared set of tales.[5]

This issue is reflected in associated myths, and enacted in rites established by them, and a great deal of those have made their way into local performances. While otherwise this study seeks to avoid all biographical considerations, Pindar's Thebanness is in all probability responsible for the respectable number of songs that survive, invaluable sources of myths and rituals in Boiotia. Boiotian choral song and dance flourished in the first half of the fifth century. Quite apart from half a dozen victory odes, Pindar records a Boiotian performance at the northern shrine of Zeus at Dodona; there are at least six songs by him for the cult of Apollo at the Ismenion in Thebes, three of them in the context of the pageant Daphnephoria at Thebes itself; possibly one in a similar context at Orkhomenos. There further features a piece for the Ptoion at Akraiphia, and, among a few songs where the addressee is unclear, possibly one for the cult of Athena Itonia near Koroneia, a deity who seems to have twice been the subject of Bacchylides' fragmentary religious poetry. The *Katabasis of Herakles* (or *Kerberos*) was a Theban dithyramb. Korinna too was keen to compose for local choral performances though we can barely work out her songs, and even Simonides may have put his

[3] Cf. pp. 52–3 above.

[4] The host of different traditions is discussed e.g. by Sordi (1966); Buck (1985); Vannicelli (1995).

[5] Note that in many versions 'Boiotians' were in Boiotia already before the Trojan War (cf. the Boiotian Catalogue *Il.* 2.494–510); they were driven out by 'Thracians and Pelasgians' to Arne and returned to Boiotia jointly with those residing in Thessaly: see esp. Ephoros *FGrH* 70 F 119 = Str. 9.2.3; Polyaen. 7.43. Cf. pp. 348–9 below. This occurred at the expense of pre-Boiotian inhabitants (of which 'Thracians and Pelasgians' might be samples too). On the 'mixed population' of Boiotia before the Boiotians came see Th. 3.61.2; Str. 9.2.3. Str. 9.2.18 mentions Kekrops' reign in Boiotia (then called Ogygia); the Hyantes were driven out by Boiotians to Hya in Phokis at the same time as Thracians etc.: Ephoros loc. cit.

mind to this area.[6] The quantity of surviving cult poems leads one to suspect that much of early fifth-century Boiotia was covered in an inextricable grid of myth-ritual performances. Even just taken as it is, extant religious song allows us to identify an elaborate picture of matters being dealt with in the *khoros.*

The picture that arises is one in which the migratory traditions are instrumental in an early fifth-century creation of a sense of 'Boiotia', even of the concept of a region Boiotia. Aetiologies tied to individual places are here deployed in the service of the merging of local and regional identities. Religious choral song had a significant share in the way such definitions were generated, perceived, and believed. Much of this, I shall argue, operates in a historical milieu leading up to the establishment of the Boiotian *koinon*, that highly problematic institution that both unified and disintegrated Boiotia for most of its history. The series of myth-ritual performances reflects the manner in which certain Boiotians in the early fifth century were keen to think, and have others think, of who had belonged to Boiotia in the past and should do so in the future. Perhaps precisely because of the memory of a complicated history in Boiotia, contested social hierarchies, questions of authority, and claims to the ultimately determining mythical tradition were constantly dealt with in the powerful illusion of harmonic dance.

This chapter will be divided into two parts. The first is concerned with a 'Boiotian' custom performed at Dodona that puts the final seal on the Boiotians' arrival in their historical home. The interpretation of the 'tripodophoric' rite comes first since despite the highly fragmented nature of the evidence, it makes the fundamental proposition for a 'Boiotian' identity based on a myth of arrival. Section 2 then looks at the plentiful remainder of Boiotian religious song, now performed in Boiotia itself, and with *khoroi* similarly embedded in the myths and rituals linked to the migratory traditions. Section 2 lends powerful proof, and greater social and historical complexity, to the conclusions reached on much shakier grounds in Section 1. Both sections reveal that the migratory myths were crucial in developing the notion, possibly even cohesion, of early fifth-century Boiotia, and in how these traditions operated particularly in the service of the early Boiotian *koinon*, not least vis-à-vis the Athenians next door. That said, despite the array of Boiotian songs that we know existed, what survives is scattered and lacunose in almost all cases. In building on the techniques and insights developed throughout this book, the aim of this chapter, deliberately placed last, is to identify the joints in the jigsaw, to suture the fragments into a cohesive historical picture.

[6] Pi. frr. 57–60; fr. 59=S8 Ruth (Dodona); *Pae.* 1, 7; poss. 7c, 9=D 1, 7; C 3; A 1 Ruth; *Parth.* 1 (fr. 94a) and 2 (fr. 94b); fr. 94c (Ismenion); fr. 104b (Galaxion); fr. *dub.* 333 (Orkhomenos); fr. 51a–d (Ptoion); frr. 106, 107a and b (?Itonia, see pp. 360–4 below); *Dith.* 2 (fr. 70b), frr. 110/109, to name just the reasonably certain ones. Cf. also hy. 1 fr. 29; Bacch. frr. 15, 15a; Korinna 654–5, 667, 670 *PMG* etc. (for a Hellenistic date for Korinna see West (1970); 1990)). For Simonides see n. 74–5.

1. *Δρῦς*, DOVES, AND *DREIFUß* AT DODONA

ἔστι καὶ Δωδωναῖον χαλκίον παροιμία ἐπὶ τῶν πολλὰ λαλούντων, ὡς μὲν ὁ Δήμων φησίν. ἀπὸ τοῦ τὸν ναὸν τοῦ Δωδωναίου Διὸς τοίχους μὴ ἔχοντα, ἀλλὰ τρίποδας πολλοὺς ἀλλήλων πλησίον, ὥστε τὸν ἑνὸς ἁπτόμενον παραπέμπειν διὰ τῆς ψαύσεως τὴν ἐπήχησιν ἑκάστῳ, καὶ διαμένειν τὸν ἦχον ἄχρις ἄν τις τοῦ ἑνὸς ἐφάψηται. (St. Byz. s.v. *Δωδώνη*[7])

The source of this *khoros* of 'babbling tripods' has been the subject of much debate. Some have thought that their talk imitated the whispering leaves of Dodona's oak-tree, where dove-women sat exercising divination, or that it represents the prophetesses' chattery cooing; or that, because bronze was thought to ward off pollution, a lustral tripod-gong introduced ritual cleansing operations, or functioned as the sanctuary's *apotropaion* and kept off pernicious influences.[8] Whatever the case may be, the tripod fortress helps us to fill the imaginative vacuum accompanying a strange rite at Dodona. This revolves around one of those guardians of the shrine, a tripod, and a *khoros.*

In a great annual, theoric procession, the Boiotians traditionally delivered a tripod to the sanctuary at Dodona. According to Proklos' generic survey of religious songs, this annual ceremony was accompanied by a 'tripod-carrying song' (*τριποδοφορικὸν μέλος*) specifically serving the mysterious escort of the tripod. Pindar's *Fragment 59* is often held to be such a tripod-carrying song. The extant text as printed in Maehler reads:

]. . ενͅε . . [. . . .]. . [
]πάτ̣ερ·
(τ)ό]θι⌋ ?]. π' Ἐλλῶν . χρο[
. . . .]ες ἑορτ[α .] κατεβα[
. . . .]ν γεδα[. .] . (.)ν· [
ἀψευδὲ̣[ς] . ε̣υ μ̣αν̣[τ]ή̣ϊον[
ἐφέπετ̣[αι]πτυχὶ Τομά̣ρου[
. . . .]ς ἁμετέρας ἄπ[ο
. . . . . . φόρμι]γγι κοινω-
σ. . . . .]ν πολυώνυμον·
ἔνθεν μὲν̣[τ]ρ̣ιπ̣όδεσ̣σ̣ί τε
καὶ θυσίαις[. . . . .]

father . . . of the Elloi . . . festival . . . came down . . . unfailing oracle . . . follows . . . the fold of Tomarus . . . from our (country?). . . share with the lyre . . . with many names . . . whence with tripods and sacrifices . . . (Pindar fr. 59 = S8 Ruth)

[7] '"Dodonaian Bronze" is a proverb about those who talk a lot, as Demon says. It comes from the fact that the shrine of Dodonaian Zeus does not have walls, but lots of tripods close to one another, so that if one touches one of them, it sends on the resonance to all the others through the contact, and the echo endures until one touches the first one again.' The same or a slightly different proverb is quoted in St. Byz. loc. cit.; in *Suda* δ 1447 s.v. *Δωδώνη*; Apostol. *Paroem. Gr.* 6.43; Eust. *Il.* 428.11–12; 524.24–7; *Od.* 72.46–73.5; Serv. *Aen.* 3.466. See A. Cook (1902).

[8] Bronze was beaten e.g. to avert lunar eclipses: e.g. *Σ* Theocr. 2.35/36a; Liv. 26.5.9; Tac. *Ann.* 1.28.2 etc.; the Kean islanders clashed weapons to ward off bad influences: *Σ* A.R. 2.498–527w; Herakl. Pont. *ap.* Cic. *De Divin.* i.130. See A. Cook (1902) 14.

Σ 1–2 uncertain traces
3 [ ]*θι τόπου ὁριστ*[*ικ*(*όν*) *ἵν*[*α* < 20] Lobel
5 *δ̣ . . ρ̣. . . . . . ἔτεκ*(*εν*)
9 *Θεσσαλοι̣*[< 20?]
11 *ἀρχ*( ) *ἀπὸ Θηβ*[*ῶν* < 20]

Related is *Π*[26] fr. 96B (a) (test. fr. 59 Maehler): *Πίνδαρος Ἑλλοί, Ὅμηρ*]*ο̣ς Σ̣ελλοί, Καλλίμα̣*[*χος ἀμφότερ*]*α̣* "*ἕδρανον Ἑλλῶ*[*ν*" (Lobel; *Ἑλλῶ*[*ν* (fr. 675 Pf)) *καὶ* "*Σελλὸς*" *ἐνὶ Τ*]*μαρίοις* (fr. 23.3 Pf)

(3) . . . determining the place where . . . (5) gave birth . . . (9) Thessalian (11) starting from Thebes.

Pindaros has (H)Elloi, Homer Selloi, Callimachus both: 'seat of the Elloi/Helloi' and 'Sellos' in the Tomaros mountains?/amongst the Tmarioi?

This rather insubstantial piece of text is the best surviving fragment of one or several songs concerned with the famous oracle at Dodona by Pindar.[9] It was a hymn to Zeus, who is addressed as *πάτερ* (l. 2). An oracle is mentioned (l. 6); both the presence of the *Ἑλλοί* (l. 3), a people associated with the area around Dodona, and the 'fold' of Mount Tomaros (l. 7), at the foot of which the sanctuary of Zeus is placed, confirm the setting. We learn of some movement towards, or in connection with, a *ἑορτά* ('festival'), and of a first-person plural whose singing is accompanied by some instrument (*-γγι* 9). What has made this fragment tripodophoric can be found in the two lines which are commonly added (as above) as verses 11–12 to fr. 59. These lines appear on the papyrus separately from the bulk of the text, but stand near to 9–10. On the grounds of what else is on the papyrus, they appear to be securely attributed.[10] Here some ritual activity is mentioned, involving combined *θυσίαι* ('sacrifices') and, in an inescapable supplement, *τ*]*ριπ̣όδεσ̣σ̣ί* ('with tripods'). If these lines belong to the song, it is highly probable that the text preceding told of events or people connected with the mythical past of the sanctuary. *Ἔνθεν* ('from there/then onwards') at the beginning of line 11 may be taken locally or temporally. In typically aetiological manner it could introduce a ritual custom continued to the time of the here and now of the performance.

The scholia provide some indications regarding the nature of the song. The Helloi or Selloi of line 3 are discussed in a related scholion; the commentator on line 11 speaks of an *ἀρχ-* ('beginn[ing') and makes an explicit reference to Thebes, suggesting Theban involvement in the performance. Line 9 is explained by something to do with *Θεσσαλοί̣*[. The presence of Thessalians here at first glance seems particularly obscure but, as we shall see, provides a key to the mystery of the rite. As far as the text is concerned, this chapter will show how the song may well have sung about what it seems to be performing: the origins of

[9] Pi. frr. 57–60.

[10] *Π*[26] fr. 96A; fr. 95 (beginning of ll. 11–12) and fr. 96B (scholia). Lobel suggested placing fr. 41a at the beginning of lines 6 and 7 (*POxy.* xxvi, 1961).

the tripodophoric rite; but it will also establish this rite's position in the myth-ritual network of the northern and central Greek migrations. The role of this rite in the wider Boiotian context will then be explained in conjunction with the other Boiotian songs in the second part of the chapter.

The cult tribute

Ephoros and Proklos provide essentially the same story of how the tripodophoric rite came into existence.[11] The aetiological myth is set at the time when the Boiotians were about to settle in Boiotia, at the crucial point when they were expelling the Pelasgians. In the midst of the irresolvable conflict both parties send *theoroi* ('pilgrims') to Dodona to inquire about the victory:

τοὺς δὲ Πελασγοὺς μένοντος ἔτι τοῦ πολέμου χρηστηριασομένους ἀπελθεῖν, ἀπελθεῖν δὲ καὶ τοὺς Βοιωτούς. τὸν μὲν οὖν τοῖς Πελασγοῖς δοθέντα χρησμὸν ἔφη μὴ ἔχειν εἰπεῖν, τοῖς δὲ Βοιωτοῖς ἀνελεῖν τὴν προφῆτιν ἀσεβήσαντας εὖ πράξειν· τοὺς δὲ θεωρούς, ὑπονοήσαντας χαριζομένην τοῖς Πελασγοῖς τὴν προφῆτιν κατὰ τὸ συγγενές, ἐπειδὴ καὶ τὸ ἱερὸν Πελασγικὸν ἐξ ἀρχῆς ὑπῆρξεν, οὕτως ἀνελεῖν, ἁρπάσαντας τὴν ἄνθρωπον εἰς πυρὰν ἐμβαλεῖν, ἐνθυμηθέντας εἴτε κακουργήσασαν εἴτε μή, πρὸς ἀμφότερα ὀρθῶς ἔχειν, εἰ μὲν παρεχρηστηρίασε κολασθείσης αὐτῆς, εἰ δ' οὐδὲν ἐκακούργησε τὸ προσταχθὲν αὐτῶν πραξάντων.

The Pelasgians, when the war was still going on, went to consult the oracle, as did also the Boeotians. Now Ephorus is unable, he says, to tell the oracular response that was given to the Pelasgians, but the prophetess replied to the Boeotians that they would prosper if they committed sacrilege; and the messengers who were sent to consult the oracle, suspecting that the prophetess responded thus out of favour to the Pelasgians, because of her kinship with them (indeed, the temple also was from the beginning Pelasgian), seized the woman and threw her upon a burning pile, for they considered that, whether she had acted falsely or had not, they were right in either case, since, if she uttered a false oracle, she had her punishment, whereas if she did not act falsely, they had only obeyed the order of the oracle.

Dodona's sacred personnel instantly avenge the burnt priestess by putting these 'pilgrims' on religious trial. But the Boiotians ask for special treatment, with lasting consequences:

τοὺς δὲ περὶ τὸ ἱερὸν τὸ μὲν ἀκρίτους κτείνειν τοὺς πράξαντας, καὶ ταῦτ' ἐν ἱερῷ, μὴ δοκιμάσαι, καθιστάναι δ' εἰς κρίσιν, καλεῖν δ' ἐπὶ τὰς ἱερείας· ταύτας δὲ εἶναι τὰς προφήτιδας, αἳ λοιπαὶ τριῶν οὐσῶν περιῆσαν· λεγόντων δ' ὡς οὐδαμοῦ νόμος εἴη δικάζειν γυναῖκας, προσελέσθαι καὶ ἄνδρας ἴσους ταῖς γυναιξὶ τὸν ἀριθμόν. τοὺς μὲν οὖν ἄνδρας ἀπογνῶναι, τὰς δὲ γυναῖκας καταγνῶναι, ἴσων δὲ τῶν ψήφων γενομένων τὰς ἀπολυούσας νικῆσαι· ἐκ δὲ τούτων Βοιωτοῖς μόνοις ἄνδρας προθεσπίζειν ἐν Δωδώνῃ.

Now those in charge of the temple, he says, did not approve of putting to death without trial—and that too in the temple—the men who did this, and therefore they brought them to trial, and summoned them before the priestesses, who were also the prophetesses, being the two survivors of the three; but when the Boeotians said that it was nowhere lawful for women to act as judges, they chose an equal number of men in addition to the women.

[11] Ephoros *FGrH* 70 F 119 = Str. 9.2.4; Procl. *ap.* Phot. *Bibl.* 239.321b32–322a.

Now the men, he says, voted for acquittal, but the women for conviction, and since the votes cast were equal, those for acquittal prevailed; and in consequence of this prophecies are uttered at Dodona by men to Boiotians only. (Ephoros *FGrH* 70 F 119 = Str. 9.2.4; tr. Jones)

Once the Boiotians are acquitted through this mysterious forgery of votes in a procedure strikingly recalling Orestes' trial at Athens, the priestesses eventually reveal what the oracle had in mind when requiring a sacrilege: 'the prophetesses, however, explain the oracle to mean that the god ordered the Boiotians to steal their own tripods and take one to Dodona every year'. The episode concludes with the aetiological punch line: 'and they actually do this, for they always take down one of the dedicated tripods by night and cover it up with garments and secretly, as it were, carry it to Dodona'.[12]

The story gives the reason why the Boiotians returned year after year with the veiled tripod trophy. Parts of this narrative, or perhaps the entire story, were known by the fifth century, and may therefore perhaps be presupposed for Pindar's times, too. It is formulated as a story of *miasma*, 'pollution'. Euripides' *Erekhtheus* recalls what seems to be a version of the same incident of a priestess set on fire, here boiling away in one of Dodona's tripod-cauldrons. The episode even became proverbial, as the 'defilement of the oak':

μίασμα δρυός· παρ' Εὐριπίδῃ ἐν Ἐρεχθεῖ αἰνιττόμενον τὸ Θηβαίων παρανόμημα εἰς τὸ ἐν Δωδώνῃ μαντεῖον. Ἠσ(ε)βεσαν γὰρ εἰς τὴν ἱέρειαν ἐμβαλόντες αὐτὴν εἰς τὸν ἐν Δωδώνῃ λέβητα ζέοντα, ἐρωτικῶς διατεθεῖσαν εἰς ἕνα τῶν θεωρῶν.

The 'Pollution of the Oak Tree': in Euripides' *Erekhtheus* riddlingly the Theban sacrilege against the oracle at Dodona. For they committed a crime against the priestess in throwing her into one of the cauldrons at Dodona into the boiling water because she had fallen for one of the *theoroi*. (Euripides *TrGF* 368 = Prov. append. 3.97)[13]

The *μίασμα δρυός*, the 'Pollution of the Oak Tree' is an instance of a sacred place being defiled by humans. Sacrilege here infects the shrine; because the gods are not violable, the pollution recoils upon its originator, and it is through

[12] Eph. *FGrH* 70 F 119 = Str. 9.2.4: *τὰς μέντοι προφήτιδας ἐξηγουμένας τὸ μαντεῖον εἰπεῖν, ὅτι προστάττοι ὁ θεὸς τοῖς Βοιωτοῖς τοὺς παρ' αὐτοῖς τρίποδας συλήσαντας ἕνα εἰς Δωδώνην πέμπειν κατ' ἔτος· καὶ δὴ καὶ ποιεῖν τοῦτο· αἰεὶ γάρ τινα τῶν ἀνακειμένων τριπόδων νύκτωρ καθαιροῦντας καὶ κατακαλύπτοντας ἱματίοις ὡς ἂν λάθρα τριποδηφορεῖν εἰς Δωδώνην.*

[13] Zenob. 2.84 (= *Paroem. Gr.* i p. 53), quoting Herakleides, adduces the story for a form of proverbial cursing: *Βοιωτοῖς μαντεύσαιο· αὕτη καταρακτή ἐστιν Ἡρακλείδης γὰρ φησὶ μαντευομένοις τοῖς Θηβαίοις περὶ πολέμου ἀπεκρίνατο ἡ προφῆτις ἡ ἐν Δωδώνῃ, νίκην αὐτοῖς ἀσεβήσασιν ἔσεσθαι. εἷς δὲ τῶν θεωρῶν ἁρπάσας Μυρτίλαν τὴν προφῆτιν, ἐνέβαλεν εἰς θερμοῦ παρακείμενον λέβητα.* 'Prophesy to the Boiotians!': a curse. For Herakleides says that the prophetess answered the Thebans who were consulting the oracle about the war, that they would be victorious if they committed sacrilege. One of the *theoroi* seized the prophetess Myrtilas and threw her into a cauldron of hot water near by.' This is followed by another tradition that suitably combines both the murder of the interpreter and the oracle with the tradition that oracles at Dodona to the Boiotians are given by men only: *Ἄλλοι δὲ δὲ φασὶν ὅτι Θηβαίοις πολεμοῦσι Βόμβος μάντις πλείους ἔφη νικήσειν, εἰ προθύσαιεν τῶν ἡγεμόνων ἕνα. οἱ ἀποκτείναντες τὸν Βόμβον ἐνίκησαν.* 'Others say that during the war Bombos the prophet said they would collectively win if they sacrificed one of their leaders in a preliminary sacrifice. The Thebans killed Bombos himself and won the battle.'

human purification that the tainted deity is cleansed.[14] Similarly, the delivery of a tripod to Dodona by the Boiotians represents the ritual compensation for the violence enacted against the oracle in myth. When we look at Boiotia's religious landscape it immediately becomes clear why the compensatory offering should be a tripod: Boiotia was the place where tripods were most at home. The Theban Ismenion is a *χρυσέων τριπόδων θησαυρός* ('treasure house of golden tripods') in Pindar; the Ptoion at Akraiphia and the sanctuary of the hero Ptoios have yielded puzzling quantities of tripods, and tripod-tributes are a recurrent phenomenon. The Itonion near Koroneia, the shrine of Athena Itonia, incidentally, has also yielded tripod bases in good numbers. It must have been known that Boiotia's shrines were submerged in these objects; this at least is suggested by the way Ephoros points to the objects in question as 'their tripods' (*οἱ παρ' αὐτοῖς τρίποδες*).[15]

In the story, one sacrilege is vindicated by another. If one entails the priestess being cooked in her own oracular tripod-cauldron, a substitute, compensatory tripod from another oracular shrine should not surprise. The Boiotians' tripod tribute 'ever since' this episode arguably represents their attempt to avoid incurring the same pollution again. By introducing the tripod every year, the Boiotians constantly renew their credit with Dodonaian Zeus for their original fault of misinterpreting the oracle. It is crucial that there *was* this misunderstanding: had the Boiotians taken the priestess's words correctly the first time round, they would have delivered a tripod straightaway and not thought about the matter again. There would have been no *tripodophoria*.

But the Boiotians return: every year they undertake the long journey all the way up to Epeiros. Why was their initial mistake worth remembering in this way? One dimension can be immediately derived from the texts. The oracle was originally consulted to settle the military conflict between the incoming Boiotians and the retreating Pelasgians. The order to deliver the tribute then marks the end of fighting over a contested spot of land, the result of which is the historical division of Boiotian territory, placing the Boiotians in Boiotia and the Pelasgians beneath Mount Hymettos in Attika. Questions such as this about victory at war (*περὶ τῆς νίκης*) are of course frequent with oracles, and are often evoked in order to produce consensus between neighbours.[16]

In this case, the process is not quite so smooth: misinterpretation and the subsequent sacrilege occurred because the answer was not unequivocal. The tradition of the Boiotian–Pelasgian conflict construes a memory of how Boiotian land was

[14] On sacrilege and pollution see Parker (1983) Ch. 5. Cf. e.g. in Soph. *OC* 466; 490–2 (quoted by Parker 145–6).

[15] Pi. *P.* 11.4–5. Tripods dedicated to the Ismenion: Paus. 9.10.4. For tripods and their bases at the Ptoion see Guillon (1943); Ducat (1971) nos. 241–51; 261; 285–7; 294; at the shrine of Athena Itonia: Amandry (1978); *PAAH* 1975, 392–414.

[16] Procl. *ap.* Phot. *Bibl.* 239.321b36; Pelasgians on Mt. Hymettos: Hdt. 6.137; Str. 9.2.3. Oracular arbitration in war: Fontenrose (1981 (1978)) 39–41, esp. as a way of creating consensus between neighbours: Osborne (1996) 326–7.

fought over for a long time and by many different groups before the people we know as Boiotians won it for themselves. The cult tribute forms a solution to a situation in which the Boiotians had rightly or wrongly claimed either victory or territory or both from the Pelasgians. This is not an unfamiliar situation: we remember the Epidaurians' religious obligation to the cult of Apollo at Asine (Chapter 3), compensation for contested territory. Or the cult of Artemis Limnatis ceremonializes the never-ending squabbles between Spartans and Messenians.[17] So the tripod tribute too may well settle a problematic territorial issue. While this in itself cannot be verified historically, the ambiguity of the situation seems to be representative of the ambiguity of the ethnic identities that it created: those of the Boiotaians, Thessalians, etc. It is the latter that can be examined, first of all through real cult practice at Dodona, and then through exploring the interlocking traditions of the people involved, Boiotians, Pelasgians, Thessalians.

Cult and catchment area

So the Boiotians sent what seems a regular *theoria* to Dodona, a religious tribute perhaps comparable to that of the islands to Delos. At first sight, this may not be surprising. Dodona in the Hellenistic period is a centre of *theoria*, where city delegations would gather.[18] As we shall see, however, regular Panhellenic *theoria* to Dodona cannot straightforwardly be presupposed for the archaic and early classical periods. The Boiotian cult obligation to Dodona celebrated in religious song seems to have special status. Why entertain such a ritual tie? And why had the Boiotians gone to Dodona in the first place, when Delphi was much closer, and perhaps more suitable for carrying out such a local conflict? The question can be tackled from two different angles: the rules governing real-life cult at Dodona, and the network of migratory myths of which the *aition* is a part.

The oracle of Zeus at Dodona lies on a high plateau in ancient Thesprotia about twenty-two kilometres south of Ioannina, at the foot of Mount Tomaros (Fig. 7.1). Considerable cult activity is attested from the Geometric period onwards, though there is no sign of monumentalization of the sanctuary until the end of the fourth century. Then Molossian control of the god accompanies the construction of the precinct, involving a small shrine to Zeus and other cult buildings. No city of Dodona seems to have existed until the second half of the fourth century, when walls enclosed what seems to have functioned as a small akropolis until Roman times.[19]

[17] See Ch. 3 p. 147–8 above. For Artemis Limnatis see Paus. 4.4.2–3 (cf. 31.3); Str. 8.4.9; Tac. *Ann.* 4.43; and the inscription, defining 'border areas' *IG* v.1 1431; see also 1371–2. Zunino (1997) 26–7, 45–68 is the first one to discuss the possibility of a '*koine* culturale' between border areas mediated through common sanctuaries and thus dissolving regional boundaries in 'real life'.

[18] e.g. a Hellenistic inscription of the Epeirote League attesting Tenian participation in the Naia festival: Etienne and Braun (1986) 102–6 (early 2nd cent. BC).

[19] Dakaris (1963) and the detailed guide by Dakaris (1995) are well-documented accounts of the ruins. See also Carapanos (1878) 1–29.

Figure 7.1 View from the theatre at Dodona across the valley on a high plateau

The most striking feature of this sanctuary is perhaps its military character. Roughly 1,000 oracular tablets provide an insight into the nature of the oracle, and even if only some 10 per cent are published, they still give us an idea of who came to the oracle, and why. Though one should not ignore the many private queries attested, in public matters, Dodonaian Zeus was consulted primarily in questions of war and battle, offering services quite similar to those of oracular Zeus at Olympia, to whom war dedications were regularly carried.[20] A series of literary inquiries to Dodona includes semi-mythical consultants on military issues, among whom feature prominent actors in Greek history; the Pelasgians, Kroisos, Themistokles, but also the fourth-century Athenians and Spartans.[21] The same concern with warfare can be deduced from Dodona's votives. Many of these dedications are not properly published but have long filled museum showcases. Tripods, a favourite object dedicated after victory in battle, dominate the early offerings, and occur in all sizes, real-life and votive. A number of high-quality warrior statuettes together with great quantities of armour, helmets, shields, spears, and arrow points add to the war-orientated image of the place.[22]

In the literary tradition Dodona was numbered among the great Panhellenic centres of divination. Even if one accepted as authentic at least some of the prophecies just mentioned, in all other respects the sanctuary preserves the character of a regional cult centre. The oracular tablets provide the best evidence for the regular catchment area of the cult in historical times. Though only a fraction of them has so far reached the public domain, it seems clear that Zeus' clientele specifically comprised consultants from all the important communities in north-western Greece.[23] Public bodies as much as private individuals, some of

[20] Sinn (1991) esp. 38–42 and 46–51; Herakles founded Olympia as an oracular site (Pi. *O.* 6.63–71), presumably to be consulted in questions of warfare when it is being marked out as a place to put ἀκρόθινα πολέμου (*O.* 2.4). Xen. *Hell.* 3.2.21.

[21] Pelasgians: D.H. 1.19.3; Kroisos: Hdt. 1.46. Themistokles: Plut. *Them.* 28.5; Athens: Paus. 7.25; Agesilaos: Plut. *Apophth. Lac.* 208f–209a; D. 21.51–3 (oracle of expiation; note the τράπεζαν χαλκῆν 53); Dinarch. 1.78 (to the Athenians after Khaironeia); cf. also Xen. *Vect.* 6.2.

[22] Dakaris (1995) 102–4 and finely crafted bronze warriors, in the Museum of Ioannina: nos. 1411, 4913–14 (Dakaris pls. 26.2 to 29.2 (*c.*550 BC)); Carapanos (1878) no. 6 (pl. xi no. 3) and vol. ii, 181 (6th cent.); no. 11 (pl. xiii no. 4) and vol. ii, 183 (7th cent.); Ashm. Mus. *JHS* 1910 pl. 12; Berl. Charl. 7470; horse riders: Athens Coll. Carap. no. 26 = Louvre MNC 1240; no. 27. Weapons: Carapanos vol. ii, 231–9. The Museum of Ioannina has a number of pieces of bronze armour on display (incl. swords, breast plates, double axes); at Athens National Museum cf. e.g. nos. 138, 166, 163, 687 (spectacular bronze helmets of the second half of the 5th cent.). The bronze statuettes are well assembled in the art historical treatments: Walter-Karyidi (1981), with bibliography on individual pieces 20–1; on the type see also Schiering (1969).

[23] Oracular tablets found at the site are often thought to have been dedicated after they had fulfilled their purpose, while in the case of public inquiry maintained tablets were 'taken home' to be shown there (Christidis–Dakaris–Vokotopoulou (1993) 55 (more tablets in (1997) and (1999)). This has led some to believe that tablets remaining on site by coincidence are not indicative, but even if that were the case these would still reflect the catchment area. It is therefore also unclear whether Dodona was primarily consulted in private matters, as is often maintained. More clues will doubtless emerge from the publication of the complete inscriptional body. Lhôte's new study (2006) appeared too late to be taken account of here.

them as early as the sixth century, name as their origins places such as Kerkyra, Epidamnos, and the Kerkyrean colony Khemara; or Apollonia and Orikos (near the gulf of Panormos) in Illyria. We meet the Khaonians from Pindos, and particularly from Onkhesmos (the port of Phoinike, the capital of Khaonia), and the northern tribe of the Bylliones (Map 7.1).[24]

Similarly, while sanctuaries of Panhellenic standing often attract dedications brought from all over Greece, Dodona's famous bronzes, for example, are purely epichoric. Comparisons to Peloponnesian bronze workshops have been made, but the distinctive patina on these objects reveals that the bulk of bronze manufacture was local.[25] The iconography of Zeus Dodonaios (*Δωδωναῖος*), prominent with these statuettes, also suggests that in practice the god served a set of north-western Greek cities, and did so first and foremost as a god concerned with warfare. At Dodona itself, bronze statues in surprising quantities and of all sizes show Zeus throwing the thunderbolt, complemented by a group of loose thunderbolts, which were part of statues of the same type or dedicated individually.[26]

The iconographic formula recurs in Zeus' catchment area, suggesting that what on the surface just seems a standard way of depicting the god, carried its own regional significance within this worshipping community. Dodonaian Zeus became the religious and political centre of the Epeirote *koinon* in the third century BC, giving thundering Zeus a regular appearance on all league coins. Even though the north-west is archaeologically the least explored region of Greece, the type still persistently occurs far earlier in the area. Apollonia has yielded a high-quality bronze statuette of about 460 BC showing Zeus throwing the thunderbolt. In Ambrakia, Zeus appears on the city's silver staters already in 360–338 BC.[27] A cult of Zeus in southern Khaonia on the 'Akrokeraunian' mountains may well derive its name from the cult or vice versa. Furthermore, the later Molossian generals were said to have taken their oaths at the sanctuary of Zeus Areios ('the

[24] The tablets are published in Christidis–Dakaris–Vokotopoulou (1993): Kerkyra M 33 (4th cent. BC, with Christidis *et al.*, ibid. 60) and Dakaris (1995) 95; Epidamnos M 4 (6th cent. BC); Khemara M 718 (4th cent.); Orikos M 526 (5th cent.); M 33 (4th cent. BC; near golf of Panormos: Hdt. 9.93.1; Hec. *FGrH* 1 F 106); Apollonia (colony of Kerkyra); M 38; 234); Khaones M 22 (4th cent. BC, one of the three tribes of Epeiros: Th. 2.80.5; 81.4); Onkhesmos M 177 (4th cent. BC); Bylliones M 827 (4th cent. BC; the tribe is located further than Apollonia: Hec. *FGrH* 1 F 102a; Str. 7.5.8). Private consultants: Christidis–Dakaris–Vokotopoulou (1993) 55 and Christidis (2001) 67 on the north-west Greek preponderance of script. Cf. the dedications to Zeus from Leukas, Zakynthos, and Lekhoion: Carapanos (1878) i. 40 no. 2 (late 6th/early 5th cent. BC); 39–40 no. 1 (4th cent.); 45 no. 4.

[25] See e.g. Schiering (1969) and Walter-Karyidi (1981).

[26] National Museum at Athens: no. 34 (750 BC); 32 (500–475 BC); 31 (480–70 BC); no. 16546; Munich 4339; Berl. Charl. 10561; Louvre 158. Museum of Ioannina: the 8th-cent. 'warrior statuettes' at Ioannina of Dakaris (1995) pls. 24–5 (*c.*750–730 BC) may in fact be thundering Zeuses; 4927. Dakaris ibid. pl. 30. Carapanos (1878) no. 13 (pl. xii no. 4) and vol. ii, 184 (archaizing). Isolated thunderbolts e.g. no. 267 (*c.*30 cm).

[27] Apollonia: *L'Arte Albanese* no. 174; *Albanien* no. 378 n. 293. Coins: Ravel (1928) 66–7; Lacroix (1949) 74. Apparently a considerable quantity of Ambrakian pottery has been found at Dodona: Tzouvara-Souli (1993) 78.

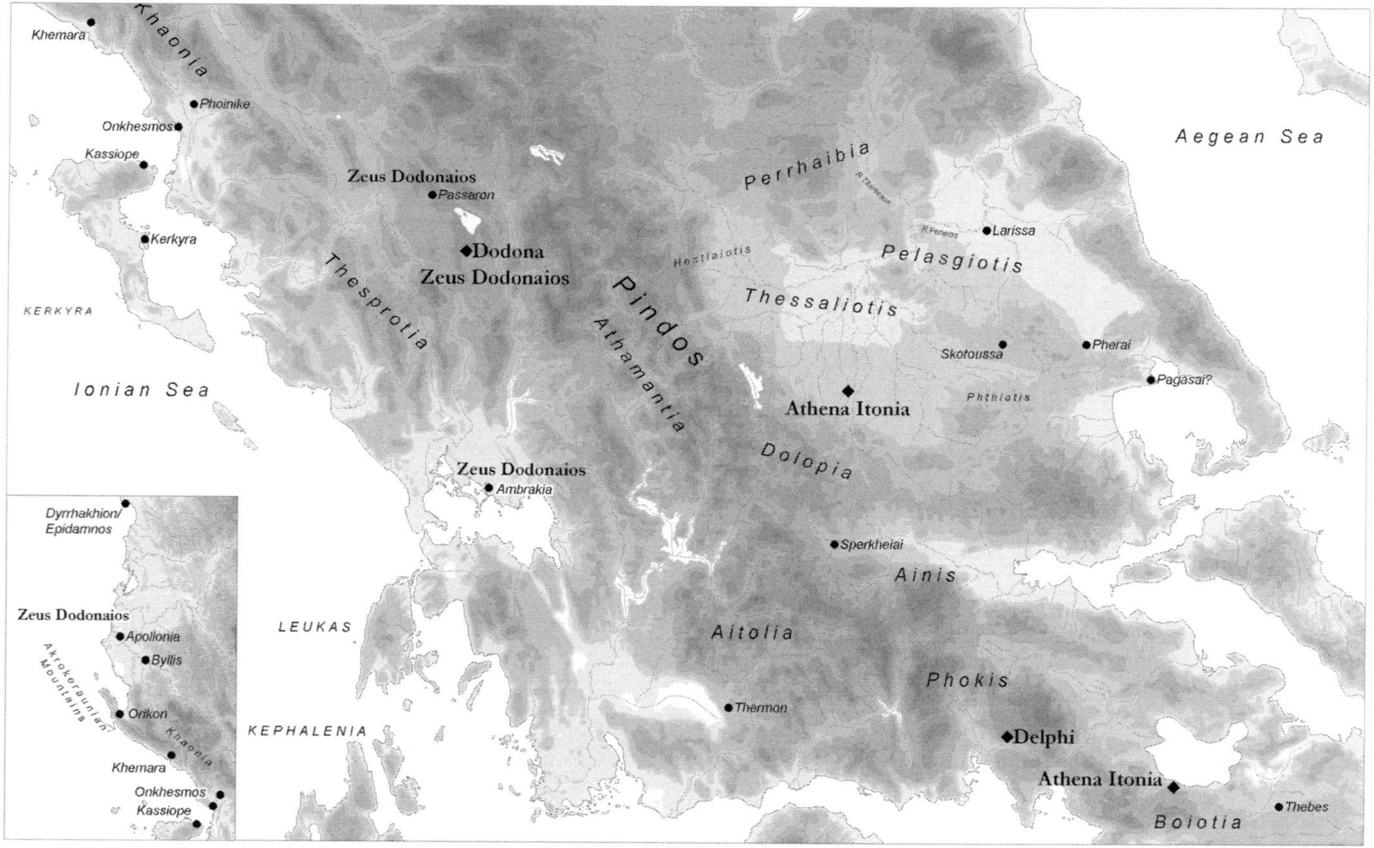

Map 7.1 The populations of central and northern Greece, the spread of Zeus Dodonaios in the north-west, and places consulting the oracle at Dodona in the sixth to fourth centuries BC. Created from digital map data © Collins Bartholomew (2004) 2007

War-God') in their capital Passaron, quite probably identified in a site near modern Ioannina and in the immediate neighbourhood of Dodona. An inscription found there clarifies almost better than any other source that the hurling of the thunderbolt was the key to this Zeus' importance (Ioannina Museum no. 8): ἀρὰ τῶι Διὶ οὗ βέλ[ος] διίπτατ[αι] 'a vow to Zeus whose missile flies'.[28]

So a Zeus concerned with warfare was worshipped at Dodona as a thrower of thunderbolts. The shrine functioned from early on as a regional theoric centre embracing a substantial part of north-western Greece. Zeus' cult correspondingly seems to have spread among the participating communities according to the model established above for other 'amphiktyonic' cults. When the Molossians in the third century turned Zeus Dodonaios into the ritual centre of the Epeirotic *koinon*, they probably adopted a long-standing local network of communications arising from a theoric centre receiving delegations and tributes from participating communities with a strong north-western Greek bias. Relations between Dodona and more distant places are attested epigraphically for Hellenistic times, but there is no unambiguous evidence for the regular reception of long-travelled *theoroi* this early.

The one exception is the annual expedition of tripod-carrying Boiotians. They frequent Zeus Dodonaios as if they were somehow part of this north-western Greek theoric network. The Boiotians' share in the cult cannot be explained through the normal behaviour of the cult, and neither dedications nor oracular service point towards a particularly close relationship between Boiotia and Dodona.[29] Why then should the Boiotians have wanted a share in this cult, and cared to keep it going?

One god for the Thessalo-Boiotian tradition

The answer lies in the maze of traditions surrounding the mobility of the populations of central and northern Greece, and the role this set of stories came to assume in fifth-century BC Boiotia. This is the intertwined network of migratory myths concerning the regions and people that are also involved in the aetiology of the tripodophoric rite, Boiotia, Epeiros, the mysterious Pelasgians, and especially the Pindaric scholiast's Thessalians (Θεσσαλοί [(l. 9)).

We remember that, at the time when the tripod tribute was believed to have been instituted, the Boiotians lived in the region known historically as Thessaly,

[28] This is the temple at Rodotovi; for the inscribed stone (uncertain dating to 4th/3rd cent.; Ioannina Museum no. 8); see Hammond (1967) 183–4, 576–7, 1st pub. by Euangelides in *Epeirotika Chronika* (1935) 260–1; Cook, *JHS* 66 (1946) 112. Cf. Plut. *Pyrrh.* 5 (295 BC). A full survey of the spread of Zeus in Epeiros in antiquity is now available in Tzouvara-Souli (2004).

[29] The Voutonissi hydria (Ioannina Museum no. 302 (*c.*480–60 BC)), adduced among others by Hammond (1967) 440, appears to be part of a group of Boiotian spoils dating from the 5th to the 3rd cent. that travelled to Epeiros: see the discussion by Dakaris in Roesch (1987) 183; cf. the Korinthian helmet (no. 4633) representing an incised Boiotian funerary stele, of the late 4th cent. BC.

just on the other side of Pindos and adjacent to Epeiros. Given the historical evidence surveyed above for regional participation in the cult of Zeus Dodonaios, one might think that from a geographical position closer to Dodona, some involvement by the Boiotians in the cult is not unlikely: the tripodophoric tribute could be tied to the Boiotians' imagined presence in or near Dodona's catchment area. It is arguably a practice through which the Boiotians maintain—and perhaps invent in the first place—their link to their migratory past, and through which they construct their arrival in Boiotia.

The curious garbling of myth and history implied in this claim can indeed be extrapolated from the surviving testimonies, revealing that the myths of the Boiotian wanderings were inextricably intertwined with those of the people around them. Despite the confused and inconsistently attested nature of the traditions, mythical personnel and place-names, for example, allow us to follow the tracks of the mythical *Boiotoi* in the three spheres concerned: Epeiros, Thessaly, Boiotia. What emerges are elements of a shared tradition among all three, conceived through mythical characters moving about in historical geography. Not all pertinent material can be cited here, but let us examine a few salient examples pertinent to the tripodophoric rite.

There is, first of all, the case of Athamas, who is best known as king of Boiotian Orkhomenos. He is one of the chief players in the Boiotian migration south, and particularly happy to travel between the three areas. Herodotus places Athamas close to Halos in eastern Thessaly, where he lends his name to the local plain.[30] He also served as the eponymous ancestor of the Athamanes, the people dwelling in south-east Epeiros, on a stretch of the Pindos mountain-range, and members of the later Epeirote *koinon*; the region always looked more towards Thessaly than to the rest of Epeiros.[31] In Boiotia an 'Athamantine plain' stretched between Athamas' city Orkhomenos along the northern shores of Lake Kopaïs up to the city of Akraiphia with its renowned cult of Apollo Ptoios (also Ptoïeus). In a piece of genealogical construction already known to Asios and Hellanikos, Athamas fastened the localities of the Kopaïs to himself. Pto(i)os and Leukon, the eponym of Lake Kopaïs itself, were Athamas' sons, forming a

[30] Athamas in Thessaly: Hdt. 7.197; Str. 9.5.8; *Σ* Pl. *Min.* 315c; *EM* 24.10 s.v. *Ἀθαμάντιον*; king of Thessaly in Hyg. *Fab.* 4. Athamas in the Kopais: Tz. Lyc. 22; St. Byz. s.v. *Ἀκραιφία* has Akraiphia founded by Athamas or by Akraipheus son of Apollo; Paus. 9.24.1; he is *Βοιωτίας δυναστεύων* ('ruling over Boiotia') and lends his name to the region Athamantia: Apollod. 1.9.1 (see also next note).

[31] Athamania being close or even part of Thessaly [Scymn.] 614: *Θεσσαλίᾳ ὅμορος* ('bordering on Thessaly') and near the Perrhaibians and Dolopes; St. Byz. s.v. *Ἀθαμανία, χώρα Ἰλλυρίας οἱ δὲ Θεσσαλίας* ('Athamania is a region of Illyria, or some say of Thessaly'); Str. 9.5.11; Ov. *Met.* 15.311 might allude to a relationship to Dodona as suggested by Plin. *NH* 2.228. Athamanes close to Epeiros: Plb. 21.25.6, 1; 6; 16.27.4; Str. 9.4.17 says that former Athamanes in Thessaly now 'had left the place' (*ἐκλελοίπασιν*); 9.5.22 names the Athamanian mountains close to Pindos. Athamanes caught between Epeiros and Thessaly come across also in Str. 7.7.1; 8; 9.4–5; 10.1–2 etc. On mountains easing communications rather than functioning as barriers see Horden and Purcell (2000) 133–4; see also Philippson (1950–9) ii. 1 218–19; 223.

grid of relations in the northern Kopaïs area and tied together by the plain that bore his name.[32]

Athamas' threefold presence in Epeiros, Thessaly, and Boiotia is only one of several such instances in the traditions. One that is directly linked to the tripodophoric rite is that of Hellopia (Ἑλλοπία). Hesiod authoritatively called Hellopia the area around Dodona. Hellopia, however, was also a city in 'Thessalian' Dolopia, just east of Pindos. Significantly, the land (χώρα) around Thespiai on the slopes of Mount Kithairon south-west of Thebes was also called by this name and is here preserved in a modern place-name too.[33] But Hellopia also ties Dodona and Boiotia together in a further significant way. The link can be traced through the movements of the Thessalians, and is probably what motivates the Thessalians' appearance in the Pindaric scholion. Thessalians, as we shall see, are the only people with a mythical claim to the name Hellopia, which in turn provides them with an intimate connection to Dodona. Working out the Thessalians' claim to Dodona will in turn throw light on the Boiotian case.

The area around Dodona, Hellopia, was known to be inhabited by Ἑλλοί, Ἐλλοί, or Σελλοί who functioned as priests and prophets at Dodona.[34] The tradition dates back at least to a much-quoted passage of the *Iliad* in which Achilles invokes Dodonaian Zeus:

Ζεῦ ἄνα, Δωδωναῖε, Πελασγικέ, τηλόθι ναίων,
Δωδώνης μεδέων δυσχειμέρου· ἀμφὶ δὲ Σελλοὶ
σοι ναίουσ' ὑποφῆται ἀνιπτόποδες χαμαιεῦναι.

High Zeus, lord of Dodona, Pelasgian, living afar off,
Brooding over wintry Dodona, your prophets about you
living, the Selloi who sleep on the ground with feet unwashed.

(*Iliad* 16.233–5, tr. Lattimore)

The ascetic Selloi prophets and their curious purity habits occur systematically in passages recording the very early oracular tradition at Dodona, notably the epics

[32] Asios fr. 3 Bernabé = Paus. 9.23.6 (Ptoios son of Athamas and Themisto, after him cult and mountain are named). See n. 95 below for the date of Asios. The sons were according to Herodorus (late 5th? cent.) *FGrH* 31 F 38 = Σ A.R. 2.1144–45a (cf. Hell. *FGrH* 4 F 127): Skhoineus, Erythr(i)os, Leukon, Ptoios (plus Phrixos, Helle from Ino); the same list appears in Apollod. 1.9.2; cf. Nonn. 9.302–20: Skhoineus, Leukon, Porphyrion, Ptoios; Σ Lyc. 966: Leukon, Erythros, Skhoineus, Titon. See Schachter (1981–94) s.v. 58–9 for the possibility that this is a late 5th-cent. tradition. Leukon eponym of the Leukonis (= Lake Kopaïs): St. Byz. s.v. *Κῶπαι*; his daughter married Andreus of Orkhomenos: Paus. 9.34.6–7.

[33] St. Byz. s.v. *Ἑλλοπία· . . . ἐλέγετο καὶ ἡ περὶ Δωδώνην χώρα Ἑλλοπία, ἧς οἱ οἰκήτορες Ἑλλοὶ καὶ Σελλοί·. . . ἔστι δὲ καὶ πόλις περὶ Δολοπίαν καὶ χώρα περὶ Θεσπιάς.* 'Hellopia: . . . the region around Dodona is called Hellopia, and its inhabitants are called Helloi and Selloi . . . there is also a city near Delopia and land around Thespiai'. Hellopia is also a region in Euboia and the island itself: St. Byz. loc. cit.; Hdt. 8.23 (Hellopia is Hestaiaia); Str. 10.1.3; Hsch. ε 2172 s.v. *Ἑλλοπιῆες* (a group of women in Chalkis on Euboia); Call. *Del.* (4) 20.

[34] Already in antiquity it was generally agreed that *Selloi* and *Helloi* as well as *Elloi* were mutations of the same people: Σ Pi. *Π*[26] fr. 96B (a) as p. 332 above.

and Hesiod, but also Sophokles' *Trakhiniai.*[35] The mysterious priests appear exclusively in reference to a mythical Dodona, and have no place at the historical oracle, which was served by a pair of doves or women, or by women who were imagined to be doves. Not even Herodotus' long legendary description of Dodona's foundation mentions the peculiar priests.[36]

While the (H)Elloi or Selloi have no relation to historical practice at the oracle, they are nevertheless related to the historical Thessalians. According to the one uncontested etymology available, they are descendants of a priestly *genos* stemming from an eponymous ancestor 'Hellos son of Thessalos', or simply from 'Hellos the Thessalian'. *Ἑλλοπία* derives from the same name.[37] This character Hellos is known from what at first seems a remote, marginal, and late tradition about the origins of the oracle in the Homeric scholia. Hellos here is a *δρυτόμος*, a woodcutter who, on one of his routine strolls around the valley of Dodona, attempted to chop down the oak destined to be the oracular tree. A dove explaining the tree's nature made sure it survived, and Hellos—the 'Thessalian'—then became its first priest and the ancestor of the relevant *genos.* The story itself

[35] Hes. fr. 240 MW = *Σ* Soph. *Trach.* 1167

ἔστι τις Ἑλλοπίη πολυλήϊος ἠδ' εὐλείμων
ἀφνειὴ μήλοισι καὶ εἰλιπόδεσσι βόεσσιν·
ἐν δ' ἄνδρες ναίουσι πολύρρηνες πολυβοῦται
πολλοὶ ἀπειρέσιοι φῦλα θνητῶν ἀνθρώπων·
ἔνθα δὲ Δωδώνη τις ἐπ' ἐσχατιῇ πεπόλισται·
τὴν δὲ Ζεὺς ἐφίλησε καὶ ὃν χρηστήριον εἶναι
τίμιον ἀνθρώποις (
) ναῖον δ' ἐν πυθμένι φηγοῦ·
ἔνθεν ἐπιχθόνιοι μαντήϊα πάντα φέρονται.
ὃς δὴ κεῖθι μολὼν θεὸν ἄμβροτον ἐξερεείνῃ
δῶρα φέρων <τ'> ἔλθησι σὺν οἰωνοῖς ἀγαθοῖσιν . . .

There is a land Ellopia with much glebe and rich meadows, and rich in flock and shambling kine. There dwell men who have many sheep and many oxen, and they are in number past telling, tribes of mortal men. And there upon its border is built a city, Dodona; and Zeus loved it and (appointed) it to be his oracle, reverenced by men . . . And they (the doves) lived in the hollow of an oak. From them men of earth carry away all kinds of prophecy—whosoever fares to that spot and questions the deathless god, and comes bringing gifts with good omens. (tr. Evelyn-White)

Cf. Soph. *Trach.* 1164–71, in which Herakles refers to an old prophecy he received from Dodona and that (1166) 'when I entered the grove of the Selli who live in the mountains and sleep upon the ground I wrote down at the dictation of the ancestral oak with many voices' (tr. Lloyd-Jones) *ἃ τῶν ὀρείων καὶ χαμαικοιτῶν ἐγὼ / Σελλῶν ἐσελθὼν ἄλσος ἐξεγραψάμην / πρὸς τῆς πατρῴας καὶ πολυγλώσσου δρυός.*

[36] Hdt. 2.54–7; Str. 7.7.10–12 and frr. of book 7. For the mantic practices at Dodona see Dakaris (1963) and De Simone (1993).

[37] *Σ Il.* 16.234d^1(T): *Ἑλλοί, ἀπὸ Ἑλλοῦ τοῦ Θεσσαλοῦ . . . ἐν Δωδώνῃ γὰρ τὸ γένος ἐστὶ τῶν ἱερέων τοῦ Διὸς κατὰ διαδοχήν*; d^2(b): *ἀπὸ †σελλοῦ† τοῦ Θεσσαλοῦ τοῦτο τὸ γένος· ὅθεν κατὰ διαδοχὴν οἱ τοῦ Διὸς ἱερεῖς ἐγένοντο.* 'Helloi, from Hellos the Thessalian . . . for in Dodona the priesthood of Zeus is hereditary'; 'this clan stems from Sellos son of Thessalos: from him the priests of Zeus have arisen by succession'. Eust. *Il.* 844.16–18: *Ἑλλοὶ τὸ ἔθνος ἀπὸ Ἑλλοῦ τοῦ Θεσσαλοῦ, ἀφ' ὧν καὶ Ἑλλοπίαν τὴν περὶ Δωδώνην τόπον καλεῖσθαι* 'the *ethnos* of the Helloi derived from Hellos the Thessalian (or the son of Thessalos), and from them the locality around Dodona is called Hellopia'.

is quoted in a scholion to Homer which also makes reference to Pindar, locking this myth directly to our song.[38] Hellos' axe (*πέλεκυς*), which according to Philostratos could still be seen lying on the ground of the precinct, is curiously replicated in a respectable quantity of both real and votive bronze axes found in the sanctuary. Dating to the late geometric and archaic periods, they may lend support to the antiquity of this myth.[39]

Hellos is only one of Thessaly's connections to Dodona. Hyginus, when listing the mythical founders of some ancient sanctuaries in Greece, maintains that Dodona was built by (Hellos' father) Thessalos. The *Catalogue of Ships* even thinks of Dodona as located in Thessaly. This tradition recurs in fourth- and third-century Thessalian historians, who were on the whole very keen to make Dodona theirs. They keep pointing out that it was this god whom Achilles invoked and Odysseus consulted. It was only 'subsequent' to epic events that Dodona moved from its initial location in Thessaly to the Dodona in question here.[40]

What might have been the origin of this Thessalian claim to Dodona? Both literally believing and sceptically dismissing the entire tradition may be a mistake. We remember that the Thessalians were thought to have dwelt in Epeiros before they settled Thessaly itself.[41] The peculiar myth that Dodona moved from there to Epeiros is a reverse journey to that of place-names who travel with the people inhabiting them, though it serves the same function. The normal process would be that Thessalian settlers had taken the Dodonaian oracle with them in the same way as, as I shall discuss below, the Boiotians took Athena Itonia from Thessaly to their new home in Boiotia. Both types of tradition validate the claim of having migrated from one place to another; in the case of the Thessalians and Dodona the retrojection lends additional antiquity to the tradition of the wanderings, perhaps subliminally accounting for the fact that historically Dodona did not yet

38 *Σ Il.* 16.234d^2 (A): *Σελλοί· Πίνδαρος Ἑλλοί χωρὶς τοῦ σ, ἀπὸ Ἑλλοῦ τοῦ δρυτόμου, ᾧ φασὶ τὴν περιστερὰν πρώτην καταδεῖξαι τὸ μαντεῖον* 'Selloi: Pindar writes Helloi without the s, from Hellos the woodcutter, to whom they say the dove first indicated the oracle'. Cf. Eust. *Od.* 14.327 = Proxenos *FGrH* 703 F 7, an analogous story involving a shepherd seeking his flocks while the oak avoids being hewed by indicating its sacredness. The notion of sacrilege is present, too, in Serv. *Aen.* 3.466.

39 Phil. *Im.* 2.33.1: *κεῖται δ' οὗτος ὁ πέλεκυς, ὃν μεθῆκεν Ἑλλὸς ὁ δρυτόμος ἀφ' οὗ κατὰ Δωδώνην οἱ Ἑλλοί* 'there lies the axe that Hellos the woodcutter left, the ancestor of the Helloi around Dodona'. The axes: Athens National Museum, Salle Carapanos nos. 173–95 (votive); 1248 (real) and Carapanos (1878) vol. ii, pl. liv, nos. 6, 7, 9, 10; cf. Museum Ioannina nos. 4918, 1690 (real axes). A group of similar such votive double axes has been found near Preveza and can be seen in the same museum (no publication). The group of unused real axes in nos. 4979–85 are of Mycenaean date. The *πέλεκυς* must have been a votive special to the early Zeus at Dodona, and therefore may well be related to Hellos the woodcutter of the myth.

40 Thessalian Dodona is supposed to be located among the Perrhaibians and Ainianes by the rivers Peneius and Titaressos, near the city of Skotoussa. *Il.* 2.748–55; cf. Souidas *FGrH* 602 F 11 = Str. 7.7.12 and Kineas *FGrH* 603 F 2 = St. Byz. s.v. *Δωδώνη* = Str. frr. of book 7.1; *Σ Il.* 16.233. Lepore (1962) 58–66 discusses the relationship between Thessaly and Dodona.

41 Hdt. 7.176.4 and n. 2 above.

exist when the migrations were supposed to have happened, at the time just after the Trojan War (in our terms in the twelfth century BC). The sanctuary in its historical shape is projected into the alleged Thessalian past, an extraordinary piece of anachronism.

On the evidence of the traditions just discussed, both Boiotians and Thessalians had some stake in the area of and around Dodona: the cases I have mentioned are the travelling toponyms associated with Athamas and the (H)elloi/Selloi, the sacred personnel at the shrine itself, on which the Thessalians seem to have a particular hold. Digging a bit further into these interlocking myths reveals that the two peoples' memories are interdependent. The link arises through a third people, also with an obscure claim to Dodona. The mythical Pelasgians, at the time of the tripodophoric aetiology, had a particular affinity with the god: thinking back to Ephoros' story, we remember that the Boiotians suspected the priestess of being biased 'because of kinship' (*κατὰ τὸ συγγενές*), in favour of the Pelasgians; he then proceeds to explain that the oracle was a Pelasgian foundation.[42]

The Pelasgian claim to the oracle will be seen as relevant for the functioning of the tripodophoric *aition*. Just how 'Pelasgian' had this cult been? The widespread idea about Pelasgians at Dodona is essentially derived from Achilles' invocation of the god at Dodona quoted above; Hesiod also calls Dodona the 'seat of the Pelasgians' (*Πελασγῶν ἕδρανον*).[43] Outside this story, however, there is no literary evidence that the Pelasgians in Greek tradition ever set foot near Mount Tomaros. Epeiros does not normally appear in the long list of places where Pelasgians spread.[44] Rather they have a strong bias towards Thessaly, which seems to be their core area. The Pelasgians featuring in the *Catalogue of Ships* and allied to the Trojans, for example, dwell in the region of Larissa. Argos Pelasgikon is part of Achilles' realm in Phthia. Pelasgiotis is one of the archaic tetrads of Thessaly, and Herodotus, in a truly confused passage, claims that the Dorians formerly 'shared a border' (*ὅμουροί κοτε ἦσαν*) with the Pelasgians when they lived just south-west, in historical Thessaliotis.[45] Whatever the explanation of the 'Pelasgian' phenomenon itself, it certainly did not counteract the tradition that saw in this area of Thessaly the heart of Pelasgian territory.[46]

[42] See pp. 333–4 above. On the Pelasgians in Greek perception see now Sourvinou-Inwood (2003*b*); 109–10 on the Pelasgians and Dodona; Briquel (1984) 73–81, 427–36, 511–12, esp. 427–36 on the link between Dodona, the Pelasgians, and Thessaly.

[43] *Il.* 16.233–5; Hes. fr. 319 MW = Str. 7.7.10.

[44] See Lochner von Hüttenbach (1960) 97–135 for a complete set of references. Dodona as refuge: D.H. 1.18.2. The traditions only invent indirect relations between the Pelasgians and the entire region of Epeiros: Str. 5.2.4; Kineas *FGrH* 603 F 1; Plut. *Pyrrh.* 1.

[45] Hdt. 1.57.

[46] For the Thessalian focus being strong, but not excluding ties to other regions in Greece see Sourvinou-Inwood (2003*b*) esp. 115–16.

Pelasgians then only settle Thessaly and not Dodona; this must suggest that the 'Pelasgian' nature of the oracle is inseparable from the tradition that makes Dodona a Thessalian foundation. In other words, only when Thessalians in later Thessaly laid claim to having owned Dodona could Epeirote Dodona turn Pelasgian. The Thessalian past and the Pelasgian past of the sanctuary were mutually dependent. This observation is of interest here because the interlocking of Pelasgian and Thessalian traditions also moves Thessalian and Boiotian pasts closer to one another. The *aition* of the Boiotians' tripodophoric rite cannot work without the Pelasgian element, essential for the original sacrilege to have been committed. The aetiology for the *tripodophoria* therefore presupposes the Thessalian claim to the sanctuary, and suggests that former Thessalian and Boiotian presences at Dodona were closely linked.

Other circumstantial bits and pieces of evidence in and around the tripodophoric *aition* confirm this observation. They attest intertwining pasts of central and northern Greece's migratory peoples and give reason to suspect that they are in fact part of one and the same, shared, or at least heavily interdependent, tradition. We remember that in Ephoros' and Proklos' stories the Boiotians refused to be tried by women priestesses. Men were summoned and acquitted the Boiotians, and ever since, 'oracles to the Boiotians were given by men only'. While the mythical tradition only knows the male, historical practice only the female prophets, the aetiological myth postulates a parallel office of both prophets and prophetesses at Dodona, and may even set them up against each other. The joint appearance of male and female priests in this story suggests an awareness at Dodona that at some point a change from male, that is the (H)Elloi/Selloi priests with their dirty feet, to female diviners, the cooing dove-women, occurred. The arrival of the dove-women at Dodona is closely connected to the move of the sanctuary from Thessaly to Dodona: 'most women, whose descendants are now the prophetesses' were said to have accompanied the shrine on its journey, and subsequently acted as priestesses for it.[47] In using the parallel male and female diviners in the story, the tripodophoric *aition* seems to imply that the Boiotians and their nascent tripodophoric rite are somehow related to the changeover.

A further piece of evidence supports the idea that the Boiotian presence at Dodona was inherently bound up with the sanctuary's previous Helloi/Selloi-Thessalian existence. Philostratos, painting his second-century picture of Dodona with yet more *spolia* of its mythical past, had pointed to Hellos' axe lying around; between this and his description of the S/(H)elloi busying themselves at the shrine he sets up a 'Theban *khoros*' for his image:

καὶ χορὸς οὑτοσὶ ἐκ Θηβῶν περιεστᾶσι τὴν δρῦν οἰκειούμενοι τὴν σοφίαν τοῦ δένδρου.

and this *khoros* from Thebes stands around the oak claiming as their own the wisdom of the tree. (Philostratos, *Imagines* 2.33.1)

Although Philostratos might have extrapolated from the Pindaric song, it is remarkable that Boiotians, or Thebans for that matter, should be sandwiched in

47 Suidas *ap.* Str. 7.7.12.

this way between the eponymous founder and the priestly *genos* of his descendants, suggesting their coexistence at the shrine. It is unclear what it means for the Theban *khoros* to 'claim as their own the tree's wisdom', but Philostratos certainly communicates that these Thebans had a special stake in Dodona. This also involved the Helloi priests. The Helloi priests in turn presuppose, as we saw above, the Thessalian claim to the oracle. It is possible that the right to special treatment which the Boiotians claim in Philostratos' image essentially relates to the same set of mythical issues as those alluded to in the aetiological myth for the tripodophoric rite, as this, too, recorded that the Boiotians alone received prophecies from men. By quoting this *khoros* Philostratos may well be drawing attention to the story of the origins of the exceptional Theban ritual searched for here, and he also fosters the notion of the rite's antiquity and highly charged traditionalism.

That the Thessalian and Boiotian traditions related to Dodona merge in the *aition* is puzzling, almost as if the tripodophoric rite could not work without this connection. The *tripodophoria* seems to embrace a memory in which Boiotia and Thessaly were tied to Dodona in similar ways at some point in the distant past, and the visible 'reminder' of this memory is the tripodophoric rite. Although any speculation about actual historical circumstances should be left aside, perhaps it is permissible to state that our *aition* may express a conflict at the oracle frequented by both, leading to major changes in oracular practice in the first instance and prompting the imaginations of the wanderings in the second—not so dissimilar to what might have happened in Delphi's remote past (Chapter 3). One way to make sense of this challenging observation is to consider the idea, hinted at in the texts but hardly ever taken seriously, that Boiotians and Thessalians had a memory of not being quite as different from each other as they came to think in historical times. This may well be related to the fact that the Greeks thought of them both as Aiolians, just as we do on the basis of their dialects. For example, the Boiotians who stayed at Arne ended up ruling together with the locals for such a long time that after all 'they were all called Boiotians'.[48] Then various passages attest an inferior relationship of Boiotians to Thessalians at that time, raising the possibility that the Boiotians in the sense of the historical people came into existence on emancipation from their overlords.[49] The Thessalians themselves claimed to have once owned Greece as far south as

[48] Ephoros *FGrH* 70 F 119 = Str. 9.2.3: *συνεστήσαντο τὴν ἀρχὴν μετὰ Ἀρναίων επὶ πολὺν χρόνον ὥστε καὶ Βοιωτοὺς κληθῆναι πάντας*. Cf. their leader 'Boiotos' *καταστήσας εἰς τὴν τότε μὲν Αἰολίδα, νῦν δὲ Θετταλίαν καλουμένην, τοὺς μεθ' ἑαυτοὺς Βοιωτοὺς ὠνόμασε* 'entering in what was then Aiolis but is now called Thessaly, he named those with him Boiotians'.

[49] The Boiotians inferior population or slaves at Arne, often at war with the Thessalians: e.g. Kharax *FGrH* 103 F 6 = St. Byz. s.v. *Δώριον*: a battle between Thessalians and Boiotians at Arne which a Thessalian general Aiatos won; Arkhemakhos *FGrH* 424 F 1 = Ath. 6.264a–b: the Boiotians were the 'slaves' of the Thessalians at Arne; Polyaen. 1.12: Thessalos evicted the Boiotians, who became suppliants of Athena Itonia. Cf. D.S. 4.67.6–7; Polyaen. 7.43. The connection with Arne is also formulated in mythical genealogy. In D.S. 4.67.2 ff. Boiotos is the son of Poseidon and Arne, the Boiotoi the people named after him; Boiotian chieftains at Troy are his grandsons. Boiotos' mother is Arne also in Nikokrates *FGrH* 376 F 5 = St. Byz. s.v. *Βοιωτία*; Euphorion *CA* 96.

Thespiai—the location of the ancient Hellopia discussed above.[50] The city of Arne itself is curiously placed in Thessaly only in the migratory traditions themselves, whereas many other texts locate it in Boiotia as if the Boiotians had never moved at all.[51] And finally, there is the Boiotians' long stay in Thessaly, during which they 'adapted' so much that they cared to take on the Thessalian cult centre of Athena Itonia—a deity also known from other areas with some Thessalian influence—and replanted her in Boiotia, which may itself be indicative of a period of perceived cohabitation.[52]

The tripodophoric rite is thus embedded in a set of myths which form part of one overarching mythical framework attesting simultaneously occurring, if irretrievable, changes in central and northern Greece that particularly involved the segregation of what were to become the later historical Thessalians and Boiotians (possibly coming out of the 'Aiolians'). With these details in mind we can glance again at Pindar's original text and its scholia. We can now provide the fragment with a mythical context, and attempt to fill it with content. There is sufficient evidence to assure us that, with this song, we move within that mythical stratum of which the tripodophoric *aition* too was part. The scholion's Thessalians' involvement in the song makes little sense other than in the context of the traditions discussed here. The explicit mention of Thebes in the scholion to line 11 cannot really be explained except in terms of the tripodophoric rite, the obvious (and only recorded) religious connection between Boiotia and Dodona.

Similarly, in the song itself, the presence of the mythical S/(H)Elloi suggests that the narrative concerned the earlier history of Dodona's prophecy practices, when there were the Hesiodic *hypophetai*, and not the Herodotean priestesses. *Μαντήϊον* ('oracle') in line 6 could refer to the oracle in general, or introduce a specific instance. The next lines speak about the ongoing ritual, and may have said something like 'from our [city, or other place of origin] with [*aulos* and] *phorminx* we come to make known the many-named seat of Zeus'. The fact that these lines seem already to imply a sense of direction through *ἀπό* . . . ('from . . .') makes it unlikely that this is repeated in the lines starting with *ἔνθεν* ('from here' ll. 11–12), which should therefore be taken temporally ('from then onwards'). *ἔνθεν* would refer back to the oracle given in l. 6 and introduce something along the lines of 'from then on, [we have been coming] with tripods and with sacrifices

[50] Cf. the semi-mythical battle of Keressos, where Thessalians threatened the Boiotians at Thespiai, and were defeated (early 6th cent. or early 5th cent. BC?): Paus. 9.14.2–3; Plut. *De Her. Mal.* 866d ff.; cf. Hdt. 7.233; Plut. *Cam.* 19.4 claims that defeating the Thessalians 'frees' the Greeks: is this an allusion to the Sacred War and 'Thessalian Hellenism' as discussed in Ch. 4?

[51] e.g. St. Byz s.v. calls Arne a city in Boiotia and a Boiotian colony; most importantly the *Catalogue of Ships*: *Il.* 2.507. Khaironeia was once called Arne according to Paus. 9.40.5; or Akraiphia was Arne: Str. 9.2.34. The relationship between Boiotos and Itonos (father of Athena Itonia (see below)) is often reversed: Boiotos can be the son of Itonos son of Amphiktyon: Paus. 9.1.1; 9.34.1; St. Byz. s.v. *Βοιωτία*; or Itonos is son of Boiotos and Arne, daughter of Aiolos: D.S. 4.67.7.

[52] See n. 72 below.

[to the shrine of Dodonaian Zeus]'. Since these lines 11 and 12 derive from a different part of the papyrus we might imagine a more elaborate tale to fit the space, one which then concluded with a reference to the dedication of tripod and sacrifice celebrated in the song's actual, early fifth-century ritual. Perhaps the *manteion* of line 6 is an allusion to the oracle of the aetiological myth leading to the tripodophoric rite. This is as far as we can go in reconstructing the content of the Pindaric lines.

I have proposed that the regular tripod tribute of the Boiotians attested by Pindar's *tripodophorikon melos* does not make sense in historical times when the Boiotians lived outside Dodona's regular catchment area as attested by the historical sources. It would make sense, however, for a time when the Boiotians lived closer to Dodona and belonged to the theoric worshipping community at this cult. And this is in fact suggested by the evidence from the migratory myths. Boiotian participation is rooted in the memory of the migrations, and furthermore closely bound up with their conflict with the Thessalians and Pelasgians. It is to this memory that we should attribute the odd fact of a Boiotian *tripodophoria* to Dodona.

While no historical relations between Dodona and Boiotia are attested, traces of links in the traditions about the wanderings of peoples in central and north-western Greece make one surmise that the tripodophoric rite emerged from a series of simultaneous changes, reconfigurations of peoples and places in the area; certainly the context of the tripodophoric *aition* is a set of delicately intertwined myths covering the whole area. The tripodophoric rite, if not generated through, at least arises from within, the intricacies of those interrelating traditions. Whether or not either Boiotians or Thessalians ever really lived in or near Dodona is irrelevant to this suggestion, while it is rather more pertinent that their imagined pasts are spread out over much of the vast space of central Greece. Rather, then, the possible important implication is that the tripodophoric rite attests to the process of regional ethnogenesis in early Greece in which these peoples were engaged.

So the Boiotian cult obligation to Dodona is interrelated with the Boiotians' own subjective memory of their physical presence in the catchment area of the sanctuary. This is an interesting phenomenon. There is at least one parallel case of a people who retain the memory of their former dwellings by sending a tribute to a cult they believed they had once participated in. This is also connected with the Epeiros of a time immemorial and irrecoverable: the Ainianes, located in Thessaly, recalled their former stay in Kassiopeia near Dodona by the annual delivery of an ox to the local Zeus (who is possibly the very same Zeus as the one we are dealing with here). The Ainianes, according to Heliodorus, also kept worshipping Neoptolemos in memory of the same stay in Molossia.[53]

[53] Plut. *QG* 293f–94c; 297b–c; cf. Str. 9.5.22 for their movements. The Ainianes also kept a cult of Zeus, and of Apollo, and worshipped Neoptolemos at Delphi. Cf. also [Arist.] *Mir. Ausc.* 133 843^{b}: the Ainianes also came through Boiotia and had trouble at the Ismenion.

That the Boiotians cared to celebrate this link in an annual ceremony in the fifth century suggests that the fact of their arrival in historical Boiotia mattered crucially to the image they had of themselves and were anxious to propagate among others. The cult tribute resolves the conflict between Boiotians and Pelasgians, and the Boiotians' victory marks the end of the wanderings. Cult obligation and final settlement in Boiotia are therefore intimately bound up with each other. By the annual performance of this ritual, the final victory over the Pelasgians and their expulsion from historical Boiotia, the turning point in Boiotian affairs, was re-enacted time and again. If the memory of this victory was unclear and in reality contested, all ambiguity was ruled out by its continuous reperformance in ritual. That this *was* problematic memory is suggested by the fact that the Boiotians had to incur pollution (the *μίασμα δρυός*, the 'pollution of the oak tree') to gain it.

Through the association with the triumphant entry of the Boiotians into Boiotia the tripod also acquires a special function. On the level of narrative it remains the compensatory gift to the god at Dodona. But when carried along in the annual celebration, the tripod takes on the role of a trophy, presented to the god who prompted the story in the first place. Offering a tripod in thanks for a victory in battle is a post-war ritual so common that it is hard to believe that this one would not have had similar connotations. The tripodophoric song (*τριποδηφορικὸν μέλος*) to accompany the glorious delivery functions as victory song, and indeed for the ancient eidographers Pindar's song seems to have qualified as a paean.[54] The *khoros* here too performs at the borderline between myth and ritual, between the victory in myth and the victory re-enacted in ritual, while the tripod itself is an essential prop that marks out the *khoros*-singing as that of a post-battle situation. The *khoros*-with-a-tripod establishes the vital link between myth and ritual.

Because it maintains so many pasts simultaneously created by the people involved in the developments in central and north-western Greece, this myth-ritual complex demonstrates aetiological practice at its extreme: aetiology is an interplay of the mythical past and the religious practice of the present. In none of the instances considered in this book has it been quite so evident how legends project elements of a contemporary cultic landscape into an imagined past: the whole functioning sanctuary of Dodona is retrojected to explain the changes that have led to the rite's contemporary, that is, its early fifth-century, shape. It is especially the priestesses in our story who document the change that produced them; because female diviners became perfectly normal after this myth had become 'true', a story without these priestesses can probably not work in a contemporary context. This presents yet another characteristic aetiological myth in which the narrative anticipates what it subsequently establishes. The priestesses as well as the tripods (surely a feature of the Boiotian cultic landscape only once the Boiotians had 'arrived' there) are anachronistic set props of the story.

[54] Its contributing papyri Π^{26} and Π^{7} included paeans: Rutherford (2001) 399.

The continuous performance of this myth-ritual complex ensures that the appreciation of the migrations remained present in the Boiotians' collective 'memory'. The tradition of the wanderings was re-enacted in ritual, and the rites themselves were performed as if the myths of the wanderings were true. The tripodophoric ritual effectively illustrates how memory is anchored, created, and maintained, in continual religious practice. It demonstrates perhaps more explicitly than other examples how different layers of myth survive in and through ritual.[55] It is of no great importance for the understanding of this process to know whether this perception of the past contained an element of true wanderings or not. Rather, such ritual landmarks play an important role in reiterating the memory of a suitable past through the creation of religious ties with the landscape left behind. Because of every *aition*'s obligation to a physical reality, the role aetiology must have played in this exercise of preserving memories of changing one's landscape can hardly be overrated. Aetiology links the real surroundings to imagined human conceptions of the past in an inherited space. Pindar's *tripodophorikon melos*—and those that followed it if we believe the antiquarian tradition—was a powerful reminder of how the Boiotians had arrived in Boiotia.

2. BECOMING BOIOTIAN IN THE *KOINON*

Thus far the tripodophoric fragment by itself. When we examine the plentiful remainder of Boiotian religious song, it quickly emerges that migratory traditions are all-pervasive, a major recurrent theme of the time. What was their role? They belonged, as we shall see, to a set of stock themes through which epichoric song-culture became operative in the definition of a regional Boiotian identity: Boiotians, in this myth, had things to share because they were allegedly immigrants from Thessaly. The creation of a notional 'Boiotia' in the second half of the sixth and early fifth centuries was in turn instrumental in the process of the constitution of the later Boiotian *koinon*, commonly termed the 'Boiotian League', a unity that became highly charged vis-à-vis the fifth-century Athenian empire.

In earlier chapters we have already seen how religious song moulded different senses of locality in different geographical and historical contexts of the early fifth century. In Boiotia, it has a part in formulating a conceptual definition of a region, which gradually takes shape as the fifth century moves on. Through the use of local aetiologies on regional ritual occasions shared by multiple localities on the one hand, of regional ones in local contexts on the other, religious song tackles the difficult problem of reconciling local and regional identities. Cult song also appears to have been operative in merging elite interest in the *koinon* with non-elite concerns for local independence, in the notion of a unified Boiotia. Within this wider Boiotian context, it furthermore attests strategies by which

[55] Cf. Chaniotis (2002) on 'ritual dynamics', interestingly also for Boiotia (above, Ch. 1, nn. 132, 134).

Thebes used the power of myth-ritual performances to create for itself a leading position within the emerging *koinon*. It achieved this by re-channelling traditional local myth and ritual into a myth-ritual grid covering much of historical Boiotia, and one in which Thebes was central. Nevertheless, the notion of 'Boiotia' remains a fragile one throughout the fifth century; the point of labouring or ignoring the concept seems to lie in justifying the existence or promoting the dissolution of the *koinon*: the idea of Boiotia is only ever as strong as the *koinon* itself.

In the second part of the chapter I deal with many different localities for the performance of religious song. I shall be concerned with the songs revolving around the sanctuary of Athena Itonia at Koroneia, that of Poseidon at Onkhestos, and that of Apollo Ptoios at Perdikovrysi near Akraiphia, the three cults sharing guardianship of matters Boiotian as future religious centres of the *koinon*. Following that I shall focus on the cult and oracle of Apollo Ismenios at Thebes and its relation to a string of oracular cults located around Lake Kopaïs and draw from this some broader conclusions about regional integration in Boiotia. As usual, the all-encompassing evidence from cult song trumps the sparse historical data for this period: the performance of myth in ritual gives tantalizing insights into how the momentum of song-dance, with its powerful illusions and pretences, actively aspires to settle contemporary questions of authority over, and contesting claims to, the mythical tradition. Fifth-century performance sets back the Boiotian clock to the beginning, rejigging the maze of the many Boiotian pasts into a new temporal framework, tied to an old religious space.

The Boiotian *koinon* and the notion of Boiotia

Before launching into the colourful early fifth-century reconstitution of Boiotia in myth and ritual, it is helpful to advance some central issues regarding the *koinon* itself, inseparably linked as they are to Theban regional hegemony.[56]

The date of the formation of what should at least provisionally be termed the Boiotian *koinon* is obscure. It is beyond doubt that by the late sixth century the Thebans had already obliged a number of cities to fight for them that were later members of the *koinon*, but how tight these links were is unclear.[57] Boiotia

[56] The key studies on the *koina* ('federal states') are Larsen (1968); Hansen (1995*a*); Corsten (1999), Beck (1997); and now Mackil (2003), embedding the phenomenon in social and economic structures in the Mediterranean along the lines of Horden and Purcell (2000). I have not seen Mafodda (1999). Specifically on the Boiotian *koinon* the most thorough account is Roesch (1965) 31–152 and (1982); Hammond (2000) gives a good overview of the complicated 5th and 4th cent. political history, see also Demand (1982) 16–47. Ducat (1973); Buck (1972) on the archaic *koinon*. On the role of Thebes see e.g. Sordi (1966); Bakhuizen (1994) for the 4th cent.

[57] Hdt. 5.79; 6.108; Th. 3.61.2. The so-called federal coinage presents the single most-cited argument in favour of a 6th-cent. *koinon*; see Hansen (1995*a*) 31 on how to handle this evidence: shared coinage need not 'be evidence of a proper federation; they may simply reflect the continued cooperation between cities belonging to the same region'. The point is now taken further by Mackil and Van Alfen (2006).

fought more or less concertedly, certainly energetically, on the Persian side during the Persian Wars. Any federal efforts, it is normally assumed, would have been thwarted after defeat by Athens at the battle of Oinophyta in 457 BC followed by a period of Athenian occupation of Boiotia lasting until the Athenians' defeat at Koroneia in 446 BC. Then 'exiles' from all over Boiotia bonded and liberated their fellow Boiotians, providing the conventional date for the *koinon*'s definite constitution. But even this date is not supported by any firm evidence. However, the *koinon* was definitely in existence by the time of the Peloponnesian War. That granted, like all the other *koina* in Greece, it still never adopted a fixed shape for long; the continuous reshuffling of the Boiotian cities' relationship to each other characterizes the long-term history of the 'federation'.[58]

The institutional problems related to the question of the *koinon*'s formation cannot be solved for the early period,[59] and are perhaps also a less fruitful field of inquiry than the quite different question that we can really tackle: that of the fostering of a particular notion of 'Boiotia' and 'Boiotians', which made possible the eventual coalescence of the *koinon* in the first place. Religious song-dance reveals how, and perhaps why, the formation of something like a regional identity took shape in the time between the Thebans' first attested call to arms and the fixed federation at some point after the middle of the fifth century. Operative in the run-up to the *koinon*'s eventual institution as it may have been, the network of myths and rituals implicated in the performance of contemporary religious song also suggests something a little broader: that 'what it means to be Boiotian' was a hot topic, probably at least from the late sixth century, and definitely throughout the fifth, and continued with just as much verve after the *koinon*'s institutional manifestation. In creating a certain vision of Boiotia, the songs were very much part of this debate.

The reason for the concept of Boiotia being so fragile in the archaic and classical periods no doubt lies in the fact that the *koinon* itself was constantly contested. Whether or not Boiotia should be unified was a continuous, burning issue in the region's history; the *koinon's* defenders always had to make a case to justify its existence. The nature of what constituted Boiotia, and how important an idea it was, kept changing with the relationships between the cities of Boiotia and later within the *koinon*. In this situation, the appropriation of the notion of

[58] Persian Wars: Hdt. *passim*. Athenian occupation of Boiotia except Thebes after 457 BC: Th. 4.92.6; 95; D.S. 11.83. No source unambiguously points to Athenian interference in individual cities: Th. 1.113; D.S. 11.81; 83; [Xen.] *Ath. Pol.* 3.1 (though cf. D.S. 12.5.6 where after the battle of Koroneia 446 BC the Boiotian cities are autonomous; cf. Th. 1.113); the events referred to in Arist. *Pol.* 1302^b29 cannot be dated. The *koinon* existed by 427/6 BC (Th. 3.91; 4.76.2 ff.; 4.91; 93.4; 5.38.2). Dull (1977) thinks of the period 457–446 BC as killing off Theban hegemonic spirits until at least 431 BC while Orkhomenos ascended, but there is no real proof of that. Cf. Larsen (1960); Buck (1970).

[59] Whether or not the Boiotians were organized as a league depends on what one thinks a 'federation' entails politically and institutionally and is irrelevant to the argument proposed here. For the view that draws a strict distinction between an institutionalized federal state and a loose, often military league, thereby neglecting non-constitutionalized forms of federal organization, see Hansen (1995*a*); Corsten (1999).

'Boiotia' was at all times an important tool in local and regional power politics. Much of this was probably prompted by, and confronted with, the growing Athenian empire, or at least a crowd of precocious Athenians next door. Just as they were keen to break up insularity at Rhodes, Athenians were probably not particularly comfortable with a unified Boiotian neighbour.[60] Their dislike of the *koinon* gives another relevant, if rather blunt, insight into Boiotian affairs. While it cannot be proved that the Athenians promoted democracies during the period of their occupation, historical texts suggest that the issue of Boiotian unity or autonomy of the cities was inseparably linked to that of oligarchy versus democracy. That is to say, the two competing models in play were those of an oligarchic Boiotian *koinon* and autonomous democratic *poleis* in Boiotia, the first arousing enmity, the second alliance with Athens. This schematic distinction is unlikely to represent reality—at best it reflects the rhetoric of intra-elite rivalry, in which individuals or groups took on one or the other case in order to further their own position in individual cities. But the fact remains that Thespiai and Plataiai, the two long-term *enfants terribles* in the long-term history of the *koinon*, were also the keenest to adopt democracies and manifestly parade their friendship with the Athenians. The resulting implication of relevance for this chapter is that at this time (though not necessarily in later centuries) the promotion of the *koinon* was the interest of a wider Boiotian and not just Theban elite, who in order to reach this goal sought to reconcile civic and regional identities; the opposite tendency, a little less visible but no less relevant, emphasizes local civic identity and, it seems, Panhellenism.[61]

So the question of Boiotia itself, and in whose interest it should be unified, was problematic. Approaching and retreating from this 'project Boiotia' was at least as old as the late sixth century, and never stopped during the classical period. In fact, the claim to Boiotianness was contested as soon as it emerged, and was used against other Boiotians. The *Boiotoi* in the *Catalogue of Ships* tellingly encompass most historical Boiotian cities, but not the Orkhomenians, who feature as Minyans with their own troops. A confident collective claiming to be the *Boiotoi* already dedicated to Athena Pronaia in the sanctuary of Apollo Ptoios at Akraiphia at around 500 BC, and it is very uncertain who these devotees to Athena were. Pindar pointedly speaks of 'customary Boiotian contests' (*ἔννομοι ἀγῶνες τῶν Βοιωτίων*)—juxtaposed with the festivals in Thebes—which ensures that a regional Boiotian awareness was both extant and perhaps provocative.[62] Fifth-

[60] D.S. 11.82.5 implies this; see e.g. Meiggs (1972) 209–10, but Athenian aggression during the 5th cent. was not necessarily directed against Thebes, which was not occupied between 457 and 446 BC.

[61] Democratic opposition, reacting to federal attempts: Th. 4.76.2 (cities hoping to introduce democracies); 4.133.1; 6.95.2 (Thespiai); Thebes' march into Plataiai was summoned by Plataiai's elite: Th. 3.65.2. Later oligarchic *koinon*: Th. 3.62.3–5; 4.76.2 ff.; 5.31.6 etc.; cf. *Hell. Oxy.* 12.32–3. Hornblower (2004) 154–66 gives a prosopography of the Boiotian elites as known from Pindar's victory odes. On Panhellenism see below, p. 387.

[62] *Il.* 2.510; Ptoion inscriptions: Ducat (1971) no. 269a, fragments of bronze vase (now lost): *Βο[ιωτοὶ Ἀθαναῖ τ]αῖ Προναίαι* 'the Boiotians to Athena Pronaia'; no. 257 (statuette base *c*.480 BC). Nos. 249 (poros colonnette *c*.500 BC) and 261 (fragment of tripod base *c*.500 BC), also to Athena, could be dedications by the *Boiotoi* as well; Pi. *O.* 7.84–5.

century Herodotus knows that in 519 BC the Thebans pursued the Plataians for their lack of interest in 'contributing to the Boiotians' (εἰς Βοιωτοὺς τελέειν), the beginning of a long history of charges launched against Plataiai for their lack of sense of Boiotianness. By contrast, the text says elsewhere, cities such as Tanagra, Koroneia, and Thespiai had 'always' fought with the Thebans—a problematic claim since certainly the later Thespians were notoriously reluctant to support the *koinon*. Plataiai and Thespiai were also the two cities who refused to join the Persians against the Greeks with all the other Boiotians. If the remaining Boiotians got off lightly after the end of the Persian Wars when only their Theban leaders were executed, this gives testimony to the idea that a Boiotia medizing as a whole was the ideal of only some Boiotians. That said, this view was a penetrating one: the memory of medism—after all Boiotia offered itself as the Persian military headquarters as much as for banqueting with the pro-Persian Greek elites—was a stigma attached to all Boiotians *qua Boiotians* for ever after.[63]

In this situation, where inter-city collaboration was not top of everyone's agenda, calling upon shared tradition was highly tactical in keeping the Boiotian idea together. An appeal to Boiotian identity was arguably difficult to resist and, if not ruthlessly, certainly systematically exploited by those with an interest in a unified Boiotia. Boiotia's 'liberation' from Athens in 446 BC may have established the formalized *koinon*, but more interestingly for us also some key themes in the rhetoric of the *koinon*'s supporters. These demonstrate how keen some Thebans in particular were to turn Boiotianness into their greatest draw. The key strategy was to declare Boiotia something that all Boiotians inevitably wanted, with the unargued assumption that there *was* something like Boiotia.

Thucydides on post-446 BC Boiotians gives an idea of what Boiotianness really was: a vague, rather vacuous sense of shared 'custom' and 'tradition' that the Thebans were predicating of themselves as much as of the nascent *koinon*. The debate held over Plataiai in the context of the Theban intervention in 432 BC brilliantly portrays Theban self-righteous notions of who was a Boiotian and what Boiotia was supposed to look like, designed to justify aggressive Theban action, even if we need to be aware of its being a piece of contrived rhetoric. So for example, Plataians already in 519 BC had been 'separating themselves from the other Boiotians, transgressing the ancestral customs' (ἔξω τῶν ἄλλων Βοιωτῶν παραβαίνοντες τὰ πάτρια Th. 3.61.2), and they repeated this in 432 BC through their alliance with Athens. Plataiai's 'first men in wealth and birth' had called in the Thebans having in mind to 'reinstate [the city] into the ancestral traditions of

[63] The situation in 519 BC: Hdt. 6.108 (on the meaning of *teleein*, not necessarily financial, in this passage see Hornblower (1991–6) ii. 251); 5.79. Execution of pro-Persian leaders: 9.86; D.S. 11.33.4: medism the eternal charge: e.g. Th. 3.62 (where it is attributed to the rule of a very tight elite); 3.64; Xen. *Hell.* 3.5.35; *Exp. Cyr.* 3.1.26. Herodotus is keen to stress Plataiai and Thespiai's commitment to the Greeks: cf. 7.132, 202, 222, 226, 132, 8.25, 50, 66, 75.

all the Boiotians' and 'to win it back into the kinship'.[64] High moral ground in the name of Boiotia also reigns when Thebans had proclaimed that 'those who want to be governed according to the hereditary customs common to all Boiotians were to come over to us [the Thebans]' (*τὸν βουλόμενον κατὰ τὰ τῶν πάντων Βοιτωτῶν πάτρια πολιτεύειν ἰέναι πρὸς ἡμᾶς*, 3.66.1). The sensitivity of this issue is uniquely brought out in Pagondas' patriotic speech before the battle of Delion between Athenians and Boiotians in 424 BC. This speech pointedly starts 'O Boiotians!' (*ὦ ἄνδρες Βοιωτοί*) and proceeds to plea for Boiotian 'freedom' from Athenian 'enslavement'. Importantly, emphasizing the tyranny of the Athenian empire in this speech as elsewhere does not just help the case of the *koinon* but above all mitigates Boiotian medism—which was arguably and ironically furthered by the very same people who later proceeded to promote the *koinon*, the elites in the individual cities.[65] Boiotianness was something to invest in—as the Athenian experience suggests and we already saw in the case of the Rhodian islanders, appealing to a shared exclusivity is the most effective way of rallying support for a disputed case.

We can conclude that the history of the *koinon* and attempting to develop a communal Boiotian identity are inextricably intertwined; the dynamic is bound up with the circumstances created by the Persian Wars and the Athenian empire and democracy, and the challenges they posed to local communities. Over the course of the fifth century certainly, it seems, the (not exclusively Theban-motivated) *koinon* appropriated the notion of Boiotia for itself and made it inaccessible to all others, as suggested by the Plataiai debate. It is this process that religious song carries along so energetically. While little or nothing is known about the relations between the Boiotian cities in the early to mid-fifth century, religious songs give insight into, and have a share in, the construction of a Boiotian identity, in which among other things Thebes was enthroned in the centre of the Boiotian map. Such a role cannot be taken for granted since despite, or because of, all the inverse rhetoric the city had no uncontested tradition of leadership in Boiotia.[66] There is a good chance that our songs, performed as they were as Boiotian 'tradition', share responsibility for the concept of Boiotia we glean from Thucydides, and with it for its emptiness: by the time he wrote, probably there *were* perceived 'Boiotian' customs, or at least everyone had been told so often that there were that it was credible: *you cannot argue with a song.*

[64] Th. 3.65.2: *ἐς δὲ τὰ κοινὰ τῶν πάντων Βοιωτῶν πάτρια καταστῆσαι*; 65.3: *ἐς τὴν συγγένειαν οἰκειοῦντες*. The debate is full of 'Boiotian' rhetoric, much of which the Theban speakers put into the mouth of pro-Theban Plataians, alluding to Hdt. 6.108 when the Plataians first did not abide by Theban concerns.

[65] Th. 4.92–4; cf. 3.62, 64.

[66] Rather Orkhomenos has a tradition of leadership in Boiotia (though historical signs of this are few): Isocr. 14.10; D.S. 15.79.3–6, and n. 68 below. On the basis of the 'Tanagra issue' of coins and Th. 1.107–8, Fowler (1957) and Dull (1977) postulate an important role for Tanagra leading to the battle of Tanagra in 457 BC.

Cultivating the Thessalian traditions of Lake Kopaïs

It is in this context that the myth of the immigration from Thessaly gains relevance in mapping out the local geography in a Boiotian way. It attests the emergence of a group of people who constantly paraded their togetherness through this myth, prompting the overwhelming number of contemporary Boiotian *khoroi*. The migratory myths, however, do not envelop the whole of Boiotia, and most conspicuously ignore Thebes. They are exclusively bound up with the places sitting around Lake Kopaïs—that shallow body of water taking up much of eastern Boiotia that every major power, from the Minyans to Nero, tried to drain (Fig. 7.2, Map 7.2). Ancient tradition unanimously believed that the 'Boiotoi' entered historical Boiotia in several instalments from the western Kopaïs, sometimes Orkhomenos, sometimes Khaironeia. From there they collectively trekked eastwards; decisive battles, myths, and associated cults mark their slow progress before they eventually settled along the northern and southwestern coast of the Kopaïs. But at Koroneia their traces vanish; into eastern Boiotia the Boiotians of the migratory traditions never came. No ancient source (with one tantalizing exception, which I shall discuss in Section 2.3) tells us that the Boiotoi ever reached Thebes during their push from Thessaly. The myth of the Boiotian wanderings simply does not cover Thebes.[67]

The set of migratory traditions is thus limited to the Kopaïs basin in western Boiotia, producing a curious dynamic. It is in this area that the collective of the Boiotoi most intensively invests in the making of community. The absence of Thebes in the relevant tradition gradually and fascinatingly adjusts itself perhaps from the late sixth century onwards, and definitely during the first half of the fifth. Boiotian cultic songs belabour the immigrant traditions and, by extension, the entire network of myths and rituals of the Kopaïs for the creation of a regional identity.

One can only speculate on the reasons why the Kopaïs basin is so specifically targeted in choral performances: why do no hymns survive, for example, for the constantly defecting Plataians? The antiquity of the problem of Boiotia's unity may provide part of an answer. The competing Bronze Age centres Orkhomenos, which dominated western Boiotia and the Kopaïs, and Thebes, overseeing the east, ensured a divided region. The rivalry could account for the lack of significant overlaps between western and eastern Boiotian mythical traditions as they are preserved. A form of rivalry certainly continued in the historical period, but there is little evidence for Orkhomenos ever having seriously engaged in matters

[67] Three basic episodes are known: the Boiotoi were believed to have first arrived at Khaironeia: Plut. *Cim.* 1.1 (NB the city was once called Arne according to Paus. 9.40.5; cf. Tz. *Lyc.* 644); then they took Orkhomenos and defeated the Thracians at Koroneia where they built the temple of Athena Itonia (Str. 9.2.29). Then the Thracians launched their surprise attack (the 'Thracian pretence') against the Boiotians, who were celebrating the festival of Athena Itonia (cf. Polyaen. 7.43) or Apollo (Procl.; Zenob. 4.37). The Thracians at various stages in the story lived on Mt. Helikon/Parnassos near Thespiai (south of Koroneia): Str. 9.2.25.

'Boiotian'. However, this city's sway over its traditional sphere of influence, the Kopaïs, was affected by Boiotian initiatives often, but not exclusively, mounted by Thebes. It is the investment in the myth-ritual network of the Kopaïs basin in the service of a unified Boiotia where Theban inspirations are most manifestly visible.[68]

The sudden explosion of activity in the previously rather sleepy Kopaïs basin of the late sixth and early fifth centuries gives a starting point for the phenomenon to be observed. The cities sitting round the lake one by one start entering the picture as if their interaction began to matter in a new or different way. Hyettos, an Orkhomenian neighbour in the Athamantine plain, was defeated by Thebes in around 500 BC, as a dedication at Olympia suggests. Another votive of about 550–525 BC knows of an Orkhomenian victory over Koroneia, one of those cities acclaimed as habitual supporters of the Thebans. A late sixth-century *horos* stone appears between Akraiphia and Kopai, a traditional Orkhomenian ally; this arrangement gains relevance considering that the Boiotoi of the *koinon* much later regulated the same border—over fishing rights in the Kopaïs basin. Somewhat later, in 480 BC, the Thebans are said to control the Ptoion at Akraiphia, possibly in the name of the, or a notional, *koinon*. Thebans were definitely up and about the Kopaïs vying with traditional Orkhomenian allegiances in the late sixth century and the early fifth, peering at what was quickly becoming the problematic heartland of 'Boiotia'.[69]

Bits and pieces of early fifth-century song-dance relating to the myths and rituals of local sanctuaries spell out more clearly what is at stake—a change of power structures less resembling aggressive territorial politics than the subtle undermining of established traditions of myth and ritual. As we have seen in earlier chapters, this was often a more cogent way of establishing relations with uncomfortable neighbours than brute military force. Three of the relevant scenes of religious activity are all part of the sixth-century Kopaïd dynamic, and the cults involved would in future become closely involved with the affairs of the *koinon*: the cult of Athena Itonia at Koroneia, Poseidon's sanctuary at Onkhestos, and Apollo's oracle at the Ptoion near the city of Akraiphia. All three are more intimately linked to western Boiotia through (partly genealogical) myth; they seem to experience a degree of monumentalization at some point in the sixth century, and in the early fifth century religious song starts tying these gods into a single network of myths and rituals, presided over by Thebes. The evidence for movement in each individual cult is scant, but the developments in all three

[68] On a possible Bronze Age rivalry between Orkhomenos and Thebes see Schachter (1989); Buck (1979*a*); others think it an early archaic conflict: Cloché (*s.d.*) 21–2. For Orkhomenos' ancestral claim to leadership of Boiotia see n. 66 above.

[69] Thebes' victory over Hyettos: Lazzarini 957 = *SEG* xxvii 48 (*c*.500 BC). Orkhomenos' victory over Koroneia: *LSAG* 95.11 = Lazzarini 994 = *SEG* xxviii 427 (550–525BC); Paus. 9.24.3 (Orkhomenian control over Hyettos and the Athamantine plain). Horos stone: *SEG* xxx 440 (around 500 BC); Roesch (1965) 64–5 links a later arbitration by 'the Boiotians' over the same boundary to a conflict over the catching area of the Boiotian eel (*IG* vii 2792). Thebans at the Ptoion: Hdt. 8.135. Schachter (1989) 80–1 discusses some of these pieces of 6th-cent. history.

Figure 7.2 The Kopaïs basin, seen from Haliartos. The ancient lake is now a fertile agricultural plain

taken together begin to open up a picture of committed investment in regional interaction enveloping the entire Kopaïs. This will be the theme of what follows immediately. The phenomenon can be taken further by considering afterwards Apollo's mantic pool, the string of oracular cults sitting around the Kopaïs, together with Apollo Ismenios at Thebes and the pageant of the Daphnephoria. The final part of this chapter will identify the role of these performances of myth and ritual in the ongoing debate over local and regional identities characteristic of the dynamics within the Boiotian *koinon*.

Athena Itonia and the making of a warrior tradition

The cult of Athena Itonia at Koroneia at the southern edge of the Kopaïs is particularly illustrative of the way in which the wanderings accumulated relevance, especially (but not exclusively) in the early fifth century. Here the Boiotian *koinon* centuries later lavishly celebrated the so-called Pamboiotia. Athena's pan-Boiotian significance is generally thought not to pre-date the first epigraphic testimony of such a role at the turn of the fourth century. By contrast, her archaeology, especially when held against other cults round the Kopaïs, and the fragments from religious song, hint that she was very much in the spotlight in the late sixth and especially during the fifth century, suggesting that her festival

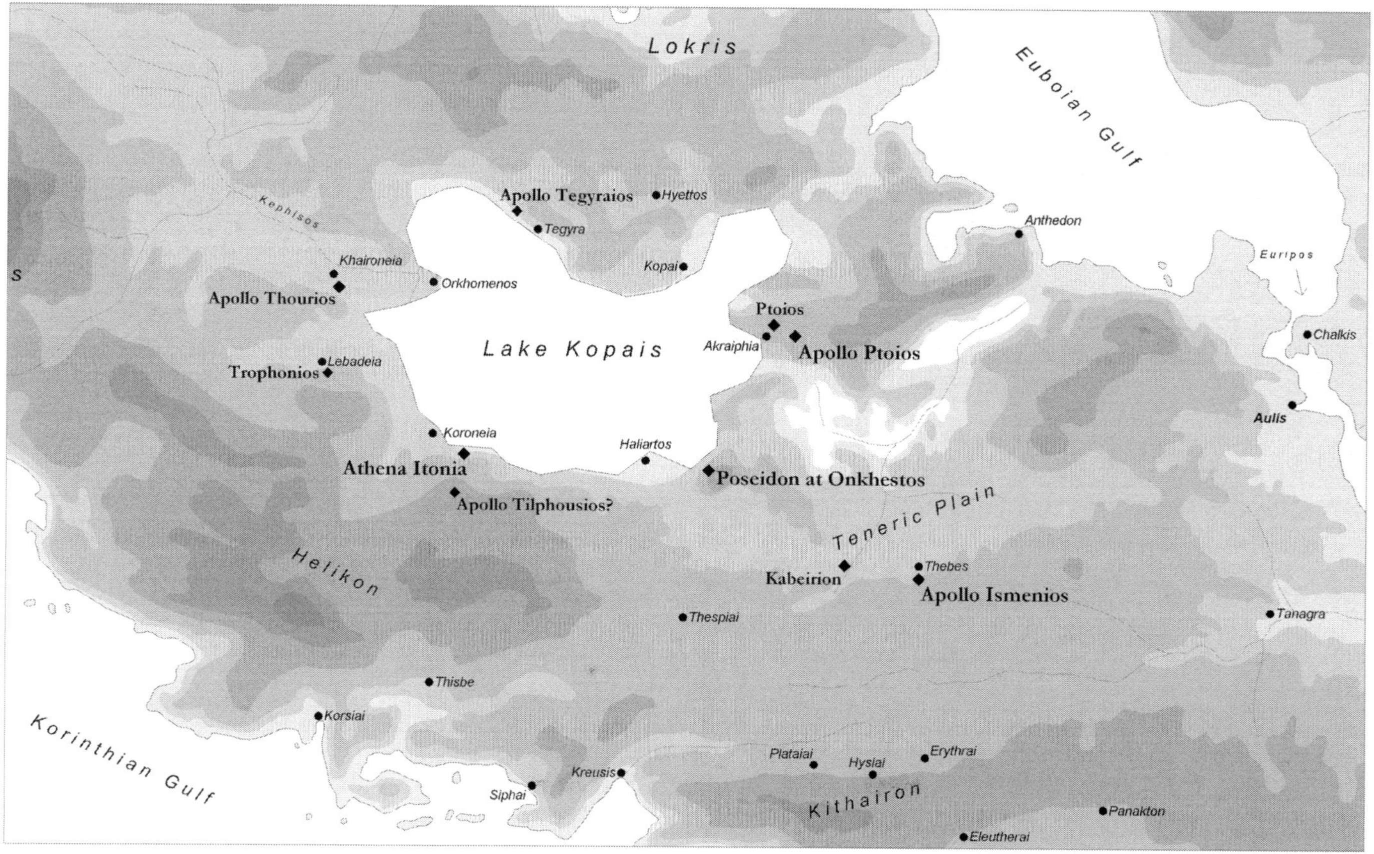

Map 7.2 Cults of Thessalian heritage: Athena Itonia, Poseidon at Onkhestos, and the mantic pool, a string of oracles, often Apolline, sitting around Lake Kopaïs. Created from digital map data © Collins Bartholomew (2004) 2007

came to be a cornerstone in the elaboration of the Boiotians' immigrant identity.[70]

Athena's precinct, identified beyond reasonable doubt in the early 1970s, lies just north of the ancient akropolis of Koroneia and in later times was sizeable, comprising as many as three major buildings of which one has a good chance of dating back to the sixth century BC. The fifth-century *eromenos* of Pheidias, Agorakritos, sculpted Athena with Zeus as a consort for the temple, an obscure cult image signalling attention for the shrine at this time.[71]

This Athena is an exemplary goddess of the Thessalo-Boiotian migratory traditions: she derives her epithet from the city of Iton in central Thessaly, and Strabo tells us that the Boiotians set her up at the Kopaïs on their way from Thessaly into Boiotia; they also named the nearby river after a Thessalian one. Athena Itonia was a warrior goddess for the Thessalians as much as for the Boiotians, and her journey from Thessaly into Boiotia was one of conquest.[72] As early as the seventh century Alkaios invoked the goddess at Koroneia as πολεμάδοκε ('war-sustaining'). Boiotian black-figure vases depict Athena as a warlike deity, often thought to be in reference to Athena Itonia. Hellenistic poets and antiquarians give her attributes such as 'well-greaved' (εὐκνήμις) and 'superbly warlike' (πολεμικωτάτην), suggesting that this Athena was always ready to strike.[73]

An Athena striding forth in battle was also what interested the fifth-century worshippers. The contemporary 'genealogos' Simonides of Keos (his relation to the choral poet is unclear)[74] tells us that Iton, eponym of Athena's Thessalian city

[70] For the traditional view see e.g. Schachter (1981–94) i. 123; but also Ziehen (1949); Ducat (1973) 60–1; Buck (1979*a*) 88–9. Pamboiotia: Str. 9.2.29; Paus. 9.34.1; Plut. *Am. Narr.* 774f–75a. The cult is mentioned in many 'pan-Boiotian' contexts, e.g. Plb. 4.25.2; Plut. *Ages.* 19.1 ff.; Polyaen. 7.43; Liv. 36.20.3; Plut. *Am. Narr.* 774. The Pamboiotia are first epigraphically attested in *IG* ix^2.1 170 (early 3rd cent.). *IG* vii 2858–69 are the later *koinon*'s proxeny decrees set up in the temple; 2711.70 ff. mentions an honorary statue put up in the shrine; 2871 is a list of victors. 3426 knows of an (imperial) priest of the *koinon* τῆς Ἰτωνίας Ἀθηνᾶς; the cult was an *asylon* in Hellenistic times (*SEG* xviii 240 and Plut. *Ages.* 19). The Pamboiotia are best discussed by Schachter (1978).

[71] Spyropoulos (1973) 385–92; *ΑΔ* 28 B.1 (1973) 271–2; (1975); cf. *BCH* 98 (1974) 643. Schachter (1981–94) i. 117–27 provides the most comprehensive treatment of the cult. Cf. Roesch (1982) 217–24 and Deacy (1995); Paus. 9.34.1–2.

[72] Str. 9.2.29; cf. 9.2.14; 17 for the Thessalo-Boiotian goddess. Settlers allegedly from Thessaly elsewhere in the Greek world claim cults of this Athena perhaps for the same reason, to state their successful establishment in a new place: Arkesine and Amorgos on the island of Amorgos: *IG* xii.7 *passim*. Cf. Athens *IG* i^2 310.216 f.; ii^2 33 (4th cent.).

[73] Alc. *PLF* 325 cf. Hekataios *FGrH* 1 F 2; Armenidas *FGrH* 278 F 1; Korinna *PMG* 667 speaks of an Athena's 'stormy shield'. The cult in Thessaly: *Σ* A.R. 1.551 = Hekataios *FGrH* 1 F 2; *Anth. Pal.* 9.743; 6.130. This is where Pyrrhus dedicates his spoils: Plut. *Pyrrh.* 26.5; Itonia important for Thessalians in battle: Paus. 1.13.2–3; cf. 10.1.10; A.R. 1.551; *Σ* A *Il.* 2.175 = Rhianos *CA* 47: ἐϋκνήμιδος Ἰτώνης; *EM* 479.47 = Simonides of Keos *FGrH* 8 F 1; Call. *Ath.* (6) 74 (Thessalian goddess together with Boiotian Athena) and *Σ*; Fest. 105.22. Boiotian ritual scenes on 6th-cent. vases with a warlike Athena: Scheffer (1992), esp. London BM B 80.

[74] This Simonides is sometimes thought to be the poet's daughter's son (θυγατριδοῦς, *Suda* σ 442 s.v.), though the older Simonides also had a conspicuous interest in Thessaly and composed for elite families there: 510 (at the house of Skopas), 529, 542 *PMG* see also 519 fr. 22. Cf. Molyneux (1992) Ch. 6.

and father of *Βοιωτός*, was father of the two girls Athena and Iodama, both such keen warriors that the goddess killed her sibling in armed battle (*ὁπλομαχία*).[75] A later story placed in Boiotia similarly connects Athena Itonia with the supersession of a local predecessor, equally called Iodama whom Athena's *aigis* turned into stone. From Pausanias we know about a rite by which every day a woman laid a piece of stone on Iodamas' altar murmuring three times that 'Iodama lives and demands fire' (i.e. sacrifice): an instance once again for an old ritual past not being swallowed up by newcomers.[76] It is also interesting that certainly the later scholarly tradition seems to confuse Athena Itonia with the local goddess known from the Homeric epics, bearing the epithet Alalkomeneis, which implies that Athena Itonia mythically speaking is a product of post-Trojan War times, thus matching the chronology of the migrations. The Homeric scholia set Alalkomeneis in the times of Kekrops, and I shall argue later that alleged pristine Athenian presence in Boiotia comes to play a role for communities wishing to distance themselves from the myth-ritual network of the Kopaïs.[77]

The most pertinent evidence for a warring Athena's allure to early fifth-century Boiotians comes from directly contemporary religious song. At least one, and probably two, *hyporkhemata* by Bacchylides were composed for performance in honour of the goddess (frr. 15, 15a); Pindar produced two rather more substantial pieces of this genre, which have a good chance of stemming from the same central Greek context (frr. 106, 107ab). Bacchylides' four lines are the least obscure, speaking of Athena 'with the golden *aigis*'—should this be in allusion to the context of conquest from which she arose in Boiotia?

Οὐχ ἕδρας ἔργον οὐδ' ἀμβολᾶς
ἀλλὰ χρυσαίγιδος Ἰτωνίας
χρὴ παρ' εὐδαίδαλον ναὸν ἐλ-
θόντας ἁβρόν τι δεῖξαι ⏑ –

This is no time for sitting or delaying: we must go to the well-crafted temple of Itonia of the golden aegis and perform a splendid [song? dance?] (Bacchylides fr. 15)

We know next to nothing about hyporchemes, except that dance was a feature more prominent than usual. In one of Pindar's songs of the same genre a

[75] Simonides *FGrH* 8 F 1 = Tz. *Lyc.* 355: *Ἰτωνὶς καὶ Ἰτωνία ἡ Ἀθηνᾶ εἴρηται παρὰ τοῖς Θετταλοῖς, ἀπό τινος πόλεως Ἴτωνος. φησὶ δὲ ὁ γενεαλόγος Σιμονίδης Ἰτώνου θυγατέρας γενέσθαι δύο, Ἀθηνᾶν καὶ Ἰοδάμαν, ἃς ἐζηλοκυίας τὴν ὁπλομαχικὴν εἰς ἔριν τὴν εἰς ἀλλήλας χωρῆσαι, ἀναιρεθῆναι τὴν Ἰοδάμαν ὑπὸ τῆς Ἀθηνᾶς.* 'Athena is called Itonis and Itonia by the Thessalians, from a city Iton. For the 'genealogue' Simonides says that there were two daughters of Itonos, Athena and Iodama, who, ambitious about martial arts, launched into single combat against each other, and Iodama was killed by Athena'. Cf. *Σ Lyc.* 355: *πολεμικωτάτην Ἀθηνᾶν Ἰτωνίου . . . θυγατέρα, Ἰοδάμας δὲ ἀδελφήν, ἣν ἀντιπολεμοῦσαν Ἀθηνᾶ ἀνεῖλεν* 'Athena daughter of Iton, the very warlike, sister of Iodama whom she killed in battle'. Iodamas' grandfather is, interestingly, Amphiktyon (ibid. 1206). Cf. *EM* 479.46–54. s.v. *Ἰτωνίς καὶ Ἰτωνία.*

[76] Paus. 9.34.

[77] e.g. Lact. ad St. *Theb.* 7.330 (where the Itonia and Alkaiomeneis are identical), attributing the confusion even to Bacchylides (fr. 15a). For Athena Alalkomeneis see *Il.* 4.8; 5.908; Paus. 9.33.5–7; Str. 9.2.36. Kekrops: *Σ Il.* 4.8.

first person compares its song-dance to the 'Amyklaian dog's whirling hunt over the Dotian plain in Thessaly' (fr. 107), and the same dog's dance, now turned 'Lakonian', features together with a Theban war-chariot in his other hyporcheme (fr. 106). Though the divine addressee of these two Pindaric pieces remains unconfirmed, Boiotian military dances staged as hunts based on some Thessalian model are a good possibility.[78]

Two songs are certainly, and two possibly, related to Athena Itonia, the latter attributed on the basis of shared genre and the peculiar 'Thessalian' dance. Should this document significant attention given to Athena in the fifth century as a warrior goddess hailing from Thessaly? Certainly we must look for a performance context for these scraps of song: this may already have been the Pamboiotia, but the more attractive interpretation in the absence of any firm evidence on an all-Boiotian gathering in this period is that spinning the yarn in religious song of her conquest of Boiotia, arriving there together with the Boiotians themselves, was producing, rather than confirming, the case of the Boiotoi, that of a community whose distinctive feature was that they were newcomers in Boiotia. Pindar cites hippic agons for Athena, as I shall argue below, as part of a pan-Boiotian rhetoric relevant to the Daphnephoria at Thebes. Just as neatly, Plutarch remembers that after the Boiotians vanquished the Athenians in 446 BC at Koroneia, they dedicated a statue to Athena, a timely memory of a victory about which pro-federalists very much cared; that battles of importance to the *koinon* tended to happen at Koroneia is a telling coincidence. The festival of the Pamboiotia at all later times integrated warrior strength with regionalism: for example third-century and later soldier contingents of cavalry, archers, slingers, peltasts, and the mysterious *epilektoi* ('the chosen') from the individual Boiotian cities fostered their sense of regional unity in military agons in Athena's honour.[79] Athena Itonia's festival cannot be separated from her military character, nor can she be untied from the Boiotians. Supposedly it paraded her Thessalian origins, re-enacting the Boiotians' arrival, and there is a good chance that this is what the hyporchemes sang and danced about.

Hijacking Poseidon at Onkhestos and Apollo Ptoios

The emphasis on a pan-Boiotian Athena Itonia hailing from Thessaly is closely matched by specifically Theban investment in the 'Thessalian' tradition, albeit

[78] Hyporchemes: Procl. *ap.* Phot. *Bibl.* 239.320b33–4. See the testimonia now assembled by E. Robbins, *DNP* 5 (1998), 815–16 s.v. On hunting komast dancers on vases see now Steinhart (2007) 204–9.

[79] Pi. *Parth.* 2, fr. 94b, ll. 41–7; Plut. *Ages.* 19.1 ff.; Polyaen. 7.34. On the military character of the festival Roesch (1965) 107–8; Schachter (1981–94) i. 119 s.v. Ares was involved in the games: *IG* vii 2871. Fascinating are the 3rd-cent. victor lists and dedications: *IG* vii 3087 (Lebadeia); *SEG* iii 354–5 (Thespiai and Thisbe); *IG* vii. 3172 (Orkhomenos). On the stereotype of the always-warring Boiotians see Vottero (1998–2001) i. 166–8. On Boiotian contemporary 'military' culture drawn from an exciting discussion of the knight Eugnotos' victory monument see now Ma (2005).

not only in that of the wanderings. Thebans can be seen to insert themselves into the mythical past, even into the aetiologies, of two sanctuaries with strong links to the Kopaïs basin, that of Poseidon at Onkhestos, and that of Apollo Ptoios at Perdikovrysi near Akraiphia. The shrines of both Onkhestian Poseidon and Ptoian Apollo are traditional venues for Erginos and Athamas, kings or sub-kings of the rival Orkhomenos and the chief mythical personnel of the Thessalo-Kopaïd heritage. They represent the so-called Minyan origins, in turn reflecting the Thessalian ancestry of Orkhomenos; these 'Minyans' are equated with the Argonauts from Iolkos in Thessaly.[80] In the context of the wanderings Erginos and Athamas prefigure the perceived later migrations of the Boiotians much as the Herakleids prefigure the Dorians of the Peloponnese. Thebans, who as we said have no share in the myth of the wanderings of the Boiotoi, are not unequivocally associated either with the mythical figures and cults foreshadowing them. However, in Pindaric song the Thessalian heritage miraculously starts to become theirs.

The Theban hero Teneros is the key figure here. He is Apollo's child and archetypal seer at the Theban Ismenion and will feature again in the discussion of Apollo's Boiotian song-world below. Teneros was the eponym of the triangular plain reaching from Thebes westwards to Onkhestos and northwards to the Ptoion (Map 7.2); the low mountain range extending between the two shrines (Phikion) separates the Teneric plain from the Kopaïs basin. In the early fifth century, this Theban hero effectively chases after the Thessalo-Kopaïd traditions, and the two sanctuaries, closely entwined with the myth-ritual network of the basin, are two of his hunting grounds. His involvement in these shrines marks interesting Theban claims to the Kopaïs traditions.[81]

Pindar's so-called *Paean 9* insists that Teneros, beyond being a major Theban hero, was the 'favourite of Poseidon' (Pi. *Pae.* 9.47–8, as cited below, p. 372). This is plausibly Poseidon of Onkhestos, who dwelt at the other end of the Teneric plain from Thebes, a direct neighbour of Teneros at the border of the Kopaïs and in charge of the major east–west route in Boiotia (Map 7.2). The Onkhesteion is the only significant cult of Poseidon's in all of Boiotia, making this local god the likely candidate for protection of Teneros in the paean. Poseidon's shrine underwent the same somewhat mysterious sixth-century monumentalization as did that of Athena Itonia. The construction at Onkhestos of a temple and an adjacent building (misleadingly called 'bouleuterion'), and a dedication of around 500 BC suggest heightened activity, though the site is too badly explored to allow major conclusions.[82]

[80] Minyans and Argonauts: Pi. *P.* 4.69; Hdt. 4.145–6; Str. 9.2.40; Paus. 7.2.2. Minyans at Orkhomenos: *Σ* A.R. 1.763–64a. It is not clear how the Bronze Age civilization of Orkhomenos relates to a 'Thessalian' ancestry.

[81] Teneros: Str. 9.2.34; Paus. 9.26.1.

[82] Spyropoulos (1973) 379–81, *AΔ* 28 B.1 (1973) 269–71 are the main accounts (with references to earlier reports); cf. *BCH* 98 (1974) 64–5 (the inscription); *Teiresias* 3 (1973), 4; Roesch (1982) 269; 272; Schachter (1981–94) ii. 207–21 s.v.

Onkhestian Poseidon has no extant chant of his own, but Teneros as Poseidon's early fifth-century page in *Paean 9* nevertheless requires scrutiny: it is unlikely to be a long-standing and unchallenged association in view of an elaborate network of myths and rituals embracing the shrine, which suggest that rule of this sanctuary was contested. Rather Teneros' appearance fits the notion that mythical Thebans were at this time keen to mingle with gods of Thessalo-Boiotian colouring of the Kopaïs, exploited for the development of an identity for the Boiotoi. Poseidon of Onkhestos was indeed an old god of the 'Boiotians', and is loosely attached to a group of this name in the *Catalogue of Ships.* He was already sitting up on the pass when Apollo came for his oracular tour in the *Homeric Hymn to Apollo,* something that I shall later explain implies a younger age for a Boiotian communality based around cults of Apollo. Importantly, Poseidon's cult itself had a curious Thessalian slant. Its inland location along a major thoroughfare of Boiotia links the Onkhestian shrine to a group of similar cults placed at the rivers and heights of Thessaly. If Onkhestos were indeed only the most southern of this central Greek cult-type, it would suggest a Theban hunt after Thessalian figures.[83]

Despite the absence of a hymn of his own, Poseidon's shrine and the mythical figures associated with it are nevertheless ubiquitous in early fifth-century cult song. If the sixth-century historical evidence quoted above intimates trouble between the two centres of Thebes and Orkhomenos, this rivalry is expressed in the legends enveloping Onkhestos and featuring the conflict between the Orkhomenian king Erginos and Theban Herakles.[84] These two heroes fought in and around Poseidon's shrine, wrapping the sanctuary in an elaborate mythical web marking Theban influence in the area.[85] The set of legends is a good example of how the notion of perceived change of local power relations was expressed in cult myths. Erginos, in the Argonautic cycle a son of Poseidon, is tied to the shrine through his mortal father Klymenos. Klymenos' accidental death in a horse race at a *heorte* ('festival') of Poseidon sparked off the war between Herakles and Erginos and left the Thebans tributary to Orkhomenos, a tribute probably connected to the shrine. Herakles struck back to release the Thebans from the obligation, and in most traditions Erginos himself and two of the Orkhomenian leaders were killed near the sanctuary. Herakles eventually received a shrine as ἱπποδέτης ('the horse tamer') near by. The set of myths presumably attempts to construe a 'memory' of the Thebans having taken control of the shrine from Orkhomenos

[83] *Il.* 2.494–510; *H. Ap.* 229–38 (on which see Schachter (1976)). The interesting suggestion that Onkhestos belonged typologically to a group of Thessalian cults is made by Schachter (1981–94) ii. 212, with references.

[84] See Schachter (1981–94) ii. 215–16 for a sixth-century stake of Orkhomenos in the shrine, citing Pseudo-Hesiod's *Aspis*, esp. 103–5 accompanying a possible Theban appropriation. The *Aspis* requires a detailed study.

[85] Herakles had just killed the lion on Mount Kithairon, and visited Thespies and his daughters. Buck (1979*a*) 59–60 accounts for the group of legends. See also Schachter (1989) 80 n. 31.

at some point in the mythical past, not unlike the Minoan–Theseian takeover discussed in Chapter 2.[86]

Some of this mythical ensemble must have been known to, and controversial for, an early- to mid-fifth century audience. The Thebans claimed that they were firmly established at Onkhestos then: in Pindar's odes Poseidon regularly protects Theban victors in particular.[87] But Theban control seems to be predicated on Erginos' death—except that he conspicuously survives the battle in all earlier traditions, as if the conflict had not yet been entirely settled. Furthermore, in *Paean 8* the elderly Erginos features as the father of Trophonios and Agamedes, the legendary builders of a mythical temple made of 'feathers' at Delphi; Trophonios himself is the eponym of the oracle in Lebadeia, known already to the *Homeric Hymn to Apollo*.[88] Erginos was alive and well in an early fifth-century paean, intimating Orkhomenos' lasting claim to Onkhestos. Who controlled the shrine—and hence the aura of Boiotianness it undoubtedly had from early on—had not been entirely established in Pindar's time.

In this context, a Theban seer Teneros privileged by Onkhestian Poseidon in *Paean 9* may well have been combative. Whether a song for Poseidon himself would have turned the establishment of the god into a feat of Theban mythical figures is impossible to say. But clearly the archetypal Theban seer of Apollo Ismenios had surreptitiously replaced Erginos' privileged role as Poseidon's favourite, at least in the Apollo-dominated world of *Paean 9*.

Appropriating Apollo Ptoios

Teneros' intrusion is remarkable since the very same hero in the early fifth century performs at yet another shrine, now at the north-eastern end of the Kopaïs basin. His presence there can equally not be taken for granted. According to some isolated lines from another Apolline paean, quite possibly for the Ptoion itself, Theban Teneros features as the seer at the oracle of Apollo Ptoios at Perdikovrysi near Akraiphia (Map. 7.2). Rescued in bits by Strabo for his outline of the Teneric plain, three Pindaric fragments attributed to a song for Apollo

[86] The Erginos of the Argonauts is the son of Poseidon and possibly the same as the Boiotian (cf. Hyg. *Fab.* 14.16): e.g. A.R. 1.185–7; Klymenos' death at the sanctuary and tribute: Apollod. 2.4.11; Paus. 9.37.1–4; Herakles' freeing the Thebans: D.S. 4.10.4; 47.3–5; Herakles Hippodetes (where the Orkhomenians had their chariot horses stolen): Paus. 9.26.1. Commemorative monuments of the conflict decorate Theban public places: Paus. 9.17.1–2; 25.4 a statue *Ῥινοκολούστης* ('nose-clipper') recalled Herakles knocking off the Orkhomenian heralds' noses when they came to exact the tribute. Herakles's victory is known to a 5th-cent. public: Pherec. *FGrH* 3 F 95 (= Σ Eur. *Phoen.* 53: Oidipous' sons were killed in the battle against Erginos); Eur. *HF* 47–50, 220 cites Herakles' victory over 'the Minyans'. Cf. Str. 9.2.40.

[87] Pi. *I.* 1.33; 3.37; *Parth.* 2 fr. 94b.46.

[88] The point about Erginos' survival is made by Schachter (1989) 80 n. 31, according to whom Erginos would only die in the mythical tradition once Orkhomenos was erased by Thebes in the 4th cent. BC. See *H. Ap.* 297–8; Pi. *O.* 4.19–21; Pi. *Pae.* 8.100–11; this is followed by Paus. 9.37; Trophonios and Agamedes: Str. 9.3.9; Paus. 10.5.13. On the role of Herakles for the Thebans see briefly Demand (1982) 49–52.

Ptoios tell of the god setting up the cult presumably on his oracle-founding voyage through Boiotia known from the *Homeric Hymn to Apollo*. The lines single out features of the somewhat alienating geography of the site at Perdikovrysi (that Teneros is the *kouros* here is clear from the context in which Strabo quotes the lines):

> καί ποτε τὸν τρικάρανον
> Πτωΐου κευθμῶνα κατέσχεθε κοῦ[ρος]
>
> and once the *kouros* inhabited the three-
> peaked hollow of Ptoïon
>
> (Pindar fr. 51b)

Teneros the seer, together with his plain, feature in another verse shortly afterwards:

> ναοπόλον μάντιν δαπέδοισιν ὁμοκλέα.
> 'the temple's attendant with the same name as the plain'
>
> (Pindar fr. 51d)[89]

The Ptoion is the place of the first material manifestation of the Boiotoi, albeit in a dedication not to Apollo but to Athena Pronaia, of around 500 BC.[90] Like Poseidon at Onkhestos, Apollo sat in splendour high up on a hill, but some ten kilometres further north. Located on the slopes above Lake Paralimni, in between the Kopaïs and the Teneric plain, his sanctuary, just like those of Athena and Poseidon, saw major building activity during the sixth century; unlike these, the Ptoion has also yielded much evidence characteristic of a place of nearly Panhellenic appeal. The Ptoion flourished as early as the late seventh century, and particularly through the sixth, and just as in the case of the other two shrines, we do not really know why. Old photographs of the now overgrown remains show vividly how impressive a site this had been, featuring two grand sixth-century stoas, extended over several terraces; larger than life-size *kouroi* sprang up from the soil, many of them from Boiotia, but just as many from elsewhere in Greece, altogether near 100 now surviving in the museums at Athens and Thebes. Big tripod bases were scattered over the site, in their complete state perhaps a chief source of the idea that Boiotians abounded in them as discussed above, in the context of the tripod-tribute to Dodona.[91]

[89] The fragments attributed to this song are Pi. frr. 51a–d; 51a, b, and d are quoted by Strabo 9.2.33; fr. 51c (n. 97 below) is a scholion to Paus. 9.23.6 and attributed to a 'hymn'. The Ptoion also features in a tiny papyrus fragment that in the line before seems to mention Poseidon: Pi. fr. 52g (f). Korinna too had an expressed interest in Apollo Ptoios, possibly inventing a genealogy that linked the Ptoion to Tanagrean figures (*PMG* 654. iii. 12–51; 694 fr. 1 (b) suppl. (Ptoios and Athena)). This is not irrelevant as her Koronides also had relations with western Boiotia (*PMG* 655).

[90] Ducat (1971) 443–4 and n. 62 above; the old excavations by Holleaux (*BCH* 11 (1887) 4–5) apparently had unearthed yet more likely dedications to Athena.

[91] Ducat's (1971) is the standard monograph of the site. Apollo first appears in inscriptions from around 650–25 BC (as *Πτωϊεύς*); *LSAG* 94.4=*IG* vii 2729; Homolle, *BCH* (1886) 77–80; other early dedications include Ducat (1971) 50a; 50b; 49. The impression of sixth-century blossoming (note also

The wealth of this sanctuary has been explained in terms of Thebans taking over the Ptoion as early as the turn of the seventh century, but this is not self-evident, nor is the idea of the oracle being served by heroic personnel from Thebes. Herodotus later in the fifth century mentions explicitly on the occasion of Mys' oracular tour on behalf of the Persian King in 480 BC that this Apollo was then in Theban hands. That he takes the trouble to say this is suggestive, since in the archaeological record there is certainly no trace of the Akraiphians themselves ceasing to administer the cult either then or indeed any time later when they did so on behalf of the *koinon*.[92] The rather remarkable additional comment is that Mys' consultation was accompanied by 'three citizens who were sent from the *koinon*'; these people later in the story are called Thebans. Herodotus associates the visit with a Theban-led *koinon* that was doubtless in existence by his time but not necessarily when the events were supposed to have taken place. The mystery around the consultation (the oracle purportedly answered in Karian), I shall argue below, may reflect the *koinon*'s later concern to gloss over Boiotian medism by cultivating a tradition of ambiguous or outright anti-Persian answers from all the region's oracles.[93] Historically, Thebans never held the Ptoion other than *qua* members of the *koinon*; the Herodotean comments reflect Theban claims to representation of Boiotia, but not their actual control of the sanctuary.[94]

Teneros' alleged guardianship, therefore, is problematic, and possibly at the centre of the debate on the identity of Thebes and Boiotia, which will be discussed in greater detail below. By contrast, the local hero Ptoios (*Πτώϊος*), one of Athamas' sons, had the more legitimate claim to being the original seer at the Ptoion. Ptoios as we remember, was one of the sons of the Thessalian immigrant Athamas who in Asios' times, in the (?) sixth century, had already covered parts of the Kopaïs basin with his family relations. So Ptoios was himself one of these Kopaïs heroes with serious Thessalian parentage.[95] And he was a prominent local

Schachter (1989) 75 on Akraiphia) is confirmed by the vast cemetery in the Moraites field just below the Akropolis and encroaching on the modern motorway, where e.g. a high-quality sixth-century grave relief has recently been discovered: *AR* (1998–90) 54–5; more recent discoveries *AR* 46 (1999–2000) 56; 47 (2000–1) 55–6; 48 (2001–2) 50–1; 49 (2002–3) 46–7; 51 (2004–5) 44–5.

[92] Akraiphian prominence at the shrine: Ducat (1971): the base no. 232, possibly to be joined with no. 233 (*c.*540–520 BC), appears to be a Theban dedication sculpted by the Akraiphian Akousilos; cf. no. 202 (*c.*500 BC). *Theorodokia* inscriptions sent out to the other Boiotian cities in the 3rd cent. make it unambiguous that the Akraiphians continued the administration of the Ptoion's main festival (Perlman (2000) index s.v.).

[93] Hdt. 8.133–5. The passage is not often discussed as relevant to the *koinon*: see Schachter (2000); cf. Mackil (2003) 276 ff. who similarly thinks of the passage as anachronistic.

[94] Different Str. 9.2.34, quite possibly led astray by the fragments for the Ptoion that he has just discussed.

[95] See n. 32 above. Asios also wrote songs for the Phokians, another people in central Greece: fr. 5 Bernabé = Paus. 2.29.4. G. Huxley (1969) 89–98; Bowra (1961) for an alleged 5th-cent. date.

figure: his own shrine lies on the slopes of the Akraiphian akropolis, on the other side of Lake Paralimni, which separates the Ptoion from the city of Akraiphia. The obscure history of the two cults and their relationship is even more obscured by scholarly dispute about the role of Thebes in their running.[96] The one remarkable coincidence, however, must be that the hero Ptoios' shrine first appears just at the time of the Ptoion's *akme*, and one way out of the conundrum is to think of a possible parallel monumentalization of the Kopaïs's Thessalian past in cult that characterized all three major sanctuaries and also hit Ptoios. Ptoios too might have been caught in the apparent sixth-century phenomenon of increased regional interaction, manifested in the embellishment of a string of shrines.

If Pindar's *paianes* put Teneros in the prophet's chair instead of the Athamantid Ptoios, the song substitutes with a Theban past the sanctuary's allegiances with Orkhomenos and the western Kopaïs, and the Thessalian tradition: we remember that Ptoios' father Athamas was a chief representative of the mythical Thessalian wanderings. It fits that Ptoios' ancestry itself is not deleted but reconfigured. Pindar, possibly even in the same song, also claims that Ptoios was the son of Apollo and Athamas his maternal grandfather. Athamantid origins are not erased but kept at a safer distance by moving Athamas up a generation and making Ptoios the stepbrother of Teneros. Ptoios receives a more noble ancestry this way but is now less clearly linked to the key figure of the Thessalian past. The Theban hero Teneros, by contrast, fills the shoes of the deposed hero of Thessalian roots.[97]

If all the different scraps belong to a single cult song for Apollo Ptoios, they would plausibly have told the story of how Teneros came to become seer at the Ptoion. That is to say, how the young man (κοῦρος) 'came to hold' (κατέσχεθε) the three-peaked hollow (κευθμών), telling and performing the story as if of old (fr. 51b, as above). Did this piece inaugurate as it were the shrine's pan-Boiotian oracle precisely by making Teneros its Ur-seer? We cannot tell but, particularly with a view to the earlier dedication by the Boiotoi in the same shrine, Teneros' appearance in a religious song for a god later to be central to the *koinon*'s affairs might well have had significance in the shaping up of a sense of Boiotianness. The possibility that the performance claimed a function for the oracle in the wider Boiotian context by having a Theban hero of myth take on a role in pan-Boiotian divinatory ritual has its attractions.[98]

So at a rather early date something that would later come to mean 'Boiotian' appears to be happening with the three cults sitting at three angles of the Kopaïs,

96 Guillon (1943); Ducat (1971), who have severe differences about who dominated the sanctuaries when.

97 Pi. fr. 51c = Σ Paus. 9.23.6: ὅτι οὗτος Ἀθάμαντος καὶ Θεμιστοῦς φησι τὸν Πτῷιον, Πίνδαρος δὲ ἐν ὕμνοις Ἀπόλλωνος καὶ τῆς Ἀθάμαντος θυγατρὸς Ζευξίππης καταγίνεται. 'he says that Ptoios was the son of Athamas and Themisto, Pindar in his hymns claims that he was the son of Apollo and Athamas' daughter Zeuxippe'.

98 The Ptoion seems to have been the *koinon*'s principal prophetic source: cf. Guillon (1943) ii. 157–65; Roesch (1982) 225–43 is the most helpful on the Hellenistic Ptoia.

Athena Itonia, Poseidon at Onkhestos, and Apollo Ptoios at Akraiphia. The sixth century already makes a perceived Thessalian past visible in religious practice at sites linked to this tradition, suggesting a new form of interaction between places in this area. All three cults undergo major building works during the sixth century and are central to early fifth-century performances; while Onkhestos had been linked to 'the Boiotians' since at least the *Catalogue of Ships*, some historical Boiotoi even visit Apollo Ptoios in this period. Athena Itonia is neatly tied to the warrior traditions of the wanderings, whereas the other two cults form part of the mythical repertoire prefiguring these wanderings, and into which Thebes claims entry through cult song.

Apollo Ismenios, the Daphnephoria, and the 'Theban Migration'

The cult of Apollo Ismenios at Thebes links the two strands of the Thessalo-Kopaïd tradition, the migrations from Thessaly on the one hand, and the 'epic' myths prefiguring them on the other. Singing for this god helped the Theban appropriation of this tradition and put it to use in the formation of a Boiotian community. Apollo Ismenios' *khoroi* also had a role in constructing a relationship between Thebes and Boiotia, more explicitly so than the cults already discussed. And finally, his songs make fascinating suggestions about a Theban attempt to integrate civic Theban affairs with those of Boiotia as a whole.[99]

Apollo Ismenios' importance is borne out by the respectable number of extant songs. Apollo Ismenios is a local Theban god, part of the city's pantheon, with no one else claiming control, something that might help to explain why so much effort is expended on turning him into a 'Boiotian' god. Pindar's *Paeans 7* and *9*, the latter better known for its depiction of an eclipse than for its mythical substance, contain episodes of Apollo's aetiology. *Paean 1* has the Ismenion in its title; *Pythian 11* seems to have been performed in the shrine itself. At least three of Pindar's *partheneia* accompanied the important ritual of the *Δαφνηφορία* (fr. 94a–c). Together these songs give a good impression of what Apollo Ismenios did for the Thebans both in a civic and a regional context.[100]

Located on a low hill some way south-west of the Kadmeia, the Ismenion was Apollo's most prominent centre in Thebes. Some superficial digging in the late 1960s, the results of which have not been properly published, complement the excavation of the site in the early decades of the twentieth century. We know that there was a geometric and an archaic temple; both were destroyed, but the few scattered dedications, as well as Pausanias' curious mention of a sixth-century sculpture of Apollo made by the Sikyonian Kanakhos, suggest one *floruit* around

[99] Quintessential Boiotians, particularly prominent Thebans, are called Ismenias after this cult: cf. Ar. *Ach.* 860 ff.; son of Timokrates: Xen. *Hell.* 3.5.1; 5.2.25–6; his son: D.S. 15.71.2; Plut. *Pelop. passim*. More on this name representing the Boiotian *koinon* see n. 127 below.

[100] For Pi. *Pae.* 7 being related to Ismenios rather than Ptoios (as assumed by Maehler) see Rutherford (2001) 343–4).

the turn of the sixth century—like the other sites implicated in regional Boiotian affairs. The temple was rebuilt in the fourth century. Apollo had a consort, Athena Pronaia, who seems to have shared his cultic space at Thebes just as she did at the Ptoion. Today the overgrown foundations of the fourth-century building survive as a small *alsos* in the modern city.[101]

Aetiology at the Ismenion

With Apollo Ismenios we re-enter the world of surviving aetiological myth, as opposed to those songs that let one suspect it, as in the case of Athena Itonia and Apollo Ptoios. The two *Paeans 7* and *9* relate the Ismenion's mythical origin. *Paean 9* is the more comprehensive:

σάματι δ'] ἐκράνθην ὑπὸ
δαιμονίῳ τινὶ
λέχει πέλας ἀμβροσίῳ Μελίας
ἀγαυὸν καλάμῳ συνάγεν θρόον
μήδεσί τε φρενὸς ὑμ[ε]ṭέραν χάριν.
λιτανεύω, ἑκαβόλε,
Μοισαίαις ἀν[α]τιθεὶς τέχνα[ι]σι
χρηστήριον . [.]. . . ο . . [. .].
ἐν ῷ Τήνερον εὐρυβίαν θεμίτ[ων ⏑ –
ἐξαίρετον προφάταν ἔτεκ[εν λέχει
κόρα μιγεῖσ' Ὠκεανοῦ Μελία σέο, Πύθι[ε. τῷ] Κάδμου στρατὸν,
καὶ Ζεάθου πό[λιν
ἀκερσεκόμα πάτερ, ἀνορέας
ἐπέτρεψας ἕκατι σαόφρονος.
καὶ γὰρ ὁ πόντιος Ὀρσ[ιτ]ρίαινά νιν
περίαλλα βροτῶν τίεν,
Εὐρίπου τε συνέτεινε χῶρον.

I have been ordained by some divine sign,
to compose, beside the immortal couch of Melia,
a noble song with the pipe
and by the skills of my mind in your honour.
I entreat you, Far-Shooting god,
as I dedicate to the Muses' arts
your oracle . . .
in which Melia, daughter of Okeanos,
having shared your bed, Pythian god,
bore mighty Teneros, chosen prophet of oracles.
To him, unshorn father, you entrusted
the people of Kadmos and Zethos' city

[101] Keramopoulos (1917). Rescue excavations in 1966: *ΑΔ* 22 (1967 [1968]). Β' 232–3; *AR* 1968–9, 18. Inscriptions: *IG* vii 2455 (*MDAI(A)* 1 (1875) 97–101 found in Chalkis, though for its Theban origin see *BCH* 3 (1879) 139): *Πτωΐων Μάστος τοὶ hΙσμενίοι ἐνέθεαν* 'Ptoion and Mastos dedicated this to Ismenios'. Keramopoulos ibid. 35 (6th-cent. bronze oinochoe): *Πολύκλετο[s] ἀνέθεκε τὀπόλ(λ)ονι τôι h[ι]σμενίοι* 'Polykletos dedicated this to Apollo Ismenios'. Paus. 9.10.2.

because of his wise courage.
For the sea god Wielder of the Trident
honoured him above all mortals,
and he sped (his chariot) to the region of Euripos . . .
(Pindar, *Paean* 9.33–49=A1 Ruth, tr. Race)

Teneros is again the main protagonist. The lines constitute the aetiological myth for the Ismenion and its oracle, a myth that Pausanias recounts in greater detail.[102] Apollo seized the nymph Melia, having shot her anxious brother Kaanthos. The product of the union was Teneros who became the first prophet of Apollo's new oracular cult. To this Pausanias adds that Melia also bore a second son Ismenos, future eponym of the nearby river and source of the names of several prominent Theban politicians. Lines 43 to 46 of the paean add the interesting detail of Apollo entrusting the city of Thebes to Teneros, giving the first hint of the idea that Theban affairs revolved around this cult and its mythical personnel. The text then makes the curious remark on Teneros being Poseidon's favourite, which I discussed above.

In this aetiology for Apollo Ismenios, the figure of Teneros brings together the threads of various mythical pasts, as he did at the Ptoion. His centrality in the cult emerges from the manner in which myth and ritual interact in all the Pindaric songs dedicated to the Ismenion. The fragments of *Paeans 1*, *7*, and *9* are almost silent about their ritual context, and the identity of the performing *khoros*. Their mythic narratives, by contrast, just like those for Apollo and Artemis on Delos, focus on the event of Teneros' birth and are helpful. His mother, the nymph Melia (*κόρα* in *Pae.* 9.43), is elaborately portrayed; the circumstances and locality of Teneros' birth are described in great detail; just setting the scene seems to have mattered much in this story: Apollo's *ἄδυτον*-to-be is turned into 'Melia's splendid hall' (*εἰς αὐλάν . . . Μελίας Pae.* 7.3–4), or her 'divine bed' (*λέχει ἀμβροσίῳ Pae.* 9.35). The portrayal of the birth's locality, Apollo's precinct, was arguably of great importance to the telling of the myth in a ritual context.

Pindar's *Pythian 11*, composed for the child victor Thrasydaios in 474 BC, also implies a narrative of Teneros' birth in the Ismenion.[103] Here there is a *khoros* which characteristically wavers between mythical and ritual performers. The singers open the ode by calling upon the daughters of the Theban Kadmos, Ino-Leukothea and Semele, as well as Herakles' mother Alkmene, to come into the Ismenion. This shrine once, they say—and here the text suggestively shifts into myth through the typical relative clause changing tenses—'Apollo honoured above all, and called it Ismenion, the true seat of prophecies' (Pi. *P.* 11.5–6). The song re-emerges from this quick flashback picturing Apollo calling upon the same *στρατὸς ἡρωΐδων* ('army of heroines', 7–8) to come to the Ismenion to join the present celebration (*ἔνθα καί νυν*, 7), and, it seems, the singers of the song being sung (*ὄφρα . . . κελαδήσετ'*, 9–10):

[102] Paus. 9.10.5–6; cf. *POxy.* 10.1241 col. iv.5–10.

[103] For the performance of this ode in the Ismenion see Angeli Bernardini (1989).

Κάδμου κόραι, Σεμέλα μὲν Ὀλυμπιάδων ἀγυιᾶτι,
Ἰνὼ δὲ Λευκοθέα
ποντιᾶν ὁμοθάλαμε Νηρηΐδων,
ἴτε σὺν Ἡρακλέος ἀριστογόνῳ
ματρὶ πὰρ Μελίαν χρυσέων ἐς ἄδυτον τριπόδων
θησαυρόν, ὃν περίαλλ᾽ ἐτίμασε Λοξίας,
Ἰσμήνιον δ᾽ ὀνύμαξεν, ἀλαθέα μαντίων θῶκον,
ὦ παῖδες Ἁρμονίας,
ἔνθα καί νυν ἐπίνομον ἡρωΐδων
στρατὸν ὁμαγερέα καλεῖ συνίμεν,
ὄφρα Θέμιν ἱερὰν Πυθῶνά τε καὶ ὀρθοδίκαν
γᾶς ὀμφαλὸν κελαδήσετ᾽ ἄκρᾳ σὺν ἑσπέρᾳ
ἑπταπύλοισι Θήβαις

Daughters of Kadmos, you, Semele, neighbour
of the Olympian goddesses, and you, Ino Leukothea,
who share the chambers of the Nereid sea nymphs,
go with the most nobly born mother of Herakles
and join Melia at the treasury of the golden tripods,
the sanctuary which Loxias especially honoured
and named the Ismenion, the true seat of seers.
O daughters of Harmonia,
there he now summons
the local host of heroines to gather together,
so that you may celebrate the holy Themis, Pytho,
and the just-judging centre of the earth at nightfall
in honour of the seven-gated Thebes . . .

(Pindar, *Pythian* 11.1–11, tr. Race)

The suggestion arising from this beginning is that just as the *khoros* of heroines had witnessed the important birth of Teneros and the designation of Apollo's oracle, so it was summoned to re-enact it again, merging with the *khoros* as they are singing, and it is this mythical nexus that the paeans and quite possibly this victory ode seek to invoke. Dancing girls were closely involved in the worship of the cult: Callimachus depicts Melia herself as a nymph dancing and singing in Apollo's cult song. Pausanias mentions two statues in the precinct commemorating Kreon's daughters Pyrrhe and Heniokhe, who once reigned over Thebes.[104] The dedication makes best sense if we take it together with the suggestions of the texts. Multiplied into a *khoros*, the girls or women acted perhaps as attendants to Teneros' birth, or as representatives of his youthful mother Melia.

The founding act of Apollo's cult through the birth of Teneros was apparently reinvoked in choral performances of varying type on ritual occasions in the Ismenion;[105] the inevitable suggestion in the case of *Pythian 11* is that the little

[104] Paus. 9.10.3.

[105] One is reminded of Pindar's *Paean 1*, a text, too insubstantial to point conclusively to another (implied or actual) birth-story, inviting Ὧραι, and the set of women, to join the δαῖτα φιλησιστέφανον ('the crown-loving feast', l. 8) (cf. fr. *dub.* 333.5).

boy-victor Thrasydaios is projected into the role of Teneros himself, carrying the burden of the city's welfare—a point to which I shall return. We might note that *Pythian 11* troubles to assemble all the important Theban heroines for Apollo's introduction at Thebes (ll. 1–6), almost as if Apollo and his seer were the late-comers in this awe-inspiring company. The issue of mythical chronology resurfaces once again in one of several intriguing and little examined Pindaric fragments dealing with musical innovation in Boiotia: in fr. 32 Kadmos 'listened to Apollo displaying the "right music"' as if Apollo was a novice at Thebes who taught his new tunes to the rest. The context in which this passage is quoted claims that Pindar was here elaborating on human suffering and upheaval, a period of 'change'. There is a hint here that Pindar's hymns were meddling with the Thebans' past, expressed in ritual music: as we shall see, Apollo Ismenios' mythical arrival at Thebes did indeed change the Thebans' life—musically, and in the direction of 'Boiotia'.[106]

Interaction in the mantic pool

Apollo Ismenios seems on the surface to form part of a group of oracular cults placed around the Kopaïs basin, the Theban god being the one outlying member in this exclusive group. Boiotia, as cultural tradition tells us, was famous for these oracles: Apollo travelled to a number of them on the way to Delphi in his *Homeric Hymn*, a tour that the Karian Mys retraces in part when the Persian general Mardonios in 480 BC sends him out to consult central Greek oracles about the fate of the Persians against the Hellenic forces. The stations of the tour from oracle to oracle undergo some variations in antiquarian tradition just as Mys' experiences alter with time, but there is little doubt that the string of cults encircling Lake Kopaïs liked to represent themselves as a highly interactive group. The Boiotian part of the oracular journey, which developed its own tradition in Greek antiquity, will occupy us through the rest of this section.[107]

The mantic pool included the Ptoion near Akraiphia, the Trophonion at Lebadeia, Apollo's oracles at the spring Tilphousa (Telphousa) near Haliartos, at Tegyra, and possibly also at Thourion (Map 7.2; Fig. 7.2). Scarcely documented though they are, striking similarities can be observed between what is attested. In one way or another every one of these Apollos reiterates the Ismenion's *aition* and the sacred locality it construes. All situated on or at the foot of a mountain-side, their stories of origin uniformly feature Apollo seizing a local nymph and a male diviner and/or priest produced by the union. Water, coming up from springs or a cave-like place, had a role in the mantic practices. So the prophet-priests Teneros and Ptoios are products of Apollo's amorous encounters with the local nymphs at the Ismenion and the Ptoion, as is Khairon, the eponym of Khaironeia,

[106] Pi. fr. 32 (*Κάδμος ἤκουσε Ἀπόλλωνος*) *μουσικὰν ὀρθὰν ἐπιδεικνυμένου*, quoted by Aristid. 3.620; cf. Plut. *Pyth. Orac.* 397a.

[107] *H. Ap.* 225–74; Hdt. 8.133–5; Plut. *De Def. Or.* 411e ff.; *Arist.* 19.1–2; Paus. 9.23.5–7. Epameinondas pursued the same *periegesis* prior to the battle of Leuktra: Paus. 4.32.5 (cf. Xen. *Hell.* 6.4.7).

of that between the god and Thero at Thourion. Springs appear in Tilphousa's romance with Apollo as well as in the transmitted topography of Tegyra, and in the myth and ritual of Trophonios' grotto-cult. A well is also situated right in the middle of the sanctuary of Apollo Ptoios. Not all the parallels are fully sustainable for all cults, but the broader case can be made for their being replicas of one and the same cult. These parallels arise from a variety of evidence (literary and archaeological), much of which goes back a fair way, suggesting a level of long-standing contact across this mantic pool possibly since the times of the *Homeric Hymn* itself. The cities of the Kopaïs liked to think that their Apollos were similar.[108]

However, despite the convincing analogies with all these cults, residing above all in the recurring aetiological pattern, the Ismenion at Thebes ultimately does not conform to the template of the cults just sketched when it comes to real-life religious practice. The site is located on a low hill (Pausanias calls it a λόφος) which would only with difficulty qualify as a mountain; no spring has been found in connection with it, and the river Ismenos does not form part of the precinct in any meaningful way. But the main argument against Apollo Ismenios belonging to the Kopaïs circle is that the fifth-century practice was not hydromancy, but oracles were given, as at Olympia, διὰ ἐμπύρων, 'from the ashes of sacrifice'.[109] Pindar's *Paean 7* quotes Teneros, the mythical prophet of the Ismenion, in connection with a sacrifice, featuring bulls, activity in front of an altar, some singing and subsequently a prophetic utterance.[110] Plutarch's image of dried-up oracles in second-century Boiotia assumes water divination, proving that oracular fluency *was* an important point.[111] Other features of the Ismenion also lead one to question the timing and nature of Apollo's arrival at Thebes, and whether this oracle was really just like the rest: the Apollo of the *Homeric Hymn*, for example, does not know of his cult at Thebes, surely an important oracular stop judging by the Ismenion's later importance. The problem of the Ismenion's dubious antiquity recurs in Herodotus, who quotes mythical oracles to Kadmos uttered by Apollo

[108] The evidence was first collected and discussed by Schachter (1967), cf. (1972), from whom I quote here, with additions: Thourion: Hes. fr. 252.5–6 MW; Hellanikos *FGrH* 4 F 81; at river Molos: Plut. *Sull.* 17.6–8; Tilphousa: *H. Ap.* 244–76; 375–87; Teiresias (epitome of the male prophet) dies drinking from the spring: Aristophanes of Boiotia *FGrH* 379 F 4 and Ephoros *FGrH* 70 F 153. Lebadeia (where it is possible to see the niches for incubation just above the springs of the river Herkynna): Trophonios is son of Erginos (according to an oracle of Apollo) and is a direct son of Apollo in late sources, e.g. Kharax *FGrH* 103 F 5; Paus. 9.39–40.2. For Tegyra see p. 109 n. 158. Georgoudi (1998) esp. 348–51 draws attention to the distinction between 'prophets' and 'priests' involved in Boiotian oracular practice.

[109] Soph. *OT* 21; cf. Hdt. 8.134.1; Philoch. *FGrH* 328 F 193 = *Σ OT* 21. Cf. also Soph. *Ant.* 998 ff. (Teiresias priest). Later texts differ even more about the channels of prophecy at the Ismenion: Plut. *Lys.* 29.10; D.S. 17.10.3; Max. Tyr. 41.1.

[110] Pi. *Pae.* 7.12–18 (= D7 Ruth): ἥρωα Τήνερον λέγομεν [/~ 8]α ταύρων ε̣ι̣[/~10]ν προβωμ[/~10]οιτ . τ . μο[. . . .]παρα̣[/~9 κελ]ά̣δησαν αὐδάν· /~6]αντεσι χρηστήριον / 'we speak of the hero Teneros / of bulls / . . . before the altar . . . / they sang a song / oracle'.

[111] Plut. *De Def. Or.* 411e compares the oracles ceasing to talk in his times to streams of water (νάματα), leading to a 'drought of prophecy' (μαντικῆς αὐχμός) befalling the land, leaving no prophecy 'to draw from' (ἀρύσασθαι).

Ismenios—as a testimony for the cult's great age (and counteracting Pindar's claim that Apollo's tunes supersede 'Kadmeian' music).[112]

This kind of evidence rather defies the idea of an overarching divinatory tradition shared by the Ismenion together with the Kopaïs oracles. Rather, we will see that local rituals of the Ismenion and the Kopaïs Apollos during the first half of the fifth century seem to create, rather than to transmit, a religious practice common to them all. This arguably happened as part of the same process of Boiotian regional integration that we have started to trace for the three sanctuaries above. The key source for this argument is what we know as the Ismenion's most glamorous festival, the Daphnephoria, an occasion featuring leading families and of chief importance for the city, furnishing, we think, the setting for what survives of Pindar's *Partheneia.* The Theban Daphnephoria was a highly charged ritual, performed by an entire 'clan' marching in an extravagant procession. According to Pausanias, a model youth, a boy of good family, beautiful stature, and healthy constitution, was made priest of Apollo Ismenios for the year. He held the title *daphnephoros* as the boys wore laurel crowns during their period of service. The late antique scholar Proklos gives a detailed description of the procession that the office entailed: a splendid *pompe* in which the laurel-bearer, also referred to as *pais amphithales* ('flourishing on both sides', see below), carried an obscure item called the *κωπώ*, a wooden stick decorated with a complicated ensemble of laurel and flowers and a number of *σφαῖραι*, astral symbols. Members of his family escorted him, as well as a maiden *khoros* singing the surviving Daphnephoric hymns.[113] Once the boy's service was over, his parents dedicated a tripod to Apollo, stimulating as it were Pindar's image of the Ismenion being the 'treasury of tripods' (*τριπόδων θησαυρός*).[114]

Pindar composed at least three *daphnephorika* (Pi. *Parth.* 1–3 frr. 94a–c) for the Ismenion, confirming the centrality of the festival to Thebes: two of these were for the prominent political actors of the Aioladadai and a boy Agasikles,

[112] *H. Ap.* 225–74; Hdt. 5.59–61. To have Athena Pronaia in the precinct may be a conscious imitation of her presence at Delphi, lending oracular authority. On Kadmos and Apollo see p. 375 above.

[113] Paus. 9.10.2–4; Procl. *ap.* Phot. *Bibl.* 239.321b (where the office seems split between two boys): *ἄρχει δὲ τῆς δαφνηφορίας παῖς ἀμφιθαλής, καὶ ὁ μάλιστα αὐτῷ οἰκεῖος βαστάζει τὸ κατεστεμμένον ξύλον ὃ κώπω καλοῦσιν. Αὐτὸς δὲ ὁ δαφνηφόρος ἑπόμενος τῆς δάφνης ἐφάπτεται, τὰς μὲν κόμας καθειμένος, χρυσοῦν δὲ στέφανον φέρων καὶ λαμπρὰν ἐσθῆτα ποδήρη ἐστολισμένος ἐπικρατίδας τὲ ὑποδεδεμένος· ᾧ χορὸς παρθένων ἐπακαλουθεῖ προτείνων κλῶνας πρὸς ἱκετηρίαν ὕμνων. Παρέπεμπον δὲ τὴν δαφνηφορίαν εἰς Ἀπόλλωνος Ἰσμηνίου καὶ Χαλαζίου.* 'at the head of the Daphnephoria walks the *pais amphithales* and his closest relative holds up the log with garlands, which they call *kopo.* The Daphnephoros himself follows holding the laurel, his hair is loose, and he wears a golden crown and a fair robe falling to his feet, and he has *epikratides* as shoes. The *khoros* of young women follows him singing, holding branches of supplication. They send the Daphnephoria to Apollo Ismenios and Khalazios.' Although there are some discrepancies between the Pindaric lines and the later antiquarians, the text should be regarded as essentially reliable, particularly with a view to its social significance: for a sensible, detailed disussion on what and what not to use of Proklos see Kurke (2007) esp. 71–6 and Schachter (2000).

[114] Pi. *P.* 11.4–5. For the Daphnephoria and the Pindaric *partheneia* fragments see Brelich (1969) 413 ff.; Calame (1997) esp. 58–63; 101–3; Schachter (1981–94) i. 83–5; Lehnus (1984); and now Kurke (2007).

and one allegedly for Pindar's own son. Deceived by these fragments, we tend to think of the Daphnephoria as a characteristically Theban occasion; this is not, however, what the analysis of either the Daphnephoria's aetiological myth, nor evidence for ritual activity in the shrine of the Kopaïs Apollos, suggests.

While Apollo's Kopaïs-type is widely thought to include the Ismenion, the inverse move to think the Daphnephoria back on to the basin has not been made.[115] But such pageants are likely to have occurred elsewhere in the Kopaïs, and there is reason to believe that the Daphnephoria are more appropriately placed in the Kopaïs basin. A fourth-century inscription from Khaironeia, for example, is dedicated to Apollo Daphnaphoros (*Δαφναφόρος*). A series of bronze laurel leaves features among the unpublished finds from the Ptoion, and some cutting of (sacred?) *δάφνη* appears in an albeit highly enigmatic votive inscription. The Ptoion at Akraiphia has yielded the greatest number of tripod bases known from any site other than Athens, as if to support an analogy with Pausanias' experience of tripods at the Ismenion. Most relevantly perhaps, the curious stick, the *κώπω* or *κωπώ*, is not known from any other context; the stem *κωπ-*, however, suggests some association with the *Κωπαΐς*. The existence of the city *Κῶπαι* at the lake similarly makes the word local to the area, supporting the idea of a geographical connection between the strange object and a widespread local ritual.[116]

A closer look at Pindar's non-Theban songs adds weight to this view. D'Alessio has alluringly suggested that the dubious fr. 333 for Ekhekrates of Orkhomenos might have been a *daphnephorikon* involving also a prophecy, and I shall discuss some aspects of this below.[117] An obscure *partheneion* 'for the Thebans to the Galaxion' (fr. 104b) is another *daphnephorikon*. To quote a merely circumstantial piece of evidence, one wonders in what ritual context Pindar talked of spring Tilphousa's 'honeysweet, immortal water' if not in that of a ritual in connection with yet another oracle: was this given in the context of the Daphnephoria (fr. 198b)?[118] And finally, as we shall see, in the Daphnephoria's aetiology the laurel-cutting for the procession took place near the future oracle at Tegyra. All in all, there is a better chance than not that the Daphnephoria was a widespread ritual in the area in the early fifth century, and daphnephoric hymns part of a shared contemporary song-culture in the Kopaïs basin. Certainly we are justified

[115] Schachter (1981–94) i. 85 rather brings in log-processions from southern Boiotia in support of the hypothesis of a pan-Boiotian rite, particularly the Plataian Daidala for Hera. It seems to me that analogous forms of worship for a variety of gods is a less stringent bond than iterated rites for the same god.

[116] Khaironeia dedication: *IG* vii 3407. On *κωπ-* see LSJ s.v. Ritual prescriptions are made on a stele from the Ptoion (Ducat (1971) no. 252. For the tripods see Guillon (1943).

[117] D'Alessio (2000).

[118] Oracles might have been given at the Daphnephoria: see Pi. *Parth.* 1 fr. 94a5–6; they certainly seem to motivate some of the paeans for Ismenios, e.g. *Paean 7*. Cf. the specifically Boiotian name Galaxidoros, analogous to Ptoiodorus, from the oracle at the Ptoion: Xen. *Hell.* 3.5.1; Plut. *De Gen. Socr.* 577a, 579f; 580f; 581e; 588b–c; 594b.

in the claim that a comparable wealth of evidence entangles all these Apollos into common aetiological and ritual patterns, and as we shall now see, the associated myth of the wanderings as well.[119]

What the Daphnephoria was about, and why the ritual came to assume particular prominence at Thebes, emerges from the festival's aetiology. And here the Boiotoi of Thessalian origins resurface. Proklos' aetiology for the Daphnephoria at the Ismenion reveals that, like the tripodophoric rite, the Daphnephoria was thought to have arrived in Boiotia together with the Boiotoi. Although the legend occurs in this late source, the wider Boiotian context as unfolded here suggests that we should take it seriously. We are again in the midst of the war between the invading Boiotoi and the then resident Pelasgians. Warfare stopped to celebrate the common feast for Apollo. *Δάφνη*, laurel, for the rituals was cut from the slopes of Helikon by the Pelasgians, and by the Boiotians from 'near the river Melas', which, as we know from Plutarch, was the river rising in Orkhomenos and flowing into the Kopaïs at Tegyra.[120] The following night the Boiotian general Polematas dreamt of a young man offering him a panoply and giving instructions to institute the enneateric Daphnephoria to Apollo. Shortly afterwards, Polematas and the Boiotoi were victorious in battle and duly set about performing the prescribed ritual, which was then conducted forever after.[121]

In this version the daphnephoric procession was, like the tripodophoric rite and the foundation of Athena Itonia at Koroneia, believed to have originated as a victory ceremony celebrating, and then regularly commemorating, the arrival of the Boiotoi in Boiotia and the conquest of the Pelasgians. But, although Proklos speaks of the Boiotoi, the context here is a fictitious sack of Thebes, and this is what marks the final victory. While Boiotoi leading future Boiotians from Thessaly into Thebes sounds plausible at first, as hinted above no role can be made out for Thebes in any of the myths on the movements of the later Boiotians towards Boiotia.[122] If in this aetiological myth Thebes is where all expeditions converge, this must be a highly controversial move with which the Thebans appropriate the festival and the migratory traditions. We have already seen how Thebes reached out to Onkhestos and the Ptoion, two cults belonging to the mythical personnel foreshadowing the Boiotian migrations from Thessaly into Boiotia. The Daphnephoria are an even more prominent manifestation of Thebes, initially absent from the traditions covering the religious world of the Kopaïs, making a sudden appearance in the world of myth and ritual pertaining to the Boiotian wanderings in the fifth century.

[119] Korinna *PMG* 690 is also sometimes thought to be a Daphnephorikon: West (1970), esp. 280 n. 5; cf. Page (1953) 27–8.

[120] Paus. 9.38.6; Plut. *Pelop.* 16.3–4; Str. 9.2.41; *Σ* Nic. *Ther.* 686a1. Melas is, significantly, also a Thessalian river: Hdt. 7.198–9, near Trakhis. For the location see Roesch (1965) 64.

[121] Procl. *ap.* Phot. *Bibl.* 239.321a–b.

[122] The same ambiguity incidentally occurs in Proklos' report on the tripod-carrying to Dodona, though contrast the generic 'Boiotians' who are the actors of the tributary *pompe* of the older source Ephoros (Procl. *ap.* Phot. *Bibl.* 239.321b–22a; Ephoros *FGrH* 70 F 119).

On this view, early fifth-century performances of the Daphnephoria throughout eastern Boiotia and at Thebes seem simultaneously to labour Thebes' leading role in this community and to forge its cohesion in the first place. What seems to be a parallel construction of a common—and lasting—performance tradition gives away that much: it validates the idea of aetiologies of Apollo's arrival and journey around the mantic pool tying together these different localities in shared practice. We have already met Kadmos succumbing to Apollo's correct music; and some of this is intriguingly picked up by another musical fragment. This claims that formerly the combined force of the river Acheloos bordering Aitolia, the Euripos strait between Euboia and Boiotia, and the streams of the river Melas 'nourished the *kalamoi* most full of song' (αἰῳδότατοι). The area outlined includes western Boiotia and the Kopaïs but not eastern Boiotia; the *aulos* which these *kalamoi* serve is *the* Boiotian instrument in the antiquarian tradition. All the songs in connection with any of the Kopaïs Apollos self-consciously refer to their auletic orchestration. Another extant tradition claims that Pindar was taught the *aulos* by one Pagondas—the father of the Aioladad Daphnephoros Agasikles? It is a likely inference from this motif that Pindar's Theban songs were implicated in the making of a Boiotian song-culture that drew heavily on what was perceived as a Thessalo-Boiotoi practice.[123]

Similarly, that this festival was about the arrival of specifically 'Boiotian' Apollo from Thessaly suggests itself when one places the Daphnephoria in its wider central Greek context, which once again stresses a Thessalian connection. It also reiterates the view that there was something that the Kopaïs Apollos had in common that Theban Ismenios was keen to seize upon. The most frequently cited comparandum, the Delphic Stepterion, at which also a *pais amphithales* headed a splendid procession, retraced Apollo's expiatory journey after the murder of Python and introduced him to his chief seat at Delphi.[124] Daphnephoria and Stepterion share the celebration of Apollo's perceived supersession of a 'local predecessor' in establishing Apollo's oracular cult, linking the traditions of the entire Kopaïs to the Thessalian north just as we saw Onkhestian Poseidon may have been the southernmost of a larger group in the area. This revives the issue of a perceived central Greek ('Aiolian') cultural unity lurking behind the mystery of the Kopaïs basin's Thessalian attachment which I avoided dwelling on in Section 1 above. Whether or not the historical process of regionalization preserved a real

[123] Pi. frr. 32, 70; cf. 191. Among Pindar's possible aulete teachers is one Pagondas: *Suda* s.v.; *Vit. Pind.* p. 1.2; 4.11 Dr. Ismenias is the name of a famous 4th-cent. aulete: Plut. *Per.* 1.5. The traditions around the Boiotian *aulos* are gathered by Roesch (1989) 211—12; new light (and more evidence) will be shed on this issue by Wilson (forthcoming). Auletic orchestration for Ismenios: Pi. *Pae.* 9.36; 7.1, 11; *Parth.* 2 fr. 94b14.

[124] The analogy between Stepterion and Daphnephoria is often made. For the Stepterion see Nilsson (1906/95) 150–7; Farnell (1896–1909) iv. 293–5; Jeanmaire (1939) 387–411; Burkert (1983) 127–30; Brelich (1969) 387–438, also on the laurel from which the future crowns for Pythian victors were woven; Grandolini (1993) Ancient testimonies: Ael. *VH* 3.1 = Theopomp. *FGrH* 115 F 80; *arg.* Pi. *P.* p. 4.11–14; Ephoros *FGrH* 70 F 31b; Call. *Aet.* frr. 87–9 Pf; Plut. *QG* 293c; *De Def. Or.* 418a ff. See Farnell (1896–1909) iv. 124 for the stages of Apollo's journey from Tempe; Blech (1982) 137–8, 221–6, arguing for an expiatory meaning.

memory of a common central Greek past, the conflict between 'local god' and newcomer seems to be a way of conceiving of religious change shared between the places of Thessalian colouring around the mantic pool. It appears to be this context of which the Ismenion becomes a part in the early fifth century when the Daphnephoria is recasted into a festival with significance for all of Boiotia, not just the Kopaïs basin.

The Daphnephoria was thus a ritual of the arriving Boiotoi, intimately connected with their conquest of Boiotia, and marking the Boiotoi's victory over the Pelasgians. It will have been a festival of pan-Boiotian significance, but performed in local contexts. The Daphnephoria apparently underwent several reorganizations in antiquity, and some transformation, virtually every time they reappear in the sources. Tellingly, these seem to occur whenever Boiotia at large is at stake: an outside force threatening Boiotia, the dissolution of the *koinon*, or the need to prop up Thebes' position within Boiotia. The Daphnephoria was clearly operational in Boiotian matters throughout Boiotian history.[125]

Together with the Tripodophoria and the celebrations that must be Athena Itonia's introduction to Koroneia, the Daphnephoria is the third festival situated in the context of the migratory myths marking the conquest of Boiotia. All three are war memorial festivals, cultivating memories of victory in battle and taking possession of the land. As discussed above, the details we have of the later festival for Athena Itonia very much convey the idea that forging a warrior identity was part of what becoming Boiotian entailed for the Boiotians. The 'warrior' Polematas is an apt leader for the introduction of Apollo's Daphnephoria—he is even attired with a special type of military footwear.[126] The affinity with the Stepterion reveals a 'Thessalian' link for which we need not rely on Boiotian myth. It gives extra force to the view that the Daphnephoria particularly tied together the places sitting round the Kopaïs basin, maintaining a fragile collective identity across the pond, a dynamic seemingly of potential for the making of Boiotia.

In enthusiastically practising this rite the Thebans slotted into this Kopaïd network their own Apollo, of a different religious tradition, as much as themselves; but by locating the final victory at Thebes itself, the Thebans emerge at the head of the conquest of Boiotia for the Boiotians from the Pelasgians. This appropriation of the Thessalo-Boiotoi tradition, if as successful as religious song seems to suggest, has enormous potential for the role of the Thebans in Boiotia: seizing sovereignty over this mythical past (possibly from Orkhomenos) must have been their most important tool in tying eastern Boiotia to themselves (and we shall see below that untying oneself from this web was a means of dissociating oneself from Boiotia and from Thebes). Rather than the physical territory of the

[125] Schachter's (2000) essay on the Daphnephoria discusses some aspects of the possible reorganizations in the late 4th and the 1st cent. BC, then again in 2nd century AD. Note for example Thebes' rebuilding of several sancturaries in the 4th cent., including the Ismenion: Symeonoglou (1985) 227–8. Kurke (2007) also argues for a pan-Boiotian role of the Daphnephoria.

[126] According to Proklos, the daphnephoros wears 'epikratides', or 'iphikratides', associated with the Athenian general Iphikrates, see Davies (1971) s.v. Kurke (2007) 83 discusses these 'military boots'.

Kopaïs, Thebes had conquered the area's mythical cornerstone, the myths and rituals recalling the immigration from Thessaly.

Even if Proklos' tradition on the Daphnephoria is not ancient enough to hold for the early fifth century, it nevertheless illustrates the same point: that Thebans were successful in putting themselves in the front line of the Boiotoi and the project Boiotia. The extent to which the Thebans became identified with Boiotia as a whole and took a central place in the Boiotian wanderings comes out for example in Thucydides, who confounds the Boiotian migrations with the conquest of the Theban Kadmeia in the passage quoted at the very beginning of this chapter (n. 2 above). Later on the Thebans themselves claim that it was they who expelled the 'mixed peoples' from Boiotia. Ismenias becomes the prototypical name of a Boiotian, symptomatic of how Apollo Ismenios and Boiotia coincided; this name and its many derivatives, other than in Thebes, are surprisingly prominent precisely amongst citizens of the cities round the Kopaïs.[127] It is just as telling that Ismenias is also the name of the *slave* who escorts (to the accompaniment of wild *aulos*-piping) the Boiotian seller of the Kopaïs-eel in Aristophanes' *Acharnians*: is this turning upside down a perceived Theban enslavement of the Kopaïs?[128]

Civic and regional identities

So the Daphnephoria, performed at Thebes and in the cities of the Kopaïs basin, had implications for the perceived and performed unity of early fifth-century Boiotia. But within individual cities, the Daphnephoria seem to have remained local civic festivals.[129] Certainly at Thebes, they arguably functioned as a kind of

[127] Th. 3.61.2. *LGPN* IIIb s.v. *Ἰσμειν-*, *Ἰσμην-*, *Ἰσμιν-* has attestations from Thebes, Hyettos, Kopai, Orkhomenos, Koroneia, Khaironeia, and Thespiai (though several attestations cannot be located); at Anthedon on the Euboian Gulf (*IG* xii.9 91, 25), a city always looking towards the Kopais (see Mackil (2003)); and an uncertain one at Tanagra (*IG* ii^2 3634.1). See above, n. 99, on prominent Boiotian figures called Ismenias. Note that the names deriving from *Πτωϊ-* reach into eastern Boiotia.

[128] Ar. *Ach.* 860 ff. Cf. the equation Boiotia-Thebes-Ismenia(s) for the 'Boiotian' woman in *Lys.* 85 ff.; 696 ff. We know from Agatharkhides *FGrH* 86 F 5 *ap.* Ath. 7.297c–d that sacrifice of the renowned and lucratively sold Kopaïs eel was an 'ancestral custom' of the Boiotians, revealing the degree to which Boiotian identity was bound up with the local economy (see Mackil (2003) *passim* for other examples). The scene in Aristophanes (cf. also the eel's occurrences in *Lys.* 36, 702; *Vesp.* 510–11; *Pax* 1005) attests this for as early as the 5th cent. and implies Lake Kopaïs as being part of a 'Theban' Boiotia.

[129] Some smaller places around Thebes, however, contributed to the Ismenion: at least one of them offered (!) tripods: Potniai: Keramopoulos (1917) 64, fig. 54 (6th cent., on a column drum):]*λονι Ποτνιε̂ς*; *SEG* xxii 417 (6th or 5th cent.; Roesch, *RPh* 29 (1965) 261–3): *Ἀπόλλων*]*ι hισμ*[*ενίοι* ...] *ει̂ες κα* (*ΑΔ* 13 (1930–1) 105–18: *-νει̂ες*). The Thebageneis' annual tripod delivery: Didymos p. 238 Schm. with Ephoros *FGrH* 70 F 21; D.S. 19.53. Potniai is amongst the towns oscillating between Thebes and Plataiai and synoikizing with Thebes, possibly in 431 BC: see *Hell. Oxy.* 12. 3–4; cf. Str. 9.2.24; 32; Paus. 9.2.1, 44; 8.1 with Demand (1990) 83–5 (including earlier bibliography). Are these indications that the Ismenion already during the 6th cent. functioned as a 'Boiotian' cult, rallying those cities who were keener on belonging to Thebes and Boiotia, rather than to Plataiai?

liturgy which leading families took on in return for public prestige much like the Athenian elite, though there is no trace of a developed institutionalization of the practice. Agasikles, the *pais amphithales* of frr. 94a and 94b, is the grandson of Aioladas and the son of a Pagondas; this Pagondas either himself masterminded the battle at Delion in 424 BC for the Boiotians, or was a relative of the Pagondas who did.[130] In view of what we have just learned about the pan-Boiotian significance of the festival, should we be surprised to find a laurel-bearer whose relations later staunchly resisted the attempt to dispel the unity of Boiotia?

On the other hand, it is overwhelmingly clear that the Daphnephoria had an important civic dimension. The Theban boys even had a respectable 'local' predecessor in the job: Herakles himself carried the laurel, commemorated with a tripod by his father Amphitryon. How does this square with the festival's overwhelmingly Boiotian character, and the role of Thebes within that? What follows will demonstrate that in considering the Daphnephoria's civic role we gain a fascinating glimpse into how a *koinon*-to-be dealt with one, perhaps the most important stumbling-block in the way of a unified Boiotia: the reconciliation of local and regional identity, that feature that in the fourth century would prompt the important theoretical discussion of the role of civic autonomy in a largely federal world.[131]

Of course only for Thebes, and to some degree for Orkhomenos (depending on how much credence we lend to D'Alessio's attribution of fr. *dub.* 333 to the Daphnephoria there), can we delve into what role the festival might have had in the *poleis*, but what one finds intriguingly suggests that the Daphnephoria helped to position the individuals and individual cities with regard to Boiotia at large. It has recently been suggested that among other things the Theban Daphnephoria controlled inter-elite *stasis* at Thebes.[132] I shall take the set of interesting observations a step further by arguing that the Daphnephoria was an occasion at which the Theban, Orkhomenian, and by implication other cities' leading citizens, were competing with each other for 'Boiotianness', for the best performance as a Boiotian in their respecive *poleis*. Turning themselves into good Boiotians was conceivably a way of rallying support for the unification of Boiotia amongst those citizens who watched. In the case of Thebes it might have served the purpose of making the *demos* (of whom more traces survive than we tend to think) part of the project Boiotia: as I said above, as far as we can work out, the project of a unified Boiotia was largely an elite concern. In developing 'Boiotianness' as a field

[130] For the possible reconstruction of the family stemma in these songs see Lehnus (1984) 83–5; for the link to the Pagondas of 424 BC cf. already von Wilamowitz-Moellendorff (1922) 432–8; cf. also Hornblower (2004) 159. See Wilson (2000) 280–1 on the Daphnephoria as a Theban liturgy; 297–8 on Boiotian *khoregiai* in general. For the *pais amphithales* see Oepke (1934); Severyns (1938–63); Robert (1969); Redfield (1982) 193. The meaning is a little obscure, literally 'blooming on both sides', of children who have both parents alive: *Il.* 22.496; Pl. *Leg.* 927d, Call. *Aet.* fr. 75.3; *Syll.*[3] 589.19 (examples taken from LSJ).

[131] For the 4th-cent. concept of *autonomia* see Hansen (1995*b*); cf. (1996*b*) for Boiotia in particular.

[132] Kurke (2007) esp. 84–97.

of contest for a competing elite in individual cities, the idea of Boiotia might itself have gained ground amongst those judging this particular agon, the Theban public. The ritual strategy for achieving this was to integrate local and regional identities in myth and ritual, of which the Daphnephoria was an important instance.

It is important for this argument to introduce a little flexibility into our rather hardened views on Thebes.[133] According to the standard view, Thebes is ruled by its aristocratic elite and is a sometimes more, sometimes less, narrow oligarchy. Although late fifth-century Thebes is oligarchically ruled as are all the cities in the *koinon*, it does not automatically follow that this was the case earlier. The evidence is too scarce to reach a definite conclusion, but the Theban *demos* does raise its voice occasionally, more than a tight oligarchy might lead one to expect: for example Thebes' chief medizers, about to be tried by the Greeks in 479 BC, claim that not just they but 'the whole Theban *demos* supported the Persians'. For the period to follow, Aristotle knows of a democracy at Thebes that was managed badly, overturned perhaps through Athenian support of the *beltistoi*; the latter piece of information derives from the *Old Oligarch* and is usually taken to refer to the period of Athenian domination between 457 and 446 BC. Democracy had a harder time at Thebes than at Athens, but it would be wrong to deny the *demos* any role in the political process. Rather, the integration of civic and elite concerns, just as on Rhodes, will have been high on the agenda of Thebes' leading figures, and with it the delicate issue of civic identity—what it means to be a Theban, as something that all Thebans share: I have already hinted above that Thebanness and Boiotianness gradually merged into each other.[134]

This ties in with another orthodox view of Thebes which needs to be overturned, the idea that the city was a safe refuge for nobles away from issues of revolt and popular concerns. By contrast, the evidence suggests that *stasis* ('strife') was as much feared as it was frequent in early to mid-fifth-century Thebes. This need not be between elite and *demos* rather than between the leading citizens and sometimes on behalf of the *demos*, just as was the case in the fourth century. Although the semantics of *stasis* are a topos in choral song, Thebes and Theban victors attract so much of the relevant vocabulary that blunt historicism is tempting: the Thebans seem in a constant state of *stasis*, much like what Thucydides claims for Boiotia as a whole during the fifth century. Strife, arrogance, and tyranny are defied in favour of 'peace' (ἡσυχία), 'justice' (δίκη) both in the victory odes and religious songs and the unattributed fragments

[133] For this 'flexibility' I am indebted to a youthful Pelling's (1970) delicate and detailed interpretation of internal Theban and Boiotian affairs.

[134] Fifth-cent. oligarchy at Thebes: Th. 3.62.3 where the claim is that rule of a very narrow elite (δυναστεία ὀλίγων) had been responsible for medism rather than an 'isonomous oligarchy' (ὀλιγαρχία ἰσόνομος) or—NB!—a democracy. Oligarchy elsewhere in the *koinon*: see n. 61 above; Theban *demos*: Hdt. 9.86–8; Arist. *Pol.* 1302^{b}29; [Xen.] *Ath. Pol.* 3.11; Theban *pleonexia* might encourage comparison with the Athenian *demos*: Xen. *Mem.* 3.5.1; *Hell.* 5.2.34. Factions at Thebes are more associated with the 4th cent. (M. Cook (1988), Buck (1985)), but inter-elite rivalry was actually a constant.

about Thebes.[135] If it is right that contemporary dithyramb cures the aches of a divided society reconstituting itself in the shared *khoros*, Pindar's 'Theban' dithyramb fr. 75 (the so-called *katabasis* of Herakles) must be placed in such a tense social context.[136]

So *stasis* in Thebes entailing different elite factions competing for local support is a plausible scenario; 'Boiotia' will have been a sticking point in such an atmosphere. The associations developed around Apollo Ismenios further this picture. He had an important role in regulating, controlling, or overseeing civic affairs. He is associated with the city's well-being, providing 'good governance' (*εὐνομία*) and 'grace' (*χάρις*); entrusting Theban happiness to Teneros in the aetiological myth makes the responsibility for civic health weigh on the daphnephoros' shoulders; and, as we saw above, Thrasydaios the boy victor was also caught in the civic responsibilities that Apollo Ismenios imposed. At the Daphnephoria, the *partheneia* praise the *pais amphithales* and his family through civic topoi much like those applied to epinikian victors, and strife and injustice feature strongly.[137]

What is striking is that the lining up of civic virtues in many Theban songs is complemented by supra-civic praise themes. *Isthmian 4* makes the link apparent in claiming that the Theban Kleonymidai 'have from the beginning been honoured by the Thebans, are *proxenoi* of the *amphiktiones*, and devoid of hubris' (Pi. *I.* 4.7–9). The formulae for Agasikles the *daphnephoros* and his family are an intriguing duplicate: 'As a faithful witness I have come to the *khoros* for Agasikles and his noble parents because of their *proxeniai* (*ἀμφὶ προξενίαισι*). For both of old and now they have been honoured by the *amphiktiones* for their celebrated victories with swift-footed horses' (Pi. *Parth.* 2 fr. 94b 38–43). These honours are then claimed to derive from the many horse-racing victories that the family achieved at the games of none other than Athena Itonia and Poseidon at Onkhestos. The song's catalogue of victories moves on to Olympia and peters out until—one or two dozen lost lines later—it arrives back at Thebes with the recommendations against civic strife already quoted (ll. 44–65). The *amphiktiones* ('neighbours') are plausibly the inhabitants of Thebes' Boiotian neighbours rallying at these two festivals. The appearance of these 'neighbours' here is I think less a reference to an amphiktyony such as at Delphi than deliberate use of this term in

[135] e.g. Pi. *I.* 4.1–9; *P.* 11.50–8; fr. 109 (any citizen who is looking for the public good should be looking out for peace's *hesykhia* and avoiding *stasis*); fr. 215 (*dike* at Thebes?). Cf. n. 137. On *hesykhia* Hornblower (2004) 60–4.

[136] On the dithyramb healing fragmented early 5th-cent. societies, often in the context of a joint cult of Demeter and Dionysos, see Wilson (2003*b*); Kowalzig (2007) 226–32. Interestingly, replicas of the cult of (often Eleusinian) Demeter notoriously protect the democratic Greeks and those who fight for their democracy, notably Plataiai, whose sanctuary of Demeter remains always unharmed: Hdt. 9.57, 62, 65 (Plataiai) (cf. 97, 101: Mykale, paralleled with Plataiai); cf. Th. 3.56.2 (Plataiai); Xen. *Hell.* 5.2.29 (Theban occupation of the Kadmeia). Cf. Ch. 4 n. 96 for 'democrats' fleeing to the sanctuary of Demeter on Aigina.

[137] Pi. *Parth.* 2 fr. 94b65 ff.; cf. the praise of the family in 1 fr. 94a; Ismenios and civic order/welfare: *Pae.* 1.10; *Parth.* 2 fr. 94b3–5; cf. also *Pae.* 9.1–20.

order to create that aura around the two cults of Athena and Poseidon.[138] The enigmatic *proxenoi*, also appearing a little earlier in the *partheneion* for the Aioladadai analogous to the passage of *Isthmian 4* implies that individual victors were judged against a pan-Boiotian scene. The use of the word and its derivatives by Pindar is obscure. But here, for the two families to be honoured as '*proxenoi* of the *amphiktiones*', or as 'honoured for the *proxeniai*' refers, I think, to their standing amongst the other Boiotians, not to their hospitality offered to strangers at home in Thebes.[139] What is intriguing about these passages is that apparently a reputation on the pan-Boiotian stage matters for one's standing in the city of Thebes. To be appreciated by the Boiotian 'neighbours' is not only something to aspire to, but is intrinsically linked to honour within the city of Thebes itself. When perusing the *epinikia*, one observes that Theban victories are linked to 'Boiotian' cults such as that of Poseidon at Onkhestos, and mythical figures from elsewhere in Boiotia are evoked, suggesting that the pan-Boiotian context is important. Religious song, on this view, was not only operative in giving Thebes a role in Boiotia, but also in making Boiotian interests part of the civic. The Daphnephoria, with its inbuilt integration of civic and Boiotian representations, must have had an overarching role in the merging of the local and the regional.[140]

The Theban elite may not have been the only ones who tried to square the individual city with the project Boiotia: Pi. fr. *dub.* 333, the possible *daphnephorikon* for a certain Ekhekrates of Orkhomenos, when put into its historical context suggests a similar practice. It is a convincing, old proposition that this Ekhekrates should be identified with the seer of Apollo's oracle at Tegyra who according to Plutarch foresaw the Greeks' defeat of the Persians at the time of Mys' mantic tour. In Herodotus, Mys does not consult Tegyra, but Plutarch's anecdote is one element in an anti-Persian thread developing in Boiotia around this final phase of the Persian Wars and already present in Herodotus. The story of the Orkhomenian Thersandros sharing a couch with a Persian warrior who fatefully anticipates doom for Mardonios' expedition is likely to be part of this tradition. Mardonios' keen interpretation of the 'Karian' words mysteriously

138 'Amphiktiones' and 'periktiones' occur frequently in Pindar: see Ch. 3, n. 4 above. Not many of the cults involved are attested as 'amphiktyonies' in the institutionalized sense of classical Delphi or Delos. It is better to think of them as cult centres (I suggested 'theoric cult centres' in (2005)) with a set of, albeit highly binding, rules based on a laboured sense of shared custom and tradition. In that sense the words *amphi-/periktiones* as they feature in Pindar can assume a rhetorical role. Onkhestos is attested as an 'amphiktyony' in Str. 9.2.33.

139 Pindar's use of the word(s) in an institutional or social sense is controversial, and the suggestion made here is merely an attempt to account for the curious parallel in the praise for the two Theban families. Cf. the uses in Pi. *N.* 7.65 (most recently discussed by Hornblower (2004) 178–80) and *O.* 9.82, which both also seem to refer to *proxenia* being granted by a (religious and political?) 'centre', the Molossians in the first, Isthmia in the second case. Cf. the use of *amphiktiones* for Isthmia at *N.* 6.39–41. Marek (1984) 121–32, 162–331 strikingly reveals how proxenies frequently emanate from cult centres (though almost always in connection with the administering city), in Hellenistic times often closely linked to *koina.* Kurke (2007) 88–91 also discusses these passages.

140 e.g. Pi. *I.* 1.32 ff.; 52 ff.; *I.* 4.19 (37) ff. Panhellenic myth in these odes seems to perform a similar function: see n. 142.

uttered by Apollo Ptoios points to an ambiguous answer rather than a foreign one.[141]

It is less fruitful to try to identify whether these oracles were attesting an authentic anti-Persian mood amongst the medizing Boiotians than to consider that Boiotia's former medism squared badly with the later fifth-century slogan 'freedom for Boiotia', the pro-federalists' most alluring draw vis-à-vis the Athenian empire. The persistent tradition of anti-Persian Thebans during Xerxes' invasion is likely to belong to the same tendency of later Thebans developing a keen interest in Hellenic affairs. It is quite possible that the tradition of an anti-Persian—that is, pro-Hellenic—Boiotian Apollo was propagated by the leading citizens in the Boiotian cities for the same reasons as victories at pan-Boiotian festivals were summoned to heighten the standing of the Theban *daphnephoros*: these are strategies by which elites tried to further, and justify, the case for a unified Boiotia in their local communities. Harping on one's Panhellenic merits was, as we saw already in Chapter 4, a popular strategy to gain support.[142] If Ekhekrates' possible *daphnephorikon* did actually accompany the alleged prophecy, it could suitably indicate that the reconciliation of Boiotianness and Panhellenism was an issue dating back right to the Persian Wars. But it is just as likely that the prophecy was later grafted onto the existing *daphnephorikon*, and belonged to the post-Persian War tradition by which one's favourable stance towards Hellas was the *sine qua non* for the acquisition of political authority, and especially so in the developing *koinon*.

One needs here to be aware of the complexities of contemporary internal politics in the whole of Boiotia. *Stasis* was tearing Boiotia apart throughout the Peloponnesian War,[143] and was often linked to democratizing tendencies; perhaps the situation of the 'Boiotian masses' (*πλῆθος Βοιωτῶν*), as Herodotus describes the great number of Persian supporters in Boiotia, was not so different from that at Thebes. Did our Daphnephoric songs reconcile local and Boiotian concerns in myth and ritual everywhere in Boiotia just as conspicuously as they did in Thebes? Religious song in Boiotia may well have prepared fundamental ground

[141] On Ekhekrates and Pi. fr. *dub.* 333 cf. e.g. already Bergk and now D'Alessio (2000) 245 ff.; Plut. *De Def. Or.* 411e–12b; Mys at the Ptoion: Hdt. 8.133–6; Thersandros' wise words: 9.16.

[142] 'Freedom of Boiotia': Th. 4.92–5; esp. 92; cf. 1.113.4. The curious tradition of anti-Persian factions specifically at Thebes: Hdt. 7.202; D.S. 11.4.7 (cf. 81 on Thebes' medism). The Plataiai debate makes clear that, at least in Thucydides' world, 'Panhellenism' was something competed for, and what individual *poleis* quoted in support of their independence: Th. 3.62.1–2; cf. the Theban answer: 63–4; 67.6 etc. claiming that the Plataians assist Greece's enslavement through their support of the Athenians. The festival of Zeus Eleutherios, apparently in the 5th cent. exclusively conducted as a 'civic' festival at Plataiai, confirms this view: Th. 2.71.2–4; 3.58.4–5; D.S. 11.29 (cf. Schachter (1981–94) iii. 125–43). Thespiai, the rebel amongst the cities of the *koinon*, is a similarly keen Panhellenist: Hdt. 7.222, 226–7; 8.25 (Thermopylai); 9.30 (Plataiai), cf. 7.132, 202; 8.50, 66, 75. Perhaps similar to Aigina (Ch. 4, n. 74 above), 'Panhellenic' myth, i.e. of the Trojan cycle, is conspicuous in Theban victory odes: e.g. Pi. *P.* 11.17 ff.; *I.* 4.35 (53a) ff. Raaflaub (2004), esp. Chs. 3 and 4, discusses the development of the notion of 'freedom' at this time from a wider Greek perspective.

[143] *Stasis* in Boiotia: Th. 3.62.5; 4.92.6; cf. 1.113; Arist. *Rhet.* 3.4, 1407^{a}4 ff.; *Pol.* 5.2, 1302^{b}27. Various Boiotians held Athenian, even hereditary, proxenies: Walbank (1978) nos. 4, 5, 7, 11, 45 (including Pindar himself: no. 5).

for the formalized *koinon*, of 446 BC or after; and with this bit of Boiotianness limited popular participation was made attractive to 'the people'.[144]

Not that this strategy was universally successful, quite the contrary, but the negative examples are those that best illustrate how tightly knit the song-dance network must have been. How effectively the 'Thessalian' myth so intimately connected to the Kopaïs basin fastened the cities into the business of Boiotia is illustrated by places which notoriously refused to play the game, notably Thespiai and Plataiai. Both of these have rocky relationships with the mythical Boiotoi as much as with the historical Boiotian *koinon*, whether in the pre- or the post-formalization period. Both cities rather look to Athens. The case of Plataiai is more difficult to explain than the Thespian gaze in the direction of the sea: the Thespians, with their well-placed harbour of Siphai at the Korinthian Gulf, probably had less to gain from the exchange networks justifying the existence of the *koinon* than from wider Mediterranean sea-traffic travelling through the Isthmos.[145]

Thucydides expresses the differences between the *koinon* and its defecting members rather simply through an oligarchic–democratic antithesis, which then also divides anti- and pro-Athenians. Whether things were in fact that straightforward is an issue needing further investigation, but the opposition handily coincides with how absconding cities construe their identities in myth and, probably, how the Boiotian *koinon* expresses its relations to the Athenian empire. The crucial point is the overlap of Boiotian and Athenian traditions in the area south of the Kopaïs and parts of western Boiotia. The Pelasgians withdrawing to Mount Hymettos above Athens in the story of the wanderings forms only the tip of a whole mound of stories claiming Athenian presence in Boiotia in mythical times: for the enigmatic Athena Alalkomeneis, Athena Itonia's epichoric counterpart at Koroneia, is said to have been founded in the time of Kekrops, the first Athenian king. Athenians are thought to have been settling the southern shores of the Kopaïs.[146] And consequently, this set of traditions is summoned for the anti-Boiotian case. Thespians take to the streets for democracy throughout Thucydides (and later), but their sustained *attikismos* goes beyond mere 'political' sympathies. Thespios is another son of the Athenian king Erekhtheus; while Apollo-shaped names are given to future Boiotian leaders, the Thespian individuals of which we hear in this period turn to Apollo's divine complement and rival Dionysos: we know of Demophilos and Dithyrambos, the latter the Thespians' best fighter at Plataiai; Themistokles tellingly made his slave Sikinnos (a satyr's name) a citizen of this city. Together with the series of Thespian

[144] Hdt. 7.202. The *koinon* is a relatively 'participatory' oligarchy (low property census): *Hell. Oxy.* 11.2. Arist. *Pol.* 1278^{a}25 (no one to hold office who had in the preceding 10 years been an artisan); Heracl. Lemb. fr. 76 (Thespiai: disgrace to work land with one's hands) point to civic arrogance and a strong civic ideology similar to that at Athens rather than to elite snobbery.

[145] Roesch (1965) is the standard monograph on the city, though it does not examine Thespiai's mythical traditions, nor an economic motivation for *stasis*. Mackil (2003) sheds light on economic concerns underlying the formation of *koina*.

[146] Paus. 9.33.5, 7, *Σ Il.* 4.8 (Alalkomeneis); Paus. 9.24.2 (Kopaïs).

attempts to break away from the *koinon* and become a democracy all this is indicative of the intertwining of political, social, and perhaps even economic distance from the *koinon*, expressed through all things that were the *koinon*'s favourites. So even this brief discussion of Thespian peculiarities makes it clear that local myth-ritual networks prompted a set of social practices beyond the performance of ritual itself, and provided an efficient means of tying and untying oneself to and from loved or less loved neighbours.[147]

On this view, the Thessalian/Apolline myth-ritual network of the Kopaïs forms a highly refined reference frame, cultivated to support a unified Boiotia; therefore, just as I argued in Chapter 2 that cities defecting from the Delian League would invent their own myth of Apollo's birth, the Kopaïs network is also forcefully denied by those who have no interest in the project Boiotia. This also clinches the case for the Boiotian idea being anti-Athenian, which was one of the side-postulations I tentatively launched at the beginning. Though looking at the songs by themselves does not necessarily yield anti-Athenian feelings amongst the Boiotoi, the atticizing myths and cults (including that of Dionysos) together with Athenian support of 'populist' inclinations suggest that Athenians liked to undermine what the Boiotian elites were so keen to promulgate through the powerful suggestions of the joint action of myth and ritual in religious song: the integration of local and regional identity, a cornerstone as much as a key concern for the *koinon* for a long time to come.

CHANTING BOIOTIAN IDENTITY

All of these disparate pieces of evidence tie into the larger picture of a highly dynamic and fiercely argumentative collection of contemporary Boiotian cities trying to come to grips with their relations to each other, torn as they are between local and regional obligations in the process of the establishment of the *koinon*. The traditions of the wanderings were an essential tool for the making, or the redefinition, of Boiotia in a grid of myths going beyond the local. These traditions were associated with places of the Thessalo-Boiotian legacy in western Boiotia and the Kopaïs area, and it is probably not least a product of the traditional rivalry with Orkhomenos that Thebes' quest for power went along with the appropriation of, and interference with, the Thessalian past in the area. The proliferation of migratory pasts in Boiotia is no doubt partly a product of the process by which Thebes established itself as the major power in Boiotia. It

[147] Thespios: Paus. 9.26.4; Thespiai pro-Greek, pro-democracy, and pro-Athenian: Hdt. 7.202: enthusiastic fighters at Thermopylai under the commander Demophilos, as opposed to unmotivated Thebans; 227: Dithyrambos; 233; 8.75: Sikinnos; resistance to the *koinon* and democratic revolts: Th. 4.89; 133; 6.95.2 (cf. 1.113). In the 4th cent. both Thespiai and Plataiai are on the Spartan (= anti-federal) side: Xen. *Hell.* 5.4.10. Four Thespian citizens were *proxenoi* of Athens: Walbank (1978) no. 11. Thespiai was littered with the oeuvre of Athenian sculptors: Paus. 9.26.4–27.4. Apollo's world was not therefore absent: cf. *LGPN* IIIb s.v. Ism-.

would, however, be wrong to make Thebes the one and only factor in a changing landscape of myths and rituals: we have seen that one can plausibly assume an interest in Boiotia outside Thebes, amongst the elites of the Boiotian cities. It is quite possible, though it cannot be proved, that elites in the Boiotian *poleis* feared the *pleonexia* of the Theban *demos* more than loss of independence in a *koinon* headed by their Theban peers. And once Theban identity had fully swallowed the Boiotian, the Theban citizenry's appetite for the territory of Boiotia might also have been satisfied. Either way, it appears that the notion of Boiotia helped to steer several counterposing tendencies into the same direction.

As migratory myths are essential to this new or newly activated Boiotian identity, their preservation must have been a prime concern. Insisting indefatigably on the same issue in continuously new configurations of myth and ritual performed in religious song, strictly obeying the principle of ritual redundancy, seems to have made sure that the message did not get lost in the rather dense forest of symbols.[148] In this, the Boiotians seem actively to make use of the widespread belief about their complicated past rather than eliminate it, or replace it by myths of the more popular autochthony. It is clear, therefore, why the Boiotians should be keen to keep the tiresome cult obligation to Dodona, or in fact might have invented it first in this period: without a continually re-enacted tie with their former homes, they could never have arrived in Boiotia; a myth of arrival makes no sense without somewhere to have arrived from. The same can be said of the travelling Athena Itonia, unfortunately so badly documented, who derives her meaningful existence from the fact that she is a foreign goddess. In this practice the people involved in central Greek migrations do not in reality behave differently from those who settle overseas and construe connections with their supposed homelands through cultivating ancestral rituals associated with this homeland.

While in command of the migrations probably by the middle or the end of the fifth century, Thebes reached this position only gradually, and religious song seems to have had an important share in this process. The investment of performances in the aetiologies of the two old shrines at the edges of the Kopaïs is no bad strategy: Poseidon's at Onkhestos and Apollo's at the Ptoion, whose mythical personnel prefigure the Boiotian migration from Thessaly. The most astonishing and richest instances of productive performance, however, are the performances at the Daphnephoria. This festival, in myth directly linked to the process by which the Boiotoi had finally arrived in historical Boiotia, was celebrated as I argued above not just in Thebes as the longer Pindaric fragments might suggest, but quite possibly at Apollo's oracles all over the Kopaïs basin. Theban Apollo Ismenios, of a different oracular tradition from these cults, was slotted into this series, by the fifth century at the latest boasting an analogous aetiology for his cult, and sharing the Daphnephoric rite. Exploiting interaction across Lake Kopaïs that might well be older, early fifth-century religious song belaboured a performance tradition that was as intimately related to a shared Boiotian con-

[148] Cf. Introduction, esp. pp. 46 ff.

quest of Boiotia as it was to Theban leadership. But the Daphnephoria did not only mediate between the different cities on behalf of Boiotia; it also served to cement the notion of Boiotia within the individual cities. By making Boiotianness a sticking point in elite competition, a way to sunder good citizens from bad, the Daphnephoria certainly at Thebes, but perhaps also elsewhere, helped the performing elite to justify the existence of Boiotia. A festival that was at once civic and Boiotian, the Daphnephoria most conspicuously merges local and regional identities.

Reconciling local and regional identities was clearly crucial to the attractions and the future success of the *koinon*. Diodorus for example preserves a memory by which already at Oinophyta in 457 BC the Boiotians rushed together to fight πανδημεί (literally 'the whole *demos* of the Boiotians') to ward off the Athenians (whose eventual triumph is then compared to that against the Persians (!)). The passage reveals a perception of a unified Boiotia at a point far too early to match reality.[149] Then, if local civic pride is something cultivated particularly in the service of the social integration of the *polis*, the merging of local and regional identities was in part related to that of elite and non-elite interests. In this, the Boiotian *koinon* is not necessarily very different from the Rhodian synoikism. Certainly performance at festivals seems to have had a similar role in the production of a mentality that looked beyond the *polis*. The case for a structural role of religious song in the making of social change as I have postulated it throughout this book is lent powerful support by the Boiotian case—here near a dozen compositions survive all revolving around the same set of mythical issues. Whilst *Olympian 7* is an isolated yet monumental survival of what may have been a huge community-making apparatus at Rhodes, in the case of Boiotia one cannot help thinking that what survives is only a glimpse of multifarious and diverse religious activity producing gradual social change. If the Boiotian *koinon* came about at some point in the second half of the fifth century, religious song reveals strategies making it, as the case may be, palatable, attractive, something to aspire to.

Because of the comparable wealth of evidence that survives for Boiotian song-dance of the period, it is here possible to observe how combined evidence from a number of sanctuaries—those of Zeus at Dodona and Poseidon at Onkhestos, the Itonion, the Ptoion, and the Ismenion—feed into one, mutually conditioning, system of myths and rituals. In curiously lending concreteness to what can only be guessed from documentary evidence, their enactment in ritual reflects mobile social and power relations in the area. The Boiotian aetiologies emerge as an extraordinary example of the way myth and ritual work in the immediate performative context of changing local configurations in myth, cult, and politics. This is perhaps how we have to imagine epichoric performance cultures all over Greece in this period when the nature of locality, the strength of local, communal identities, and the feasibility of the *polis*-world were very much an issue in a rapidly changing society.

[149] D.S. 11.81–3 (conflating the battles of Tanagra (Th. 1.108, where Athens was defeated) and of Oionophyta).

Epilogue

κύριός εἰμι θροεῖν ὅδιον κράτος αἴσιον ἀνδρῶν
ἐκτελέων· ἔτι γὰρ θεόθεν καταπνείει
Πειθώ, μολπὰν ἀλκὰν σύμφυτος αἰών·
ὅπως Ἀχαιῶν δίθρονον κράτος, Ἑλλάδος ἥβας
ξύμφρονα ταγάν,
πέμπει ξὺν δορὶ καὶ χερὶ πράκτορι
θούριος ὄρνις Τευκρίδ' ἐπ' αἶαν,
οἰωνῶν βασιλεὺς βασιλεῦσι νε-
ῶν, ὁ κελαινὸς ὅ τ' ἐξόπιν ἀργᾶς,
φανέντες ἴκταρ μελάθρων χερὸς ἐκ δοριπάλτου
παμπρέπτοις ἐν ἕδραισιν,
βοσκομένω λαγίναν ἐρικύμονα φέρματι γένναν,
βλάψαντε λοισθίων δρόμων·
αἴλινον αἴλινον εἰπέ, τὸ δ' εὖ νικάτω.

(Aeschylus, *Agamemnon* 104–21 Page)

I have the power to tell of the auspicious command of the
expedition, the command of men in authority: for still from the gods am I inspired
with persuasive power, my strength in song, by the life that has grown up with me:
to tell how the two-throned command of the Achaeans, of the youth of Hellas
the concordant leadership,
was sped with avenging spear and arm
by the warlike bird of omen to the Teucrian land,
the king of birds appearing to the kings of the ships,
the black eagle and behind it the white one,
appearing near the palace on the hand in which the spear is brandished,
in seats conspicuous,
feeding upon the hare, her womb teeming with young,
checked from running her final course.
Sing sorrow, sorrow, but may the good prevail.

(tr. H. Lloyd-Jones)

The powerful language of the bird-omen, combined with typically Aeschylean enigmatic Greek, and mysterious and somehow fateful metaphors, has simultaneously confounded and enthused generations of students of Greek literature. What has attracted less attention is the baroque context in which this passage stands. The scene is Argos, the moment is the Greeks' glorious return from Troy. In a jubilant city, the altars are set alight everywhere, steaming and blazing with offerings, torches are flashing, quantities of unguents and ointments are running.

The entire pantheon—Olympian, khthonian, private and public—is receiving its sacrifice as Argos embarks on victory celebrations.[1] In this highly ritualized environment, the story of the omen itself almost acquires the function of a cult song, confidently performed by the old men's chorus. Their curious authority (κύριός εἰμι), oddly contrasting with their feeble physique lamented earlier in the ode, seems to lie in the fact that this narrative of ten years ago is something that the old men have so often gone over and over that it has already become a kind of folksong whose authority and shape are determined by its continuous reperformance. The passage bears witness to the process of how a story of the past is becoming a myth through performance in ritual. Indeed, this performance at the moment of victory is the ultimate proof that the story is telling the truth: 'you cannot argue with this song'. The mesmerizing quality of ritual orchestration forms part and parcel of the song's context, almost as if the whole passage were about how ritual changes one's perception of reality. The *Πειθώ* that the old men quote as their source of wisdom is the 'Persuasion' that comes with ritual involvement. The passage, exploiting religious convention for its tragic narrative, suggests how the ritual context of a story can propel a community into belief about the past through the momentum of performance.

This book has argued for a basic principle of Greek religion: 'myth and ritual' typically interact through performance, perhaps cannot even relate without a performative element. It is in choral performance that they become closely bound up with one another, and it is through choral performance that myth and ritual become socially effective, for it offers a medium for myth and ritual to come together. I have tried to show, on the basis of some concrete instances, that choral performances, in hosting the dialogue between these two fundamentals, emerge as a creative means for the delineation of worshipping communities by allowing for a constant reconfiguration of mythical pasts and ritual presents. Religious song, performances of myth and ritual, turn out to be a productive activity with a full and dynamic share in historical processes and social change, above all through the way it opens up new social realities formulated through the myth-ritual interface. That Greek religion, and hence certain aspects of Greek history, cannot work without such performances may be an intriguing consequence.

I have argued that in order to establish the relationship between myth and ritual the workings of each must be taken into account; it is because of their shared strategies and shared purpose, geared towards correlating, or even merging, past and present, that they form such a powerful and productive ensemble.

[1] Aesch. *Ag.* 88 ff.: 'The altars of all the gods that guide the city, gods on high and gods below the earth, gods of the doors and of the market-place, blaze with offerings; and from this side and that as high as heaven torches send up their light, charmed by the hallowed unguent's soft guileless coaxing (μαλακαῖς ἀδόλοισι παρηγορίαις), the royal offering from the inmost store. Of these matters tell us what you can and may and become the healer of this anxiety. Now it carries thoughts of ill, and now from the sacrifices you reveal springs hope that gives protection (ll. 101–2 ἐκ θυσιῶν ἃς ἀναφαίνεις ἐλπίς), so that worry insufferable cannot grieve my heart'.

Instead of deriving myth from ritual or vice versa, or looking for parallels or opposites between them, myth and ritual can be related to each other in a carefully built-up nexus; the crux lies in the ritual moment orchestrated by the contemporary performance. It is in such ritual moments during performance that the narrative of the past and the ritual activity of the present blend into one another, as is demonstrated most clearly in the case of the choruses on Delos. Rather than thinking about myth and ritual in a linear relationship, we should therefore imagine processes of interaction between myth and ritual. The image of 'interaction' avoids ideas of close correspondence, replacing them by a more flexible and irregular interrelationship between the two, at individual moments rather than throughout the entire unfolding of the myths and rituals.

Since the circularity in aetiological myth and transcendence of time are essential to the workings of myth in ritual, it follows that myth that bears a relation to ritual is always in some way aetiological. The distinction between aetiological myth and non-aetiological myth thus collapses, or at the very least the proportion of one to the other requires adjustment. In fact, we have seen throughout this study that many origins of cults are not formulated as aetiologies in the strict sense, but nevertheless result in cult foundations. To pin down the difference, one could postulate that myths that have lost their ritual context are socially inactive, or are active in a different way. Though one must take into account the literary fixing of myth through writing, it would be very difficult to find the cut-off point where myths 'stop' being aetiological: there is enough evidence that myth and ritual worked in choral performance in later times just as in the period under consideration here.

While it would be excessive to claim that the chorus lies at the foundation of all action in Greek ritual, its role is nevertheless conspicuous, and it is clear from the instances discussed that myth-ritual performances encompass entire landscapes with a density that contrasts oddly with the patchiness of the surviving evidence. The singing chorus provides the hinge between myth and ritual, that element that brings the myth into the present. This oscillation of the chorus between mythical past and ritual present is made literal when past and present choruses join at the end of the aetiological myth, as if to illustrate their (almost mechanical) function at the transition between the two realms: the chorus carries itself from mythical narrative into performative ritual.

How deeply intertwined the performing chorus is with the myth it recounts emerges most clearly in Bacchylides' *Ode 11* (Chapter 6), when the Arkadian women's chorus (χορὸς γυναικῶν) of the subsequent ritual established through the myth is the direct successor of the girls who, in what seems to be a rite of transition, had imagined themselves to be wild animals hunted by Artemis. Generally, the members of the chorus are (sometimes in a less direct way) the multiplied protagonists of actors in cult myth: of the local Delian women, of the warriors at the cult of Apollo at Asine, of the Panhellenic ambassadors, the Heliadai, or the military troops of the migrating Boiotoi.

The chorus thus supplies the fundamental communal aspect of religious ritual, and perhaps of many other aspects of Greek religion *and* history. Since the chorus is in the myth, it provides access to the mythical past. The members of the singing and dancing chorus are representatives of the worshipping community and through their performance make the re-enactment of the myth relevant to the community; without the chorus, neither community nor communal re-enactment could exist. The choral 'tribute', so conspicuous in some cases of aetiological myth, is none other than the obligatory offering to the deity, manifesting both a community's propitiation of a crime committed against its future divine patron, and the worshipping group that this divine patron once guarded.

Many choral aetiologies, such as those establishing the Dryopians at Asine, the Proitids at Metapontion, or the Boiotians in Boiotia, point to some form of conflict within the local community (often caused by the arrival of outsiders): the implication is that much of Greek cult is concerned with the justification of unjustly acquired social power. I can only allude here to the vast number of aetiological myths in antiquarian and other literature that illustrate precisely this relation.[2] The choral nature of these rituals therefore clearly implies that questions of social solidarity and community identity are at stake in these performances; the chorus-dancing lies at the heart of the social nature of these rituals. That choral performances are an essentially aristocratic institution fits this configuration well but in a way different from what one might imagine: the fierce formulation of new or alternative group identities through song, for example at Metapontion, on Rhodes or in Boiotia, shows effectively how delineating a worshipping community in myth-ritual performance is always a process of exclusion, not always and not necessarily, however, to the sole benefit of an aristocratic elite.

To look at these choral compositions without their ritual context misses the way they are a part of community activity. This approach raises the issue of that other choral event with a strong, if obscure, relation to ritual: Athens' dramatic *khoroi*, the ubiquity of which is often attributed to the perhaps questionable observation that in this city of choruses, there are no choruses other than those of male citizens and of, or similar to those of, Dionysos.[3] The way I have dealt with choral song encourages us to think of drama as a form of ritual, namely as *creative* ritual, and similar to the earlier *khoroi* as productive in social and historical processes. Drama's affinity with choral song is only beginning to be more closely examined. Quite apart from the fact, for example, that the way dramatic choruses refer to their own dancing looks suspiciously like what lyric dithyrambic choruses do,[4] it is probably no coincidence that aetiology features so prominently in drama and that many plays are actually a large-scale aetiology. The transition between myth and real-life cult at the end of a play is achieved through aetiology just as in our lyric examples, almost as if to orchestrate the myth-ritual nexus, the

[2] Kowalzig (2004).

[3] Even some female choral ritual can be discovered on closer inspection: the *arktoi* for Artemis at Brauron; *parthenoi* dancing for the Erekhtheids (Eur. *TrGF* 65; though the context of the *pannykhis* is problematic); mystery cult at Eleusis also features female dance (Paus. 1.38.6); the Athenians' annual κόραι ἱλασόμεναι sent to the Delphinion (Plut. *Thes.* 18).

[4] I discuss some facets of this in (2007).

moment when dramatic myth becomes *polis*-ritual. So the dramatic *khoros* no less than the lyric *khoros* imperceptibly moves between myth and ritual. It would be counter-intuitive (and a *lectio difficilior*) to assume that the choral ritual which for many centuries had functioned so effectively as a form of social interaction should suddenly cease to do so; rather, one might wonder what it is in the social and political conditions of Athens' democratic fifth century that made their choral ritual take a different shape.[5]

Performance catapults ritual participants into a kind of limbo-state. Time-levels blend and notions of space are blurred through the aesthetic involution in which the associations of myth and ritual are pooled: mixed and confused (what I called synaesthesia above) to create a powerful, overwhelming, and vastly redundant, set of closely interrelated ideas and associations. This effect is fundamental for the way in which performances of myth and ritual create, maintain, and transform worshipping communities, in other words how these performances become productive rituals. Much of this book has sought to establish the 'state of mind' which performers would have been in at a particular time and place in a Greek community, and to determine the multiple associations that would have been made, or, rather, felt by ritual participants.

Eliade's old elusive 'abolition of time', the transcendence of historical time in ritual, is the prerequisite by which the state of affairs evoked by whatever associations the ritual carries can be made relevant, can be projected into the moment of performance. The mythical past is productive in the working of Greek ritual in a present historical reality; the idea of a routine interaction between myth and ritual as illustrated in this book might explain one aspect of why and how the mythical past is quite such a powerful tool throughout Greek history. At the same time I have throughout insisted on the transcendence of time being intimately linked to a reshuffling of cultic places and a reconstitution of sacred spaces. Both myth and ritual define religious localities and map out ritual spaces, structured ceremonial environments; and it is the configuration between mythical time and religious space (religious 'place') that is continuously altered through myth-ritual interaction. Greek history has been much concerned with the anthropology of time, much less with that of space, and even less with their dynamic correlation, but the case of the Boiotian *koinon* with its transformation of the Kopaïs basin from a Thessalian into a Boiotian ambience through performances of myth and ritual (Chapter 7), should indicate that it is in malleable traditional religious spaces that Greek history *Takes Place.*[6]

The interaction of myth, ritual, time, and space becomes particularly creative when performances associate myths and rituals that are not normally, or not before that point in history, thrown together in quite this way: tying a collection of gods and heroes to Argos when really they belong to the Eastern Plain (Chapter 3); or giving a role to the tiny locality of Aigina in the wider Greek world through an

[5] I experiment with this set of ideas in Kowalzig (2006), various of them now addressed in Sourvinou-Inwood (2003*a*).

[6] The allusion is to J. Z. Smith's important study (1987).

association of myths and rituals of Aiginetan Zeus *Hellanios* to a Panhellenic festival at Delphi (Chapter 4). Some cases are more striking than others, but all the performances considered have turned out to show how myth and ritual exist in a dynamic, rather than in a stable, relationship. Our sacred chants exploit this dynamism to the extreme and fully benefit from the modalities of reinterpretation. Religious song thus lends new meanings to old configurations of myth and ritual. Perhaps it is also for this reason that we sometimes feel that myth and ritual meander freely through the forest of possible representations of religious activity.

The key point is that religious song of the variety investigated here exploits the perceived conservatism of both myth and ritual in order to redefine a given worshipping group. The interaction of myth and ritual allows for authoritative illusions about the relationship between participants in religious spectacles. It is for this reason that they can become a powerful tool in society, and play a role in historical and social change. All the songs' cult groups are themselves in crisis or involved in conflicts with others: the Delian theoric community in its songs reveals a deep ambiguity about the constituency of that community; the Argives undergo a kind of reformation of their divine patrons and mythical ancestors; Aigina looks for a role on the greater Panhellenic stage. The ever-chanting Boiotians reveal that they are in search of a regional identity while the Akhaians wander between different ethnic allegiances; and the Rhodian chorus give away a rivalry with Athens over 'which was the better island'. The case of the Boiotians, but also that of the Rhodians, perhaps illustrates well how the illusion of tradition generated by myth-ritual performances provides a powerful, but essentially conservative, context for eventual change.

The dynamics of mythical past, ritual present, and social change are an interesting topic. For it addresses that other pressing issue that has been exposed in the working together of tradition and immediacy in performance. While no myth or ritual can be traced back to its origins, myths and rituals are still marked by their own past. Myth and ritual carry both the weight of, and profit from, the potential that lies in their own continuity. The paradox formulated at the beginning, that in these two categories the recounting of origins or beginnings does not play a role, that neither aetiology nor ritual care to explain a real past, is throughout fruitful. Nevertheless it does not tell the whole story. I hope to have shown that a certain dimension of the past—one beyond facts and dates, solely preserved in actual or imagined long-standing associations of cult places with worshipping communities, of religious place with religious space—does make a contribution to the uninterrupted continuum from mythical times that is so relevant for the authority of myth-ritual performances in a historical context. To cite the case of Apollo at Asine again, the catchment area of Apollo Pythaieus goes back to a perceived pre-Dorian grouping of these same cities, and probably for this reason the cult can exercise a level of social integration when supposed Dorians enter the scene—all that of course within the Greeks' made-up past, in which the so-called Dorian migration may not have been more than a significant social upheaval. What a participant overwhelmed by the powerful evocation of tradition at the Delia in 426/5 BC was supposed to have picked up is a confidence in Ionian unity, inextricably linked with this cult through continuous practice, no matter how many times the worshipping community itself had been disrupted and redefined, and whether or not it really contained Ionians, or exclusively Ionians. Or, as the case of the Hyperboreans at Delos has laid bare, previous associations of Delos with Artemis incontestably feed into how the fifth-century cult community on Delos represents itself. The past, while itself irretrievable, can nevertheless be seen as shaping the character of the continuum between present and past (Chapter 2).

Commissioners of these songs must have internalized and sought to exploit the opportunities of the generation of social change in the community that choral rituals can offer. We shall never know who commissioned the songs, and what the mechanism of commissioning was. It is clear that the Daphnephoric hymns were not primarily a public charge, nor, probably, were the victory odes. What is, however, of interest not least in pinning down the actors in our scenarios a little more closely, is that these songs *always* work with and for a community: a community that exists is in the process of being formulated, or stipulated in the cult song. Either way, the songs work with a sense of community—and its exclusivity. That is not to say that they were intrinsically populist, quite the contrary. But the case of *Olympian 7* (Chapter 5) makes it abundantly clear how powerful aristocrats exploited notions of community and civic identity not just at Athens—where we consider it a normality—but throughout the Greek world.

Several historically relevant conclusions should be drawn from this. This world of song was probably more participatory than elitist, where localism and local pride were bargains that a commissioning elite exploited to enhance its position within a city, always under the guise of public commitment. A recent study of the social context of victory odes has yet further emphasized the public dimension of athletic victory in the cities of this period.[7] Investment in local identity might not be a remnant of a sixth-century archaic world, but rather a vigorous continuation, even sophistication, of 'popular politics' and rather fulsome attempts at social integration. But the question of why the tiny communities monumentalize in song also relates back to a point I aired at the very beginning, that the role of individual localities in the wider Greek world was a hotly and widely debated matter during the fifth century: cult songs were an expression of this concern. That Athens features grandly throughout the chapters—with the exception of the song-dance world of the Argolid—is part of the same phenomenon: it is in confrontation with the emerging Athenian empire that the question of the role of individual cities is most seen to be disputed. The varied responses the Athenian empire prompts in the Kykladic island world is a good illustration of this situation, as are the debates on Panhellenism that also took place in cultic song, as illustrated by Pindar's *Paean 6*. A prosperous song-culture in the early fifth century thus gives testimony to a self-aware, proud, and thriving local Greek

[7] Thomas (2007).

world which did not necessarily make its choices out of financial, or even military, necessity.

In such a world of continuous redefinition of community identity, myths and rituals are not codified; they are constantly adapted. I introduced at the beginning the notion of myth and ritual as an 'open system'—as opposed to a closed ensemble where myth and ritual exist in a static, one-to-one relationship. Myth and ritual relate to each other in an extremely malleable system in which meanings can be attributed to, and taken away from, both myths and rituals in a performative situation. The dynamic of the interaction between myth and ritual lies in the constant reconfiguration of their interrelationship, making the concept of 'ritualization' as introduced above helpful: on the ground, the interaction of myth and ritual entails a continuously changing ritualization of social relations within the religious community of an individual cult or a bigger cultic web through religious ceremony. The case of Boiotia may exemplify this best, where it seems that the cities of the Kopaïs develop an ever closer tie to Thebes by belabouring the migratory tradition in shared practices at all the cult places relating to this tradition.

The phenomenon of myths and rituals interacting in an open texture also ties in with the fact that throughout this book myth and ritual operate within networks, which in turn define and redefine communities. Because of their repetition, the theoric choruses sent to Delos depict most vividly how performances of myth and ritual deploy the myth-ritual network of a particular cult for the forging and splitting of a religious group, and how important the notion of a myth-ritual network is for the configuration of the catchment area of a particular cult. Through the way they can jumble up and fuse notions of centre and locality, myth-ritual performances thus allow for the reconstitution of social spaces, expressed in the ordered environments of cultic practice. It is in the effect of these performances on a worshipping group that their power lies in a historical context.

A by-product of this book is to have engaged in a little more detail with the workings of local and regional cult centres—the phenomenon technical language calls 'amphiktyonies', a term better avoided in order not to evoke an image of strict and hierarchical organization. Local cult centres, such as those of Delos, Asine, or Dodona, send us on the tracks of extremely mobile cities: the catchment areas of these cults function as an alternative social network, operating according to their own rules and alongside other forms of social relations such as politico-military agreements. When communities aligned themselves through shared religious practice, they went beyond such immediately apparent forms of tying people together. These ritualized relations were not pragmatic arrangements but worked through the power of tradition; common belief in a shared past kept them together, and breaking with this tradition required as much effort as keeping it up.[8] Perhaps for this reason cult song features regularly at such local inter-state cult centres.

[8] Phlegon of Tralles *FGrH* 257 F 1 (Ch. 2, n. 60 above) may be cited once again here in demonstration of how it was thought that every time Olympia was abandoned by its worshippers, war erupted amongst them.

The working of such cults mirrors a system of relations expressed through myth and ritual, the great variation within which can be explained by the fast-changing social and power relations between places. It reflects, more broadly speaking, the elaborate web of connectivity of the ancient world. If one drew on the map I set up at the beginning of this study concentric circles around cults and their catchment areas, one would quickly discover groups overlapping in members but probably rarely identical; each individual locality could be part of many such religious networks. Their relationship to political alliances is ever ambiguous, and this did not escape the Greeks—it is for this reason that we find the two types of association continuously interacting without ever quite sorting out the extension or the limits of the overlap. Common worship in this sense presents a forum for social discussion and negotiation of, most often, power relations. Theoric cults, whether local or 'Panhellenic', whether on Delos or at Asine, are an extreme example of this general truth, in which the participating communities tie or untie themselves from the basic aetiological myth for the cult in question. I have tried to uncover matters which were dealt with in cult-song more forcefully than through any other means. Its force lies exclusively in the ambiguity, indirectness, and oblique associations enabled through sensual involvement.

The notion of shared aetiology suggests a second aetiological paradox: not only is the claim to relate origins in time a pretence, but aetiology's local tie also needs to be put into question. Aetiological myth pretends to be bound to locality and to local performances, but that clearly does not mean that it is a local phenomenon, or that Greek religion restricts itself to a local level. Aetiologies always form part of a larger cluster of stories, and local aetiologies are a way of tying oneself to this cluster; it is only through reference to a broader framework that aetiological myths can work socially. The performances of myth and ritual on Delos have perhaps shown most explicitly how aetiology lies at the interface between the local and the non-local.

The resulting view that no myth and no ritual is either local or Panhellenic raises interesting questions about the extent to which one unifying aspect of Greek religion lies in its essentially 'theoric' nature. While I have already hinted at the possibility of circumscribing social mobility through religion, larger questions of the reverse nature arise as well. As students of Greek polytheism know well, Greek religion manoeuvres between an overriding set of Panhellenic gods and a varying set of local practices. How in the decentralized Greek world they mediated between one and the other—in other words, how they developed a homogeneous pantheon—is mysterious: the space in between no one has ever tried to cover; it has remained conceptually empty. Many of the cults discussed here lie in that intermediary space, suggesting that aetiological myth and ritual were basic to the process of inventing common gods; more broadly, however, it also suggests that the essential features of Greek polytheism were probably addressed through, and became a product of, religious, and therefore social, mobility.

Forging ties through aetiological myth and ritual in performance lies at the very heart of such social interactions. In a fundamental way the nature of these associations is not so different from the economic relations which are more and more argued for at the moment: the unconnected *polis* does not exist; no place in the Mediterranean is likely to have no relation of this kind (a form of religious self-sufficiency), just as not one would be part of all.[9] The malleability of these different interrelating systems is what creates the complexity in the world of the ancient Greek *polis*.

9 Horden and Purcell (2000).

Bibliography

PUBLICATIONS of inscriptions and excavation reports are generally referred to in the notes by journal name only; the bibliography only contains substantial epigraphical and archaeological publications.

ACCAME, S. (1938). 'Un nuovo decreto di Lindo del V sec. a.C.', *Clara Rhodos* 9, 209–29.

ACKERMAN, R. (1991). *The Myth and Ritual School: J. G. Frazer and the Cambridge Ritualists.* Theorists of Myth 2. Garland Reference Library of the Humanities 1282. London–New York.

ADAMESTEANU, D. (1974). *La Basilicata antica. Storia e Monumenti.* Cava dei Tirreni.

—— (1986). 'Incoronata—Scavi della Soprintendenza archeologica della Basilicata (1971–2)', in *I Greci sul Basento*, 25–8.

ADCOCK, F. E. (1930). 'The Peloponnesian League. The New Spartan Policy', *CAH* iv. Cambridge, 71–5.

ADSHEAD, K. (1989). *Politics of the Archaic Peloponnese: The Transition from Archaic to Classical Politics.* Hampshire—Vermont (1st pub. Aldershot, 1986).

Albanien: Schätze aus dem Land der Skipetaren (Mainz a. Rhein, 1988).

ALBRIGHT, W. F. (1939). 'The Israelite Conquest of Canaan in the Light of Archaeology', *BASOR* 74, 11–23.

—— (1946). *From the Stone Age to Christianity: Monotheism and the Historical Process.* 2nd edn. Baltimore.

ALCOCK, S. E. (2002). *Archaeologies of the Greek Past: Landscape, Monuments, and Memories.* Cambridge.

—— and OSBORNE, R. G., eds. (1994). *Placing the Gods: Sanctuaries and Sacred Space in Ancient Greece.* Oxford.

—— and van DYKE, R. M., eds. (2003). *Archaeologies of Memory.* Oxford.

ALLAN, W. (2000). *The Andromache and Euripidean Tragedy.* Oxford.

ALROTH, B. (1989). *Greek Gods and Figurines: Aspects of the Anthropomorphic Dedications.* Boreas 18. Uppsala–Stockholm.

ALT, A. G. (1953). *Kleine Schriften zur Geschichte des Volkes Israels*, vol. i. Munich.

AMANDRY, P. (1939). 'Convention religieuse conclue entre Delphes et Skiathos', *BCH* 63, 183–219.

—— (1978). 'Bases de trépied à Coronée', *BCH* 102, 565–9.

—— (1980). 'Sur les concours argiens', in *Études Argiennes*, 211–53.

AMERUOSO, M. (1996). *Megale Hellas. Genesi, storia ed estensione del nome.* Studi pubblicati dall'Istituto italiano per la storia antica 61. Rome.

ANDERSEN, H. D. (1992–3). 'The Origin of Potnia Theron in Southern Italy', *Hamburger Beiträge zur Archäologie* 19, 73–107.

ANGELI BERNARDINI, P. (1977). 'Le Halieia di Rodi e lo scolio a Pind. O. 7, 146ab (p. 229 Dr.)', *Stadion* 3, 1–3.

—— (1983). *Mito e attualità nelle odi di Pindaro. La Nemea 4, l'Olimpica 9, l'Olimpica 7.* Rome.

—— (1989). 'Il proemio della Pitica xi di Pindaro e culti tebani', in BEISTER and BUCKLER (1989), 39–47.

Angeli Bernardini, P. ed. (2000). *Presenza e funzione della città di Tebe nella cultura greca* (Conference, Urbino, 7–9 July 1997). Pisa–Rome.

—— ed. (2004*a*). *La città di Argo. Mito, storia, tradizioni poetiche* (Conference, Urbino, 13–15 June 2002). Rome.

—— (2004*b*). 'La città e i suoi miti nella lirica corale: l'Argolide e Bacchilide', in (2004*a*), 127–45.

Antonaccio, C. (2001). 'Ethnicity and Colonization', in Malkin (2001), 113–57.

Antonetti, C., ed. (1997). *Il dinamismo della colonizzazione greca. Atti della tavola rotonda Espansione e colonizzazione greca di età arcaica: metodologie e problemi a confronto (Venezia, 10–11/11/1995).* Con la collaborazione di P. Lévêque. Naples.

Appel, W., and Schechner, R., eds. (1990). *By Means of Performance: Intercultural Studies of Theatre and Ritual.* Cambridge.

Aron, R. (1967). *Les Étapes de la pensée sociologique. Montesquieu, Comte, Marx, Tocqueville, Durkheim, Pareto, Weber.* Paris.

Arrighetti, G. (1987). 'I problemi dell'esegesi pindarica fra originalità e tradizione: la Nemea VII', in S. Boldrini *et al.*, eds., *Filologia e forme letterarie. Studi offerti a Francesco della Corte*, 5 vols. Urbino, i. 79–105.

Arrigoni, G. (1999). 'Perseo contro Dioniso a Lerna', in F. Conca, ed. *Ricordando Raffaele Cantarella. Miscellanea di studi.* Bologna, 9–70.

L'Arte Albanese nei Secoli: Museo Nazionale Preistorico Etnografico «Luigi Pigorini» Piazzale Marconi 14, Roma, EUR. Feb.–Apr. 1985 (Rome, 1985).

Asad, T. (1993). *Genealogies of Religion: Discipline and Reasons of Power in Christianity and Islam.* Baltimore.

Athanassaki, L. (2003). 'Transformations of Colonial Disruption into Narrative Continuity in Pindar's Epinician Odes', *HSPh* 101, 93–128.

—— Martin, R., and Miller, J. F., eds. (forthcoming). *Apolline Politics and Poetics* (Conference, Delphi, 4–11 July 2003).

Auffarth, Ch. (1994). *Hera und ihre Stadt Argos. Methodische und historische Untersuchungen zur Polis-Religion im frühen Griechenland.* Habilitationsschrift Tübingen.

Austin, J. L. (1962). *How to Do Things with Words: The William James Lectures 1955.* Oxford.

Austin, M. M. (1990). 'Greek Tyrants and the Persians, 546–479 B.C.', *CQ* 40, 289–306.

Avezzù, G. (2004). 'Mappe di Argo', in Angeli Bernardini (2004*a*), 149–61.

Bagordo, A., and Zimmermann, B., eds. (2000). *Bakchylides. 100 Jahre nach seiner Wiederentdeckung.* Zetemata 106. Munich.

Bakewell, G. W. (1997). 'Metoikia in the Supplices of Aeschylus', *ClAnt* 16, 209–28.

Bakhtin, M. M. (1968). *Rabelais and his World*, trans. H. Iswolsky. Cambridge, Mass.

Bakhuizen, S. C. (1994). 'Thebes and Boeotia in the Fourth Century B.C.', *Phoenix* 48, 307–30.

Balcer, J. M. (1995). *The Persian Conquest of the Greeks 545–450 B.C.* Xenia 38. Konstanz.

Bammer, A. (2002). 'Aigeira e Hypereresia', in Greco (2002), 235–56.

Barchiesi, A. (1994). 'Immovable Delos: Aeneid 3.73–98 and the Hymns of Callimachus', *CQ* 44, 438–43.

Barkhuisen, J. H. (1968). 'Structural Patterns in Pindar's Seventh Olympian Ode', *AClass* 11, 25–37.

Barletta, B. (1990). 'An "Ionian Sea" Style in Archaic Doric Architecture', *AJA* 94, 45–72.

Barrett, W. S. (1954). 'Bacchylides, Asine, and Apollo Pythaieus', *Hermes* 82, 421–44.

Barron, J. P. (1964). 'Religious Propaganda of the Delian League', *JHS* 84, 35–48.

—— (1980). 'Bakchylides, Theseus and a Wooly Cloak', *BICS* 27, 1–8.

BAUMANN, H. (1959). 'Der Mythos in ethnologischer Sicht, 1–2', *Studium Generale* 12, 1–17; 583–97.

BEAN, G. E., and COOK, J. M. (1957). 'The Carian Coast III', *ABSA* 52, 58–146.

BEARD, M. (1988). 'Rituel, Texts, Temps: Les *Parilia* Romains', in A.-M. BLONDEAU and K. SCHIPPER, eds., *Essais sur le rituel I*. Louvain–Paris, 15–29.

—— (2000). *The Invention of Jane Harrison*. Revealing Antiquity 14. Cambridge, Mass.

BECK, H. (1997). *Polis und Koinon. Untersuchungen zur Geschichte und Struktur der griechischen Bundesstaaten im 4. Jahrhundert v. Chr.* Historia ES 114. Stuttgart.

BEISTER, H. and BUCKLER, J., eds. (1989). *Boiotika: Vorträge vom 5. Internationalen Böotien-Kolloquium zu Ehren von Professor Dr. Siegfried Lauffer* (Conference, Munich, 13–17 June, 1986). Munich.

BÉLIS, A. (1998). 'Les Fabricants d'auloi en Grèce: l'exemple de Délos', *Topoi* 8, 777–90.

BELL, C. (1988). 'Ritualization of Texts and the Textualisation of Ritual in the Codification of Taoist Liturgy', *History of Religions* 27, 366–92.

—— (1989). 'Ritual, Change and Changing Rituals', *Worship* 63, 31–41.

—— (1992). *Ritual Theory, Ritual Practice*. New York–Oxford.

—— (1997). *Ritual. Perspectives and Dimensions*. New York–Oxford.

BELOCH, K. J. (1894). 'Siris', *Hermes* 29, 604–8.

—— (1912–27). *Griechische Geschichte*, 4 vols. 2nd edn. Strasbourg.

BEN-AMOS, D., and GOLDSTEIN, K. S., eds. (1975). *Folklore: Performance and Communication*. The Hague.

BENDIX, R. (1978). *Kings or People. Power and the Mandate to Rule*. Berkeley–London.

BENGTSON, H. (1969). *Griechische Geschichte. Von den Anfängen bis in die römische Kaiserzeit*. 4th edn. Munich.

BENZI, M. (1988). 'Mycenaean Pottery Later than LH IIIA:1 from the Italian Excavations at Trianda on Rhodes'; 'Mycenaean Rhodes: A Summary', in DIETZ and PAPACHRISTODOULOU (1988), 39–55; 59–72.

—— (1992). *Rodi e la civiltà micenena*, 2 vols. Incunabula Graeca 99. Rome.

La Béotie antique. Lyon-Saint-Etienne, 16–20 mai 1983 (Paris, 1985).

BÉRARD, J. (1957). *La Colonisation grecque de l'Italie méridionale et de la Sicile dans l'antiquité. L'Histoire et la légende*. 2nd edn. Paris.

BERGER, S. Z. (1989). 'Democracy in the Greek West and the Athenian Example', *Hermes* 117, 303–14.

—— (1992). *Revolution and Society in Greek Sicily and Southern Italy*. Historia ES 71. Stuttgart.

BERGQUIST, B. (1988). 'The Archaeology of Sacrifice: Minoan-Mycenaean versus Greek. A Brief Survey into two Sites with Contrary Evidence', in HÄGG *et al.* (1988), 21–34.

—— (1993). 'Bronze Age Sacrificial *Koine* in the Eastern Mediterranean?', in J. QUAEGEBEUER, ed., *Ritual and Sacrifice in the Ancient Near East* (Conference, Leuven, 17–20 Apr., 1991). Orientalia Lovaniensia Analecta 55. Leuven, 11–43.

BERTHOLD, R. M. (1980). 'Fourth Century Rhodes', *Historia* 29, 32–49.

—— (1984). *Rhodes in the Hellenistic Age*. Ithaca.

BETH, K. (1927–42). 'Aitiologie', in E. HOFFMANN-KRAYER and H. BÄCHTHOLD-STÄUBLI, eds., *Handwörterbuch des deutschen Aberglaubens*, vols. 1–10. Berlin, vol. i, 647–66.

BIERL, A. (2001). *Der Chor in der Alten Komödie: Ritual und Performativität (unter besonderer Berücksichtigung von Aristophanes' "Thesmophoriazusen" und der Phalloslieder fr. 851 PMG)*. BzA 126. Munich.

BILLOT, M.-F. (1989–90). 'Apollon Pythéen et l'Argolide archaïque. Histoire et mythes', *Αρχαιογνωσία* 6, 35–98.

BILLOT, M.-F. (1997). 'Recherches archéologiques récentes à l'Héraion d'Argos avec une annexe: propositions pour une restitution du temple archaïque (avec la collaboration de M.-G. Foidevaux)', in DE LA GENIÈRE (1997), 11–56.

BLAU, H. (1990). 'Universals of Performance; or Amortizing Play', in APPEL and SCHECHNER (1990), 250–72.

BLECH, M. (1982). *Studien zum Kranz bei den Griechen.* RGVV 38. Berlin–New York.

BLINKENBERG, Ch. (1915*a*). *Die lindische Tempelchronik.* Kleine Texte für Vorlesungen und Übungen 131. Bonn.

—— (1915*b*). 'Rhodische Urvölker', *Hermes* 50, 271–303.

—— (1917). *L'Image d'Athana Lindia.* Det Kgl. danske videnskabernes selskab. Historisk-filologiske meddelelser i, 2. Copenhagen.

—— (1930). 'La Déesse de Lindos', *ARW* 28, 154–65.

—— (1939). 'Règlements de sacrifices rhodiens', in DRAGMA *Martino P. Nilsson a.d. IV Id.Iul. anno MCMXXXIX dedicatum.* Lund, 96–113.

BLOCH, M. (1974). 'Symbols, Song, Dance and Features of Articulation: Is Religion an Extra Form of Authority?', *Archives Européennes de Sociologie* 15, 55–81.

BLUMENTHAL, A. v. (1942). 'Paian', *RE* xvi, 2340–62, s.v.

BOARDMAN, J. (1980). *The Greeks Overseas: Their Early Colonies and Trade.* Enlarg. edn. London.

—— and PARKE, H. W. (1957). 'The Struggle for the Tripod and the First Sacred War', *JHS* 77, 276–82.

BOEDEKER, D. A. (1993). 'Hero Cult and Politics in Herodotus: The Bones of Orestes', in DOUGHERTY and KURKE (1993), 164–77.

—— and RAAFLAUB, K. A., eds. (1998). *Democracy, Empire, and the Arts in Fifth-Century Athens.* Cambridge, Mass.–London.

BOERSMA, J. S. (1970). *Athenian Building Policy from 561/0 to 405/4 B.C.* Groningen.

BOL, P. C. (1988). 'Die "Artemis von Lusoi". Eine klassische Wiedergabe eines früh-griechischen Kultbildes', in M. SCHMIDT, ed., *Kanon. Festschrift Ernst Berger zum 60. Geburtstag am 26. Februar 1988 gewidmet*, 2 vols. Antike Kunst Beiheft 15. Basel, 76–80.

BOMMELAER, J.-F. (1991). *Guide de Delphes. Le Site.* Athens–Paris.

BONACCI, E. (2002). 'La difesa di una polis: Metaponto e i Lucani tra V e IV secolo a.C.', in MOSCATI CASTELNUOVO (2002), 63–90.

BOTTINI, A., and GUZZO, P. G. (1986). 'Greci e indigeni nel sud della penisola dall'VIII sec. a.C. alla conquista romana', in *Popoli e civiltà dell'Italia antica* viii. Rome, 9–390.

BOUDEWIJNSE, B. (1995). 'The Conceptualization of Ritual. A History of its Problematic Aspects', *Jaarboek voor Liturgie-Onderzoek* 11, 31–56.

BOURDIEU, P. (1977). *Outline of a Theory of Practice*, trans. R. Nice. Cambridge.

BOWIE, E. L. (1986). 'Early Greek Elegy, Symposium, and Public Festival', *JHS* 106, 13–35.

—— (2006) 'Choral performances', in D. KONSTAN and S. SAID, eds., *Greeks on Greekness: Viewing the Greek Past under the Roman Empire.* PCPhS suppl. 29, 61–92.

BOWRA, C. M. (1957). 'Asius and the Old-Fashioned Samians', *Hermes* 85, 391–401.

—— (1961). *Greek Lyric Poetry: From Alcman to Simonides.* 2nd edn. Oxford.

—— (1964). *Pindar.* Oxford.

BRANDT, H. (1992). 'IG IV 554: aus Argos oder Halieis?', *Chiron* 22, 83–90.

BRASWELL, B. K. (1976). 'Notes on the Prooemium to Pindar's Seventh Olympian Ode', *Mnemosyne* 29, 232–42.

—— (1988). *A Commentary on the Fourth Pythian Ode of Pindar.* Berlin.

BRAVO, B., and FRONTISI-DUCROUX, F. (1997). *Pannychis e simposio: feste private notturne*

di donne e uomini nei testi letterari e nel culto. Con uno studio iconografico di Françoise Frontisi-Ducroux. Filologia e critica 79. Pisa.
Brelich, A. (1958). *Gli eroi greci. Un problema storico-religioso.* Rome. Repr. 1978.
—— (1959).'I figli di Medeia', *SMSR* 30, 213–54.
—— (1961). *Guerre, agoni e culti nella Grecia arcaica.* Antiquitas 1, Abhandlungen zur alten Geschichte 7. Bonn.
—— (1969). *Paides e parthenoi.* Incunabula Graeca 36. Rome.
Bremer, J. M. (1998). 'Greek Cultic Poetry: Some Ideas behind a Forthcoming Edition', *Mnemosyne* ser. 4, 51, 513–24.
—— (2000). 'Der dithyrambische Agon: ein kompetitiver Gottesdienst oder gar keiner?', in Bagordo and Zimmermann (2000), 59–67.
—— and Furley, W. D., eds. (2001). *Greek Hymns: Selected Cult Songs from the Archaic to the Hellenistic Period, 1. The Texts in Translation; 2. Greek Texts and Commentary.* Studien und Texte zu Antike und Christentum 9, 10. Tübingen.
Bremmer, J. (1978). 'Heroes, Ritual and the Trojan War', *SSR* 2, 5–38.
—— ed. (1987). *Interpretations of Greek Mythology.* London.
—— (1998). '"Religion", "Ritual" and the Opposition "Sacred and Profane": Notes towards a Terminological "Genealogy"', in Graf (1998), 9–32.
—— (2001*a*). 'Sacrificing a Child in Ancient Greece: The Case of Iphigeneia', in E. Noort and E. J. C. Tigchelaar, eds., *The Sacrifice of Isaac. The Aqedah (Genesis 22) and its Interpretations.* Leiden, 21–43.
—— (2001*b*). 'Myth and History in the Foundation of Cyrene', in P. Azara *et al.*, eds., *Mites de fundació de ciutats al món antic (Mestpotàmia, Grècia i Roma). Actes del Colloqui.* Barcelona, 155–63.
—— (2005*a*). 'Myth and Ritual in Ancient Greece', in R. v. Haehling, ed., *Griechische Mythologie und frühes Christentum.* Darmstadt, 21–43.
—— (2005*b*). 'Anaphe, Aeschrology and Apollo Aigletes', in A. Harder and M. Cuypers, eds., *Beginning from Apollo. Studies in Apollonius Rhodius and the Argonautic Tradition.* Leuven, 18–34.
Bresson, A. (1979). *Mythe et contradiction. Analyse de la VIIe Olympique de Pindare.* Centre de recherches d'histoire ancienne 29. Annales littéraires de l'Université de Besançon 230. Paris.
—— (1980). 'Rhodes, l'Hellénion et le statut de Naucratis (vi–iv s. a.C.)', *DHA* 6, 291–349.
—— (1986). 'Deux légendes rhodiennes', in *Les Grandes Figures religieuses. Fonctionnement pratique et symbolique dans l'antiquité* (Conference, Besançon, 25–6 Apr. 1984). Annales littéraires de l'Université de Besançon 329. Paris, 411–21.
—— (1999). 'Rhodes and Lykia in Hellenistic Times', in Gabrielsen *et al.* (1999), 98–131.
Briquel, D. (1984). *Les Pélasges en Italie. Recherches sur l'histoire de la légende.* Bibliothèque des Écoles françaises d'Athènes et de Rome 252. Athens–Rome.
Brock, R. (1996). 'Thucydides and the Athenian Purification of Delos', *Mnemosyne* ser. 4, 49, 321–7.
—— and Hodkinson, S., eds. (2000). *Alternatives to Athens: Varieties of Political Organization and Community in Ancient Greece.* Oxford.
Brommer, F. (1984). *Herakles II. Die zwölf unkanonischen Taten des Helden.* 2nd edn. Darmstadt.
Brown, C. (1984). 'The Bridegroom and the Athlete: The Proem to Pindar's Seventh Olympian', in D. E. Gerber, ed., *Greek Poetry and Philosophy: Studies in Honour of Leonard Woodbury.* Chicago, 37–50.
Bruce, I. A. F. (1961). 'The Democratic Revolution at Rhodes', *CQ* 11, 166–70.

Bruit, L. (1984). 'Sacrifice à Delphes: sur deux figures d'Apollon', *RHR* 201, 339–67.
—— (1989). 'Les Dieux aux festins des mortels. Théoxénies et "xeniae" ', in A.-F. Laurens, ed., *Entre hommes et dieux. Le Convive, le héros, le prophète.* Centre de recherches d'histoire ancienne, 86. Lire les polythéismes, 2. Annales littéraires de l'Université de Besançon 391. Paris, 13–25.
—— (1990). 'The Meal at the Hyakinthia: Ritual Consumption and Offering', in Murray (1990), 162–74.
Bruit-Zaidman, L. (2005). 'Repas des dieux et repas des hommes en Grèce ancienne', in S. Georgoudi, R. Koch-Piettre, and F. Schmidt, eds., *La Cuisine et l'autel: Les Sacrifices en questions dans les sociétés de la Méditerranée ancienne.* Bibliothèque de l'École des Hautes Études, Sciences Religieuses 124 (Turnhout, 2005), 31–46.
—— and Schmitt Pantel, P. (1992). *Religion in the Ancient Greek City*, trans. P. Cartledge. Cambridge (orig. *La Religion dans la cité grecque.* 2nd edn. Paris, 1991).
Brun, P. (1989). 'L'Île de Kéos et ses cités au iv s. av. J. C.', *ZPE* 76, 121–38.
—— (1993). 'La Faiblesse insulaire: histoire d'un topos', *ZPE* 99, 163–83.
—— (1996). *Les Archipels égéens dans l' antiquité grecque (Ve–IIe siècles av. notre ère).* Paris.
—— (1998). 'Pauvreté et impuissance de Kythnos: essai pour un jugement équilibré', in Mazarakis Ainian and Mendone (1998), 657–67.
Bruneau, Ph. (1970). *Recherches sur les cultes de Délos à l'époque hellénistique et à l'époque impériale.* Paris.
—— (1995). 'L'Autel de cornes à Délos', *CRAI*, 321–39.
—— (1997). 'Le Portrait littéraire de Délos', *REA* 99, 299–304.
—— and Ducat, J. (1983). *Guide de Délos.* 3rd edn. Paris.
Buc, P. (2000). 'Political Ritual: Medieval, and Modern Interpretations', in H.-W. Goetz, ed., *Die Aktualitaet des Mittelalters.* Bochum, 255–72.
—— (2001). *The Dangers of Ritual. Between Early Medieval Texts and Social Scientific Theory.* Princeton.
Buchholz, H. G. (1991). 'Hammon und Zeus Ammon auf Zypern', *MDAI* (A) 106, 85–128.
Buck, R. J. (1968). 'The Aeolic Dialect in Boeotia', *CPh* 63, 268–80.
—— (1970). 'The Athenian Domination of Boeotia', *CPh* 65, 217–27.
—— (1972). 'The Formation of the Boeotian League', *CPh* 67, 94–101.
—— (1979*a*). *A History of Boeotia.* Edmonton, Alberta.
—— (1979*b*). 'The Historical Traditions of Early Boiotia', in J. M. Fossey and A. Schachter, eds., *Proceedings of the Second International Conference on Boiotian Antiquities (McGill University Montréal 2–4 November, 1973).* Teiresias suppl. 2. Montreal, 21–4.
—— (1985). 'Boeotia, its Development of Institutions and Oligarchic and Democratic Theory in the Fifth and Fourth Centuries B.C.', in *La Béotie antique*, 291–5.
—— (1994). *Boiotia and the Boiotian League, 432–371* B.C. Edmonton, Alberta.
Bundy, E. L. (1986). *Studia Pindarica.* Berkeley (1st pub. 1962 as University of California Publications in Classical Philology 18.1/2).
Burke, P. (1987). 'The Repudiation of Ritual in Early Modern Europe', repr. in *The Historical Anthropology of Early Modern Italy: Essays on Perception and Communication.* Cambridge, 223–38; 258–60.
Burkert, W. (1966). 'Kekropidensage und Arrhephoria', *Hermes* 94, 1–25.
—— (1970). 'Jason, Hypsipyle and New Fire at Lemnos: A Study in Myth and Ritual', *CQ* 20, 1–16. Repr. in Buxton (2000), 227–49.
—— (1979*a*). *Structure and History in Greek Mythology and Ritual.* Berkeley.

—— (1979*b*). 'Mythisches Denken. Versuch einer Definition an Hand des griechischen Befundes', in H. POSER, ed., *Philosophie und Mythos. Ein Kolloquium*. Berlin, 16–39.

—— (1979*c*). 'Kynaithos, Polycrates, and the Homeric Hymn to Apollo', in G. W. BOWERSOCK *et al.*, eds., *Arktouros: Hellenic Studies Presented to Bernard M. W. Knox on the Occasion of his 65th Birthday*. Berlin, 53–62.

—— (1980). 'Griechische Mythologie in der Geistesgeschichte der Moderne', in W. de BOER *et al.*, eds., *Les Études classiques au xixe et xxe siècles. Leur place dans l'histoire des idées: huit exposés suivis de discussions*. Entr. Hardt 26. Vandoeuvres, 159–99.

—— (1983). *Homo Necans: The Anthropology of Ancient Greek Sacrificial Ritual and Myth*. trans. P. Bing. Berkeley–London (orig. *Homo Necans. Interpretationen altgriechischer Opferriten und Mythen*. Berlin–New York, 1972).

—— (1985). *Greek Religion: Archaic and Classical*, trans. J. Raffan. Oxford.

—— (1987). *Ancient Mystery Cults*. Cambridge, Mass.

—— (1988). 'Katagógia-Anagógia and the Goddess of Knossos', in HÄGG *et al.* (1988), 81–7.

—— (1996). *Creation of the Sacred: Tracks of Biology in Early Religions*. Cambridge, Mass.

—— (1998). 'La Cité d'Argos entre la tradition mycénienne, dorienne et homérique', in V. PIRENNE-DELFORGE, ed., *Les Panthéons des cités. Des origines à la «Périégèse» de Pausanias* (part ii, Conference, Liège, 15–17 May 1997). Kernos suppl. 8. Liège, 47–59.

—— (2002) 'Mythos und Ritual: im Wechselwind der Moderne', in HORSTMANNSHOFF *et al.* (2002), 1–22.

BURNETT, A. P. (1985). *The Art of Bacchylides*. Cambridge, Mass.

—— (1989). 'Performing Pindar's Odes', *CPh* 84, 283–93.

—— (1998). 'Spontaneity, Savaging, and Praise in Pindar's Sixth Paean', *AJPh* 119, 493–520.

—— (2005). *Pindar's Songs for Young Athletes of Aigina*. Oxford.

BURSIAN, C. (1862–72). *Geographie von Griechenland*, 2 vols. Leipzig.

BUXTON, R. G. A. (1994). *Imaginary Greece. The Contexts of Mythology*. Cambridge.

—— ed. (2000). *Oxford Readings in Greek Religion*. Oxford.

CABANES, P., ed. (1987). *L'Illyrie méridionale et l'Épire dans l'antiquité I* (Conference, Clermont-Ferrand, 22–5 Oct. 1984). Clermont-Ferrand.

—— ed. (1993). *L'Illyrie méridionale et l'Épire dans l'Antiquité II* (Conference, Clermont-Ferrand, 25–7 Oct. 1990). Paris.

—— and LAMBOLEY, J.-L., eds. (2004). *L'Illyrie mériodionale et l'Épire dans l'Antiquité IV.* (Conference, Grenoble, 10–12 Oct. 2002). Paris.

CAIRNS, D. (2005). 'Myth and Polis in Bacchylides' Eleventh Ode', *JHS* 125, 35–48.

CAIRNS, F. (2005). 'Pindar. Olympian 7: Rhodes, Athens, and the Diagorids', *Eikasmos* 16, 63–91.

CALAME, C. (1977). *Les Chœurs de jeunes filles en Grèce archaïque*, i. *Morphologie, fonction religieuse et sociale*; ii. *Alcman*. Filologia e critica 20 and 21. Rome.

—— (1983). 'Entre oralité et écriture. Énonciation et énoncé dans la poésie grecque archaïque', *Semiotica* 43, 245–73.

—— (1991). '"Mythe" et "rite" en Grèce: des catégories indigènes?', *Kernos* 4, 179–204.

—— (1996*a*). *Thésée et l'imaginaire athénien. Légende et culte en Grèce classique*. 2nd rev. and enlarg. edn. Lausanne.

—— (1996*b*). *Mythe et histoire dans l'antiquité grecque. La Création symbolique d'une colonie*. Lausanne.

—— (1997). *Choruses of Young Women in Ancient Greece. Their Morphology, Religious Role, and Social Function*, trans. D. B. Collins and J. Orion. Lanham.

CALAME, C. (1999). 'Tempo del racconto e tempo del rito nella poesia greca: Bacchilide tra mito, storia e culto', *QUCC* 62, 63–83.

—— (2003). 'Fabrications du genre et identités politiques en comparaison: la création poétique de Thésée par Bacchylides', in U. HEIDMANN, ed., *Poétiques comparées des mythes. De l'antiquité à la modernité: en hommage à Claude Calame*. Études de Lettres 3. Lausanne, 13–45.

—— (2004). 'Le funzioni di un racconto geneaologico: Acusilao di Argo e la nascita della storiografia', in ANGELI BERNARDINI (2004*a*), 229–43.

—— (2006*a*). *Pratiques poétiques de la mémoire. Représentations de l'espace-temps en Grèce ancienne*. Paris.

—— (2006*b*). 'Le Passé poétique des cités grecques classiques: récit mythique et pratique religieuse', in *Annales HSS*, 527–51.

—— (forthcoming). 'Apollon à Delphes et à Délos', in ATHANASSAKI, MARTIN, and MILLER eds. (forthcoming).

CAMASSA, G. (1993). 'I culti', *AttTar* 32 (1992), 573–94.

CAMPBELL, D. A. (1982–93). *Greek Lyric*. With an English translation. 5 vols. Loeb Classical Library. Cambridge, Mass.

CANCIK-LINDEMAIER, H. (1988). 'Ätiologie', in H. CANCIK, B. GLADIGOW, and M. S. LAUBSCHER, eds., *Handbuch religionswissenschaftlicher Grundbegriffe* i. Stuttgart, 390–4.

CANNADINE, D. (1982). 'The Transformation of Civic Ritual in Modern Britain: The Colchester Oyster Feast', *Past and Present* 94, 107–30.

—— (1983). 'The Context, Performance and Meaning of Religion: The British Monarchy and the "Invention of Tradition"', in HOBSBAWM and RANGER (1983), 101–64.

—— (1987). 'Introduction: Divine Rites of Kings', in CANNADINE and PRICE (1987), 1–19.

—— and PRICE, S. R. F., eds. (1987). *Rituals of Royalty: Power and Ceremonial in Traditional Societies*. Cambridge.

CANTILENA, M. (1987). 'Due studi sulla VII Olimpica di Pindaro: 1. Quando cade la pioggia d'oro', *Prometheus* 13, 209–16.

—— (1990). 'Due studi sulla VII Olimpica di Pindaro: 2. I significati della pioggia d'oro', *Prometheus* 16, 111–35.

CAPODICASA, R. (1997). 'Apollo Oulios, Teseo e i Filaïdi nell'Atene di V sec. a.C.', *PP* 52, 177–89.

CARAPANOS, K. (1878). *Dodone et ses ruines*, 2 vols. Paris.

CAREY, C. (1980). 'Bacchylides' Experiments: Ode XI', *Mnemosyne* ser. 4, 33, 225–43.

—— (1989). 'The Performance of the Victory Ode', *AJPh* 110, 545–65.

—— (1991). 'The Victory Ode in Performance. The Case for the Chorus', *CPh* 86, 192–200.

—— (1994). 'Comic Ridicule and Democracy', in HORNBLOWER and OSBORNE (1994), 69–83.

CARRUTHERS, M. J. (1990). *The Book of Memory: A Study of Memory in Medieval Culture*. Cambridge.

—— and ZIOLKOWSKI, J. M., eds. (2002). *The Medieval Craft of Memory: An Anthology of Texts and Pictures*. Philadelphia, Pa.

CARTER, J. C. (1990). 'Metapontum—Land, Wealth and Population', in DESCŒUDRES (1990), 405–41.

—— (1994). 'Sanctuaries in the Chora of Metaponto', in ALCOCK and OSBORNE (1994), 161–98.

—— (2004). 'The Greek Identity at Metaponto', in LOMAS (2004), 363–90.

Carpenter, T. H., and Faraone, C. A., eds. (1993). *Masks of Dionysus.* Ithaca.
Cartledge, P. (1979). *Sparta and Lakonia. A Regional History 1300–362 B.C.* London.
Casadio, G. (1982–3). 'Per un' indagine storico-religiosa sui culti di Dioniso in relazione alla fenomenologia dei misteri', I: *SSR* 6, 209–34; II: *SMSR* 7, 123–49.
—— (1994). *Storia del culto di Dioniso in Argolide.* Filologia e critica 71. Rome.
—— (1999). *Il vino dell'anima: storia del culto di Dioniso a Corinto, Sicione, Trezene.* Biblioteca di storia delle religioni 1. Rome.
Caskey, M. E. (1976). 'Notes on Relief Pithoi of the Tenian-Boiotian Group', *AJA* 80, 19–41.
—— (1998). 'A Relief Pithos from Koresia, Kea', in Mazarakis Ainian and Mendone (1998), 477–86.
Cawkwell, G. (2005). *The Greek Wars: The Failure of Persia.* Oxford.
Cazzaniga, I. (1953). 'A Callimaco, fr. 100, 4 Pfeiffer', *SCO* 3, 9–13.
Ceccarelli, P. (1993). 'Sans thalassocratie, pas de démocratie? Le Rapport entre thalassocratie et démocratie à Athènes dans la discussion du Ve et IVe siècle av. J.-C.', *Historia* 42, 444–70.
—— (1998). *La pirrica nell'antichità greco romana: studi sulla danza armata.* Filologia e critica 83. Pisa.
Chaniotis, A. (2002). 'Ritual Dynamics: The Boiotian Festival of the Daidala', in Horstmanshoff (2002), 23–48.
—— (2005). 'Ritual Dynamics in the Eastern Mediterranean: Case Studies in Ancient Greece and Asia Minor', in Harris (2005), 141–66
Chankowski, V. (2001). 'Athènes, Délos et les Cyclades à l'époque classique: un réseau économique?', *REA* 103, 83–102.
Childs, B. S. (1963). 'A Study of the Formula "Until this Day"', *JBL* 82, 279–92.
—— (1974). 'The Etiological Tale Re-examined', *VT* 24, 387–97.
Chirassi Colombo, I. (1964). *Miti e culti arcaici di Artemis nel Peloponneso e nella Grecia centrale.* Trieste.
Christian, W. A., Jr. (1981). *Local Religion in Sixteenth-Century Spain.* Princeton.
Christidis, A.-P. (2001). *Ιστορία της Ελληνικής γλώσσας. Από τις αρχές έως την ύστερη αρχαιότητα. Επιστημονική επιμέλεια.* Thessaloniki.
—— Dakaris, S., and Vokotopoulou, I. (1993). 'Les Lamelles oraculaires de Dodone et les villes de l'Épire du nord', in Cabanes (1993), 55–60.
—— —— —— (1997). 'Oracular Tablets from Dodona', in C. Brixhe, ed., *Poikila epigraphika.* Études d'archéologie classique 9. Nancy–Paris, 103–10.
—— —— —— (1999). 'Magic in the Oracular Tablets from Dodona', in D. R. Jordan, H. Montgomery, and E. Thomasson, eds., *The World of Ancient Magic* (Conference, Athens, 4–8 May 1997). Papers from the Norwegian Institute at Athens 4. Bergen, 67–72.
Cingano, E. (2004). 'Tradizioni epiche intorno ad Argo da omero al VI sec. a.C.', in Angeli Bernardini (2004*a*), 59–78.
Cipriani, M. (1997). 'Il ruolo di Hera nel santuario meridionale di Poseidonia', in De La Genière (1997), 211–25.
Clarke, K. J. (1999). *Between Geography and History. Hellenistic Constructions of the Roman World.* Oxford.
Cloché, P. (*s.d.*). *Thèbes de Béotie. Des origines à la conquête romaine.* Namur.
Codrignani, G. (1958). 'L'aition nella poesia greca prima di Callimaco', *Convivium* NS 26, 527–45.
Cohen, A. (1993). *Masquerade Politics: Explorations in the Structure of Urban Cultural Movements.* Oxford.

COLDSTREAM, J. N. (1969). 'The Phoenicians of Ialysos', *BICS* 16, 1–8.
COLE, S. G. (1980). 'New Evidence for the Mysteries of Dionysos', *GRBS* 21, 223–38.
—— (2003). 'Landscapes of Dionysos and Elysian Fields', in M. B. COSMOPOULOS, ed., *Greek Mysteries: The Archaeology and Ritual of Ancient Greek Secret Cults*. London, 193–217.
COLE, T. (1992). *Pindar's Feasts or the Music of Power*. Rome.
COMBS-SCHILLING, M. E. (1989). *Sacred Performances: Islam, Sexuality, and Sacrifice*. New York.
CONNOR, W. R. (1987). 'Tribes, Festivals and Processions: Civic Ceremonial and Political Manipulation in Archaic Greece', *JHS* 107, 40–50.
—— (1993). 'The Ionian Era of Athenian Civic Identity', in *PAPhS* 137, 194–206.
CONSTANTAKOPOULOU, C. (2002). 'The Dance of the Islands: Perceptions of Insularity in Classical Greece' D.Phil. dissertation. Oxford.
—— (2005). 'Proud to be an Islander: Island Identity in Multi-Polis Islands in the Classical and Hellenistic Aegean', *MHR* 20, 1–34.
COOK, A. B. (1902). 'The Gong and Dodona', *JHS* 22, 5–28.
—— (1964–5). *Zeus: A Study in Ancient Religion*, 3 vols. Repr. New York (orig. Cambridge, 1914–40).
COOK, J. M. (1962). *The Greeks in Ionia and the East*. New York.
COOK, M. (1988). 'Ancient Political Factions: Boiotia 404–395', *TAPhA* 118, 57–85.
COOPER, N. K. (1989). *The Development of Roof Revetment in the Peloponnese*. Jonsered.
CORCELLA, A., *et al.* (1993). *Erodoto. Le storie. Libro 4. La Scizia e la Libia*. Milan.
CORNFORD, F. M. (1912). 'The Origin of the Olympic Games', in HARRISON (1912), 212–59.
CORSTEN, T. (1999). *Vom Stamm zum Bund: Gründung und territoriale Organisation griechischer Bundesstaaten*. Munich.
COURBIN, P. (1966). *La Céramique géométrique de l'Argolide*. Bibliothèque des Écoles françaises d'Athènes et de Rome 208. Paris.
—— (1979). 'Délos. L'Oikos des Naxiens', *RA*, 182–5.
—— (1980). *L'Oikos des Naxiens. ED* 33. Paris.
—— (1987). 'Le Temple archaïque de Délos', *BCH* 111, 63–78.
COZZOLI, U. (1968). 'Siris', in *Seconda miscellanea greca e romana*. Rome, 1–35.
CRAIK, E. M. (1980). *The Dorian Aegean*. London.
CROON, J. H. (1967). 'Hot Springs and Healing Gods', *Mnemosyne* 20, 225–46.
CSAPO, E. (2004). 'Some Social and Economic Conditions behind the Rise of the Acting Profession in the Fifth and Fourth Centuries BC', in C. HUGONIOT, F. HURLET, and S. MILANEZI, eds., *Le Statut de l'acteur dans l'antiquité grecque et romaine* (Conference, Tours, 3–4 May 2002). Perspectives historiques 9. Tours, 53–76.
—— (2005). *Theories of Mythology*. Oxford.
—— and MILLER, M., eds. (2007). *The Origins of Theater in Ancient Greece and Beyond: From Ritual to Drama*. Cambridge.
CULASSO GASTALDI, E. (1996). 'I Filaidi tra Milziade e Cimone. Per una lettura del decennio 490–480 a.C.', *Athenaeum* 84, 493–526.
CURRIE, B. (2004). 'Reperformance Scenarios for Pindar's Odes', in C. J. MACKIE, ed., *Oral Performance and its Context*. Orality and Literacy in Ancient Greece 5. Mnemos. suppl. 248. Leiden–Boston–Cologne, 49–69.
—— (2005). *Pindar and the Cult of Heroes*. Oxford.
DÄHNHARDT, O. (1907–12). *Natursagen. Eine Sammlung naturdeutender Sagen, Märchen, Fabeln und Legenden*, 4 vols. Leipzig–Berlin.

Dakaris, S. (1963). 'Das Taubenorakel in Dodona und das Totenorakel bei Ephyra', in *Neue Ausgrabungen in Griechenland.* Antike Kunst Beiheft 1. Olten, 35–55.

—— (1995). *Δωδώνη. Αρχαιολογικός οδηγός.* 4th edn. Ioannina.

D'Alessio, G. B. (1991). 'Osservazioni e paralipomeni ad una nuova edizione dei frammenti di Pindaro', *RFIC* 119, 91–117.

—— (1994*a*). 'First-Person Problems in Pindar', *BICS* 39, 117–39.

—— (1994*b*). Review of L. Käppel, *Paian. Studien zur Geschichte einer Gattung* (Berlin, 1992), *CR* 44, 62–5.

—— (1995). Review of M. J. H. Van der Weiden, *The Dithyrambs of Pindar. Introduction, Text and Commentary* (Amsterdam, 1991), *JEA* 81, 270–3.

—— (1997). 'Pindar's *Prosodia* and the Classification of Pindaric Papyrus Fragments', *ZPE* 118, 23–60.

—— (2000). '«Tra gli dèi ad Apollo, e tra gli uomini ad Echecrate» *P. Louvre* E 7734 + 7733 (Pind. fr. dub. 333 S.-M.)', in M. Cannatà Fera and S. Grandolini, eds., *Poesia e religione in Grecia. Studi in onore di G. Aurelio Privitera*, 2 vols. Naples, i. 233–62.

—— (2001). *Callimaco. Introduzione, traduzione e note*, 2 vols. 3rd edn. Milan.

—— (2004). 'Argo e l'Argolide nei canti cultuali di Pindaro', in Angeli Bernardini (2004*a*), 107–25.

—— (2005). 'Il primo Inno di Pindaro', in S. Grandolini, ed., *Lirica e Teatro in Grecia. Il testo e la sua ricezione* (Conference, Perugia, 23–4 Jan. 2003). Naples, 113–49.

—— (forthcoming *a*). 'Re-Constructing Pindar's First Hymn: The Theban "Theogony" and the Birth of Apollo', in Athanassaki, Martin, and Miller (forthcoming).

—— (forthcoming *b*). 'Defining Local Identities in Greek Lyric Poetry', in R. Hunter and I. Rutherford, eds., *Poeti Vaganti.* Cambridge.

—— and Ferrari, F. (1988). 'Pindaro, Peana 6, 175–83: Una ricostruzione', *SCO* 38, 159–79.

D'Angour, A. (1997). 'How the Dithyramb got its Shape', *CQ* 47, 331–51.

David, E. (1984). 'The Oligarchic Revolution at Rhodes 391–389 b.c.', *CPh* 79, 271–84.

—— (1986). 'The Diagoreans and the Defection of Rhodes from Athens in 411 b.c.', *Eranos* 84, 157–64.

Davies, J. K. (1971). *Athenian Propertied Families 600–300 B.C.* Oxford.

—— (1994). 'The Tradition of the First Sacred War', in S. Hornblower, ed., *Greek Historiography.* Oxford, 193–212.

Davies, M. (1988). 'Monody, Choral Lyric and the Tyranny of the Handbook', *CQ* 38, 52–64.

Davis, N. Z. (1975). *Society and Culture in Early Modern France: Eight Essays.* Stanford.

—— (1981*a*). 'The Possibilities of the Past', *Journal of Interdisciplinary History* 12, 267–75.

—— (1981*b*). 'The Sacred and the Body Social in Sixteenth-Century Lyon', *Past and Present* 90, 40–70.

Deacy, S. (1995). 'Athena in Boiotia: Local Tradition and Cultural Identity', in J. M. Fossey, ed., *Boeotia Antiqua, v. Studies on Boiotian Topography, Cults and Terracottas.* Amsterdam, 91–103.

Defradas, J. (1972). *Les Thèmes de la propagande delphique.* 2nd rev. edn. Paris.

—— (1974). '*Διορθῶσαι λόγον*: La Septième Olympique', in J. L. Heller, ed., *Serta Turyniana. Studies in Greek Literature and Palaeography in Honor of Alexander Turyn.* Urbana, 34–50.

De Juliis, E. M. (2000). *Taranto.* Bari.

DE LA GENIÈRE, J., ed. (1991). *Epéios et Philoctète en Italie: données archéologiques et traditions légendaires* (Conference, Lille, 23–4 Nov. 1987). Cahiers du Centre Jean Bérard 16. Naples.

DE LA GENIÈRE, J. (1997). *Héra. Images, espaces, cultes* (Conference, Lille, 29–30 Nov., 1993). Collection du Centre Jean Bérard 15, Naples.

DEMAND, N. H. (1982). *Thebes in the Fifth Century: Heracles Resurgent.* London.

—— (1990). *Urban Relocation in Archaic and Classical Greece: Flight and Consolidation.* Bristol.

DENEKEN, F. (1881). *De Theoxeniis.* Diss. Berlin.

DE POLIGNAC, F. (1994). 'Mediation, Competition and Sovereignty: The Evolution of Rural Sanctuaries in Geometric Greece', in ALCOCK and OSBORNE (1994), 3–18.

—— (1995). *Cults, Territory, and the Origins of the Greek City-State*, trans. J. Lloyd. Chicago–London (orig. *La Naissance de la cité grecque: cultes, espace et société, VIIIe–VIIe siècles avant J.-C.* Paris, 1984).

DEROW, P., and PARKER, R., eds. (2003). *Herodotus and his World: Essays from a Conference in Memory of George Forrest.* Oxford.

DE STE. CROIX, G. E. M. (1954). 'The Character of the Athenian Empire', *Historia* 3, 1–41.

—— (2004*a*). *Athenian Democratic Origins and other Essays*, ed. D. HARVEY and R. C. T. PARKER, with the assistance of P. J. Thonemann. Oxford.

—— (2004*b*). 'But What about Aegina?', in (2004*a*), 371–411.

DESAN, S. (1989). 'Crowds, Community and Ritual in the Work of E. P. Thompson and Natalie Davis', in L. HUNT, ed., *The New Cultural History.* Berkeley, 47–71.

DESCŒUDRES, J.-P., ed. (1990). *Greek Colonists and Native Populations. Proceedings of the First Australian Congress of Classical Archaeology Held in Honour of A. D. Trendall* (Sydney, 9–14 July 1985). Oxford.

DE SENSI SESTITO, G. (1987). 'La Calabria in età arcaica e classica. Storia, economia, società', in S. SETTIS, ed., *Storia della Calabria*, vol. i: *La Calabria antica.* Rome 227–303.

DESHOURS, N. (1999). 'Les Messéniens, le règlement des mystères et la consultation de l'oracle d'Apollon Pythéen à Argos', *REG* 112, 463–84.

DE SIENA, A. (1986*a*). 'Metaponto. Nuove scoperte in proprietà Andrisani', in *Siris-Polieion*, 135–56.

—— (1986*b*). 'Scavi in località Incoronata ed a Metaponto: nuove scoperte', in *I Greci Sul Basento*, 199–212.

—— (1990). 'Contributi archeologici alla definizione della fase protocoloniale del Metapontino', *Bollettino storico della Basilicata* 6, 71–88.

—— (1998). 'Metaponto. Problemi urbanistici e scoperte recenti', in *Siritide e Metapontino*, 141–70.

DE SIMONE, C. (1993). 'Il santuario di Dodona e la mantica greca più antica: considerazioni linguistico-culturali', in CABANES (1993), 51–4.

DETIENNE, M. (1977). 'Mythes grecs et analyse structurale: controverses et problèmes', in B. GENTILI and B. PAIONI, eds., *Il mito greco* (Conference, Urbino, 7–12 May 1973). Rome, 69–89.

—— (1986). *The Creation of Mythology*, trans. M. Cook. Chicago (orig. *L'Invention de la mythologie.* Paris, 1981).

DEUBNER, L. (1932). *Attische Feste.* Berlin. 2nd edn. rev. by B. Doer, Darmstadt, 1966.

—— (1941). 'Ololyge und Verwandtes', *APAW* 1, 1–28. Repr. in *Kleine Schriften zur klassischen Altertumskunde* (Königstein, 1982), 607–34.

DIAMOND, E. (1996). 'Introduction', to *Performance and Cultural Politics.* London–New York, 1–12.

DIETZ, S., and PAPACHRISTODOULOU, I., eds. (1988). *Archaeology in the Dodecanese.* Copenhagen.

DIGNAS, B. (2002). *Economy of the Sacred in Hellenistic and Roman Asia Minor.* Oxford.

—— (2003). 'Rhodian Priests after the Synoikism', *Ancient Society* 33, 35–51.

DILLERY, J. (1996). 'Reconfiguring the Past: Thyrea, Thermopylae, and Narrative Patterns in Herodotus', *AJPh* 117, 217–54.

DILTHEY, H. (1980). 'Sorgenti, acque, luoghi sacri in Basilicata', in PADULA (1980), 539–57.

DITTENBERGER, W. (1886–7). *De sacris Rhodiorum commentati.* Halle.

DONOHUE, A. A. (1988). *Xoana and the Origins of Greek Sculpture.* Atlanta.

DORATI, M. (2004). 'Pausania, le Pretidi e la triarchia argiva', in ANGELI BERNARDINI (2004*a*), 295–320.

DOUGHERTY, C. (1993). *The Poetics of Colonization. From City to Text in Archaic Greece.* New York–Oxford.

—— and KURKE, L., eds. (1993). *Cultural Poetics in Archaic Greece: Cult, Performance, Politics.* Cambridge. Repr. Oxford, 1998.

—— —— (2003). *The Cultures within Ancient Greek Culture. Contact, Conflict, Collaboration.* Cambridge.

DOWDEN, K. (1989). *Death and the Maiden: Girls' Initiation Rites in Greek Mythology.* London.

—— (1992). *The Uses of Greek Mythology.* London.

DUBISCH, J. (1995). *In a Different Place: Pilgrimage, Gender, and Politics at a Greek Island Shrine.* Princeton.

DUCAT, J. (1971). *Les Kouroi du Ptoion: le sanctuaire d'Apollon Ptoieus à l'époque archaïque.* Bibliothèque des Écoles françaises d'Athènes et de Rome 219. Paris.

—— (1973). 'La Confèderation béotienne et l'expansion thébaine à l'époque archaïque', *BCH* 97, 59–73.

DUCHEMIN, J. (1983). 'Pindare et l'Orient. Le Mythe de la VIIe Olympique. Essai d'interprétation', in *Mélanges Edouard Delebecque.* Aix-en-Provence, 109–30.

DULL, C. J. (1977). 'Thucydides 1.113 and the Leadership of Orchomenus', *CPh* 72, 305–14.

DUNBABIN, T. J. (1948). *The Western Greeks. The History of Sicily and South Italy from the Foundation of the Greek Colonies to 480 B.C.* Oxford.

DURKHEIM, É. (1915). *The Elementary Forms of Religious Life. A Study in Religious Sociology*, trans. J. W. Swain. London (orig. *Les Formes élémentaires de la vie religieuse. Le Système totémique en Australie.* Paris, 1912).

EADE, J., and SALLNOW, M., eds. (1991). *Contesting the Sacred: The Anthropology of Christian Pilgrimage.* London.

EDLUND, I. E. M. (1987). *The Gods and the Place. Location and Function of Sanctuaries in the Countryside of Etruria and Magna Graecia (700–400 B.C.).* Stockholm.

EKROTH, G. (2002). *The Sacrificial Rituals of Greek Heroes in the Archaic to the Early Hellenistic Periods.* Kernos suppl. 12. Liège.

ELIADE, M. (1949). *Le Mythe de l'éternel retour. Archétypes et répétition.* Paris. Eng. *The Myth of the Eternal Return or, Cosmos and History*, trans. W. R. Trask (London, 1955).

—— (1965). *Le Sacré et le profane.* Paris.

—— (1969). 'Cosmogonic Myth and "Sacred History"', in *The Quest: History and Meaning in Religion.* Chicago, 72–87. Repr. in A. DUNDES, ed., *Sacred Narrative: Readings in the Theory of Myth* (Berkeley, 1984), 137–51.

ELLINGER, P. (1993). *La Légende nationale phocidienne: Artémis, les situations extrèmes et les récits de guerre d'anéantissement.* BCH suppl. 27. Athens–Paris.

ELSNER, J. (1998). *Imperial Rome and Christian Triumph: The Art of the Roman Empire, AD 100–450*. Oxford.

—— and RUTHERFORD, I., eds. (2005). *Pilgrimage in Graeco-Roman and Early Christian Antiquity: Seeing the Gods*. Oxford.

ENGNELL, K. I. A. (1943). *Studies in Divine Kingship in the Ancient Near East*. Uppsala.

ERIKSON, E. H. (1966). 'Ontogeny of Ritualization in Man', in HUXLEY (1966*a*), 337–49.

ÉTIENNE, R., and BRAUN, J. P. (1986). *Ténos I. Le Sanctuaire de Poséidon et d'Amphitrite*. Bibliothèque des Écoles françaises d'Athènes et de Rome 263. Paris.

—— and FRAISSE, P. (1989). 'L'Autel archaïque de l'Artémision de Délos', *BCH* 113, 451–66.

Études Argiennes. École française d'Athènes. BCH suppl. 6 (Athens–Paris, 1980).

Études Déliennes, publiées à l'occasion du centième anniversiare du début des fouilles de l'École française d'Athènes à Délos. BCH suppl. 1 (Athens–Paris, 1973).

EVANS-PRITCHARD, E. E. (1974 (1957)). *Nuer Religion*. Oxford (1st pub. 1957).

FABRE, P. (1981). *Les Grecs et la connaissance de l'occident*. Diss. Paris 1977, Lille.

FAIRBANKS, A. (1900). *A Study of the Greek Paean*. Cornell Studies in Classical Philology 12. New York.

FARAONE, C. A. (1987). 'Hephaestus the Magician and Near Eastern Parallels for Alcinous' Watchdogs', *GRBS* 28, 257–80.

FARNELL, L. E. (1896–1909). *The Cults of the Greek States*, 5 vols. Oxford.

—— (1921). *Greek Hero Cults and Ideas of Immortality*. Oxford.

FEARN, D. (2003). 'Mapping Phleious: Politics and Myth-Making in Bacchylides 9', *CQ* 53, 347–67.

FIGUEIRA, T. J. (1981). *Aegina: Society and Politics*. Salem, NH.

—— (1990). 'Aigina and the Naval Strategy of the Late Fifth and Early Fourth Centuries', *RhM* 133, 15–51.

—— (1993*a*). *Excursions in Epichoric History: Aiginetan Essays*. Lanham, Md.

—— (1993*b*). 'Aeginetan Membership in the Peloponnesian League', in (1993*a*), 87–112. Repr. from *CPh* 76 (1981), 1–24.

—— (1993*c*). 'Aeginetan Independence', in (1993*a*), 9–33. Repr. from *CJ* 79 (1983–4) 8–29.

—— (1993*d*). 'Herodotus on the Early Hostilities Between Aegina and Athens', in (1993*a*), 35–60. Repr. from *AJPh* 106 (1985), 49–74.

—— (1993*e*). 'The Chronology of the Conflict between Athens and Aegina in Herodotus Bk. 6', in (1993*a*), 113–49. Repr. from *QUCC* 28 (1988), 49–89.

FILENI, M. G. (1987). *Senocrito di Locri e Pindaro (fr. 140b Sn.-Maehl.)*. Biblioteca di Quaderni di Cultura Classica 2. Rome.

FINKELBERG, M. (1988). 'Ajax's Entry in the Hesiodic Catalogue of Women', *CQ* 38, 31–41.

FINLEY, M. I. (1978). 'The Fifth-Century Athenian Empire: A Balance Sheet', in P. D. A. GARNSEY and C. R. WHITTAKER, eds., *Imperialism in the Ancient World*. Cambridge, 103–26. Repr. in B. D. SHAW and R. P. SALLER, eds., *Economy and Society in Ancient Greece* (London, 1981), 41–61.

FISCHER-LICHTE, E. (2004). *Ästhetik des Performativen*. Frankfurt.

FISHER, N., and van WEES, H., eds. (1998). *Archaic Greece: New Approaches and New Evidence*. London.

FLENSTED-JENSEN, P., NIELSEN, T. H., and RUBINSTEIN, L., eds. (2000). *Polis & Politics: Studies in Ancient Greek History Presented to Mogens Herman Hansen on his Sixtieth Birthday, August 20, 2000*. Copenhagen.

Flower, M. (2000). 'From Simonides to Isocrates: The Fifth-Century Origins of Fourth-Century Panhellenism', *ClAnt* 19.1, 65–101.

Fogelmark, S. (1972). *Studies in Pindar. With Particular Reference to Paean VI and Nemean VII.* Lund.

Foley, A. (1988). *The Argolid, 800–600 B.C.: An Archaeological Survey.* SIMA 80. Gothenburg.

Fontenrose, J. E. (1959). *Python: A Study of Delphic Myth and its Origins.* Berkeley.

—— (1960). *The Cult and Myth of Pyrros at Delphi.* University of California Publications in Classical Archaeology iv.3. Berkeley.

—— (1966). *The Ritual Theory of Myth.* University of California Publications. Folklore Studies 18. Berkeley.

—— (1981 (1978)). *The Delphic Oracle: Its Responses and Operations, with a Catalogue of Responses.* 2nd edn. Berkeley.

Fornara, C. W. (1966). 'Some Aspects of the Career of Pausanias of Sparta', *Historia* 15, 257–71.

Forrest, W. G. (1956). 'The First Sacred War', *BCH* 86, 33–52.

—— (1960). 'Themistokles and Argos', *CQ* 10, 221–41.

—— (1968). *A History of Sparta, 950–192 B.C.* London. Amended edn. London, 1995. Repr. Bristol, 1995.

Fossey, J. M. (1973–4). 'The End of the Bronze Age in the South West Copaic', *Euphrosyne* 6, 7–21.

—— (1987). 'The Cults of Artemis in Argolis', *Euphrosyne* 15, 71–88.

—— (2001). 'Theophoric Names in Central Greece and a Particular Case', *AncW* 32.2, 139–46.

Foucault, M. (1975). *Surveiller et punir: naissance de la prison.* Paris. Eng. *Discipline and Punish: The Birth of the Prison*, trans. A. Sheridan (London, 1977).

—— (1980). *Power/Knowledge: Selected Interviews and Other Writings, 1972–1977*, ed. and trans. C. Gordon *et al.* Brighton.

—— (1982). 'The Subject and Power', in H. L. Dreyfus and P. Rabinow, eds., *Michel Foucault: Beyond Structuralism and Hermeneutics.* With an afterword by Michel Foucault. Brighton, 208–26.

Fourgous, D. (1989). 'Les Dryopes. Peuple sauvage ou divin?', *Métis* 4, 5–32.

Fowler, B. H. (1957). 'Thucydides 1.107–8 and the Tanagran Federal Issues', *Phoenix* 11, 164–70.

Fowler, R. L. (1998). 'Genealogical Thinking, Hesiod's Catalogue, and the Creation of the Hellenes', *PCPhS* 44, 1–19.

—— (2000). *Early Greek Mythography.* Oxford.

Francis, E. D., and Vickers, M. (1984). 'Amasis and Lindos', *BICS* 31, 119–30.

François, E., Siegrist, H., and Vogel, J., eds. (1995). *Nation und Emotion: Deutschland und Frankreich im Vergleich 19. und 20. Jahrhundert.* Göttingen.

Fraser, P. M., and Bean, G. E. (1954). *The Rhodian Peraea and Islands.* Oxford.

Frazer, J. G. (1890). *The Golden Bough: A Study in Magic and Religion.* 2 vols. London (1st edn., subsequently revised, enlarged, and reprinted multiple times).

—— (1898). *Pausanias's Description of Greece.* Translated with a commentary, 6 vols. London.

Fritz, K. von (1940). *Pythagorean Politics in Southern Italy. An Analysis of the Sources*: New York.

Frödin, O., and Persson, A. W. (1938). *Asine: Results of the Swedish Institute Excavations 1922–30.* Stockholm.

Frontisi-Ducroux, F. (1975). *Dédale. Mythologie de l'artisan en Grèce ancienne.* Paris.
—— (1981). 'Artémis bucolique', *RHR* 198, 29–56.
—— , Lissarrague, F., and Veyne, P. (1998). *Les Mystères du gynécée.* Paris.
Furtwängler, A., *et al.* (1906). *Ägina. Das Heiligtum der Aphaia*, 2 vols. Munich.
Gabrielsen, V. (1997). *The Naval Aristocracy of Hellenistic Rhodes.* Studies in Hellenistic Civilisation 6. Aarhus.
—— *et al.*, eds. (1999). *Hellenistic Rhodes: Politics, Culture, and Society.* Aarhus.
—— (2000*a*). 'The Synoikized *Polis* of Rhodes', in Flensted-Jensen, Nielsen, and Rubinstein (2000), 177–205.
—— (2000*b*). 'The Rhodian Peraia in the Third and Second Centuries B.C.' *C&M* 51, 129–83.
Gallet de Santerre, H. (1946). 'Héra et Léto à Délos', *BCH* 70, 208–15.
—— (1958). *Délos primitive et archaïque.* Bibliothèque des Écoles françaises d'Athènes et de Rome 192. Paris.
—— (1984). 'L'Oikos des Naxien à Délos – était-il un temple?', *BCH* 108, 671–93.
García Romero, F. (2000). 'The Dithyrambs of Bacchylides: Their Position in the Evolution of the Genre', in Bagordo and Zimmermann (2000), 47–57.
Garner, R. (1992). 'Countless Deeds of Valour: Bacchyl. 11', *CQ* 42, 523–5.
Garnsey, P. (1988). *Famine and Food Supply in the Greco-Roman World: Responses to Risk and Crisis.* Cambridge.
—— (1999). *Food and Society in Classical Antiquity.* Cambridge.
Gates, C. (1983). *From Cremation to Inhumation: Burial Practices at Ialysos and Kameiros during the Mid-Archaic Period ca. 625–525 B.C.* Los Angeles.
Gauer, W. (1968). *Weihgeschenke aus den Perserkriegen.* Istanbuler Mitteilungen Beiheft 2. Tübingen.
Geertz, C. (1966). 'Religion as a Cultural System', in M. Banton, ed., *Anthropological Approaches to the Study of Religion.* London, 1–46. Repr. in (1973), 87–125.
—— (1973). *The Interpretation of Cultures: Selected Essays.* London.
—— (1980). *Negara: The Theater State in Nineteenth-Century Bali*, Princeton.
Gehrke, H.-J. (1985). *Stasis. Untersuchungen zu den inneren Kriegen in den griechischen Staaten des 5. und 4. Jahrhunderts v. Chr.* Vestigia 35. Munich.
—— (1986). *Jenseits von Athen und Sparta. Das dritte Griechenland und seine Staatenwelt.* Munich.
Gelder, H. van (1900). *Geschichte der alten Rhodier.* The Hague.
Gell, A. (1992). *The Anthropology of Time. Cultural Construction of Temporal Maps and Images.* Oxford.
Gennep, A. van (1909). *Les Rites de passage.* Paris.
Gentili, B. (1958). *Bacchilide. Studi.* Urbino.
—— (1981). 'L'effigie bifronte di Neottolemo nel sesto Peana e nella settima Nemea di Pindar', in *Letterature comparate: Problemi e metodo. Studi in onore di E. Paratore.* Bologna, 103–9.
—— (1988). *Poetry and its Public in Ancient Greece: From Homer to the Fifth Century*, trans. A. T. Cole. Baltimore–London (orig. *Poesia e pubblico nella Grecia antica. Da Omero al V secolo.* Rome, 1984).
Georges, P. (1994). *Barbarian Asia and the Greek Experience: From the Archaic Period to the Age of Xenophon.* Baltimore.
Georgoudi, S. (1998). 'Les Porte-parole des dieux: réflexions sur le personnel des oracles grecs', in I. Chirassi Colombo and T. Seppilli, eds., *Sibille e linguaggi oracolari. Mito, storia, tradizione* (Conference, Macerata–Norcia, Sept. 1994). Ichnia 3. Pisa, 315–65.

GIACOMETTI, D. (1990–1). 'Melanippe e i Neleidi a Metaponto. La versione ateniese di Euripide e quella italiota di Antioco', *AFLPer* 28, 277–96.
—— (1999). 'Il culto di Artemis a Metaponto', *Ostraka* 8, 407–26.
—— (2001). 'L'Acaia tra VI e V sec. a. C.', *RSA* 31, 7–41.
GIANGIULIO, M. (1981). 'Deformità eroiche e tradizioni di fondazione. Batto, Miscello e l'oracolo delfico', *ASNP* 11, 1–24.
—— (1982). 'Per la storia dei culti di Crotone antica. Il santuario di Hera Lacinia. Strutture e funzioni cultuali, origini storiche e mitiche', *ASCL* 49, 5–69.
—— (1989). *Ricerche su Crotone arcaica.* Scuola Normale Superiore. Pubblicazioni della Classe di lettere e filosofia 6. Pisa.
—— (1992).'La φιλότης tra Sibariti e Serdaioi (Meiggs–Lewis, 10)', *ZPE* 93, 31–44.
—— (2002). 'I culti delle colonie achee d'Occidente. Strutture religiose e matrici metropolitane', in GRECO (2002), 283–313.
GIANNELLI, G. (1963). *Culti e miti della Magna Grecia. Contributo alla storia più antica delle colonie greche in Occidente.* 2nd edn. Florence.
GIESEKAM, G. J. (1977). 'The Portrayal of Minos in Bacchylides 17', *PLLS* 1, 237–52.
GILDERSLEEVE, S. L. (1908). *The Olympian and Pythian Odes.* 2nd edn. London.
GILL, D. H. (1974). 'Trapezomata: A Neglected Aspect of Greek Sacrifice', *HThR* 67, 117–37.
—— (1991). *Greek Cult Tables.* New York–London.
GILL, D. W. J. (1993). 'The Temple of Aphaia on Aegina: Further Thoughts on the Date of the Reconstruction', *ABSA* 88, 173–81.
GILLIS, D. (1979). *Collaboration with the Persians.* Wiesbaden.
GINOUVÈS, R. (1962). *Balaneutike. Recherches sur le bain dans l'antiquité grecque.* Bibliothèque des Écoles françaises d'Athènes et de Rome, ser. 1, 200. Paris.
GLASER, F. (1983). *Antike Brunnenbauten (*krēnai*) in Griechenland.* Denkschriften Österreichische Akademie der Wissenschaften. Phil.-hist. Klasse 161. Vienna.
GLUCKMAN, M., ed. (1962*a*), *Essays on the Ritual of Social Relations.* Manchester.
—— (1962*b*). 'Les Rites de Passage', in GLUCKMAN (1962*a*), 1–52.
—— (1963). *Order and Rebellion in Tribal Africa. Collected Essays with an Autobiographical Introduction.* London.
—— (1965). *Politics, Law, and Ritual in Tribal Society.* Oxford.
—— (1977). 'On Drama, and Games, and Athletic Contests', in MOORE and MYERHOFF (1977*a*), 227–43.
GOEGEBEUR, W. (1985). 'Hérodote et la fondation achéenne de Crotone', *AC* 54, 116–51.
GOFFMAN, E. (1967). *Interaction Ritual: Essays in Face-to-Face Behaviour.* Chicago.
GOLDHILL, S. D. (1986). *Reading Greek Tragedy.* Cambridge.
—— (1987/90). 'The Great City Dionysia and Civic Ideology', *JHS* 107, 58–76, expanded version in WINKLER and ZEITLIN (1990), 97–129.
—— (1991). *The Poet's Voice: Essays on Poetics and Greek Literature.* Cambridge.
—— (1999). 'Programme Notes', in GOLDHILL and OSBORNE (1999), 1–28.
—— and OSBORNE, R. G., eds. (1999). *Performance Culture and Athenian Democracy.* Cambridge.
GOLKA, F. W. (1970). 'Zur Erforschung der Ätiologien im Alten Testament', *VT* 20, 90–8.
—— (1972). *Die Ätiologien im Alten Testament.* Typed MS. Diss. Heidelberg.
—— (1976). 'The Aetiologies in the Old Testament. Part I', *VT* 26, 410–28.
—— (1977).'The Aetiologies in the Old Testament. Part II', *VT* 27, 36–47.
GOMME, A. W. (1945–81). *A Historical Commentary on Thucydides*, 5 vols. Oxford.

González de Tobia, A. M. (2004). 'El pensamiento moral de Baquílides, entre ὄλβος y ἀρετή' in ead., ed., *Ética y estética. De Grecia a la modernidad.* La Plata, 59–73.
Goody, J. R. (1977). 'Against Ritual: Loosely Structured Thoughts on a Loosely Defined Topic', in Moore and Myerhoff (1977*a*), 25–35.
Gordon, R. L., ed. (1981). *Myth, Religion and Society. Structuralist Essays by M. Detienne et al.* London.
Graf, F. W. (1979). 'Das Götterbildnis aus dem Taurerland', *Antike Welt* 10, 33–41.
—— (1980). 'Milch, Honig und Wein', in *Perennitas. Studi in onore di Angelo Brelich.* Rome, 209–21.
—— (1982). 'Culti e credenze religiose della Magna Grecia', *AttTar* 21 (1981), 157–85.
—— (1985). *Nordionische Kulte. Religionsgeschichtliche und epigraphische Untersuchungen zu den Kulten von Chios, Erythrai, Klazomenai und Phokaia.* Bibliotheca Helvetica Romana 21. Zurich.
—— (1993*a*). *Greek Mythology: An Introduction*, trans. T. Marier. Baltimore–London.
—— (1993*b*). 'Der Mythos bei den Römern. Forschungs- und Problemgeschichte', in id., ed., *Mythos in mythenloser Gesellschaft. Das Paradigma Roms.* Conference Rauricum 3. Stuttgart, 25–43.
—— ed. (1998). *Ansichten griechischer Rituale. Geburtstags-Symposium für Walter Burkert: Castelen bei Basel, 15. bis 18. März 1996.* Stuttgart.
—— (2000). 'The Locrian Maidens' in Buxton (2000), 250–70 (orig. 'Die lokrischen Mädchen', *SSR* 2 (1978), 61–79).
Graham, A. J. (1964). *Colony and Mother City in Ancient Greece.* Manchester.
Grandolini, S. (1993). 'Canto processionale e culto nell'antica Grecia', in A. C. Cassio and G. Cerri, eds., *L'inno tra rituale e letteratura nel mondo antico* (Conference, Naples, 21–4 Oct. 1991). AION (filol.) 13. Rome, 125–40.
I Greci sul Basento. Mostra degli scavi archeologici all'Incoronata di Metaponto 1971–84. Milano. Galleria del sagrato-piazza Duomo, 16 gennaio–28 febbraio 1986. Como, 1986.
Greco, E. (1998). 'Le fondazioni degli Achei in Occidente', in *Helike 2. Αρχαία Ελίκη και Αιγιάλεια* (Conference, Aigion, 1–3 Dec. 1995). Athens, 335–43.
—— ed. (2002). *Gli Achei e l'identità etnica degli Achei d'occidente* (Conference, Paestum, 23–5 Feb. 2001). Tekmeria 3. Paestum–Athens.
Greco, G. (1998). 'Da Hera argiva ad Hera pestana, trasformazioni di un'iconografia', in *I Culti della Campania antica. Scritti in onore di Nazarena Valenza Mele* (Conference, Naples, 15–17 May 1995). Rome, 45–62.
Greco, M. (1990). 'Serdaioi', *AION* (archeol.) 12, 39–57.
Green, P. (1996). 'The Metamorphosis of the Barbarian: Athenian Panhellenism in a Changing World', in E. M. Harris and R. W. Wallace, eds., *Transitions to Empire: Essays in Greco-Roman History, 360–146 B.C. in Honor of E. Badian.* London, 5–36.
Grimes, R. L. (1985). *Research in Ritual Studies: A Programmatic Engaged Bibliography.* Chicago-Metuchen.
—— (1990). *Ritual Criticism: Case Studies in its Practice, Essays on its Theory.* New York.
Groningen, B. van (1960). *La Composition littéraire archaïque grecque. Procédés et réalisation.* 2nd edn. Amsterdam.
Grote, G. (1846–56). *History of Greece*, 12 vols. London.
Gruben, G. (1984). *Die Tempel der Griechen.* 4th rev. edn. Munich (1st pub. in 1966).
—— (1997). 'Naxos und Delos. Studien zur archaischen Architektur der Kykladen', *JdI* 112, 261–416.
Guillon, P. (1943). *Les Trépieds du Ptoion*, 2 vols. Bibliothèque des Écoles françaises d'Athènes et de Rome 153. Paris.

Gundert, H. (1935). *Pindar und sein Dichterberuf.* Frankfurter Studien zur Religion und Kultur der Antike 10. Frankfurt.

Gunkel, J. F. H. (1910). *Genesis.* 3rd edn. Göttinger Handkommentar zum Alten Testament i.1. Göttingen.

Guzzo, P. G. (1987). 'L'archeologia delle colonie arcaiche', in S. Settis, ed., *Storia della Calabria,* i. *La Calabria antica.* Rome, 137–226.

Gzella, S. (1981). 'Pindar and Aegina', *Eos* 69, 5–19.

Hadzisteliou-Price, T. (1978). *Kourotrophos: Cults and Representations of the Greek Nursing Deities.* Studies of the Dutch Archaeological and Historical Society 8. Leiden.

Hägg, R. (1965). 'Geometrische Gräber von Asine', *OAth* 6, 117–38.

—— (1992*a*). 'Geometric Sanctuaries in the Argolid', in Piérart (1992*b*), 9–35.

—— ed. (1992*b*). *The Iconography of Greek Cult in the Archaic and Classical Periods* (Conference, Delphi, 16–18 Nov. 1990). Kernos suppl. 1. Athens–Liège.

—— ed. (1994). *Ancient Greek Cult Practice from the Epigraphical Evidence* (Conference, Athens, 22–4 Nov. 1991). Skrifter utgivna av Svenska institutet i Athen 8.13. Stockholm.

—— (1998). 'Ritual in Mycenaean Greece', in Graf (1998), 99–113.

—— and Laffineur, R. (2001). *Potnia: Deities and Religion in the Aegean Bronze Age* (Conference, Gothenburg University, 12–15 Apr. 2000). Aegeum 22. Brussels–Austin.

—— and Marinatos, N., eds. (1993). *Greek Sanctuaries: New Approaches.* London–New York.

—— and Nordquist, C., eds. (1990). *Celebrations of Death and Divinity in the Bronze Age Argolid* (Conference, Athens, 11–13 June 1988). Skrifter utgivna av Svenska institutet i Athen 4.40. Stockholm.

—— Marinatos, N., and Nordquist, G., eds. (1988). *Early Greek Cult Practice* (Conference, Athens, 26–9 June 1986). Skrifter utgivna av Svenska institutet i Athen 4.38. Stockholm.

Hahland, W. (1964). 'Didyma im 5. Jahrhundert v. Chr.', *JDAI* 79, 142–240.

Halbwachs, M. (1980). *The Collective Memory,* trans. F. J. Ditter and V. Y. Ditter. New York (orig. *La Mémoire collective.* 2nd edn. Paris, 1968).

Hall, E. (1989). *Inventing the Barbarian: Greek Self-Definition through Tragedy.* Oxford.

Hall, J. M. (1995). 'How Argive was the "Argive" Heraion? The Political and Cultic Geography of the Argive Plain, 900–400 bc', *AJA* 99, 577–613.

—— (1997). *Ethnic Identity in Greek Antiquity.* Cambridge.

—— (2002). *Hellenicity: Between Ethnicity and Culture.* Chicago.

—— and Morgan, C. (1996). 'Achaean Poleis and Achaean Colonization', in Hansen (1996*b*), 164–232.

Halliday, W. R. (1909–10). 'A Note on Herodotus VI.83, and the Hybristika', *ABSA* 16, 212–19.

Hallof, L., Hallof, K., and Habicht, Ch. (1998). 'Aus der Arbeit der "Inscriptiones Graecae" 2. Ehrendekrete aus dem Asklepieion von Kos', *Chiron* 28, 101–42.

Halstead, P. and Isaakidou, V. (2004). 'Faunal Evidence for Feasting: Burnt Offerings from the Palace of Nestor at Pylos', in P. Halstead and J. C. Barrett, eds., *Food, Cuisine and Society in Prehistoric Greece.* Sheffield Studies in Aegean Archaeology 5. Oxford, 136–54.

Hambly, W. D. (1926). *Tribal Dancing and Social Development.* London.

Hamilakis, Y., and Konsolaki, E. (2004). 'Pigs for the Gods: Burnt Animal Sacrifices as Embodied Rituals at a Mycenaean Sanctuary', *OJA* 23, 135–51.

Hamilton, R. (1974). *Epinikion. General Form in the Odes of Pindar.* The Hague.

Hammond, N. G. L. (1967). *Epirus. The Geography, the Ancient Remains, the History, and the Topography of Epirus and Adjacent Areas.* Oxford.

—— (2000). 'Political Developments in Boeotia', *CQ* 50, 80–93.
HANAWALT, B. A., and REYERSON, K. L., eds. (1994). *City and Spectacle in Medieval Europe.* Minneapolis.
HANELL, K. (1934). *Megarische Studien.* Lund.
HANSEN, M. H. (1995*a*). 'Boiotian Poleis – A Test Case', in (1995*c*), 13–63.
—— (1995*b*). 'The "Autonomous City-State". Ancient Fact or Modern Fiction?', in HANSEN and RAAFLAUB (1995), 21–43.
—— ed. (1995*c*). *Sources for the Ancient Greek City-State.* Acts of the Copenhagen Polis Centre 2. Copenhagen.
—— (1996*a*). 'Were the Boiotian Poleis Deprived of their *autonomia* during the First and Second Boiotian Federations? A Reply', in HANSEN and RAAFLAUB (1996), 127–36.
—— ed. (1996*b*). *Introduction to an Inventory of Poleis: Symposium August, 23–26 1995.* Historisk-filosofiske Meddelelser, 74. Acts of the Copenhagen Polis Centre 3. Copenhagen.
—— ed. (1997). *The Polis as an Urban Centre and as a Political Community: Symposium August, 29–31 1996.* Acts of the Copenhagen Polis Centre 4. Copenhagen.
—— and RAAFLAUB, K., eds. (1995), *Studies in the Ancient Greek Polis.* Historia ES 95, Stuttgart.
—— —— eds. (1996). *More Studies in the Ancient Greek Polis.* Historia ES 108. Stuttgart.
HARRIS, M. (1977). *Cannibals and Kings: The Origins of Cultures.* New York.
HARRIS, W. V., ed. (2005). *Rethinking the Mediterranean.* Oxford.
HARRISON, J. E. (1890). *Mythology and Monuments of Ancient Athens: Being a Translation of a Portion of the 'Attica' of Pausanias.* By Margaret de G. Verral; with introductory essay and archaeological commentary by Jane E. Harrison. London.
—— (1903). *Prolegomena to the Study of Greek Religion.* Cambridge.
—— (1912). *Themis. A Study of the Social Origins of Greek Religion.* Cambridge.
HARRISON, T. (2000*a*). *Divinity and History: The Religion of Herodotus.* Oxford.
—— (2000*b*). *The Emptiness of Asia: Aeschylus' Persians and the History of the Fifth Century.* London.
HAUBEN, H. (1977). 'Rhodes, Alexander and the Diadochi from 333–332 to 304 BC', *Historia* 26, 307–39.
HEATH, M., and LEFKOWITZ, M. R. (1991). 'Epinician Performance', *CPh* 86, 173–91.
HEFFTER, F. (1827–33). *Die Götterdienste auf Rhodus im Alterthume.* Zerbst.
HEGYI, D. (1969). 'Athens and Aigina on the Eve of the Battle of Marathon.' *AAntHung* 17, 171–81
HEICHELHEIM, F. M. (1953). 'The Bacchylides Paian in Toronto', *SO* 30, 77–81.
HENRICHS, A. (1974). 'Die Proitiden im hesiodischen Katalog', *ZPE* 15, 297–301.
—— (1996). 'Dancing in Athens, Dancing on Delos: Some Patterns of Choral Projection in Euripides', *Philologus* 140.1, 48–62.
—— (2000). 'Drama and Dromena. Bloodshed, Violence, and Sacrificial Metaphor in Euripides', *HSPh* 100, 173–88.
HERINGTON, C. J. (1985). *Poetry into Drama: Early Tragedy and the Greek Poetic Tradition.* Berkeley.
HERMARY, A. (1984). *La Sculpture archaïque et classique, i. Catalogue des sculptures classiques de Délos. ED* 34. Paris.
HERTER, H. (1934). 'Telchinen', *RE* v.1, 197–224.
HERZOG, R. (1895). 'Koios und Kos', *Hermes* 30, 154–5.
HIGBIE, C. (2003). *The Lindian Chronicle and the Greek Creation of their Past.* Oxford.

HOBSBAWM, E. (1983). 'Introduction: Inventing Tradition', in HOBSBAWM and RANGER (1983), 1–14.

—— and RANGER, T., eds. (1983). *The Invention of Tradition*. Cambridge.

HOEKSTRA, A. (1962). 'The Absence of the Aeginetans (On the Interpretation of Pindar's Sixth Paean)', *Mnemosyne* ser. 4, 15, 1–14.

HOLLEAUX, M. (1893). 'Notes sur l'épigraphie et l'histoire de Rhodes', *BCH* 17, 52–69.

—— (1894). 'Notes épigraphiques', *BCH* 18, 390–407.

HOMMEL, P., KLEINER, G., and MÜLLER-WIENER, W. (1967). *Panionion und Melie*. Berlin.

HOMOLLE, T. (1885). *De antiquissimis Dianae simulacris Deliacis*. Paris.

HOOKE, S. H. (1933). *Myth and Ritual: Essays on the Myth and Ritual of the Hebrews in Relation to the Culture Pattern of the Ancient East*. London.

—— (1935). 'The Myth and Ritual Pattern in Jewish and Christian Apocalyptic', in *The Labyrinth: Further Studies in the Relation between Myth and Ritual in the Ancient World*. London, 211–33.

—— (1956). *The Siege Perilous: Essays in Biblical Anthropology and Kindred Subjects*. London.

—— (1958*a*). *Myth, Ritual and Kingship. Essays in the Theory and Practice of Kingship in the Ancient Near East and in Israel*. Oxford.

—— (1958*b*).'Myth and Ritual: Past and Present', in HOOKE (1958*a*), 1–21.

HOOKER, J. T. (1985). 'A Reading of the Seventh *Olympian*', *BICS* 32, 63–70.

HORDEN, P., and PURCELL, N. (2000). *The Corrupting Sea: A Study of Mediterranean History*. Oxford.

HORDERN, J. (2002). *The Fragments of Timotheos of Miletus*. Oxford.

HORNBLOWER, S. (1982*a*). *Mausolus*. Oxford.

—— (1982*b*). 'Thucydides, the Panionian Festival and the Ephesia (iii.104)', *Historia* 31, 241–5.

—— (1991–6). *A Commentary on Thucydides*, vols. i–ii. Oxford.

—— (1992). 'The Religious Dimension of the Peloponnesian War, or, what Thucydides does not Tell us', *HSPh* 94, 169–97.

—— (2002). *The Greek World 478–323 B.C.* 3rd edn. London.

—— (2004). *Thucydides and Pindar: Historical Narrative and the World of Epinikian Poetry*. Oxford.

—— (2007). '"Dolphins in the Sea" (*Isthmian* 9.7): Pindar and the Aeginetans', in HORNBLOWER and MORGAN (2007), 287–308.

—— and MORGAN, C. A., eds. (2007). *Pindar's Poetry, Patrons and Festivals: From Archaic Greece to the Roman Empire*. Oxford.

—— and OSBORNE, R. G., eds. (1994). *Ritual, Finance, Politics: Athenian Democratic Accounts Presented to David Lewis*. Oxford.

HORSTMANSHOFF, H. F. J., *et al.* (2002). *Kykeon: Studies in Honour of H. S. Versnel*. Religions in the Graeco-Roman World 142. Leiden.

HOW, W. W., and WELLS, J. (1928). *A Commentary on Herodotus*, 2 vols. 2nd edn. Oxford (1st pub. 1912).

HUBBARD, T. K. (1985). *The Pindaric Mind: A Study of Logical Structure in Early Greek Poetry*. Mnemosyne suppl. 85. Leiden.

—— (2001). 'Pindar and Athens after the Persian Wars', in *Gab es das griechische Wunder? Griechenland zwischen dem Ende des 6. und der Mitte des 5. Jahrhunderts v. Chr.* (Conference, Freiburg im Breisgau, 5–9 Apr. 1999), 387–97.

HUGH-JONES, S. (1979). *The Palm and the Pleiades: Initiation and Cosmology in Northwest Amazonia*. Cambridge.

Humphrey, C., and Laidlaw, J. (1994). *The Archetypal Actions of Ritual: A Theory of Ritual Illustrated by the Jain Rite of Worship.* Oxford.
Hunter, R., ed. (2005). *The Hesiodic Catalogue of Women. Constructions and Reconstructions.* Cambridge.
Hurst, A. (1983). 'Temps du récit chez Pindare (Pyth. 4) et Bacchylide (11)', *MH* 40, 154–68.
Hutchinson, G. O. (2001). *Greek Lyric Poetry: A Commentary on Selected Larger Pieces.* Oxford.
Huxley, G. L. (1965). 'Xenomedes of Keos', *GRBS* 6, 235–45.
—— (1969). *Greek Epic Poetry from Eumelos to Panyassis.* London.
—— (1972). *The Early Ionians.* Shannon (1st pub. London, 1966).
Huxley, J. (1963). 'Eight Ages of Man', in E. H. Erikson, ed., *Childhood and Society.* 2nd edn. New York, 247–74.
—— ed. (1966*a*). *A Discussion on Ritualization of Behaviour in Animals and Man.* Philosophical Transactions of the Royal Society of London, ser. B, vol. 251. London.
—— (1966*b*). 'Introduction', in (1966*a*), 249–71.
Ieranò, G. (1989). 'Il ditirambo XVII di Bacchilide e le feste apollinee di Delo', *Quaderni di Storia* 30, 157–83.
—— (1997). *Il ditirambo di Dioniso. Le testimonianze antiche.* Pisa–Rome.
Irigoin, J., Duchemin, J., and Bardollet, L., eds. (1993). *Bacchylide. Dithyrambes—Épinicies—Fragments.* Collection des Universités de France. Paris.
Isaakidou, V., Halstead, P., Davis, J., and Stocker, S. (2002). 'Burnt Animal Sacrifice at the Mycenaean "Palace of Nestor", Pylos', *Antiquity* 76, 86–92.
Isager, S. (1992). 'Sacred Animals in Classical and Hellenistic Greece', in T. Linders and B. Alroth, eds., *Economics of Cult in the Ancient Greek World.* Uppsala, 15–20.
Jackson, S. (1996). 'Callimachus, Istrus and the Statue of Delian Apollo', *ZPE* 110, 43–8.
—— (1999). 'Callimachean Istrus and the Helieia on Rhodes', *Eikasmos* 10, 119–24.
Jacquemin, A. (2000). 'Pausanias à Délos, ou: Un chapitre recomposé du livre imaginé des "Kykladika"', *Ktema* 25, 19–36.
—— (2001). 'Delphes au Ve siècle ou un panhellénisme difficile à concrétiser', *Pallas* 57, 93–110.
Jameson, M. H. (1974). 'A Treasury of Athena in the Argolid (IG IV 554)', in D. W. Bradeen and M. F. McGregor, eds., *Phoros. Tribute to Benjamin Dean Meritt.* Locus Valley, 67–75.
—— (1990). 'Perseus, the Hero of Mykenai', in Hägg and Nordquist (1990), 213–23.
—— (1991). 'Sacrifice before Battle', in V. D. Hanson, ed., *Hoplites: The Classical Greek Battle Experience.* London, 97–227.
—— (1994). 'Theoxenia', in Hägg (1994), 35–57.
Jameson, M. H., Runnels, C. N., and van Andel, T. H. (1994). *A Greek Countryside. The Southern Argolid from Prehistory to the Present Day.* With a register of sites by C. N. Runnels, M. H. Munn. Stanford.
Jantzen, U., ed. (1976). *Neue Forschungen in griechischen Heiligtümern. Internationales Symposion in Olympia vom 10. bis 12. Oktober 1974 anlässl. der Hundertjahrfeier der Abteilung Athen und der deutschen Ausgrabungen in Olympia.* Tübingen.
Jeanmaire, H. (1939). *Couroi et courètes: essai sur l'éducation spartiate et sur les rites d'adolescence dans l'antiquité hellénique.* Lille.
Jebb, R. C. (1905). *Bacchylides: The Poems and Fragments.* Cambridge.
Jeffery, L. H. (1976). *Archaic Greece: The City-States, c. 700–500 B.C.* London.

Jensen, A. E. (1960). *Mythos und Kult bei Naturvölkern.* 2nd edn. Studien zur Kulturkunde 10. Wiesbaden.

Jockey, P. (1996). 'Le Sanctuaire de Délos à l'époque archaïque. Bilan historiographique et bibliographique', *Topoi* 6, 159–97.

Johnston, A. (1977). 'Rhodes, Sunny Side up', *ZPE* 26, 157–8.

Jost, M. (1985). *Sanctuaires et cultes d'Arcadie.* École Française d'Athènes. Études péloponnésiaques 9. Paris.

—— (1992). 'La Légende de Mélampus en Argolide et dans le Péloponnèse', in Piérart (1992*b*), 173–84.

—— (1994). 'The Distribution of Sanctuaries in Civic Space', in Alcock and Osborne (1994), 217–30.

Jourdain-Annequin, C. (1989). *Héraclès aux portes du soir: mythe et histoire.* Annales littéraires de l'Université de Besançon 402. Centre de recherches d'histoire ancienne 89. Paris.

Just, R. (2000). *A Greek Island Cosmos: Kinship and Community on Meganisi.* Oxford.

Kadletz, E. (1978). 'The Cult of Apollo Deiradiotes', *TAPhA* 108, 93–101.

Kakavogianni, O. (1984). "*Πορτο Ράφτη (Πρασιές)*", *ΑΔ* 39 B—*Χρονικά* (1989), 45.

—— (1985). "*Πορτο Ράφτη (Πρασιές)*", *ΑΔ* 40 *B*—*Χρονικά* (1990), 66.

—— (1986). "*Δύο νέα μνημεία υστεροαρχαικής πλαστική από τις Πρασιές*", in H. Kyrieleis, ed., *Archaische und klassische griechische Plastik* (Conference, Athens, 22–5 Apr. 1985), 2 vols. Mainz, i. 171–5.

Kallet-Marx, L. (1993). *Money, Expense and Naval Power in Thucydides' History 1–5.24.* Berkeley.

Kalpaxis, A. (1989). 'Der Oikos der Naxier', in *FS B. Neutsch.* Innsbruck, 237–42.

Käppel, L. (1992). *Paian. Studien zur Geschichte einer Gattung.* UaLG 37. Berlin–New York.

Kästner, V. (1990). 'Scheibenförmige Akrotere in Griechenland und Italien', *Hesperia* 59, 251–64.

Katsonopoulou, D. (2002). 'Helike and her Territory in the Light of New Discoveries', in Greco (2002), 205–16.

Kearns, E. (1994). 'Cakes in Greek Sacrifice Regulations', in Hägg (1994), 65–70.

Kelly, Th. (1967). 'The Argive Destruction of Asine', *Historia* 16, 422–31.

—— (1974). 'Argive Foreign Policy in the Fifth Century B.C.', *CPh* 69, 81–99.

—— (1976). *A History of Argos to 500 B.C.* Minneapolis.

Keramopoulos, A. (1917). "*Ὁ Ναὸς τοῦ Ἰσμηνίου Ἀπόλλωνος*", *ΑΔ* 3, 33–98.

Kertzer, D. I. (1988). *Ritual, Politics and Power.* New Haven–London.

Kipling, G. (1998). *Enter the King: Theatre, Liturgy, and Ritual in the Medieval Civic Triumph.* Oxford.

Kirchhoff, A. (1887). *Studien zur Geschichte des griechischen Alphabets.* 4th edn. Gütersloh.

Kirigin, B., and Cace, S. (1998). 'Archaeological Evidence for the Cult of Diomedes in the Adriatic', *Hesperia* 9, 63–110.

Kirk, G. S. (1970). *Myth: Its Meaning and Function in Ancient and other Cultures.* London–Cambridge–Berkeley.

—— (1972). 'Aetiology, Ritual, Charter: Three Equivocal Terms in the Study of Myth', *YClS* 22, 83–102.

—— (1974). *The Nature of Greek Myths.* Harmondsworth.

Kirkwood, G. (1982). *Selections from Pindar.* Edited with an Introduction and Commentary. American Philological Association Textbook ser. 7. Chicago.

Kluckhohn, C. (1942). 'Myths and Rituals: A General Theory', *HThR* 35, 45–79.

KNAUSS, J. (1987). *Die Melioration des Kopaisbeckens durch die Minyer im 2. Jt. v. Chr.* Kopais 2. Wasserbau und Siedlungsbedingungen im Altertum. Versuchsanstalt für Wasserbau und Wassermengenwirtschaft 57. Oskar v. Müller-Institut (Technische Universität München). Munich–Obernach.

—— (1990). *Wasserbau und Geschichte. Minysche Epoche—Bayerische Zeit (vier Jahrhunderte—ein Jahrzehnt).* Versuchsanstalt für Wasserbau und Wassermengenwirtschaft 63. Oskar v. Müller-Institut (Technische Universität München). Munich–Obernach.

—— HEINRICH, B., and KALCYK, H. (1984). *Die Wasserbauten der Minyer in der Kopais: die älteste Flussregulierung Europas: Untersuchungsergebnisse 1984.* Versuchsanstalt für Wasserbau und Wassermengenwirtschaft 50. Oskar v. Müller-Institut (Technische Universität München). Munich–Obernach.

KOERNER, R. (1987). 'Zur Landaufteilung in griechischen Poleis in älterer Zeit', *Klio* 69, 443–9.

KÖHNKEN, A. (1971). *Die Funktion des Mythos bei Pindar. Interpretationen zu sechs Pindargedichten.* UaLG 12. Berlin.

—— (1976). 'Hemerasien- oder Pythiensieg? Zu Bakchylides, ep. 11', *WJA* 2, 49–51.

KOKKOROU-ALEWRAS, G. (1975). *Archaische naxische Plastik.* Munich.

KOLF, M. C. VAN DER (1928). *Quaeritur quomodo Pindarus fabulas tractaverit et quidque in eis mutaverit.* Rotterdam.

KORFMANN, M. (1986). 'Troy, Topography and Navigation', in M. J. MELLINK, ed., *Troy and the Trojan War* (Conference, Bryn Mawr, Oct. 1984). Bryn Mawr, 1–16.

—— (1995). 'Troia: A Residential and Trading City at the Dardanelles', in R. LAFFINEUR and W. D. NIEMEIER, eds., *Politeia: Society and State in the Aegean Bronze Age*, vol. i. Aegaeum 12. Liège–Austin, 173–83.

KOSTOGLOU-DESPINI, A. (1979). *Προβλήματα της παριανής γλυπτικής.* Thessaloniki.

KOSTOMITSOPOULOU, P. (1988). 'Lindian Sacrifice: An Evaluation of the Evidence Based on New Inscriptions', in DIETZ and PAPACHRISTODOULOU (1988), 121–8.

KOURAYOS, Y. (2005). 'Despotiko Mandra: A Sanctuary Dedicated to Apollo', in M. STAMATOPOULOU and M. YEROULANOU, eds., *Archaeology and Architecture in the Cyclades. Essays in Honour of J. J. Coulton.* Oxford, 105–33.

—— (2006). "*Δεσποτικό* 2005: *Η ανασκαφική δραστηριότητα στο ιερό του Απόλλωνα*", in N. STAMPOLIDES, ed., *Γενέθλιον: αναμνηστικός τόμος για την συμπλήρωση είκοσι χρόνων λειτουργίας του Μουσείου Κυκλαδικής Τέχνης.* Athens, 147–58.

KOURETAS, D. (1977). "*Αγχοπλημμιριστική θεραπεία της μανίας των Προιτίδων υπό του Μελάμποδος*", *Platon* 29, 110–17.

KOWALZIG, B. (2004). 'Changing Choral Worlds: Song-Dance and Society in Athens and Beyond', in MURRAY and WILSON (2004), 39–65.

—— (2005). 'Mapping out *Communitas*: *Theoria* in its Sacred and Political Context', in ELSNER and RUTHERFORD (2005), 41–72.

—— (2006). 'The Aetiology of Empire? Hero-Cult and Athenian Tragedy', in J. DAVIDSON, F. MUECKE, and P. WILSON, eds., *Greek Drama*, iii. *Studies in Honour of Kevin Lee.* BICS suppl. 87, London, 78–98.

—— (2007). '"And Now All the World Shall Dance" (Eur. *Bacch.* 114): Dionysus' Choroi between Ritual and Drama', in CSAPO and MILLER (2007), 221–51.

KRITZAS, C. (1992). 'Aspects de la vie politique et économique d'Argos au V siècle avant J.-C.', in PIÉRART (1992*b*), 231–40.

KRUMMEN, E. (1990). *Pyrsos Hymnon. Festliche Gegenwart und mythisch-rituelle Tradition als Voraussetzung einer Pindarinterpretation (Isthmie 4, Pythie 5, Olympie 1 und 3).* UaLG 35. Berlin–New York.

KRUMMEN, E. (1998). 'Ritual und Katastrophe: rituelle Handlung und Bildersprache bei Sophokles und Euripides', in GRAF (1998), 296–325.
KULLMANN, W. (1960). *Die Quellen der Ilias (troischer Sagenkreis).* Hermes ES 14. Wiesbaden.
—— (1974). *Wissenschaft und Methode. Interpretationen zur aristotelischen Theorie der Naturwissenschaft.* Berlin–New York.
KURKE, L. V. (1991). *The Traffic in Praise: Pindar and the Poetics of Social Economy.* Ithaca–London.
—— (1993). 'The Economy of *kudos*', in DOUGHERTY and KURKE (1993), 131–63.
—— (1999). *Coins, Bodies, Games and Gold: The Politics of Meaning in Archaic Greece.* Princeton.
—— (2003). 'Aesop and the Contestation of Delphic Authority', in DOUGHERTY and KURKE (2003), 77–100.
—— (2005). 'Choral Lyric as "Ritualization": Poetic Sacrifice and Poetic Ego in Pindar's Sixth Paian', *ClAnt* 24, 81–130.
—— (2007). 'Visualizing the Choral: Epichoric Poetry, Ritual and Elite Negotiation in Fifth-Century Thebes', in J. ELSNER, H. FOLEY, S. GOLDHILL, and C. KRAUS, eds., *Visualizing the Tragic: Drama, Myth, and Ritual in Greek Art and Literature.* Oxford, 63–101.
LAAGER, J. (1957). *Geburt und Kindheit des Gottes in der griechischen Mythologie.* Winterthur.
LACROIX, L. (1949). *Les Reproductions des statues sur les monnaies grecques. La Statuaire archaïque et classique.* Liège.
LADA-RICHARDS, I. (1999). *Initiating Dionysus: Ritual and Theatre in Aristophanes' Frogs.* Oxford.
LA FONTAINE, J. (1986). 'Invisible Custom: Public Lectures as Ceremonials', *Anthropology Today* 2.5, 3–9.
LAGOS, C. (2001). 'Athena Itonia at Koroneia (Boiotia) and in Cilicia', *NC* 161, 1–10.
LANGDON, M. K. (1976). *A Sanctuary of Zeus on Mount Hymettos.* Hesperia suppl. 16. Princeton.
LANGER, S. (1953). *Feeling and Form: A Theory of Art Developed from Philosophy in a New Key.* London.
LARSEN, J. A. O. (1960). 'Orchomenus and the Formation of the Boeotian Confederacy in 447 B.C.', *CPh* 55, 9–18.
—— (1968). *Greek Federal States: Their Institutions and History.* Oxford.
LA TORRE, G. F. (2002). *Un tempio arcaico nel territorio dell'antica Temesa. L'edificio sacro in località di Campora San Giovanni.* Rome.
LATTE, K. (1960). *Römische Religionsgeschichte.* HAW v.4. Munich.
LAUMONIER, A. (1956). *Les Figurines de terre cuite. ED* 33. Paris.
LAVECCHIA, S. (1994). 'Il "Secondo Ditirambo" di Pindaro e i culti tebani', *SCO* 44, 33–93.
—— (1996). 'P. Oxy. 2622 e il "Secondo Ditirambo" di Pindaro', *ZPE* 110, 1–26.
—— (2000). *Pindari Dithyramborum fragmenta. Introduzione, testo critico, traduzione e commento.* Lyricorum Graecorum quae exstant. Collana di testi critici. 13. Rome–Pisa.
LAWALL, G. (1961). 'The Cup, the Rose, and the Winds in Pindar's Seventh Olympian', *RFIC* NS 39, 33–47.
LAWLER, L. (1978). *The Dance in Ancient Greece.* Middletown, Conn. (1st edn. London, 1964).
LAWSON, J. C. (1910). *Modern Greek Folklore and Ancient Greek Religion, a Study in Survivals.* Cambridge.

LEACH, E. R. (1954). *Political Systems of Highland Burma: A Study of Kachin Social Structure.* London.
—— (1966). 'Ritualization in Man in Relation to Conceptual and Social Development', in J. HUXLEY (1966*a*), 403–27.
—— (1976) *Culture and Communication: The Logic by which Symbols are Connected: An Introduction to the Use of Structuralist Analysis in Social Anthropology.* Cambridge.
—— (1981). 'A Poetics of Power': A Review of Geertz' *Negara*', *New Republic* 184, 30–3.
LEAHY, D. M. (1954). 'Aegina and the Peloponnesian League', *CPh* 49, 232–43.
LEFKOWITZ, M. R. (1963). '*Τῶ καὶ εγώ*: The First Person in Pindar', *HSPh* 67, 177–253. Repr. in (1991), 1–71.
—— (1988). 'Who sang Pindar's Victory Odes', *AJPh* 109, 1–11. Repr. in (1991), 191–201.
—— (1991). *First Person Fictions. Pindar's Poetic 'I'.* Oxford.
LE GOFF, J. (1980). 'The Symbolic Ritual of Vassalage', in *Time, Work and Culture*, trans. A. Goldhammer. Chicago–London, 237–87.
LEHNUS, L. (1977). 'Da una nuova ispezione di P.Oxy. IV 659 (Pindaro, Partheneia)', *MPhL* 2, 227–31.
—— (1984). 'Il Dafneforico per Agasicle (Fr. 94b Sn-M)', *BICS* 31, 61–92.
LEPORE, E. (1962). *Ricerche sull'antico Epiro. Le origini storiche e gli interessi greci.* Naples.
—— (1977). 'Fiumi e città nella colonizzazione greca dell'Occidente, con speciale riguardo alla Magna Grecia', in P. M. DUVAL and E. FRÉZOULS, eds., *Thèmes de recherches sur les villes antiques d'Occident* (Conference, Strasbourg, 1–4 Oct. 1971). Paris, 267–72.
—— (1980). 'L'Italia dal punto di vista ionico. Tra Ecateo ed Erodoto', in M. J. FONTANA *et al.*, eds., *Φιλίας Χάριν. Miscellanea di studi classici in onore di Eugenio Manni*, 4 vols. Rome, iv. 1329–44.
—— (1990). 'Parallelismi, riflessi e incidenza degli avvenimenti del contesto mediterraneo in Italia', in *Crise et transformation des sociétés archaïques de l'Italie antique au Ve siècle av. J.-C.* Collection de l'École Française de Rome 137. Rome, 289–97.
LEPPIN, H. (1999). 'Argos. Eine griechische Demokratie des fünften Jahrhunderts v. Chr.', *Ktema* 24, 297–312.
LE ROY, C. (1974). 'Deux notes déliennes', *BCH* 98, 383–96.
—— (1983).'La Naissance d'Apollon et les palmiers déliens', in *Études Déliennes*, 263–86.
LESCHHORN, W. (1984). *Gründer der Stadt. Studien zu einem politisch-religiösen Phänomen der griechischen Geschichte.* Palingenesia 20. Stuttgart.
LÉVI-STRAUSS, C. (1970). *Introduction to a Science of Mythology*, trans. J. and D. Weightman. Vol. 1: *The Raw and the Cooked.* London (orig. *Le Cru et le cuit.* Paris, 1964).
—— (1973). Vol. 2: *From Honey to Ashes.* London (orig. *Du miel aux cendres.* Paris, 1964).
—— (1978). Vol. 4: *The Origin of Table Manners.* London (orig. *L'Origine des manières de table.* Paris, 1971).
—— (1981). Vol. 3: *The Naked Man.* London (orig. *L'Homme nu.* Paris, 1968).
LÉVY, E. (1991). 'Apparition des notions de Grèce et de Grecs', in S. SAID, ed., *ELLENISMOS. Quelques jalons pour une histoire de l'identité grecque.* Leiden, 49–69.
LEWIS, D. M. (1981). 'The Origin of the First Peloponnesian War', in G. S. SHRIMPTON and D. J. MCCARGAR, eds., *Classical Contributions: Studies in Honour of Malcolm Francis McGregor*, New York, 71–8.
—— (1992*a*). 'Mainland Greece', *CAH* v². Cambridge, 96–120.
—— (1992*b*). 'Chronological Notes', *CAH* v². Cambridge, 499–505.
LEWIS, G. (1980). *Day of Shining Red: An Essay on Understanding Ritual.* Cambridge.
LHÔTE, E. (2006). *Les Lamelles oraculaires de Dodone.* Hautes études du monde greco-romain 35. Geneva.

LINDERS, T. (1987). 'Gods, Gifts, Society', in T. LINDERS and G. NORDQUIST, eds., *Gifts to the Gods* (Conference, Uppsala, 1985). Stockholm, 115–22.

LIPPOLIS, E. (1988–9). 'Il santuario di Athana a Lindo', *ASAA* 66–7, 97–157 (pub. in 1993).

—— (1996) 'Lindo. L'acropoli. 1. Il santuario. 2. La riscoperta archeologica e il restauro', in LIVADIOTTI and ROCCO (1996), 52–60.

LIVADIOTTI, M. (1996). 'Gli scavi sull'acropoli', in LIVADIOTTI and ROCCO (1996), 40–2.

—— and ROCCO, G., eds. (1996). *La presenza italiana nel Dodecaneso tra il 1912 e il 1948: la ricerca archeologica, la conservazione, le scelte progettuali.* Catania.

LIXFELD, H. (1977). 'Aitiologie', in K. RANKE, ed., *Enzyklopädie des Märchens. Handwörterbuch zur historischen und vergleichenden Erzählforschung.* Berlin–New York, vol. i. s.v.

LLOYD, A. B. (1975–88). *Herodotus Book II*, 3 vols. Leiden.

LLOYD-JONES, H. (1973). 'Modern Interpretation of Pindar: The Second Pythian and Seventh Nemean Odes', *JHS* 93, 109–37. Repr. in *The Academic Papers of Sir Hugh Lloyd-Jones* (Oxford, 1990), 110–53.

LOBEL, G. (1961). *POxy xxvi.*

LOCHNER VON HÜTTENBACH, F. (1960). *Die Pelasger.* Vienna.

LOEFFLER, I. (1963). *Die Melampodie. Versuch einer Rekonstruktion des Inhalts.* Beiträge zur Klassischen Philologie 7. Meisenheim am Glan.

LOEHR, J. (1996). *Ovids Mehrfacherklärungen in der Tradition aitiologischen Dichtens.* BzA 74. Stuttgart–Leipzig.

LOMAS, K., ed. (2004). *Greek Identity in the Western Mediterranean. Papers in Honour of Brian Shefton.* Mnemosyne suppl. 246. Leiden.

LOMBARDO, M. (1982). 'Antileon tirannicida nella tradizione metapontina ed eracleota', *SAL* 3, 189–205.

—— (1986). 'Fonti letterarie, documentazione archeologica e problemi storici', in *Siris-Polieion*, 55–86.

—— (1998). 'La democrazia in Magna Grecia: aspetti e problemi', in E. GRECO, L. CANFORA, *et al.*, *Venticinque secoli dopo l'invenzione della democrazia.* Paestum, 77–106.

LONG, B. O. (1968). *The Problem of Etiological Narrative in the Old Testament.* BZAW 108. Berlin.

LONG, C. R. (1958). 'Greeks, Carians, and the Purification of Delos', *AJA* 62, 297–306.

LONSDALE, S. (1993). *Dance and Ritual Play in Greek Religion.* London–Baltimore.

LO PORTO, F. G. (1987). 'Due iscrizioni votive dai dintorni di Taranto', *PP* 42, 39–50.

LORAUX, N. (1986). *The Invention of Athens: The Funeral Oration in the Classical City.* Cambridge, Mass. (orig. *L'Invention d'Athènes. Histoire de l'oraison funèbre dans la cité classique.* Paris, 1981).

LORENZ, K. Z. (1966). 'Evolution of Ritualization in the Biological and Cultural Spheres', in J. HUXLEY (1966*a*), 273–84.

LO SCALZO, D. (1998). 'Neottolemo Boathoos a Delfi', *QS* 47, 119–31.

LOTZE, D. (1971). 'Zur Verfassung von Argos nach der Schlacht bei Sepeia (Aristoteles Politik 5, 1303a6–8)', *Chiron* 1, 95–109.

LOWELL, E., ed. (1990). *Approaches to Greek Myth.* Baltimore–London.

LUKES, S. (1973). *Emile Durkheim: His Life and his Work. A Historical and Critical Study.* London.

LURAGHI, N. (1994). *Tirannidi arcaiche in Sicilia e Magna Grecia. Da Panezio di Leontini alla caduta dei Dinomenidi.* Florence.

—— (2002). 'Becoming Messenian', *JHS* 122, 45–69.

Ma, J. (2005). 'The Many Lives of Eugnotos of Akraiphia', in B. Virgilio, ed., *Studi ellenistici*, XVI. Pisa, 141–91.

MacAloon, J. J., ed. (1984*a*). *Rite, Drama, Festival, Spectacle: Rehearsals towards a Theory of Cultural Performance.* Philadelphia.

—— (1984*b*). 'Olympic Games and the Theory of Spectacle in Modern Societies', in MacAloon (1984*a*), 241–80.

MacDowell, D. M. (1960). 'Aigina and the Delian League', *JHS* 80, 118–21.

McInerney, J. (1999). *The Folds of Parnassos: Land and Ethnicity in Ancient Phokis.* Austin.

MacKay, A. (1985). 'Ritual and Propaganda in Fifteenth-Century Castile', *Past and Present* 107, 3–43.

Mackil, E. (2003). '*Koinon* and *Koinonia*: Mechanisms and Structures of Political Collectivity in Classical and Hellenistic Greece'. Ph.D. diss. Princeton.

—— and Van Alfen, P. G. (2006). 'Cooperative Coinage', in *Agoranomia: Studies in Money and Exchange Presented to John H. Kroll.* New York, 201–46.

McMullin, R. (2001–2). 'Aspects of Medizing: Themistocles, Simonides, and Timocreon of Rhodes', *CJ* 97, 55–67.

Maddoli, G. F. (1982). 'Megále Hellás: genesi di un concetto e realtà storico-politiche', *AttTar* 21 (1981), 9–32.

—— (1984). 'I culti di Crotone', *AttTar* 23 (1983), 313–43.

—— and Saladino, V. (1995). *Pausania. Guida della Grecia. Libro V: L'Elide e Olimpia.* Milan.

—— Nafissi, M., and Saladino, V. (1999). *Pausania. Guida della Grecia. Libro VI: L'Elide e Olimpia.* Milan.

Maehler, H. (1963). *Die Auffassung des Dichterberufs im frühen Griechentum bis zur Zeit Pindars.* Göttingen.

—— (1982–97). *Die Lieder des Bakchylides*, 2 vols. Mnemosyne suppl. 62, 167. Leiden.

—— (1991). 'Theseus' Kretafahrt und Bacchylides 17', *MH* 48, 114–26.

—— (2004). *Bacchylides: A Selection.* Greek and Latin Classics. Cambridge.

Mafodda, G. (2000). *Il koinon beotico in età arcaica e classica. Storia e istituzioni.* SEIA ns iv. Rome.

Maiuri, A. (1916–20*a*). 'Lavori della Missione archeologica italiana a Rodi. Ricerche nella necropoli di Jalisos', *ASAA* 3, 252–9.

—— (1916–20*b*). 'Note sulla topografia antica di Rodi', *ASAA* 3, 259–62.

Malinowski, B. (1948 (1926)). *Myth in Primitive Psychology.* London, 1926. Repr. in *Magic, Science and Religion and Other Essays by Bronislaw Malinowski.* Selected, and with an introduction by R. Redfield (Boston, 1948), 72–124.

Malkin, I. (1987). *Religion and Colonization in Ancient Greece.* Leiden.

—— (1993). 'Colonisation spartiate dans la mer Egée: tradition et archéologie', *REA* 95.3–4, 365–81.

—— (1994). *Myth and Territory in the Spartan Mediterranean.* Cambridge.

—— (1997). 'Categories of Early Greek Colonization: The Case of the Dorian Aegean', in C. Antonetti, ed., *Il dinamismo della colonizzazione greca. Atti della tavola rotonda «Espansione e colonizzazione greca di età arcaica: metodologie e problemi a confronto»* (Venice, 10–11 Nov. 1995). Naples, 25–38.

—— (1998*a*). 'The Middle Ground: Philoktetes in Italy'. *Kernos* 11, 131–41.

—— (1998*b*). *The Returns of Odysseus. Colonization and Ethnicity.* Berkeley–London.

—— ed. (2001). *Ancient Perceptions of Greek Ethnicity.* CHS Colloquia 5. Cambridge, Mass.

Malten, L. (1912). 'Heliadai', *RE* vii.2, 2849–52.

Maniet, A. (1941). 'Le Caractère de Minos dans l'Ode XVII de Bacchylides', *LEC* 10, 35–54.

Mann, C. (2001). *Athlet und Polis im archaischen und frühklassischen Griechenland.* Hypomnemata 138. Göttingen.

Mannhardt, W. (1875–7). *Wald- und Feldkulte*, 2 vols. Berlin.

Marankou, L. I. (2002). *Amorgos*, vol. 1. *Βιβλιοθήκη της εν Αθήναις Αρχαιολογικής Εταιρείας* 228. Athens.

Marchetti, P. (1977). 'A propos de l'archonte delphien de 344/3', in *Études Delphiques.* BCH suppl. 4. Athens, 67–89.

Marek, C. (1984). *Die Proxenie.* Frankfurt.

Marinatos, N. (1988). 'The Imagery of Sacrifice: Minoan and Greek', in Hägg *et al.* (1988), 9–20.

Marketou, T. (1998). 'Excavations at Trianda (Ialysos) on Rhodes: New Evidence for the Late Bronze Age I Period', *RAL* 9, 39–82.

Martelli, M. (1988). 'La stipe votiva dell'Athenaion di Jalysos: un primo bilancio', in Dietz and Papachristodoulou (1988), 104–20.

—— (1996). 'La stipe votiva dell'Athenaion di Ialisos', in Livadiotti and Rocco (1996), 46–50.

Martin, R. P. (1987). 'Fire on the Mountain: Lysistrata and the Lemnian Women', *ClAnt* 6, 77–105.

—— (1989). *The Language of Heroes: Speech and Performance in the Iliad.* Ithaca.

Marton, L. (1997). 'Le tradizioni sui Rodii in Occidente in età pre-olimpiadica: tra realtà storica e propaganda', in Antonetti (1997), 135–44.

Masson, O. (1988). 'Le Culte ionien d'Apollon Oulios, d'après des données onomastiques nouvelles', *JS*, 173–83.

Mattes, J. (1970). *Der Wahnsinn im griechischen Mythos und in der Dichtung bis zum Drama des fünften Jahrhunderts.* Bibliothek der Klassischen Altertumswissenschaften 2. Reihe 36. Heidelberg.

Matthaiou, A. P. (2003). "*Ἀπόλλων Δήλιος ἐν Ἀθήναις*", in D. Jordan and J. Traill, eds., *Lettered Attica: A Day of Attic Epigraphy* (Conference, Athens, 8 Mar. 2000). Athens.

Mazarakis Ainian, A. (1997). *From Rulers to Temples: Architecture, Religion and Society in Early Iron Age Greece (1100–700 B.C).* Studies in Mediterranean Archaeology 121. Jonsered.

—— and Mendone, L. G., eds. (1998). *Κέα-Κύθνος. Ιστορία και αρχαιολογία. Πρακτικά του διεθνούς συμποσίου. Κέα-Κύθνος, 22–25 Ιουνίου 1994.* Meletemata 27. Athens–Paris.

Mazzarino, S. (1964). 'Metropoli e colonie', *AttTar* 3 (1963), 51–85.

Mee, C. (1982). *Rhodes in the Bronze Age: An Archaeological Survey.* Warminster.

Méheust, B. (1990). 'Les Occidentaux du XXe siècle, ont-ils cru à leur mythes?', *Communications* 52, 337–56.

Meiggs, R. (1972). *The Athenian Empire.* Oxford.

Mele, A. (1982). 'La Megale Hellás pitagorica: aspetti politici, economici e sociali', *AttTar* 21 (1981), 33–80.

—— (1995). 'Tradizioni eroiche e colonizzazione greca: le colonie achee', in A. Storchi Marino, ed., *L'incidenza dell'antico. Studi in memoria di Ettore Lepore* (Conference, Anacapri, 24–8 Mar. 1991). Naples, vol. i, 427–50.

—— (1998). 'Culti e miti nella storia di Metaponto', in *Siritide e Metapontino*, 67–90.

—— (2000). '"Megale Hellas" e pitagorismo', in M. Tortorelli *et al.*, eds., *Tra Orfeo e Pitagora. Origini e incontri di culture nell'antichità. Atti dei seminari napoletani 1996–1998.* Naples, 297–333.

Merkelbach, R. (1973*a*). 'Bakchylides auf einen Sieger in den Ἡμεράσια zu Lousoi', *ZPE* 11, 257–60.

—— (1973*b*). 'Bakchylides Fr. 4.45', *ZPE* 12, 44.

Mertens, D. (1974). 'L'architettura', *AttTar* 13 (1973), 187–235.

—— (1976). 'Zur archaischen Architektur der achäischen Kolonien in Unteritalien', in Jantzen (1976), 167–97.

—— (1980). 'Parallelismi strutturali nell'architettura della Magna Grecia e dell'Italia centrale in età archaica', in Padula (1980), 37–82.

—— (1982). 'Per l'urbanistica e l'architettura della Magna Grecia', *AttTar* 21 (1981), 97–141.

—— (1993). *Der alte Heratempel in Paestum und die archaische Baukunst in Unteritalien.* Mainz.

—— (2002). 'L'architettura delle colonie achee d' Occidente', in Greco (2002), 315–22.

Mertens-Horn, M. (1992). 'Die archaischen Baufriese aus Metapont', *MDAI(R)* 99, 1–122.

Metzger, H. (1940–1). 'Le Sanctuaire de Glanitsa (Gortynie)', *BCH* 64–5, 5–33.

Miller, A. M. (1986). *From Delos to Delphi: A Literary Study of the Homeric Hymn to Apollo.* Mnemosyne suppl. 93. Leiden.

Mingarelli, S. (2003). 'Eracle a Cos: una lettura del fr. 33a Sn.-M. di Pindaro', in R. Nicolai, ed., *Rhysmos. Studi di poesia, metrica e musica greca offerti dagli allievi a Luigi Enrico Rossi per i suoi settant'anni.* Rome, 117–32.

Mitsopoulos-Leon, V. (1990). 'Kästchen für Artemis', in J.-P. Descoeudres, ed., *ΕΥΜΟΥΣΙΑ. Ceramic and Iconographic Studies in Honour of Alexander Cambitoglou,* 1. suppl. med. A, 137–40.

—— (1992). 'Artémis de Lousoi. Les fouilles autrichiennes', *Kernos* 5, 97–108.

—— (1993). 'The Statue of Artemis at Lousoi: Some Thoughts', in O. Palagia and W. Coulson, eds., *Sculpture from Arcadia and Laconia* (Conference, Athens, 10–14 Apr. 1992). Oxbow Monograph 30. Oxford, 33–9.

—— ed. (2001*a*). *Forschungen in der Peloponnes: Akten des Symposions anläßlich der Feier "100 Jahre Österreichisches Archäeologisches Institut Athen", Athen 5.3–7.3.1998.* Sonderschriften des Österreichischen Archäologischen Instituts 38. Athens.

—— (2001*b*). 'Lousoi nach hundert Jahren', in (2001*a*), 132–42.

Mitsos, Th. (1949). 'Inscriptions of the Eastern Peloponnese', *Hesperia* 18, 73–7.

Moggi, M. (1974). 'I sinecismi di Argo e le annessioni territoriali nel v secolo a.C.', *ASNP* ser. 3, 4, 1249–63.

—— (1976*a*). *I sinecismi interstatali greci,* vol. i. *Dalle origini al 338 a.C.* Relazioni interstatali nel mondo antico. Fonti e studi 2. Pisa.

—— (1976*b*). 'Il sinecismo di Tebe e la costituzione federale della Beozia nel V sec. a. C.', *CS* 13, 193–206.

—— and Osanna, M. (2000). *Pausania. Guida della Grecia. Libro VII. L'Acaia.* Milan.

Molyneux, J. H. (1992). *Simonides. A Historical Study.* Wauconda Il.

Momigliano, A. D. (1929/75). "*Η Μεγάλη Ελλάς*", *Bollettino di Filologia Classica* 36 (1929–30), 47–9. Repr. in *Quinto contributo alla storia degli studi classici e del mondo antico,* vol. ii (Rome, 1975), 843–5.

—— (1936*a*). 'Rodi', in *Enciclopedia Italiana.* Rome, vol. xxix, 547–62 s.v.

—— (1936*b*). 'Note sulla storia di Rodi', *RFIC* 14, 49–63.

Montepaone, C. (1986). 'L'apologia di Alexidamos, "l'avventura del cavaliere"', *Métis* 1, 219–35.

Moore, S. F., and Myerhoff, B. G., eds. (1977*a*). *Secular Ritual.* Assen.
—— —— (1977*b*). 'Introduction: Secular Ritual: Forms and Meanings', in Moore and Myerhoff (1977*a*), 3–24.
Morelli, D. (1959). *I culti di Rodi.* SCO 8. Pisa.
Moreno, A. (2003). 'The Athenian Grain Supply in the Fifth and Fourth Centuries B.C.' D.Phil. thesis. Oxford.
Moretti, J.-C. (1998), 'L'Implantation du théâtre d'Argos dans un lieu plein de sanctuaires', in Pariente and Touchais (1998), 233–59.
Morgan, C. A. (1990). *Athletes and Oracles: The Transformation of Olympia and Delphi in the Eighth Century B.C.* Cambridge.
—— (1991). 'Ethnicity and Early Greek States: Historical and Material Perspectives', *PCPhS* 37, 131–63.
—— (1997). 'The Archaeology of Sanctuaries in Early Iron Age and Archaic Ethne', in L. G. Mitchell and P. J. Rhodes, eds., *The Development of the Polis in Archaic Greece.* London–New York, 168–98.
—— (1999). 'Cultural Subzones in Early Iron Age and Archaic Arkadia?', in Nielsen and Roy (1999), 382–456.
—— (2000). 'Politics without the Polis: Cities and the Achaean Ethnos, *c.*800–500 BC', in Brock and Hodkinson (2000), 189–211.
—— (2001). 'Ethne, Ethnicity and Early Greek States, ca. 1200–480 B.C.: An Archaeological Perspective', in Malkin (2001), 75–112.
—— (2002). 'Ethnicity: The Example of Achaia', in Greco (2002), 95–116.
—— (2003). *Early Greek States beyond the Polis.* London.
—— and Whitelaw, T. (1991). 'Pots and Politics: Ceramic Evidence for the Rise of the Argive State', *AJA* 95, 79–108.
Morris, B. (1987). *Anthropological Studies of Religion: An Introductory Text.* Cambridge.
Morris, I. (2000). *Archaeology as Cultural History: Words and Things in Iron Age Greece.* Oxford.
Morris, S. P. (1992). *Daidalos and the Origins of Greek Art.* Princeton.
Moscati Castelnuovo, L. (1989). *Siris: tradizione storiografica e momenti della storia di una città della Magna Grecia.* Collection Latomus 207. Brussels.
—— ed. (2002). *Identità e prassi storica nel Mediterraneo greco.* Milan.
Most, G. (1985). 'Pindar, *Nemean* 7.64–6', *GRBS* 26, 315–31.
—— (1986). 'Pindar, Fr. 94b19–20 Sn.-M.', *ZPE* 64, 33–8.
—— (1987). *The Measures of Praise: Structure and Function in Pindar's Second Pythian and Seventh Nemean Odes.* Hypomnemata 83. Göttingen.
Mowinckel, S. (1921–4). *Psalmenstudien*, 6 vols., ii: *Das Thronbesteigungsfest Jahwähs und der Ursprung der Eschatologie* (Kristiania, 1923).
Mühll, P. von der (1976). 'Weitere pindarische Notizen', in B. Wyss, ed., *Ausgewählte Kleine Schriften.* Schweizerische Beiträge zur Altertumswissenschaft 12. Basel, 1976, 203–15. Repr. from *MH* 20 (1963), 101–2; 197–202.
Muir, E. (1981). *Civic Ritual in Renaissance Venice.* Princeton.
—— (1997). *Ritual in Early Modern Europe.* New Approaches to European History 11. Cambridge.
Mullen, W. (1982). *Choreia: Pindar and Dance.* Princeton.
Müller, K. O. (1830). *The History and Antiquity of the Doric Race.* Oxford.
Munn, N. D. (1992). 'The Cultural Anthropology of Time: A Critical Essay', *Annual Review of Anthropology* 21, 93–123.

MURRAY, G. (1912). 'Excursus on the Ritual Forms Preserved in Greek Tragedy', in HARRISON (1912), 341–63.
—— (1914). 'Hamlet and Orestes: A Study in Traditional Types'. Annual Shakespeare Lecture for the British Academy 1914. London.
MURRAY, O. (1988). 'The Ionian Revolt', *CAH* iv. 2nd edn. Cambridge, 461–90.
—— ed. (1990). *Sympotica: A Symposium on the Symposion.* Oxford.
—— (1993). *Early Greece.* 2nd edn. London.
—— and PRICE, S. F. G., eds. (1990). *The Greek City from Homer to Alexander.* Oxford.
MURRAY, P. (1981). 'Poetic Inspiration in Early Greece', *JHS* 101, 87–100.
—— and WILSON, P., eds. (2004). *Music and the Muses: The Culture of* Mousike *in the Classical Athenian City.* Oxford.
MUSTI, D. (1985*a*). 'Continuità e discontinuità tra Achei e Dori nelle tradizioni storiche', in (1985*b*), 37–71
—— ed. (1985*b*). *Le origini dei Greci. Dori e mondo egeo* (Conference, Rome, 11–13 Apr. 1983). Rome-Bari.
—— (1994*a*). *Strabone e la Magna Grecia. Città e popoli dell'Italia antica.* 2nd edn. Saggi di antichità e tradizione classica 8. Padua.
—— (1994*b*). 'Metaponto: Note sulla tradizione storica', in (1994*a*), 123–49. Repr. from *RFIC* 111 (1983), 265–91.
—— (1994*c*). '"Una città simile a Troia". Città troiane da Siri a Lavinio', in (1994*a*), 95–122. Repr. from *ArchClass* 33 (1981) 1–26.
—— (1994*d*). 'L'idea di *ΜΕΓΑΛΗ ΕΛΛΑΣ*', in (1994*a*), 61–94. Repr. from *RFIC* 114 (1986), 286–319.
—— (2004). 'Argo, il "nuovo che avanza"', in ANGELI BERNARDINI (2004*a*), 263–78.
—— and BESCHI, L. (1987). *Pausania. Guida della Grecia, Libro I. L'Attica.* 2nd edn. Milan.
—— and TORELLI, M. (1986). *Pausania. Guida della Grecia. Libro II. La Corinzia e l'Argolide.* Milan.
—— (1991). *Pausania. Guida della Grecia. Libro III. La Laconia; Libro IV. La Messenia.* Milan.
MUTH, R. (1988). *Einführung in die griechische und römische Religion.* Darmstadt.
MUTHMANN, F. (1975). *Mutter und Quelle. Studien zur Quellenverehrung im Alterum und im Mittelalter.* Basel.
MYERHOFF, B. G. (1977). 'We Don't Wrap Herring in a Printed Page: Fusion, Fictions and Continuity', in MOORE and MYERHOFF (1977*a*), 199–224.
—— (1990). 'Transformation of Consciousness in Ritual Performance: Some Thoughts and Questions', in APPEL and SCHECHNER (1990), 245–9.
NAEREBOUT, F. G. (1997). *Attractive Performances: Ancient Greek Dance: Three Preliminary Studies.* Amsterdam.
NAFISSI, M. (1997). 'Atene e Metaponto: Ancora sulla "Melanippe Desmotis" e i Neleidi', *Ostraka* 6, 337–57.
NAGY, G. (1979). *The Best of the Achaeans: Concepts of the Hero in Archaic Greek Poetry.* Baltimore.
—— (1990). *Pindar's Homer: The Lyric Possession of an Epic Past.* Baltimore.
NIELSEN, T. H. (1999). 'The Concept of Arkadia—The People, their Land, and their Organisation', in NIELSEN and ROY (1999), 16–79.
—— (2002). *Arkadia and its Poleis in the Archaic and Classical Periods.* Hypomnemata 140. Göttingen.
—— and ROY, J. (1998). 'The Azanians of Northern Arkadia', *C&M* 49, 5–44.

Nielsen, T. H. and Roy, J. eds. (1999). *Defining Ancient Arkadia. Symposium, April, 1–4, 1998.* Historisk-filosofiske Meddelelser 78. Acts of the Copenhagen Polis Centre 6. Copenhagen.

Nilsson, M. P. (1906/95). *Griechische Feste von religiöser Bedeutung (mit Ausschluß der attischen)* (Leipzig, 1906). 2nd edn., with an introd. by F. Graf. Stuttgart.

—— (1951). *Cults, Myths, Oracles and Politics in Ancient Greece.* With two appendices: the Ionian phylae, the phratries. Skrifter utgivna av Svenska institutet i Athen 8.1. Lund.

—— (1967–74). *Geschichte der griechischen Religion.* 2 vols. HAW v. 2. 3rd rev. edn. Munich.

Nixon, L., and Price, S. F. G. (1990). 'The Size and Resources of Greek Cities', in Murray and Price (1990), 137–70.

Norwood, G. (1945). *Pindar.* Berkeley.

Noth, M. (1960). 'Der Beitrag der Archäologie zur Geschichte Israels', *VT* suppl. 7, 262–82.

Oepke, A. (1934). '*ΑΜΦΙΘΑΛΕΙΣ* im griechischen und hellenistischen Kult', *Archiv für Religionswissenschaft* 31, 42–56.

Ohly, D. (1976–2001). *Die Aegineten. Die Marmorskulpturen des Tempels der Aphaia auf Aegina. Ein Katalog der Glyptothek München*, 3 vols. Munich.

Olbrich, G. (1976). 'Ein Heiligtum der Artemis Metapontina? Zur Ikonographie der Terrakotta-Figuren von S. Biagio bei Metapont', *PP* 31, 376–408.

—— (1979). *Archaische Statuetten eines Metapontiner Heiligtums.* Studia archaeologica 23. Rome.

Olson, S. D. (1998). *Aristophanes: Peace.* Ed. with intro. and comm. Oxford.

O'Neil, J. L. (1981). 'How Democratic was Hellenistic Rhodes?', *Athenaeum* 59, 468–73.

Orlandini, P. (1986). 'Incoronata—Scavi dell'Università Statale di Milano (1974–84)', in *I Greci sul Basento*, 29–56.

—— (1992). *Ricerche archeologiche all'Incoronata di Metaponto*, ii. *Dal villaggio indigeno all'emporio greco. Le strutture e i materiali del saggio T.* Milan (non vidi).

—— (1998). 'Scavi e scoperte all'Incoronata di Metaponto', in *Siritide e Metapontino* 91–4.

Osanna, M. (1992). *Chorai coloniali da Taranto a Locri: documentazione archeologica e ricostruzione storica.* Rome.

—— (1996). *Santuari e culti dell'Acaia antica.* Naples.

Osborne, R. G. (1996). *Greece in the Making 1200–479 bc.* London.

—— (1997). 'The Ecstasy and the Tragedy: Varieties of Religious Experience in Art, Drama, and Society', in Pelling (1997), 187–211.

—— (1998). 'Early Greek Colonization? The Nature of Greek Settlement in the West', in Fisher and van Wees (1998), 251–69.

—— (2004). *The Old Oligarch: Pseudo-Xenophon's Constitution of the Athenians.* Introd., trans. and comm. LACTOR 2. 2nd edn. London.

O'Sullivan, P. (2005). 'Pindar and the Statues of Rhodes', *CQ* 55, 96–104.

Padula, M., ed. (1980). *Attività archeologica in Basilicata 1964–77. Scritti in onore di Dinu Admesteanu.* Matera.

Page, D. L. (1953). *Corinna.* London.

Pais, E. (1894). *Storia della Sicilia e della Magna Grecia.* Turin.

Panzeri-Pozzetti, P. (1986). 'Ceramica di produzione coloniale', in *I Greci sul Basento*, 144–6.

Papachristodoulou, J. (1989). *Οι αρχαίοι ροδιακοί δήμοι. Ιστορική επισκόπηση. Η Ιαλυσία. Βιβλιοθήκη της εν Αθήναις Εταιρείας* 121. Athens.
—— (1992). 'Città e santuari di Rodi', *AttTar* 31 (1991), 249–73.
Papadopoulos, J. K. (2001). 'Magna Achaea: Akhaian Late Geometric and Archaic Pottery in South Italy and Sicily', *Hesperia* 70, 373–460.
—— (2002). 'Minting Identity: Coinage, Ideology and the Economics of Colonization in Akhaian Magna Graecia', *Cambridge Archaeological Journal* 12, 21–55.
—— (2003). *La dea di Sibari e il santuario ritrovato: studi sui rinvenimenti dal Timpone Motta di Francavilla Marittima*. Bollettino d'arte, volume speciale. Rome.
—— (2005). Review of G. F. la Torre, *Un tempio arcaico nel territorio dell'antica Temesa: L'edificio sacro in località di Campora San Giovanni* (Rome, 2002), *BMCR* 22 Nov. 2005.
Papapostolou, I. (1982). "*Ἀνασκαφὴ ὑστερογεωμετρικοῦ ἀποθέτη στὴ Ῥακίτα Παναχαϊκοῦ*", *PAAE*, 187–8.
Pariente, A. (1992). 'Le Monument argien des "Sept contre Thèbes"', in Piérart (1992*b*), 195–229.
—— and Touchais, G., eds. (1998), *Argos et l'Argolide. Topographie et urbanisme* (Conference, Athens–Argos 28 Apr.–1 May 1990). Athens.
—— Piérart, M., and Thalmann, J.-P. (1986). 'Argos', *BCH* 77, 763–73.
Parke, H. W. (1948). 'Consecration to Apollo. *Δεκατεύειν τῷ ἐν Δελφοῖς θεῷ*', *Hermathena* 72, 82–114.
Parker, R. (1983). *Miasma: Pollution and Purification in Early Greek Religion*. Oxford.
—— (1989). 'Spartan Religion', in A. Powell, ed., *Classical Sparta: Techniques behind her Success*. London, 142–72.
—— (1996). *Athenian Religion: A History*. Oxford.
—— (1997). 'Gods Cruel and Kind: Tragic and Civic Ideology', in Pelling (1997), 143–60.
—— (1998*a*). *Cleomenes on the Acropolis*. An Inaugural Lecture Delivered before the University of Oxford on 12 May 1997. Oxford.
—— (1998*b*). 'Pleasing Thighs: Reciprocity in Greek Religion', in C. Gill, N. Postlethwaite, and R. Seaford, eds., *Reciprocity in Ancient Greece*. Oxford, 105–25.
—— (2004*a*). 'Afterword', in De Ste. Croix (2004*a*), 411–20.
—— (2004*b*). 'Formulae of Dedication', *ThesCRA* 1, 274–6.
—— (2005). *Polytheism and Society at Athens*. Oxford.
—— (forthcoming). 'Subjection, Synoecism and Religious Life'.
—— and Obbink, D. (2001). 'Aus der Arbeit der "Inscriptiones Graecae" VIII: Three Further Inscriptions Concerning Coan Cults', *Chiron* 31, 253–75.
Peacock, J. L. (1968). *Rites of Modernization: Symbolic and Social Aspects of Indonesian Proletarian Drama*. Chicago.
Pelliccia, H. (1989). 'Pindar, *Nemean* 7.31–36 and the Syntax of Aetiology', *HSPh* 92, 71–101.
Pelling, C. B. R. (1970). *Divisions in Boeotian Politics 457–387* bc. Arnold Ancient History Prize Essay, University of Oxford.
—— ed. (1997). *Greek Tragedy and the Historian*. Oxford.
—— (2002). *Plutarch and History: Eighteen Studies*. London.
—— (2005), 'Tragedy, Rhetoric and Performance Culture', in J. Gregory, ed., *A Companion to Greek Tragedy*. Oxford, 83–102.
—— (2007). 'Ion's *Epidemiai* and Plutarch's *Ion*', in V. Jennings and A. Katsaros, eds., *The World of Ion of Chios. Mnemos.* Suppl. 288. Leiden–Boston, 75–109.

Perlman, P. J. (2000). *City and Sanctuary in Ancient Greece: The Theorodokia in the Peloponnese.* Hypomnemata 121. Göttingen.

Perrot, G., and Chipiez, C. (1882–1914). *Histoire de l'art dans l'antiquité.* 10 vols. Paris.

Petropoulos, M. (1987–8). "*Τρίτη ανασκαφική περίοδος στο Άνω Μαζαράκι (Ρακίτα) Αχαΐας*", in *Πρακτικά του Γ' Διεθνούς Συνεδρίου Πελοποννησιακών Σπουδών*. Athens, 81–96.

—— (1992–3). "*Περίπτερος αψιδωτός γεωμετρικός ναός στο Άνω Μαζαράκι (Ρακίτα) Πατρών*", in *Πρακτικά του Δ' Διεθνούς Συνεδρίου Πελοποννησιακών Σπουδών, Κόρινθος*, 9–16 *Σεπτεμβρίου* 1990. vol. ii. Athens, 141–58.

—— (1997). "*Νεώτερα στοιχεία από την ανασκαφή του γεωμετρικού ναού στο Άνω Μαζαράκι (Ρακίτα) Πατρών*", in *Πρακτικά του Ε' Διεθνούς Συνεδρίου Πελοποννησιακών Σπουδών, Ναύπλιον*, 6–10 *Σεπτεμβρίου* 1995. Athens, 165–92.

—— (2001). "*Γεωμετρικός ναός Ρακίτας — Λατρευόμενη θεότητα*", in Mitsopoulos-Leon (2001*a*), 39–45.

—— (2002). 'The Geometric Temple of Ano Mazaraki (Rakita) in Achaia during the Period of Colonisation', in Greco (2002), 143–64.

Pettersson, M. (1992). *Cults of Apollo at Sparta: The Hyakinthia, the Gymnopaidiai and the Karneia.* Skrifter utgivna av Svenska institutet i Athen 12. Stockholm.

Pfeijffer, I. L. (1999). *Three Aeginetan Odes of Pindar: A Commentary on Nemean V, Nemean II & Pythian VIII.* Mnemosyne suppl. 197. Leiden.

Pfister, F. (1974). *Der Reliquienkult im Altertum*, 2 vols. Berlin (orig. Giessen, 1909–12).

Phaklares, P. W. (1990). *Αρχαία Κυνουρία. Ανθρώπινη δραστηριότητα και περιβάλλον. Δημοσιεύματα του Αρχαιολογικού Δελτίου* 43. Athens.

Philipp, H. (1968). *Tektonon Daidala. Der bildende Künstler und sein Werk im vorplatonischen Schrifttum.* Quellen und Schriften zur bildenden Kunst 2. Berlin.

—— (1994). 'Olympia, die Peloponnes und die Westgriechen', *JDAI* 109, 77–92.

Philippson, A. (1950–9). *Die griechischen Landschaften: eine Landeskunde*, 4 vols. ed. H. Lehmann and E. Kirsten. Frankfurt.

Phythian-Adams, Ch. (1972). 'Ceremony and the Citizen: The Communal Year at Coventry, 1450–1550', in P. Clark and P. Slack, eds., *Crisis and Order in English Towns, 1500–1700.* London, 57–85.

Picard, C. (1959). 'Oracles et sanctuaires. Les Deux Temples et la purification à Délos', *CRAI*, 321–34.

—— (1992). 'Recherches récentes autour du temple d'Apollon à Délos', *AttTar* 31 (1991), 231–47.

Pickering, W. S. F. (1984). *Durkheim's Sociology of Religion: Themes and Theories.* London.

Piérart, M. (1985*a*). 'Le tradizioni epiche e il loro rapporto con la questione dorica: Argo e l'Argolide', in Musti (1985*b*), 277–92.

—— (1985*b*). 'A propos des subdivisions de la population argienne', *BCH* 109, 345–56.

—— (1990). 'Un oracle d'Apollon à Argos', *Kernos* 3, 319–33.

—— (1992*a*). 'Les Honneurs de Persée et d'Héraclès', in C. Bonnet and C. Jourdain-Annequin, eds., *Héraclès d'une rive à l'autre de la Méditerranée. Bilan et perspectives* (Conference, Rome, 15–16 Sept., 1989). Brussels–Rome, 223–44.

—— ed. (1992*b*). *Polydipsion Argos. Argos de la fin des palais mycéniens à la constitution de l'état classique* (Conference, Fribourg (Switzerland), 7–9 May 1987). BCH suppl. 22. Paris.

—— (1996). 'Le Culte de Dionysos à Argos', *Kernos* 9, 423–9.

PIÉRART, M. (1997). 'L'Attitude d'Argos à l'égard des autres cités d'Argolide', in HANSEN (1997), 321–51.
—— (2000). 'Argos. Une autre démocratie?', in FLENSTED-JENSEN, NIELSEN, and RUBINSTEIN (2000), 297–314.
—— (2003). 'The Common Oracle of the Milesians and the Argives (Herodotus 6.19 and 77)', in DEROW and PARKER (2003), 275–96.
—— (2004). 'Deux voisins: Argos et Épidaure (mythes, société, histoire)', in ANGELI BERNARDINI (2004*a*), 19–34.
PIKOULAS, G. A. (1981–2). "*Η Αρκαδική Αζανία*", in *Πρακτικά Β' Διεθνοῦς Συνεδρίου Πελοποννησιακών Σπουδών*. Athens, 269–81.
PILAFIDIS-WILLIAMS, K. (1995). 'A Mycenaean Terracotta Figure from Mount Oros on Aigina', in C. MORRIS, ed., *Klados. Essays in Honour of J. N. Coldstream*. BICS suppl. 63. London, 229–34.
PINGIATOGLOU, S. (1981). *Eileithyia*. Würzburg.
POLITES, N. G. (1994 (1904)). *Παραδώσεις. Μελετὰ περὶ τοῦ βίου καὶ τῆς γλώσσης τοῦ ἑλληνικοῦ λαοῦ*, 2 vols. Athens.
PÖTSCHER, W. (1996–7). 'Das Hera-Fest im Heraion von Argos, (Hdt. 1, 31 und Eur. El. 169 ff.)', *AAntHung* 37, 25–36.
POUILLOUX, J. (1970). 'Callianax, gendre de Diagoras de Rhodes. A propos de la VIIe Olympique de Pindare', *RPh* ser. 3, 44, 206–14.
POULSEN, E. (1994). *Asine II. Results of the Excavations East of the Acropolis 1970–1974.* Fasc. 6.2. *The Post-Geometric Settlement Material and Tombs of the Hellenistic Period.* Skrifter utgivna av Svenska institutet i Athen 4. 24.6.2.
PRICE, S. R. F. (1984). *Rituals and Power: The Roman Imperial Cult in Asia Minor.* Cambridge.
PRINZ, F. (1979). *Gründungsmythen und Sagenchronologie.* Zetemata 72. Munich.
PRITCHETT, W. K. (1971–91). *The Greek State at War*, 5 vols. Berkeley–London.
PRODI, P. (1987). *The Papal Prince, One Body and Two Souls: The Papal Monarchy in Early Modern Europe*, trans. S. Haskins. Cambridge.
PROST, F. (1999). 'La Statue cultuelle d'Apollon à Délos', *REG* 112, 37–60.
PUGLIESE CARRATELLI, G. (1951). 'La formazione dello stato rodio', *SCO* 1, 77–88.
—— (1953). 'Culti aniconici a Rodi e Lesbo', *SCO* 3, 5–8.
—— (1952–4) 'Supplemento epigrafico rodio. Documenti sulle feste', *ASAA* 30–2, 247–316 (pub. in 1955).
PURCELL, N. (2005). 'The View from the Customs House', in HARRIS (2005), 200–32.
RAAFLAUB, K. A. (2004). *The Discovery of Freedom in Ancient Greece*, trans. R. Franciscono; ed., rev. and updated. Chicago–London.
RADCLIFFE-BROWN, A. R. (1964 (1933)). *The Andaman Islanders.* New York (orig. Cambridge, 1933).
RADERMACHER, L. (1950). 'Die Mädchen aus dem Hyperboreerland', *RhM* 92, 325–9.
RADT, S. L. (1958). *Pindars zweiter und sechster Paian: Text, Scholien und Kommentar.* Amsterdam.
RAPPAPORT, R. (1979). *Ecology, Meaning, and Religion.* 2nd edn. Berkeley.
—— (1999). *Ritual and Religion in the Making of Humanity.* Cambridge.
RATINAUD-LACHKAR, I. (2004). 'Insoumise Asiné? Pour une mise en perspective des sources littéraires et archéologiques relatives à la destruction d'Asiné par Argos in 715 avant notre ère', *OAth* 29, 73–88.
RAVEL, O. (1928). *The Colts of Ambracia.* Numismatic Notes and Monographs 37. New York.

Realacci, P. (1976). 'I Telchines, "maghi" nel segno della trasformazione', in P. Xella, ed., *Magia. Studi di storia delle religioni in memoria di Raffaella Garosi*. Rome, 197–206.

Rechenauer, G. (1991). *Thukydides und die hippokratischen Schriften. Der Einfluß der Medizin auf Zielsetzung und Darstellung des Geschichtswerks*. Zurich–New York.

Redfield, J. (1982). 'Notes on the Greek Wedding', *Arethusa* 15, 181–201.

—— (2003). *The Locrian Maidens: Love and Death in Greek Italy*. Princeton.

Regenbogen, O. (1931). 'Die Naturwissenschaft der Peripatetiker', *Scientia* 50, 345–54. Repr. in *Kleine Schriften*, ed. F. Dirlmeier (Munich, 1961), 141–94; 286–95.

Reger, G. (1994). *Regionalism and Change in the Economy of Independent Delos, 314–167 B.C.* Berkeley–Oxford.

—— (1997). 'Islands with One Polis versus Islands with Several Poleis', in Hansen (1997), 450–92.

—— (2001). 'The Mykonian Synoikismos', *REA* 103, 157–81.

Reichel, W., and Wilhelm, A. (1901). 'Das Heiligthum der Artemis zu Lusoi', *JÖAI* 4, 1–89.

Revermann, M. (2006). *Comic Business: Theatricality, Dramatic Technique, and Performance Contexts of Aristophanic Comedy*. Oxford.

Riccioni, G. (1966). 'Delos e i Letoidi offerenti in una pyxis di Spina. Nuovo contributo alla conoscenza del culto di Apollo Delio', *Arte antica e moderna* 9, 34–6, 173–81.

Riedweg, C. (2002). *Pythagoras. Leben. Lehre. Nachwirkung. Eine Einführung*. Munich.

Ringwood, I. C. (1927). *Agonistic Features of Local Greek Festivals Chiefly from Inscriptional Evidence*. Poughkeepsie.

Riu, X. (1999). *Dionysism and Comedy*. Lanham.

Rizakis, A. D. (2002). 'L'Achaie péloponnésienne: structure spatiale et géographie historique', in Greco (2002), 43–66.

Robert, L. (1934). 'Diodore, xiv, 84, 3', *RPh* 60, 43–8. Repr. in *Opera Minora Selecta*, vol. i (Amsterdam, 1969), 569–74.

—— (1940–65). *Hellenica. Recueil d'épigraphie, de numismatique et d'antiquités grecques*. 12 vols. Limoges.

—— (1969). '*ΑΜΦΙΘΑΛΗΣ*' in *Opera Minora Selecta*, vol. i. Amsterdam, 633–43.

Roberts, E. S. (1887–1905). *An Introduction to Greek Epigraphy*. Cambridge.

Robertson, N. (1978). 'The Myth of the First Sacred War', *CQ* 28, 38–73.

—— (1980*a*). 'The True Nature of the "Delian League" 478–461 B.C.', *AJAH* 5, 64–96, 110–33.

—— (1980*b*). 'The Dorian Migration and Corinthian Ritual', *CPh* 75, 1–22.

—— (1980*c*). 'Timocreon and Themistocles', *AJPh* 101, 61–78.

—— (1992). *Festivals and Legends: The Formation of Greek Cities in the Light of Public Ritual*. Toronto.

—— (1995). 'The Magic Properties of Female Age-Groups in Greek Ritual', *AncW* 26.2, 193–203.

—— (1996). 'New Light on Demeter's Mysteries: The Festival Proerosia', *GRBS* 37, 319–75.

Robertson Smith, W. (1889). *Lectures on the Religion of the Semites*. Edinburgh.

Robinson, A. (2002). *The Life and Work of Jane Ellen Harrison*. Oxford.

Robinson, R. (1942). 'New Greek Bronze Vases. A Commentary on Pindar', *AJA* 46, 172–97.

Rocco, G. (1996), 'Il tempio di Athana Polias e Zeus Polieus', in Livadiotti and Rocco (1996), 43–6.

Roesch, P. (1965). *Thespies et la confédération béotienne*. Paris.

—— (1982). *Études Béotiennes*. Paris.

ROESCH, P. (1987). 'Y eut-il des rapports entre les Béotiens, les Épirotes et les Illyriens', in CABANES (1987), 179–83.
—— (1989). 'L'Aulos et les aulètes en Béotie', in BEISTER and BUCKLER (1989), 203–14.
RÖHRICH, L. (1964). *Märchen und Wirklichkeit.* 2nd edn. Wiesbaden (1st edn. 1956).
ROMM, J. (1989). 'Herodotus and Mythic Geography: The Case of the Hyperboreans', *TAPhA* 119, 97–113.
RONCONI, L. (1997). 'La terra chiamata Italia', in ANTONETTI (1997), 109–19.
ROSALDO, R. (1993). *Culture and Truth: The Remaking of Social Analysis.* London (1st edn. Boston, 1989).
ROSENBLOOM, D. (1993). 'Shouting "Fire" in a Crowded Theater: Phrynichos's Capture of Miletos and the Politics of Fear in Early Attic Tragedy', *Philologus* 137, 159–96.
RÖSLER, W. (1980). *Dichter und Gruppe: eine Untersuchung zu den Bedingungen und zur historischen Funktion früher griechischer Lyrik am Beispiel Alkaios.* Theorie und Geschichte der Literatur und der schönen Künste. Texte und Abhandlungen 50. Munich.
ROSTOVTZEFF, M. (1937). 'Alexandrien und Rhodos', *Klio* 30, 70–6.
ROUSSEL, P. (1987). *Délos, colonie athénienne.* Rev. and enl. edn. Bibliothèque des Écoles françaises d'Athènes et de Rome 111. Paris.
ROUX, G. (1957). 'Le Sanctuaire argien d'Apollon Pythéen', *REG* 70, 474–87.
—— (1961). *L'Architecture de l'Argolide aux IVe et IIIe siècle avant J.-C.* Paris.
—— (1976). *Delphes, son oracle et ses dieux.* Paris.
—— (1977/9). 'Le Vrai Temple d'Apollon à Délos', *REG* 90 (1977), xxii–xxiv; *BCH* 103 (1979), 109–35.
—— (1984). 'Politique et religion. Delphes et Délos à l'époque archaïque', in J. HARMATTA, ed., *Actes du vii*[e] *Congrès de la Fédération internationale des Associations d'Études classiques.* Budapest, 97–105.
RUBENSOHN, O. (1949). 'Paros', *RE* xxxvi, 1781–872.
—— (1962). *Das Delion von Paros.* Wiesbaden.
RUBIN, N. F. (1980–1). 'Pindar's Creation of Epinician Symbols: *Olympians* 7 and 6', *CW* 74, 67–87.
RUSCHENBUSCH, E. (1982). 'Stasis und politischer Umsturz in Rhodos', *Hermes* 110, 495–8.
RUTHERFORD, I. C. (1988).'Pindar on the Birth of Apollo', *CQ* 38, 65–75.
—— (1990). 'Paeans by Simonides', *HSPh* 93, 169–209.
—— (1997). 'For the Aeginetans to Aiakos a Prosodion: An Unnoticed Title at Pindar, Paean 6, 123, and its Significance for the Poem', *ZPE* 118, 1–21.
—— (2000). 'Keos or Delos? State-Pilgrimage and the Performance of Paean 4', in M. CANNATÀ FERA and S. GRANDOLINI, eds., *Poesia e religione in Grecia: studi in onore di G. Aurelio Privitera,* 2 vols. Naples, 605–12.
—— (2001). *Pindar's Paeans: A Reading of the Fragments with a Survey of the Genre.* Oxford.
—— (2004). '*Χορὸς εἷς ἐκ τῆσδε τῆς πόλεως* (Xen. *Mem.* 3.3.12): Song-Dance and State-Pilgrimage at Athens', in MURRAY and WILSON (2004), 67–90.
—— (2005). 'Mestra at Athens: Hesiod fr. 43 and the Poetics of Panhellenism', in HUNTER (2005), 99–117.
—— (forthcoming). 'The Koan-Dalian Ritual Complex: Apollo and *theoria* in a Sacred Law from Kos', in ATHANASSAKI, MARTIN, and MILLER (forthcoming).
SAHLINS, M. (1976). *Culture and Practical Reason.* Chicago.
SAÏD, S. (1993). 'Tragic Argos', in SOMMERSTEIN *et al.* (1993), 167–89.
SAKELLARIOU, M. B. (1977). *Peuples préhelléniques d'origine indoeuropéenne.* Athens.

Sakellariou, M. B. (1984). 'La Migration des Aenianes', in *Aux origines de l'hellénisme: La Crète et la Grèce: hommage à Henri van Effenterre*. Publications de la Sorbonne. Série Histoire ancienne et médiévale 15, 173–80.

—— (1990). *Between Memory and Oblivion: The Transmission of Early Greek Historical Traditions*. Meletemata 12. Paris.

Sale, W. (1961). 'The Hyperborean Maidens and Delos', *HThR* 54, 70–89.

Samuel, A. E. (1972). *Greek and Roman Chonology: Calendars and Years in Classical Antiquity*. HAW i.7. Munich.

Sanchez, P. (2001). *L'Amphictionie des Pyles et de Delphes: recherches sur son rôle historique, des origines au IIe siècle de notre ère*. Historia ES 148. Stuttgart.

Santi Amantini, L. (1977). 'L'inno omerico ad Apollo e l'origine dell'arcaica anfizionia delica', in *Contributi di storia antica in onore di A. Garzetti*. Genoa, 31–60.

Savignoni, L. (1913 (1915)). 'La purificazione delle Pretidi', *Ausonia* 8, 145–78.

Sbordone, F. (1940). 'Parteni pindarici e dafneforie tebane', *Athenaeum* 18, 26–50.

Schachter, A. (1967). 'A Boeotian Cult Type', *BICS* 14, 1–16.

—— (1972). 'Some Underlying Cult Patterns in Boeotia', in *Proceedings of the First International Congress on Boiotian Antiquities McGill University Montréal 18 March 1972*. Teiresias suppl. 1, 17–30.

—— (1976). 'Homeric Hymn to Apollo, lines 229–38 (the Onchestos episode): Another Interpretation', *BICS* 23, 102–13.

—— (1978). 'La Fête des Pamboiotia. Le dossier épigraphique', *CEA* 8, 81–107.

—— (1981–94). *Cults of Boiotia*, 4 vols. BICS suppl. 38. London.

—— (1989). 'Boiotia in the Sixth Century', in Beister and Buckler (1989), 73–86.

—— (1994). 'The Politics of Dedication: Athenian Dedications at the Sanctuary of Apollo Ptoieus in Boeotia', in Hornblower and Osborne (1994), 291–306.

—— (2000). 'The Daphnephoria of Thebes', in Angeli Bernardini (2000), 99–123.

Schaefer, J. (1957). *Studien zu den griechischen Reliefpithoi des 8.–6. Jahrhunderts v. Chr. aus Kreta, Rhodos, Tenos und Boiotien*. Kallmünz.

Schauer, C. (1998). "*Κεραμεική από το αρχαϊκό ιερό της Αρτέμιδος στους Λουσούς*", in *Πρακτικά του Ε′ Διεθνούς Συνεδρίου Πελοποννησιακών Σπουδών*. Athens, 257–71.

—— (2001). 'Zur frühen Keramik aus dem Artemisheiligtum von Lousoi', in Mitsopoulos-Leon (2001*a*), 155–9.

Schechner, R. (1988). *Essays on Performance Theory 1970–1976*. Rev. and expanded edn. New York (orig. 1977).

Scheer, T. S. (1993). *Mythische Vorväter: zur Bedeutung griechischer Heroenmythen im Selbstverständnis kleinasiatischer Städte*. Münchener Arbeiten zur alten Geschichte 7. Munich.

Scheffer, C. (1992). 'Boiotian Festival Scenes: Competition, Consumption and Cult in Archaic Black Figure', in Hägg (1992*b*), 117–41.

Scheid, J. (2005). *Quand faire, c'est croire. Les rites sacrificiels des Romains*. Paris.

Schiering, W. (1969). *Die Bronzestatuette des Zeus von Dodona: Einführung*. Werkmonographien zur bildenden Kunst 134. Stuttgart.

Schlesier, R. (1994). *Kulte, Mythen und Gelehrte. Anthropologie der Antike seit 1800*. Frankfurt.

Schmid, W., and Staehlin, O. (1934). *Geschichte der griechischen Litteratur*, i.2. *Die griechische Literatur zur Zeit der attischen Hegemonie nach dem Eingreifen der Sophistik*. HAW vii.1.3. Munich.

Schmidt, D. (1999). 'An Unusual Victory List from Keos: IG XII, 5, 608 and the Dating of Bakchylides', *JHS* 119, 67–85.

SCHMITT, J.-C. (1999). 'Rites', in J. Le FOGG and J.-C. SCHMITT, *Dictionnaire raisonné de l'occident médiéval*. Paris, 965–84.

SCHMITT PANTEL, P. (1985). 'Banquet et cité grecque. Quelques questions suscités par les recherches récentes ', *MEFRA* 97, 135–58.

SCHMITT PANTEL, P. (1990). 'Sacrificial Meal and Symposium: Two Models of Civic Institutions in the Archaic City', in MURRAY (1990), 14–33.

—— (1992). *La Cité au banquet: histoire des repas publics dans les cités grecques*. Collection de l'École française de Rome 157. Paris–Rome.

SCHÖNBERGER, J. K. (1942). "Κωπώ", *Glotta* 29, 87–9.

SCHRÖDER, S. (1999). *Geschichte und Theorie der Gattung Paian. Eine kritische Untersuchung mit einem Ausblick auf Behandlungen und Auffassung der lyrischen Gattungen bei den alexandrinischen Philologen*. BzA 121. Stuttgart.

SCHUIR, M. (1930–40). 'Aitiologischer Schluß', in J. BOLTE and L. MACKENSEN, eds., *Handwörterbuch des deutschen Märchens*, vol. i. Berlin, 46–7.

SCHULLER, M. (1982). 'Der Artemistempel im Delion auf Paros', *AA* 231–44.

—— (1985). 'Die dorische Architektur der Kykladen in spätarchaischer Zeit', *JdI* 100, 319–98.

—— and OHNESORG, A. (1991). *Der Artemistempel im Delion auf Paros*. Berlin.

SCHUMACHER, R. W. M. (1993). 'Three Related Sanctuaries of Poseidon: Geraistos, Kalaureia and Tainaron', in HÄGG and MARINATOS (1993), 62–87.

SCODEL, R. (1983). 'Timocreon's Encomium of Aristides', *ClAnt* 2, 102–7.

—— ed. (1993). *Theater and Society in the Classical World*. Ann Arbor.

SEAFORD, R. (1988). 'The Eleventh Ode of Bacchylides: Hera, Artemis and the Absence of Dionysos', *JHS* 108, 118–36.

—— (1994). *Reciprocity and Ritual: Homer and Tragedy in the Developing City-State*. Oxford.

—— (1996). *Euripides Bacchae*. With an introduction, translation, and commentary, Warminster.

SEAGER, R., and TUPLIN, C. J. (1980). 'The Freedom of the Greeks in Asia: On the Origins of a Concept and the Creation of a Slogan', *JHS* 100, 141–54.

SEALEY, R. (1966). 'The Origins of the Delian League', in E. BADIAN *et al.*, *Ancient Societies and Institutions. Studies Presented to Victor Ehrenberg on his 75th Birthday*. Oxford, 233–55.

SEELIGMANN, J. L. (1961). 'Aetiological Elements in Biblical Historiography', *Zion* 26, 141–69.

SEGAL, C. P. (1967). 'Pindar's Seventh Nemean', *TAPhA* 98, 431–80.

—— (1976). 'Bacchylides Reconsidered: Epithets and the Dynamics of Lyric Narrative', *QUCC* 22, 99–130; revised in (1998), 251–80.

—— (1998). *Aglaia: The Poetry of Alcman, Sappho, Pindar, Bacchylides, and Corinna*. Lanham–Oxford.

SEGAL, R. A. (1980). 'The Myth-Ritualist Theory of Religion', *Journal for the Scientific Study of Religion* 19, 173–85.

—— ed. (1998). *The Myth and Ritual Theory: An Anthology*. Oxford.

SEGRE, M. (1951). 'Rituali rodii di sacrifici', *PP* 6, 139–53.

SELTMAN, C. T. (1928). 'The Offerings of the Hyperboreans', *CQ* 22, 155–9.

SEVERYNS, A. (1938–63). *Recherches sur la Chrestomathie de Proclos*, 4 vols. Bibliothèque de la Faculté de Philosophie et Lettres de l'Université de Liège, fasc. 78–9, 132, 170. Paris.

SFYOERAS, P. (1993). 'Fireless Sacrifices: Pindar *Olympian* 7 and the Panathenaic Festival', *AJPh* 114, 1–26.

SHEAR, T. L. (1987). 'Tax Angle, Ancient Style', *ASCS Newsletter*, Spring 1987, 8.

SHERWIN-WHITE, S. (1978). *Ancient Cos: An Historical Study from the Dorian Settlement to the Imperial Period.* Hypomnemata 51. Göttingen.

SIMON, E. (1997). 'Pindar und Delos', *JDAI* 112, 247–59.

SINATRA, D. (1994). 'Amitaonidi e Pelopidi in Argolide', *RCCM* 36, 87–95.

SINGER, M., ed. (1959). *Traditional India: Structure and Change.* Philadelphia.

SINN, U. (1980). 'Ein Fundkomplex aus dem Artemis-Heiligtum von Lousoi im Badischen Landesmuseum', *Jahrbuch der Staatlichen Kunstsammlungen in Baden-Württemberg* 17, 25–40.

—— (1991). 'Olympia. Die Stellung der Wettkämpfe im Kult des Zeus Olympios', *Nikephoros* 4, 31–54.

—— (1992). 'The Sacred Herd of Artemis at Lousoi', in HÄGG (1992*b*), 177–87.

—— (2000). 'Greek Sanctuaries as Places of Refuge', in HÄGG and MARINATOS (1993) 88–109. Repr. in BUXTON (2000), 155–79.

Siris-Polieion. Fonti letterarie e nuova documentazione archeologica (Conference, Policoro, 8–10 June 1984). Galatina.

Siritide e Metapontino. Storie di due territori coloniali (Conference, Policoro, 31 Oct.–2 Nov. 1991). Cahiers du Centre Jean Bérard 20 (Naples, 1998).

SITZLER, J. (1911). 'Zum sechsten Päan Pindars', *Wochenschrift für Klassische Philologie* 28, 1015–18.

SKINNER, Q. (1981). 'The World as Stage', *New York Review of Books*, 16 Apr. 1981.

SMARCZYK, B. (1990). *Untersuchungen zur Religionspolitik und politischen Propaganda Athens im Delisch-Attischen Seebund.* Quellen und Forschungen zur antiken Welt 5. Munich.

SMEND, R. (1968). *Elemente alttestamentlichen Geschichtsdenkens.* Theologische Studien 95. Zurich.

—— (1984). *Die Entstehung des alten Testaments.* 3rd edn. Theologische Wissensschaft 1. Stuttgart (1st edn. Stuttgart, 1978).

SMITH, J. Z. (1987). *To Take Place: Toward Theory in Ritual.* Chicago.

—— (1998). 'Constructing a Small Place', in B. Z. KEDAR and R. J. ZWI WERBLOWSKY, eds., *Sacred Space: Shrine, City, Land. Proceedings of the International Conference in Memory of Joshua Prawer.* London, 18–31.

SMITH, O. (1967). 'An Interpretation of Pindar's Seventh Olympian Ode', *C&M* 28, 172–85.

SMITH, P. (1992). Review of C. Bell, *Ritual Theory, Ritual Practice* (New York–Oxford, 1992), *American Journal of Sociology* 98, 420–2.

SNELL. B. (1932). 'Das Bruchstück eines Paians von Bakchylides', *Hermes* 67, 1–13.

—— (1965). *Dichtung und Gesellschaft. Studien zum Einfluß der Dichter auf das Soziale Denken und Verhalten im alten Griechenland.* Hamburg.

SNODGRASS, A. M. (1988). *Cyprus and Early Greek History: Fourth Annual Lecture on History and Archaeology.* Cyprus.

SOMMERSTEIN, A. H., *et al.* eds. (1993). *Tragedy, Comedy and the Polis: Papers from the Greek Drama Conference. Nottingham, 18–20 July 1990.* Bari.

—— (1998). *Aristophanes: Ecclesiazusae.* Ed. with transl. and notes. Warminster.

SORDI, M. (1966). 'Mitologia e propaganda nella Beozia antica', *A&R* 11, 15–24.

SOURVINOU-INWOOD, C. (1979). *Theseus as Son and Stepson: A Tentative Illustration of Greek Mythological Mentality.* London.

—— (1987). 'Myth as History: The Previous Owners of the Delphic Oracle', in BREMMER (1987), 215–41.

Sourvinou-Inwood, C. (1988). *Studies in Girls' Transitions: Aspects of the Arkteia and Age Representation in Attic Iconography.* Athens.

—— (1990). 'What is Polis Religion?' in Murray and Price (1990), 295–322. Repr. in Buxton (2000), 1–37.

—— (1991*a*). *Reading Greek Culture: Texts and Images, Ritual and Myths.* Oxford.

—— (1991*b*). 'Persephone and Aphrodite at Locri: A Model for Personality Definitions in Greek Religion', in (1991*a*), 147–88.

—— (1994). 'Something to Do with Athens: Tragedy and Ritual', in Hornblower and Osborne (1994), 269–90.

—— (2003*a*). *Tragedy and Athenian Religion.* Lanham–Oxford.

—— (2003*b*). 'Herodotus (and others) on Pelasgians: Some Perceptions of Ethnicity', in Derow and Parker (2003), 103–44.

—— (2005). *Hylas, the Nymphs, Dionysos and Others: Myth, Ritual, Ethnicity: Martin P. Nilsson Lecture on Greek Religion, delivered 1997 at the Swedish Institute at Athens.* Skrifter utgivna av Svenska institutet i Athen. 8.19. Stockholm.

Spadea, R. (1996). *Il Tesoro di Hera. Scoperte nel santuario di Hera Lacinia a Capo Colonna di Crotone.* Museo Baracco, 28 Mar.–30 June 1996. Milan.

—— (1997). 'Santuari di Hera a Crotone', in De la Genière (1997), 235–59.

Spencer, P. (1985). *Society and the Dance: The Social Anthropology of Process and Performance.* Cambridge.

Sperber, D. (1975). *Rethinking Symbolism*, trans. A. Morton. Cambridge (orig. *Symbolisme en général.* Paris, 1974).

Spyropoulos, T. (1973). "*Εἰδήσεις ἐκ Βοιωτίας*", *AAA* 6, 375–95.

—— (1975). "*Ἀνασκαφὴ παρὰ τὴν Κορωνείαν Βοιωτίας*", *PAAE*, 392–414.

Stadter, Ph. (1965). *Plutarch's Historical Methods: An Analysis of the Mulierum Virtutes.* Cambridge.

—— (1989). *A Commentary on Plutarch's Pericles.* Chapel Hill–London.

Stazio, A. (1983). 'Moneta e scambi', in G. Pugliese Carratelli, ed., *Megale Hellas: storia e civiltà della Magna Grecia.* Milan, 103–69.

Stehle, E. (1997). *Performance and Gender in Ancient Greece: Nondramatic Poetry in its Setting.* Princeton.

Steinbrecher, M. (1985). *Der delisch-attische Seebund und die athenisch-spartanischen Beziehungen in der Kimonischen Ära* (ca. 478/7–462/1). Palingenesia 21. Stuttgart.

Steinhart, M. (2007). ''From Ritual to Narrative', in Csapo and Miller (2007), 196–220.

Stern, J. (1965). 'Bestial Imagery in Bacchylides' Ode 11', *GRBS* 6, 275–82.

Stewart, A. (1982). 'Dionysos at Delphi: The Pediments of the Sixth Temple of Apollo and Religious Reform in the Age of Alexander', in B. Barr-Sharrar and E. N. Borza, eds., *Macedonia and Greece in Late Classical and Early Hellenistic Times.* Studies in the History of Art 10. Washington, 205–27.

Stiglitz, R. (1967). *Die grossen Göttinnen Arkadiens. Der Kultname ΜΕΓΑΛΑΙ ΘΕΑΙ und seine Grundlagen.* Sonderschriften des Österreichischen Archäologischen Instituts in Wien 15. Vienna.

Storey, I. C. (2003). *Eupolis: Poet of Old Comedy.* Oxford.

Straten, F. T. van (1995). *Hiera Kala: Images of Animal Sacrifice in Archaic and Classical Greece.* Religions in the Graeco-Roman World 127. Leiden.

Strid, O. (1999). *Die Dryoper. Eine Untersuchung der Überlieferung,* Acta Universitatis Upsaliensis. Studia Graeca Upsaliensia 20. Uppsala.

Strøm, I. (1988). 'The Early Sanctuary of the Argive Heraion and its external relations (8th–early 6th cent. B.C.): The Monumental Architecture', *AArch* 59, 173–203.

STRØM, I. (1995). 'The Early Sanctuary of the Argive Heraion and its External Relations (8th–early 6th Century B.C.)', *Proceedings of the Danish Institute at Athens* 1, 37–128.

—— (1998). 'The Early Sanctuary of the Argive Heraion and its External Relations (8th–early 6th cent. B.C.). Bronze Imports and Archaic Greek Bronzes', *Proceedings of the Danish Institute at Athens* 2, 37–125.

STROUD, R. S. (1998). *The Athenian Grain-Tax Law of 374/3 B.C.* Hesperia suppl. 29. Princeton.

STYLIANOU, P. J. (1983). 'Thucydides, the Panionian Festival and the Ephesia (iii.104), Again', *Historia* 32, 245–9.

STYRENIUS, C.-G. (1998). *Asine : en svensk utgrävningsplats i Grekland.* Stockholm

SUAREZ DE LA TORRE, E. (1992). 'Les Pouvoirs des devins et les récits mythiques. L'Exemple de Mélampous', *LEC* 60, 3–21.

—— (1997). 'Neoptolemos at Delphi', *Kernos* 10, 153–76.

SULLIVAN, A. E. (1986). 'Sound and Senses: Towards a Hermeneutics of Performance', *History of Religions* 26, 1–33.

SULLIVAN, S. D. (1982). 'A Strand of Thought in Pindar, Olympians 7', *TAPhA* 112, 215–23.

SUSINI, G. (1963–4). 'Supplemento epigrafico di Caso, Scarpanto, Saro, Calchi, Alinnia e Tilo', *ASAA* 41–2, 203–92.

SYMEONOGLOU, S. (1985). *The Topography of Thebes from the Bronze Age to Modern Times.* Princeton.

TAMBIAH, S. J. (1968). 'The Magical Power of Words', *Man* NS 3, no. 2, 175–208. Repr. in (1985), 17–59.

—— (1970). *Buddhism and the Spirit Cults in North-East Thailand.* Cambridge.

—— (1985 (1981)). *A Performative Approach to Ritual.* Radcliffe Brown Lecture in Social Anthropology 1979. Oxford. Repr. in (1985) 123–66.

—— (1985). *Culture, Thought and Social Action: An Anthropological Perspective.* Cambridge–London.

—— (1990). *Magic, Science, Religion, and the Scope of Rationality.* Lewis Henry Morgan Lectures 1984. Cambridge.

TAPLIN, O. (1999). 'Spreading the Word through Performance', in GOLDHILL and OSBORNE (1999), 33–57.

—— (2007). *Pots and Plays: Interactions between Tragedy and Greek Vase-Painting of the Fourth Century B.C.* Oxford–New York.

TAUSEND, K. (1992). *Amphiktyonie und Symmachie. Formen zwischenstaatlicher Beziehungen im archaischen Griechenland.* Stuttgart.

—— (1993). 'Zur Bedeutung von Lousoi in archaischer Zeit', *JÖAI* 62, Beiblatt, 13–26.

—— (1995*a*). 'Von Artemis zu Artemis? Der antike Weg von Lousoi nach Pheneos', *JÖAI* 64, Beiblatt, 1–20.

—— (1995*b*). 'Pheidon von Argos und das argolische Aigina', *GB* 21, 1–5.

—— (1999). 'Die Topographie des nordostarkadischen Raumes', in id., ed., *Pheneos und Lousoi. Untersuchungen zu Geschichte und Topographie Nordostarkadiens.* Grazer Altertumskundliche Studien 5. Frankfurt a. M., 17–27.

TERPSTRA, N. (1995). *Lay Confraternities and Civic Religion in Renaissance Bologna.* Cambridge.

—— ed. (2000). *The Politics of Ritual Kinship: Confraternities and Social Order in Early Modern Italy.* Cambridge.

THEMELIS, P. (1971). *Mykonos, Delos. Archaeological Guide.* Athens.

Thiersch, H. (1928). *Äginetische Studien*. Göttingen.
Thomas, R. (1989). *Oral Tradition and Written Record in Classical Athens*. Cambridge.
—— (1992). *Literacy and Orality in Ancient Greece*. Cambridge.
—— (2007). 'Fame, Memorial and Choral Poetry: The Origins of Epinician Poetry. A Historical Study', in Hornblower and Morgan (2007), 141–66.
Thummer, E. (1957). *Die Religiosität Pindars*. Commentationes Aenipotanae 13. Innsbruck.
Tigerstedt, E. N. (1965–78). *The Legend of Sparta in Classical Antiquity*. 3 vols. Stockholm. Vol. i.
Tocco Sciarelli, G. (1997). 'Il culto di Hera ad Elea', in De la Genière (1997), 227–34.
Tomlinson, R. A. (1972). *Argos and the Argolid: From the End of the Bronze Age to the Roman Occupation*. London.
Torelli, M. (1988). 'Paestum romana', *AttTar* 27 (1987), 33–115.
Torr, C. (1885). *Rhodes in Ancient Times*. Cambridge.
Torre, A. (1985). 'Il consumo di devozioni: rituale e potere nelle campagne piemontesi nella prima metà del Settecento', *Quaderni Storici* 58, 181–223.
—— (1992). 'Politics Cloaked in Worship: State, Church and Local Power in Piedmont 1550–1770', *Past and Present* 134, 42–92.
Tosi, T. (1908). 'Sul sesto peana di Pindaro', *A&R* 11, 201–20.
Trammell, E. P. (1949). 'The Grave of Neoptolemos', *CJ* 44, 270–3.
Trexler, R. C. (1980). *Public Life in Renaissance Florence*. New York–London.
Tugendhat, E. (1960). 'Zum Rechtfertigungsproblem in Pindars 7. Nemeischen Gedicht', *Hermes* 88, 385–409.
Turner, V. W. (1967). *The Forest of Symbols: Aspects of Ndembu Ritual*. Ithaca–London.
—— (1969). *The Ritual Process: Structure and Anti-Structure*. London.
—— (1974*a*). *Dramas, Fields and Metaphors: Symbolic Action in Human Society*. Ithaca–London.
—— (1974*b*). 'Pilgrimage as Social Processes', in (1974*a*), 166–230.
—— (1982). *From Ritual to Theatre: The Human Seriousness of Play*. Performance studies series 1. New York.
—— (1986). *The Anthropology of Performance*. Performance studies series 4. New York–Baltimore.
—— (1990). 'Are there Universals of Performance in Myth, Ritual and Drama?', in Appel and Schechner (1990), 8–18.
Tylor, E. B. (1958 (1871)). *Primitive Culture: Research into the Development of Mythology, Philosophy, Religion, Art, and Custom*, 2 vols. Repr. New York (1st pub. London, 1871).
Tzouvara-Souli, C. (1993).'Common Cults in Epirus and Albania', in Cabanes (1993), 65–82.
—— (2004). 'The Cults of Zeus in Ancient Epirus', in Cabanes and Lamboley (2004), 515–47.
Ugolini, D. (1983). 'Tra perirrhanteria, louteria e thymiateria. Note su una classe ceramica da S. Biagio della Venella (Metaponto)', *MEFRA* 95, 449–72.
Usener, H. (1912–13). *Kleine Schriften*, vol. 4: *Arbeiten zur Religionsgeschichte*. Repr. Osnabrück, 1965.
Vallet, G. (1968). 'La Cité et son territoire dans les colonies grecques', *AttTar* 7 (1967), 67–141.
Vallois, R. (1966–78). *L' Architecture hellénique et hellénistique à Délos jusqu'à l'éviction des Déliens (166 av. J.-C.)*, 2 vols. Bibliothèque des Écoles françaises d'Athènes et de Rome 157. Paris.

Van Dyke, R., and Alcock, S. E., eds. (2003). *Archaeologies of Memory*. Oxford.

Vannicelli, P. (1989). 'Il nome "Ἕλληνες" in Omero', *RFIC* 117, 34–48.

—— (1995). 'La fuga da Tebe dei Cadmei dopo la spedizione degli Epigoni', in M. Sordi, ed., *Coercizione e mobilità umana nel mondo antico*. Vita e Pensiero, Contributi dell'Istituto di Storia Antica 21. Milan, 17–26.

—— (1996). 'Problemi della Beozia omerica', in E. De Miro *et al.*, eds., *Atti e memorie del secondo congresso internazionale di micenologia: Roma–Napoli 20 ottobre 1991*. Incunabula Graeca 98. Rome, 939–45.

—— (2004). 'Eraclidi e Perseidi: aspetti del conflitto tra Sparta e Argo nel V sec. a.C.', in Angeli Bernardini (2004*a*), 279–94.

Vanotti, G. (1979). 'Sofocle e l'Occidente', in *I tragici greci e l'Occidente*. Bologna, 93–125.

Verdenius, W. J. (1968). *Commentaries on Pindar*, vol. i. *Olympian Odes 3, 7, 12, 14*. Mnemosyne suppl. 97. Leiden.

—— (1976). 'Pindar's Seventh Olympian Ode: Supplementary Comments', *Mnemosyne* ser. 4, 29, 243–53.

Vermeule, E. T. (1960). 'The Mycenaeans in Achaea', *AJA* 64, 1–21.

Vernant, J.-P. (1979). *Myth and Society in Ancient Greece*, trans. J. Lloyd. Brighton (orig. *Mythe et société en Grèce ancienne*. Paris, 1974).

—— (1983). *Myth and Thought among the Greeks*. London (orig. *Mythe et pensée chez les Grecs. Études de psychologie historique*. Paris, 1965).

—— (1991). *Mortals and Immortals*. Collected Essays ed. F. I. Zeitlin. Princeton.

Versnel, H. S. (1970). *Triumphus: An Inquiry into the Origin, Development and Meaning of the Roman Triumph*. Leiden

—— (1987). 'Greek Myth and Ritual. The Case of Kronos', in Bremmer (1987), 121–32.

—— (1990). 'What's Sauce for the Goose is Sauce for the Gander: Myth and Ritual, Old and New', in Lowell (1990), 25–90. Revised in (1993), 15–88.

—— (1993). *Inconsistencies in Greek and Roman Religion*, ii. *Transition and Reversal in Myth and Ritual*. Leiden.

Veyne, P. (1988). *Did the Greeks Believe in their Myths? An Essay on the Constitutive Imagination*, trans. P. Wissing. Chicago (orig. *Les Grecs ont-ils cru à leurs mythes: essai sur l'imagination constituante*. Paris, 1983).

Vian, F. (1965). 'Mélampous et les Proitides', *REA* 67, 25–30.

Vidal-Naquet, P. (1986). *The Black Hunter: Forms of Thought and Forms of Society in the Greek World*, trans. A. Szegedy-Maszak; with a foreword by B. Knox. Baltimore–London (orig. *Le Chasseur noir: formes de pensée et formes de société dans le monde grec*. Paris, 1981).

Villarrubia, A. (1987–8). 'Una lectura del pean a Apolo Piteo de Baquílides (fr. 4 Snell–Maehler)', *Habis* 18–19, 59–78.

Visser, E. (1997). *Homers Katalog der Schiffe*. Stuttgart–Leipzig.

Vokotopoulou, I. (1987). "*Η δημοσίευση των μολυβδίνων πινακίων της Δωδώνης*", *Πρακτικά του Η' Συνεδρίου Έλλην. και Λατιν. Επιγρ. Β*. Athens, 82–6.

Vollgraff, C. W. (1956). *Le Sanctuaire d'Apollon Pythéen à Argos*. École Française d'Athènes. Études Péloponnésiennes 1. Paris.

Vordos, A. G. (2002). 'Rhypes. A la recherche de la métropole achéenne', in Greco (2002), 217–34.

Vottero, G. (1998–2001). *Le Dialecte béotien (7e s.–2es. Av. J.-C.)*, 2 vols. Études anciennes 18 and 23. Nancy.

Voyatzis, M. E. (1990). *The Early Sanctuary of Athena Alea at Tegea and other Archaic Sanctuaries in Arcadia.* Studies in Mediterranean Archaeology and Literature. Pocket-book 97. Gothenburg.

—— (1999). 'The Role of Temple Building in Consolidating Arkadian Communities', in Nielsen and Roy (1999), 130–68.

Walbank, F. W. (1957–79). *A Historical Commentary to Polybius*, 3 vols. Oxford.

Walbank, M. B. (1978). *Athenian Proxenies of the Fifth Century B.C.* Toronto–Sarasota.

Walter, H. (1993). *Ägina. Die archäologische Geschichte einer Insel.* Munich.

Walter-Karyidi, E. (1981). 'Eine epirotische Erzbildnerschule', *JbBerlMus.* 23, 11–48.

Wathelet, P. (1992). 'Argos et l'Argolide dans l'épopée, spécialement dans le Catalogue des vaisseaux', in Piérart (1992*b*), 99–116.

Wells, B. (1987–8). 'Apollo at Asine', in *Πρακτικά του Γ' Διεθνούς Συνεδρίου Πελοποννησιακών Σπουδών, Καλαμάτα,* 8–15 *Σεπτεμβρίου* 1985, *II. Αρχαιότης και Βυζάντιον.* Athens, 349–52.

—— (1988). 'Early Greek Building Sacrifice', in Hägg *et al.* (1988), 259–66.

—— (1990). 'The Asine Sima', *Hesperia* 59, 157–61.

—— ed. (2002*a*). *New Research on Old Material From Asine and Berbati: In Celebration of the Fiftieth Anniversary of the Swedish Institute at Athens.* Stockholm.

—— (2002*b*). 'Evidence for Cult at the Acropolis of Asine from Late Geometric through Archaic and Classical Times', in (2002*a*), 95–133.

Welter, G. (1938*a*). *Aigina.* Berlin.

—— (1938*b*). 'Aeginetica I–XII', *AA*, 1–33.

West, M. L. (1970). 'Corinna', *CQ* 20, 277–87.

—— (1985). *The Hesiodic Catalogue of Women: Its Nature, Structure and Origins.* Oxford.

—— (1990). 'Dating Corinna', *CQ* 40, 553–7.

—— (1992). *Ancient Greek Music.* Oxford.

—— (1995). 'The Date of the Iliad', *MH* 52, 203–19.

—— (1997). *The East Face of Helicon: West Asiatic Elements in Greek Poetry and Myth.* Oxford.

Westermann, C. (1964). 'Arten der Erzählung in der Genesis', in *Forschung am Alten Testament. Gesammelte Studien*, vol. i. Theologische Bücherei 24. Munich, 9–91.

Westlake, H. D. (1983). 'Conon of Rhodes: The Troubled Aftermath of Synoecism', *GRBS* 24, 333–44.

Whitby, M. (1998). 'An International Symposium? Ion of Chios fr. 27 and the Margins of the Delian League', in E. Dabrowa, ed., *Ancient Iran and the Mediterranean World.* Electrum, Studies in Ancient History 2. Krakow, 207–24.

Widengren, G. (1955). *Sakrales Königtum im Alten Testament und im Judentum.* Stuttgart.

—— (1969). *Religionsphänomenologie.* Berlin.

Wilamowitz-Moellendorff, U. v. (1883). 'Phaethon', *Hermes* 18, 396–434.

—— (1921). 'Melanippe', in *Kleine Schriften* (Berlin, 1935), vol. i, 440–60. Repr. from *SbBerlin* (1921), 63–80.

—— (1922). *Pindaros.* Berlin.

—— (1931–2). *Der Glaube der Hellenen*, 2 vols. Berlin.

Willcock, M. M. (1995). *Pindar: Victory Odes. Olympians 2, 7 and 11; Nemean 4; Isthmians 3, 4 and 7.* Cambridge.

Wilson, P. J. (1999). 'The Aulos in Athens', in Goldhill and Osborne (1999), 58–95.

—— (2000). *The Athenian Institution of the Khoregia: The Chorus, the City, and the Stage.* Cambridge.

WILSON, P. J. (2003*a*). 'The Sound of Cultural Conflict: Kritias and the Culture of mousike in Athens', in DOUGHERTY and KURKE (2003), 181–206.

—— (2003*b*). 'The Politics of Dance: Dithyrambic Contest and Social Order in Ancient Greece', in D. PHILLIPS and D. PRITCHARD, eds., *Sport and Festival in the Ancient Greek World*. Swansea, 163–96.

—— (2007). 'The Athenian Thargelia', in P. WILSON, ed., *The Greek Theatre and Festivals: Documentary Studies*. Oxford, 150–84.

—— (forthcoming). 'The Musical World of Pronomos', Paper Given on a Day on the Pronomos Vase, Oxford, Sept. 2006.

WINKLER, J. (1990). 'The Ephebes' Song: *Tragoidia* and *Polis*', in id. and ZEITLIN (1990), 20–62.

—— and ZEITLIN, F. I., eds. (1990). *Nothing to Do with Dionysos? Athenian Drama in its Social Context*. Princeton.

WIRTH, U., ed. (2000). *Performanz. Zwischen Sprachphilosophie und Kulturwissenschaften*. Frankfurt.

WISSOWA, G. (1912). *Religion und Kultus der Römer*. HAW v.4. Munich (1st edn. 1902).

WOLSKI, J. (1973). '*Μηδισμός* et son importance en Grèce à l'époque des guerres médiques', *Historia* 22, 3–15.

WOODBURY, L. (1979). 'Neoptolemus at Delphi: Pindar, *Nem*. 7. 30 ff.', *Phoenix* 33, 95–133.

WÖRRLE, M. (1964). *Untersuchungen zur Verfassungsgeschichte von Argos im 5. Jahrhundert vor Christus*. Erlangen.

WÜST, E. (1967). *Pindar als geschichtsschreibender Dichter. Interpretation der 12 vorsizilischen Siegeslieder, des sechsten Paians und der zehnten olympischen Ode*. Diss. Tübingen.

YOUNG, D. C. (1968). *Three Odes of Pindar: A Literary Study of Pythian 11, Pythian 3, and Olympian 7*. Mnemosyne suppl. 9. Leiden.

—— (1987). 'Pindar and Horace against the Telchines (*Ol*. 7.53 & *Carm*. 4.4.33)', *AJPh* 108, 152–7.

WYCHERLEY, R. E. (1957). *Literary and Epigraphical Testimonia*. Athenian Agora 3. Princeton.

ZAMBELLI, M. (1971–4). 'Per la storia di Argo nella prima metà del V secolo a.C.', i: *RFIC* 99, 148–58; ii: *RFIC* 102, 442–53.

ZANGGER, E. (1994). 'The Island of Asine: A Palaeogeographic Reconstruction', *OAth* 20, 221–39.

ZAPHEIROPOULOU, Ph. (1988). *Naxos: Monuments and Museum*. Athens.

—— (1998). *Paros*. Athens.

ZEITLIN, F. I. (1990). 'Thebes: Theater of Self and Society in Athenian Drama', in WINKLER and ZEITLIN (1990), 130–67.

—— (1993). 'Staging Dionysus between Thebes and Athens', in CARPENTER and FARAONE (1993), 147–82.

—— (1996). *Playing the Other: Gender and Society in Classical Greek Literature*. Chicago.

ZIEBARTH, E. (1932). 'Zur Handelsgeschichte der Insel Rhodos', in *Mélanges Gustave Glotz* II. Paris, 909–24.

ZIEHEN, L. (1949). 'Pamboiotia', *RE* xxxviii, 288–9.

ZIMMERMANN, B. (1992). *Dithyrambos. Geschichte einer Gattung*. Hypomnemata 98. Göttingen.

ZUNINO, M. L. (1997). *Hiera Messeniaka: la storia religiosa della Messenia dall'età micenea all'età ellenistica*. Udine.

ZUNKER, A. (1988). *Untersuchungen zur Aiakidensage auf Aigina*. Dissertationen Philosophische Reihe 4. Diss. Tübingen.

Index Locorum

This index aims to include all passages cited from classical and Hellenistic sources, as well as inscriptions; it is selective with later texts and lexicographers, such as Pausanias or St. Byz. Note too the entries under individual authors in the subject index.

A. Literary Texts

Subject Index

Page numbers in italics indicate the main treatment of a subject, numbers in bold refer to an image or a map. Modern authors forming part of the argument in Chapter 1 are also indexed.